George Szell

MUSIC IN AMERICAN LIFE

A list of books in the series appears at the end of this book.

George Szell

A Life of Music

Michael Charry

UNIVERSITY OF ILLINOIS PRESS
Urbana, Chicago, and Springfield

Frontispiece: Photograph by Geoffrey Landsman,
courtesy of The Cleveland Orchestra Archives.

Publication of this book was supported by a grant from the Henry and Edna Binkele Classical Music Fund.

Manufactured in the United States of America
C 5 4 3 2 1
♾ This book is printed on acid-free paper.

Library of Congress Cataloging-in-Publication Data
Charry, Michael.
George Szell : a life of music / Michael Charry.
p. cm. — (Music in American life)
Includes bibliographical references and index.
Discography.
ISBN 978-0-252-03616-3 (cloth)
1. Szell, George, 1897–1970. 2. Conductors (Music)—United States—Biography.
I. Title.
ML422.S99C43 2011
784.2092—dc22 [B] 2011006825

To Jane

Contents

Preface

My years with George Szell and the Cleveland Orchestra were a life-changing experience that I could not have imagined a decade earlier when I first heard the orchestra under Szell. I was a freshman piano major and oboe minor at Oberlin College's Conservatory of Music in 1950. The Cleveland Orchestra then gave four concerts a season in Oberlin's Spanish-style Finney Chapel. Each of these concerts, and a few that I heard in the orchestra's Cleveland home, Severance Hall, were spellbinding, searing events that left me shaken, elated, inspired.

By the spring of 1952 I had decided to pursue a conducting career and was about to leave Oberlin to transfer to the Juilliard School of Music. David Robertson, the dean of the conservatory, called me in to discuss my decision and told me of the apprentice program Szell had established in Cleveland, and that a former Oberlin student had been an apprentice in 1946–47. He advised me to finish my piano studies in Oberlin, saying that I would need to be an excellent pianist to have a chance for that scholarship.

But by then I had made up my mind. Oberlin did not offer a conducting major at that time and, having taken all of Oberlin's conducting courses, I transferred to Juilliard. However, I never forgot Robertson's advice, and kept up piano study while continuing oboe study and majoring in conducting at Juilliard.

Having heard the Cleveland Orchestra and having studied oboe at Oberlin with Robert Zupnick, the orchestra's assistant principal oboist, I already knew of the orchestra's greatness and Szell's awesome talent, legendary memory, phenomenal ear, and highest standards. When in 1959 I read of Szell's revival of the apprentice conductor program, only the encouragement of my wife gave me sufficient nerve to apply.

The audition was typical Szell. All the requirements were spelled out in a bulletin published by the American Symphony Orchestra League (appendix C). Arriving at

Severance Hall at the appointed day and time, I was ushered to Szell's office, where we spoke for several minutes before he took me in the little elevator up one floor to his spacious study, furnished with a grand piano. He began the comprehensive musical exam with a test of my musical hearing. Szell played a complex chord at the piano of seven dissonant notes, and asked, "How many?" Passing that, we followed the announced audition list for the next hour and a half. At the end he said that I had acquitted myself well and that he would consider me; "acquitted," I thought, in the ancient civilian law tradition of guilty until proven innocent. But he was right to be skeptical of aspiring young conductors, having found many without sufficient training or talent for a professional career. I knew that he did not mince words and meant exactly what he said.

Months later I received a telegram from Szell on a Friday, asking me to telephone him the following Monday at 9:30 A.M. I timed my call so that his secretary would connect me with his office phone at exactly 9:30 A.M. He said, "If I were in a position to offer you the apprenticeship of the Cleveland Orchestra, would you be in a position to accept?" Again, he covered himself in not directly offering me the apprenticeship so that if I had said no, I would not have turned down his offer. Of course I immediately said yes, to which he replied, "Mr. Barksdale [the orchestra manager] will send you a letter of confirmation with the repertoire for next season." He told me to study it and to take some lessons in percussion, as I would be helping out that section, and that he would see me in October.

In Szell's last decade the orchestra was in its glory. The level of playing astounded me. The first Monday rehearsal I heard as apprentice conductor was a nonstop reading of Brahms's Second Symphony that struck me as the greatest performance I had ever heard or could conceive of. By the Thursday subscription performance, the music was even more magnificent.

The next nine years were the greatest education I could imagine. My apprenticeship scholarship was renewed for an unprecedented four years, during which time I assisted Szell in transmitting his markings to the orchestra librarians, who marked the parts from which the orchestra would play; I played all keyboard instruments as needed, and I joined the percussion section frequently.

I observed all the orchestra's rehearsals and concerts at home and on tour, and attended recording sessions. Gradually, under the generous mentoring of Szell's assistant, Louis Lane, I took over pieces in children's concerts, became assistant conductor to Lane in the summer Pops, and drew an assignment to conduct full children's concerts. The term of apprenticeship was initially for one year. I stayed with the orchestra eleven years, four as apprentice conductor and then as assistant conductor; the first nine years were under Szell, the last two were after he died. Szell asked me to conduct one piece on some of his subscription concerts, and eventually

I conducted full subscription concerts of my own. Lane and I initiated opera with the orchestra for seven seasons.

Every day observing Szell rehearse and perform was the greatest lesson. Szell's rehearsals dealt with the infinite tiny details of balance, phrasing, intonation, and ensemble that were the foundation on which he molded his grand design of work after work in run-throughs, dress rehearsals, and performances. They were never static. Szell constantly refined and polished the already near-perfect gems of stylish music making.

Besides assisting in keyboard and other sections of the orchestra, the "job" of apprentice conductors was to learn. Szell did not give lessons except by daily example, but each time that we apprentices or assistants were assigned to conduct pieces on concerts, we had a coaching session with Szell in which one of us played piano for the other, who conducted his piece. In our rehearsals with the orchestra, Szell took an active part. Facing that orchestra was scary, but with Szell behind us in the auditorium, the pressure increased geometrically. Survival between a rock and a hard place served as a lesson itself.

Of thousands of priceless moments with Szell and the orchestra, one unusual experience stands among the most memorable. On the East Coast tour with the orchestra in February 1963, Szell enjoyed a free day in Northampton, Massachusetts. After conducting the concert at Smith College the night before, Szell told me and the Kulas Fellow that year, Yoshimi Takeda, to meet him in the lobby the next morning to play some score with him at the piano, four hands. When I asked what I thought was a simple question of which score, he grinned and said emphatically, "I'll bring the score," in his way that meant the point was final and the subject closed for then. It would be sight reading for me, which is exactly what he wanted. Takeda, not being a pianist, would observe.

After a restless night, I met Szell, who greeted me cheerfully. He brought one large score with him, beautifully bound. I tried to tell from the cover what it might be, but he held it tightly tucked under his arm so that I could not see. He enjoyed hiding the score like a little boy, with a grin from ear to ear.

We traveled in his chauffeured car to the Smith College music building, he still hiding the score from me. Only when we had arrived in the practice studio he had reserved did he prop open the score on the piano's music rack, and I saw what it was. I should have guessed.

One of the major works on the tour that year was Mahler's beautiful Fourth Symphony, with the soprano soloist in the last movement. Our soprano was the wonderful Judith Raskin. We had performed it in Severance Hall that January as preparation for the tour. The orchestra had presented it earlier on the tour, and it would be done twice more, in Hartford and, most important, in Carnegie Hall.

As perfectly as he knew every note by memory and as often and as recently as he had conducted it, in true Szell style he was always studying. Here, on his busman's holiday, I figured into his plan. I felt flattered, delighted, and scared out of my senses. Szell's score-playing prowess at the piano was legendary.

He, at the upper end of the piano, gestured to me to sit at the lower. With his left hand he drew an imaginary line at middle "C" and told me to play any instruments with notes below that, and he would play all those above. That meant reading the score from top to bottom, winds, brass, percussion, harp, and strings and deciding in every split second which instruments to play and which to leave to him.

Szell was sixty-six years old and had been conducting that score for almost half a century. Mahler's score is very contrapuntal and has many independent lines. In some of the composer's most complex moments, even Szell did not have enough fingers to play all the parts, although the way he played that day, it seemed to me that he had three hands.

We began from the beginning. Szell dominated the keyboard. When he began a musical phrase that went over his imaginary line, he just ignored his own restriction and went deep into my territory, for which I was infinitely grateful. I, of course, never went a semitone above the border line, although today I realize he would have admired a bit of aggression on my part. But that day I was having a delightful time being flattered and scared, and found that I could hold my own with him for the most part because he, becoming thoroughly engrossed in the music, was roaring up and down the keyboard.

At a few points, I was playing some tricky transpositions really cleverly, perhaps the French horns in F in bass clef, and Szell, all the while grabbing fistfuls of notes, looked down from his Olympian heights and murmured approvingly yet a little begrudgingly, "Hmm, not bad, not bad." And so it went to the glorious end of the symphony.

Between movements he gave me some of his score-reading techniques. I had felt from the first that he seemed to have more than two hands. In effect, he did. He showed me how he used his two thumbs together as an almost independent third hand. At times he alternated his thumbs, passing notes back and forth to each other. At other times they crossed over each other, depending on the shape of the passage. I tried the trick, somewhat awkwardly, and found even in my first fumblings that there was more potential there for score reading than pianists think to use, and that practice could produce great improvement.

After the Asian tour in 1970, I went on holiday with my family for a month in Europe, and only learned of Szell's illness from Lane while en route to Cleveland in July. My first visit with Szell in the hospital showed no indication of the seriousness of his condition. He was sitting up and we conversed for about ten minutes. I told him that I had seen Mrs. Hansen, of the publishing house Wilhelm Hansen, in

Copenhagen. Remembering that two sisters were running the firm, he immediately asked, "Which one?" On my next visit he was lying down, sedated, half awake. His face was relaxed, his lips pursed as if he were whistling a favorite score, but he made no sound. Szell's right forearm was raised and he was conducting something in his mind. It was an eerie sight, coming so soon after seeing him with all his powers, conducting the touring orchestra in concert after triumphant concert. We did not speak, and that was the last time I saw him.

After Szell died I stayed on with Lane and Pierre Boulez to maintain stability after the loss. I left when the orchestra appointed a new music director.

Helene Szell, George's widow, proposed the idea of a biography and approached contacts she knew in Europe, but without success. I offered to assist with research and to search for a writer to undertake the task, also without success. After a time, I came to realize that this important life and career needed to be documented and, with no sign anywhere that anyone else was taking it on, and with trepidation but determination, I began the odyssey of researching and writing Szell's biography, described in the acknowledgments. At long last, this is the result.

Acknowledgments

Many people over many years have helped me with their support, memories, expertise, and guidance. I wish to thank them all, and if I have omitted any, I beg to be forgiven. Mrs. Helene Szell gave me encouragement and tangible support over the years. I received grants from the Mather Foundation in Cleveland, headed by James D. Ireland III, and benefitted from the editorial assistance of Sedgwick Clark. The first publisher to whom I submitted the manuscript advised me to cut and polish it with further editorial help. For this next step I received guidance by gifted author and editor Barbara Heyman.

Donald Rosenberg, music critic for the *Cleveland Plain Dealer*, who wrote a history of the Cleveland Orchestra, told the excellent longtime archivist of the Cleveland Orchestra, Carol Jacobs, that he would be glad to help me, and I gratefully accepted. In an amazingly short time, Donald read the manuscript twice, providing many insightful and important suggestions and corrections large and small. Carol's predecessor as archivist, Nancy Parish, and two successors, Amy Dankowski and Deborah Hefling, have all given their time and expertise, for which I am infinitely grateful. Conductor colleagues Louis Lane and John Canarina read the manuscript and made welcome contributions, as did my wonderful daughter, Barbara Charry, and John supplied me with material from the Scottish Orchestra when he was conducting in Britain. The late, renowned conductor, scholar, and teacher Max Rudolf, who had been Szell's associate since 1929 and friend for life, gave invaluable advice over many years.

A friend from Fulbright Scholarship days, Professor Bruno Nettl at the University of Illinois, recommended that I consult with Judy McCulloh at the University of Illinois Press, who advised me to cut further. With the enthusiastic and wise guidance and support of her successor, Laurie Matheson, and the extraordinary expert editing of Manuela Kruger in New York City, the book took final shape. I am grateful to all the people who helped make this book possible, who are listed separately.

My most heartfelt thanks go to my wife, Jane Charry, who has been involved every step of the way over these many years, and without whom this work would simply not exist. The love and support of my family has been of the greatest importance, and I want to name them all with my love and thanks. Our son Stephen Charry (1958–2008) was with me all the way and always will be. He accompanied Jane and me on our first visit to the University of Illinois Press in 2005, and knew that the book would be published by that distinguished institution. His family includes his wife, Karin, and their children, Kaylyn, Benjamin, and Genevieve. And our daughter Barbara, her husband, and daughter, Iver, and Diana—all are ever in our hearts.

Thanks also to:

Elinore Barber, A. Beverly Barksdale, Myron Bloom, Emily (Mrs. Dudley S.) Blossom Jr., Martin Bookspan, Pierre Boulez, Helen (Mrs. Percy) Brown, Theodore Brown, John Browning, James Buswell, Robert B. Cantrick, Gaby and Robert Casadesus, Alice Chalifoux, Schuyler Chapin, Robert Conrad, Marcel Dick, Rafael Druian, Cloyd Duff, Anita Duquette, John S. Edwards, Philip Farkas, Robert Finn, Rudolf Firkusny, Dietrich Fischer-Dieskau, Leon Fleisher, Jean Fonda Fournier, Zino Francescatti, Hans Gal, Joseph Gingold, Margaret Glove, Saul Goodman, Gary Graffman, Kenneth Haas, Lynn Harrell, Olga Heifetz, Hans Heinzheimer, Frank Hruby, Christopher Jaffe, Frank E. Joseph, Andrew Kazdin, Eugene Kilinski, Joseph Koch, Alan Kofsky, Paul Henry Lang, Edward A. Lanyi, Rosalie (Mrs. Edgar M.) Leventritt, James Levine, Seymour Lipkin, David Loebel, Kurt Loebel, Joseph Machlis, Daniel Majeske, Vladimir Maleckar, Ursula Mamlok, Robert Marcellus, Robert C. Marsh, Robert Matson, Michael Maxwell, Peter Mennin, Erica Morini, Carlos Moseley, Edward Murphy, Paul Myers, Richard Oliver, Edith Peinemann, Murray Perahia, Maurice Peress, Martin Perlich, Frank Peters, Richard Pittschke, Eunice Podis, Peter Poltun, Jacques Posell, Alfred Rankin, Judith Raskin, Peter Reed, Rudolf Ringwall, George Rochberg, Halina (Mrs. Artur) Rodzinski, Leonard Rose, Klaus G. Roy, Harvey Sachs, Samuel Salkin, Felix Salzer, Hedwig (Mrs. Felix) Salzer, Leonard Samuels, Jack Saul, Jerzy Semkow, Rudolf Serkin, Robert Shankland, Harold Shapero, Robert Shaw, Mrs. Thomas B. Sherman, George Silfies, Ernst Silberstein, Abraham Skernick, Martin Sokoloff, Noel Sokoloff, Risë Stevens Surovy, David J. Stiller, George Sturm, Ethel (Mrs. Irvin) Talbot, John G. Teltsch, Henri Temianka, Olin Trogdon, Paul Vermel, Edgar Vincent, Frederic Waldman, Richard Weiner, Evan Whallon, Thomas Willis, Nancy Coe Wixom, Rachel de W. Wixom, Martyn Zagwijn, David Zauder, and Alfred Zetzer.

Australian Broadcasting Corporation, Rex E. Ellis, federal director of concerts/controller, Administrative Services, Patricia Kelly, archivist, Documents, 1983.

Extracts from memoranda and correspondence reproduced by permission of the Australian Broadcasting Corporation ©2010, ABC. All rights reserved.

British Broadcasting Corporation, for permission to quote from television interview of George Szell by John Culshaw, licensed courtesy of BBC Worldwide.

Budapest Opera

Budapest Central Synagogue

The Cleveland Orchestra, Nancy Parrish, Carol S. Jacobs, Amy Dankowski, Deborah Hefling, archivists

Chicago Symphony Orchestra, Henry Fogel, executive director, Evelyn Meine, Special Services; Robert Kular, Public Relations

Royal Concertgebouw Orchestra, Marius Flothuis, Piet Heuweckemeijer

Mannes College of Music, Charles Kaufman, president

Metropolitan Opera, Robert Tuggle, archivist

New York Philharmonic, Barbara Haws, archivist

Archives of the St. Louis Symphony

Northwestern University Music Library, Don L. Roberts, head music librarian

Archives of the Residence Orchestra of The Hague

Fleisher Collection of the Free Library of Philadelphia

Newberry Library, Diana Haskell, curator of Special Collections

New York Public Library

The Philadelphia Orchestra Archives

Vancouver Maritime Museum, Frank Brayard

Copies of the author's research materials, including printed and recorded items, will be deposited in The Cleveland Orchestra Archives.

I take responsibility for any inaccuracies or omissions, unintended and regretted, and welcome with thanks any and all suggestions, additions, and/or corrections.

Abbreviations

All citations from the Musical Arts Association (Cleveland Orchestra) unless otherwise noted.

CHSP	*Cleveland Heights Sun-Press*
CN	*Cleveland News*
CP	*Cleveland Press*
MA	*Musical America*
MAA	Musical Arts Association Archives (when multiple sources are cited in an endnote)
MC	*Musical Courier*
MCA	The author's archives
MCB	The author's taped reports from the Soviet Union
MOA	Metropolitan Opera Archives
NYDN	*New York Daily News*
NYHT	*New York Herald Tribune*
NYJA	*New York Journal American*
NYP	*New York Post*
NYPhA	New York Philharmonic Archives
NYPL	New York Public Library
NYS	*New York Sun*
NYT	*New York Times*
NWA	Northwestern University Archives
NYWT	*New York World-Telegram and Sun*
PD	*Cleveland Plain Dealer*
RCO	The Royal Concertgebouw Orchestra Archives

SLPD	*St. Louis Post-Dispatch*
SR	*Saturday Review*
TNY	*The New Yorker*

Frequently cited book sources

FM	Fellers & Meyers, see bibliography
GB	Le Grand Baton, see bibliography

Chronology

1897	Born June 7 in Budapest
1903–1904	Begins musical studies in Vienna: composition and theory with Mandyczewski; piano with Richard Robert
1908	Debut as pianist/composer, Vienna Tonkünstler Orchestra
1909–10	European concert tour, study with Max Reger
1912	Ten-year composition contract with Universal Edition
1914	Conducting debut, Blüthner Orchestra, Berlin
1915–17	Assistant conductor, Berlin Royal Opera; begins association with Richard Strauss
1917–18	First conductor, Strasbourg Opera, under Hans Pfitzner
1919–20	Assistant conductor, German Opera House, Prague
1920	Marries Olga Band (divorced ca. 1926)
1924–29	First conductor, Berlin State Opera, under Erich Kleiber
1927–29	Professor, Hochschule für Musik, Berlin
1929–37	Leading conductor, German Opera House, Prague; guest conductor in Europe, U.S.S.R, England, and St. Louis
1933	Debut Residence Orchestra, The Hague
1936	Debut Royal Concertgebouw Orchestra, Amsterdam
1937–39	Conductor, Scottish Orchestra, Glasgow; Residence Orchestra, The Hague
1939	Marries Helene Schultz Teltsch, Glasgow
1938, 1939	Australian Broadcasting Corporation orchestras
1939	New York; teaches at New School for Social Research; composition and advanced theory at Mannes School of Music

1941–42	Guest conducts Detroit Symphony, NBC Symphony, Los Angeles Philharmonic, and Ravinia Festival
1942–46	Conductor, Metropolitan Opera; guest conducts Philadelphia Orchestra, Chicago Symphony, Boston Symphony, New York Philharmonic, and Cleveland Orchestra
1946	Musical director of the Cleveland Orchestra Becomes American citizen
1949–69	Festivals: Holland, Salzburg, and Zurich
1957	First Cleveland Orchestra European tour
1957–60	Vienna Opera; La Scala concerts
1958–61	Co-conductor, Royal Concertgebouw Orchestra
1965	Cleveland Orchestra tour of U.S.S.R. and Europe
1967	Cleveland Orchestra three-festivals tour: Salzburg, Edinburgh, and Lucerne
1969	Senior music advisor and principal guest conductor, New York Philharmonic
1970	Cleveland Orchestra tour of Japan, Korea, and Alaska; dies in Cleveland, July 30

George Szell

Introduction

When George Szell died in 1970, Irving Kolodin wrote, "The size of his figure will grow as time recedes and the magnitude of his accomplishment emerges in ever greater grandeur against its background." Szell, born in 1897, was one of the greatest orchestra and opera conductors of his time. He has been the subject of numerous newspaper and magazine articles. This is his first biography.

Szell's most significant life accomplishment was as musical director of the Cleveland Orchestra. He raised it from the ranks of respected second-tier ensembles to the highest level of world class. The Szell/Cleveland Orchestra combination is legendary. Szell's Cleveland performances from 1965 to 1970 are preserved in broadcast recordings, and his commercial recordings with the Cleveland and concerts and recordings with other orchestras are continually being reissued on compact disc.

A product of central Europe at the turn of the twentieth century, Szell was a child prodigy pianist and composer, but in his mid-twenties he gave up both for conducting. He served as a protégé of composer-conductor Richard Strauss at the Berlin Opera, and Strauss recommended him for his first musical post at the Strasbourg Opera when Szell was twenty years old.

Szell is known throughout the musical world. He was a guest conductor of the most prestigious orchestras and festivals in North America, Austria, Australia, France, Germany, Great Britain, Italy, the Netherlands, and Switzerland. On tours, he led the Cleveland Orchestra throughout the United States, to Canada, Europe, the Soviet Union, Korea, and Japan. Coming from Prague, where he was chief conductor of the German Opera House (1929–1937), Szell made his United States debut in 1930 with the St. Louis Symphony, returning in 1931. He made his New York orchestral debut with the NBC Symphony Orchestra in 1941, at the invitation of Arturo Toscanini, with whom he has often been compared.

Szell was one of the chief conductors of the Metropolitan Opera from 1942 until he assumed leadership of the Cleveland Orchestra in 1946. From 1936 until the end of his life, Szell was a regular guest conductor of the Royal Concertgebouw Orchestra of Amsterdam. Until his death, he served as musical director in Cleveland, and in 1969 was named "music advisor and senior guest conductor" of the New York Philharmonic, of which he had been a regular guest conductor since 1943.

From early on and throughout his career, Szell championed the music of numerous living composers, including Béla Bartók, Paul Hindemith, Rolf Liebermann, Peter Mennin, and William Walton. Szell's support of Pierre Boulez and Stanislaw Skrowaczewski helped establish their international conducting careers.

Szell was born in Budapest of Jewish parents. His family converted from Judaism and moved to Vienna when he was three, and there he was raised a Catholic. Throughout his life Szell felt ambivalent about his Hungarian origin, claiming Czech ancestry through his mother's side. He became a citizen of the newly formed Czechoslovakia in 1919 and of the United States in 1946, the year he became musical director in Cleveland. *Time* magazine quoted him as saying, "I'm so damned normal," but many would dispute that vigorously. "No one is indifferent to George Szell," wrote Joseph Wechsberg in a long profile in *The New Yorker*. In 1953–54 Szell returned briefly to the Metropolitan Opera and departed abruptly after conducting half of his contracted performances, because of a dispute with the Met's general manager, Rudolf Bing. When Szell died, it was said that some musicians celebrated. On the other hand, when the dying Szell's deteriorating condition prevented Leonard Bernstein from visiting him in the hospital, Bernstein, knowing he would never see Szell alive again, cried. He was not alone.

* * *

Mindful of the effect of Szell's powerful personality, I have sought to give a balanced portrayal of this enormously gifted musician and complex human being. In the course of researching this biography, I have interviewed numerous soloists, orchestra musicians, and many others associated with Szell over many years. Many of the photographs are unique and never before published. An appendix lists Szell's conducting repertoire and important world premieres. Also included is a discography of Szell's original recordings, with a selection of live concerts on CD and DVD.

1

The New Mozart (1897–1929)

At one o'clock in the afternoon on June 7, 1897, György Endre Szél was born in Budapest, Hungary, the only child of Kálman and Malvin Szél.[1] Kálman Szél, a successful businessman, called himself an "entrepreneur." He was born in Marczali, in Somogyi County, south of the great Lake Balaton. György's mother hailed from Ipolyság, northwest of Budapest on the Ipoly River, which formed a border with Slovakia. After World War I, Slovakia, Moravia, and Bohemia were joined to form Czechoslovakia. The connection to this area in which many ethnic Czechs lived formed the basis of Szell's later claim to Czech ancestry on his mother's side. The language spoken in the Szell home, however, was Hungarian.[2]

The city of Budapest was formed in 1873 by incorporating the towns of Buda and Óbuda on the west bank of the Danube River with Pest on the east. Budapest was a growing city; by 1900 its population reached 700,000. The Szells lived in an elegant neighborhood north of the old town center of Pest at 34 Nádor utca (Nádor Street), at the corner of Garibaldi utca, two blocks from the Danube.

At the end of the nineteenth century, the neighborhood was becoming a center of commerce and government. The Szells lived in a four-story stone apartment building on the block between the old Stock Exchange and the Parliament building. Iron-grill doors frame its entrance passageway, leading to a square central courtyard. On the left in the passageway is the concierge's apartment; on the right are mailboxes and a stairway to balconies along the two interior back walls of the courtyard. Off the balconies are entrances to the apartments, which face Nádor and Garibaldi Streets.[3]

After the turn of the century, Szell's father moved the family to Vienna, where he established the city's first security-guard firm (*Wach- und Schliessgesellschaft*). A pioneering venture that depended on liaison with the police, the company held a virtual monopoly in the thriving city. As commerce grew, so did the need for such a service.[4]

Tied by the bonds of empire, Austria and Hungary shared a border, and their capitals lay only 130 miles apart. Roads and the Danube, one of the world's longest and most important commercial waterways, connected the cities. Budapest wielded strong economic and political influence, but Vienna held the center of power, as it had for centuries under the Hapsburg dynasty.

Vienna was a magnet for talent and ambition, and Kálman Szél possessed both. The city offered him the opportunity to elevate his family's status. They converted to Catholicism, obligatory for a business dealing closely with the government. A second *l* was added to the family name—suggesting a more aristocratic origin—and first names were Germanicized: György Endre became Georg Andreas, Kálman became Karl or Carl, and Malvin was changed to Margarete. Szell's maternal grandfather changed his family name from Hirschbein to Harmat.[5] Young George was brought up as a Catholic and taken regularly to Mass. He readily assimilated German as his mother tongue, and adopted the negative attitudes toward Hungary prevalent in Vienna.

Contrary to the nature of his business, Szell's father was relaxed and easygoing at home. To illustrate, a crystal chandelier once fell from the ceiling and smashed to pieces, fortunately harming no one. Mrs. Szell became excited and screamed, but Mr. Szell calmly said, "God gave it, God took it away."[6]

Karl Szell's business prospered, and routine affairs were left to his father-in-law. This arrangement freed him to indulge his interests in shopping for food and dressing meticulously, as well as pursuing his love of music. Father Szell placed much time and importance on the preparation and consumption of the main meal at midday, sometimes spending hours searching for exactly the right piece of meat. Visitors, including their son's young musician friends, received frequent invitations to enjoy the warmth and hospitality of the Szell family's dinners.[7] Everyone was expected to spend hours in conversation at mealtimes.[8]

More significant was Karl Szell's passion for music, especially opera. As a student in Paris, he often traveled to London and back solely to hear a favorite opera or singer at Covent Garden.[9] Later, in Vienna, he attended operas and concerts, taking young George along with him. Near the end of his life, Szell recalled attending his first opera: "I remember that in the so-called Volksoper, which was the second rank opera in Vienna, I was taken to a performance of *Carmen* and I had to be taken home after the second act because I was so bored; 'Oh, always these old love stories,' I said. Well, I hope you'll be indulgent, I was just six at that time."[10]

Szell's precocity was evident at a very early age, amazing his parents. He began to talk at nine months, and his musical talent was evident shortly after, when he began to correctly hum songs he heard. By the age of one George was singing the words as well; at two he could sing folk songs in Hungarian, German, French, and Czech.

His mother's account suggests that George's critical faculties also developed early: "I was playing the piano one day while Georg crawled, on the carpet, at my feet. . . .

Suddenly he looked up, held his ears, and shouted frantically, 'It's false, mother, it's false!' Fancy having one's playing criticized by a boy of two! But Georg was quite right—and ever since I have had to be very careful about my music, for my memory, my reading, and touch are not infallible—but Georg's ear certainly is."[11]

Szell himself recalled that when he was two-and-a-half, he would slap his mother's hands if she played a wrong note.[12] She began to teach him the rudiments of music when he was five. He was astonishingly quick, learning to read the treble clef in three days. She soon taught him all she could. "A year later I had very little to teach him," she said, "Not only could he read almost any music, but he improvised and composed well, which I was unable to do."

George's parents had the time and means to devote themselves to the development of his talent, which they did happily. They sought the advice of one of the most famous piano teachers in Vienna, Theodor Leschetizky. He heard the child but declined to take him on; Leschetizky was not interested in another prodigy, nor did he think Szell's talent was sufficient. His mother recalled: "A few days after the audition for Leschetizky he had the toothache. I took him to a dentist. While I was explaining his case, Georg, having found a piano in the waiting-room, had of course, opened it and was improvising. The doctor heard him and begged me to let him take the boy to a friend of his who taught piano." Young George's talent *was* extraordinary. The friend turned out to be Richard Robert, who, "as soon as he had heard and tested Georg, grew wild with excitement, and forthwith became his master." "With him," Szell's mother claimed, "our son has learned all he knows."[13]

An inspired teacher, Robert followed no routine or system and sought to teach his pupils to their individual needs. He was a shrewd judge of musical potential, but his chief virtue was an incomparable energy in imparting to his pupils the essentials of musical training, especially with regard to articulation, breathing, and "the whole organization of great music and everything included in a really authentic, stylistically impeccable interpretation."[14]

Robert's influence was immeasurable. In later life Szell expressed wonder that his parents had taken him to this teacher. Robert took the young Szell to chamber music sessions at the home of Arnold Rosé, concertmaster of the Vienna Philharmonic. Szell's musical education was supplemented with lessons from prominent teachers of composition and theory, among who were J. B. Förster, Karl Prohaska, and the famous Brahms scholar Eusebius Mandyczewski. Lessons with composer Max Reger in Leipzig were not as successful, according to Szell: "I did know of Reger's music because my teacher Robert thought very highly of him and also had his pupils play some of [his] piano music. . . . I was not very warmly attracted by it. I tended more towards Strauss but I had to admire the wonderful workmanship. These three months at the class of Reger were not terribly productive for me."

Reger had a rather cavalier attitude toward teaching, sending the thirteen-year-old pupil home after the very first lesson with an impossible assignment: "Well, this is Tuesday," Szell quoted Reger as saying, "next class is Friday. Until then write thirty minuets and fifteen chorales for me." Szell could not, and came back with "half a minuet and one chorale or something like that." Reger frequently told his class "the filthiest stories." But before he began, he would send Szell, the youngest pupil, out of the room. Reger's class in analysis, however, proved "unforgettable"; in particular, an analysis of Bruckner's Eighth Symphony that was "very, very profound, very imaginative, not simply dissecting." Curiously enough, Reger's piano playing left a more positive and lasting impression on Szell than his teaching of composition: "He was a huge uncouth-looking man . . . and when he went to the piano, you heard the most velvety touch, and the greatest delicacy in the treatment of the instrument I've ever experienced."[15]

Young George, full of fun, highly intelligent, and enormously talented, was adored and pampered by his parents. Reveling in his accomplishments, they kept display cases containing mementos of his achievements. Committed to his musical education, the parents arranged for private tutoring instead of school. As an only child, George lived in an adult world and had little opportunity for the company of his contemporaries. This could have contributed to Szell's often evidenced lack of awareness of others' feelings. Eventually, however, he found companions among his fellow students in Robert's piano class: Rudolf Serkin, Hans Gal, Clara Haskil, and Olga Band—whom Szell would later marry.

Seven years his senior, Gal befriended Szell on equal terms. This was possible, Gal recalled, because the "youngster was a marvelous, mature musician with stupendous intelligence, an insatiable, incredibly precocious reader, and a human being burning with curiosity." Gal's recollection of their first encounter offers insight into the youthful Szell's playful character: "George was a handsome boy in a sailor suit, nine years old, blue-eyed and fair-haired, very lively and talkative. . . . Both George's parents had come with him. He was just struggling, seemingly sight-reading, through a difficult piece, Chopin's Polonaise in G Sharp Minor, Robert patiently correcting every mistake. When George had finished with a resounding wrong chord, Robert took away the music and said: 'Now try and play it from memory!' It went off like a bombshell. The boy played with incredible fluency. It turned out that he had practiced the piece, surreptitiously, as a birthday surprise for his father, who adored Chopin. There were hugs and thanks to the successful teacher, and the proud father had tears in his eyes."[16]

Robert's love of music and pursuit of the highest goals became deeply ingrained in the young musician. The teacher's own words best convey the warmth and depth of this association. Written on the flyleaf of a presentation volume of the scores of Mozart's last six symphonies:

> Dear Georg! The first word that I let you speak in public was devoted to Mozart! With it I wished, symbolically, to place you under the protection of our divine Wolfgang Amadeus. Mozart—the combination of soul and naturalness, of grace and depth—*is music itself*. May he be the beacon to which you should look up all your life, for its light will always remind you whether you have distanced yourself from the ideal of artistic beauty or whether you have approached it. Therefore: Mozart forever!
>
> Your faithful friend and teacher, Rich. Robert.[17]

Under Robert's guidance, Szell made his public debut at age ten-and-a-half on January 30, 1908, in Vienna's fabled Musikvereinsaal. The Tonkünstler Orchestra, led by Oscar Nedbal, one of Vienna's most prominent musicians, played Szell's first orchestral composition, an overture; additionally, Mozart's Piano Concerto in A Major, K. 488, with Szell as soloist playing his own cadenza; a concert piece for piano and orchestra; and a group of solo pieces by Szell.

One of the most powerful critics of the day, Julius Korngold, wrote in the *Neue Freie Presse* that Szell's "piano playing . . . has the soul and the expression of a musically mature pianist." He continued:

> One miracle here practically overwhelms the other. To be sure, the precocity of creative talent must inspire especial astonishment because it is far rarer.
>
> One considers that this ten-year-old boy not only knows what he is doing, as for example in the form of the overture, not merely binds together logical tonal thoughts, organizes, rounds off into a whole, but also already begins to find his way in orchestral technique, in the distribution of his phrases to an orchestral choir, whose sound and essence differs from his familiar piano, but which lives in only his imagination. . . . What Széll has given us in his musical pieces are certainly mostly emulation of recognizable models; but he already shows independently formed melodic ideas as in the second theme of the overture.

Korngold properly credits Szell's teacher Robert for guiding his talent in the right direction, and concludes, "We only know what Georg Széll can accomplish at ten years, and know that the treasure is in the best of hands. What Széll in perhaps five years will have to say—for that one must wait in all eagerness but with all patience."[18]

Szell's debut caused such a sensation that his parents were deluged with offers for appearances of their son, soon referred to as "the new Mozart."[19] Szell's parents, however, permitted only one concert tour of prestigious musical centers—London, Berlin, Dresden, Cologne, Hamburg, and Leipzig. Following Robert's advice, they turned down most other offers. Szell would later comment, "My parents just wanted me to drop my calling card in the big cities of Europe and then continue my studies."[20]

The fourth concert he played in London, on Sunday November 22, (1908), was on a series sponsored by the National Sunday League, conducted by H. Lyell-Tayler.

The program credit announced the "special engagement" of Szell, the "Marvelous Boy Composer and Pianist, aged 11 years." Among works by Wagner, Tchaikovsky, Beethoven, and Offenbach, Szell played Mendelssohn's Capriccio in B Minor, several solo pieces of Chopin, and, for an encore, his own *Aria e Polacca.* The program also included an overture composed by Szell; both compositions now appear lost.

Even as a child, Szell recalled many years later, he had a keen sense of the ridiculous: "I remember that at one concert, I think it was in the Albert Hall, when the orchestra played an overture I had composed, I was required to sit like a dummy at the piano for exhibition purposes I suppose—there was no piano obbligato in the piece—and I didn't know what to do."[21]

London critics were dazzled by the child's virtuosity. R. de Chateleux's article in the *Daily Mail,* quoted above, took nearly a full page. Generously illustrated with photos of the "Wunderkind" against a background of one of his own piano compositions, the article recounted in florid prose an interview with the Szell family at their hotel. To his "astonishment," the child was not "delicate, emaciated and nerve-wracked, pale, haggard-looking, with the Promethean bumpy forehead of a Beethoven, the mane of a Liszt, the sunken eyes of a [Anton] Rubinstein, and the devilish expression of a Paganini," but rather "a fine, big, strong, healthy boy, with pink cheeks and mischievous eyes, simple, and totally unaware of his genius." "When the photographer attempted to photograph him," Chateleux wrote, the lad "would not keep quiet, argued humorously, refused to have his hair combed, and behaved altogether as all children do at his age." Every time the photographer attempted to close the shutter, Szell would either put out his tongue or take a piece of cake out of his pocket and begin to eat it.

Only when asked about his music was Szell attentive. Szell's early preference for Bach, Beethoven, and Mozart was expressed strongly, even snobbishly: "They have something to say," he said with a mouthful of cake, "you never get tired of them. I hate vulgar music. Anyone can write it. But there is only one Beethoven . . . I love Chopin, too—he is not so great, but who could help loving Chopin?"

When Chateleux asked him to improvise at the piano, the boy insisted that the journalist give him a theme. "His face grew serious at once," Chateleux reported, "as if another personality was taking possession of him. His eyes were now half-closed, as if in a semi-conscious dream, and his lips were set."

"Is this for piano only, or for orchestra?" the reporter asked softly.

"For orchestra—I am 'hearing' all the instruments."

"Tell me about them as you play."

"And then this wonderful child played, played—and as his fingers wandered over the keyboard, then striking with great power, then touching it with incredible lightness, he whispered, 'Horns—'cello solo—all the strings—tuba—full orchestra—oboe—harp—strings again.'"

Such anecdotes suggest that, already at eleven, Szell had the instincts of a conductor. He possessed a keen musical memory. When asked if he remembered everything he heard, Szell replied, "Always—when it is real music. I cannot always play it when I return from the concert, but I can write it all straight away—every note I have heard—and I never forget what I have once heard." And when asked about his plans for the future, he said, "I will learn the violin, the 'cello, one wooden and one brass instrument; and then . . . well, I will be a conductor and a composer."[22]

One London critic was highly impressed with Szell's "talent, instinctive knowledge of graceful and musical phrasing, a true sense of crisp and spontaneous rhythm, and a most sympathetic singing tone."[23] It was reported that by eleven he had composed some three hundred compositions—overtures, string quartets, instrumental pieces, songs, and even a comic opera, *Der kleine Roland*. "This little modern Mozart," wrote one reviewer, "scores with the greatest ease for the fullest and most up to date modern orchestra and improvises with extraordinary versatility upon any theme given him."[24]

Offers followed the tour and, to act as a protective buffer, Szell's parents engaged a concert manager, Emil Gutmann. His promotional brochure provided biographical material about Szell, a history of his concert career, extracts of dozens of reviews, and the assurance that he was not the "dreadful type of prodigy whose promotion in the music world today must rightly be vehemently resisted." "His achievements at the piano had nothing to do with the forced drill of an outward virtuosity of immature prodigies which were, so to speak, developed under the whip of the animal trainer. It was much more the playing of a musician, self-confident in his musical gifts, who had already found his own form of expression."[25]

After Szell's initial debut and tour, he took only a few engagements each year. By devoting his time to studying composition and continuing under Robert's wise guidance, George was protected from the exploitation and burnout that is too often the ruin of child prodigies. The development of a composer requires an intense, comprehensive study of music fundamentals, more so than the specialized training required by a piano virtuoso. Nevertheless, during the next five years, a limited number of important engagements took place in which Szell performed his own pieces as well as standard piano repertoire. But during that period, his talent took a direction that would eventually overshadow his career as pianist and curtail his role as composer.

The Adolescent Prodigy

Prodigious talents are fragile, with their greatest vulnerability appearing in adolescence. During his teen years, Szell had personal storms to weather, forces within him that threatened his talent and shifted the course of his life. Szell's musical development continued under the guidance of Richard Robert and a succession of teachers of composition and theory. The healthy boyishness reported by R. de Chateleux in

1908 gave way to darker forces within him, as noted by his close friend Hans Gal: "With puberty, he entered a period of incredible rowdyism. He became the terror of teachers and servants, and the despair of his parents. . . . His nature was to react with violence to any physical or mental strain. . . . At their wits' end, his parents sent him to [Carl] Jung, in Zurich, for psychoanalytical treatment. He came back quite unchanged but with a rich vocabulary of psychoanalytical terms to amuse his friends and exasperate his parents."

These were turbulent years for the young prodigy. To the natural internal pressures of adolescence were added those of performance, even if carefully restricted. His sheltered upbringing exacerbated this troubled period, and private tutoring ruled out the socializing influence of interaction with his contemporaries.

Szell's talent survived and matured, however, undoubtedly to the credit of Robert and of his supportive family, as well as to his innate strengths and overriding passion for music. He never had to struggle against poverty or parental resistance to a musical career as did many artists. Nevertheless, during these years, certain traits emerged—a tendency toward cruel practical jokes and gluttony—that would appear in his adult life as well.

Though Gal professed to be perhaps the "only friend who had never to suffer under George's pranks," there were many victims of Szell's mischievous, even sadistic tricks, and "if one tried to explain to him how he had hurt somebody's feelings, he would be amazed, but hardly repentant." Gal recalled of Szell's gluttony: "At the time of his first activity in Prague, in his early twenties, it was difficult to prevent him from entering every grocer's shop in order to eat another pair of those delicious sausages that were sold there. Later in life he became anxious not to put on too much weight, but not without rueful regrets."

Here Szell was engaging in the classic pattern of the child prodigy—the negative reaction toward his talent and the enormous strain it puts on normal development. Many of the most gifted never survive this period as artists. Others come through it poorly, and as adults, struggle in vain to compete with their own precocious reputations. In his fourteenth year, the most serious symptom of Szell's adolescent crisis was his refusal to do any kind of systematic work, and this, of course, profoundly affected his musical studies. "George played scores with unparalleled virtuosity, but he could not be induced to practice or to write contrapuntal studies," Gal observed.[26]

Before Szell was fifteen, Universal Edition awarded him a "general publication contract," which obligated him to offer all his music to the venerable Viennese publishing house. In effect, they held exclusive rights to his compositions for ten years from the date of the agreement, April 22, 1912. Under this contract, four of his works were published: Variations on an Original Theme (1918); Lyric Overture, op. 5 (1921); 3 Little Piano Pieces, op. 6 (1921); and Piano Quintet, op. 2 (1929).[27]

It may be a curious paradox that the rebellion against work removed the possibility of Szell's prodigy appearances from becoming excessive. During that time of enforced idleness, his emotional development could catch up with his musical one. After the period of contrary behavior, Szell was able to continue studying and developing. Yet the calling for which he seemed to be so extraordinarily gifted—that of composition—was the true casualty of his prodigy crisis. In his twenties Szell chose to curtail his career as a composer. When, at the suggestion of their teacher Richard Robert, Rudolf Serkin played one of Szell's piano pieces as a surprise for his twentieth birthday, Szell angrily said, "Serkin, how can you waste your time learning that trash!"[28]

As Szell's interest in the orchestra itself grew stronger, his desire for composing and performing as a pianist diminished. Early on as a composer, Szell had indicated a strong affinity for the orchestra: in improvisations at the piano, he named the instruments of the orchestra as he played. Playing orchestral scores at the piano became a lifelong hobby, as well as a study tool. Perhaps wisely, Szell recognized that he would not fulfill the promise of his early compositional talent and, as he would later reflect, "gave up composing very soon. . . . I wasn't good enough by my own standards," he said, "but I still believe it's advantageous—almost indispensable, in fact—for an interpreter to have tried his hand at composing. At least he will have a feel for what the musical universe looks like from the composer's vantage point."[29] Szell, however, had more than "tried his hand at composing"; he ended a fifteen-year composing career at age twenty-three. The "new Mozart" had his compositions performed frequently by the leading musicians of the day. This is a far cry from those who turn out competent but meaningless compositions—*Kapellmeister Musik* (conductor's music), as the Germans call it.

Sixty years later, in a BBC interview, Szell vividly recalled one of his early works, the overture that was played in London on his first tour in 1908: "During the development section, which was not a real development section but a sort of a free fantasia, there was a very passionate recitative melody by the clarinet over a tremolo of strings [Szell played the theme on the piano], which probably was influenced by a very similar place [in] the first movement of the F-minor piano concerto by Chopin . . . of course it's very difficult to say whether *I* wrote it; I rewrote it, I suppose. But after all, all composers started under some influence."[30]

Although it is not unusual for young composers to use models—and Szell chose excellent ones—reviewers of these early works recognized that in his pieces, Szell displayed a distinctive voice.[31] Variations on an Original Theme, written when Szell was seventeen, earned considerable popularity. It was first performed by the Vienna Philharmonic, conducted by Ferdinand Löwe. Richard Strauss conducted its Berlin premiere with the Royal Opera Orchestra, and Nikisch, Weingartner, and Furtwängler, among others, performed it. Szell himself conducted it in his debut season in St. Louis in February 1930 and in two concerts with the Residence Orchestra of The Hague in March 1938.

Szell became less and less tolerant of his own compositions and, whenever possible, suppressed their performances. It seemed not to matter to him that several of his compositions had been highly successful. His orchestration of Smetana's first string quartet was a great success in his debut season with the NBC Symphony in 1941 and when he first appeared as guest conductor with the Cleveland Orchestra in 1944.

He later rejected all his compositions, speaking deprecatingly about them. When Louis Lane, associate conductor of the Cleveland Orchestra, proposed performing Szell's *Lyric Overture* with the orchestra in the 1960s, Szell sharply rebuffed him. Although his Piano Quintet in E Major is clearly eclectic, with overtones of such first-rate influences as Brahms, Dvořák, and Schumann, it is a fully formed work of mature craftsmanship, demonstrating a well-developed concept of structure and adept handling of the musical materials. Lane eventually performed and recorded the *Lyric Overture* in Cleveland in 1992 with the orchestra of the Cleveland Institute of Music.[32]

From Composer to Conductor

Conducting became an inevitability. Szell claimed he was simply following the precepts of his parents and teachers to become "an all-round musician": "I kept on taking engagements as a pianist and I kept on writing music. But I was always so interested in the orchestra that probably very soon afterwards, I would say around the age of twelve or thirteen, it was pretty clear that eventually I would become a conductor."[33] His practice sessions were usually no more than four hours a day. He began to familiarize himself with the whole symphonic literature by playing it on the piano. In the summer of 1913 an opportunity presented itself that would influence the direction of his life. He was vacationing with his parents in Bad Kissingen, where the Vienna Symphony gave regular evening concerts. As might be expected, the young Szell was always "hanging around the bandroom pestering the players." It happened that, one morning, when the regular conductor, Martin Spörr, was indisposed, Szell was invited to conduct the evening concert, a program of seven pieces, including the overture to Peter Cornelius's *The Barber of Baghdad,* a Strauss waltz, and the overture to Rossini's *William Tell.* Apparently the sixteen-year-old Szell came through "with flying colors, and that settled it: he was going to be a conductor."[34]

Hans Gal confirmed Szell's innate conducting talent around this time: "His father had hired an orchestra for a rehearsal in order to give George a chance of hearing his music. He was sixteen, a tall, rather hefty boy, and it was his first opportunity to handle a baton. His self-confidence was as amazing as the exact control of his hands and his ears. It was obvious, he was a born conductor."[35]

A concert with the Blüthner Orchestra at the Royal Academy of Music in Berlin then displayed Szell as pianist, composer, and now, conductor. He was piano soloist in the "Emperor" Concerto and conducted *Till Eulenspiegel*, as well as some of his own compositions. Szell's relatively protected period of musical training was essentially over, and the multitalented young musician needed to establish a career path. A second brochure published around 1914 seems aimed at securing professional opportunities that might lead to a permanent conducting position.[36] Organized into three sections, it presented Szell as pianist, composer, and conductor and included two photographs: Szell, pencil poised, seated at a desk stacked with scores, and Szell conducting the Blüthner Orchestra. The brochure quotes highlights from reviews of each of Szell's musical activities.

Longer and more elaborate than the first brochure, of 1909, the 1914 version notes that "Georg Széll is no longer a novice in the world of music despite his youth . . . he has risen to this artistic height in an uncannily short span of time. . . . The recognition he has received from the public and press as a consequence of his threefold artistic attributes indicates that he has garnered an exceptional place in contemporary musical life and assures a future of the greatest expectations."

Szell's Mentor, Richard Strauss

The path to a conducting career in central Europe, then, went through the opera house. A large pool of pianist-coaches *(repetiteurs)* assisted singers in learning their roles, substituted for the orchestra in the tedious, stop-and-start staging rehearsals, and accompanied chorus rehearsals. Those who had the gift for conducting eventually rose through the ranks to assistant and then to full-fledged conductor. From 1915 to 1917 Szell began to climb that musical ladder in a top institution: the Berlin State Opera. Its director and chief conductor was the renowned Richard Strauss. Near the end of his life, Szell told of how that opportunity came about: "I met Strauss after I had joined the Berlin State Opera, then Royal Opera, as repetiteur. He didn't actually engage me. The man who engaged me was his second-in-command, Leo Blech, a very versatile and very knowledgeable, eminently practical conductor whose most economic rehearsing technique I have admired and adopted. He really did his homework beautifully. When I actually was already in service at the opera, Strauss met me and sort of took the protectorate away from Leo Blech . . . and he apparently found pleasure in using me and my talent."[37]

Strauss, as a young composer, had gained international prominence in the 1880s and '90s with his brilliant tone poems and, later, operas. Strauss was also a truly great conductor. At the time Szell met him, in 1915, Strauss was approaching fifty, had already composed *Salome*, *Elektra*, *Der Rosenkavalier*, and *Ariadne auf Naxos*, and was working on *Die Frau ohne Schatten*. Szell's brilliant transcription of *Till Eulenspiegel*, which he played in many of his piano recitals, ingratiated him with the composer. In it Szell made a striking effect. At a climactic moment, the score called for a ratchet to add to the din of the full orchestra. Szell wore a pair of heavy gold cufflinks. To simulate the noise of the ratchet, Szell scraped a cufflink over the black keys of the piano. Unknown to Szell, Strauss heard one of Szell's performances of his *Till* transcription. When Szell performed the ratchet passage, Strauss laughed out loud and was then and there taken with Szell.[38]

Szell remembered the eight pages of house regulations that accompanied the contract for his services as *repetiteur*, which "will not be paid." Years later, Szell remarked that he considered the arrangement "perfectly proper," because "my value to the organization was smaller than the organization's value to me." During his two years in Berlin, he coached singers, played piano and celesta in the orchestra, conducted backstage orchestras, and occasionally conducted rehearsals for Strauss. From Strauss he gained a "deep understanding of Mozart and Wagner, a feeling for drama and climax in conducting opera, and a precise, spare baton technique."[39]

Szell described Strauss's beat as "a very small clickety, precise beat with always another little upbeat inside his wrist,"[40] probably the origin of a similar beat that Szell himself occasionally used. Yet, from his very small gesture, Strauss could elicit pandemonium from an orchestra.[41] Szell was impressed by Strauss's strong sense of line and balance and clarity of rhythm as an objective approach to the score.

"There were two Strausses as a conductor," Szell observed, "the one who was interested and the one who was not interested. Very often you had the feeling that he was just serving time earning his fee and waiting for the card game that came after the performance." Yet, at other times, when he prepared a Mozart opera, or if he "was in the mood [with] a performance of *Walküre* or *Tristan*, it could really be most exciting. Curiously enough, he gave short shrift to his own works." Even so, one "hair-raising" performance of *Elektra* by Strauss in Vienna left a lasting impression on Szell.

Szell obviously made a strong impression on Strauss, and their relationship provided Szell with the opportunity to be one of the earliest—though uncredited—recorded conductors and the first to conduct *Don Juan* on record. Szell recalled that in the fall of 1916,

> [There] was a session of his *Don Juan* scheduled . . . very early in the morning, a terrible, unpleasant November morning in Berlin, and Strauss had instructed me to go there and rehearse the orchestra so he [could] sleep an hour longer and then take over. . . . At that time pieces were split up into four-minute [segments],—and *Don Juan* was a sixteen-minute piece, therefore [in] four parts.

> I rehearsed the first part and then the second part . . . incidentally . . . from memory . . . and everybody was quite pleased. . . . Some time had lapsed and the producer got nervous . . . and said, "Dr. Strauss isn't here yet, you have to conduct the first take." So I conducted the first four minutes, no Strauss visible. Then I was forced to conduct the second four minutes. And after having finished those, I turned around and saw Strauss, who had just arrived, in his big fur coat grinning all over his face and saying something which I might translate into, "Well, in this case one can cheerfully bite the dust if one sees such a young generation coming along," and directed that these two first parts were plenty good enough to go out under his name, he didn't care to repeat them. So the very first record of *Don Juan* if it is still available somewhere, which was made in I think '16, it must have been November '16, were conducted by me, the first two sides, under his name.[42]

On another occasion, Szell reportedly conducted a rehearsal of Strauss's *Ariadne auf Naxos* so ably that the orchestra sent a delegation to the intendant, Count Hülsen-Haeseler, asking him to make Szell a full conductor and to dismiss one of the regulars, whom the orchestra members did not like.[43] Although Hülsen-Haeseler was ready to agree, Strauss evidently had other plans for his young assistant. In mid-season 1917, it was announced that Otto Klemperer would leave Strasbourg for the Cologne Opera. Klemperer made a trip to Zurich to hear Strauss conduct *Ariadne auf Naxos* that he was preparing for performances in Strasbourg. He was impressed with Szell, who played the important piano part in *Ariadne*. Szell "was already regarded as a possible candidate for the vacancy in Strasbourg."[44] He was invited to conduct guest performances of *Carmen* and *Ariadne* in Strasbourg, and was offered the job. Strasbourg did not accept Szell's age without some difficulty, and questioned Strauss after receiving his recommendation. Strauss replied by telegraph: "*Mit Szell zieht man das grosse Los*" (With Szell you win the jackpot).[45] Szell was twenty, but it was thought more politic to announce his age as twenty-two.

Szell also welcomed a move to Strasbourg for other reasons. As Szell later told Louis Lane, on tour over a shared sandwich on a train, "You should have been with me in 1916 in Berlin. Already toward the summer of 1916 food was becoming scarce and you didn't know when you would get something to eat." A violinist friend received an invitation to play a recital in Breslau, Poland, and asked Szell to accompany him. Szell was reluctant at first, until the violinist explained that Breslau was the center of the meat-packing industry and that food was abundant there. They played three Beethoven violin and piano sonatas and spent their paltry fee entirely on food. Among other things, Szell took two hams home with him.[46] Presumably, food was also more abundant in Strasbourg than in Berlin.

Szell's tenure in Strasbourg—his first independent post—was cut short when France reclaimed Alsace after World War I. The opera was closed and Szell left.

Intrigue at the Vienna Opera

During the years 1918–19, Strauss anticipated taking over the Vienna Opera and wanted Szell as his assistant there. He energetically tried to overcome strong resistance against Szell, grounded in characteristic and historic Viennese intrigue, and fascinatingly documented in the correspondence between Strauss and the conductor Franz Schalk, at the Vienna Opera.[47]

Strauss's appointment was a delicate matter and Schalk's agenda clearly did not include adding Szell, with whatever problems, real or fictitious, that he posed. After Strasbourg, Szell freelanced as conductor and pianist and was, judging from Strauss's and Schalk's correspondence, as eager to be bottom man in Vienna as Strauss was to have him. Although Schalk claimed no personal objections, he nevertheless expressed one reservation after another about Szell—his obvious youth and the powerful critic Julius K. Korngold's opposition both to Strauss and to Szell (as a prodigy composer, he had been a rival to Korngold's son, Erich Wolfgang).

In late 1918, Strauss's own position vis-à-vis the Vienna Opera was far from secure. Vienna had a reputation for cruelty and intolerance toward its greatest talents. The opera had become neglected during the war and needed new blood to restore its glories. Although famous and viewed as the right man, Strauss faced resistance from factions: met with Strauss's announced plan to make a clean sweep, they feared losing their jobs. Coached by Schalk, Strauss tactically stayed away from Vienna until his contract was ratified. Eventually, in 1919, he assumed the post, which he held for five years.

Early in December 1918, Strauss wrote to Schalk of his preference for Szell, whom he presented as talented, while malleable: "In my view we need a young, very talented man such as Szell who will work his way into things completely to our taste and who, without too strong personal aspirations, is suited to prepare the operas which I conduct and to take them over in my way when I am away."[48] Responding promptly, Schalk wrote to Strauss: "I fear that [Szell] would be accepted by the orchestra with difficulty because of his extreme youth." Then, as if to assure Strauss of his loyalty, Schalk concluded, "I never cease to rejoice over your [future] presence in Vienna. . . . Art and Knowledge must make good here what Business and Politics have corrupted."[49] Three days later, Strauss ceded, "For the time being, I relinquish Szell under the weight of your objections," to which Schalk replied, "for the present we will put Szell into cold storage. He is young enough for that."[50] On Christmas day, Szell paid a call on Schalk at his home.

Apparently concerned that his position on Szell may have been too dismissive, later that day, Schalk sent Strauss a telegram marked "*Most Confidential!*" (*Vertraulichst!*), softening his stand:

> I know Szell, if not as intimately as you do, through collaboration, but well enough to be, by all means, *for* him. He is an excellent, thoroughly lively, indeed brilliant musician, as a human being reliable and of amazing earnestness for his youth. From this side, therefore, no reasonable objection is to be raised against him. This case is, however, not like any other. . . . There are . . . serious misgivings of a political nature that I, unfortunately, can't explain in writing. And it could easily happen that by engaging Szell, we might bring difficulties down on our heads perhaps not in any reasonable proportion to the profit he would bring us. I propose to you therefore that for the present we leave this thing undecided until the proverbial psychological moment arrives.

In the telegram, Schalk stresses the need for secrecy lest the spies in the opera use Szell's possible appointment against Strauss's engagement: "Just now Szell was with me. We talked for an hour.—I completely agree with you; he is a bright, lively fellow and is full of music.—The most important thing now is absolute secrecy. Not a sound will come from me about it.—I have pretty much halted spying in the Opera; but in Szell's case I won't even have a telegram sent from there."[51]

Strauss finally came to a decision:

> Szell was with me yesterday and again so pleased me that I, assuming your assent, have firmly decided, to push him through in Vienna . . . against the Orchestra (whose approval I expect as with the experience with the Berlin Orchestra, which Szell took by assault in two rehearsals), and in spite of his youth. I think: we wish to let ourselves be led . . . by artistic considerations, and they are—in my opinion—all for Szell. Besides the lad is much more mature than one would suppose for his age: intelligent, prudent, and tactful. I am completely sure of him! I have sent him to you; please talk with him. I am strongly convinced that he will also win you over.

Strauss had cautioned Szell against talking to anyone except Schalk about his prospective appointment until Strauss's own contract had been confirmed by Parliament. While holding his cards close to his chest—his letter to Schalk is marked up and down the left margin, "Please don't leave my letter lying around, the spies in the Court Opera overlook no indiscretion"—Strauss revealed his plan to Schalk. He would engage Szell without an audition once his own position was firmly established. He would introduce him in August, when he could help Strauss prepare *Lohengrin* and *Così fan tutte*, and assist Schalk with *Die Frau ohne Schatten*. As if to nail down his point, the next day, in the context of a long letter, Strauss wrote to Schalk: "*Don't* reengage Reichwein, but instead *Szell and again Szell*."[52]

Strauss had drawn his conclusions about what Schalk could not put into writing and suggested the then-current standard solution: "Sz. must immediately get himself baptized!"[53] The issue was in the open. Strauss did not know that Szell's family had converted years ago. Schalk, however, denied that was the problem: "Sz is a political issue—it is absolutely not the question of religion that tips the scale there. Please believe me, because I know the local conditions.—Once it is possible to foretell who rules here, then indeed all the difficulties that appear insurmountable today might disappear."[54] If not religion, what was the "political issue"? Strauss never pinned Schalk down on this in writing but evidently did not fully accept Schalk's disclaimer about religion.

Strauss's last allusion to the matter comes more than a year after he first suggested Szell to Schalk. It was again New Year's Eve: "But cannot one let oneself be baptized any more in Vienna? With Mahler it almost worked! Yes, but—?" Strauss was concerned about Germany's imminent bankruptcy and Austria's being rescued by the United States! He included two musical examples from Rossini's *The Barber of Seville*—the theme of the allegro of the trio "Zitti, zitti, piano, piano," (Quiet, quiet, that we escape the danger) and a short motive from the quintet "Buona sera" (Good night, everybody), wishing Schalk and his wife "a right good New Year without a coal shortage."[55]

The five years that Strauss led the Vienna Opera (1919–24) saw great musical achievements. The seed of the conflict that grew between Strauss and Schalk can be detected in their correspondence. A codirectorship is an unwieldy beast. Schalk, who was only a year older than Strauss, may have been jealous of his world-famous colleague. He had been there first and was entrenched with his power. Szell would have been Strauss's man, a possible reason for Schalk's resistance. When the friction between Strauss and Schalk grew to the point that it became clear that one or the other must go, Strauss resigned and Schalk's contract was renewed. Vienna held true to form.[56]

The year from December 1918 to December 1919 must have been difficult for Szell, shuttling back and forth between Strauss and Schalk, with the secrecy, the waiting, and eventual disappointment. But he soon would be making his way successfully elsewhere and his association with Strauss would always stand him in good stead.

Climbing the Opera House Ladder

After leaving Strasbourg, Szell continued to develop his career in the German-speaking opera world along the time-honored pattern, advancing during 1919–29 in quick succession from subordinate to higher posts in smaller opera houses. Szell did, however, encounter one other setback: he again sought a post he did not win.

From 1919 to 1920 he was staff conductor and coach at the Deutsches Theater in Prague. In February 1920, as an audition for a staff position in the city of his birth, Szell conducted two performances of *Carmen* and one of *Tannhäuser*. He also conducted his Variations on an Original Theme in a concert by the Budapest Philharmonic, of which the rest of the concert was conducted by Ernst von Dohnányi. In March he and Dohnányi gave a two-piano and four-hand piano recital. Yet the Budapest Opera filled the position by persuading an older former conductor, István Kerner, to return.

Szell's being given two orchestra rehearsals for each opera provides evidence that he was held in high esteem; it was most unusual, according to a musical eyewitness, Marcel Dick, a member of the first violin section. More than fifty years later, Dick remembered Szell's rehearsals and the results he got from them:

> [He] transformed that orchestra, entirely different. It was absolutely unbelievable in such a short time how he got what he wanted and what he wanted was something extraordinary. [Asked, how?] By telling how you should play. To the strings that you play at the frog, play downbow here, change the bow here but not there, the winds should attack that way, the horn I suggest that other fingering of the valves. Things like that. The two performances were extraordinary and so was the orchestra concert that he gave in connection with that guest appearance. He didn't get the position, for which he never forgave Hungary and Hungarians. He turned his back on them. He never had a good word about Hungary and Hungarians.[57]

Szell spoke fluent Hungarian, according to Dick, but after he came to America and met a Hungarian, he almost always refused to speak the language.

Szell went on with his career elsewhere, holding posts at the Hessisches Landestheater Darmstadt (1921) and the Municipal Opera in Düsseldorf (1922–24). With each move, he acquired greater responsibilities for productions, added to his repertoire, and honed his craft and conducting technique.[58]

In 1920, Szell married the Viennese pianist Olga Band, a former fellow student of Richard Robert's. They gave duo-piano concerts and spent many leisure hours together reading through scores. Their marriage lasted a stormy six years, near the end of which they performed a concert without speaking to each other, communicating in rehearsal through a mutual friend.[59] Perhaps Szell's contact with attractive female singers contributed to the eventual dissolution of his marriage. As likely, however, their divorce was precipitated by a romantic triangle that included him, his wife, and the couple's mutual friend, the violinist Josef Wolfsthal, concertmaster at the State Opera and a faculty member at the Hochschule. Apparently, Wolfsthal was secretly in love with Olga.

All was revealed when Olga visited her parents in Vienna. Szell—with Wolfsthal at his side—received a cable intending to report that she had been "spoken to" (*gesprochen*). But through a misunderstanding by a telegraph agent, it read that she had died (*gestorben*). In his mistaken grief, Wolfsthal confessed his true feelings for his friend's wife. Olga's actual state of health was eventually made known, but the cat was out of the bag.[60]

In 1924, nearly ten years after beginning his career in Berlin with Strauss, Szell returned there to begin what would become a five-year tenure at the State Opera as "first conductor," which, although a respectable position, is actually second in command. He served under the general music director, Erich Kleiber, who at thirty-four was seven years Szell's senior.

The pace of life and work in Berlin was intense. Called there suddenly in mid-season, Szell conducted Wagner's *Die Meistersinger von Nürnberg* and the complete *Der Ring des Nibelungen* in his first week in Berlin, without an orchestra rehearsal. Although Kleiber took such plums as the premiere of Berg's *Wozzeck* for himself, Szell received the prestigious assignment of the first Berlin performance of Erich Wolfgang Korngold's *Die tote Stadt*. Szell still had formidable competition in the city, including Wilhelm Furtwängler, conductor of the Philharmonic Orchestra, Bruno Walter at the City Opera, Klemperer at the Kroll Opera, and Leo Blech at the State Opera. Hans Gal witnessed brilliant Szell performances of *Der Barbier von Bagdad*, by Peter Cornelius, and Franz Schreker's *Der ferne Klang*, but opined: "There is no doubt that he did not move into the front rank and that he did not rise to achievements that would have placed him comfortably alongside his prominent colleagues."[61]

On April 1, 1927, Szell joined the composition and theory faculty of Berlin's Staatliche Akademie Hochschule für Musik, one of Germany's leading conservatories. Directed by Franz Schreker, with assistant director Georg Schünemann, the faculty included Artur Schnabel, Emil Nikolaus Freiherr von Reznicek, and Curt Sachs.[62] In 1927 Szell took an apartment at Schillerstrasse 3, a quiet residential street near the Hochschule. Schnabel also lived in that area. In 1928 Szell moved to Kaiserdamm 11, a broad boulevard a little farther away. At the Hochschule, Szell taught instrumentation and *Partiturspiel* (score playing), at which he was especially brilliant, performing full orchestral and operatic scores on the piano at sight.

An eyewitness to Szell's pianistic brilliance attended a private house concert in Berlin at the "palatial home" of the banker Robert von Mendelssohn, "surrounded by glorious paintings by van Dyck, Velásquez, Goya, Breughel, as well as countless impressionistic masterpieces, performing for piano solo his own transcription of R. Strauss *Till Eulenspiegel* in a glittering, plastic, brilliant and full of charm way."[63]

As early as 1922, in Düsseldorf and continuing in Berlin, Szell was beset by echoes of his adolescent emotional problems. There Szell at times shirked his rehearsals and would sit for half a day at a time "in the shop of one of his friends, the bookseller Worm, poring over books of all kinds." Szell's talent, which covered up for his indolence, "proved to be a treacherous gift." His marriage, which undoubtedly added to his stress, had by then broken down and ended in 1926. "In the end (1928)," Gal wrote, "he escaped into a severe illness: a violent attack of sciatica invalided him for half a year and put an end to his activities in Berlin." Szell was absent from the Berlin Opera from July 5, 1928 until March 19, 1929.

He retreated to his parents' home in Vienna, barely speaking of Berlin, and "seemed to be more interested in literature or philosophy than music." But, through one means or another—"maybe by his doctors, maybe by his strong nature," or perhaps the inevitable process of maturation—he recovered, and in the spring of 1929 returned to Berlin.[64] There he conducted a busy season of twenty-five performances of seven operas, including *Boris Godunov, Der Rosenkavalier*, and *Salome*. In all, Szell conducted 371 performances of thirty-four operas at the Berlin Opera between January 20, 1924, and July 19, 1929.[65] He was also one of the four pianists in a performance of Stravinsky's cantata *Les noces* on June 17, 1929, conducted at the Staatsoper by Otto Klemperer.

In the fall of 1929 "he took up an appointment as first conductor of the German Theater in Prague, where he had served as second in command eight years before."[66] He followed Hans Wilhelm Steinberg, who had left for a similar post in Frankfurt.[67] As chief conductor, Szell had the responsibility of selecting his own first conductor, and after hearing Max Rudolf conduct a *Tannhaüser* in Darmstadt, Szell chose him. Szell charged Rudolf to freely criticize his performances, an indication of Szell's respect for Rudolf's knowledge and his own fierce desire for self-improvement. After one performance, Rudolf found Szell literally beating his head against a wall, raging against himself for what he considered some musical stupidity he had just perpetrated.

Organized along the lines of the provincial theaters in Germany, the Neues Deutsches Theater (New German Theater) in Prague had two houses. Designers modeled the larger one on the classical Italian opera house, with three rows of boxes gracefully curved around the main floor and a seating capacity of 1,130. The small hall hosted straight plays.

The orchestra, typical of the German provincial model of the time, was not large. There were ten first violins, three of whom were designated as concertmasters, seven second violins, five violas, five cellos, and four double basses. The regular staff also included three each of flutes, oboes, bassoons, trumpets, and percussionists, four clarinets, and four trombones, six French horns, a tuba, and a harp. A roster of thirty-five to forty singers and thirty to thirty-five actors, dancers, directors, ballet masters, prompters, administrators, and technical staff maintained a full schedule of opera, operetta, and play productions.[68]

In a typical year (1928–29), the combined performing schedule of opera, operetta, and theater from the beginning of September until the end of July listed 744 performances. The opera repertoire encompassed 129 performances of forty-five different works, including world premieres, first performances at the theater, new productions, and revivals. There were 168 performances of twenty-seven operettas and six Philharmonic Orchestra concerts.[69] Besides Szell and Rudolf, the conducting staff included George Schick, Kurt Adler, Walter Susskind, and Laszlo Halasz, all of whom would later become active in the United States.[70]

In addition to standard opera repertoire during Szell's tenure in Prague were some of the latest works, including Dohnányi's *The Tenor*, Hindemith's *Hin und Zurück*, Toch's *The Princess and the Pea*, and Brecht/Weill's *Mahagonny*.[71] Soloists in the Philharmonic concerts included Joseph Szigeti, Rudolf Serkin, Paul Hindemith (viola), and Paul Wittgenstein, the pianist who lost his right arm in World War I, playing Strauss's *Panathenäenzug*, which he commissioned. Through conducting the Philharmonic concerts, Szell found a practical means for developing his orchestra repertoire.[72]

Prague enchanted Szell, with its lively arts and artistic heritage—*Don Giovanni* had its premiere there—its wine cellars, beer *stube*, restaurants, and shops. Szell lived in a series of hotels in the city; an office and studio were provided at the theater. He practiced the French horn regularly in his studio.[73] It is not surprising that he never mastered the precarious instrument, and undoubtedly that is why he never claimed to have played it. Szell's encyclopedic knowledge of every orchestral instrument is well known; however, he felt that as a conductor, it was important for him to have hands-on experience with at least one orchestral instrument. Szell's choice of horn may have been influenced by his association with Strauss, whose father had been a superb horn player, and who wrote lovingly for the instrument.

2

The Conductor Spreads His Wings (1930–38)

In the spring of 1927, George Szell was on the staff of the Berlin State Opera and beginning his tenure as professor at the Hochschule für Musik. At the same time, an American orchestra, the St. Louis Symphony, was searching for a new conductor. By the time Szell became a leading candidate in that search, he had become musical head of the German Opera House in Prague.

The St. Louis Symphony was looking forward to celebrating its golden jubilee fiftieth anniversary season in 1929–30, but all was not well. The orchestra faced artistic and financial crises. It was in the throes of finding both a new conductor and a new manager. With the collapse of the stock market in 1929, the orchestra's Board of Control (as its governing body was then called) questioned whether to continue or to go out of business after the 1929–30 season.

In March 1927 the board voted not to renew the contract of the incumbent conductor, Rudolf Ganz, and he resigned. There was general agreement that the music critic for the *St. Louis Post-Dispatch*, Thomas B. Sherman, was justified in his negative opinion of Ganz's conducting. He described it as producing ragged ensemble and unblended sound, and he also pointed to Ganz's "drillmaster" interpretations, which lacked "subtle differentiation of dynamics and rhythm which give a soul to an orchestra." To clinch his argument, Sherman referred to a statement by Richard Strauss during his 1921 musical tour in America: "There is no such thing as a good or bad orchestra—there are only good or bad conductors."[1]

The board named William E. Walter manager on March 7, 1927.[2] To Walter fell the responsibility of finding a permanent conductor. Instead of accepting the recommendation of noted conductors or the decree of the omnipotent Arthur Judson, then the most powerful concert manager in America, Walter invited candidates to guest conduct in St. Louis. They came not for one or two weeks but for a minimum of four weeks. This provided the orchestra with a measure of stability and the opportunity for serious evaluation of each candidate. Walter had, in effect, carte blanche in the scouting and hiring of candidates. The board would eventually vote on which conductor to engage permanently.

It was a foregone conclusion that the new conductor would be European; the only remaining choice concerned which nationality. Thus Walter selected one conductor from each of several countries, omitting the United States as a matter of course.

A European in St. Louis (1930, 1931)

Two seasons and six guest conductors later, Szell came on the scene.[3] In the spring of 1929, with a Spanish, Italian, and British conductor already engaged for the next season, Walter traveled to Germany, where he observed more than two dozen conductors. Szell's *Figaro* and *Boris Godunov* at the Berlin State Opera convinced Walter that his search was at an end. He described Szell as "a musician in a very deep sense and a man of wide culture besides. For a young man—he is only thirty-two—he has a sound reputation. He should do well in America."[4]

Szell's programs sparked considerable interest. He gave numerous local premieres and both conducted and played the solo part in Mozart's A Major Piano Concerto, K. 488. Each program included a twentieth-century work: Szell's own youthful Variations on an Original Theme (1916); Ravel's *Le Tombeau de Couperin* (1917); Hindemith's Concerto for Orchestra; and the suite from Kodály's opera *Háry János* (1925); and Gershwin's *An American in Paris* (1928).

Young, with only opera positions under his belt, and trained in the German School, Szell showed a particularly wide range of repertoire. That his programs included the works of Beethoven, Brahms, Mendelssohn, Mozart, Wagner, and Weber is not surprising. More unusual then—and even generations later—was Szell's knowledge of French music. His bold self-confidence in tackling such an idiomatically American work as the Gershwin, however, was also remarkable, if not audacious.

Szell's Variations and his appearance as piano soloist were calculated to present him as a musician of depth and scope and an instrumentalist of concert caliber. From the start, his programs were devised to impress, with major works such as Tchaikovsky's Fifth Symphony and Beethoven's Seventh, and to keep St. Louis aware of his prestigious opera position, from the *Oberon* Overture to the *Meistersinger* Prelude.

Szell's St. Louis debut, on January 24, 1930, was, in general, favorably received by the public. Thomas B. Sherman, chief music critic of the *St. Louis Post-Dispatch,* commended Szell for including Hindemith's *Concerto for Orchestra,* which earned only a polite scattering of applause, even though Szell made an explanatory speech before the performance. Though Sherman found the *Oberon* "stiff and academic," the Tchaikovsky conveyed the "right emotional approach as well as scholarly understanding of the musical structure. . . . If first impressions count for anything," he concluded, Szell "is a forceful musical personality and during his stay here should make an important contribution to the city's musical experience."[5] On Szell's second program he performed the Mozart concerto with a reduced orchestra and an "apartment-sized grand piano," impressing Sherman greatly as "one of those rare occasions when an authentic Mozart was presented to a modern audience . . . [and was] managed in the spirit of chamber music."

In a subsequent review, Sherman stated, "Szell's performance at the piano was made such an inextricable part of the whole presentation that any discussion of his mastery of the piano has to be limited to his use of that instrument in an ensemble. A certain polished smartness and ease of execution were plainly in evidence, as well as a pearly legato that might be used as a model by several keyboard lions that I could name. But it was the playing of the ensemble, with each unit acutely aware of the other, which made the concerto so thoroughly delightful. Its prevailing characteristic was a starched and fluted elegance."[6]

Szell felt confident that he was winning the hearts of the St. Louis audience. In his second week, he wrote to his friend and colleague Max Rudolf in Prague, "My most unusual, gratifying success entails such a relentless social preoccupation that time permits nothing more than this short greeting to you and your wife. It is going brilliantly."[7] Szell's last concert, with Vladimir Horowitz as soloist in Brahms's B-flat Concerto, also included Gershwin's *An American in Paris,* which had premiered a little more than a year earlier by the New York Philharmonic under Walter Damrosch.

In preparation for a work as idiomatically American, Szell had listened to the work's vibrant first recording under Nathaniel Shilkret, house conductor for RCA Victor. His authentic reading of the score may account for Szell's "surprisingly sympathetic" interpretation, in which he "indulged the players in that idiomatic freedom of dynamics and rhythm which the music demanded," noted the critic.[8] Sherman, who had been critical of Horowitz's "badly mannered Chopin" and serious interpretive weaknesses in his earlier solo recital, wrote of his collaboration with Szell in the Brahms that the pianist's skill was "never put to better service" and that his beautiful tone had no "taint of exhibitionistic virtuosity about it." Horowitz undoubtedly was positively influenced by Szell's good taste and strong hand.

Sherman attended not only the first playing of a work but also the second and sometimes the third. More thoroughly, he could observe, for example, that although Szell's performances "had not been invariably of the best . . . [they] reached a high level often enough to justify optimistic predictions for his future." Or that Beethoven's Seventh Symphony was "the worst performance of his engagement," but that he had "corrected his original mistake within 24 hours, giving on the evening of the next day an effective and well-balanced performance in contrast to one that had been uncouth and hysterical." He further noted steady improvements in performances of Ravel's *Le Tombeau de Couperin* and Weber's *Oberon* Overture.

Sherman pinpointed Szell's capacity for "self-criticism," and such modification of his musical interpretation would characterize Szell's performances to the end of his life. He never clung to musical habits when he found evidence of the composer's wishes to the contrary.[9] Sherman said that "one technical fault" was "his tendency to allow ragged entrances." But he conceded that "crispness of ensemble is not an outstanding characteristic of European orchestras and Mr. Szell may be somewhat under the influence of the idea that other things are more important. . . . At the age of 32," Sherman pronounced, "Mr. Szell is undoubtedly one of the best of the young German conductors. . . . [He] combines a catholic outlook, one that comprehends the new and the old in one brotherhood, with a sound education, a broad general culture, an unflagging vitality and a musical conscience that is rare in these times."[10]

Sherman's greater tolerance of poor ensemble with Szell than with Rudolf Ganz owed perhaps to the critic's long exposure to Ganz's many other faults and Szell's overwhelming musicality and mastery of the scores. Szell undoubtedly respected Sherman's criticism, for they remained friends for life. Szell returned to Prague believing he was a strong candidate for St. Louis, and confident that he would be invited back the following season. Evidently the board was not ready to commit to Szell without further consideration, however, so a fourth season of guests was announced. Szell would conduct after the New Year and the Russian Emil Cooper would end the season.[11]

Four days after that announcement, Szell—his ego perhaps bruised—cabled the St. Louis management from Prague that he would not be returning.[12] It is not precisely known why Szell took this action. It may be because he had heard that St. Louis offered the post to Eugene Goossens, conductor of the Rochester Philharmonic, who had followed Szell as guest conductor. As Sherman put it at the end of the month, "This did not necessarily mean that other conductors who had performed here were not strong enough but that Mr. Goossens offered the best combination of youth, experience, energy, ability and temperament." But Goossens did not accept the offer; "certain contractual relations between Mr. Goossens and the Rochester orchestra intervened at the last moment. . . ." Sherman summed up Szell's candidacy to that point: "It is perfectly possible, of course, that Szell will develop into an extraordinary leader and it is certainly true that he gave one or two superb performances when he was here. But . . . he has not yet shown enough to make a permanent offer advisable."[13]

Whether Goossens's rejection of the offer was enough to soften Szell's decision or whether Walter had a hand in soothing his ruffled feathers, Szell did return to St. Louis. There he faced a changed lineup: Szell would end the season following Cooper's replacement, Vladimir Golschmann, called by Walter Damrosch "a natural born conductor, with a magnetic personality and a flair for the German classics as well as the French moderns."[14]

In February 1931, apparently still confident of his chances with St. Louis, Szell set sail for America. A photograph shows him on board the steamer *Adalbert Ballin.*[15] Nattily dressed in a wide-brimmed hat, fur-collared coat, gray-striped suit, and white spats, with his left hand casually in his pocket, his head is jauntily tilted, yet his expression is sober, suggesting serious contemplation.

The switch of order affected Szell's fate adversely. Aware of who he was up against, Golschmann had pulled out all the stops in his four weeks, directly challenging Szell. Golschmann programmed Beethoven's Seventh, not a Szell success, and ended with a Szell specialty: the Prelude to *Die Meistersinger.* He hit another mark with Strauss's *Tod und Verklärung.* In spite of Szell's connection to the composer, he had not played any Strauss in his first St. Louis season.

Beginning with Siloti's arrangement of Vivaldi's D-Minor Concerto Grosso and including *Deux Gymnopedies* by Satie (orchestrated by Debussy), Golschmann covered almost all the bases in his opener. According to Sherman, it was a successful debut: "The audience that greeted the young Parisian musician was larger and warmer than the usual Friday afternoon assemblage. . . . It is certainly true that his musicianship was sound beyond dispute."[16] Sherman also praised Golschmann's control of the orchestra and his sense of balance throughout. Audience enthusiasm for Golschmann's third program of Dvořák's "New World" Symphony and Ravel's *La valse* was "unrestrained," according to Sherman, scoring a "triumph."[17]

Golschmann's last program was less successful, but by this time, Sherman reported, "Golschmann's already faithful following, which was present in large numbers, applauded everything impartially and filed out of the auditorium breathing prayers for his safe return next year."[18] Three days after Golschmann's finale, the local newspaper carried news of William Walter's resignation and of the already settled engagement for the next season of his successor, Arthur J. Gaines.[19]

Szell found himself in an untenable position. If he was saving his strong suit for last, it was too late. His tasteful but not overwhelming opening concert, of Schumann's "Rhenish" Symphony, Stravinsky's *Pulcinella,* and Beethoven's *Leonore* Overture no. 2 followed Golschmann's powerhouse four. Sherman was not impressed with the Schumann or the Beethoven, nor, as he wrote, was the public, which was "polite but hardly demonstrative."[20] In spite of Szell's retouches, the critic was not convinced by the Schumann and found the Beethoven interesting only insofar as it showed how much he improved the next version, the immensely popular masterpiece, *Leonore* Overture no. 3. Szell might have fared better if his concerts had been in the middle of the season, as originally planned. Most likely, though, Golschmann's flair and sex appeal had been the deciding factors, no matter what Szell might have done.

John S. Edwards, a St. Louis native, later acknowledged as the dean of American orchestra managers, recalled the events after Szell's first season: "There was no doubt in anybody's mind that Szell was hands-down winner. It was arranged by [Arthur] Judson, since the Board had previously decided that [Szell] would be the new conductor. When he arrived for the following season, the appointment would be announced."

Edwards added that the symphony was planning to move to a newly constructed municipal auditorium that would seat 3,535, and that they had "to gear up to something very flashy to sell twice the number of seats. When Golschmann came, he seemed like the answer to every prayer." Edwards pointed out that Golschmann "was exceedingly good looking, and had a very romantic limp, which St. Louisans immediately attributed to World War I. . . . It turned out later not to be the case. He was injured in a motorcycle accident, just buzzing down the highway in southern France, and it wasn't set properly and therefore it created a permanent limp." Edwards believed that a deciding factor was the powerful Women's Committee, which "was absolutely crazy [about Golschmann] and they went to the Board and said, 'Now this is our candidate. With this gentleman, we will sell the house.'"[21]

Thirty years later, this remained a sore point for Szell. When he told Arthur Judson in 1960 that he wanted to leave his management, Judson traveled to Cleveland to try to change Szell's mind. They met for lunch. Szell, in supporting his reasons for this impending action, brought up St. Louis as a case where Judson did not serve him properly. In reply, Judson told Szell: "But George, St. Louis wasn't right for you—Golschmann was just what they deserved." Judson was unsuccessful in convincing Szell to stay with him. When Szell returned from lunch, he told Louis Lane, "I believe I have just relieved myself of an incubus."[22]

Golschmann's two-year appointment beginning the coming fall was publicly announced on March 22, during Szell's fourth concert week.[23] After his third pair of concerts, a week before the announcement, Szell sent a postcard to Rudolf, saying, "It's going dazzlingly for me—everything that could be desired without qualifications—in spite of which I'm looking forward to Europe and Prague."[24] It is not known exactly when Szell was told of St. Louis's decision.

Whether or not Szell wanted St. Louis, it was his first setback in the decade since not being appointed Strauss's assistant in Vienna. Aware that Golschmann had the job, Szell performed brilliantly. He showed his ire, however, by making the orchestra's life "sheer hell," according to Edwards. Sherman reported that the final concert, on March 28, 1931, was "the highlight of Szell's engagement in Saint Louis and one of the best performances of the year. If tonight's repetition is as successful as it should be, the Viennese conductor will return to his permanent post in Prague trailing visible clouds of glory."[25]

As a personal benefit of Szell's St. Louis sojourns, he became acquainted with Irma von Starkloff Rombauer, author-to-be of *The Joy of Cooking*, a much-loved and authoritative cookbook. Mrs. Rombauer had been active with the St. Louis Symphony for years, and became president of its Women's Committee in 1929. The brilliant young conductor would have been attractive to the music-loving matron. At the time they met, Rombauer was fifty-four and Szell thirty-three. Her vivacious personality, her love for music, and her interest in cooking would have made her attractive to Szell. Rombauer's German heritage and ability to speak the language provided another bond between them.

Rombauer's husband, Edgar, had been in poor physical and mental health for a long time. To escape the severe St. Louis winter, they traveled to South Carolina in December 1929, returning on January 23, 1930, just a day before Szell's debut. On February 3, unexpectedly, Edgar Rombauer succumbed to his recurring depression and committed suicide.

Years later, visiting Szell at home in Cleveland, Louis Lane thought it odd to see a copy of *The Joy of Cooking* in Szell's music library, and asked Szell about it. Szell answered, "It was written by an old friend of mine. She was living in St. Louis when I went there to conduct and we became very friendly. That was one of the reasons I went back the second year. You know how it is when people live far apart. Nothing came of it but I'm still very fond of her." Szell told Lane, "Some of the recipes she got from me."[26] In 1936, five years after Szell left St. Louis for the last time, Irma Rombauer toured Europe, and visited Prague. Szell was still working at the opera.

Remembering Szell in St. Louis

Forty years later, a former St. Louis Symphony first horn player, Edward Murphy, remembered Szell:

> Szell . . . was such an incredible man. We started with *Oberon* and the first thing he said was, "Horn, a little broader." I knew what he wanted right away. We became very good friends. He invited me to come to Prague. I didn't expect—you know people say, "Come and I'll show you around"—he didn't only show me around, we wandered all over Prague for four weeks together. I went to every rehearsal with him in the morning [and] I went every night. He was very frank. When he thought the performance at his German Opera would be dull, he would say, don't go tonight but go to the *Barber of Seville* at the other theater, the one in which *Don Giovanni* was first performed.

Murphy saw a very different side of Szell than did most orchestra players: "Szell . . . had a kind of sweetness about him; as much as he could be kind of a terror, he really wasn't." There had been some personnel changes in the orchestra between Szell's engagements, which, Murphy recalled, Szell regretted. "He had taken a slight fancy to the first oboe player, [Ermete] Simonazzi, who was an old Italian, style a little slow. I think Szell felt badly that Sim had made a change; he didn't see his old friends, which I thought was very nice."[27]

If Golschmann's charismatic performances had won the St. Louis audiences, Szell's last performance left a good memory. But Golschmann's immense Gallic charm overshadowed Szell's more restrained public persona. Golschmann's tenure with St. Louis, from 1931 to 1958, was a long and respectable one. Szell returned to Prague and to engagements in Europe, Great Britain, and Australia.

William Walter did not forget Szell. When, in 1932, he learned that Nikolai Sokoloff was going to leave the Cleveland Orchestra the following year, he recommended Szell to a friend with connections to the orchestra. "He is one of the finest musicians it has been my fortune to know," Walter wrote. "His knowledge of the literature of music is simply appalling. There seems to be nothing he cannot play from memory, from the latest jazz to the latest Berg and Hindemith." In his scouting missions, Walter had seen and heard many conductors, yet he unreservedly expressed his opinion that Szell was "destined to become one of the really great conductors of our time. Certainly he was head and shoulders above all the others I heard [in Europe], not excluding Kleiber, Kraus, Klemperer or Blech." "I should like to see him in America where I think he would become a power for the good of the art," he wrote.[28]

Walter's friend passed his letter on to Adella Prentiss Hughes, one of the Cleveland Orchestra's founders and then its manager. In a letter to Walter, Hughes mentioned that politics played a part in Golschmann's appointment. Walter denied it absolutely: "He is a type which makes instant appeal to the American public, especially the feminine part of it. He does some things extraordinarily well and lots of things not so well. He has a very decided charm of personality and, what is more, a most attractive and clever young wife." With obvious regret, he added, "Yet he did not stir the outburst of enthusiasm which followed Szell's Fourth Brahms at the latter's concluding concert. It was then that the powers-that-be were filled with misgivings that a contract had been given to Golschmann."[29] Walter's effort did not succeed then, but World War II would bring Szell permanently to the United States, and he and Golschmann would once again cross swords in competition—for the Cleveland Orchestra.

Holland, England, and Scotland (1931–37)

In April 1931, Szell returned to Prague, where the opera season continued until the end of July. His immediate future was clear—he would not go to America but would remain there and continue to build his career in Europe. The two St. Louis engagements had taken large chunks of time from Szell's first two seasons as musical director at Prague's German Opera House, two months for the first trip and even longer for the second.

At thirty-four, Szell was well known in Vienna and Berlin and occupied a top musical position in a well-known opera house. In Prague he was responsible for conducting the Philharmonic concerts, few in number but prestigious. Szell established his reputation, fostered contacts with soloists, and began recording, including concertos and arias with the great soloists of the day.

In 1933, twenty-five years after appearing in London in 1908 as an eleven-year-old prodigy composer/pianist, Szell was reintroduced to London audiences as a mature conductor. Mrs. Samuel Courtauld, a patron of the Covent Garden Opera, and Malcolm Sargent, the conductor, established the Courtauld-Sargent concert series, subsidized concerts that gave office workers of limited means the opportunity to attend orchestral performances of serious music. Artur Schnabel recommended that Szell be invited to conduct a concert. Its success led to invitations from other British orchestras—in London, Liverpool, and the Hallé in Manchester. Concerts with the Scottish Orchestra in Glasgow in 1936 led to Szell's becoming its permanent conductor the following season.

In Holland he made his debut with the Residence Orchestra in The Hague on Christmas Day in 1933 and with the Concertgebouw Orchestra of Amsterdam on February 6, 1936. Szell's Hague debut marked his first collaboration with Arthur Rubinstein, then forty-seven years old, in an all-Beethoven program. Rubinstein's recollection, fifty years later, of his first collaboration with Szell, on the Beethoven Piano Concerto no. 4, is not an entirely happy one. Szell felt no qualms about giving lessons to a world-renowned artist thirteen years his senior: "I was delighted to meet him and to play with him," Rubinstein wrote, "remembering how he impressed me at the Prague Opera." Before the rehearsal, Szell already appeared to Rubinstein as more a Germanic type, "rather than a Czech with a Hungarian name." The concerto begins with a quiet, sublimely beautiful five-bar introduction by the solo piano instead of the usual orchestral tutti. When Rubinstein finished this brief opening, Szell stopped him "and said loudly, Artur Schnabel took it slower." Rubinstein was not pleased. During the break, Szell began to instruct Rubinstein on how to play the concerto the way Schnabel had played it. Rubinstein told him "very angrily, 'Tell your Artur that this Artur feels it in a different way,'" and stopped speaking to Szell. Rubinstein conceded that Szell conducted the concerto well at the concert, but he left the hall at intermission. The next day, Misia Sert, a friend of Rubinstein's heard the concert and, after the concerto, "insisted on our staying with her for the *Eroica* and here came a revelation. I had never heard the symphony played as beautifully before or since that performance; the Funeral March made me cry."[30]

The power of Szell's Beethoven interpretation was also evident to the Hague orchestra authorities. Conductors have long been judged by their interpretation of the classics—Haydn, Mozart, and especially Beethoven. Szell's identification with and masterly performance of Beethoven's music struck a responsive chord in Holland and deeply rooted his involvement with music there.[31]

In the mid-1930s, Szell appeared as guest with orchestras throughout Europe and Soviet Russia. He conducted the Vienna Symphony Orchestra in an extended Italian tour in 1935, the Vienna Philharmonic, the Berlin Philharmonic, the Frankfurt Museum Orchestra, the Copenhagen Radio Orchestra, the Stockholm Konsertforenigen, and the Leningrad Philharmonic. With the last, he had a brush with authorities over his programming of the Bruckner Ninth Symphony, because their musicological staff said that Bruckner had intended to dedicate it to God, if he was allowed to finish it. Szell pointed out that Bruckner had never finished the symphony, and that the printed score included no dedication whatever. Eventually the matter was referred to the musical authorities in Moscow, perhaps even to Stalin himself, who agreed with Szell, and the performances were allowed.[32]

The World in Turmoil

With Hitler's election as German chancellor in 1933, Europe was heading toward disaster. By the mid-1930s, Szell saw war as inevitable, and decided to leave Prague.[33] The 1936–37 Prague season was his last. Szell had become disenchanted with aspects of opera routine. After twenty years of it, he began to feel "tired of telling singer after singer the same things,"[34] and by 1937 he was fortunate to be able to concentrate his musical activities in Great Britain and the Netherlands. In Prague, Szell's acquaintance with an attractive, intelligent, and strong-willed young woman, Helene Schultz Teltsch, had developed into a serious relationship. She was married and had two young sons. Szell's leaving Prague considerably eased a complicated situation while they concluded the necessary civil and religious requirements for their marriage.

A series of "musical-chair" moves in 1936 presented an opportunity for Szell. Arturo Toscanini resigned from the New York Philharmonic; John Barbirolli, conductor of the Scottish Orchestra since 1933, was called to New York; and officials in Scotland asked Szell to take Barbirolli's place. He arrived in Glasgow in early November. From its beginning, the Scottish Orchestra and its audiences had been accustomed to distinguished guest conductors, who, during the orchestra's early years, included Arthur Sullivan and Hans von Bülow, and later, Edouard Colonne, Fritz Steinbach, Henry Wood, Richard Strauss, Emil Mlynarski, Vaclav Talich, Serge Koussevitzky, Adrian Boult, Felix Weingartner, Vladimir Golschmann, Issay Dobrowen, Constant Lambert, Albert Coates, and Nikolay Malko.

The Scottish Orchestra gave one performance of two different subscription programs per week during its fourteen-week season, from November through February: one series on Saturdays, the other on Tuesdays. The programs were of generous length and difficulty, which made for two brief but strenuous rehearsal periods each week. In addition, there were repeats of the programs in Edinburgh and other Scottish cities, as well as a large number of children's concerts. The season was short, but sustaining the effort that the schedule required must have been exhausting for all concerned. The orchestra traditionally depended on the energy and enthusiasm of younger players not yet established with the larger London orchestras.

Szell conducted nineteen of the subscription concerts. The repertoire was rich, varied, and rigorous. He introduced Mahler's Fourth and Bizet's Symphony to Scotland. New works for the orchestra included Smetana's tone poem *Výšehrad*, Dohnányi's suite from *Ruralia Hungarica*, and Suk's suite *Raduz and Mahulena*. Standards such as Beethoven's and Tchaikovsky's Fifth Symphonies were balanced by Reger's Variations and Fugue on a Theme by Mozart, Liszt's symphonic poem *Tasso*, and Glazunov's *Stenka Razin*. There was also an all-Wagner program. To a number of local vocal and instrumental soloists were added Benno Moiseiwitsch, Solomon, Carl Flesch, and Bronislav Huberman.

Szell's debut concert was ambitious—Beethoven: *Egmont* Overture and Symphony no. 7, Bach: *Brandenburg* Concerto no. 1, Strauss: Serenade for Winds, Smetana: *The Moldau*, and Brahms: *Academic Festival* Overture. The glowing reviews indicated that Szell's results were greater than the customary. But he probably learned from that experience to demand extra rehearsal time at the beginning of a season, especially if it was his first with an orchestra. Szell had met the orchestra only two days before the concert, a condition he would not accept later in his career.

Many Scottish critics pointed to Szell's musical attributes that remained distinctive in his maturity. His restrained podium demeanor received praise, as did the results he achieved with economy of gesture.[35] Szell possessed a total architectural awareness, never allowing attention to meticulous detail to obscure the overall design of a work. His grasp of the whole gave his performances a feeling of inevitability. The finale of the Beethoven Seventh, for example, generates such a driving force that conductors often fall into the trap of giving the maximum early on, robbing the climax. Not Szell, for whom holding something in reserve until the right moment was a conscious principle. The *Glasgow Herald* found his interpretation "sensitive and excellently planned . . . in all the bigness of presentation of the last movement, there was still a touch of vitality in reserve for a final emphasis at the close."[36]

His performance of Brahms's Third drew similar comments: "The grasp with which each movement was presented as a well-defined whole, his power of maintaining a clear and unbroken line of development, stamped him as a conductor of great qualities of intellect and imagination."[37] The *Glasgow Herald* referred to "a fine clarity," suggesting another important Szell characteristic: skillfully maintaining a transparent orchestral texture. Szell could imbue familiar music with a sense of freshness; a review of the Prelude to *Die Meistersinger* recognized his performance as "a moving example of the familiar made wonderful."[38]

Though Szell's Scottish Orchestra schedule was demanding, he sandwiched in a performance with the London Symphony Orchestra on Thursday, November 26, only two nights before a subscription program in Glasgow. The London program—an all-Beethoven concert, in which Benno Moiseiwitsch played the "Emperor" Concerto—garnered an enthusiastic reception. Again, reviewers recognized Szell's personal trademarks: "His beat is precise and clear. . . . Mr. Szell also has that imaginative insight into the composer's work that results in the type of performance commonly—and rather weakly—called 'faithful.' . . . In the *Eroica* symphony . . . the effect was rather as though some masterpiece of the painter's art had been newly cleaned and restored to its original state."[39]

The London Symphony Orchestra was in the process of "reconstruction," to restore its reputation. Szell's performance demonstrated the orchestra's capability of really fine work. A London newspaper mentioned Szell inheriting the "mantle of Toscanini," and prophetically advised: "Any really good English orchestra looking for a conductor had better snap up Mr. Szell . . . before America gets him."[40]

W. J. Turner, a writer of great distinction, viewed Szell's *Eroica* as "one of the finest performances of this work I have ever heard in my life." He considered Szell "one of the finest of living conductors."[41] Critics had noted his poetry, passion, and power. According to one, Brahms's First was not only "in his head," but "in his heart, . . . charged with emotion without . . . the slightest risk of being over-sentimentalised."[42]

Szell's final program of the Scottish season, on January 16, 1937, included Berlioz's *Roman Carnival* Overture, Respighi's suite *The Birds*, and Beethoven's *Leonore* Overture no. 3, with Schubert's great C Major Symphony as its centerpiece. The farewells were sincere and heartfelt. At the conclusion of the season, according to the orchestra's tradition, the conductor was expected to say a few words to the audience. The custom gave Szell the opportunity to tell the Scottish public how much he had been touched by their kindness. "He thanked the orchestra very warmly for its splendid spirit of co-operation throughout the nine or ten weeks of his engagement, and then asked the audience if they fully appreciated the importance of such an orchestra and such a scheme of concerts." Szell believed that in time the public would realize the value of the orchestra to the city and "would devise ways and means of securing a longer annual season of concerts," to "give orchestral music its due place in the life of the community."[43]

When Barbirolli returned to finish the Scottish Orchestra's 1936–37 season, he informed its board of directors that he would return to New York and would not be available at all in Glasgow. They signed Szell on for the next two years.

Scotland, The Hague, and Toscanini (1937–38)

On the way to The Hague in January 1937, Szell passed through London, where Stefan Zweig introduced him to the violinist Henri Temianka. The two played a few sonatas together, and Szell was sufficiently impressed to invite Temianka to serve as concertmaster next season in Scotland. They got along famously, sharing, besides concerts, a fondness for good food, bad jokes, and concern for each other's futures. The two maintained their friendship in America, writing and visiting each other.

Szell conducted a series of concerts in The Hague from early February to early March 1937, returning to Prague for the next-to-last time. In London in June, he and Temianka held auditions for the Scottish Orchestra's 1937–38 season. From the middle of July to the middle of August, Szell vacationed in Tremezzo, a picturesque Italian village on Lake Como. Temianka joined him to rehearse for recitals and to go over bowings and prepare scores for the coming Scottish season. Szell, Helene Teltsch, and Temianka stayed at the Grand Hotel, next door to Schnabel and his family. After the summer, Helene went home to Prague, and Szell and Temianka took up adjoining rooms in More's Hotel in Glasgow, very close to Saint Andrews Hall, where they lived as "inseparable bachelor friends for several months." Temianka recalled: "I remember we both were very fond of cream and we ordered cream every morning with our fruit compote and then after the first week we got the bill and there was added 4 shillings and 6 pence for the cream. Szell was highly indignant and discontinued the cream from then on because of the expense."

Temianka's parents were Polish but he was born and grew up in Scotland. Szell's English, Temianka recalled, "was very good for a foreigner," but Temianka remembered some humorous mistakes with affection. On one occasion, Szell began a speech in which he wanted to say that he was greatly absorbed by this idea; he said, "I am pregnant . . ." As Szell paused, not knowing how to continue the sentence, "there was dead silence and then an explosion of laughter." Another time, Szell and Temianka were arguing whether to walk or pay to take a streetcar. Temianka favored walking, "Szell wanted to take the streetcar, so of course we took the streetcar," Temianka narrated. As they got on and Temianka took out change to pay, Szell said, "No, I seduced you, and I'm going to pay for it."[44]

At the end of September 1937 Szell took a five-day trip to Budapest and Vienna and returned briefly for his last performances in Prague. In October he traveled to Paris and then London. By November 18, Szell was in Glasgow, where, except for brief trips to London, he would stay through February 12.

Marriage in Scotland

Szell and Helene Teltsch were married in a civil ceremony in Glasgow on January 25, 1938. Because they were Catholic and it would be the second marriage for both, they had waited until they received a papal dispensation to remarry.[45] Szell professed that they had "married on the Continent some time ago," and were "confirming" their marriage in accordance with the laws of Scotland. If he hoped that the event could be kept quiet, he was mistaken, for their marriage was reported on the front page of the local newspaper. As usual, the couple dressed very fashionably: "The Bride was wearing a light tweed coat with fur collar and small fur hat. She had also gold earrings and wore brown Russian boots. Mr. Szell had a black coat with astrakhan collar and carried a grey soft hat in his hand."

An official called them back to the sheriff clerk's office, where the ceremony had taken place, because in their haste they had not signed the marriage register. The registrar, completely out of breath, caught up with them a few blocks away. "It was a scene worthy of a Billy Wilder comedy," Temianka remarked.[46]

Szell and Temianka carried on a running banter of friendly insults on stage. When they finished a piece, they would shake hands in the traditional conductor-concertmaster ritual while smilingly, covered by applause, exchange such insults as *Schwein* (pig) or *Dackel* (dachshund). After the concert, the focus centered on food. Temianka wrote,

> George Szell was so addicted to good food that he couldn't bear the thought of entrusting the choice and preparation of the menu to a mere railway chef. We often traveled by train from Glasgow to Edinburgh for an evening concert, and Szell arrived at the railway station almost collapsing under the weight of bottles of the finest wines, caviar, lobster, French sourdough bread, Viennese apple strudel, and all the things that make the life of a virtuoso bearable. Behind him staggered the orchestra's factotum, carrying buckets of ice, dishes, glasses, etc. . . . Of course, we did not consume these treasures prior to the concert. They were carefully deposited in the dressing room backstage to await the return train trip. Throughout the concert we worried about the gradually melting ice supply, rearranging the bottles and tins between the overture and the symphony and again during the intermission. The last piece on the program always seemed endless. But it was worth all the trouble. No banquet at the Ritz ever compared with our supper on the midnight train home.[47]

Szell always contrived to make life "bearable." Humor served as another means, and Szell's was earthy, after the Austrian fashion.[48] In a letter to Temianka, Szell wrote,

> Dear Friend,
>
> Just now I bought a new bottle of Shaeffer's fountain pen ink (the kind you tip before opening so as to let some ink flow into a small compartment—which makes it easier to fill the pen). There's a label on the bottle with the following admonition:
>
> SCREW TIGHTLY BEFORE TIPPING
>
> What would you think of making it obligatory to hang this sign around the necks of all hotel chambermaids?
>
> Yours very cordially,
>
> Szell

Szell and Temianka were soul mates in pranks: "[We performed] the Mendelssohn concerto as it had possibly never been performed before. Standing behind me, Szell would hold my bow, coordinating his up and down strokes with the movements of my left hand on the strings. To make this spectacular stunt more plausible, I once had a doctor friend put my right arm in a plaster case and explained to our audience that, unwilling to disappoint them despite a recent accident, I had called upon George Szell to save the evening. Grinning from ear to ear, George thereupon plowed into the Mendelssohn concerto with diabolical zest."[49]

But Temianka's accounts often confirmed Szell's reputation as self-centered: "There were two flying doors that you went into—the back doors of St. Andrews Hall. Szell would go through there with Helene following behind him and let those doors fly back in her face, totally thoughtless of the fact that she was with him. Whatever he was thinking about, he couldn't be bothered."

In rehearsals, Szell was often insensitive of musicians' feelings. "Well, actually he could be irritatingly pedagogical. . . . I mean he would almost wait for something that he could pounce on. . . . I heard him myself with the Scottish Orchestra tell the winds or percussion 'You sound like a chamberpot.'" According to Temianka, Szell was "ruthless" and "detested" by every orchestra member with whom the violinist spoke. Yet everybody greatly respected him. The composer Karol Rathaus said, "Szell has been chemically cleansed of all charm."[50]

Szell introduced works new to the Scottish audience, including Janáček's *Sinfonietta;* Shostakovich's First Symphony; Hindemith's Viola Concerto, with the composer as soloist; Martinů's Piano Concerto; and Suk's Fantasy for Violin, with Carl Flesch, who also played Mozart's A Major Concerto. Rudolf Firkusny played Dvořák's Piano Concerto; the mono-nomic British pianist, Solomon, played the "Emperor" Concerto; Schnabel played the Brahms B-flat; and Huberman Brahms's Violin Concerto. Works by Bantock and Delius represented English music. Risë Stevens, who had sung with Szell in Prague, sang arias and songs. Szell also conducted his Variations on an Original Theme.

Szell the Programmer

The 1937–38 Scottish season ended on February 12. Later that month Szell conducted the London Philharmonic on the Courtauld-Sargent series, and on March 1, he led the first of three concerts in The Hague.

The archives of The Hague's Residence Orchestra reveal Szell's strategy with regard to programming. This is one of the more mysterious, perilous, and least understood processes in performance: the subtleties of juxtaposition of works into a cohesive program of sixty-five to ninety minutes duration, and the coordination of several programs into what becomes a season. However promising it appears on paper, the success of a program or season is proven only in performance. Programming includes selecting soloists and their repertoire, introducing appropriate new works to the audiences, and avoiding repeats of recently played standard works. Conductors want to perform favorite pieces, and managers want variety within boundaries—translated, that means some, but not too much, new music.

The intricacies and subtleties of programming decisions depend to a great extent on the relationship between the conductor and the orchestra's manager. Szell developed warm friendships with some managers with whom there was a meeting of minds, such as S. Rodriguez, the artistic administrator of The Hague Residence Orchestra.

Planning for the coming February began in October 1936, after Szell's summer vacation. They looked to a first performance in Holland of orchestral excerpts from Ernst Krenek's opera *Jonny spielt auf*, which was enjoying considerable popularity after its 1927 premiere in Leipzig. Rodriguez suggested two program possibilities for February 17 and 18 involving the Krenek and the Fourth Symphony of Dvořák. Rodriguez was concerned that the Krenek performance royalty might exceed his budget. Szell reassured him: "I don't believe that Universal Edition demands too much for the Krenek fragment. Should they, nevertheless try to, I ask you to write me a line about it and I will set the gentlemen in Vienna's heads straight."[51]

Rodriguez proposed that Szell begin a program with Beethoven's *Fidelio* overture, which Szell rejected and gave his reasons: "For the overture I should like to give you the choice of CORIOLAN or EGMONT, as I do not care to do the Fidelio Overture in concert; it belongs to the Opera and fails completely as I have so often observed."[52] Szell reminded Rodriguez that they had been considering both the Brahms and Dvořák Fourths for different programs. Szell by that time already had his own edited orchestra parts for both those works.[53]

As Rodriguez began to feel more secure with Szell, he felt freer to advise the conductor with regard to the predilections of local audiences, and to offer suggestions: "I consider it very good if you perform a Dutch composition on the concerts of 7 and 10 February and [suggest] indeed an overture by [Johan] Wagenaar. The overture is very brilliant and successful and I have reserved the piece for you until now. I send the score with this letter." Referring to the Brahms and Dvořák Fourth Symphonies, Rodriguez wrote: "Believe me, I am sure that you would do a great service with Dvořák. Firstly, Brahms is naturally often played and Dvořák hardly at all. Secondly, all the newspapers have already written that you will be playing the unknown Dvořák and I am sure it will be a great disappointment if that is given up." Rodriguez then offered an esthetic judgment that Szell could well have appreciated: "For the Beethoven program the Coriolan Overture appears to be better, because Egmont is more dramatic and we will already have the Eroica after intermission. Therefore I find the elegiac Coriolan better."[54]

Szell felt a special affinity for Dvořák, and the G Major Symphony was a work with which he was identified throughout his life. The reference to the "unknown Dvořák" informs us that it was relatively obscure then. Szell did his part for making that genial work popular, conducting it numerous times over many years and recording it twice with the Cleveland Orchestra and once with the Concertgebouw.[55]

Reviews never ceased to matter to Szell:

> Please excuse my scandalously delayed answer to your letter of 31 October; but when I tell you that in 8½ weeks in this country I had to conduct no less than 45 concerts, you can imagine in what an insane chase in which I am living. The work is, however, richly rewarding through an unbroken chain of triumphant successes - if you are interested in completely extraordinary press opinions for purposes of publication, I'll gladly send them to you.

Regarding the programs, Szell graciously programmed Wagenaar's Overture to *Cyrano de Bergerac*, but told Rodriguez that "in no way" would he give up the Brahms Fourth as the major work of the most important concerts. The Dvořák Fourth, he agreed, was "a heavenly, golden piece, but it doesn't have enough weight for this program." He planned to include it in a matinee program in Rotterdam, but for the more weighty concerts he ended with either Brahms's Fourth or Beethoven's *Eroica*. Szell wrote, "I am convinced that the programs are right and can just see (and hear) them!"

Perhaps recalling the difficulty of beginning his first Scottish Orchestra season after only a few days of rehearsals, Szell brought up the issue with Rodriguez: "As for the rehearsals, I discovered through close examination of your schedule that I have a bit too few rehearsals at the beginning of my activities and too many later," and asked for an adjustment.

Szell's standard practice was to have all parts marked before the first rehearsal. Evidently the orchestra had its own set of parts to the Dvořák Symphony, for Szell also replied: "I am happy to hear that you have the material for the Dvořák 4th and I shall very soon send you my pocket score with my detailed markings with the request that you have a copyist transfer my bowings, dynamic indications, etc. into the orchestra parts; that will vastly simplify and shorten the rehearsals and contribute to their increased pleasantness."[56]

The opening program in Leiden on February 4 and The Hague on the sixth was all Beethoven: *Coriolan* Overture, the "Emperor" Concerto, with Scottish pianist Frederic Lamond, and the *Eroica*. Following concerts included the Tchaikovsky Piano Concerto no. 1, with Benno Moiseivitch, and the Mozart A Major Violin Concerto, with Carl Flesch. Haydn's Symphony no. 88 in G, Schumann's Second Symphony, and Berlioz's Three Pieces from *The Damnation of Faust* were works with which Szell came to have a lifelong association.

After his concerts, Szell was offered the permanent conductorship of The Hague Residence Orchestra, but he felt he could not accept because of the commitment he had just made to the Scottish Orchestra. He nevertheless worked out a part-time arrangement that included appearances in the coming seasons, as well as some involvement in the process of selection and replacement of players. He returned to The Hague in March and October 1938 and from January to February 1939. The outbreak of war prevented his engagement planned for January 1940.

Szell and Toscanini

Arturo Toscanini conducted The Hague Orchestra on March 6 and 8, 1937, following Szell's first season there, and again followed Szell in March 1938. Toscanini was so impressed with the orchestra's improvement, as a result of Szell's work, that he invited him to guest conduct the newly formed NBC Symphony in New York. Prior engagements in Australia and Europe prevented Szell from accepting Toscanini's invitations for 1939 and 1940. The opportunity was finally realized in one of Szell's darkest hours.

Szell admired few conductors—he occasionally mentioned Nikisch and Strauss, and seldom spoke at all of others of his contemporaries. Szell heard Toscanini conduct La Scala's ensemble in *Aida* on tour in Europe in 1929 and performances of *Tannhäuser* and *Parsifal* at Bayreuth in the thirties. Hearing him conduct the New York Philharmonic in Berlin and Prague in 1930 was, in his words, "the first real Toscanini-shock." "This was orchestral performance of a kind new to all of us. The clarity of texture; the precision of ensemble; the rightness of balances; the virtuosity of every section, every solo-player of the orchestra—then at its peak—in the service of an interpretive concept of evident, self-effacing integrity, enforced with irresistible will power and unflagging ardor, set new, undreamed-of standards literally overnight."

Toscanini revealed new heights of technique, yet his greatest influence on Szell was spiritual: the composer was to be revered above the conductor. The sheer brilliance of Toscanini's personality, Szell believed, swept away accumulations of tradition:

> Toscanini's interpretations . . . have influenced all of us, whether we accepted them in every detail or not. . . . Too many contemporaries of Toscanini (conductors and instrumentalists alike) overlooked the difference between emulation and imitation, thus putting themselves in a strait jacket. . . . In attempting to imitate the inimitable, these literalistic followers failed to recognize Toscanini's historic mission as the Great Purifier, his essential character as a truth seeker. . . . He considered himself the advocate and servant of the composer; he never spared

> himself, not even during rehearsals; he was completely involved at every moment and rightfully demanded the same of the orchestra he conducted.
>
> Do not ask "What can *I* do with this piece"; but "what does the *composer* want me to do with this piece?"[57]

To Szell, Toscanini was much more than a time-beater, he was "a truth-seeker." Toscanini's most impressive characteristics, Szell thought, were "his artistic ethics. . . . The complete humility in the face of the masterworks and the self-effacing devotion to the task is something that has influenced all of us. And without him none of us will be the same."[58]

Szell himself was not the same after his exposure to the white heat of Toscanini's music making. Szell was then in his thirties, and Toscanini's example set a new standard to which he aspired for the rest of his life.

3

Musical Pioneering in Australia (1938, 1939)

Szell received an invitation from the Australian Broadcasting Commission (ABC, now the Australian Broadcasting Corporation) to lead the Celebrity Concerts, the most prestigious subscription series of their winter season, with five of their orchestras from May to August 1938. They would take place in the major cities of Melbourne and Sydney, as well as in Brisbane, Adelaide, and Perth. The orchestras were conducted by resident Australian conductors and distinguished guests from Great Britain and the Continent, such as Maurice De Abravanel (as Maurice Abravanel was then known), Hamilton Harty, George Schneevoigt, and Malcolm Sargent.

Szell's musical life was divided between London, Scotland, and The Hague, but the reversal of seasons in the Southern Hemisphere would afford him year-round musical activity. There, he would stand as a pioneer in a remote and exotic land. And he and Helene could enjoy new surroundings.

Sargent may have proposed Szell to the ABC, or also Arthur Rubinstein or Bronislaw Huberman, who had performed with Szell and had made successful concert tours of Australia in the early thirties. The ABC, patterned after Great Britain's BBC, supported orchestras for local concert and national broadcasting purposes. The concerts ensured employment for local musicians, and the broadcasts enhanced the cultural life of far-flung areas of that huge country. Some of the orchestras were small and their proficiency low, so the ABC looked earnestly for conductors who could raise their level. Szell's reputation in Scotland made him a natural choice.

Considerable press coverage preceded the arrival of artists. Szell's engagement was announced six months in advance.[1] An article from London about one of his Courtauld-Sargent concerts, picked up by the Australian press, reported: "Szell is well known in London, his appearance as guest-conductor having been frequent, and his work is appreciated for its soundness and skill. He always gets from his orchestra satisfying performances by reason of a conducting artistry, conspicuous for its close touch with the music in hand, an impressive vitality of style, insight and imaginativeness."[2]

Expectations were high, and interest was great. In the Australian newspapers, Szell's name sometimes appeared as "Czell," and even "Snell," and journalists put forth suggestions for proper pronunciation: "you may safely leave out the 'z,'" or, "Show off your knowledge at your next bridge party, and casually refer to the delightful conductorship of 'Gay-org' Sell (note the z is silent in the surname), and watch the impression you make!"[3] We are also told that the Szells brought with them "16 large trunks of clothes, which included 15 of the Professor's suits, and 12 evening frocks Mrs. Szell bought in Paris."[4]

The extended cruise on the *Strathallen* from Marseilles to Australia was a welcome respite. The ship arrived in Melbourne on the twenty-third, docking in Sydney four days later.[5] The Szells were a colorful pair—cosmopolitan, cultured, multilingual, well-traveled, and newly wed. In each city, the press photographed and interviewed them, and their attendance at luncheons and other entertainments made the news. The couple were photographed on shipboard, in their hotel rooms, and on golf courses. The Szells had just learned the game in Scotland, and had brought with them the "most up-to-date kits" available.[6] The Szells also stated a fondness for contract bridge and motoring. "They drive their own autos." Mrs. Szell's sporting activities also included tennis and skiing, while Mr. Szell declared that he loved his work, music, and that his work and his hobby were one and the same.

The press gave much attention to the attractive, bright, and stylishly dressed conductor's wife, yet she longed for her own home. She missed cooking and she brought many old family recipes. Szell boasted to the press about his gourmet cooking—not of Czech food, even though he thought very highly of that cuisine, but of the subtler French style. "My cooking is best when I am at a party," he said. "I like to go into the kitchen and cook for all of my friends."[7]

Even their courtship was not off limits. "CONDUCTOR CZELL [*sic*], CAVEMAN," brought out intimate details of their early relationship, and they must have been shocked to see them in print. It begins simply, with Szell's debut the previous evening, the concert's broadcast schedule, and future Melbourne concerts. The article continued:

> The most interested—and most decorative—member of last night's audience was the conductor's charming Czech wife. But it was not always thus.
>
> Mr. Czell can laugh about it now, but, for eight years, Mrs. Czell would not listen to his matrimonial plea.

> They met first in the Austrian Alps and felt mutually antagonistic. The conductor thought the lovely young girl just a spoilt darling, and determined to teach her a lesson. Her teasing tactics reached a crisis, after a week or two, when Mr. Czell seized her, smacked her soundly and threw her into the adjacent swimming pool.
>
> It took him just eight years to wear down the prejudice occasioned by those caveman tactics.
>
> But "he who laughs last—." And now, following a secret wedding in Scotland five months ago, Mr. and Mrs. Czell are enjoying a delayed honeymoon.[8]

When the Szells realized how their statements might be reported, they never again divulged personal information. Szell directed interviews as much as possible toward musical matters: his background, his busy schedule in Britain and Holland (eighty concerts in the preceding four months), his prior radio experience, and his recent recordings. He declared that his musical mission in Australia was to develop orchestras and audiences through programming the classics and playing them as well as possible. It seemed logical to him to present only a few novelties to an audience that—for instance in Sydney, a city of a million and a quarter—heard only ten symphony concerts a year. He told his Australian audience that "some folk hold that the classics are dull," only because "they hear so many dull performances."[9]

Radio had only recently emerged in Australia, although Szell himself was a veteran radio performer. Since 1923 he had conducted radio concerts in London, Prague, Vienna, and Scandinavia.[10] And though he believed radio could "never replace the community enjoyment of performances in the concert hall," and warned that it "seemed to be displacing the making of music by families at home," he recognized "the value of broadcasting concerts to the remotest regions of the country where there was no live music at all."[11]

For Szell's first program, in Melbourne, on May 7, he conducted the *Oberon* Overture; "Ella giammai m'amo," from *Don Carlo*, sung by Russian basso Alexander Kipnis; the *Moldau;* and Beethoven's Symphony no. 7. As a prepared encore, Kipnis sang the Catalog Aria from *Don Giovanni*. Part of the concert was broadcast live. The next day they played *Oberon* and the Beethoven symphony in a studio broadcast.

An eyewitness report of the dress rehearsal observed:

> Australian orchestral players will always remember Georg Szell for his courtesy and politeness. He has all the authority of his predecessors . . . their confidence, their insistence that a work shall be played only as he wants it . . . and, more than any of them, a meticulous regard for detail. But he differs from them in his manner of going about getting what he wants.
>
> "If you would be so kind. . . ." "I am very sorry, but would you please play that section again for me." "I would very much appreciate it if you would. . . ." "I should

> like it if you would. . . ." These are the phrases that punctuate a Szell rehearsal. Then, when he gets what he wants: "That is nice, thank you. . . . That could not be better."
>
> If he had studied the psychology of Australian players for years he could not have found a better recipe for success. As one player said at the interval in the first rehearsal: "He's so jolly nice about things that you simply must try to do what he wants."

Yet, for all Szell's gentleness, he gave the players one of the best music lessons they had ever had, conveying to them the urgency of cooperation in successful symphony playing. "There are things the baton cannot do. Only you can do them," he explained. "You must feel for the melodic line and enunciate it clearly. Listen to the other fellows—that is most important. And, while you are not playing during the symphony, I beg you not to turn yourselves off intellectually and emotionally. If you do the spirit of our work is destroyed."

In this early time in Australia, Szell seemed infused with British good manners, even worrying about the orchestra's opinion of him. When he left the podium, he asked a journalist, "Do you think they like me? Did you think we got on well?" Astonished, the writer pondered "And this is the man who has worked with Richard Strauss. . . . Who has conducted performances in some of Europe's greatest opera houses. . . . Australians like celebrities like that."[12] This was a far cry from Temianka's report of Szell's bad treatment of his Scottish musicians.

Reviews of the opening concert were unanimously favorable. The *Hobart Mercury* noted the "unusual sight of the 'house full' sign," and Melbourne's *Argus* described Szell's "immediate personal and artistic success," acknowledged at the conclusion of the concert by "deafening applause" from players and audience. The reviewer continued:

> His work reveals no hint of pedantry, but combines the authoritative maturity of long experience with spontaneous gaiety of colour and enjoyable flexibility and buoyancy of rhythm. Never flurried, dictatorial, or at a loss, he has the happy knack of propelling his associates over and through technical difficulties with the maximum degree of efficiency and the minimum of fuss. Most important of all qualifications, when dealing with a comparatively unfamiliar orchestra, he has these scores from memory and can literally, as well as figuratively, keep his eye on his players.[13]

At a press luncheon, Szell noted the absence of opera houses in the country, and proposed a novel solution: "as all [Australia's] big cities were on the sea, a floating opera house would be an admirable and economic project. . . . Mr. Kipnis is an enthusiastic supporter of the idea," reported the *Melbourne Herald*.[14] The novelty on the second Melbourne concert was Elgar's symphonic poem *Falstaff*. The reviewers were impressed with Szell's undertaking this large and complex work with so few rehearsals.[15] His greatest triumph came on May 21, in the third and last Melbourne concert, with the First Symphony of Brahms. Said a reviewer: "probably the greatest performance of a Brahms symphony ever heard in this country—one which would rival those of almost any famous combination in Europe or America. Virtually it was flawless in execution and in expression."[16]

The Melbourne concerts took place on Saturday evenings. A portion of each concert was broadcast live, and on the following day the orchestra played a studio broadcast of the remaining works. For the last studio concert, Szell directed not only the orchestra but the placement of microphones. Even with fifteen years of broadcasting experience, he evidently miscalculated. The day after the concert, C. C. Wickes, the acting manager for Victoria, sent a memo complaining of the violin sound to the general manager of the ABC, Charles Moses. He concluded that "had the microphones not been lowered, and had the angle of forty-five degrees been maintained, the tone from the string section would have been quite satisfactory."[17] Reports and memos such as this helped the ABC keep track of its far-flung activities.

During the next month, Szell gave four public and four studio concerts with the Sydney orchestra. With the exception of one vitriolic review by "J.R.," who found the concert "not very thrilling,"[18] the Sydney press was highly complimentary. Tossy Spivakovsky performed as soloist in Beethoven's Violin Concerto. To present a more authentic performance than was customary at the time, the violinist played according to a copy of the original manuscript he had made. Szell practiced such scholarship himself.

Several reviewers adhered to the conventional wisdom that Schumann's symphonies were poorly orchestrated and structurally weak. Of the Fourth, which Szell performed, one wrote, "the conductor made it sound like a great symphony . . . and [one] was carried along irresistibly to a tremendous climax."[19] The following week, Szell's harshest critic, J.R., in character, wrote, "It is possible that Szell himself may find it amusing to see the simpler critics betrayed into open-mouthed amazement at his conducting standard works without a score." But he evidently softened somewhat, conceding that Szell "has a fine sense of climax, and accompanies sensitively in concertos." And he found himself "admiring the many refinements in Szell's treatment of the rambling score" of Schubert's "heavenly long" C Major Symphony, and that "under Szell's direction the orchestra has acquired a nice precision of attack." The final word was, however, negative: "But I have yet to be thrilled by Szell's undoubtedly expert direction."[20]

The day after Szell's first Sydney concert, an internal report noted his satisfaction with the orchestra's "excellent performance." To the woodwind section, however, he had mentioned that "although at times their intonation was faultless, they sometimes allowed themselves to relax, with the consequence that, through not concentrating on the tone they were to produce, they were slightly, but almost imperceptibly out of tune."[21]

As in Melbourne, Szell's rehearsals were covered by the Sydney press. Again, reports noted his "firm but always polite" demeanor with the musicians. Sydney's concertmaster, Lionel Lawson, was lavish in his appreciation of Szell: "The most amazing conductor I have ever played under. He has such a prodigious knowledge of music that it is a musical experience, and at the same time, a pleasure to work under him. He will have nothing but the best. . . . Some of his performances in the South have been amazing. He has re-created works that some critics thought were dull. They were dull . . . to them, until he came and played them. And yet he is very kind with it all."[22] The appreciation was mutual: in a letter to the ABC evaluating the Sydney and Melbourne orchestras, Szell found Lawson "a very good leader indeed; head and shoulders above the leaders in the other States."[23]

An unidentified writer observed Szell rehearsing in Sydney and interviewed him for a Brisbane newspaper. Appearing a week before the conductor was due, it added to the Brisbane Orchestra's positive expectations of Szell:

> I had heard him go over and over a passage in the Scherzo of a Beethoven Symphony [the Sixth]—patient, kindly, encouraging, but firm, in his quest of perfection.
>
> I had heard him ask for "a little accent" from the strings and watched him cock his head to one side, listening carefully, before he enjoined the oboes to "make it speak softly."
>
> I had to listen to the soft, long drawn hiss with which he invited a pianissimo, reinforcing the invitation with a cautionary raised hand and the vivid and poetic suggestion—"Make it like a shadow."
>
> "There is 100 per cent difference between piano and pianissimo," he told the listening players. To the woodwind, he recommended "a tiny imperceptible pause" before each chord. To the brass he said: "Play your staccato notes just a little shorter."
>
> And to the trumpet he said once: "You are playing G Flat there?" Then, very sympathetically: "An awful note, G Flat. But try to get it."
>
> Details, the exact nuance of tone, just the right stress and value of a note—these things are so important in a performance. They can make or mar it, he told me afterwards.[24]

After Szell played in Sydney, a reviewer considered him "the most promising conductor for the difficult task of building competent orchestras. . . . Szell is one of those rare musicians who can teach and yet rise to the heights of musical expression—the kind of man so vitally necessary for the proper foundation of symphony music in Australia." Australians expected that he would return to their country under "a long-term contract that is two or three years," following his coming European engagements.[25]

A Different Challenge

The smaller orchestras of Brisbane, Adelaide, and Perth presented a major challenge to Szell. The nucleus of regular players in Melbourne (thirty-five) and Sydney (forty-five) had been brought up to full strength by augmenting each orchestra with players from the other, and supplementing further with freelance players. But the Brisbane, Adelaide, and Perth orchestras had a considerably smaller core of players. Their supply of local freelance talent was correspondingly meager. The financial burden of transporting musicians from Sydney to Perth, a distance of 2,700 miles, prohibited bringing a large number of musicians to bolster the local forces. The ABC sent twelve key players from Sydney to Brisbane, the first of the smaller cities Szell visited.

There, he faced his first difficulties. Resistance to importing players from other cities stemmed not only from financial considerations but also from local pride. For want of a clearance card from the Sydney union, the Brisbane union exacerbated the situation and refused to allow Lawson, the most important import, to take his seat as concertmaster, delaying the start of the first rehearsal fifteen minutes.[26] Such nitpicking could only have irritated Szell, and the level of playing, which did not meet Sydney's or Melbourne's standard, frustrated him further.

And so, the Szell who up to then had been polite, patient, and deferential—almost insecure in wondering and caring about how the musicians in the orchestra perceived him—now demonstrated his alter persona. Perhaps the contrasting abilities of the orchestras governed the change in demeanor. In Adelaide and Perth, where the orchestras were smaller and less proficient than those in Melbourne and Sydney, he showed signs of frazzling. In Brisbane Szell was impatient, indifferent, even careless about musical details.

An official of the Brisbane Orchestra wrote in a memorandum: "The demeanour of Professor Szell to the members of the orchestra was not conducive to happy relations between players and conductor. Professor Szell adopted an attitude that more than bordered on rudeness and lack of courtesy."[27] Writing from Perth, Szell expressed that, "In Brisbane things are aggravated by an astounding lack of keenness, so contrary to all my experiences in other Australian cites."[28] Szell proved diplomatic, however, when the press asked him to comment on the orchestras and musicians, not mentioning his unpleasant experience in Brisbane: "I have found the Australian orchestral player pleasant to work with, keen to learn and to improve, and prepared to give of his best if he is working with a conductor whom he can respect."[29]

The results in Brisbane appeared better than might have been expected, considering the friction in the rehearsals. Szell's will and musicality won out, and something better than the orchestra's norm emerged. Reviews were generally positive, although showing some effects of the difficulties. And the Brisbane public, which at first had been slow to purchase tickets, attended the concerts.

Szell arrived in Adelaide on July 5 and conducted his first rehearsal that evening. Word of the troubles in Brisbane had preceded his arrival, compelling the local management to take considerable care to offset any similar problems. An ABC official reported: "He told me that 'after my terrible experiences in Brisbane' he felt that the orchestra here was considerably better and that he could do something with them." Szell suggested to the regular conductor, William R. Cade, "that two of the second violins on the last desk should be told that their services were not required," adding "that some orchestras were strengthened by the omission of certain players." Szell "was in an excellent good humour," the official continued, "and we arranged a game of golf for his wife and himself this morning. . . . I feel that he will settle down well."[30] The Adelaide situation differed because Cade had wisely begun rehearsing the orchestra three weeks before Szell's arrival.[31]

Reviews were good, although both local critics faulted his programming, calling for "better material, more suited to his undoubted ability and more in line with the programmes he has conducted in other capitals." There was no Beethoven or Brahms in Adelaide, and Schubert's "Unfinished" instead of the great C Major Symphony. Szell tailored his programs for the smaller orchestras, likely guided by ABC management, and the critics might have understood that.[32]

On November 7, the manager for South Australia summed up Szell's Adelaide stand:

> Professor Szell made a great impression on the audiences in Adelaide at his concerts but I do not feel that he was as helpful to the orchestra itself. . . .
>
> My personal impression was that he came here a little against his will and rather tired of the Commission's smaller orchestras. At the same time it was a very great privilege to have a man of his distinction amongst us.[33]

Szell's flight to Perth was an ordeal: "It was the worst trip of my experience," Szell remarked. They were so indisposed on arrival that they deferred interviews until the following day.

A review of Szell's first concert in Perth, by a critic with the colorful *nom de plume* "Fidelio," mentioned "striking performances" that "rose to high levels of eloquence; yet one felt, too, that he did not draw forth always the utmost which (we have had reason to believe) the forces under his command could give."[34] Perhaps the reviewer was observing his frustration with the orchestra, as suggested by the following memo from James to Moses:

> This was not a very happy week for the players, as I am afraid Professor Szell did not get on very well with them, and many could not do justice to their playing. He was rather disinterested and did not help them very much, as he seemed to have the idea that none of the Australian Orchestras were very good. Professor Szell also generally finished his rehearsals one hour before time.
>
> I think he loses sight of the fact that 75 per cent of our Orchestras are semi-professionals, and have to be patiently instructed. Not-withstanding all this, the performances at both Concerts were very good, and Szell is a fine conductor, although he must have first class musicians to make him interested.[35]

Another in-house report to Moses about Szell's Perth concerts complained: "Only two movements of the L'Arlesienne No. 2 Suite were given, and played at a furious tempo which robbed the work of its beauty. I fear that Mr. Szell was not particularly interested in our orchestra as he rarely utilised more than two thirds of his rehearsal time."[36]

Szell had lost heart and given up on them. He was not sparing of the Perth musicians' feelings in the process. In his report to Moses, C. Charlton mentioned Szell's "caustic criticism" of the players in rehearsal and opined, "It struck me that he could only be interested in orchestras which were of the highest standard and could not be bothered with a small combination which had been augmented by casual players to form a symphony orchestra."[37]

Szell expressed his admiration "for the way in which the Australian Broadcasting Commission is attempting to foster and develop orchestral music in Australia." Although he was "impressed by the sincerity of its purpose," he could not avoid feeling that "there are many obstacles which would appear to be almost insurmountable in the quest of achieving a reasonable standard of symphonic music in six centres simultaneously."

He rated each section of the Sydney and Melbourne orchestras from "good" ("1st violins: some even very good") to "impossible" ("1st oboe in Sydney, and Tuba quite impossible"), expressed his appreciation for "the splendid assistance" he received from the commission's staff, and noted the "remarkable smoothness" of tour arrangements. Szell found Australian musicians "anxious to learn and very amenable to orchestral discipline," and acknowledged that even when he was unable to reach his "minimum standard," he found the work interesting and derived "considerable pleasure" from it.[38]

After two rehearsals with the Perth orchestra, Szell reported, "It is simply horrible, most particularly the strings—if it is possible at all to make so subtle differentiations on such deplorable a level. As most of the players can neither read the notes properly nor play their instruments, any attempt to get at least a fair amount of right notes—let alone everything else—is quite futile." He summed up his experiences in the smaller orchestras: "I knew perfectly well what I was up against and yet I am almost amused to see how the reality beats imagination ever again."[39]

Charles Moses expressed his gratitude for Szell's contribution to Australia's musical life and invited him to return the next year. "You have made our orchestras play better than they know," he wrote.[40]

Interlude in Europe

The Szells sailed from Perth on August 1, 1938, bound for Marseilles. Arriving on August 25, the couple traveled to Switzerland for vacation. In September, Britain and France, at the infamous Munich Conference, sought to appease Hitler to prevent war, agreeing to let him have the Sudetenland, the part of Czechoslovakia with a majority of German-speaking inhabitants. In October, Germany occupied the Sudeten territories.

In this ominous atmosphere, Szell was conducting in Scotland, Holland, and England. He wrote Moses from Glasgow in November:

> I have never stopped keeping the interests of the Australian Broadcasting Commission and the problem of musical development in Australia in my mind, and since my return to Europe, I have taken many steps to find out what first-class European orchestral players would be available for a permanent engagement in Australia. My enquiries were very successful and I could establish already, within the short time I have had at my disposal, that about a dozen or a score of first-rate players would be available.

Noting that the Australian musicians' union placed restrictions against imported players, Szell exhorted Moses to try to make them realize the importance of admitting skilled musicians and issue the necessary permits. "The paramount standard of American orchestras has been achieved only by the influx of European players, one or two generations ago," he pointed out, "and now the Americans can dispense with European musicians. This is the state of things which I would wish for Australia in the near future." In fact, Szell had on file specific recommendations on fifteen or twenty players that he stood ready to forward to the ABC as soon as they "succeeded in breaking the ban on the Unions."[41]

Szell's Scottish season began in November 1938 and ended in the following February. By March 1939 he had traveled twice to The Hague and went to Brussels for concerts on the eighteenth and nineteenth—just days after Hitler formally dissolved Czechoslovakia, his adopted homeland. Szell returned to The Hague and on April 1 traveled to London for concerts at the BBC. The cataclysm of world events prevented the Szells from setting foot again in Europe for eight years.

Szell's Second Australian Season

The Szells flew to Australia on an Empire "flying boat," arriving in Sydney at the end of April. The plane made frequent refueling stops, some overnight. It passed through Cairo, Calcutta, and Bangkok, and the passengers spent a night in Townsville on Australia's east coast, hundreds of miles north of Brisbane, before the last leg to Sydney. Somehow Szell knew that Alan McCristal, one of his piano soloists from 1938, had moved from Sydney to Townsville. To McCristal's surprise and delight, Szell phoned him on arrival and they had dinner together. McCristal told a journalist: "I had to smile when he said: 'This is Professor Szell. I wonder if you remember I conducted the orchestra when you played last season?' As if I could ever forget," he concluded, "but what thrilled me was to think he remembered me."[42]

Shortly before the Szells' first trip to Australia, on March 13, 1938, the German *Anschluss* of Austria had taken place. While on their first Australian tour, they were questioned about conditions in Europe, and Czechoslovakia in particular. Helene Szell occasionally alluded to the situation, but her husband usually changed the subject immediately. He said then that if people would turn more to the pursuit of music, the world would be a much better place.[43]

By the time the Szells returned to Australia, the world was a much worse place and they were less reluctant to speak about the state of Europe. Of their Swiss holiday, he remarked, "We had a little rest, not much. It was considerably disturbed by the crisis,"[44] a reference to the Munich Conference. Szell reported that the European situation had not affected the Scottish season, which had enjoyed record attendance. But, he said: "Even art in Europe is suffering in the hands of the dictators. There is no freedom left. . . . When I was arranging to leave London a fortnight ago, I had to discuss alternative routes for Australia if the flying-boats were unable to cross the Mediterranean in the next few days."

Szell responded gravely when asked if he could visit Czechoslovakia: "I have not been able to, and even if I were able I should not care to go. . . . It is a grief-stricken land."[45] He told the press: "Guns and planes, rather than music, are being created in Central Europe. . . . You in Australia can have no idea of the mental tension under which people live in European countries."[46] Far from the events, people in Australia could breathe easier—for the time being at least. The Szells were on familiar ground there: "My wife and I are delighted to be back in Australia," he said on arrival, "It is just like being home."[47] Szell excitedly told of being asked to conduct Toscanini's newly formed NBC Symphony in New York for six weeks, just before the opening of the World's Fair. Their Australian hosts were flattered that he turned down the prestigious invitation because of his existing contract with the ABC.

Szell looked forward to the 1939 season in Australia, no longer a stranger but returning to old friends. He had agreed that he would conduct twenty concerts in twelve weeks, "limited to Sydney and Melbourne," with a single concert in Adelaide. Instead of the mix of full-time and part-time players—the professional nuclei of each orchestra augmented by the same from the other orchestra—Melbourne's players would go to Sydney and Sydney's to Melbourne, adding only the best "casual" players to fill out the ranks in either city. That and the offer to add ten of the better players in Adelaide made the 1939 season a significant improvement over that of 1938. Accordingly, Szell could program more ambitiously. For instance, cellist Edmund Kurtz was available to perform a work Szell would not have considered the previous year, Strauss's *Don Quixote;* Kurtz had played it with him in Prague a few years before. Szell also brought Artur Schnabel to Australia for five concerts. The conductor took into account "the different musical tastes of the Melbourne and Sydney audiences." He scheduled Walton and Stravinsky in Sydney, Strauss and Bruckner in Melbourne. Both would hear Beethoven. Szell's goals for this second season were to present "important standard works, but at the same time to introduce works which Australians have not heard before, although they have high standing on the other side of the world," to gradually enlarge the standard Australian repertory.[48]

Szell felt more confident of his ground now, and he held the promise of the best soloists and strengthened orchestras, so he programmed more freely. But perhaps he miscalculated the readiness of Australian audiences to embrace adventurous works. When Szell essayed the Bruckner Third on a nonsubscription program, for example, attendance fell noticeably. This was its Australian debut, sixty years after its composition. The performance evidently went extremely well. The *Melbourne Herald*'s critic, however, remarked that the work might better have been placed on the subscription series. But he was nevertheless sensitive to the monumental design of the work and to Szell's interpretation of it, especially his "vast ascent," beginning in the first movement and climaxing in the fourth. "The effect here was terrific," wrote the reviewer, "yet with all the power and weight of the orchestra, the ensemble was of unusual musical richness."[49] The concert included the Australian composer Margaret Sutherland's *Suite on a Theme by Purcell,* which Szell had premiered in suburban Coburg.

For *Don Quixote,* Szell agreed to go along with the percussionists' suggestion of using the sound of compressed oxygen escaping from a cylinder to augment the insufficient sound of their wind machine for the passage depicting the Don's ride through the air. This was the Australian debut of the Strauss, forty years after its composition. Szell played one of his favorites, the Haydn Eighty-eighth Symphony. In an earlier interview he remarked that there was "much left for discovery about Haydn, [the] least-known composer."[50] He revealed his awareness that manuscript scores of previously unknown Haydn works were being discovered in Europe.

Highlights of the season in Sydney included first Australian performances of William Walton's First Symphony and *Jeu de cartes* by Stravinsky. By that time

Stravinsky had become firmly established in the international musical world, but he was known in Australia only for *The Firebird* and *Petrouchka*. Szell's performance received praise for capturing the music's "spirit of parody," and "wayward playfulness with a fine sense of smartness and sophistication."[51]

Walton, at thirty-seven, was relatively unknown in Australia. A music critic observed about the symphony, "although the audience marvelled at its intricacies of orchestration and admired Szell's faultless shepherding of the orchestra through its complex measures, the majority of listeners were in a daze as to the meaning of this music." He attributed it to the times: "If such music has a meaning, it can only be to reflect the troubled state of the modern world and the chaos of its mass thought."[52]

Szell championed Walton's music throughout his life. He appreciated its superb craftsmanship and its technical virtuosity. It was challenging in a way he could relate to—rhythmic vitality and complexity without constantly changing meters, and with dissonance rooted in tonality. Many conductors have championed the music of one or more of their contemporaries and have thus been identified with them by posterity: Richter with Wagner, Walter with Mahler, Toscanini with Puccini and Verdi, Beecham with Sibelius and Delius, Monteux and Ansermet with Stravinsky and Ravel, Koussevitzky with Bartók, and Szell with Walton.[53]

Farewell to Australia

In the Sydney suburb of Marrickville, Szell said a musical goodbye to Australia. The program was a mixture from several of his previous downtown concerts: Smetana's *Bartered Bride* Overture, the Grieg Piano Concerto, with Lawrence Godfrey Smith, who had played it in the July 10 Celebrity Concert, Delius's Prelude to *Irmelin*, Haydn's Symphony no. 88, and Dvořák's *Carnival* Overture. "Between 1,100 and 1,200 packed the hall to overflowing," reported the *Daily News*. "Well after the time for the concert was due to commence eager crowds were still arriving." At the end of the performance, "Even after the lights were switched on, the audience refused to go, calling for the conductor, amid vigorous acclamation." Szell said: "This is one of the most happy and successful nights of my stay in Australia. The acoustics of the hall are wonderful, the audience true music-lovers, and as for the orchestra—I have never seen it work harder or to such good purpose."[54]

Szell might have been reminded of a previous "happiest day," at the end of his first Scottish season. It would be a long time before he would enjoy another. The world outlook was increasingly bleak. The Szells decided it would not be safe to return to England on the *Strathallen*, as planned. Instead they went eastward on the *Aorangi* to Canada.

Moses had to go to Adelaide and Szell missed saying goodbye in person. He wrote a farewell letter to Szell, and the conductor responded:

> I and my wife are very sorry indeed that we have had no opportunity to see you before you left for Adelaide. I would have welcomed the chance to tell you personally once more how much I have enjoyed my second visit to Australia and to express my deep appreciation of the Commission's activities for the musical development of this happy country. I should like to add that I have had the greatest pleasure again in dealing with all and any sections and departments of the ABC and that the courtesy, knowledge and understanding of your officers will always stick in my mind as a model to be presented to many organisations overseas.[55]

Szell's contribution to its musical development would not be forgotten by Australia. Newspapers frequently carried items about him over the years, and Szell was prominently mentioned in a history that the ABC published about itself.[56] An article in the *Brisbane Telegraph* near the end of 1939 aptly characterized the impression Szell left on one listener:

> Oddly enough, there were a few musical know-alls in Australia who turned up their noses and sneered at this fine conductor. As far as I could make out their main objection was that he was so quiet and unobtrusive about everything. Perhaps it was because Dr. Malcolm Sargent has quite a different technique and no one disputes that he is a great conductor. But just as Schnabel produces his effects in one way and Paderewski in another, so does Szell control his orchestra by one method and Sargent by another. That however is not to say that one is superior to the other.[57]

With happy memories of Australia and sad thoughts of and for Europe, the Szells embarked on a new life in a new world. Truly out of work, Szell had turned down Toscanini's first invitation to conduct the NBC Symphony because of his commitment to Australia in 1939 and a second invitation in 1940 because of European engagements now cancelled. Events were turning grim. On August 23, 1939, the Nazi-Soviet Nonaggression Pact was signed and on September 1, Germany attacked Poland. Britain and France declared war on Germany on September 3. As the world faced the inevitable, the Szells settled in New York.

4

New World, New Beginnings (1939–46)

The luxury liner *Aorangi* landed in Vancouver on August 25, 1939, and the Szells made their way to New York City. Friends from Prague lived in an apartment building at 7 Park Avenue, and by October the Szells were settled there.[1]

Szell immediately took in New York's concert life. On October 21, he wrote to Henri Temianka, his "dear old friend," then living in California: "Your limericks were properly *schweinisch*," using a term of their old familiar banter, "but by far not so *schweinisch* as a performance of the 7th Beethoven by my Glasgow predecessor [John Barbirolli, conductor of the New York Philharmonic]. It was unimaginably helpless, and the orchestra took not the slightest notice of the conductor." To the typewritten letter he added in pen, "Please keep this completely between us!"[2]

Hopes of returning to Europe were soon dashed. On November 17, Szell received a cable from the manager of the Hague Orchestra, saying "situation in holland normal stop count on your coming stop when will you arrive stop answer by night letter answer paid stop best wishes." Szell's answer, sent the next day, read "intend arriving end january will advise further in time cordially."[3] The situation was anything but normal. That month Russia attacked Finland. Hitler was preparing to seize Denmark and the Low Countries. Szell stayed put.

The Szells faced new problems in the New World. Most ties with the Old World were cut and the rest soon would be. Money was evidently not a pressing matter for the Szells, but inactivity alone was oppressive. A hiatus of almost thirteen months fell between Szell's last performance in Australia, on July 27, 1939, and his debut season at the Hollywood Bowl, on August 16 and 23, 1940. In Australia, he had conducted twenty concerts in three months; before that, in Scotland and Holland, eighty concerts in five months. Accustomed to constant rehearsals and performances as he had been for nearly twenty years, uncertainty and musical inactivity took its emotional toll. On top of that, both Szells were despondent about the world situation, and that of their beloved Czechoslovakia. The fate of their relatives weighed especially heavily on them. George Szell's parents had fled from Vienna to southern France, believing it a safe haven from the advancing German army. It was not, and for the rest of his life Szell would regret that he did not extricate them when he had a chance.[4] Helene Szell's former husband, Ernest Teltsch, left Prague in April 1939 for France. In Paris he met Rudolf Firkusny, who he had known in Prague, and invited him to join him on the Brittany coast, where he had rented a house with his sons for the summer, thinking it safe. Instead, Firkusny escaped to Spain only a few days before the Germans occupied Paris, and he later settled in America.[5] The Szells did not know the fate of Helene's former family until war's end, but feared the worst.

In April 1940, Szell wrote to Temianka about his bad conscience regarding his long silence. He said he had been in a state of inertia caused by depression, from which he was only then recovering. Now the prospect of future conducting engagements, however vague, and playing the piano, engaging in chamber music, and, to a limited extent, even composing, opened up. But two months later he told Temianka, "It is impossible for me to write at this moment anything of a more personal character—I am sure you will know how we feel and share our feelings."[6]

The Russian basso Alexander Kipnis, a mainstay at the Metropolitan Opera, and his wife threw parties—soirées, they called them—to which the Szells were invited so that they could meet people. Szell had last seen Kipnis at their 1938 concert in Australia. The singer's son, harpsichordist Igor Kipnis, remembered the beautiful experience of hearing his father singing lieder, accompanied at the piano by Szell.[7] Mrs. Edgar M. Leventritt, a patron of the arts, regularly hosted parties at which some of the greatest artists of the time performed. There Szell played chamber music with Adolf Busch, Emanuel Feuermann, Zino Francescatti, Erica Morini, Joseph Szigeti, and others. The majority of them had been soloists with Szell in Europe.

With time on his hands, in 1939–40 Szell undertook a number of projects. He orchestrated Smetana's First String Quartet, *From My Life*. Boosey & Hawkes published the score in 1941, along with his transcription of Weber's *Perpetuum mobile*, which he first performed with the Los Angeles Philharmonic at the Hollywood Bowl in August 1940. Commissioned by Hans Heinsheimer, of Boosey & Hawkes, Szell edited several of Dvořák's Slavonic Dances. He also provided timings and instrumentation for a book on favorite orchestral works.[8]

On September 12, 1940, three weeks after Szell's debut at the Hollywood Bowl, he and his wife crossed the United States–Mexico border at Calexico, California, and entered Mexicali, returning to Calexico the next day. This was not a sightseeing trip: the Immigration Act of 1924 required them to reenter the United States as legal immigrants. As such, they could remain in the country, and soon thereafter they applied for citizenship. In 1946, after the usual waiting period, they became U.S. citizens.

In 1940 in New York, Szell taught at the Mannes School of Music; Carl Bamberger already conducted there, so Szell taught instrumentation, composition, and, along with the noted Felix Salzer, advanced theory. He remained on the Mannes faculty for five years, through the 1944–45 season, giving it up because of time pressure in his fourth and last year at the Metropolitan Opera. In 1941–42, Szell also taught courses at the New School for Social Research, one a "Symposium on Current Musical Issues" with fellow faculty members Henry Cowell, Hanns Eisler, Ernst T. Ferand, Jascha Horenstein, and Rudolf Kolisch.[9]

Among Szell's composition students were George Rochberg and Ursula Mamlok. Rochberg characterized Szell as a "monolith"; Mamlok remembers fear-inspired stomachaches before her composition lessons with him. Studying with Szell, Rochberg completed a set of piano variations that he performed at a concert Szell attended. Rochberg had "vague memories of certain places where Szell was quite pleased and expressed pleasure" in what he had done. "Well, naturally, that tickled me no end," he said, "because I knew that he was a tough cookie and that his standards were what they should be. Those were the standards I wanted—I didn't want anything less than that." Rochberg looked forward to his lessons with Szell but at the same time was somewhat intimidated by his imposing presence. Szell's powerful voice "could express very real and direct impatience if things weren't quite right," he recalled.

One day Rochberg came for a lesson and found Szell playing *Der Rosenkavalier* on the piano. Rochberg said of that moment, "When they speak of the blinding light that Paul had experienced on the road to Damascus, I had that experience. Listening to this man play, watching him, it was more than the piano. This thing was alive. Listening was tantamount to this blinding light. It was one of the great experiences of my musical life."[10]

In his composition lessons, Szell talked about structure and harmony but had no methodology that Rochberg recalls. He remembered a conversation with Szell about performance as having vital importance. Rochberg has applied a guiding principle of Szell's to every one of his compositions since that moment. Szell told him, "You must always hold something in reserve, always! You must never give everything away. Always hold something in reserve so that at the right moment you can release it."[11]

The Berlin-born Mamlok's first impression of Szell was of his resonant voice, which she heard as she waited for her first interview. She began talking in German, but he cut her off immediately, "Oh, no, my child," he said, "you better speak English. I only speak English." At one lesson there happened to be a harp in the room, and Szell gave her a thorough demonstration of how it was played and how its mechanism worked. He invited her to his New York Philharmonic rehearsals, to learn more about the orchestra. Sometime later they became closed to visitors. She believed it was because Szell occasionally insulted the orchestra, and they did not want that heard by outsiders.

He taught her harmony and counterpoint. Whenever Szell found a mistake, such as parallel fifths, he would get angry and lapse into German. *Schweinerei!* he would exclaim. If she attempted to give an excuse, he would shout at her, "You're lying!" But she learned. When Mamlok came to Mannes for lessons, she always saw Szell's little red car parked out front. Rochberg remembered Szell's Homburg hat and his coat with its fur collar.

Mamlok felt more than a little attracted to Szell the man, with his resonant voice and commanding presence, always immaculately dressed, his suits tailor-made. Looking over her compositions at a desk together or at the piano, she could observe his fingernails, which were neatly manicured. He was then still a chain smoker. Mamlok remembers cigarette ashes falling as he played. This appears rather paradoxical for such an otherwise fastidious person, but cigarette smoking was fashionable then.

Szell generously gave Mamlok extra lessons in counterpoint. At one time, when she had the possibility of publishing some piano compositions for children, he offered to give her one lesson a week for a month after school ended in June. She could not afford to pay and was fumbling for words when he, equally embarrassed, blurted out, "There is no fee."[12]

One of Szell's closest colleagues was Felix Salzer, to whom he often turned for sincere and informed criticism. Salzer was an authority on theory and the teachings of Heinrich Schenker, for whom Szell also had great respect. Szell and Salzer enjoyed long discussions on large and small musical issues, sometimes extending over several months. Their discussion about a rhythm in the Trio of Beethoven's Ninth Symphony, for example, was resumed a summer later in Switzerland. Szell tapped his version of the controversial rhythm on the body of a parked auto, which, in the heat of their renewed argument, Salzer took up in opposition.[13]

Szell's Hollywood Bowl concerts on August 18 and 23, 1940, served to ameliorate the dry period somewhat. They seem to have shown signs of his strain—Isabel Morse Jones, of the *Los Angeles Times*, was not impressed. "George Szell," she wrote, "made his debut as conductor in the Hollywood Bowl last night and was received judiciously. He is a martinet. That much was clear in 'The Star-Spangled Banner.'" Szell reminded her of Artur Rodzinski when he first came to Los Angeles. They conducted "like Viennese Conservatory directors used to think Americans liked. Rodzinski knows better now and it is quite possible that Szell will also, before he conducts many orchestras in the United States."[14] Carl Bronson, writing in the *Los Angeles Evening Herald and Express*, was not totally without reservations, but found Szell's Tchaikovsky Sixth, which "had taken an unforgettable grip upon our musical consciousness," the success of the evening.[15] Szell returned for several succeeding summers. His next engagement was a pair of concerts with the Detroit Symphony on January 23 and 30, 1941, with brilliant soloists Vladimir Horowitz and Zino Francescatti.

Six weeks later the long-delayed NBC Symphony engagement materialized. Szell had called on Toscanini soon after arriving in New York to remind him of his earlier invitations to conduct the orchestra. As Szell told it:

> We met at the house of the president [of the Hague Orchestra in 1938] and had a very nice chat at dinner, and nothing further happened except that a few months later there came the invitation from New York to conduct his orchestra in 1939, which I unfortunately couldn't accept because I was already booked in Australia for that summer.
>
> But when, on my way back to Europe, I was marooned in New York by the beginning of the war, I paid my respects to Toscanini and said to him, "Maestro, unfortunately I couldn't then, but now I can." Whereupon he said, "That's very well, but for this season everything is already booked. But for next season I renew my invitation." And so I conducted for the first time, I think it was 1941.[16]

Szell conducted four concerts with the NBC Symphony Orchestra in March 1941. At forty-three, severed from his European ties, this engagement was crucial for his career. He had been successful in Los Angeles and Detroit, but in New York, with the fabled orchestra created especially for Arturo Toscanini, the concerts would be broadcast live to the entire country.

Szell chose his programs carefully, dealing from strength to strength. Four programs could show his breadth and depth. He began with a Schumann symphony, the Fourth, a bold choice. More surefire would have been Beethoven, Brahms, or Tchaikovsky, but they were more frequently played. Beethoven's *Eroica* he saved for last.

Schumann's symphonies were not often played at that time. They were not well understood and their orchestration was considered weak. But Szell had his personal insights and solutions, and the Fourth was the least problematical in that respect. It is also shorter than the others, compact and intense, while lyrical. Szell loved it and played it with conviction and the insight of a lifetime of acquaintance. He balanced the Schumann with two other "specialties of the house," Haydn (Symphony no. 97 in C) and Strauss (*Till Eulenspiegel*). His Haydn was fresh and vibrant, his Strauss authentic and exciting.

Szell's NBC concerts took place in Studio 8-H at Radio City. The audience gave him a "rousing welcome," and reviews were nearly unanimous in their praise. Noel Straus, of the *New York Times*, appreciated that Szell, in his debut concert, had devised a program aimed at displaying his talents in the classical, romantic, and modern fields. He noted Szell's "grateful economy of gesture," and that he "incited his men to a type of performance characterized by immaculateness of tone and attack and by its enthusiasm and vitality." The Schumann gamble evidently paid off, but not without a cavil from Straus: "If his interpretation of the Schumann symphony was not memorable for subtlety or emotional depth, it was invariably alive, and dominated the attention by its virility and eloquence." Though recognizing Szell's "important stature" in the classical realm, Straus found parts of the Haydn ponderous. Straus noted, "Mr. Szell made his deepest impression, however, in a brilliant and highly colored presentation of Strauss's 'Till Eulenspiegel.' It was vividly set forth with great technical virtuosity and led to a climax of thundering power with the trial episode. . . . By this masterly accomplishment," Straus wrote, "Mr. Szell established himself as a conductor of truly distinguished abilities.[17]

Szell's orchestra transcription of *From My Life* received its premiere on a program of all-Czech music. He had "pondered" such a transcription for two years: "I considered all of the objections to such tampering with a composer's work and I arrived at the conclusion that far from being a crime, it was almost a duty to arrange 'From My Life' for orchestra," he said. "The thematic material seems to me to call for the bigger, richer, symphonic treatment. And Smetana, you know, once said he had no quarrel with any one who thought 'From My Life' was better suited to other forms than the quartet."[18]

Interest in Szell's concerts mounted. The all-Czech program received numerous reviews in the local newspapers as well as in *Musical America,* which judged the performances as "played with a fervor and a devotion. . . . Other conductors have made 'The Moldau' sing superbly," the writer remarked, "but Mr. Szell's performance had a lyrical beauty which those who heard it will not quickly forget." The reviewer questioned the wisdom of orchestrating Smetana's string quartet. Though he judged the scoring as admittedly "expert and the results can justly be termed brilliant," the "work of poetic imagery" was converted to one of "clangorous realism."[19]

Robert Lawrence extolled "Mr. Szell's rhythms [as] perfect, his grasp of the ensemble amazing."[20] Olin Downes commended Szell's *Roman Carnival* Overture: "Almost anyone can make an exhilarating noise with the 'Carnaval Romain' overture. But there are different ways of making that noise. . . . He played the allegro with wholly exceptional esprit, not merely loud and fast, but with glinting color and the 'flair' which inhabits the music. The orchestra played here with a special brilliancy." The reading of the *Eroica* "was the accomplishment of a musician who has made his success here by the most legitimate means and whose knowledge and sincerity are never in question. . . ." Downes believed that "intensities in the funeral march . . . were not wholly fulfilled," and the Scherzo "was taken too fast," blurring the syncopated accents and causing "the horns to bobble in the trio." The worst fault consisted of Szell missing "the hush and mystery of this movement . . . by a too literal treatment." Downes concluded, "He is a musician of a fine culture and broad horizons, and the public has been the richer by his engagement."[21]

Szell had been tested on the highest level and had succeeded brilliantly. In Europe and Great Britain he had been recognized as a worthy bearer of Toscanini's mantle.

But Szell had a serious falling out with Toscanini. The older conductor came to one of Szell's rehearsals of the *Eroica* and became enraged. Jack Berv, who played French horn under Toscanini in the NBC for seventeen years, gave his account of the incident in a letter to the *Saturday Review* in 1967:

> One day, Toscanini entered Studio 8H and sat down to listen to the rehearsal. Szell was rehearsing us in such a way that we would never know what a number would sound like until the performance. He repeated specific passages many times. Abe Reines, a contra-bassoon player who was sitting directly in front of me, was taking count of the number of times Szell stopped to repeat a passage. The final count was forty-four repetitions. . . .
>
> Toscanini came rushing up to the podium. He yelled at Szell, "What are you doing to my orchestra? They are my orchestra and you are rehearsing them like they are just-born babies! You do not know how to rehearse." With that, Toscanini ran out of the studio. Szell tried to continue. After that concert, he never again conducted the NBC Symphony Orchestra.[22]

Although Berv's account is suspect in some details—for example, there is no contrabassoon in the *Eroica*—the event did occur two days before the concert. Another NBC eyewitness, Alan Shulman, counted that Szell stopped fifty-four times in the slow movement. Shulman recalled that at intermission, Toscanini berated Szell for "having the audacity to wear out his orchestra. . . . I am sure it was water off Szell's back," Shulman recalled. "He was an intellectual conductor, but the ice flowed through his veins."[23]

Szell took Toscanini's displeasure very seriously. That same day he wrote the older conductor a conciliatory letter:

> 20th March 1941
> Illustrissimo Maestro,
> Please allow me to thank you once more for the criticism and advice you gave me this afternoon. Your benevolent frankness is a great honor and privilege for me and what you said, of unique importance. I shall remember every word you said and act accordingly. Please favor me again by telling what you don't like.
> Most gratefully
> Yours,
> George Szell
> Maestro Arturo Toscanini
> Riverdale N.Y.[24]

Szell's rehearsal methods vastly differed from Toscanini's. Later, with the New York Philharmonic, Szell felt it a special challenge to shape them up in his way. He may have felt that same challenge even more strongly with Toscanini's orchestra:

> Those who knew Toscanini only from his performances with the [NBC] Orchestra and never heard him with the New York Philharmonic, the Vienna Philharmonic, or the BBC Symphony during those earlier years can have but a very incomplete idea of his real greatness. Not only was Toscanini then at the very height of his powers, but his collaboration with those orchestras in public performances with live audiences seemed to inspire him more. The artificial, antiseptic atmosphere of Studio 8H with its small invited audience; and the Orchestra—which at its best was rather the finest collection of virtuosic players money could assemble, not an orchestra in the sense of an integrated organism—left more than a little to be desired.[25]

Toscanini's displeasure during the *Eroica* rehearsal could have shaken Szell so sufficiently that he was not at his best in its performance. That concert was not, as Berv asserted, the last time that he conducted the NBC. Szell tried to assuage Toscanini's wrath, but by his nature he could not play the role of sycophant and could not have fit in with the entourage that formed around the older conductor.

One wonders why NBC engaged Szell for two more concerts in January 1942. Harvey Sachs reported that Toscanini had a blowup with the NBC management and resigned for the 1941–42 season.[26] Leopold Stokowski was music director for that season and would have had no reason to block Szell's second engagement. Toscanini returned the following season, and after 1942 Szell did not conduct the NBC again.

Szell's Personal Side

The New Friends of Music invited Szell to conduct an all-Mozart concert in New York's Town Hall on March 1, 1942. The society, then in its fourth year, sponsored a modest season of concerts, some of chamber music and others for chamber orchestra. Many of its organizers were members of a small group of central European émigrés sometimes sarcastically referred to as "The Old Friends of Schnabel." The New Friends' Orchestra had been organized by Fritz Stiedry, like Szell an expatriate European conductor. Szell's debut was so successful that the orchestra's board hired him to replace Stiedry, who had invited him. A colleague of Stiedry, who was also a close friend of Szell, was warned by an embittered Stiedry, "Just wait until you are in his way." When Stiedry was the conductor of the Leningrad Philharmonic in the 1930s, he had invited Szell to be a guest conductor. When Szell left the Metropolitan Opera in 1946 to go to the Cleveland Orchestra, "he talked Edward Johnson into engaging [Stiedry] out of bad conscience."[27]

Between March 12 and April 10, 1942, Szell conducted three subscription pairs with the Los Angeles Philharmonic. During the summer, there were concerts at

Ravinia and the Hollywood Bowl. That summer he also made his debut at the Robin Hood Dell with the Philadelphia Orchestra, and he would conduct there in following summers. The engagements necessitated several cross-country trips, but this posed no hardship for Szell, who loved to travel and had an insatiable curiosity about his newly adopted country.

The Szells drove across the continent in the summer of 1940, a year after their arrival from Australia, and in many subsequent summers. Helene Szell remembered that they bought a secondhand Packard for $400. After 1943, however, the couple traveled mostly by rail. They may have tired of the long drives and had already seen many sights, but more likely, wartime gasoline rationing contributed to the change, and at the time, trains were luxurious.

His youthful fondness for practical jokes had ended, but Szell still liked to surprise. Just as he had dropped in unannounced on pianist Allen McCristal in Australia in 1939, he did something similar on one of his trans-U.S. drives. In his third NBC Symphony concert in March 1941, Szell had conducted Schubert's Symphony no. 9 in C, "The Great." A Mrs. Nellie Luthold in Spokane, Washington, had heard the broadcast and wrote Szell a fan letter. Not since hearing the Schubert conducted by Artur Nikisch in Berlin, she wrote, had she heard any performance as good. Szell was flattered by the comparison, for in his youthful Berlin days he had also been under Nikisch's spell. He saw on a map that he could pass through Spokane on his way to Los Angeles. It would require a detour, but he decided to make it for the fun of surprising Luthold, and also to see a new part of his adopted country. One afternoon Szell drove up to Luthold's house in Spokane and knocked on the door. When she answered, he said, "Are you Nellie Luthold? I'm George Szell." Amazed and thrilled, Luthold invited the Szells in for tea. She told the story for the rest of her life.[28]

Szell and the Metropolitan Opera

The Metropolitan Opera had its eye on Szell as early as 1926. Edward Ziegler, assistant manager of the company since 1916, considered Szell one of the "younger men" among European opera conductors who might someday be suitable for the Met. When Szell was beginning his St. Louis engagement, Ziegler wrote to Otto H. Kahn, president of the Met board and its chief stockholder:[29] "He is a most excellent musician. I heard him conduct an opera and thought he lacked authority, but that was three years ago and I am told he has improved very much."[30]

Artur Bodanzky, the Met's chief conductor, knew and respected Szell. In 1934 he recommended that Kirsten Flagstad coach with Szell for her forthcoming Met debut roles. She spent ten tense but productive days with the young conductor in Prague. When they finished, Szell wrote Bodanzky of his satisfaction with her knowledge of the roles. Flagstad's Met debut as Sieglinde in February 1935 caused an instant sensation.

While in Prague in 1935, Szell was offered and accepted an engagement with the Metropolitan by Herbert Witherspoon, the manager of the Met in 1934–35, that was never consummated. It was to have been for fourteen weeks with an option for the tour, and a salary of $400 per week. Witherspoon, who had been a Met singer under Toscanini and manager after Gatti-Casazza in 1935, had initiated hiring Szell. Selection of the conducting staff held a high priority. The Met retained Bodanzky as chief conductor in spite of much criticism; among new prospects was Fritz Reiner, an excellent conductor, though "difficult to get on with." Witherspoon's notes say: "Szell is especially desirable, because he has conducted in Italy, France, England, Germany, etc., Italian, French and German repertoire, and could therefore substitute for either Bodanzky or Panizza in case of illness."

But Witherspoon died suddenly of a heart attack in May 1935 and was succeeded by his assistant, Edward Johnson (another former singer), who had his own agenda for the Met. Martin Mayer wrote: "The most striking change Johnson made in Witherspoon's plans was the abandonment of the arrangement with Szell (which had never been announced); instead, Johnson rehired Gennaro Papi, whom Gatti had dropped in 1928. . . . It is fascinating to speculate on what might have happened at the Met if that ferociously intelligent musician had come on the scene in 1935 rather than in 1942."[31]

Szell began his operatic career in the United States at the Metropolitan with a revival of *Salome* on December 9, 1942, thirty-seven years to the day since its premiere in Dresden. The distinguished cast included Lily Djanel in the title role, making her American debut, Frederick Jagel as Herod, Herbert Janssen as Jokanaan, Karin Branzell as Herodias, and John Garris as Narraboth. The young American baritone Mack Harrell, who would become a favorite of Szell, sang the small role of First Soldier. Szell had *Salome* in his bones. As he later wrote:

> I conducted Salome for the first time in 1925 at the Berlin State Opera. How many times I have conducted it I cannot tell, but I must have conducted at least sixty or seventy performances all told, if not more, in Berlin, in Prague and at the Met.
>
> My earliest contact with that work, however, dates back to 1915 when I was serving my apprenticeship under Richard Strauss at the then Royal Opera in Berlin. I played the celesta part of Salome in performances conducted by Strauss himself at least fifty times during two seasons.
>
> My first contact with Salome as a listener, not as a performer, goes even further back. I heard this opera for the first time in my life in 1910 [while studying with Max Reger] in Leipzig under Egon Pollak, with Aline Sanden as Salome. She was at that time quite a famous representative of this particular work. I was only

> thirteen at that time but already a pretty completely equipped musician and was so fascinated and intoxicated by this opera that when I left the theatre after an hour and a half, it seemed to me as if I had spent only five minutes in there. I can experience this sensation of time-compressing, breathless tension to this day in listening to a good performance of Salome and that is one of the reasons, why, quite subjectively, I prefer it to the other Strauss operas.
>
> [Underline added by Szell in pen.][32]

Szell knew *Salome* inside and out; he understood how to pace it, and knew all its difficulties of execution and how to overcome them in preparation. He had the Met schedule twenty-one hours of orchestra rehearsal. The results bore out his effort, as Olin Downes attested: "The audience gained a different impression of the opera than it could have had in any recent seasons. . . . It was clear as soon as he started that Mr. Szell had the score secure in his brain and his hand, that he was reading it with authority and a true sense of the theatre."[33]

Virgil Thomson, critical curmudgeon, wrote:

> The score was squeezed for every effect, and yet the great line of it was kept intact and the sonorities remained within the domain of "legitimate" musical sounds. Mr. Szell did a virtuoso job on a difficult and complex work. He did not force the singers or the brasses; he made all the music sound and sound well. So vigorous an hour and a half of musical experience is not to be met with every week.

Thomson had especially noted that "the brilliant performance of the polytonal quintet of the Jews was one of the outstanding movements of the evening," a mark of Szell's mastery of ensemble complexities.[34] Szell's technical virtuosity and architectural grasp of the most complicated musical structures and orchestral fabrics would be recognized throughout his career.

On December 19, ten days after his debut, Szell conducted the first of six *Tannhäusers* of the season and received much critical praise. Irving Kolodin found Szell's interpretation "the most interesting *Tannhäuser* in years." He especially noted the fine articulation Szell brought to the festal scene in the Hall of Song, in which "soloists, chorus, on and off-stage musicians were balanced with an energy and artistic sensibility which made a fresh experience of this more than familiar music."[35]

Downes praised Szell's performance as a realization of Wagner's intentions: "The sense of form which characterized each moment of this reading was exceptionally communicative of the drama as well as the music structure. . . . The orchestra not only underscored but often anticipated what was to come, revealed the thought in the character's mind, as Wagner more than once intends, before it becomes visible in action."[36]

On December 30, Szell conducted *Boris Godunov*.[37] Toscanini had introduced Mussorgsky's magnificent tapestry of old Russia at the Met in 1913, and the opera had presented it with great regularity since. The Rimsky-Korsakov version had always been used and, except for Chaliapin, who sang his part in the original Russian, the opera was sung in Italian. The sets, acquired in Paris for the Met premiere twenty-seven years before and judiciously repainted, remained in use. Ezio Pinza sang the title role, with other key roles played by Irra Petina, Marita Farell, Alessio De Paolis, Nicola Moscona, René Maison, Kerstin Thorborg, Leonard Warren, Salvatore Baccaloni, and Mack Harrell.

Press commentary was again unanimous. Szell's conducting was the new element and his firm control, overall concept, and thorough preparation laid the foundation of a powerful and expressive performance. As Downes put it, "The opera came again and at long last into its own."[38] Thomson found Szell "full of fire."[39]

Revelations in Boston

Late in January, Szell made a brilliantly successful debut with the Boston Symphony Orchestra. His first program was Schubert's C Major Symphony, Smetana's *Moldau*, and his own orchestration of the "From My Life" String Quartet. Critics observed that Szell used no scores. Some noted that he reseated the violins, placing the seconds on the conductor's right, "according to the so-called 'classical' plan," one wrote.[40] "Whether he had reseated the orchestra or not," another remarked, "Mr. Szell would have achieved a highly individual performance of Schubert's beautiful C major symphony. From the outset, his conception of the work was individual and arresting, filled with contrast, and romantic flavor."[41]

Szell, in turn, found the orchestra "altogether unique," and the concert, he said, was "the crowning event of [his] life."[42] He thought that Boston's orchestra was unequalled by any he had conducted thus far in Europe or America. Back in New York, he wrote to Henri Temianka: "Boston was a great experience for me—quite apart from the really tremendous success with Audience, Press, and—last but not least, the orchestra, which gave me ovation after ovation—already at the rehearsals. The greatest thing about it was, that I met an orchestra that has been trained to make its daily routine to give its best![43]

Szell put his foot in his mouth in Boston by telling the *Globe*'s Cyrus Durgin that he could make him a good clam chowder . . . New York style! "This reporter feebly observed," Durgin answered, "that New York clam chowder is not discussed in these parts."[44] Szell's gaffe was not fatal—the orchestra invited him back for the season-after-next for two programs and several out-of-town dates. On his return to Boston in 1945, Szell made a culinary turnabout which, although assuaging the New England pride, might have been taken as an insult by his hometown. He told Cyrus Durgin that he now liked the New England–style clam chowder better.[45] An editorial in the *New York Sun* picked up on that: "Mr. Durgin remarked that

Manhattan clam chowder was not even discussed in those parts. This year, when Mr. Szell returned to serve as guest conductor of the Boston orchestra, he gave proof of good memory and a talent for diplomacy. Meeting the same interviewer, he asked whether he had been forgiven for the Manhattan clam chowder and went on to say that now he liked New England style better. Manhattan will not hold this against Mr. Szell."[46]

Finishing out the Met season, Szell conducted fifteen performances of the three operas with which he had so auspiciously begun: six of *Boris*, three of *Salome*, and six of *Tannhäuser*. *Boris* toured to Philadelphia and *Boris* and *Tannhäuser* to Chicago. This *Tannhäuser* featured Lauritz Melchior in the title role, Rose Bampton as Elizabeth, Lawrence Tibbett as Wolfram, and the brave Marjorie Lawrence as Venus. Lawrence, who had recently recovered from polio, brought great dramatic, as well as vocal, force to her portrayal, while reclining throughout her scene on a specially constructed couch.

The *Chicago Tribune*'s notoriously venomous Claudia Cassidy gave a review that could well be called ecstatic, referring to the opera as "admirably cast and brilliantly conducted. . . . With a crackling performance of the overture." Szell "captured the warring elements of the score in remarkable fusion, strumming its pagan fire and its mystical tenderness with notable conviction."[47] With *Boris* in Chicago on April 2, 1943, Szell's first Met season ended.

The Hometown Band

In 1943 Szell began a long-term association with his then-hometown orchestra, the New York Philharmonic, that would span twenty-seven years. His conducting debut with the orchestra took place on July 4 and 11, 1943, on its new summer series of Sundays in Carnegie Hall. Broadcast nationally by CBS over a network of 118 stations and sponsored by U.S. Rubber, listeners could hear the Philharmonic on the radio every week throughout the year, a first. Besides Szell, the roster of distinguished conductors for the new series included Bruno Walter, Pierre Monteux, Eugene Ormandy, José Iturbi, Fritz Reiner, Dimitri Mitropoulos, Howard Barlow, Vladimir Golschmann, and Wilhelm Steinberg.[48] The list of soloists was equally notable, including Claudio Arrau, Robert Casadesus, Josef Hofmann, Arthur Rubinstein, Artur Schnabel, Adolf Busch, Nathan Milstein, and Marjorie Lawrence.

Szell's first program bowed to the patriotic holiday with Sousa's march *Stars and Stripes Forever*. For his second program, he also included an American work, Gershwin's *Rhapsody in Blue*. Eugene List, then a sergeant in the U.S. Army, was soloist.

In June and July 1943 Szell commuted between New York and Philadelphia and returned to Ravinia in July and August. He seemed to have struck a comfortable professional balance, conducting opera during the winter season in New York from

November to May, and then leading prestigious orchestra festivals in the summers, usually ending at the Hollywood Bowl, followed by a restful vacation in Santa Monica.

During the 1943–44 season, Erich Leinsdorf left the Met for the Cleveland Orchestra. Szell took over the German repertoire, conducting twenty-three performances of eight operas: *Boris* (3), *Der Rosenkavalier* (5), *Salome* (4), and two complete cycles of Wagner's *Ring*, in addition to three separate performances of *Die Walküre*. In 1942, his first season at the Met, Szell had been engaged for the first part of the season and gradually received extensions taking him to the end of the season. In 1943 the Met engaged him for a full twenty weeks in advance. Szell's compensation was markedly improved, indicative of his growing responsibilities and value to the company. He received $12,500 for the season, increasing his average per performance fee by $200, to $568.

Szell opened the Met's diamond jubilee season with *Boris Godunov* on November 22, 1943. Four days later he led *Der Rosenkavalier*, and, on December 2, his first Met *Die Walküre*, which "unrolled a panorama of myth and fantasy at the Metropolitan last night," Louis Biancolli wrote, "in a tight-knit reading":

> With all due respect to a sound vocal staff, Mr. Szell, like Mr. Walter the night before, was in the big news last night. Wagnerism is in the man's blood. No detail was too puny for sharp attention, and the musico-dramatic unity was never lost sight of. . . . Mr. Szell's rendering was steeped in expressive style. Fervor and conviction pulsed through, and there seemed to be a god of music last night—Richard Wagner—and his prophet was George Szell.[49]

On February 8, 1944, Szell began the first of two *Ring* cycles. Since 1887–88, except for the years of the First World War, when German opera was not performed, the *Ring* cycle had often been heard in New York. Separately impressive, four massive operas given consecutively cohere into a whole of near superhuman proportions. They invariably generate a frenzy of anticipation and excitement. Their presentation demands talent, energy, and endurance; the latter is also required of the audience. Szell's understanding and mastery of the *Ring* was complete and of long standing, and fully justified the fervor. According to Max Rudolf, Szell knew the fifteen-hour score so well that he could play and sing the entire cycle at the piano from memory, and his interpretation was superior to any Rudolf had ever experienced. Herbert F. Peyser believed Szell's first complete *Ring* cycle to be "the greatest heard at the Metropolitan in a generation." For this, he attributed "the overwhelming share of credit . . . to George Szell, a Wagnerian conductor of the stripe of Seidl, Mottl and Mahler, who at long last has restored in New York the authentic Wagner tradition obscured for so many years by a false, irreverent, cynical and small-scale one. . . . But if a new spirit seemed repeatedly to possess them it emanated beyond question from the conductor's stand."

Peyser's analysis of Szell's contribution suggests Szell's particular strengths:

> Something more potent and pervasive than questions of tempi or problems of phrasing, rhythm and balance lay at the root of Mr. Szell's achievement, something which governs and determines all these and related considerations—the element of love, the spirit of enthusiasm, which in Wagner intuitively resolves deep secrets and conquers myriad difficulties. . . . The *Rheingold* which the conductor piloted on Feb. 8 was irrespective of shabby scenery, weakness of casting and freaks of stage management—quite the finest, most poetic and animated heard at this theater in a blue moon.[50]

Several music critics noted that the orchestra, while mostly playing very well, made numerous technical slips. But, as one critic put it, "so much of the playing was eloquent that they were quickly forgotten."[51] The Met gave Szell the responsibility of improving the orchestra. In the spring of 1944 Helene Szell wrote a friend, "This season was quite thrilling. Now with the season over George has daily for hours auditions as there will be quite some changes for the better in the orchestra."[52] The number of new players in the 1944–45 season was high, twenty or more. Early in that season one reviewer felt that even with the new players, the orchestra sounded "thin," a possible result of a wartime shortage of qualified personnel. At the end of the season, Downes proclaimed that George Szell "simply transformed the works he directed by some new preparation and grasp of his scores.[53]

Social and artistic changes at the Met also reflected a turn of events brought about by the war. A larger, more affluent public than ever before was seeking entertainment. The Metropolitan Opera enjoyed a very well-attended season even though it had been lengthened from sixteen to twenty weeks. Moreover, at that time the Met was enjoying a golden age of conductors. In addition to Szell, operagoers heard performances led by Bruno Walter, Fritz Busch, and Sir Thomas Beecham.

Reviews of Szell's Met performances enumerate the recurrent themes of strong leadership and sweeping sense of the music's architecture, as well as minute attention to nuance and detail. Critics noted that he inspired and supported the singers so that they gave their best, and he balanced the orchestra so that they were always heard. The Met's stage settings were sometimes ancient and tired, and the level of singing was not always first-rate, but Szell usually transcended this. By the end of his second Met season, *Time* magazine hailed his success in Wagner and Moussorgsky as "remarkable in its power and drama." *Time* pictured the Szells at home:

> Szell lives with his striking, chestnut-haired Czech wife in a Manhattan apartment so scrupulously kept that visitors are almost afraid to sit down in it. A devout gourmet, he frequently terrifies his wife by tying an apron around his muscular torso and assuming autocratic control of the kitchen.[54] He resents all imputations of artistic temperament. Says George Szell: "There is nothing in-

teresting about me. I have no hobbies. I am not melancholy. My accounts are all in perfect order. I am so damn normal. . . ."

"I am so damn normal" was the photo caption for a frontal view of Szell's face. Unsmiling, his mouth was set, and his eyes, precisely centered within his thick glasses, looked straight out at the reader. His thinning hair seemed even thinner, emphasizing his forehead. It was a pose of confidence and satisfaction. He may have meant that he lived a life of routine and discipline, of hard work, without being eccentric. Szell's daily business just happened to be the sublime art of music. His businesslike exterior belied the fact that he was a performing artist. For him the trappings of an international career were not in themselves glamorous. Gourmet food and first-class travel and hotels were a way of life for any successful businessman. But artists' private lives as a kind of public entertainment was not his way. The *Time* article spoke of him as "a Jewish refugee from Nazi Europe and a fervent Hitler-hater," but said that "his outward manner suggests the average American idea of the typical Nazi," that "he fixes his orchestra with a thick-spectacled stare that would do credit to a cinema Prussian," and that he was "one of the most coldly efficient tyrants who ever stood in the Metropolitan's orchestra pit."[55]

In the summer of 1944, after two broadcast concerts with the Detroit Symphony, Szell returned to the Robin Hood Dell, Ravinia, and the Hollywood Bowl, for his third, fourth, and fifth seasons, respectively. After the Hollywood Bowl concerts, Szell again vacationed in Santa Monica. He wrote his friend Eric Oldberg that the condition of the Bowl orchestra "has disintegrated almost completely." He attributed the "47 changes" partly to players defecting to the more lucrative film studios, but also to the "whims" of Los Angeles Philharmonic conductor Alfred Wallenstein. "They sounded like a Kurkapelle in a minor European summer resort," he wrote, but "when I took over they did their damndest."[56]

Szell's third season at the Metropolitan Opera (1944–45) was interspersed with concerts with the Boston Symphony, for the second and last time, and his debut in the regular subscription season of the New York Philharmonic. His winter season began with a pair of concerts with the Montreal Symphony on October 17 and 18. Conducting a standard program of works by Weber, Beethoven, and Brahms, he received glowing reviews. At the Metropolitan Opera, he conducted two *Ring* cycles and added two new operas: *Die Meistersinger* and *Don Giovanni*. Ezio Pinza, one of the great Dons, who led the cast on opening night, and Szell, who had identified with Mozart's music since his childhood piano studies with Richard Robert, made a brilliant combination. Szell had conducted the opera often in Prague, the city for which it was composed and premiered. Virgil Thomson called their collaboration "the liveliest performance of Mozart's *Don Giovanni* this city has witnessed in quite some years."[57]

Szell squeezed in his first guest engagement with the Cleveland Orchestra between Metropolitan Opera performances for two weeks in early November. His enormous success led to an invitation to return for three weeks the following season. Beginning on December 14, 1944, Szell conducted two weeks of concerts with the New York Philharmonic. He had been engaged by Artur Rodzinski, former Cleveland Orchestra conductor and then music director of the Philharmonic, and planning had been under way for almost a year. In mid-February 1944, Rodzinski had requested that Szell submit a list of works he wished to play, to ensure that there were no duplications on other guests' programs. A champion of American music, he asked Szell to include at least two works by American composers. Although his first program was vintage Szell—Weber, Beethoven, Smetana, and Strauss—he included Barber's *Second Essay for Orchestra* on his second program and, on his return for two weeks in March, Lukas Foss's *Ode*. "Contemporary composers in this country," Szell said, "are as good as anywhere in the world."[58] When he criticized Foss's piece in rehearsal in front of the orchestra, the feisty young composer countered by saying, "Maybe it's the way you're conducting it!"[59]

Three years earlier, Olin Downes had been lukewarm about Szell's *Eroica* with the NBC Symphony Orchestra, but now he judged his reading "superbly realized, and surcharged with that master's rugged power . . . an *Eroica* to be remembered with gratitude and admiration."[60] When Szell returned in March, the critic found him wanting. Of his performance of Haydn's Symphony no. 97, Downes wrote "too coarse-grained . . . too precise and too much domineered. . . . The winged flight was not there." He credited Szell for his Metropolitan opera performances, which "have made history there," but plainly stated that, "In view of his exceptional musical mind, and brilliant musicianship, in symphonic music he seldom convinces us." Downes allowed that "sentiment there was and plenty of energy, swiftness, rhythm and fine dynamics, too," but "for all that, there was the impression of the didactic."[61] Szell never did completely escape from that perception, although to many his interpretations in the two and a half decades with the Cleveland Orchestra were informed by a passion that rose to great heights. But it was rarely characterized by relaxation.

At the Met, *Die Meistersinger* was a staggering success. *Newsweek* called Szell a "windmill on the podium" who brought the opera "back to buoyant, glowing life." A description of his podium antics could have applied to Gustav Mahler: "When the music soared, he too, soared so fervently he carried principals, orchestra, and chorus with him. His arms waved like a limber windmill; his spare body scrunched down when he quieted the music, rose on tiptoe as the sound poured forth in crashing crescendos. And when the audience several times applauded in the wrong place, he shushed it with one arm while he kept right on conducting with the other."[62]

Musical America pointed out a paradox. It listed the orchestra's many shortcomings ("roughness of tone was not uncommon, woodwind counterpoint . . . was sometimes thin and ragged, and the strings occasionally wanted richness") and those of a number of the singers, but the overall impression was favorable. Owing to the cohesive quality that Szell brought to it, "Mr. Szell was the mainspring of the performance. His viable tempos, his fastidious insistence upon the phrase and the details of design brought the score up off its heels and gave it a fleetness and plasticity that few conductors even try to achieve where Wagner is concerned."[63]

Szell thrived on activity. On Sunday afternoon, February 25, 1945, he made his New York debut as a pianist in a memorable concert of the New Friends of Music in Town Hall, playing the two piano quartets of Mozart with three members of the Budapest String Quartet. The reviews cited his "extraordinary sense of ensemble," "singing tone," and "skill in building climaxes." Moreover, a reviewer recognized Szell as a "musician concerned only with the veracious conveyance of the composer's message," even while "the strength of his personality indubitably dominated" his performance.[64] Szell and the Budapest instrumentalists would further hone their interpretations of the two quartets at the Library of Congress in 1945 and eventually make a historic recording of both in August 1946. On March 13 he performed Beethoven's Quintet for Piano and Winds at a special concert for Philharmonic patrons, with four principal winds: Harold Gomberg, oboe; Simeon Bellison, clarinet; William Polisi, bassoon; and Joseph Singer, French horn. Szell could not help being pleased with the lavish critical acclaim coming his way, yet he remained objective and exacting with self-criticism. "The press has been so unanimously and monotonously panegyric about everything I touched that it is getting most embarrassing," he wrote to Hilda Oldberg. "Fortunately I myself know best when things ain't that good.[65]

Returning to the Met after the second Philharmonic fortnight, he conducted *Die Walküre* on March 17, 1945, *Die Meistersinger* on the twenty-second, *Siegfried* on the twenty-fourth, *Der Rosenkavalier* on the twenty-ninth, and, ending the Saturday cycle he began on the tenth, *Götterdämmerung* on the thirty-first. He was scheduled to conduct the Strauss in Cleveland in April but became ill and canceled; this rarely occurred with him. Cleveland especially looked forward to the engagement after his extremely successful debut with the orchestra.

Szell's will was so strong that it was always a surprise to be reminded that his body was vulnerable. Cumulative activity had weakened him, and he contracted measles. This posed a serious threat to Szell's musical career, for he suffered what at first he minimized as "a silly middle-ear-abscess" in both ears: it did not cause pain but obstructed his hearing considerably.[66] He came to realize the seriousness of his condition. While Max Rudolf was visiting, Szell played a piano chord and asked Rudolf what he heard. When Rudolf instantly and correctly identified the chord and its notes, Szell said, "I don't hear it that way." He was frightened. For a performing musician this was tantamount to life-threatening.

Szell's physician was a fellow refugee with whom he felt comfortable, but when his condition did not improve, he finally saw a specialist, who operated on one ear and, later, on the other. Szell endured three weeks in the hospital, visited nearly every day by Rudolf, with whom he played gin rummy. Fortunately, Szell's hearing was fully restored.

Helene's younger son, John Teltsch, who had lived with his father and older brother in Brittany during the Nazi occupation, was the only one to survive. He had been taken in by a French family. John knew his uncle and aunt's address in England and, after the liberation of France, was able to contact them; his aunt and uncle, in turn, informed Szell and Helene. Szell arranged for the boy's admission to the United States, obtaining for him the first postwar entry visa from France.[67]

A day after his forty-eighth birthday, on June 8, 1945, Szell felt ready to conduct the New York Philharmonic in the first of four Sunday concerts. He took the rest of the summer off to fully recuperate. In mid-October Szell played the Brahms F Minor Piano Quintet with the Budapest Quartet at the Library of Congress. About the Brahms, Szell had written to the chief of the Library of Congress Music Division that "after a period of being fed up with it and a subsequent period of rest, [the work] turns out not to be such a bad piece after all."[68]

The 1945–46 season proved pivotal for Szell's career. His heavy schedule now precluded teaching at Mannes. At the Met for a fourth and final season—twenty-five performances of five operas, including tour performances in Boston, Cleveland, and Chicago—he inserted concerts with the New York Philharmonic, beginning on November 1 and 2, 1945.

Bruno Zirato, associate manager of the Philharmonic, asked Szell to change his rehearsal schedule from five two-and-a-half-hour sessions to four three-hour rehearsals. Szell agreed, although he wrote to Zirato, "This works very much to my disadvantage in the first week as I would need most of the available time for the 1st program with the [Strauss] Don Quixote which has not been played for some years and the new Schoenberg piece [Theme and Variations, op. 43]." In return, he asked that the players familiarize themselves individually with their parts of the Schönberg "so we don't waste any time at the first rehearsal with mere deciphering."[69] This request, rendered diplomatically, would be mandatory when Szell ruled his own orchestra. Throughout his career, Szell sought to make first rehearsals a musical, rather than purely technical, experience. With this head start, his orchestra could reach higher by the end of any rehearsal period. It was one factor that permitted Szell to say later of the Cleveland Orchestra, "We start rehearsing where the vast majority of orchestras finish performing."[70]

Rodzinski vetoed Szell's proposed season opener, Tchaikovsky's Symphony no. 6, *Pathétique*. He had recently made a recording of it and felt he should be "identified" with the work himself. "I feel it is a poor business," Rodzinski wrote to Zirato, "so I am awfully sorry I can't do that." Rodzinski had also been reluctant to honor Szell's request to conduct Strauss's *Don Quixote*, as he planned it for his own program that season. Szell, however, must not have accepted the double veto without protest, for two weeks later, Zirato informed him that Rodzinski had agreed to give him *Don Quixote*.[71] The program would begin with the Schoenberg Variations, op. 43, and include Mozart's "Jupiter" Symphony.

Szell chose the Philharmonic's principal cellist, Leonard Rose, to perform the solo role in the Strauss. Backstage before one of Szell's previous Philharmonic concerts, Szell had heard Rose practicing the Dvořák concerto, which he was going to perform with the orchestra a few weeks later. "He said 'come to my room,'" Rose recalled, "and he sits down at the piano and begins to play from memory the Dvořák concerto—from beginning to end, and he was extremely complimentary when we finished." When the twenty-six-year-old cellist found out that Szell later requested him for the *Don Quixote* role, he was thrilled.[72]

Although all critics respected Szell's musicianship and control of the orchestra, sides were drawn pro and con. The cons, led by the *Times*' Olin Downes, did not begrudge Szell those qualities, but found Szell's "Jupiter" performance "clean and somewhat didactic." Downes was fair, however, and praised the *Quixote* accordingly: "This work has been played by every conductor of pretensions for nearly half a century. But we do not recall any previous performance of it when it had such a completely illuminating interpretation."

Irving Kolodin in the *Sun* praised Rose and violist William Lincer for their solo parts, but emphasized that "the responsibility [for this re-creation] rested squarely on the conductor's shoulders, and Szell's did not sag." Kolodin found qualities in Szell's Mozart that Downes did not: "Having succumbed to this spell of Jumboism—regarding the largest thing on the program as the most important—one may add that Szell was an even more admirable musician in the 'Jupiter.' This was musicianship incarnate . . . producing a warm amount of supple, animated and clean-contoured Mozart."[73]

Szell's final full season at the Met began with a *Rosenkavalier*, revived from the previous season, in Philadelphia on November 27, 1945. The *Ring* was given a rest but *Götterdämmerung* was retained this season, as well as *Die Meistersinger*. Szell conducted Verdi's *Otello*, his first of the standard Italian repertoire at the Met. Downes commended Szell for "the finest reading we have heard of the score. He conducted not only with knowledge and authority, but with passion that made the music blaze." Kolodin praised Leonard Warren (as Iago) for his magnificent vocal resources, and "under the menacing baton of Szell, more tonal variety than he usually bothers about."[74]

From December 20, 1945, to January 5, 1946, Szell made his second guest appearance with the Cleveland Orchestra. In mid-January, he met with members of the Cleveland Orchestra's board, resulting in a three-year engagement as musical director.

On the twenty-eighth Szell conducted another *Don Giovanni* at the Met, and he returned to the Philharmonic for a week. Perhaps he felt a "new sense of security" as a "full-fledged conductor," no longer "a menial," in the words of Kolodin. A visibly energized Szell returned to the Philharmonic.[75] He presented its first reading of Bartók's *Concerto for Orchestra*. Szell had conducted that virtuosic work in Cleveland just a month before; this was only its second New York performance. Edward O'Gorman observed that Szell, "in rather more animated spirits than usual, but still the unrelenting orchestral disciplinarian, turned out a program that at times threatened to raise the roof with its sheer brilliance and vitality."[76]

Although Virgil Thomson called it an "impeccable concert," he nevertheless found Szell's style unconvincing. "If the concert was lacking in that flamelike quality that makes the difference between a merely good evening and a memorable one, the fault lies probably with Mr. Szell's temperament, which is neither poetic nor passionate." More important, however, was Thomson's recognition that Szell's inclusion of the Bartók among standard repertoire—Brahms and Berlioz—represented Szell's new confidence:

> Ever since his arrival in this country, he has stuck to the warhorses of symphonic repertory with a tenacity that has shown more strength of character than liveliness of understanding. His conducting technique is thoroughly contemporary, even advanced; but his taste (if his programs represent his taste, as we must suppose) has been shown to us consistently nineteenth century. We have no reason to know that he has ever, up till now, considered the music of his own century as having anything to do with either his obligations or his opportunities as a conductor. Not even Toscanini or Bruno Walter, whose programs are also reactionary but who are, after all, some thirty years his senior, has pursued so willful a line.
>
> Last night's deviation from this line was the Concerto for Orchestra by his late fellow-countryman, Béla Bartók. It is not on record that Mr. Szell ever conducted a piece by Bartók in this city, where he has conducted a good deal, during that composer's lifetime. I find the fact regrettable, because I have never heard in my lifetime so admirable a rendering of any work by Bartók.
>
> That Mr. Szell should turn his back on the world that he (at least) still lives in and become a sort of archeologist of Romanticism would be a charming gesture, if only there were any evidence that his interest in the nineteenth century included any of that vast landscape that lies beyond its chestnut trees.[77]

Thomson evidently did not know of Szell's international performances of contemporary music, but his criticism was valid at that time in Szell's recent American career. Kolodin, on the other hand, found "much to listen to both in Berlioz and Brahms." "Szell," he perceptively wrote, "is one of the few conductors of the day who has been vivified rather than paralyzed by the Hiroshimian energy released by Arturo Toscanini. Such qualities as clarity of texture, niceness of balance and forward-pressing energy that never allows a work to lag have not often been evident in the Toscaninian degree they were last night."[78]

Szell returned to the Met for the end of his last full season, conducting more *Meistersingers* and *Rosenkavaliers*, *Otellos*, and *Götterdämmerungs*, and a *Don Giovanni*. In all, Szell conducted twenty-five performances of five operas that season. On January 24, 1946, the appointment of Szell as conductor of the Cleveland Orchestra was announced. He finally conducted the Met on tour in Cleveland, a performance of *Der Rosenkavalier* on April 26. With a performance in Chicago on May 11, 1946, Szell ended his four years at the Met, with its blessing. The Met press release stated, "His loss to the Metropolitan public is tempered by the hope, as expressed by both Mr. Szell and Mr. Johnson, that the conductor will keep in close touch with the Opera House and that guest performances may be arranged at some future time if compatible with his symphonic schedule."[79] During four seasons, Szell conducted a total of eighty-five performances of eleven operas—seventy-two in New York and thirteen on tour.[80] The bare statistics tell just a small part of his enormous impact on the Met.

5

Cleveland

Contest and Commitment (1942–47)

The Cleveland Orchestra's twenty-fifth anniversary season, 1942–43, was Artur Rodzinski's tenth with the orchestra, a double cause for celebration. Instead, the orchestra faced a major disappointment: Rodzinski announced that he would be leaving Cleveland after the season to succeed John Barbirolli at the New York Philharmonic. A search for a new conductor began.

Hiring an American conductor received considerable support, as the president of the board of trustees of the Musical Arts Association, Thomas Sidlo, acknowledged: "We'd like nothing so much as to engage an American, but the number of available American conductors with the proper experience is very low."[1] Rodzinski, too, had much to say about choosing his successor, naming Alfred Wallenstein, Howard Barlow, Frank Black, Albert Stoessel, and Izler Solomon as qualified American conductors. He emphasized that the board should assess musical qualifications in at least four pairs of guest concerts lest a one- or two-program star fizzle out under closer scrutiny. Rodzinski also advised that the opinions of orchestra musicians be considered, as they had been earlier in Los Angeles, when he had been selected, and as in Chicago, the orchestra there seeking a successor to the late Frederick Stock.[2] Arthur Loesser supported this method, writing, "the most important thing is that he have the respect and admiration of the players."[3] Most of this good advice was ignored.

The trustees narrowed the choice to Wallenstein, music director of New York radio station WOR; Stoessel, head of the Juilliard School of Music; and Metropolitan Opera conductor Erich Leinsdorf. Wallenstein soon faded from the picture. Stoessel made a good impression as guest conductor in 1938. He had the support of a minority faction led by Percy W. Brown, a vice president of the Musical Arts Association, and leading Cleveland musical figures such as composer and music critic Herbert Elwell; composer, teacher, and former Cleveland Orchestra assistant conductor Arthur Shepherd; pianist and music critic Arthur Loesser; and pianist Beryl Rubinstein, director of the Cleveland Institute of Music.[4]

Leinsdorf had never conducted the Cleveland Orchestra, but he had an effective champion in Constance Hope, his publicist and manager. Among her other important Cleveland connections, Hope had the ear of the orchestra's founder, Adella Prentiss Hughes, then in her seventies but still a powerful presence on the orchestra's board. "Della," wrote Hope in a letter seen by Percy Brown, "let us conspire together to bring Erich Leinsdorf to Cleveland."[5]

The Vienna-born Leinsdorf had come to the United States in 1936, fresh from assisting Toscanini and Bruno Walter at the Salzburg Festival, and, with the help of Constance Hope, quickly found his way into the Metropolitan Opera. He was thirty-one years old and his orchestral conducting experience was limited, but the cachet of the Met carried much weight in Cleveland and he used it to good advantage. Leinsdorf spoke at the annual Chamber of Commerce spring opera luncheon on March 23, flanked by the Met's general manager, Edward Johnson. Speculation ran high that Sidlo arranged this opportunity to boost Leinsdorf's candidacy, as Sidlo was also chairman of the Northern Ohio Opera Association, local sponsor of the Met tour.[6]

The Contest

March 1943 proved fateful for the Cleveland Orchestra. The selection committee would make its recommendation to the Musical Arts Association's Trustees on the thirty-first. Leinsdorf met with the selection committee on the eleventh, and then stayed a day for a luncheon meeting with Sidlo and Brown, who had been out of town the day before. Goddard Lieberson, an executive of Columbia Masterworks, met with them on the seventeenth on behalf of Fritz Reiner, then conductor in Pittsburgh, who recorded for Columbia; Stoessel met with them on the nineteenth.

Into this political cauldron George Szell's name entered the Cleveland arena for the second time in a decade.[7] Against the advice of Arthur Judson, who surely had an inside track on the situation, Szell quietly went to Cleveland on March 9 to meet with members of the committee. A number of newspaper articles listed him as a contender, along with Dimitri Mitropoulos, who was not.[8]

Hughes felt determined to further Leinsdorf's cause, but she was even more determined to block Szell's. For unknown reasons, she had taken a strong dislike to him and did not hesitate to make it generally known. She was formidable as champion or opponent. Sidlo and Hughes made a powerful team, and their faction prevailed. The board of trustees approved the appointment of Leinsdorf, who had the selection committee's vote of four to one in his favor. Percy Brown cast the dissenting vote, for Albert Stoessel. He wrote in his diary, "Tom Sidlo railroaded E. L. through and offended the women." On April 1, the orchestra announced Leinsdorf's appointment.

In his first Cleveland season, 1943–44, Leinsdorf was scheduled to conduct sixteen out of the twenty subscription pairs. Following the dynamic Rodzinski, Leinsdorf needed all the breaks he could get; unfortunately for him, they were all bad ones. He had come to the post not without controversy, and had been selected without proving himself among a field of eligible candidates in guest engagements, and indeed, without even having conducted the orchestra. Leinsdorf, the talented young conductor, was denied the necessary tranquility to grow into the job.

His newly conferred citizenship made Leinsdorf eligible for induction into the U.S. Army, and this invitation was forthcoming. Because of the high visibility of his position, an effort by influential trustees to have him exempted was criticized as unpatriotic. Leinsdorf was inducted on January 21, 1944. He was eventually found unfit for duty on legitimate physical grounds—his flat feet—and he received an honorable discharge that September. However, wheels were set in motion at that crucial beginning of his tenure, forces that in his absence he was powerless to halt.

Cleveland's new season resembled a three-ring circus. Private, later Corporal, Leinsdorf's replacements for the rest of his first season were Frank Black, Eugene Goossens, Vladimir Golschmann, Sir Thomas Beecham, and the associate conductor, Rudolph Ringwall. The orchestra's board assumed that Leinsdorf would remain in the military for the war's duration, so they engaged conductors for what would have been his second season, 1944–45. The lion's share of programs went to Golschmann, with appearances by Reiner, Ringwall, Black, Goossens, and Szell. Nevertheless, Leinsdorf was squeezed in for the final pair of concerts. Until the end of that season, subscribers might well have asked "Erich Who?" but for the heavy press speculation as to his future in Cleveland and news of his musical activities elsewhere, including a month's conducting in Havana and fifteen performances at the Metropolitan Opera.[9]

Golschmann began the season with three weeks of concerts, followed by two with Szell, who did not mention the incumbent Leinsdorf. Instead, he referred to his predecessor, whom he publicly commended: "I am looking forward to working with the Cleveland Orchestra, which Artur Rodzinski has brought to such a high standard of excellence, a feat he is duplicating with the New York Philharmonic." Szell's guest engagements with the New York orchestra depended on Rodzinski's good graces.

Szell's first concert began with Beethoven's *Pastoral* Symphony. Where Golschmann had opted for the kinetic Seventh, Szell performed his magic with the more subtle Sixth. Principal violist Marcel Dick, who was impressed with Szell at the Budapest Opera in 1921 and with one of his NBC Symphony broadcasts in 1941, wondered how it would go in Cleveland in 1944. Szell began the first rehearsal with the *Pastoral*. "That is a very difficult beginning for any conductor, for any orchestra," Dick said, "no matter how well he knows it."

> He started and everything was perfection. For once in a long time, months and months, we were together in the beginning, the first violins knew what they were supposed to do and they did it. This is how it started, the first rehearsal with Szell. So now I said, "this is going to be something fantastic," and by golly, it was! On Thursday evening the orchestra played the way Szell's orchestra played when it was the NBC Orchestra or the Budapest Philharmonic. It was that orchestra, that precision, that transparency. The audience went wild and the press followed suit.[10]

The Beethoven stood alone in the first half of the concert. During intermission, the orchestra's former assistant conductor and former music critic for the *Cleveland Press*, Arthur Shepherd, shouted in the hallways, "Beethoven lives again!" Shepherd's enthusiasm for Szell led him to say to the newspaper's music editor, "I wish I had your job just for tonight." His wish granted, he wrote:

> In Mr. Szell, one suddenly becomes aware of a conductor who has escaped the dead hand of the "metrical" beat and who is not content to whip up a neat ensemble through the metronomic line of least resistance in rehearsal. Under his vitalizing baton one becomes aware of the fusion of expressive rhythmic inflection and sensitive phrasing. What is still more unique, he actually avows and discloses the romantic nuance that is the very life-pulse of every symphonic masterpiece from Beethoven to Sibelius.[11]

Szell completely won over Shepherd, who had previously favored the hiring of an American conductor.[12] The genial Beethoven symphony earned Szell six curtain calls, and decades later many still held fond memories of it. Following intermission, Szell conducted his orchestral arrangement of Smetana's "From My Life," a first performance in Cleveland. The concert concluded with *Till Eulenspiegel*, a reminder of Szell's direct link to Strauss.

Although Golschmann had earlier made a generally favorable impression, the power of Szell's music-making swept all before it. The resounding ovation gave recognition that he had brought the orchestra to new heights. Herbert Elwell, Cleveland's leading music critic, whose admiration for Golschmann had been steadily growing, recognized Szell's "brilliant artistic and personal success. . . . He conducts without score and without eccentricities, and there is something warm and friendly, as well as authoritative, in his approach to the music and to the orchestra, a fact which seemed to cause the musicians to work as they have not worked for some time." Elwell found in Szell's interpretation of Beethoven's *Pastoral*, "sparkling rhythmic delineation, logically advancing development, arresting contrasts in dynamics, and a human, genial touch that made the music sing with a full, glad heart."[13]

On November 9 and 11, Arthur Rubinstein was soloist in Mozart's A Major Concerto (K. 488) and Rachmaninoff's *Rhapsody on a Theme by Paganini*. The program included Smetana's Overture to *The Bartered Bride* and the first Cleveland performance of Hindemith's *Symphonic Metamorphosis on Themes by Carl Maria von Weber*. This program reinforced the impressions made by Szell's first concert. Critics and audiences were again overwhelmed, and the box office reported standing room only. Elwell poured forth extravagant praise:

> Szell's splendid musical integrity and astonishing skill were again apparent in everything he did, from Smetana's *Bartered Bride* Overture, done with amazing speed, vigor and precision, to the new work by Paul Hindemith, *Symphonic Metamorphosis on Themes by* C. M. *von Weber*, which unlike most modern music played here for the first time obtained a cordial reception. . . . One can feel with assurance that in the two short weeks he has been here he has brought our orchestra to a most complete and illuminating realization of its splendid potentialities.[14]

Elmore Bacon was the first to publicly state what must have been already on many minds: "We join in the opinion of many that the Cleveland Orchestra in all its history has not had such vitalizing, fervent and virtuosic leadership as under the magic baton of director Szell. Sir Thomas Beecham, Dr. Artur Rodzinski, at times, and one or two other guest conductors have come close to matching the Szell artistry. But none has excelled it."[15]

The *Cleveland News* reported that at Szell's Saturday night concert in Severance Hall, there had been more than 150 standees and that the box office receipts were the second largest in the orchestra's history, exceeded only by one concert in the early years directed by Rachmaninoff. Prompted by the ovation at the close, the orchestra and Rubinstein broke precedent, with an encore. The next day, Sunday, November 12, Szell conducted the orchestra in Ann Arbor, Michigan, with an attendance of two thousand and many standees. "An ovation at the close brought forth an encore. In saying farewell to the orchestra—it was Szell's final appearance—the director declared it a sheer delight to direct the orchestra and expressed the hope that he might be invited to guest conduct again next season."[16]

The next season, 1945–46, Leinsdorf conducted twelve out of twenty subscription pairs. Ringwall conducted two and Golschmann and Szell each conducted three. Leinsdorf presided over seventy-nine of the 148 concerts that season, and Szell and Golschmann each weighed in with seven. Leinsdorf found himself in the unenviable position of being a candidate for his own job. He could not overcome the bad timing of his absence, his orchestral inexperience, and the behind-the-scenes pressures of the Szell and Golschmann factions.

Szell's chief rival for the Cleveland post was the man who had snatched St. Louis away at the eleventh hour in 1931. Golschmann was now an even more formidable opponent. After fifteen successful years with St. Louis, he seemed ripe for a change.

It would be insufferable for Szell to lose again to Golschmann; but victory would taste doubly sweet.

Golschmann and Szell, now on equal terms, followed Leinsdorf with three programs apiece. Golschmann ended each of his programs with a winner: Sibelius's Symphony no. 2; Tchaikovsky's *Francesca da Rimini;* and Brahms's Symphony no. 2. Newer works included Khrennikov's Symphony no. 1 and Antheil's Nocturne from the Suite *Decatur at Algiers* in the first program, Schoenberg's *Verklärte Nacht* in the second, and Debussy's *Ibéria* in the final. The one solo work was Khachaturian's piano concerto in the middle program.

The Antheil, Khrennikov, and Khachaturian were first performances in Cleveland. The Khachaturian concerto, in a post-romantic idiom and with the enormously gifted twenty-three-year-old William Kapell, was bound to succeed. But the Antheil and Khrennikov were less accessible music and risky choices for a candidate. The Schoenberg had been a success when Golschmann introduced it to Cleveland the previous season in March. The variety appeared admirable, but he was risking comparison with the previous interpreters of the Mozart and Brahms: Beecham and Reiner, respectively, merely a year earlier.

The Szells came to Cleveland with Helene's fifteen-year-old son, John Teltsch, then on Christmas holiday. They stayed at the Wade Park Manor, across from Severance Hall, and they were guests of the Browns at Christmas dinner.[17]

Szell's programs were varied and solid. The opening consisted of all Beethoven: *Egmont* Overture, Piano Concerto no. 5 with Rudolf Serkin, and the Symphony no. 7. Next came Tchaikovsky's Symphony no. 6, *Pathétique*, Stravinsky's Suite from *L'Oiseau de Feu*, and Ravel's *La Valse*. The last pair contained only two works: Bartók's Concerto for Orchestra—a Cleveland first—and Brahms's Symphony no. 1.

Except for the daring new Bartók, Szell avoided the unfamiliar, opting for masterpieces that could demonstrate his interpretive power. Szell had been living with the music of Beethoven since his piano prodigy years, and all-Beethoven programs had been one of his great strengths as a conductor for more than a decade. The Ravel and Stravinsky bowed to the twentieth century, and the Ravel showed that his vocabulary also included French.

Bartók's dazzlingly inventive Concerto for Orchestra (1943) had a powerful impact, with its fiendish string writing, its exposed and taxing parts for all other sections of the orchestra, and its profound originality. Szell heard the Bartók when Koussevitzky and the Boston Symphony first presented it in Carnegie Hall on January 13, 1945. Cleveland Orchestra manager Carl J. Vosburgh and Szell met in New York that morning to plan for his first concert, in December. Shortly afterward, Szell left for his second season as guest conductor in Boston, where he could peruse the Bartók score. From Boston, Szell wrote Vosburgh that he reserved the right from its publisher to conduct the Bartók's first performances with the Cleveland Orchestra and New York Philharmonic next season, and considered it "one of the most important compositions written during the past 25 years."[18]

Szell's pairing of Brahms's First Symphony with the Bartók was well calculated. He had been refining his powerful interpretation of the Brahms for years, and at the end of his final Cleveland concert, it proved stunning, earning unanimous praise from the critics. Elwell wrote of Szell's "firmness of a master hand," and his "exceptional musical personality in which every fiber is intensely alive with the most dynamic energy":

> He gives forth a sense of authority, assurance and fiery animation. Yet to dwell on him as a personality would be wrong, for he makes himself so transparent that no part of his own shadow falls upon the score. Literally this would be impossible anyway, for there is no score for it to fall upon. The score is in his head, which is filled also with the kind of wisdom and insight which bring us very close to the fountainhead of the greatest musical inspiration.[19]

"Not since Artur Rodzinski came here from Los Angeles 13 years ago . . . have Cleveland audiences been so enthusiastic or have symphonic patrons been so interested in conductorial matters," wrote the critic in the *Cleveland Press*.[20]

Szell's Conquest

Months before the board had to decide on a successor to Leinsdorf, Sidlo and Brown had orchestrated a coup to prevent a repeat of the board struggle three years earlier. They forced the orchestra's founder, Adella Prentiss Hughes, to retire from full board status and assume the title "honorary vice-president." Brown confided to his diary in January 1945, six months prior: "She must stop her smear campaign of Szell and Golschmann as with Stoessel, and stop interviewing trustees secretly. Orchestra no longer her baby." In July, he wrote: "Meeting (election) at Severance Hall. We . . . retired Adella Hughes (on full pay). It took 5 or 6 big strong men to oust one lone woman, aged 75, but we did it and a great victory was the result." Brown, who had opposed Leinsdorf's candidacy on the grounds of his draft eligibility and had wanted Stoessel as conductor in 1942, was now an ardent Szell supporter. This cleared the deck to choose a new conductor, made all the easier by Szell's smashing success.

After Cleveland, Szell traveled to the Met to conduct *Die Meistersinger* and *Don Giovanni* (on January 9 and 12). He returned to Cleveland for a crucial meeting with a board committee on January 15. Although he maintained that Cleveland needed him more than he needed Cleveland—"I didn't have to make a change, and I did not need it"[21]—in a letter to Eric Oldberg, Szell reveals a state of tension at the prospect of change:

> I have to tell you something that has to remain a secret until Friday morning. I have accepted the Musical Directorship of the Cleveland Orchestra. It was no easy decision to make. I had taken root in New York and I had been enjoying my work at the Met more and more and this in conjunction with Guest Conducting the finest orchestras had given me a life full of artistic interest and satisfaction without the headaches that go with the running of an organization. But the temptation to have an orchestra of my own that I can mould according to my ideals was strong and became irresistible when I discovered that the people in Cleveland had gone completely wild and were prepared to give me anything I wanted on a golden platter.

Szell told Oldberg that he had put off talking with the Cleveland board "for weeks" unless "they approached me with the fullest authority." The Operating Committee finally gave Sidlo complete authority to negotiate with Szell. Szell met with Sidlo, two vice presidents, and the manager, "in [the] presence of a stenographer with a typewriter," and "virtually dictated" his conditions, which the group unqualifiedly accepted. The terms agreed on gave Szell "ideal working conditions" and complete musical authority. They also included a salary "they never paid before," which was "second only to those of the 3 Eastern Orchestras." Szell would have six to eight weeks' leave during the season, for guest conducting elsewhere. He made sure to tell Oldberg, "I kept some time free for Chicago."[22] Because Cleveland would occupy him for only twenty weeks a season, he kept the New York apartment. Maintaining a presence there was logistically practical and professionally wise.

Hughes chose not to attend the annual meeting of the Musical Arts Association, on January 24, 1946. "For the first time in the entire history of the orchestra," Sidlo said, "the task of choosing a regular conductor was virtually taken out of our hands and the choice made for us by audience and public. . . . Cleveland has never before received a conductor with such universal favor." Szell would meet only with a committee fully empowered to speak for the Musical Arts Association. It was striking that Szell handled the face-to-face negotiations without either his manager, Arthur Judson, or a legal representative as an intermediary. Apparently, the board had sought Judson's opinion: in a report to the board of trustees in March, Sidlo quoted Judson as saying that Szell was "the ablest conductor in America at this moment."[23]

Orchestral Goals

Szell controlled the process from the start; he orchestrated each step, confident in the strength of his position. He set forth his conditions "one by one," salary or term of engagement last, as there would be no point in discussing those unless Szell's conditions were accepted.

Szell planned to transform the orchestra into a great one. To accomplish this, he secured complete authority in all musical matters, including choice of programs, soloists, guest conductors, and hiring orchestra musicians. The committee readily agreed to Szell's request to enlarge the orchestra by eight players, probably to be divided equally between strings and woodwinds. Rodzinski had long sought an increase, but the board had staunchly resisted. Now they readily acceded to Szell, partly because of the positive climate prevailing after the Depression and the war. It was also a sign of confidence that the musical and fiscal results of Szell's leadership would more than justify the increase.

Szell secured the resources to attract and keep the best first-chair players available. The recent loss of four principal players, he felt, had weakened the orchestra. He stipulated that "every reasonable effort" be made to reengage them, and three returned. In his meticulous manner, Szell covered all details of his duties. He specified the number of weeks and concerts he would conduct and the time off he would take during the season. Before the opening week of concerts, he required an unprecedented extra week of rehearsals without concerts. Szell accepted that the board would negotiate with the musicians' union the number of rehearsals and the players' salaries for that week.

Szell acknowledged that recording and radio broadcasting would benefit the orchestra, but he cautioned that he would begin recording only when he felt the orchestra was ready, and that it probably would not occur his first season. Radio broadcasts, however, could begin the first season; his fee would depend on the sponsor. Every aesthetic detail was important to Szell. The stage would require repainting, "as it would be difficult for [Szell] to face the existing highly stylized background week after week and do his best work." He preferred a "neutral shade like ivory, with the understanding that the color chosen should be in harmony with the color scheme of the rest of the hall."

Szell negotiated a three-year contract, with salary commensurate with his current earnings, considerably more than the board had paid Rodzinski. He asked them to make an offer, which he rejected. Szell then proposed a nonnegotiable salary, and announced that he would withdraw his candidacy unless it was met. By policy his salary was never officially announced. It was $40,000, a substantial increase over Rodzinski's salary of $30,000 and more than twice Leinsdorf's $18,000, but lower than the current salaries of other major orchestra conductors.[24] The cost of Szell's salary appeared small compared with the cost of reshaping the orchestra according to his design.

Sidlo concluded:

> The undertaking we have entered into is going to require work and contribution from every Trustee. Dr. Szell is no easy-going person. He is a worker, a terrific

worker, an artist so dedicated to his art as to be unwilling to give anything but his best, and equally unwilling to accept anything but the best from others. Of this though I feel certain, - that if we will do our part, he will do his, and that with good will, determined purpose, and everyone co-operating, it will not be long before we shall see results that will open our eyes and gladden our hearts. We have taken the step we have in response to the verdict of our audience and the music-loving public of Cleveland. But I feel that we are also taking it out of a sense of duty and loyalty to those [who say] "Let us have nothing but the best. Nothing but the best will do!"[25]

Second to None

Sidlo's report "received enthusiastic applause," and the trustees voted unanimously to "approve and endorse the action taken by the President, the operating committee and the negotiating committee" to hire Szell. Szell's concise reply would be quoted often in the years to come: "I am most happy to come to Cleveland. I shall do my best to justify the confidence and warm affection the Cleveland public has so generously showered upon me. The Musical Arts Association has expressed its desire to make the Cleveland Orchestra second to none in quality of performance. To this end I shall dedicate all my efforts."[26]

Hail, the Conquering Hero

After his last *Rosenkavalier* in Chicago on May 11, Szell returned to New York, where a Cleveland reporter interviewed him at the Lotos Club, then down the street from Carnegie Hall. The journalist had to wait to speak to Szell while well-wishers "gathered to congratulate him on his new position in Cleveland." They included Dimitri Mitropoulos, conductor of the Minneapolis Symphony, composer Aaron Copland, composer-conductor Morton Gould, and violinist Joseph Fuchs, former concertmaster of the Cleveland Orchestra.[27] Szell told the interviewer of Cleveland's campaign to raise $100,000 for the orchestra. "Upon the generosity of the Friends of the Cleveland Orchestra as well as their numbers," Szell said, "will depend the future of this fine organization," perhaps implying also that his future in Cleveland depended on the community's support of the orchestra.

Next he played two concerts with the Budapest String Quartet at the Library of Congress. On three Sundays in June, Szell conducted radio broadcast concerts with the Detroit Symphony, dovetailing his debut at the Lewisohn Stadium in upper Manhattan on June 18 and 20 between the second and third Detroit concerts. In Detroit, Szell renewed his acquaintance (from the NBC Symphony) with the concertmaster, Josef Gingold, who he felt would be his ideal concertmaster for

Cleveland. Szell had already hired Samuel Thaviu away from Pittsburgh for that position in Cleveland, and Gingold had a year remaining on his Detroit contract, so they made a secret agreement for the following year.

Szell next conducted the two opening weeks of the Ravinia Festival in the Chicago suburb Highland Park, leading five concerts with the Chicago Symphony in the last week of June and the first week of July. Three concerts with the Philadelphia Orchestra at the Robin Hood Dell in as many days in mid-July rounded off Szell's summer performances.

The Szells rested for a month in Santa Monica. Helene's son joined them there, but did not move to Cleveland with them. Until graduation, John boarded at a private high school in the Riverdale section of New York City. Szell ended his California idyll to record the two Mozart Piano Quartets with members of the Budapest String Quartet on August 19 and 20 in Liederkranz Hall in New York City. In mid-September, he returned to Cleveland.

Szell's First Cleveland Season

The Cleveland Orchestra became the focus of George Szell's life and his greatest achievement. Born exceptionally talented and thoroughly trained in his early teens, by age forty-nine Szell possessed the ability and experience to build a major orchestra in all its complexities. During the quarter-century of his Cleveland tenure, Szell had associations with many other musical organizations. A number of these were ongoing, as with the New York Philharmonic and the Royal Concertgebouw Orchestra of Amsterdam, and others intermittent, such as with the Chicago Symphony Orchestra and the Salzburg Festival; still others consisted of short occasional engagements, such as with the Los Angeles Philharmonic, the San Francisco Symphony, the Ravinia Festival, and the Metropolitan Opera.

In summers, Szell established a pattern that, with small variations, he followed for the rest of his life. He conducted in all seasons, but in summers he made time for rest, golf, and caring for his health. After his youthful culinary excesses, Szell became increasingly aware of the importance of a healthy diet and controlling his weight to maintain his taxing physical and mental regimen.

From the start, Szell set making Cleveland a world-class ensemble as a goal. With the enthusiastic support given him by his board, he immediately took charge of building the orchestra's personnel, its repertoire, its soloists and guest conductors, and its musical and administrative staff. His new position promised great potential, but leaving New York for Cleveland was "no easy decision to make."[28] Szell's American career was beginning to flourish, so a move away from the musical center of the country posed an undoubted risk. It had been a little more than six years since his career had been interrupted, forcing him to relocate. The uncertainties of starting over surely remained fresh in his mind, and his potential for loss appeared considerable.

As a member of the Metropolitan Opera staff and a regular guest conductor of the Philharmonic, Szell had established a presence in New York's musical life. He did not know if the move to Cleveland would weaken his ties with the Philharmonic or how it would affect his career. Between his departure from Prague in 1937 and his debut at the Met in 1942, Szell had not conducted opera, nor did he regret it. "In the course of time the demands on my time away from my regular work were so great," he said, "that I gave up the regular appointment as operatic conductor. . . . I had tired of opera conducting. After 20 years of it, one becomes tired of telling singer after singer the same things, and so I concentrated more on concert work."[29] But Szell had been happy at the Met: performing with world-class singers, its location in New York City, its international prestige, and his increasing responsibilities there. He was leaving that behind.

The Szells enjoyed a wide circle of acquaintances in New York, not only musicians but some of the city's leading citizens and patrons of the arts. They lived comfortably in their lower Park Avenue apartment, a short taxi ride to the Met or Carnegie Hall. Helene Szell told a friend, "When I learned that we were going to Cleveland, I cried for a whole day."[30]

Szell was cautious about his commitment in Cleveland; he waited several seasons before buying a house there. At first he stayed at the then-fashionable Wade Park Manor Hotel or occupied houses of orchestra patrons who were away for the winter. He could leave with little personal inconvenience if insurmountable obstacles arose. High accomplishments remained possible but were by no means certain.

As a guest conductor, Szell had experienced the effects of wartime disruption on the orchestra. He did not underestimate the work required to bring back an orchestra that, in his opinion, had "slipped markedly" during the past two years.[31] On the other hand, he knew that Cleveland was a wealthy and proud city, which had proven its commitment to its orchestra by providing it with a beautiful concert hall of its own, Severance Hall. As it had been after the First World War, Cleveland was ripe for growth in all areas, during this time of natural optimism and rebirth. Cleveland held a long-established tradition of quality in the arts, and it longed for musical leadership. As critic Herbert Elwell wrote before Szell's first season, "There is . . . a strong determination within the Musical Arts Association to promote the orchestra to a deserved position close to the top among the great orchestras of the world."[32]

Szell visualized an orchestra tightly disciplined from within, yet flexible, one that would "combine the best qualities of the fine European orchestras' prewar period, even pre–First World War period, with the finest qualities of the American orchestras in their best period, that is the impeccable intonation, the impeccable virtuosity, the brilliance, the smoothness of execution, which very often in America was an end in itself," but with "the spontaneity, the warmth, the flexibility of the best European orchestras and the tradition, consciousness, and the familiarity with the good musical habits . . . of the best European orchestras during their best period."[33] How could he have known that it would be possible to make a great orchestra? This one had been in existence for barely thirty years in a moderate-sized midwestern American city. It would be a calculated gamble.[34]

Szell immediately addressed the task of strengthening the orchestra: first, seeking the return of key players, recruiting new principal and section players, and enlarging the orchestra; second, increasing the number of concerts; and third, brightening Severance Hall's subdued acoustics. Szell recognized the importance of the visual stage picture. He had the dark-blue-patterned shell repainted a plain, light beige. This was mostly an aesthetic gesture, as it had not been acoustically designed—the shell served mainly to hide the backstage area from the audience's view—although Szell had specified in his contract for the application of "3–5 coats of hard paint," to help reflect the sound. But it also had a psychological effect—the new look would symbolize a new beginning. These changes demonstrated his authority in a tangible and visible manner.[35]

Acoustical design, somewhere between alchemy and science, is mysterious and elusive at best, but is of crucial importance for an orchestral performance space. Szell once said that history does not record any great orchestra that did not have a good hall, because in a bad hall you cannot really develop a good orchestra. He had to work within Severance Hall's original acoustics, however, for a dozen years.

Between "very good," which the Cleveland Orchestra had been under Rodzinski, and "great" lies a vast territory made up of seemingly endless, minute details in which every inch gained comes at considerable effort and cost. Rodzinski was known as a builder. (Toscanini, who had known Rodzinski in Europe, chose him to select and prepare the musicians for the new NBC Symphony in advance of his arrival in 1937.) Rodzinski had drilled the Cleveland thoroughly. Years later, players recalled the grinding rehearsals, in which he might ask the members of a string section to play a difficult passage *one at a time*. They called them "Black Mondays."[36] Szell did not need to follow Rodzinski's practice; his sharp ears and eyes could detect minute infractions of ensemble and pitch by individual string players.

Throughout the spring, Szell planned his first season's programs, chose soloists and guest conductors, and made changes in the orchestra's personnel. Seventeen players did not return for his first season, some, but not all, because they had taken other jobs or were drafted. By the fifth season, however, the number of nonreturnees was smaller. Musicians who returned from military service were legally entitled to reclaim their former positions. All who did so were welcomed, but some not for long. "If they weren't excellent," Szell would later say of his musicians, "they wouldn't be in the Cleveland Orchestra." If Szell could hire the best musicians, he knew that he could make the Cleveland Orchestra the equal of any. He had the authority to offer competitive salaries to new members, and recruited key players from the Metropolitan Opera and orchestras of which he had been a guest conductor. Many orchestras accused him of pirating.[37]

Szell had clear priorities: in his first year he concentrated on filling leadership positions; in the strings, the most important was the concertmaster. For that he first hired Samuel Thaviu away from the Pittsburgh Symphony. Szell enlarged the orchestra by seven players, bringing the total to ninety-two. He added two players to each of the violin sections and increased the flute, oboe, and clarinet sections by one player each, to the standard complement of four per section.

Next, he worked to train the orchestra, to realize and increase its potential. The time allotted to rehearsals was generous then, in contrast to present conditions, where rehearsal time has been steadily eroded by pressure from union contractual demands and market forces. Even then, however, there existed a give and take. To offset the cost for the extra week of nine rehearsals before the first week of concerts, the orchestra dropped a week of touring.

In 1946–47, Szell's first season as musical director (a title he preferred to music director), audiences heard a diverse mixture of old and new music. It was solidly weighted with Brahms, in honor of the fiftieth anniversary of his death, and Beethoven. Szell conducted seven Brahms works including the Second, Third, and Fourth Symphonies.

Performances represented thirty composers; fifteen works were first Cleveland performances, two of which consisted of world premieres. More than half were by living composers, including seven by Americans—Samuel Barber's First Essay, Aaron Copland's *Danzón Cubano* and *Letter from Home*, Norman Dello Joio's *Ricercari*, David Diamond's *Rounds for String Orchestra*, Arthur Foote's *A Night Piece*, and William Grant Still's *In Memoriam: The Colored Soldiers Who Died for Democracy*. Other works given their Cleveland premieres were by composers as varied as Bach, Britten, Hindemith, Janáček, Schoenberg, and Vaughan Williams.

Szell was discriminating in his choice of soloists, including Erica Morini, Joseph Szigeti, Artur Schnabel, Rudolf Serkin, and Arthur Rubinstein. Others included the brothers Adolf and Hermann Busch in the Brahms Double Concerto, present and former Cleveland Orchestra concertmasters Samuel Thaviu and Joseph Knitzer, and the orchestra's principal flutist, Maurice Sharp. With one program each, guest conductors that season were Georges Enesco, Igor Stravinsky, and Bruno Walter. Szell conducted fifteen of the twenty subscription concert pairs, and associate conductor Rudolph Ringwall, two.

Szell also devoted time and energy to establish an advanced training program for young conductors—called apprentices—supported by the Kulas Foundation of Cleveland.[38] A press release announced a nationwide search for candidates in 1946.

Szell would choose two "master students" to observe the daily functioning of a great orchestra and conductor for one year. They would take part in the activities of the orchestra, playing keyboard and/or another instrument, and assist Szell, working with the orchestra under his guidance, and in the orchestra library.[39] The initial program ran for three years. Szell revived and expanded it from 1959 to 1968. Over the years there were seven Kulas Apprentice Conductors and eleven Kulas Fellow Conductors, who shared a concert with the orchestra under Szell's supervision each year. The program was unique. Serge Koussevitzky's class for conductors at Tanglewood had begun in 1940 and Pierre Monteux's Domaine School for Conductors, transferred from Paris to his residence in Hancock, Maine, in 1943 were admirable. Koussevitsky's and Monteux's programs operated during the summer, but Szell's ran for a full season.

The Szells were guests of honor at the annual fall meeting of the Women's Committee, the orchestra's volunteer support group. Szell took the stage to receive his first standing ovation as musical director. In his remarks, "he gave his respects to the entire committee for its contribution to the orchestra and to good music," and "asked them to extend their influence by giving music the important place it deserves by encouraging their children and other children to play some kind of instrument." Following his speech, orchestra harpist Alice Chalifoux gave a recital.[40]

The Work Begins: Training the Orchestra

He immediately began working toward his goal, planning repertoire to give the orchestra repeated contact with the great masterpieces of the literature. The symphonic works of Beethoven and Brahms alternately played season after season. For example, Szell programmed Brahms's Symphony no. 1 in fourteen of his twenty-four seasons. For the lightness and precision demanded by the classical style, Szell frequently played the late symphonies of Mozart and Haydn and delved into their earlier ones, as well. He programmed a series of Mozart piano concertos played by the greatest interpreters of the day, including Artur Schnabel, Rudolf Serkin, Robert Casadesus, Rudolf Firkusny, and, in two seasons, Szell himself.

Szell placed importance on what music and with which soloists the orchestra played, and how it played was vital. As Szell saw it, "his greatest achievement in Cleveland is the habit he has instilled into the players of listening to each other. . . . Whether the orchestral musician is actually playing or not, he must always be 'involved in the totality' of the music."[41] This did not mean passive participation. Rather, Szell directed his players to notice everything that was being played: phrasing, the subtle shaping of a musical idea, its inflection, high and low points; intonation—the constant straining toward perfect tuning; ensemble—the seamless fitting together of all instruments sounding at the same time regardless of distance on stage from each other; balance—seeing that each note had the exact weight in relation to its importance in the overall fabric of the piece at that moment; and style—to differentiate tone, vibrato, phrasing, and dynamics in the proper proportions according to the musical period. Each musician was made to feel responsible for all these qualities, and Szell would instruct and then constantly remind them of those responsibilities.

Szell likened this to chamber music: not "that the volume of sound emitted is a small one. . . ." however. "It is a large orchestra with a very considerable power output of sound but at the same time they play like a string quartet. In other words, they listen to each other, they don't just play their parts and follow the beat but they follow the music. And follow, while they are playing, with their ears, the other voices in the orchestra."[42] Szell believed that what distinguishes that sound was "a fantastic homogeneity of style, of approach, and a fantastic awareness of the most important aspects of music making which are so often overlooked . . . articulation and phrasing, which is so much more important than anything else because it means absolutely the delivery of the music for the proper understanding on the part of the listener."[43]

From the first day of Szell's extra preseason rehearsal week to the last concert he conducted, Szell had a master plan and set of musical goals for the orchestra to achieve. He consciously instilled these through constant repetition over the years so that they became a deeply ingrained habit for every musician and the orchestra as a whole. When asked once what were the five most important elements in music, Szell answered, "Well, the first four are rhythm and after that comes everything else." After the concentration on rhythm and its corollary, ensemble, came other aspects, balance chief among them. Then came articulation and phrasing. He told the strings to breathe between phrases, saying, "You have to take a breath there. The music takes a breath there. The wind players have to do that. You must do it because that's the way the music is, so you might as well breathe at the right spot."[44]

Szell's First Concert as Musical Director

For his first program, on October 17, 1946, Szell chose works with which he was closely identified: Weber's Overture to *Oberon*, *Don Juan* of Strauss, and Beethoven's Symphony no. 3, *Eroica*. Between them sat Debussy's *Prélude à "L'Après-midi d'un faune."* This program displayed his and the orchestra's stylistic versatility, and served to draw attention to the return of principal flutist Maurice Sharp.

Cleveland critic Arthur Loesser described the audience "in a mood of high expectancy, which soon changed to one of elation. . . . It did not require many phrases of Weber's *Oberon* Overture to establish the fact that the orchestra was in the hands of a man of outstanding knowledge," Loesser wrote, "of authority born of a lifetime of successful experience in directing musicians, as well as of unusual capacity for projecting musical and dramatic values." Debussy's "fanciful pastel tints exerted their magic more intensely as the composition progressed," Loesser wrote. He found the "lush ardors" of *Don Juan* "never more convincingly presented. . . . Particularly remarkable was Szell's sense of climax." Beethoven's Third Symphony was "full of vigor and dignity." A fine musician in his own right, Loesser found that Szell's solving "the difficult problem of the Funeral March: that of maintaining the mood of slow somber tragedy without permitting it to degenerate into a mere depressed sluggishness," was "admirable." The *Eroica*'s scherzo and finale, Loesser reported, "brought to a triumphant close one of the most exhilarating concerts heard here in some time."[45]

Elwell was unrestrained: "This is it, the kind of Cleveland Orchestra we have been waiting for, the kind that was promised us when George Szell was made its permanent conductor, the kind which will unquestionably be able to hold its head high and go out and make a name for itself among the finest orchestras of the world. . . . Szell has accomplished wonders in his two weeks' preseason rehearsals." "Here, indeed," Elwell noted, "is a conductor, a challenging artist whom the musicians can respect. He comes to the stand with the enthusiasm of a novice and the mastery of a veteran." A side of Szell's music making often ignored by critics was chief among his virtues, according to Elwell: "Above all," he wrote, "Szell is not afraid to inject romantic feeling into music which calls for it, yet when the rigidity of classic architecture is demanded, it is there in the full glory of finely delineated proportions." The *Eroica* held the attention "so completely as to leave an impression of brevity where there was actually great length."[46] New York, too, was watching. Reviews of the opening concert in the *New York Times* and the *Herald Tribune* mentioned the sold-out house with two hundred extra chairs and many standees, and took notice of the exuberant audience and the enlarged orchestra.[47] Szell expressed his appraisal of the concert in a letter to Bruno Zirato: "The opening night went splendidly and the orchestra played simply magnificently; in fact, as beautifully and as well integrated as I had expected them to play after a year's work."[48]

A moment of personal importance took place between the two subscription concerts. On October 18, 1946, George and Helene Szell became naturalized citizens of the United States, thus completing the process they had begun with their one-night trip to Mexico in 1940.

An unqualified triumphant beginning—a sold-out house, enthusiastic audience, and unanimously extravagant reviews. What more could Szell ask for? How to follow the difficult first act that he had so well fashioned and executed? As a bold feature, the second program introduced the eighteen-year-old Leon Fleisher, playing the Schumann Piano Concerto. Fleisher, a student of Szell's friend and colleague Artur Schnabel, had already appeared with Monteux in 1944, with Bernstein in 1945, and with Szell in 1946, the summer before his Cleveland debut. Because of Schnabel's influence, Fleisher said, his musical approach appeared so similar to Szell's that there occurred very little talk or correction of the music before or during rehearsals. This was highly unusual for Szell but not unexpected, considering their recent performance together. Szell told Fleisher that it was unnecessary to have a piano rehearsal before they rehearsed with the orchestra, saying, "I know how you play this. My orchestra is so trained as to whatever you do they will just follow."

In the rehearsal, the first movement went without incident. The second movement, the lyrical *Romanze,* begins with a dialogue between piano and orchestra. The mood is gentle, the F major tonality contrasts with the intense A Minor of the first movement, and the tempo is moderate, marked *Andantino grazioso.* For some unfathomable reason, Fleisher began twice as fast as usual. "I don't know what got into me," he said, "a dybbuk [a malicious spirit of medieval Jewish legend], perhaps." But the strings followed without hesitation, picking right up on his completely unexpected tempo so that there was no break between piano and orchestra in spite of the surprising tempo. Szell was so stunned that his baton remained motionless. Puzzled at first, he then realized that Fleisher was just testing what Szell had boasted of in the dressing room. Instead of being furious, he just beamed at how his orchestra had proved his faith in them.[49] In the concert Fleisher, of course, played at the normal tempo.

The performance proved a great success, firmly establishing a musical collaboration that would stretch nearly twenty years, until an ailment affecting Fleisher's right hand forced his premature retirement from two-hand pianism, although not before several of his youthful dreams had been realized.[50] This second program—including also Berlioz's *Roman Carnival* Overture, Brahms's Symphony no. 2, and the first Cleveland performances of three of the *Four Sea Interludes* from Benjamin Britten's opera, *Peter Grimes*—drew critical accolades, though opinions were mixed on the merits of the Britten.[51]

That season, the orchestra inaugurated live, hour-long radio broadcasts over the Mutual Network before the Saturday concerts. The twenty-six concerts garnered revenues of $26,000. Audiences purchased tickets at thirty-six cents, including a six-cent wartime entertainment tax. A number of the orchestra's board of trustees bought blocs of tickets for workers in their companies. These broadcasts received high ratings, comparing favorably with broadcasts of the NBC with Toscanini, the New York Philharmonic with Rodzinski, and the Boston Symphony with Koussevitzky. Cleveland radio station WHK carried the broadcasts live from 6:00 to 7:00 P.M. The schedule did not fit all the network's affiliates, so the concerts were recorded on acetate discs for later broadcast.[52]

Among the surviving recordings of Szell's first season is Berlioz's *Roman Carnival* Overture. His interpretation of this piece was fairly well established by then. Its duration was 8 minutes and 43 seconds, only a few seconds faster than the last two times he conducted it on subscription concerts in his last season, twenty-four years later (8'45" and 8'49," respectively). Szell and the orchestra attacked its difficulties with gusto. Although it lacked the uncanny precision they later achieved, it was nevertheless a stunning performance.

Although some individual solos and sections were outstanding, others were not. For example, the trombones played in a breathless style, lacking nobility of line. But the orchestra in general, "acquitted itself well"—to use a favorite phrase of Szell's—and the spirit is evident. There was obvious room for improvement in intonation and ensemble, but considering that this was only the second concert of Szell's first season, one can recognize the orchestra's potential and how much Szell had already attained.

The same impression holds for other works played early that season. In Sibelius's Third Symphony, Szell's sole traversal of the work in Cleveland, the conductor demonstrated a sweeping understanding of the composer's broad architecture and conveyed a rhythmic strength that was one of Szell's strongest traits. Yet there are flaws—scrappy passagework in various string sections and small ensemble imperfections that simply did not happen in later years.

A performance of *Till Eulenspiegel* suggests that whereas with the Berlioz, Szell had found his tempi by 1946, the Strauss was constantly in process. Philip Farkas's horn playing, though solid and exciting, did not have the go-for-broke brilliance that Myron Bloom would later display. The strings were not yet up to Szell's driving tempo. Over the years with this work, Szell would become more expansive. His 1946 performance ran fifteen seconds longer than it had two years earlier in 1944, and by 1969 the work's duration measured a minute-and-a-half longer than in 1946. In his two commercial recordings of *Till,* Szell broadened by a half minute between 1949 and 1957 (13'51" and 14'23", respectively). Perhaps as the orchestra developed, Szell could convey excitement through rhythmic precision rather than merely through speed.

The third program dwelt on the music of the land of Szell's deepest affinity, Czechoslovakia. As a guest conductor he had presented a dramatic reading of his orchestration of Smetana's first string quartet, *From My Life.* He opened his second guest program with that composer's overture to *The Bartered Bride.* Now, as musical director, he was continuing the bohemianizing of his orchestra.

Výšehrad, the first symphonic poem in Smetana's cycle *Má Vlast* ("My country"), opened the program. Dvořák's "New World" Symphony, which concluded the concert, received extended ovations and stamping in the balcony, "an unusual feature at these concerts," wrote one reviewer.[53] On the other hand, a spirited performance of Janáček's *Sinfonietta*—a first performance in Cleveland—while making a grand effect on the audience, exposed the weakness of the strings in their highest register. In the 1940s the talent pool of extra trumpets available in the city was not up to the demands of Janáček's score, and the low brass players were hard pressed in technical agility and weak in intonation. Also, some of the many abrupt meter and tempo changes were hesitant, revealing one of Szell's rare technical difficulties. The contrast between how the orchestra played the Janáček in 1946 and in their 1965 Columbia recording is enormous. They had by then made the piece theirs. It is precision itself, with flawless tempo changes and virtuosic brilliance; the violins play with verve and accuracy in the stratosphere, the rhythmic irregularities are executed with ease, and the tubas are dead in tune.

Although Szell had cautioned the board that the orchestra might not be ready to make commercial recordings for some time, by the end of November he agreed to three recording dates with Columbia Records in April. At the end of November, Szell took the orchestra on the first of many tours, to smaller cities in Michigan and Indiana, returning to Cleveland for the Saturday broadcast. Szell admonished them to always give their best, saying, "Remember, gentlemen, great music is great music no matter where it is played."[54] After the tour, Szell departed to guest conduct the Chicago Symphony for two weeks.

Szell's Chicago Symphony connection posed a potential threat to Cleveland. He had conducted that orchestra at Ravinia in five out of the previous six summers; these were his first winter subscription concerts there. Between 1946 and 1967 Szell served as guest conductor for six winter seasons, with a sixth return to Ravinia in 1956. The 1946–47 season was Chicago conductor Desiré Defauw's last. Since his early days at Ravinia, Szell had a powerful champion on the Chicago Symphony board, Eric Oldberg. Defauw's successor, Artur Rodzinski, left after a single season, followed by two seasons of guest conductors, Szell among them.

In Szell's first Christmas in Cleveland, he began a tradition of giving a gift to the orchestra members, a leather-bound pocket calendar for the coming year. These diaries, from the English firm of Frank Smythson, which Szell himself used, had a purpose—the players could write their concert and rehearsal schedules in them.

Just after Christmas, the ninth program began with another Cleveland first, Barber's (First) Essay for Orchestra, and ended with what was then a regular in Szell's repertoire, Tchaikovsky's Fifth Symphony. Szell's involvement with that symphony gradually diminished over the years. He played it often early in his career—the piece had been a favorite of Arthur Nikisch, whom Szell admired and heard in Berlin in his youth.[55] Concertmaster Samuel Thaviu served as soloist in the Dvořák Violin Concerto.

The Szells spent the holidays in New York and enjoyed a "quiet New Year's Eve." The *Cleveland Press* reported that Szell "played chamber music with Adolf Busch and Joseph Fuchs, violinists, at the home of Mrs. Edgar Leventritt."[56] After the New Year, Szell conducted the Philadelphia Orchestra; then it was back to Cleveland for the rest of his first season. On Tuesday, January 14, 1947, he attended a meeting of the board of trustees. Ticket sales, audience enthusiasm, and critical response during Szell's first half year were the best in the orchestra's history, board president Sidlo reported. Szell discussed his recommendation to lengthen the coming season, 1947–48, from twenty-eight to thirty weeks.

The conductor's presence at a board meeting is in itself not unusual, but it was highly unusual that he had met with the orchestra committee about the contract. "He had pointed out to the musicians that a longer season would be of more benefit to them than an increase in the minimum pay scale." Szell told the board that the musicians were willing to accept this.[57] He also sought authorization to engage up to ten players from out of town, if necessary, to fill vacancies or make replacements. Local chapters of the Musicians' Union are protective of their members. Hometown musicians had to be considered first for every opening. Szell pointed out that the longer season would attract first-class players, thus improving the quality and prestige of the orchestra, while enhancing its earning capacity. The board yielded to Szell's request, demonstrating the strong position he had already established.

In February Szell led the orchestra on a tour of New York, Pennsylvania, Massachusetts, and Connecticut, after which Szell took a week of rest in New York City. While he was there, a scandal that drew national attention erupted. Cleveland concertmaster Samuel Thaviu had resigned in January shortly after learning that in November, Szell had secretly signed Josef Gingold for the next season.[58] Szell apparently had not told Thaviu that his appointment was an interim one. He also enraged Detroit Symphony conductor Karl Krueger by hiring away his prized concertmaster. The nationwide press picked up the story, including *Billboard*.[59] "The attitude of the Detroit gentlemen, in their helpless fury, is too ridiculous to be worthy of serious comment," Szell said. "Any organization is entitled to approach any artist, in perfectly good faith, for a time for which he is not legally committed to another organization." Cleveland manager Carl Vosburgh added, "There has been nothing unusual in our signing of Mr. Gingold. . . . If a musician prefers to play under another conductor with another orchestra he should not be barred from that opportunity."[60]

The Cleveland position offered Gingold an artistic advantage, more money, and help with housing, which had been a problem for him in Detroit.[61] The warmly outgoing Gingold and the reserved Szell balanced each other musically. Their personal relationship became very close, but that did not prevent Szell from being severely critical whenever he felt he had cause. Once, when Szell became extremely upset over what Gingold felt was a trivial slip, Gingold said, "But George, an eighth note isn't a matter of life and death," to which Szell replied, "It is, in Mozart."[62]

Thaviu's resignation coincided with that of first horn Philip Farkas, who left to help with his family's business in Chicago.[63] At the same time, there were deep rumblings over Szell's dismissals of several orchestra members, many of long tenure. In his unrelenting pursuit of improvement, he was pushing hard, and now the reaction was setting in. First cellist Harry Fuchs resigned while on the eastern tour; Philip Kirchner, first oboist of twenty-nine years, also departed at the end of the season.[64]

An anonymous writer in the *Cleveland Press* asked, "Is it absolutely necessary [for Mr. Szell] to rip up the personnel of the orchestra to achieve another extra measure of perfection," to put the orchestra personnel "on pins and needles of fear for their jobs in the pursuit of . . . [the] mirage of perfection?"[65] This landed close to the mark in describing the constant pressure Szell kept up on everyone. Yet it did produce results.

Szell faced real repercussions, however. A meeting between Szell and the orchestra committee was called to discuss "forced 'resignations' and general bad feeling created by [his] methods of dismissal." The meeting turned out to be a short speech by Szell, "at the end of which the conductor stalked out of the room, not giving the orchestra men a chance to talk."[66] This was a typical Szell reaction to being challenged: firing off his broadside and abruptly ending the "argument."

Szell felt justified in his actions to build the orchestra. Firing players was a part of the process. He once told his principal violist, Marcel Dick, "A good orchestra does not depend on who plays, but who does not play."[67] In the early years, Szell exhibited a collegial, considerate, and amiable demeanor on the podium. In a rehearsal following a concert, he would thank the orchestra for their good work. In 1947 he enjoyed a rapport with the players, so they were unusually willing to discuss their contract with him and take his advice. Their vote for that contract demonstrated their trust, even after he berated them for criticizing his firing the players. Times were indeed different then.

Though Szell felt dead sure of his musical ground, he was not so adept in his social dealings, especially in difficult situations. He perceived the criticism over his firing players as a threat to his authority. Accusations such as those leveled by Carlton K. Matson, a personal friend of Thomas Sidlo, that "a great artist like Mr. Szell may possibly be overlooking some human values," may have rankled the conductor. Matson believed "we have a great conductor in George Szell," but he concluded that there existed "an almost brutal finality to Szell's disposal of human material in the orchestra, which is not necessary in any institution, even one which aspires continually to high artistry." Matson found it difficult to understand Szell showing "apparent coldness, arbitrariness and precise brutality. . . . We hope the union will put the brakes on this sort of thing."[68]

Nearly two decades later, Szell cited Rodzinski's firing of New York Philharmonic players in 1943, overstating the number as thirty—actually it was fourteen—to diminish the magnitude of his own firing of seventeen musicians during his first season in Cleveland. When he discussed the issue with John Culshaw in 1969, Szell asked, rhetorically: "What is the purpose of a symphony orchestra for which so many people give, without compensation, their time? . . . Is it the purpose [to produce] the best . . . music or is [it] . . . to give their members the easiest and unchallengeably permanent jobs?"[69]

On the other side of the coin, unknown to the public and most of the orchestra, was that Szell sometimes kept players past their prime for humane reasons. One case told me by the orchestra's longtime personnel manager, Olin Trogdon, concerned a violinist who had been with the orchestra a long time, and whose playing had deteriorated because he was losing his eyesight. Szell told Trogdon that he would have to let the musician go at the end of the season. Trogdon pointed out that the man had two years to go to retire on his full pension and that if he had to leave the orchestra this year, his pension would be drastically less. Szell said, "Oh, I didn't know that," and kept the man until his retirement "so it won't be a hardship on him."[70] Even today there is no simple solution about firing players but, to use Matson's words, the union has indeed "put the brakes on this sort of thing."[71] Firing for cause is still possible by strictly defined procedures, but the absolute power of a Toscanini, Reiner, or Szell, or any number of minor maestros, is a thing of the past.

Still another major change occurred in April 1947, when during the Metropolitan Opera's Cleveland visit in April, the announcement came that its first cellist, Ernst Silberstein, had been hired as principal cellist for the Cleveland Orchestra the following season.[72] Silberstein had played under Szell in the NBC Symphony, and Szell recommended him for the Met position. In Cleveland he replaced Harry Fuchs, who resigned rather than move into the second chair. Fuchs rejoined the orchestra a few years later, but he, like Thaviu, would never forgive Szell. Some players, on the other hand, were able to take stepping down philosophically; for example, when Szell replaced Silberstein as principal in 1959, he gracefully accepted second chair.[73]

In spite of such contretemps, high-quality concerts continued. Many new works, called "novelties" at the time were presented: the world premiere of Hindemith's Piano Concerto, with soloist Jesús María Sanromá; *Ricercari*, with its composer Norman Dello Joio as piano soloist; two premieres of Copland works, *Letter from Home* and *Danzón Cubano;* the Symphony no. 5 of Vaughan Williams; and Schoenberg's Theme and Variations, op. 43b. Hindemith was present for the premiere of his concerto. Attending the Copland premieres was Hans W. Heinsheimer, director of the American branch of Boosey and Hawkes, their publisher. The orchestra also performed the edition of six Dvořák Slavonic Dances that Boosey and Hawkes had commissioned from the unemployed Szell when he first came to America. A belated subscription series "first" was Bach's Suite no. 3 in D.

Because the Prokofiev Fifth Symphony had aroused great interest in its first performance in January, Szell repeated the work in March. "This is something rather new at Severance Hall, but a practice followed by the Boston and some other symphonies with new musical works," explained Elmore Bacon.

It was then customary to reward subscribers and supporters of the orchestra, called "Friends," with a special free concert. Because there were far more than could fit into Severance Hall, the concert took place in the cavernous Public Hall, the orchestra's Pops home. An audience of 9,547 heard the Prelude to *Die Meistersinger*, Tchaikovsky's Fifth, and the Schumann Piano Concerto, with Cleveland pianist Beryl Rubinstein. "It was one of those rare occasions," Elwell wrote, "when the size and enthusiasm of the audience spurs all the performers to their best efforts." The critic saw the "quality of performance," and the "tremendous ovation," as an "overwhelming vote of confidence, a warm-hearted testimonial to [Szell's] magnificent achievement in one season as musical director."

Szell's first season concluded in triumph on April 17 and 19. Elwell wrote, "A Beethoven program last night at Severance Hall brought to a brilliant close the Thursday night series of the most successful season in the orchestra's history," putting to rest all doubts that Szell could sustain "the level of enthusiasm aroused by [his] first appearance" in Cleveland. Elwell clearly stated, "Difficult as the task may have been, Szell has done it." He wrote, "Uppermost stands the fact that he remains a musician of uncompromising integrity. His achievement could only be that of a conductor whose intelligence is as keen as his feelings are warm and pure."[74]

Szell attended a board meeting, at which President Sidlo "said that he wanted Mr. Szell to know that the board felt that the step taken a year ago had been fully justified and vindicated, and that hopes were high for the future. Mr. Szell replied by thanking the President and the Board of Trustees for their cooperation and sympathy during the past year, which, he stated, was one of the happiest periods in his life."[75]

At the annual meeting of the Musical Arts Association in June, Sidlo reported that Szell's first season had produced "the largest subscription sales of season tickets, the largest attendance and the largest earned income in the twenty-nine years of the orchestra's existence." Manager Vosburgh announced that the Thursday night series was almost sold out and that the orchestra would play in Carnegie Hall the coming season, "for the first time in seven years."[76]

Szell scheduled a two-and-a-half-hour session with the orchestra to test the recording set-up and refresh the pieces to be recorded the next week for Columbia Records. His first recording sessions with the orchestra took place the week after the final subscription pair in April.

If, years later, Helene Szell remembered that she cried all day when she learned that they were going to move to Cleveland, she could rightly have added that it turned out well. George Szell's achievement with the Cleveland Orchestra enhanced his reputation worldwide. He kept contact with New York through regular returns to the Philharmonic and by maintaining a residence there. During winters and summers, his international career flourished, bringing him recognition and honors. In the winter seasons, the Szells settled down in Cleveland, where a small circle of friends drawn from the orchestra's board made life pleasant for them, and from 1947 on they spent their summers in Europe.

After the Cleveland season, Szell joined the New York Philharmonic's tour of seventeen states to conduct concerts in Memphis, Louisville, St. Louis, and Chicago.[77] On May 28, 1947, the Szells sailed to Europe on the *S.S. America,* their first return since leaving for Australia in April 1939. They would rest in Switzerland, where Szell would celebrate his fiftieth birthday, then return to England for rehearsals at Glyndebourne for *Le nozze di Figaro* and *Macbeth* in preparation for performances at the first Edinburgh Festival later that summer.

The Glyndebourne Fiasco

In 1947, Rudolf Bing was general manager of the Glyndebourne Festival in England. Bing grew up in Vienna and worked his way up in the administration of various German opera houses. He had served under Intendant Carl Ebert in Darmstadt, and, when Ebert was engaged to co-head the new Glyndebourne Festival in 1934, with conductor Fritz Busch, he first hired Bing as a stage assistant and, eventually, general manager.

By 1939, John Christie, Glyndebourne's founder, who "had spent about £100,000 of his own money on his Sussex opera festival," realized that if Glyndebourne were to resume its operation after its wartime suspension, an additional source of income would have to be found. Bing conceived the idea to establish a music festival "organized in association with Glyndebourne." After Oxford rejected the proposal, Henry Harvey Wood, the Scottish representative on the British Council, suggested Edinburgh. In 1947, after much politicking, the Edinburgh Festival was established.[78]

For that first season, Bing engaged Szell to conduct the Glyndebourne Opera's Edinburgh performances of *Le Nozze di Figaro* and *Macbeth*. Bing knew of Szell's prewar affiliation with the Scottish Orchestra; his cable to Szell in November 1946 refers to "your Scottish Orchestra," suggesting that Szell would have welcomed a return to an orchestra with which he had been so happy.[79] But events did not work out well.

According to Bing:

> We had imported a young American soprano. Unfortunately, the girl had never played the role before, and she arrived knowing only Susanna's arias and her lines in the concerted numbers. As the recitatives in Susanna's role are almost as long as all the rest put together, she was seriously unprepared. Szell made a terrible scene, announced that he could not possibly work with an artist who

> didn't know her role, and to our amazement abandoned both productions. I always felt that he had believed he was going to work with a London orchestra of the quality we had engaged for Glyndebourne before the war, and having heard some negative comments about the Scottish Orchestra that would be in the pit in Edinburgh he decided to seize on the soprano's failings as his excuse to quit. He undoubtedly could have taught the girl her recitatives if he had wished to do so. But he did quit; it would not be the last time George Szell walked out on me.[80]

Considering that Szell had been told he would have the Scottish Orchestra, Bing's explanation that Szell had expected a London orchestra is false, and the late arrival of many other singers could have been reason enough to quit. Szell's detailed account of the episode in a letter to Artur Schnabel clearly shows that the singers, rather than the orchestra, were the problem:

> I wish to emphasize that I did not act in a sudden outburst of ill humour or in snooty superiority in the face of low standards, but after two and a half weeks of honest endeavour against impossible odds and after duly weighing the course of action to take under given circumstances.
>
> To make it short: an incredible muddle due to incompetent management made us waste more than two out of three available weeks of rehearsals. When I arrived at Glyndebourne, we had ahead of us three weeks of rehearsals, the first of which was supposed to be devoted to musical rehearsals with the singers the other two for stage rehearsals with singers & chorus. After these three weeks we were to go up to Edinburgh and I was to rehearse for two weeks twice daily the orchestra, first alone, then with stage & cast. This was a very good schedule, providing the operas were in shape so far as the singers and the stage were concerned before moving up to Edinburgh. What actually happened in Glyndebourne was, that, for "Figaro" during the first week there was no Susanna, no Countess, no Cherubino, no Count. Basilio, Bartolo, Marzellina etc. were present (very weak local talent) but they had either not sung their parts before at all or not in Italian and at any rate did not know them by heart. I proceeded all the same cheerfully to rehearse what could be rehearsed, waiting for the arrivals of the principal singers which were staggered during the coming 2–3 weeks.

Irritated by delays and incompetent understudies, who temporarily took the place of the absent principals but who also did not know their parts, Szell worked with what he had. When the Susanna, Virginia McWatters, arrived, three days before beginning the staging and "WITHOUT KNOWING HER PART AT ALL," it made Szell "slightly worried." He asked that management call in someone who knew the demanding role (Susanna is one of the longest parts in opera, with long recitatives as well as arias and many intricate ensembles). Six days later, McWatters confessed that she could not learn the role in time.

Ebert then suggested a Turkish girl he had heard, but she turned out "just as hopeless" as Szell had anticipated. "There were only three days left and 'Figaro' not yet rehearsed before the Orchestra rehearsals were to start, and still no Countess present and a Susanna and a Cherubino only expected from Italy by every train,—in brief, a complete mess. This was so disgusting and hopeless that I would have withdrawn even if Ebert's stage-directing had not been as antimusical, provincial and wrongheaded as it proved to be during the few rehearsals that could be done with whatever was there in the way of casts. . . . But in view of the complete destruction of the whole rehearsal time-table I could not even face 'Macbeth' and so I dropped out."[81]

Szell's account seems well-reasoned and plausible. After twenty years of professional opera experience in Europe and four years at the Met, Szell had shown considerable patience with the amateur conditions he encountered at Glyndebourne. As a consequence, Szell enjoyed a longer vacation than expected. The Szells spent a restful time in the English countryside visiting Helene Szell's sister and brother-in-law at Walton-on-Thames, near London. There, Szell could prepare for his second season in Cleveland.

Szell, in a sailor suit, age twelve. Signed November 11, 1909.
Courtesy of Dover Publications, Inc.

Publicity photo for Odeon Record Company, mid-1920s. Caption reads: "Odeon Artist, Georg Szell, First conductor at the Berlin State Opera. Photo by Franz Löwy, Vienna." During his tenure at the Berlin State Opera (1924–29) Szell conducted several recordings for the Odeon Record Company. Courtesy of The Cleveland Orchestra Archives.

Szell in St. Louis 1930/31.
Author's collection.

"Gag" photo, Prague, 1930s. Szell is "driving," man wearing beret is St. Louis music critic Robert B. Sherman, third man is unidentified. Author's collection.

Szell made his debut at the Metropolitan Opera in *Salome* in 1942. Rehearsing with René Maison, Lily Djanel, and stage director Herbert Graf. Courtesy of the Metropolitan Opera Archives.

Szell returned to the Metropolitan Opera in 1953, conducting *Tannhäuser*. Rehearsing on stage, left to right: Herbert Graf, Ramon Vinay, George London, Margaret Harshaw, George Szell. Courtesy of the Metropolitan Opera Archives.

Rehearsing chorus and cast members for *Tannhäuser*, 1953. Ramon Vinay is center first row, across the aisle are Brian Sullivan and Paul Franke. Chorusmaster Kurt Adler is at Szell's left. Courtesy of the Metropolitan Opera Archives.

Philadelphia Academy of Music, 1956. Philadelphia Orchestra cellist/photographer Adrian Siegel wrote about the circumstances of this photo: "When Szell saw the photograph of Stravinsky on the dressing room wall, he asked me to take his picture because they had often been mistaken for each other." Szell enjoyed a joke even if sometimes it was on himself. The Adrian Siegel Collection/ The Philadelphia Orchestra Association Archives.

Helene Szell admires George Szell wearing the Commander's Cross of the Federal Republic of Germany, bestowed on him after a Severance Hall concert, 1959. Photograph by Ed Nano, used by permission.

Szell and the author, at Severance Hall, ca. 1963. Courtesy of photographer Thomas Beiswenger.

Leon Fleisher and Szell, at a recording session of the Beethoven Piano concertos, ca. 1959–61. Courtesy of Sony Music Entertainment.

Rehearsing with frequent collaborator Clifford Curzon, with whom Szell also had a warm personal friendship. Photograph by Peter Hastings, Courtesy of The Cleveland Orchestra Archives.

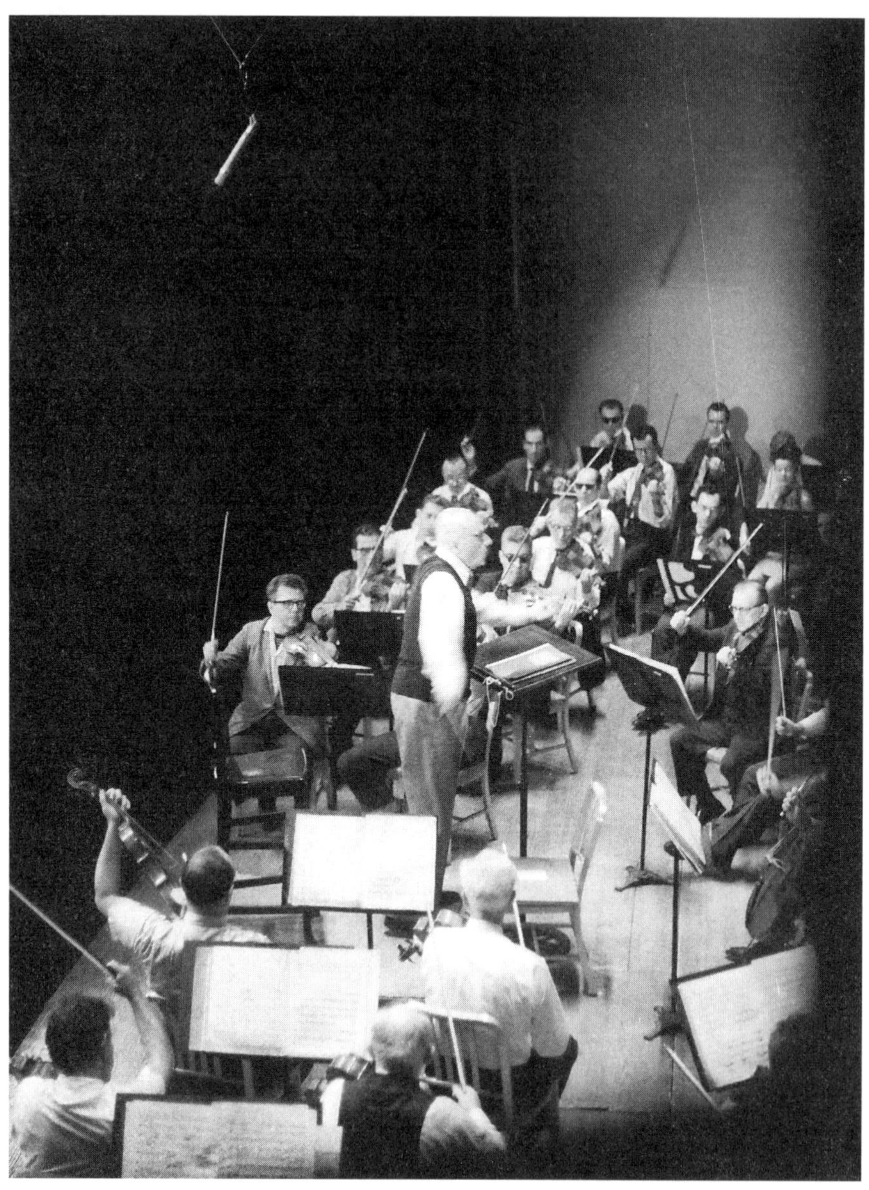

A dramatic ending to Sibelius's Second Symphony, television rehearsal for season's opening concert October 1963. Photograph by the author.

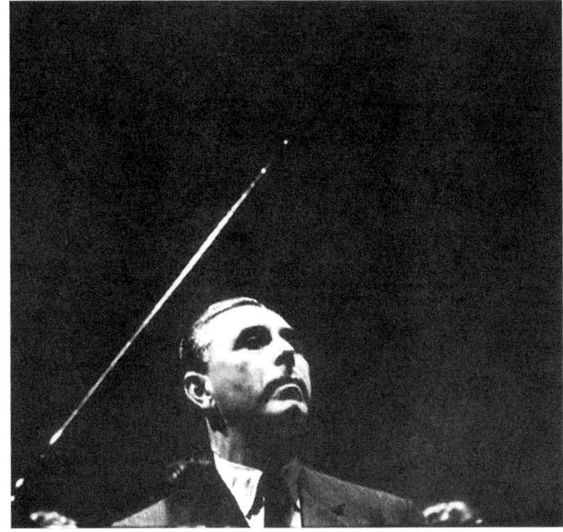

Rudolf Firkusny, a former student of Szell's friend and colleague Artur Schnabel, appeared with Szell widely (undated). Photograph by Peter Hastings, Courtesy of The Cleveland Orchestra Archives.

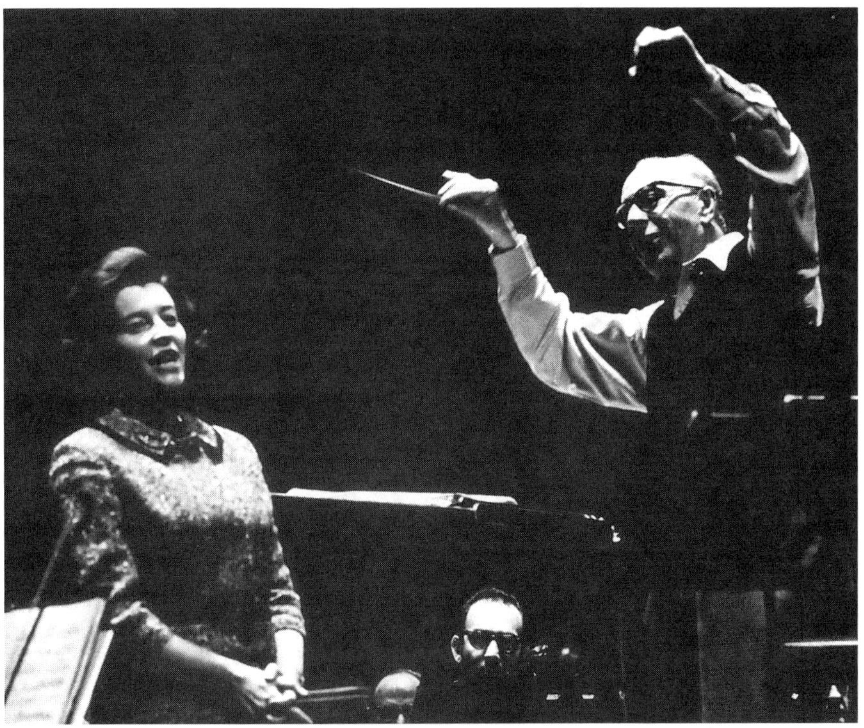

Metropolitan Opera soprano Judith Raskin sang a heavenly final movement of Mahler's Fourth Symphony. In a review, a music critic suggested she be named the orchestra's "First Soprano," 1963. Photograph by Peter Hastings, Courtesy of The Cleveland Orchestra Archives.

Listening to playback of their recording of William Schuman's *A Song of Orpheus*, left to right: Paul Myers, Columbia Records' audio producer; concertmaster Rafael Druian; George Szell; cello soloist Leonard Rose, 1964. Photograph by the author.

The young German violinist Edith Peinemann joined the circle of Szell's favorite soloists, 1965. Photograph by Peter Hastings, Courtesy of The Cleveland Orchestra Archives.

Szell with Rudolf Serkin, his oldest friend and colleague—they met in Vienna as young piano students of Richard Robert. Taken in Szell's office in Severance Hall after a concert (undated). Courtesy of Sony Music Entertainment.

Rehearsing with Arthur Rubinstein, ca. 1963. Photograph by the author.

Szell conducting the Cleveland Orchestra in Leningrad's Philharmonic Hall, on the historic eleven-week tour, 1965. Photograph by Oleg Makarov.

After concert banquet in Tbilisi, Georgia, USSR. Szell giving speech of thanks, translated by Anatole Heller, European tour manager for the U.S. State Department. Helene Szell is on George Szell's left, 1965. Photograph by the author.

The author, George Szell, and Louis Lane in Paris after lunch with Szell on the Left Bank. Taken by a Parisian passer-by. Signed by Szell, inscribed: "An unforgettable moment with unforgettable associates. En souvenir, GSz," 1965. Author's collection.

Taping a segment for "The Bell Telephone Hour, One Man's Triumph." Left to right: Stephen Portman, Kulas Fellow; George Szell; the author and James Levine, assistant conductors, 1966. Photograph by Peter Hastings, Courtesy of The Cleveland Orchestra Archives.

Official posed photo of the Cleveland Orchestra and George Szell. The author is at the piano, James Levine is at the celesta, 1966. Photograph by Hastings-Willinger & Associates, courtesy of the Cleveland Orchestra Archives.

Severance Hall, the elegant home of the Cleveland Orchestra, opened in 1932 (undated). Photograph by Peter Hastings, courtesy of The Cleveland Orchestra Archives.

The striking summer home of the Cleveland Orchestra, Blossom Music Center, opened in 1968. Its excellent acoustics require no amplification for an audience of more than four thousand seated under the roof, its sight lines uninterrupted by internal supports (undated). Photograph by Peter Hastings, courtesy of The Cleveland Orchestra Archives.

Szell rehearsing principal cellist Lynn Harrell and principal oboist John Mack, backstage before a concert on tour in Seattle, 1970. Photograph by Peter Hastings, courtesy of The Cleveland Orchestra Archives.

Conducting concert in Tokyo, 1970. Photograph by Peter Hastings, courtesy of The Cleveland Orchestra Archives.

Live television broadcast of the Tokyo concert. At the high point of the finale of Sibelius's Symphony no. 2, Szell's image is superimposed over the orchestra, 1970. Photograph by the author.

Bows at the end of the Tokyo concert. Szell holding hands of two young Japanese girls who presented flowers, with musicians beaming at the girls, 1970. Photograph by Peter Hastings, courtesy of The Cleveland Orchestra Archives.

Szell on plane en route home. The strain of the tour and of his terminal disease shows in his face, 1970. Photograph by Peter Hastings, courtesy of The Cleveland Orchestra Archives.

Triple photo-montage by Peter Hastings, of Szell conducting Beethoven's Symphony no. 3, *Eroica* (undated). Szell conducted it in twelve of his twenty-four seasons in Cleveland and conducted it on his first and last concerts as musical director—1946 and 1970—and on the last concert he ever conducted, with the Cleveland Orchestra, in Anchorage, Alaska, on May 29, 1970. Photograph by Peter Hastings, courtesy of The Cleveland Orchestra Archives.

6

Szell, the Orchestra Builder (1947–54)

Szell was a hands-on musical director in Cleveland, involving himself in every aspect of the orchestra's operation. To make the orchestra "second to none," he devoted as much time and hard work as necessary. Szell's talent, experience, and energy well equipped him for the task.

He had the full support of the board's president, Thomas Sidlo, and the orchestra's capable manager, Carl J. Vosburgh. Sidlo kept the trustees informed of Szell's accomplishments and guided their decisions to meet his musical needs. Year-round, Szell, Vosburgh, and George Henry Lovett Smith, the manager's assistant, remained in constant communication. No detail was too small for Szell's involvement, from the font size of the programs ("While I hate to appear interfering with what is eminently your work, I hope you won't mind my saying frankly that I find the type of the programs much too small") to the pricing of the cheapest seats ("Sticking my nose into what is not my business in the strict sense of the word, I feel that 2.40 Dollars for the extra chair is much too low an entrance fee"[1]) to the radio broadcast quality ("which was last year too poor to be of prestige value to us"[2]). Szell acceded to the practical: larger font size would leave an awkward number of blank folio pages, Vosburgh explained. Szell's influence had far-reaching effects, from the Severance Hall stage and administrative offices all the way to the janitorial staff. Even the hallways seemed to have an extra sparkle when Szell was in residence.

Cautious at first, Szell and Vosburgh developed a warm working relationship, ameliorating the onus that the manager had been a protégé of Adella Prentiss Hughes, a strong opponent of Szell. Vosburgh was his own man, a calming influence on Szell. Louis Lane and Seymour Lipkin served as Kulas Apprentice Conductors in the 1947–48 season. One morning, Lane recalled, they overheard Szell screaming at someone in his office. Vosburgh emerged, saying "I don't like to be shouted at and when you think about it you won't like having shouted at me. Call me when you feel better." Lipkin was shocked and asked Lane what they should do. The unflappable Lane answered, "We will apologize to Mr. Szell for being a little late for our appointment."[3]

Szell came to realize that Vosburgh had the complete confidence of the trustees. He was very good at what he did and never made musical judgments or decisions, only business ones. In time Mrs. Hughes came to appreciate Szell. She asked Lane one day how he liked Szell. Lane answered that "like" was beside the point. "He is so far my superior in gifts, knowledge, and command, that it's not a question of 'like.' It is an education for me." The formidable grande dame replied, "For me, too."[4]

Szell's second season as musical director, 1947–48, was the Cleveland Orchestra's thirtieth. But Szell was not ready for celebration so early in his tenure. He had committed to twenty-two weeks of the thirty-week season, including all the major tour concerts. Guest conductors, no matter how excellent, cannot replace the constant artistic imprint and discipline of a resident music director. Szell took charge of three-quarters of his orchestra's winter season.

His first five subscription programs included a few major works he had conducted as a guest, works dear to him and his audience that would stay in the Cleveland Orchestra's repertoire. Szell challenged the orchestra to keep these pieces fresh while delving ever deeper into their mysteries. He programmed works such as the first two of the three *Nocturnes* of Debussy and Smetana's *The Moldau* to cultivate and, at the same time, demonstrate the orchestra's versatility. Repeats from Szell's guest programs included Brahms's First Symphony, Tchaikovsky's *Pathétique* Symphony, and Beethoven's Sixth and Seventh. Hindemith's *Symphonic Metamorphosis of Themes by Carl Maria von Weber* became a brilliant signature showpiece.

The perceptive Arthur Loesser appreciated Szell's subtle tempo modifications in the Brahms: "They were worked into unobtrusively and with great finesse, avoiding the crude draggings and sprintings that one occasionally hears."[5] A review by Herbert Elwell recognized that the larger orchestral forces needed time "to age, mellow, and integrate themselves." Such refinements as tone quality and blend, he believed, "will not be long in arriving."[6] The critics showed great interest in the new concertmaster, Josef Gingold, noting that his fine musicianship and leadership boded well for the orchestra's future. That season, Szell replaced sixteen players including the principal cellist and three principal winds: horn, clarinet, and oboe.[7] The previous season, Szell had added five new positions; this season the number of players remained stable at ninety-five. Former concertmaster Joseph Fuchs made his sixteenth solo appearance with the orchestra. Other soloists included violinists Zino Francescatti, Josef Gingold, and Joseph Szigeti, pianists Rudolf Firkusny and Alexander Brailowsky, and apprentice conductor Seymour Lipkin.

After the tour de force, Mahler's *Das Lied von der Erde*,[8] Szell and the orchestra followed with a two-week tour to Ann Arbor, Detroit, Jackson, Muskegon, and

Kalamazoo, Michigan; Beverly Hills, Chicago, Bloomington, and Joliet, Illinois; Muncie, Indiana; and Toledo and Lima, Ohio. Szell explored much new territory this season: third symphonies of Aaron Copland and Peter Mennin, Sibelius's Seventh Symphony, Messiaen's *L'Ascension*, and Arthur Shepherd's *Fantasy on Down-East Spirituals*.[9] World premieres given during the 1947–48 season were *Pastorale* by Cleveland composer (and *Plain Dealer* music critic) Herbert Elwell, Artur Schnabel's *Rhapsody for Orchestra* (1946), and *Hyperion* by Ernest Toch.[10]

Under Szell the orchestra musically electrified the Cleveland community. But it also faced the sobering reality of its "first red ink in a long time," according to Sidlo. The deficit, $12,000, accounted for only 2 percent of the budget, but concerned the trustees, who were unaccustomed to any deficit.[11]

After Szell's Second Season

The Szells drove to New York soon after the orchestra season. Helene's son, John Teltsch, graduated from high school in New York on June 4. Szell wrote letters to friends in Chicago for advice on ranches, but John, armed with a supply of travelers checks, went west on his own that summer. The day after John's graduation, the Szells sailed for their second postwar summer in Europe. Szell celebrated his fifty-first birthday on board.

In England they visited Helene's sister, Marianne. The sisters had married brothers, Ernst and Emo Teltsch. In Prague, George and Emo had been close friends. After Helene's divorce from Ernst and her marriage to George, her sister and brother-in-law remained friendly, welcoming the Szells' visits. After George's death, Helene continued to visit her sister yearly.

Rudolf Bing contacted Szell in London. Bing was in negotiations with the New York Philharmonic for the third Edinburgh Festival in 1949 and wanted a backup. Szell prepared a minutely detailed budget for Cleveland's appearance there, estimating expenses, such as for "pocket money of, say, $20. per man a week whilst in Great Britain, for cigarettes, drinks, etc," fees for soloists, and marine insurance rates for musical instruments. He had consulted the Cunard Line sailing schedules around the dates in question. Szell suggested that they figure out several budgets, based on whether they stayed two or three weeks and whether the orchestra would insist on being paid for the two weeks of ocean crossing ("I trust we can convince the orchestra to accept the passage as a pleasure trip, but at any rate we have to consider the other possibilities"). Neither the Cleveland Orchestra nor the New York Philharmonic appeared in Edinburgh in 1949, but both did in later seasons.[12]

Szell reserved a summer month for golf at his favorite resort, the Hotel du Golf at Crans-sur-sierre in Valais, Switzerland. In a fertile valley amid moderate-sized, snow-capped mountains, the retreat offered pure air, warm days, and cool evenings, a healing tonic after strenuous winters. This year the couple borrowed a Jaguar sedan from Helene's relatives, and in later years they kept a Cadillac in a garage in Paris for their summer forays.

In September, while in New York, Szell attended to business—auditioning players and conferring with Vosburgh and Smith by letter and telephone. That year, he made the acquaintance of violist Abraham Skernick, who had played two seasons with the St. Louis Symphony and recently joined the Baltimore as principal. In December, with flattering politeness and a hint of secrecy—perhaps the flap over Gingold made him cautious—Szell wrote to him: "I should like to follow up the conversation we had in New York . . . and I should prefer to do so personally instead of by correspondence."[13] They met on January 11, and at the end of the season Skernick played several concerts in Cleveland under Szell. He joined the orchestra as principal the following season.

Other significant changes during the 1948–49 season included the acquisition of a new principal trombone, Robert Boyd, whose tenure would outlast Szell's. To make a place for Boyd, the redoubtable Merritt Dittert moved from first to bass trombone. Szell reappointed Louis Lane as sole apprentice conductor, because "none of the applicants whom [Szell] interviewed for that position seemed to possess the necessary qualifications."[14]

Szell's contract would expire at the end of the 1948–49 season. Cleveland audiences, as well as the orchestra's board, wanted Szell to stay on—and he himself seemed to be of that mind—but serious obstacles loomed. Although the musical results of Szell's tenure were unparalleled—the orchestra had improved very rapidly and ticket sales reached a new high—growth bore financial consequences: the fund drive fell $30,000 short of its goal of $120,000.[15] The press reported the possibility that "the Szell continuance depends upon the outcome of the present financing campaign."[16]

The 1948–49 season began with Wagner and Haydn but also included a French work not ordinarily associated with Szell: Ravel's *La Valse*. For the first time in Cleveland, Szell conducted Tchaikovsky's Symphony no. 4, which eventually surpassed the Fifth in Szell's Cleveland repertoire. Szell scheduled Howard Hanson's suite from the opera *Merry Mount* in 1948. Hanson, since 1924 head of the Eastman School of Music, and a powerful figure in the musical world, remarked to Thomas Sidlo at a luncheon at the Metropolitan Opera that Szell "had not been playing very much American music or works by modern composers since coming to Cleveland." To correct Hanson's misperception, and to prevent his spreading it about, Sidlo sent the composer the current season brochure and a repertoire list of Szell's previous seasons. Hanson responded that he "was delighted to see the representation of American music on these programs," sending to Szell and Ringwall his "congratulations and kindest regards." Sidlo wrote Vosburgh about this, including a copy of

Hanson's letter, telling him to show the correspondence to Szell. Recognizing the continued importance of defusing Hanson, Szell scheduled his composition early the following season.[17]

The fourth and fifth programs contained two of the lengthiest works in the symphonic repertoire: Schubert's C Major Symphony, "The Great," and the first Cleveland performance of Mahler's Symphony no. 9. Szell might have seen the well-known Schubert's legendary "heavenly length" as a preparation for the further stretch the audience would need to make in the next concert. As part of the orchestra's educational effort and probably at Szell's suggestion, the program book contained an article to prepare the audience: "The Length of Mahler," which concluded by saying "Patience! The rewards are immense!"[18]

Smith's duties included scheduling the orchestra's programs and those of visiting orchestras sponsored by the Musical Arts Association. For the 1948–49 season, the Association presented a Boston Symphony concert in the public music hall, on a tour celebrating Koussevitzky's twenty-fifth anniversary as its conductor. In the course of arranging for this concert, Smith proudly wrote his Boston counterpart, John N. Burk: "Szell made a killing with the Mahler Ninth last night, and we are already getting many requests to repeat it this season. . . . I should add that Szell has done two performances of the Prokofieff Fifth in the last two years, and that 'Till' brought down the house here last week. . . . What Szell is accomplishing here is so magnificent that I wish you could come, not for one concert only, but for several."[19]

A New Contract

While Szell and the orchestra were on an eight-concert tour of the Midwest—reportedly playing to "packed houses, wild applause, exuberant press notices"—the Cleveland Orchestra's board of trustees met to decide on the renewal of his contract. Szell's triumphant tours gave him much exposure, raising the possibility of other orchestras recruiting him. In fact, he was then very close to being offered the Chicago Symphony. This, of course, should have put him in a strong position in negotiating a new contract. Szell told Percy Brown of the splendid reception he had received in Chicago and also mentioned that his friend, Eric Oldberg, was promoted to vice president of the Chicago Symphony board, with the "presidency ahead."[20] Concerned over the possibility of losing Szell, Brown suggested to Sidlo a two-year contract, but the board, worried about the orchestra's financial situation, felt they could only offer one year. This Szell accepted, but asked for an increase in salary "as he had done all he had been called upon to do and believed that his regime as conductor had been a definite success." At its next meeting, the board approved a "small increase in salary," less than 10 percent. Sidlo pointed out that Szell's was below that of the conductors of the orchestras in Boston, New York, Philadelphia, and Chicago, which ranged from $50,000 to $100,000.[21] In his announcement of Szell's contract extension, Sidlo cited the uncertainty of the financial situation and attributed the one-year idea to Szell. Szell was "more than delighted at the prospect of continuing [his] work with the Cleveland Orchestra," and declared his gratitude to the trustees, musicians, and public.[22] Szell knew full well, however, that there was no guarantee that Cleveland's finances would strengthen, and he might be without an orchestra in a year: "everything is open after 49–50," he confided to Oldberg.

The Chicago Symphony would have been a challenge. But in his last guest appearance there in March 1948, after he conducted the Bruckner Third, Szell relinquished some of his prior reservations about the orchestra's condition: "Given the proper arrangements and adjustments," he wrote Oldberg, "it might not take very long to have them back to the fine standard they used to have and ought to have." His concluding words were warmly appreciative: "Neither Lene [diminutive for Helene] nor I are of the demonstrative kind, but I think you must feel all the same what those weeks in your house and in close touch with you and Hilda meant and mean to us. We simply think of you both as exceptional human beings and you are our most beloved friends of all, anywhere in the world."[23]

The tenth program featured an old friend, Rudolf Serkin, playing the Brahms Piano Concerto no. 1, and the first Cleveland performance of the *Symphony for Classical Orchestra*, by twenty-seven-year-old Harold Shapero. Loesser extolled Serkin for his "truly wonderful realization of the Brahms Concerto."[24] "Spurred by Szell's inspired conducting," Elwell wrote, "the orchestra contributed mightily to the grandeur of Brahms's vast tonal landscape. Few pianists ever seem quite so completely consumed by the Brahmsian fire as Serkin, and few are better equipped to communicate its warmth." Yet he was annoyed by Serkin's "stamping so loudly on the pedal and flinging his arms so high in the air."[25] The Koussevitzky Foundation commissioned Shapero's work. Aaron Copland viewed Shapero as, "at the same time the most gifted and the most baffling composer of his generation," noting the young composer's "technical adroitness . . . put at the service of a wonderfully spontaneous musical gift."[26]

Some forty years later, a critic for the *New York Times* wrote of the composer's dispiriting Cleveland experience:

> Szell had pretty much had his arm twisted by the publisher [Hans Heinsheimer] to perform the score. And the autocratic maestro proved condescending, at best, in Mr. Shapero's view. After playing the score at the piano for Szell, Mr. Shapero says the conductor "complained about the piece, about this and that. I don't know how to modulate. I should study Strauss. Where did I learn to orchestrate?" He just kept it up. I was a young kid and I was full of sass, and I said, "Look, if you've got that many doubts about the piece, don't play it." Szell did play it, and the trip to Cleveland proved a nightmare for the young composer. As Mr.

> Shapero recalls it, the conductor continued to lecture him on how to compose and humiliated him in public rehearsal. And while Mr. Shapero concedes that the performance came out fairly well, because, in the end, Szell was such a fine musician, the reviews were totally hostile. "So I didn't enjoy that week. I hated it. It was so bad I didn't even stay for the second performance."[27]

On balance, the 1948 reviews may have been more negative than positive, but surely not "totally hostile." Loesser liked its "many attractive qualities, among which are the neat clarity of its patterns in which all its movements are cast; a logic which even extends to the maintenance of the classical principle of tonality, certainly an anchor of comfort in a work of any length." Although he considered the forty-two-minute work too long for its subject, he cited "brisk humor, vivacious rhythms . . . amusing whimsy of orchestration economically achieved."[28]

The sympathetic Smith wrote Shapero a few days later that the Saturday performance was "much more relaxed and brilliant and had a good success."[29] Shapero replied: "I certainly was pleased with the way my work was presented. The younger composers are not often given such painstaking attention and such quantities of rehearsal time. I remember clearly the excellence and willingness of the orchestra, and I told Mr. Szell in person after the concert how grateful I was for his help, artistic and financial [!]. He knew every note of my long score and is a most precise musician, anxious to reproduce the intentions of the composer, exactly."[30]

If Szell had judged the work poor, Heinsheimer would never have been able to persuade him to play it. Szell had perceived a degree of talent in Shapero or he would not have bothered to criticize him. His blunt approach with Shapero was his way, according to Louis Lane. Szell told him he was impressed with Shapero, and encouraged him to write another work, a commission never realized.[31]

Other high points of the season included a magnificent performance of Hindemith's symphony *Mathis der Maler*, and, in its first time in subscription concerts, Bach's Brandenburg Concerto no. 1. For the traditional Viennese New Year's subscription concert that season, Szell included *The Barber of Baghdad* Overture, by Peter Cornelius, a piece with which he made his conducting debut in 1913, and Johann Strauss Jr.'s musical joke, *Perpetuum Mobile*. True to its title, the piece concludes on a "vamp" figure that is repeated ad libitum for as long as conductor and orchestra can prolong a fade-out. Finally at the end, someone, usually the conductor, says out loud, "and so forth." Szell's voice and inimitable accent are immortalized in a recording of the work made some years later.

Szell conducted the U.S. premiere of *A Pickwickian Overture*, by his boyhood friend, Hans Gal; the Dvořák 'Cello Concerto, with the new principal cellist, Ernst Silberstein; the first subscription performances of Smetana's tone poem *From Bohemia's Meadows and Forests;* and the first Cleveland performance of Samuel Barber's revised Symphony no. 1. Szell had conducted Gal's concert music in Europe and the world premiere of his opera *Die Heilige Ente* in 1923 in Düsseldorf. Gal's presence made for a joyous reunion.

Audiences and critics received the Barber Symphony enthusiastically. Brahms's Fourth was "magnificently done," Loesser wrote, with "prolonged enthusiasm at the close; the orchestra stood up to accept its share of it. But at the final recall the men refused to stand, and joined the applause for Szell."[32] This sign of respect sometimes happens with a guest conductor, but for a musical director it is rare.

At the end of January the National Arts Foundation named Szell to its advisory board. The new organization formed as "a public education movement to get 'people to give themselves to the arts,'" according to its director, Carleton Smith. He explained, "Szell was selected because of his contribution to American music through his system of apprentice conductors with the Cleveland Orchestra."[33] The orchestra departed for a two-week tour, playing in Connecticut, Massachusetts, New Jersey, and New York. Reviews of the Carnegie Hall concert, reprinted in the *Cleveland News*, claimed that the Cleveland Orchestra had brought to New York some of "the most satisfying music making of the season." Olin Downes in the *New York Times* noted that the orchestra had "developed conspicuously in point of sonority and of technical finish, compared to their visit the previous season."[34]

While Szell returned to the Chicago Symphony, Eleazar de Carvalho made his debut on the Severance Hall podium. He agreed to include on his program William Schuman's Symphony for Strings, which Szell had originally planned to perform, along with Robert Schumann's *Manfred* Overture. Szell had written Smith in June, "Add the Manfred Overture to the 21st program (as first item on the program, preceding the mono-n-ic Schuman. Let Bill follow Bob.)"[35]

In Chicago Szell led the first local performance of Mahler's monumental Symphony no. 8, which he never conducted in Cleveland. Adding to the length of the program (the Mahler runs eighty minutes) was the Mendelssohn Violin Concerto, played by Zino Francescatti. While in Chicago, Szell auditioned prospective players for Cleveland. Szell offered violinist Samuel Epstein minimum scale. Emanuel Tivin, hired as first oboist, haggled with Szell for a larger salary than offered. Szell held high hopes for Tivin: "He is gifted and I am hoping that before long we shall not miss the present incumbent too much," he wrote to Vosburgh.[36] But after one season, he replaced Tivin with the oboist of his dreams, Marc Lifschey. Epstein remained until he retired more than thirty years later.

At the Crossroads

The trustees addressed an issue: would the orchestra maintain the standard Szell had set, or slide backward? Vosburgh, and eventually Sidlo, had been meeting with union representatives since the New Year. The union stood firm on two issues:

to raise the minimum scale from $93 to $98 per week, and to double the number of summer Pops concert weeks from six to twelve. To resolve the summer point, the union had offered to underwrite half of the deficit incurred by the Pops, up to $7,500. But by early March they seemed to have reached an impasse, with Sidlo and Vosburgh holding the line against a raise. In March 1949, Cleveland's budget stood at less than two-thirds that of New York, Boston, or Philadelphia; and its weekly salary rate was seventeen dollars less than the lowest of the others. Management calculated that each dollar of salary increase would result in an increase of from $5,000 to $6,000 in operating expenses.

Cleveland had grown accustomed to a first-class orchestra and might not support less than that. The trustees were apprehensive that Szell might opt out of his contract. Any further delay might jeopardize the signing of the orchestra's first-chair players and even result in the loss of key musicians.[37] The trustees moved to meet the union's financial demands. In return, Szell gave up the preseason week of nine rehearsals, although he gained an additional rehearsal in the first week of the following season. Szell made these concessions calculating that if the orchestra could turn this corner, its future would be bright.[38]

Szell concluded the season by continuing to include American works, programming a second reading in the same season of Barber's Symphony in One Movement (Symphony no. 1) and the first Cleveland performance of Walter Piston's Toccata.[39] The national musicians' union's ban on recordings having been lifted, Szell and the orchestra made three recordings following the final concerts of the season. In later years, Szell would record works only in their subscription performance weeks.

The Szells flew to London for the first time. Szell conducted eight concerts in England, two in Holland, and one in Zurich in the summer of 1949. There were only two weeks for golf before Salzburg, where Szell conducted three performances of *Der Rosenkavalier* and a concert with the Vienna Philharmonic. Then the Szells motored leisurely through Switzerland and France for a week before returning to England.

In June, Szell's concert with the London Philharmonic Orchestra overcame "the acoustic eccentricities of enormous Albert Hall." The *Cleveland Plain Dealer* published a long article and interview with Szell by its London correspondent. Knowing the interview was intended for home consumption, Szell made some rather exaggerated statements: "It is nice to be in England again, and I have a very heavy European schedule," said Szell. "I enjoy touring overseas and there is one particular fact I get out of it. It is when I am with other orchestras and playing in other halls that I certainly realize more than ever what a magnificent instrument the Cleveland Orchestra is, and what a splendid hall we ourselves have—the best in the world so far as I know."[40]

The artistic head of the "best known recording company" in London remarked to Szell, "Why do you come over to conduct our orchestra here when you have this one at home I cannot see." Szell admitted that he derived satisfaction from European audiences for their "rapturous concentration and motionless attentiveness." Szell said, patronizingly, that he felt impelled to conduct in Europe in summer as "a feeling of obligation to make music for Europeans, who for ten years were deprived of the best," and "who just now have started to realize how their standards have dropped while ours have gone up."[41]

He could well be proud of his orchestra, but he knew better about Severance Hall. Szell had been exploring acoustical improvement since 1947. After having conducted in Carnegie Hall, Boston's Symphony Hall, the Concertgebouw in Amsterdam, and the Musikvereinsaal in Vienna, he well knew the difference. "I really enjoyed this Albert Hall concert. There was one thing which struck me particularly. That was the large number of young people in the audience. It did me more good than anything. It is something that does not happen in the United States. Oh, yes, a few come to concerts. But the majority want baseball, song-and-dance films, ice revues or what have you. Don't think I am criticizing that, but sometimes I feel sad that they haven't more time for great composers. Coming back to England it is good to see you still have pretty much the same type of audience one finds on the continent."[42]

Szell compared the present LPO with the one he knew when he was living in England in the thirties: "The London Philharmonic is getting back to the standards it had in 1936 when Sir Thomas Beecham was permanently in charge. The personnel are keen and interested. The trouble with most British orchestras is that they cannot rehearse adequately. They never have. They haven't the financial resources. The London Philharmonic is improving almost out of recognition because it does rehearse sufficiently. It can do this because it gets a subsidy. . . . On the other hand, British orchestral players are the best sight readers in the world. Any visiting conductor will tell you that."[43]

A few days later, Clevelanders read of Thomas Sidlo's reelection as president of the Musical Arts Association. It marked a vote of confidence for the man who had led the orchestra through a decade of difficulties to its present success. Although the artistic outlook looked bright, as of June 1949 finances appeared "cloudy." Income had reached an all-time high—$4,000 over the previous year—and next season's tour was fully booked a year in advance. But contributions to the maintenance fund were less than one-third of the goal of $150,000 needed to balance the budget. "If we do not reach our goal and keep the orchestra at its present high level," Sidlo warned, "some very serious questions will be raised as to the size and quality of orchestra and the caliber of conductor Cleveland will have to be content with in the future."[44]

Szell conducted two concerts with the Concertgebouw in the Holland Festival on June 30 and July 1. In Zurich he conducted a concert on July 5, "a special thrill for me," he wrote Oldberg, "as [I] had not played for that reverently attentive, discriminating audience before—which in spite of beastly heat in the hall crowded the place and stayed long after the end." He acknowledged that he had "stopped trying to make European orchestras play with the finish and lushness of American orchestras, but make them do the best they can and that gives results which seem unusual—to judge from the public's reaction."[45]

Szell wrote to Vosburgh from Salzburg, "Opera performances as well as my concert here day before yesterday were stunning successes—all the more surprising as I must have been unknown to the public in these parts—or so I thought, but we were wrong."[46] A letter from Vosburgh carried the bad news that the National and the Columbia Broadcasting System would not broadcast Cleveland concerts. "Columbia informs me that they have gone completely commercial due to the fact that they are losing their shirts on television and must make it up on AM. Mutual would be very happy to broadcast us for free. . . . Please cable me as soon as possible, 'yes' or 'no.'"[47] (Szell answered "no.")

Szell spent a week in New York, serving on the Leventritt Competition jury, which chose twenty-year-old Gary Graffman as the 1949 winner.[48] The pianist had also received a special award in the Rachmaninoff Competition for appearances with the New York and Buffalo Philharmonics and the Cleveland Orchestra.[49] Graffman performed with Szell and the orchestra often over the coming years, and made some brilliant recordings with them.[50]

Szell's Fourth Season

Szell returned to Cleveland in "an exuberant mood" to begin the 1949–50 season. With his conducting of several top European orchestras fresh in mind, "Szell held with more conviction than ever that the Cleveland Orchestra ranks among the five or six finest orchestras in the world." He boasted, "The standards of perfection in technique and reliability, in intonation, precision and balance and in general polish in ensemble playing, which are taken for granted among leading American orchestras, are not matched by European orchestras." With candor, Szell added that European orchestras "often have a warmth . . . a joy in making music and a deep familiarity with repertoire, which, to a certain extent, compensates for their inferior technical finish."[51]

The extra week of rehearsal, which Szell had given up, was clearly no longer a necessity: reviews of the orchestra's first concert of the season—Szell's fourth and the orchestra's thirty-second—were excellent. Szell intended for the program—*Eroica*, *Firebird*, *Till*—to make an impression, and it did. After three seasons, Szell had his orchestra close to where he wanted it. Elwell noted "ample evidence of the great strides that have been made in the balance of sonority, the refinement of tone quality, particularly in the singing strings, the just intonation, precision, blend and all that makes for expertness in the manner of presentation." He compared the orchestra to a gem of "living radiance."[52]

The fiscal situation remained a problem. To avert another "financial flop," Sidlo reminded subscribers that the maintenance fund was still far short of its goal: less than half of the $150,000 needed for the present season had been pledged. Not only the season was at stake, but Szell's contract, indeed his continuance with the orchestra, had to be settled again before its end.[53] The question "could Cleveland support a first-rate orchestra and conductor?" would soon be answered.

Works played for the first time included Delius's *Brigg Fair*, Norman Dello Joio's *Serenade for Orchestra*, David Diamond's *The Enormous Room* (after e.e. cummings), Alvin Etler's Passacaglia and Fugue, Hindemith's *Concert Music for Strings and Brass*, Poulenc's *Sinfonietta* (first U.S. performance), Arthur Shepherd's *Overture to a Drama*, Josef Suk's *A Fairy Tale*, Randall Thompson's Symphony no. 3, and the Suite from the documentary film *Louisiana Story* by Virgil Thomson. Szell may have preferred the great classics, but to his credit, he gave new works thorough preparation. In the case of the Thomson, Elwell wrote, "it was not played with conspicuous conviction, [but] the music itself is to blame. . . . This had some good descriptive spots and some charming folk-tune fragments," the critic observed, "but it was all in short segments and there was little sense of continuity or growth of ideas, except in the final fugue, which was concocted with amateurish counterpoint."[54]

As chief music critic for the *New York Herald-Tribune*, Thomson held a powerful position. His reviews of Szell had not been especially appreciative. At the beginning of the 1949–50 season, Louis Lane was surprised to see the *Louisiana Story* Suite listed in the prospectus. He told Szell that he could not understand how Szell could play a composition, one of whose movements was titled "Boy Fights Alligator." Szell's reply was: "Let's just call this our Louisiana Purchase."[55]

Szell's performance of Mozart's "Jupiter" Symphony must have been a marvel, for his musicians burst into spontaneous applause "in sheer admiration of his superb interpretation."[56] Soloists that season included pianists Robert Casadesus, Clifford Curzon, Gary Graffman, Eugene Istomin, Leonard Shure, Artur Schnabel, and Rudolf Serkin, and violinists Josef Gingold, Szymon Goldberg, Jacob Krachmalnick, Erica Morini, and Joseph Szigeti. Many of these soloists could justifiably be called "the old and new friends of Szell." They appeared with him season after season in Cleveland, with the New York Philharmonic and other United States orchestras, and in Europe. Concertmaster Gingold and Assistant Concertmaster Krachmalnick appeared by dint of their positions in the orchestra, and Graffman as a Leventritt winner. Shure headed the piano department of the Cleveland Music School Settlement.

Musical and personal compatibility was essential to break into the charmed circle of Szell's soloists. A musical profile of his soloists displayed a nature given to probing for the depths in musical expression, total musical honesty, and technical perfection. Personally, a performer had to be open to Szell's frequent lessons—for after all, there was much to be learned from him—and with strong enough ego or nerves to prevent being shattered by his sometimes overriding manner. Rudolf Serkin, for example, said, "I've never been able to get over that feeling that he is a big boy and I am a little one."[57]

That season, Curzon played the Beethoven Fifth Piano Concerto at Severance Hall and the Fourth in Carnegie Hall. We cannot know if Virgil Thomson's review of that Carnegie Hall concert—"Jupiter," Bartók's *Concerto for Orchestra*, Beethoven's Fourth Piano Concerto—might have been as positive without Szell's having played his music earlier that season. Thomson found "Mr. Szell's sensitivity in drawing from his excellent orchestra sounds and curves no less noble [than Curzon], no less constantly fresh and surprising, completed, filled out one of the loveliest musical executions it has been my pleasure to hear in some time. . . . The Cleveland Orchestra, long an excellent one, seems to have taken on added musical quality under this conductor. . . . The Cleveland Orchestra . . . bears comparison with the best we know."[58]

Cleveland's guest conductors in 1949–50 were Dimitri Mitropoulos, William Steinberg, and Bruno Walter.[59] Mitropoulos offered his usual hyperbolic appreciation of the orchestra: "I really honestly believe that the Cleveland Orchestra today is one of the greatest in our country, without any doubt, and this is certainly due to the invaluable efforts and greatness of an artist like Mr. George Szell. I am sure that the community spirit of the people of Cleveland must be proud of having such an orchestra and such a conductor, and that they will make even superhuman efforts to keep that torch alive, which is not only to the glory of the city of Cleveland itself, but to the whole country. With such orchestras existing, America can really compete with the whole world in matters of cultural achievement."[60]

In a letter to Sidlo, Walter complimented Szell's work without actually naming him: "I feel I must write and express the great pleasure and satisfaction that last week's concerts and rehearsals with the Cleveland Orchestra have given me. Let me congratulate you upon the excellent work by which this orchestra has been raised to its present high rank among the finest in the musical world. I am sure your audiences and citizens in general will be proud of such achievement and recognize its importance for Cleveland as a musical center and thereby for the culture of our country."[61] This kind of reassurance bolstered the orchestra's commitment to Szell's vision, and these expressions of approval provided ammunition for Sidlo in the coming battle of the budget.

Mid-December 1949 found Szell as guest conductor with the National Symphony in Washington, D.C. The National was happy with Szell—that is, until he lured away two of their best players—oboist Marc Lifschey in 1950, and clarinetist Robert Marcellus in 1953. This did not make national headlines, as had the flap over concertmaster Josef Gingold, but it was no less strongly felt by the orchestra. As might be expected, the National never again invited Szell.[62]

A Three-Year Contract

By March it was time to settle Szell's contract. The maintenance fund drive had raised well over $123,000, the contract with the musicians' union for the next season had been signed "without change," recording royalties were higher than had been expected, and the association had received additional income from the commercial broadcasts of the Twilight Concerts. The budget, around $600,000, was nearly balanced—a $15,000 projected deficit owed mostly to losses incurred by the Pops concerts.

Szell was reengaged with a three-year contract at the same salary. He could afford to wait for a raise; his salary had already reached a respectable level, and he earned recording royalties as well as extra income from guest appearances. Szell and the board added an escape clause to the contract. It would permit both parties their release "if, in the case of the Association, it was faced with immoderate salary or working-condition demands [by the musicians], and if, in the case of the Conductor, it were proposed to reduce the size or the standards of the orchestra."[63]

At the end of the season, the trustees held a reception for the Szells in the board room. Sidlo presented the conductor with an attaché case, "as a symbol of the Trustees' appreciation of four years of distinguished service." Szell told Sidlo his goal of making the orchestra "second to none" was "nearly at that point now, and would definitely be there before the expiration of his new contract."[64]

The Szells spent most of May in New York, then flew to England, where Szell conducted at the Hastings Festival. Later he conducted a concert in Zurich and, at the end of the summer, one with the Bournemouth Symphony Orchestra. He had previously expressed a desire to be bothered with as little Cleveland Orchestra business as possible while on vacation, but matters large and small were the subject of a lively exchange of letters that summer. The business of recording remained unsettled. The coming season's programs and brochure had to be proofread before going to press. Schnabel's schedule and repertoire on the November Cleveland tour needed finalizing. A keyboard glockenspiel—a set of bells played by a keyboard mechanism instead of mallets—was the elusive object of this season's instrument acquisition. Vosburgh and Szell kept tabs on each other's weight and Szell encouraged Vosburgh about keeping to his diet. Szell advised Vosburgh to again use T. Roland Berner as a go-between for the orchestra in its recording plans.

In late June, in Switzerland, Szell and Schnabel agreed they would play Beethoven's Third and Fifth concertos on tour and at two special concerts in Severance Hall immediately afterward. While Schnabel believed that playing concertos by the same composer on two successive nights in the same venue was not a good idea, and had suggested the "Emperor" and the Mozart G Major, he nevertheless pointed out this was more demanding than just repeating one concerto, and asked for an increase in fee. As Szell thought that was reasonable, he asked Vosburgh to sweeten the fee with an additional $250, as "it would be nice for the old man."[65] This Vosburgh did.

After two weeks of golf in Crans, the Szells moved to the Suvretta House in St. Moritz. In mid-August they made their way back to England, returning the "speedy English Jaguar sedan" they had borrowed from relatives.[66] Although Szell had already made reservations at the Wade Park Manor for the beginning of the season, specifying a suite with "a long ante-room" and "a full-size icebox," similar to the one in which they had stayed two years before, he asked Vosburgh to ensure the reservation was still in order, as "it will be safer to check again!" The next day, he began work on recording the Tchaikovsky concerto with Clifford Curzon, "just to get my conducting arms into condition for the season!" he wrote to Vosburgh.[67]

The 1950–51 season began on a solemn note; Adella Prentiss Hughes had died in August at the age of eighty, and Szell added the little Mozart gem, the *Masonic Funeral Music*, K. 477, as a tribute to her. Szell spoke to the audience of Mrs. Hughes, "to whom every Cleveland music lover owes a debt of gratitude," and asked for a minute of silence instead of applause.[68] She had been Szell's nemesis, but came to appreciate him; the circle closed.

Alfredo Casella's *Paganiniana* received its first Cleveland performance.[69] Local music critics recognized that the Cleveland Orchestra had now attained the level of virtuoso orchestra. Szell had clearly designed the initial program of the 1950–51 season, which included Brahms's *Variations on a Theme by Haydn*, to show off the orchestra as a whole and its solo players individually. The conductor may have allowed the virtuosity of the orchestra to run away with the music, suggested by Loesser: "Some day before I die I should like to hear variations 2, 5 and 8 [of the Brahms] done at a speed not so breathlessly brilliant as to obscure practically all of their structural finesses."[70]

New members of the orchestra included four strings and four principal winds. On the deep end were Chester Roberts, tuba, and bass clarinetist Alfred Zetzer, a Clevelander. Ross Taylor, from the New York Philharmonic, replaced Frank Brouk as first horn. Both Roberts and Zetzer would have long tenures. Taylor stayed a respectable six seasons. Oboist Marc Lifschey was the object of Szell's first raid on the National Symphony. Lifschey had studied with the legendary Marcel Tabuteau at the Curtis Institute of Music, played in the NBC Symphony under Toscanini, and been first oboist of the National Symphony. Lifschey was a feisty and difficult artist, and his constant struggle to improve what was already exquisite challenged the entire orchestra. Except for one year with the Metropolitan Opera Orchestra, he remained principal oboist in Cleveland until his dramatic departure in 1965.

Earlier, Szell secured the return of Maurice Sharp, principal flutist, who had a brilliant, clear tone and incisive musicianship, coupled with a quiet, mature personality. The lower end of the woodwinds was strongly led by first bassoonist George Goslee. Sharp and Goslee together framed the woodwinds' leadership. Between them existed a gap that Szell would need more time to fill: just the right first clarinetist, and his ideal principal French horn.

A solo player of such distinction and personality as Lifschey would have a strong effect in any orchestra, but in Cleveland, thoroughly trained to listen to itself, the fusion reached extraordinary levels. With players the caliber of Sharp and Goslee, Lifschey was electric, soaring to extraordinary heights and taking the orchestra along with him.

Szell could be hard on his first-chair players, but with Lifschey he used velvet gloves. Colleagues who bore the brunt of Szell's drive for perfection resented the gentle treatment Lifschey received. When Szell's and Lifschey's volatile, love-hate relationship—a mingling of respect and fear—erupted, other members of the orchestra tried to keep a low profile. Szell had met his match, for the oboist was as deadly serious about music and equally self-critical as he. In rehearsal, Lifschey would play the most elegant phrase and then vigorously shake his head in dissatisfaction. Szell, completely taken in, would shout over the orchestra, "Marc, stop shaking your head, that was good!"[71]

The October board meeting included a serious discussion, initiated by Szell, on the need for improving concert attendance. Szell urged that "every effort be made to make the Cleveland public aware of what a priceless possession it has in the Cleveland Orchestra." The minutes recorded: "He was very happy with the orchestra, more so this year than ever before, and that he looked forward to a bright future for it, provided that the necessary funds be forthcoming, and the draft not damaging. He remarked that he was greatly pleased by the division of labor that had been established at the time of his appointment between the conductor and the board, and added that he was available for counsel at any time."[72] The "division of labor" to which Szell referred was that the board raised the funds and Szell, within the budget, had complete artistic autonomy. He could well be "greatly pleased."

Szell fell ill for one subscription pair, which Ringwall took over. It proved no minor ailment—Szell, twenty-one members of the orchestra, and numerous Clevelanders were laid low by a flu epidemic. The season's winter weather was severe, necessitating the rescheduling of three subscription concerts, all made up at the end of the season.

For three years, Szell had been asking the board to support the establishment of the orchestra's own chorus, but the board viewed the expense as prohibitive. He suggested that there were a number of outstandingly beautiful and impressive choral works that ought to be performed, and called attention to Beethoven's Ninth

Symphony, which he had scheduled that season "to see what the response would be."[73] Another year passed, however, before the dream would be realized.

Three of the four vocal soloists for the Ninth, the soprano Frances Yeend, mezzo-soprano Jane Hobson, and tenor David Lloyd, formed a team that came near to monopolizing performances of that work with major orchestras. Together with a variety of bass singers—this time it was Oscar Natzka—they jokingly called themselves the First Beethoven Quartet, after the then well-known First Piano Quartet. It was a triumph for Szell. Elwell wrote, "No more thrilling event has taken place in Severance Hall than the Cleveland Orchestra's performance last night of Beethoven's Ninth Symphony." Loesser called it "a rarely exalting experience," and Bacon reported, "An audience that filled every nook and corner of the hall was thrilled."[74]

Other highlights of the season included Artur Schnabel's final appearances before his retirement; Rudolf Firkusny playing Martinů's Third Piano Concerto, written for him; and sterling performances by Rudolf Serkin, Clifford Curzon, and Jascha Heifetz. One month before his fifteenth birthday the violin phenomenon Michael Rabin made his debut with Vieuxtemps's Fifth Concerto. Szell considered him "one of the most extraordinary talents I have ever come across."[75] William Steinberg and Dimitri Mitropoulos returned as guest conductors, and Erik Tuxen conducted the Cleveland premiere of Nielsen's Symphony no. 5. The amazing Mitropoulos conducted the premiere of Marcel Dick's nearly hour-long twelve-tone symphony from memory.[76]

While Szell was conducting the New York Philharmonic, he met Vosburgh in New York to plan the coming season. "With the world turmoil, television, and the difficulties of raising maintenance fund," Vosburgh wrote to Szell afterward, "it will be necessary for us to arrange the very strongest season possible. Four items are of the utmost importance to accomplish this end: namely, orchestra, soloists, guest conductors and programs." Vosburgh felt confident that they could hold all salaries except those guaranteed by contract to receive raises. The soloist list included Milstein, Morini, Serkin, Casadesus, Leonard Rose, Kirsten Flagstad, and Joseph Fuchs; the orchestra's Gingold, Krachmalnick, and Silberstein; and Cleveland pianist and critic Arthur Loesser.

As for conductors, Vosburgh wrote: "Naturally your presence here as much as possible is our very strongest setup. Furthermore, the shorter the period you are away the better. Six successive weeks is not good business for us. Four and two would be much better. I have had many questions from not only members of the board but from many of our audiences as to why our conductor is away for such an extended period. If we have had these complaints, rest assured that many other members of the board have had similar ones."[77]

The letter made such an impact on Szell that he replied on the morning of a New York Philharmonic matinee: "Your long letter . . . is certainly one of the best letters you have ever written, both as to clarity of thought and as to expression. I was impressed by it and shall do everything I can to follow up its implications."[78] In the future Szell would try to break his six weeks away into two periods of four and two weeks.

In February 1951, Western Reserve University conferred an honorary doctorate on Szell, "for having devoted your great talents of mind and musicianship to a career as a teacher, and symphonic director"; it read, "because your untiring efforts have created a truly great symphony orchestra for Cleveland; because you have brought joy and inspiration to the citizens of our community."[79]

Szell made his public debut as a pianist in Cleveland in the Dvořák Quintet with Gingold, Krachmalnick, Skernick, and Silberstein. The highlight of the season had been Beethoven's Ninth. But the final concert, the make-up for a snow cancellation in November, was a fitting end to a Szell season: the Overture to *The Bartered Bride*, *La Mer* (a repeat from earlier that season), and the "Great" C Major Symphony of Schubert.

At the end of May, the Szells bought the home they would occupy for the rest of their time in Cleveland, a fourteen-room, brick-and-stone, English-style house on Larchmere Boulevard in Shaker Heights. The Szells paid between $36,000 and $42,000 for the four-bedroom, two-bath house with a library and an attached two-car garage.[80] They flew to England at the end of May. Szell could be sure that he had accomplished the most important changes in the orchestra. Now came the continually demanding task of honing and polishing the gem of his creation.

The summer of 1951 was a quiet one for the Szells. In Europe Szell conducted only two performances, with the Concertgebouw at the end of June. In Cleveland the news was good. Not only had the season been a great artistic success, but it ended in the black in spite of an ever-increasing budget. That summer, Columbia Records released Szell's recording with the New York Philharmonic of Smetana's tone poems *From Bohemia's Forests and Meadows* and *The Moldau*. And, after a two-year hiatus, the Cleveland Orchestra signed a two-year contract with Columbia to begin recording, in January 1952, Dvořák's *New World* Symphony, Liszt's Piano Concerto no. 2, and Weber's *Konzertstück*, with Robert Casadesus.

A Young Conductor Plays a Key Role

Szell's befriending and mentoring of a young conductor became a catalyst for his and the orchestra's involvement in three future conducting workshops. In Crans in July, Szell received a letter from Robert Cantrick, thirty-four-year-old band and orchestra conductor at the Carnegie Institute of Technology in Pittsburgh, who conceived the enterprising idea for a one-season residency to observe Szell and the orchestra. For that he obtained the financial resources for the project, and found the courage to ask Szell for his approval.[81] Szell replied promptly: "First, my congratulations to your Ford-Fellowship. As to your suggestion to move to Cleveland for the winter to attend rehearsals, etc., I think this can be done and may be very useful for your further development. I am sure we can work out quite easily a schedule. Please let me know at your leisure what you have decided."[82] Cantrick settled in for a season in 1951–52.

Cantrick made the most of the opportunity, sitting on stage at rehearsals, talking with members of the orchestra, and enjoying free access to Szell. He asked Szell numerous questions, the answers to which he documented in writing, often presenting his notes to Szell for editing. His questions ranged from Szell's thoughts on solfège to questions of bowing in specific passages, to Mozart style in Szell's playing of the A Major Piano Concerto.

Afterward, Cantrick wrote Helen M. Thompson, executive secretary of the American Symphony Orchestra League, of his year with Szell. That inspired her to write Szell of the League's plans for "developing additional study opportunities for community symphony conductors." [83] Szell answered immediately and set up a meeting in New York in December.[84] The three Cleveland workshops were a result of Cantrick's initiative, and Thompson wrote that he "should have a very large star studded with diamonds in [his] symphony orchestra record."[85] Cantrick, who did not conduct the orchestra during his entire residency, did take part in the second of the workshops, in which he had the opportunity to conduct. He found the experience daunting and inspiring. He continued to write during the coming years, and Szell's replies show a respect and fondness for the young conductor.[86]

Stability in Cleveland: Szell's Sixth Season

During the fifties, stability in the orchestra and in Szell's relation to it grew. He signed a series of three-year contracts with minor modifications, maintaining his control of the orchestra's growth. There were only nine personnel changes during the 1951–52 season, just one involving a principal chair: Berl Senofsky was appointed assistant concertmaster, replacing Jacob Krachmalnick, who became concertmaster of the Philadelphia Orchestra.[87]

Krachmalnick had begun as assistant concertmaster in Szell's first season. Szell tolerated Krachmalnick's brashness because he was talented. As a stand partner, he made Gingold uncomfortable. Krachmalnick's aggressive temperament did not make for a good supporting partner. Gingold complained to Szell about him and Szell told Krachmalnick, "You know, Jake, you make Joe nervous." He answered, "I can easily understand that, I play better than he does." Szell replied, "We're not going to discuss that."[88]

Szell supported Krachmalnick's move to Philadelphia and advised him so that he got the best possible contract. He told Krachmalnick to call Philadelphia and say, "Mr. Szell might consider releasing me under suitable circumstances." A scene witnessed by Louis Lane illustrates the good-natured dynamics of the relationship:

> In February of 1952, as the Cleveland Orchestra was getting ready to play its Carnegie Hall concert, I was in the dressing room with the Szells when Jake burst in—his train from Philadelphia had been late, and he wanted to wish Mr. Szell all the best for the concert. Szell said, "Jake, I have the most remarkable piece of news about your new boss." Jake asked, "What's that." Szell continued, "I have just heard secretly, but on the best authority, that your new boss has begun to study the bass clef." Great laughter. Mrs. Szell chimed in, "George, that is very naughty, and is perhaps untrue." More laughter. An usher announced, "Time to go on stage, Mr. Szell." Smashing concert.[89]

Later, when Krachmalnick was eager to leave Philadelphia, Szell happily recommended him for the concertmaster position of the Concertgebouw.[90]

The 1951–52 season saw the debuts of two distinguished guest conductors: Pierre Monteux and Leopold Stokowski. Eleazar de Carvalho returned, as did Vladimir Golschmann, substituting for Charles Munch, who had canceled. The usually fine list of visiting soloists included Erica Morini, Nathan Milstein, Arthur Grumiaux, Leonard Rose, Robert Casadesus, Rudolf Serkin, and the great soprano Kirsten Flagstad. For the first time, Szell programmed himself as soloist in his youthful calling card, Mozart's A Major Piano Concerto, K. 488.

The season opened with the Overture to *Euryanthe* of Weber, the suite from Stravinsky's *Pulcinella*, Respighi's *Fountains of Rome*, and Brahms's Second Symphony. Music played for the first time by the orchestra included Szell's one and only Cleveland *Ein Heldenleben*, his second and final traversal there of Elgar's *Enigma* Variations, the *Comedy Overture on Negro Themes* by Henry F. Gilbert, Robert Kelly's *A Miniature Symphony*, the symphonic poem *Over the Hills and Far Away* by Delius, William Schuman's Symphony no. 3, the Symphony no. 4 of David Diamond, Bruckner's Ninth Symphony, Hindemith's *Concerto for Orchestra*, and Bernard Wagenaar's *Song of Mourning*.[91]

Ein Heldenleben, the major work on the second program, began a series of Strauss's works in commemoration of the composer, who had died in 1949. Included were *Also sprach Zarathustra*, *Till Eulenspiegel*, the Suite from his incidental music to Molière's *Le bourgeois gentilhomme*, the Serenade for Wind Instruments, op. 7, and three of the *Four Last Songs*, with Kirsten Flagstad. Szell programmed *Ein Heldenleben* at Gingold's request and the concertmaster played the solo role of Mrs. Strauss superbly. But when Szell came off stage at the end, he said, "Never again," and kept his promise.[92]

In the third program, Szell played and conducted the Mozart piano concerto. First oboist Marc Lifschey was featured in Howard Hanson's *Pastorale*, which Hanson conducted. In addition to his role as guest composer/conductor, Hanson, as a representative of the National Music Council, presented Szell with a citation for distinguished service to American Music in 1949–50.[93] This was the same Hanson who, four years earlier, had asserted that Szell neglected contemporary repertoire. The honorees were not typical. According to a National Music Council report entitled "The Decline in Performances of American Orchestral Works," less American music was played by major American orchestras in 1950–51 than in any season since 1941–42. Szell performed more than his share, as the award testified.

Szell wrote Zirato: "Last Thursday's concert was something of a special occasion and instead of making you read a tedious report of mine I am enclosing press notices from which you will see what might interest you." Szell always kept his eye on the box office, adding, "The second concert of the pair has taken place. Door sales for the pair $2195.—/ all we can sell, incl. standing room." Zirato wrote back, "I am delighted at the single sale in Cleveland. More power to you." He picked up on the Mozart concerto and made a bid for a similar appearance with the Philharmonic as a replacement for Artur Schnabel, who died in August. Szell answered: "Regarding the replacement for Schnabel, please let us discuss this when we meet in December. I am not reluctant any more as a matter of principle to play a concerto and conduct at the same time, but I can do it only at a certain time of the year as long as my arms have not become too heavy from too much conducting."[94] Zirato was not able to get Szell to play and conduct that season, but did not let the matter rest, and Szell kept open the possibility.

The fifth program received warm reviews. Elwell raised his appreciation of Bartók's *Divertimento*, repeated from the previous season. "Szell has as fine a command of this score as one could ever wish to hear," he wrote. "It receives from him the same kind of emotional and intellectual penetration that he gives to the classics."[95] Szell might have repeated the Bartók in two successive seasons because he had committed to do it with the New York Philharmonic in December. It was its first time for the Philharmonic and a last time for Szell.

Szell wrote to Zirato about upcoming Philharmonic programs and soloists, and closed: "I think I mentioned already that I am leaving tomorrow for a rather extended tour and I assume our office has sent you our itinerary, just in case you want to reach me."[96] "Rather extended" was highly understated. In those days, the orchestra endured a schedule that did not give them another free day until they had played one rehearsal, sixteen full concerts, and four one-hour children's concerts, in fifteen days of travel. They toured cities in Michigan, Ohio, West Virginia, Kentucky, Iowa, Illinois, and Wisconsin, concluding in Toledo with a children's concert at 3:00 and an evening concert at 8:30. The orchestra arrived in Cleveland at 1:15A.M. on Tuesday, and rehearsed from 1:00P.M. to 4:00P.M. that same day. With two rehearsals on Wednesday and the dress rehearsal and subscription concert on Thursday, Friday would be their first day off since the Friday three weeks earlier.

While the orchestra was making a name for itself and attempting to balance the budget, this strenuous schedule was seen as necessary. In years to come, the reduction of orchestral services and restrictions on the number of concerts when touring—gradually won by union contract, coupled with Szell's wish to make touring less strenuous for himself and his orchestra—made that kind of madness a thing of the past.

A New York Philharmonic Milestone

Zirato wrote Szell on tour that the first concert of his second week—Thursday December 13, 1951—would mark the Philharmonic's 5000th concert, calling for a special program. A ceremony would involve the mayor and orchestra officials, and "The Star-Spangled Banner" would begin the concert. The Philharmonic had invited President Harry S. Truman and, to ensure his acceptance, asked his daughter, Margaret, to sing the national anthem.

For the occasion, Zirato suggested to Szell that he include a long-forgotten work from the Philharmonic's first concert, December 7, 1842: an overture by Johann Wenzel Kalliwoda. Kalliwoda (1801–66) was a Bohemian composer of some distinction in his time, however long past. Szell wrote that he would be "happy to co-operate in 'dramatizing' [as Zirato had put it] the 5000th Concert of the Philharmonic," but cautioned, "The Kalliwoda Overture as such, the putrid piece of an utterly imitative, 5th-rate composer, is only ridiculous today. But there is *one* excuse to include it and give the public at the same time something to think (and chuckle) about: if one puts it in antithesis to the Bartók Divertimento, discreetly indicating what 'New Music' was at the Philharmonic's first concert and what it is today."

Zirato replied: "Thank you . . . for the brilliant answer to my letter. We certainly had a very good time reading it and your remarks on the music of Kalliwoda amused us tremendously. I am always pleased by your tremendous sense of humor." Zirato added that the orchestra only would play "The Star-Spangled Banner" "because Miss Truman is not available and we don't think there is any sense in inviting anybody else."[97]

Szell's month with the Philharmonic began on December 6, 1951. The soloist, Brazilian pianist Guiomar Novaës, made a fine success with the Philharmonic and with Szell. She asked that if she were to be reinvited that it be with Szell. Szell on his part readily agreed, and engaged her for Cleveland as well.

Szell recorded a promotional LP with the New York Philharmonic, whose sale would benefit the orchestra's pension fund. While Szell was in New York, Leopold Stokowski sent him an enthusiastic telegram after his guest appearance in Cleveland: "YOUR ORCHESTRA IS SUPERB. MY FIRST REHEARSAL WAS A JOY. YOU HAVE CREATED A TRULY MARVELOUS INSTRUMENT. SINCERE CONGRATULATIONS ON YOUR GREAT ACHIEVEMENT."[98]

Szell's Shuttle Diplomacy

Szell returned to Cleveland after four weeks with the Philharmonic. After one week of concerts, Szell again traveled to New York to conduct the Philharmonic's pension fund concert. This gave rise to rumors. A small newspaper article told of his "triumphant month" in New York, of the 5000th Philharmonic concert, of recording with the Philharmonic and former Clevelander Leonard Rose, and of his flying back for the pension fund concert. "Regarding rumors about his leaving Cleveland to direct the New Yorkers, Szell emphatically said, 'I have no intention of leaving Cleveland.' Stories about Szell's taking New York have been so strong that Zirato met with the Philharmonic musicians and said there will be no change in the orchestra's leadership next season."[99]

Szell seemed such a tower of strength that Cleveland Orchestra members interviewed years later would swear that he never missed a rehearsal, much less a concert. That winter he succumbed for a time to the flu. This did not disrupt the Cleveland Orchestra as much as it did the New York Philharmonic. Szell's illness forced him to cancel the first of his two remaining guest weeks. This was no ordinary program—it would have closed with a concert version of the final scene from *Salome*, but was postponed until the next season. In Szell's absence, Dimitri Mitropoulos conducted, and Szell recovered in time to lead the following week.

Back in Cleveland in mid-March, Szell led a concert with Kirsten Flagstad as soloist, one of the great events of the season. It was a reunion after seventeen years, when he was in Prague and prepared her, intensely and sometimes harshly, for her triumphant Metropolitan Opera debut.[100] Now, in 1952, she sang Wagner—the "Liebestod" from *Tristan und Isolde* and the "Immolation Scene" from *Götterdämmerung*—and three of Strauss's "Four Last Songs." The songs, a first performance in Cleveland, were preceded by two other Strauss works, part of the season's memorial celebration—the Serenade for Winds, op. 7, and the Orchestral Suite from *Der Bürger als Edelmann* (*Le bourgeois gentilhomme*). The packed house gave Szell and Flagstad "the greatest ovation of the season. . . . An overflow audience . . . accorded the great Norwegian soprano one of the warmest receptions ever given at a symphony concert." Rumors of a political protest when she came on stage—her husband had been suspected of being a Quisling (Norwegian collaborator with the Nazis)—did not materialize. There were a few "subdued boos" on entrance, but "she was given a two-minute ovation before she had sung a note."

Flagstad's voice had extraordinary beauty, combined with equally extraordinary power. Loesser characterized it "the mightiest, truest, most vibrant female voice of our time." She could soar effortlessly over the orchestra without sacrificing quality of sound. In Wagner and Strauss, Szell was an ideal collaborator. He was a thoughtful accompanist, aware of a voice's strengths and weaknesses, although one reviewer felt that either he or she may have miscalculated a few low-lying passages in the Strauss. The fact was that she did not yet have the Strauss in her voice. The contrast with the Wagner was striking—the orchestra "retreated to somewhere in Lake Erie" (four miles north of Severance Hall), was Lane's impression. Elwell admired Szell, the old opera hand, who "was at one with the singer in promoting the full impact of the exalted mood, the rich pallet of orchestral color which surrounds and warms the voice."[101]

Six more subscription concerts, ending with Beethoven's Ninth, brought the season to a close. The week before, the Met came to town on its annual tour. Szell attended *Salome*, conducted by Fritz Reiner. He timed the segment of the final scene of the opera that he would conduct with the New York Philharmonic the following season. "It took exactly 40 minutes," he informed the Philharmonic, "I dare say I might be a little faster than Mr. Reiner, so there is not the slightest danger of exceeding this time."[102]

This season's Beethoven Ninth saw the return of three of the previous year's four soloists—Frances Yeend, Jane Hobson, and David Lloyd, with Hans Hotter replacing Oscar Natzka, who had died. An artist of international stature, Hotter had sung with Szell in Prague in the thirties. The Beethoven worked its perennial magic: "There was a glory at Severance Hall last night," Loesser wrote, "We remember the extraordinary exaltation that this work aroused a year ago and it would seem difficult to imagine that such an exceptional state of feeling could be resurrected so soon. Yet, we can say that in some ways last night's performance was superior to the previous one." The opening work, Beethoven's First Symphony, was no throwaway, curtain-raiser: "It, too, was superlatively played, as it only can be by a group of first-rate artists working together under a conductor of surpassing knowledge, skill and authority."[103] With a sold-out extra performance on Sunday, April 27, the thirty-fourth season (1951–52) ended.

Boding still better for the future was the union contract's peaceful settlement for the coming two years. The season remained at thirty weeks but the pay scale went from $98 a week to $108 in the first year, with an additional two-dollar increase in the second.

Lane Steps Up as Ringwall Steps Down; The Parental Szell

In a major change for the orchestra, the twenty-eight-year-old Louis Lane replaced Rudolf Ringwall as head of the Summer Pops. Besides being the Cleveland Orchestra pianist, Lane conducted the Canton Symphony. He received the title "resident conductor" of the Pops. Lane would conduct three programs. The rest were led by five guest conductors: Robert Zeller, Howard Barlow, Franz Allers, Alexander Smallens, and Lorin Maazel. Maazel had conducted the Pops ten years earlier as a thirteen-year-old child prodigy. Twenty years later, he would become Szell's successor.

Saturday, June 7, 1952, Szell's fifty-fifth birthday, did not find him in Europe, as usual. He took in his young protégé's debut as head of the Pops that night, and two days later received an honorary doctorate from Oberlin College, at the commencement ceremony in which his stepson, John Teltsch, received his bachelor of arts degree.[104] Szell had established a strong parental relationship with his stepson. Relations between John and his mother had been difficult since their reunion in America. The hurt of abandonment at a young age had left scars that would take until Helene Szell's last years to heal. Sensing that, Szell willingly and effectively took on the important role of surrogate father. While John attended high school at Riverdale Country Day School in the Bronx and the Szells were living in Manhattan, Helene complained that John's musical education was being neglected and insisted that Szell teach him piano. As John recalled:

> There was a piano in the living room and George and I would sit at the piano. I'm sure at a scheduled time every day. I think about the third time, the keyboard cover came down on my hand. He and I had a very short chat that I remember in this fashion: He said, "John, you don't want to learn to read notes, you don't want to learn to play the piano, and I don't want to teach you. So our job is to convince your mother that it's two against one, and we're not going to do it." The upshot was, after I stopped crying, I thought it was a wonderful idea. We shook hands on it, and we never spoke of it again. Every once in a while Mother would say, "Well?" We'd say, "Yes, everything's fine."

With all that John had been through—his mother leaving the family, hiding in Nazi-occupied France during the war, and the loss of his father and brother—he was rambunctious and difficult. John spent his last high school summer (1947) on a ranch in Elgin, Arizona. Although he began as a paying guest, he worked as a regular ranch hand and received the standard wages, a dollar a day. He loved it so much that he wanted to stay there. Szell handled the situation masterfully.

"George called me on a Sunday noon," John wrote, " . . . he spoke of senior year at Riverdale, the prep school I had attended in NY; how important education was." Szell asked John to come back to New York "to discuss the problem." Szell promised John a return ticket if, after their meeting, he wanted to go back. John replied, "if we met, I'd never go back," to which Szell answered, "That's a risk you'll have to take, John, but as a favor to me I ask you to return to NY and meet with me." "I finished Riverdale," John wrote, "and went on to a different life." If Szell had not intervened, John might not have finished high school nor graduated from Oberlin in 1952. The phrase "That was George at his best" comes up often in John's reminiscences.[105]

A Not-So-Quiet Summer

In July 1952, after an absence of five years, Szell made his sixth and final appearance at the Chicago Symphony's Ravinia Festival, conducting four concerts with soloists Rudolf Firkusny, Erica Morini, Leonard Rose, and Eugene Istomin. After Ravinia, the Szells left for a quiet vacation in Europe. Helene stayed with her sister in England, while George went to Crans for golf and rest.

His letters from there show the deep affection he felt for her and that he missed her physically: "Otherwise nothing new—except I miss you and love you very much," and, "Hab schon sehnsucht nach Dir! [I already long for you!]. Prepare to meet me in Zurich August 4th and order plane ticket now." The letters are full of gossip and humor and often repeat the nicknames they had for each other, "Muggi" (she) and "Pussi" or "Teddy Bear" (he). He loved it there, as evidently she did not: "It is as gorgeous here as ever and nobody can understand why you don't like the place."

Szell paid careful attention to his weight and diet: "You will be pleased to hear that this morning I weighed only 170 lbs," he wrote Helene. "This is 4 lbs. less than last weight in Cleveland and only 2½ over my lowest weight ever (which really is too little). For lunch today there was a Raclette party in the garden—very nice!" He admonished her, "Be sure to arrive in Zurich on August 4th! I shall arrive there on the 3rd." He enjoyed fussing with the car: "On the 4th I want the car looked over before going to Austria. Although she goes pretty well I feel that the carburetor should be adjusted, etc. for best performance especially in the Austrian mountains. On the way here I had very little mountain driving so I could not test her really. On the 5th we would leave for St. Moritz."

He retained some old-fashioned, central European attitudes: "At bridge I met some very nice people, among others a family from Brussels. Father, mother, and son of 15, so charming that one can lose all prejudice agin them Belgians. Then there is a Mr. Rizzo at Bridge, the Eyetalian Ambassador to Bonn, a rather quiet fellow. And some more quite nice Belgians and Eyetalians."[106]

Later in July, Szell and Zirato worked on repertoire changes for the coming Philharmonic season. He relinquished the Mozart Fortieth to Bruno Walter, but not without a quid pro quo: "Your letter of July 17th has not upset me greatly; if Bruno Walter needs the Mozart G minor for recording, va bene, and I shall substitute the 'Jupiter' for it.—But please don't tell me now that this is already pre-empted by somebody else; in this case this somebody else has to be as reasonable as I am and to make the change; capito?" Zirato understood and confirmed that the "Jupiter" was free for Szell.[107]

As planned, Helene joined Szell in Zurich. In Salzburg on the fourteenth, they heard the posthumous premiere of Strauss's opera *Die Liebe der Danae*.[108] Furtwängler had cancelled all his summer concerts. Szell was asked to conduct one of his concerts at the Lucerne Festival, but he refused, saying, "it would have torn apart completely my summer schedule." Later, Szell received a telephone call from the head of the Salzburg Festival, who had spotted him at the Strauss opera and who then drove to see him. "Before I could even ask him to share our lunch," Szell continued, "he almost went down on his knees asking me to help him out and conduct the final concert of the Vienna Philharmonic on Aug. 31, which was another of Furtwängler's commitments." Szell accepted with the understanding that, as he had not been expecting to conduct in Europe, he did not have his tails with him, only a white dinner jacket. That was acceptable under the circumstances, and so Szell set a Salzburg precedent for dress in the concert.[109] Szell left Salzburg the next day, drove back to Paris, spent a few days in England with his in-laws, returned to New York in the middle of September, and went on to Cleveland shortly after.

A Celebratory Season

Rehearsals for the 1952–53 season, Szell's seventh and the orchestra's thirty-fifth, began on October 6. The season was gala, in keeping with its significant number; the music of Brahms and Stravinsky was featured and the roster of soloists and guest conductors was stellar. Stokowski returned for two weeks and Igor Stravinsky and William Steinberg each had a week. Szell conducted Brahms's First and Third Symphonies and the *Variations on a Theme by Haydn*. Serkin and Rubinstein soloed in the Piano Concertos, Menuhin in the Violin Concerto, and the orchestra's Gingold and Silberstein in the Double Concerto. Szell conducted and played in a Mozart piano concerto and Heifetz appeared in a special nonsubscription concert.

Elmore Bacon interviewed Szell at Severance Hall before rehearsals began. The journalist loved the human touches. Szell sported a beret but asked the photographer, "Just please don't snap me wearing this beret. You know Mrs. Szell completely detests this headwear." Szell said:

> They are knee deep in music festivals in Europe, and while I found satisfaction in directing the Vienna Philharmonic at the Salzburg festival, I found it in many ways not up to the standard set by our own musicians in Cleveland.
>
> The orchestra there serves several purposes—opera, theater and symphony entertainment. It is sloppy in some respects with a warmth of tone most engaging, but lacking in brilliance.
>
> The Philharmonic is so large that we get one set of musicians in some of the sections one night and a different set the next. Musicians are under civil service. Unless they steal or murder they can't be fired.
>
> We had good food and plenty of it all over Europe. In Milan the rebuilding of war-damaged sections is fairly miraculous.[110]

Szell played Mozart's Piano Concerto in B-flat, K. 595, and had been considering repeating it with the New York Philharmonic, but decided he could not. He felt he owed it to Zirato to explain his reasons, which were more than just "having a heavy arm":

> I felt that I have to tell you that I shall not be able to play and conduct the Mozart Concerto during these weeks in New York, although I had hinted that I might do it. It is with great regret that I say this, but I have just done it here and while it came off perfectly beautifully in every respect and was a huge success, I felt that it was a very great strain on me and also that the splendid outcome was very much the result of long and leisurely rehearsing with the orchestra. We actually rehearsed it six times over a period of two or three weeks, until every player was as secure and as free and played with as much initiative yet regard to the others as a member of a first-rate string quartet would do. You know yourself that the time and the working schedule of the Philharmonic does not permit this type of preparation, at least not if the guest conductor is there only for two weeks, so to my great regret we shall have to abandon this idea and hope for a better opportunity in the future.[111]

After playing two concertos in Cleveland, Szell played one on only two other occasions: K. 488 in all-Mozart programs with the Tonhalle Orchestra of Zurich in January 1955, and with the Vienna Philharmonic in Salzburg in August 1956.

On Thursday, November 27, Szell used the dress rehearsal for the sixth concert efficiently as a prerecording test as well as run-through of the program. The stage was set and microphones arranged as they would be for the recordings to be made on Friday and Sunday.[112] The orchestra was moved forward onto the stage extension and the risers were removed, as were all sound-absorbing drapes, and all doors of the hall stood wide open (of questionable acoustical value).

Szell next spent two weeks with the New York Philharmonic. His soloists included Firkusny, Novaës, Morini, and, in the final portion of *Salome*—postponed from last season because of Szell's illness—Astrid Varnay, Blanche Thebom, and Set Svanholm. Szell began at the "Dance of the Seven Veils," and went to the end of the opera.

Back in Cleveland, Szell made a bow to Christmas with the "Shepherds' Music" (Sinfonia) from Bach's *Christmas Oratorio*, followed by Hindemith's *Symphonic Metamorphosis*, the Chopin Piano Concerto no. 2 with Novaës, and the *Pastoral*. Szell was not averse to programming the same work with two different orchestras only two weeks apart. The challenge of the great works of the repertoire provided him endless fascination, and he would have been intrigued by the differences in the orchestras.

In the New Year Szell signed a three-year contract for the seasons 1953–54, 1954–55, and 1955–56. It was his fourth contract. "The trustees fully expected that

Mr. Szell would make the Cleveland Orchestra the peer of the greatest orchestras in the world," Sidlo said, "but we never anticipated it would be done so quickly."[113] This further dispelled rumors that Szell would take over the New York Philharmonic or the Metropolitan Opera. The Philharmonic rumor originated not only because of Szell's annual lengthy guesting but also by his substituting for Mitropoulos when he was ill. The Metropolitan rumor started with the announcement of Szell's return in December and January for *Tannhäuser*.

The *New York Times* and *Time* magazine reported on Szell's contract:

> During his annual mid-season vacations from the Cleveland Orchestra, Conductor George Szell (pronounced sell) can be seen on some of the U.S.'s most famed podiums; the New York Philharmonic, the Chicago Symphony, the Philadelphia Orchestra, and starting next season, the Metropolitan Opera. To judge by the enthusiasm of critics and audiences, he could probably land himself an even more impressive berth than the one he has. But the story of Szell and Cleveland is the story of a happy musical partnership. . . .
>
> "We aim," says Szell, "at combining the virtuosity and polish and opulence that are characteristic of top-ranking American orchestras with the expressive abandon of typically European orchestras in their best days [a typically Szellian qualifier]." And he adds: "If you give me a week, I might think of a gripe."[114]

Szell was in New York beginning two weeks with the Philharmonic, including a pension fund benefit marking the silver anniversary of Vladimir Horowitz's debut. Szell had performed with Horowitz in St. Louis in 1930 and in Detroit in 1941, but not since. To commemorate the occasion, Horowitz played Tchaikovsky's First Concerto, as he had in his Philharmonic debut. With an eye to maximum popular appeal, Szell made it an all-Tchaikovsky program, devoting the first half of the concert to the Symphony no. 4. From the beginning of the concerto's last movement, Horowitz set a breathtaking pace that only became more exciting as the movement progressed. Szell and the orchestra stayed with him and the piece ended in a flourish that provoked tumultuous applause.

Szell's next-to-last Philharmonic program included Berlioz, Haydn, Strauss, and Brahms. According to Olin Downes, "Mr. Szell achieved the last detail of masterly exposition. Nothing that he did was less than the offering of a first-class musician, projecting music in which he utterly believed." He had some reservations, however: "Was it the atmosphere of a rainy evening, was it one individual's mood that made the performance of the symphony, authoritative and finished as it was, on the heavy-footed side, and the reading of the Strauss one of microscopic clarity and understanding, yet didactic?"[115]

Clifford Curzon was one among the small number of soloists with whom Szell frequently performed, appearing in ten of Szell's twenty-four Cleveland seasons.

Their collaborations were not without friction. Both men were sensitive artists with strong egos. The British pianist Gerald Moore wrote of a rehearsal, possibly in 1954, for Falla's *Nights in the Gardens of Spain* and the Mozart C Minor Concerto:

> After the Spanish piece, Curzon felt quite happy but suggested the whole performance would be improved if they adopted a slightly faster movement throughout when they played it in the evening. So far apparently so good. The theme with variations movement in the Mozart led to ructions. After the orchestra announces the theme, the piano's first variation is in urgent quavers to a sustained string accompaniment. When Clifford had finished it, Szell turned to him "You take a quicker tempo than I took with the theme." The pianist agreed but suggested that was of no significance since not all the variations need be identical in pace. "Are you giving me a lesson?" repeated Szell. "Get another pianist" said Curzon rising to his feet and throwing the score at the conductor. (It did not reach him but was traveling well on the way towards Szell.) Curzon walked off to the artists' room, followed by the conductor who was roaring with rage at every step. The racket continued (the orchestra could hear the [fortississimo] passages and were glad to be out of it) but Curzon, who had been just as angry as his friend, kept silent until the other paused for breath; he then said very quietly "I refuse to talk to you until you cease shouting, until we can speak to one another like civilised human beings." There was a long silence. Szell looked long at his companion, then came a transformation. He then said "Will you make me a promise?" "I cannot make a promise without knowing the conditions."
>
> "Will you do me a favour?"
>
> "You know I will if I possibly can."
>
> "Please say nothing to Helena about this."[116]

They went back to finish the rehearsal. In August 1953 the Szells were guests of the Curzons at their summer home in Austria. That these two high-strung artists were close personal friends did not prevent flare-ups within the intense situation of rehearsal, which they took equally seriously.

In 1953, after Curzon and Szell performed together with the New York Philharmonic, they found themselves again in Carnegie Hall with the Cleveland Orchestra in Beethoven's Fifth Piano Concerto.[117] Downes wrote of the "noble breadth and virility of his reading. . . . And in Mr. Szell, Mr. Curzon had a wonderful collaborator." The Schubert C Major Symphony "had everything in point of justness of tempo and style of phrase that the music asks. . . . The logic and proportion of the interpretation were everywhere evident. But a dryness of color, for which the orchestra itself could not be blamed, obtained through most of the performance, and the exactness of the reading weighed down in some degree the lyrical flight of the music and too often deprived the instrumentation of its native shimmer and glow of tone."

Tone for its own sake was not a high Szell priority—the orchestra produced a powerful sound in Severance Hall and had immediate presence but, with an audience, it was a trifle dry. Touring in other halls, the orchestra preserved all its notable qualities—elegance of phrasing, near perfection in balances and ensemble—but the acoustical qualities of the various halls influenced the sound. The orchestra always sounded richer in sonority when it played in Carnegie Hall, Symphony Hall in Boston, or in the 1870 gem of a hall in the Troy (New York) Savings Bank. Downes particularly mentioned the orchestra's sound: "The string tone is now rich and full and sensuous. The individual excellence of first-desk wind players is companioned by the admirable balances of the choirs and the fusion of the ensemble tone." He was not sure what to credit this to: "Mr. Szell groups his instruments in a way that is unusual and that seems conducive to the sonorous effect—all the violins on the left, the lower strings on the right of the conductor, and the brass toward the back center. How much this grouping of instruments and how much the improvement of the orchestra's virtuosity and tonal excellence were responsible for the sound of last night's performance need not be determined here; but there was the fact of an orchestra, which now ranks high among the half-dozen leading symphonic bodies of the nation; an orchestra, furthermore, which Mr. Szell has under the most exact discipline and control."[118] What seemed unusual to Downes then, placing all the violins together on the conductor's left, has become the norm for orchestras since the second half of the twentieth century.[119]

Jay S. Harrison had much good to say about Szell's control of the orchestra, but regretted that "Mr. Szell himself did not appear to be in top form. In the Schubert, actually there was only one thing wrong. It rarely sang. And what does this imply? Simply that it was not really Schubert. . . . Szell is a scrupulous musician and a man of high conscience," Harrison noted, "he is diligent, devoted, crafty and wise," but "he is also a bit cold."[120] Fueled by Szell's hard driving, that image stuck for a long time.

In March 1953 Szell made his debut with the San Francisco Symphony, then between conductors, leading his arrangement of Smetana's *From My Life* and the Schubert C Major Symphony.[121] In contrast to New York, the Schubert made a stunning impression in San Francisco. Alfred Frankenstein, in the *San Francisco Chronicle*, saw the man and his musical approach as one, but more positively:

> George Szell is a tall, broad-shouldered man who looks like a well-tailored giant when he steps on the podium to conduct a symphony orchestra. That is indicative of his style. It is big, broadly conceived, full-bodied and three dimensional in sonority. . . .
>
> Schubert's last symphony is not called "the great" without reason, but it demands a conductor of genuine stature to cope with its extraordinary length, the tricky, delicately poised contrasts of pace without which it is ruined, and its frequently

> treacherous balance of instrumental forces. Mr. Szell's interpretation was not only vivid, rich and vital in rhythm, but also possessed a creative quality which is not too easy to define. Often one grows a little tired of interpreters, their airs and vanities, and then a man like Szell comes along and reassures us that the performance of music is a major art after all.[122]

Szell returned to Cleveland to close the 1952–53 season. Its finale was the Verdi Requiem, with the newly formed orchestra chorus.[123] Soloists were Herva Nelli, Nell Rankin, Jan Peerce, and Nicola Moscona. The performance was "a high point in the history of the Cleveland Orchestra," wrote Elwell. "The 320 performers on stage made an impressive sound and received at the end 'a tumult of applause.'"[124] It represented a remarkable triumph for the spirit of the players and Szell's leadership in that the music did not suffer in any apparent way by the fact that, the night before the first of the three Verdi performances, the orchestra rehearsed at the baseball stadium, playing a test in the setup it would use for the Pops. The thirty-fifth season concluded.

The orchestra was assured of Szell's musical leadership for the next three years. It now faced a change in leadership of the board of trustees. Thomas Sidlo stepped down after fourteen years as president. The board created a new title for him: honorary president. The move was expected; Sidlo was reelected in 1952 with the understanding that it would be his final year. At the meeting on June 24, 1953, the board elected Sidlo's successor; as expected, it named Percy W. Brown. This constituted the first major change of officers since 1939.

Brown was a natural successor. He had been a trustee of the Musical Arts Association since 1934 and vice president under Sidlo. He was a successful businessman—a resident partner of the investment firm of Hornblower & Weeks, Brown had long held high standing as a community leader. He was not a musician but grew up loving music since his boyhood in Boston, where he regularly attended symphony and opera performances. Brown and his wife, Helen, had been close friends of the Szells since the conductor's first guest concerts.

At this time, Szell was with the Zurich Tonhalle Orchestra conducting a concert of the Festival Weeks. Szell felt close to the Zurich musical public and felt at home in that city: it was culturally and economically vital, beautifully set between mountains and lake, and clean and well-ordered in inimitable Swiss fashion. The Szells were beginning to look for a permanent residence in Switzerland, and would eventually choose Zurich.

While in Zurich, Szell visited composer Rolf Liebermann, then head of music at the Swiss Radio. Szell would conduct premieres of two of his operas at the Salzburg Festival: *Penelope* in 1954 and *School for Wives* in 1957. After the concert, Szell retreated to his favorite vacation spot in Crans, driving very slowly in his new automobile for the first 1,500 kilometers (nine hundred–plus miles; autos had a "break-in" period in those days). His route, Basel-Grenoble, was once taken by Napoleon. Szell paused to get a flat tire fixed, then traveled via Marseilles up the Rhone Valley to Aix-en-Provence, Lyon, Bourg, and Lausanne, and made his way to Saint Raphael, where he swam in the ocean.

In Crans, Szell explored alternatives to hotel living with a local real-estate agent. He found the rental situation impossible. Building was not a much more attractive prospect; he found the cost of any well-located piece of land prohibitive, even before the building costs themselves. Szell spoke with his bridge partners and acquaintances at the hotel about houses and wrote Helene about it. He learned that one house on the golf course ("You know, the fine big one at the 3rd hole") had been sold by the owner, a Paris banker, for 400,000 Francs. They let the matter rest for the time.

Szell described his daily regimen: "Have ½ hr. massage every morning at 7, breakfast at 8 then golf. At 12 a lunch of cold meat, salad and fruit in his room. Afternoon rest then scores or letters, later some more golf, another hot bath before dinner. After dinner bridge. No drinks—except citron pressé au vichy and 3/10 [of a liter] red wine with dinner. Have a deep tan and albino hair."[125]

Helene joined Szell in August, when they paid a visit to the Curzon family on Lake Attersee at Litzlberg, Austria. After the visit, Szell sent Curzon a present—a copy of Schubert's four-hand piano music and a large box of Salzburg "Mozart Kugeln," chocolate candies, which the Curzon children demolished. Curzon wrote his thanks: "You can't imagine—but of course you can, or you wouldn't have sent them—how much pleasure it gave me to receive the Schubert 4 hand pieces. But what a pity you weren't attached to them! (on the bass side, where the better musician must always sit!)." Curzon alluded to the Mozart D Minor Piano Concerto, which he and Szell evidently had gone over together: "It was such a help + privilege to go through the Mozart . . . with you," Curzon wrote, "There is no one like you for me, now that Schnabel has gone."[126] The rest of Curzon's letter is filled with the kind of family news one shares with an old friend with whom one is completely comfortable.

After the summer, Szell compared European and American attitudes toward the arts. He put his foot in his mouth in a Cleveland interview, comparing the good manners of the Europeans with the "vulgar" ones of the United States.[127] A reader wrote an irate letter to the editor, objecting to Szell's bad manners in making that remark: "I'm sure that none of us would be so vulgar as to point out to Szell that we support and admire our conductors in this country even though we spell our culture with a small c. But any well-trained, 10-year-old, American child might point out to him that it is rude to sneer at those who have applauded you. We might even call it vulgar."[128]

This rough beginning aside, 1953–54 had all the makings of a banner season for Szell, his eighth in Cleveland. He would conduct the New York Philharmonic for four weeks, and return to the Metropolitan Opera to conduct a new production of *Tannhäuser*. In the middle of the season, Szell would lead a ten-day workshop for conductors sponsored by the American Symphony Orchestra League. Debuts of major artists, soprano Maria Stader and French cellist Paul Tortelier, and a host of works new to Cleveland, by Blacher, Bloch, Hindemith, and Prokofiev, among others, were to be presented.

Meanwhile, new president Percy Brown was lining up his team of board committeemen and generating enthusiasm and optimism with his energy and ideas. "Each member has a specific assignment." Edgar A. Hahn took charge of the summer season; orchestra manager Carl Vosburgh headed it. It had been a separate entity up to that time. Building up the summer season would help attract the best players. "If you want a top-flight musician," Brown said, "you still have to go to New York, and we have to attract them here." He was not satisfied with only two recording sessions a year for the orchestra, which he ranked "with Boston and Philadelphia as best in the land."

The hall received some attention: architect Alexander Robinson III oversaw the installation of a new $7,000 stage sound reflector to improve the acoustics. The new treasurer, Carl N. Osborne, reported an increase in subscription sales, even as some other major orchestras' sales had dropped. Brown felt the pressures. "A $6,000,000 endowment fund, a $3,000,000 hall—worth $5,500,000 now, even with depreciation—and one of the top three symphonies are an awful responsibility."[129] Szell and Brown made a team, with warm personal relations that extended from the concert hall and board room to their homes and the golf links. For the moment, all prospects appeared rosy.

Szell and Gingold played Beethoven's A Major Sonata for four hundred members of the Women's Committee. The orchestra announced nine new players. This was about the average number of changes at that time. Szell hired two new wind players this year: Elden Gatwood, in the sensitive chair of second oboe to the superb but mercurial Lifschey, and the equally superb first clarinetist Robert Marcellus. The key woodwinds were in place and would remain so for the next dozen years.

Szell demonstrated his confidence in the orchestra when he presented a difficult new piece, Boris Blacher's *Variations for Orchestra on a Theme by Paganini*, on the opening concert of the season. Elwell marked that fact and wrote, "There was a stronger feeling of stability in the continuance of a grand tradition at Severance Hall last night than I have ever before sensed at an opening of the Cleveland Orchestra. There seemed to be fewer changes than usual in the personnel of the orchestra, fewer changes in the seating of regular patrons. . . . George Szell now has such a dependable organization that little rehearsing is needed to open the new season at the same artistic level on which he closed last spring."

The Blacher was a first performance in America. Starting with a solo violin (Gingold) playing the famous Twenty-fourth Caprice, the piece ruminates on fragments of the theme. Elwell thought it "imaginative and effective," and it made a hit with the audience. Stravinsky's *Firebird* Suite came after the Blacher and before intermission. The program opened "on a lofty plane," with Beethoven's Overture to *Egmont*, "that impressed by its dignity and assurance," and closed with Brahms's Second, "with that warmth and grandeur which Szell unfailingly feels toward the masters."[130]

Old and new works, and old and new soloists, were presented: the *Eroica*, Tchaikovsky's Fourth, *Daphnis et Chloé* Suite no. 2, Prokofiev's Seventh, the world premiere of Elwell's *The Forever Young*, with Cleveland soprano Marie Semmelink Kraft, and Robert Casadesus playing Franck's *Symphonic Variations* and the Ravel *Concerto for the Left Hand*. The first of fourteen works by American composers that season, the Elwell was composed at Szell's suggestion. Arthur Loesser was moved by his colleague's setting of Pauline Hanson's powerful antiwar poem and called it "the greatest work that Elwell has produced thus far. . . ."[131] The last concert before the tour was all-Wagner—*Siegfried Idyll* and Act I of *Die Walküre*—a first performance by the orchestra—with Astrid Varnay as Sieglinde, Ramón Vinay as Siegmund, and Lubomir Vichegonov as Hunding. This dramatic change from standard concert fare gave the Cleveland audience a taste of the Szell they had not seen for a decade in his Met tour performances. Elwell, temperamentally not disposed toward the composer, amended his assessment: "So compelling was the performance by this orchestra and in these surroundings that it almost necessitates a re-evaluation of Wagner's music, its strength and its weaknesses." It was Szell's "broad experience as an opera conductor" and "his command of the score [that] made this performance one of the most stirring and musically arresting we have heard. He conveyed a sense of depth, nobility and urgency that one seldom enjoys in an opera house."[132] During Thanksgiving week, Guiomar Novaës was soloist in the Schumann piano concerto, and the premiere of Ernest Bloch's *Sinfonia Breve* was flanked by *Eine kleine Nachtmusik* and three pieces from Berlioz's *The Damnation of Faust*.

Szell resided in New York for the next month and a half, an exception to his four-week time away from Cleveland, because of his engagement with the Philharmonic and the Metropolitan Opera. After his first two Philharmonic weeks, its board asked him to increase his annual engagement for the coming season by two weeks. Szell wrote Zirato: "It is always a joy for me to conduct such a wonderful orchestra as yours," but "Unfortunately . . . my commitments with the Cleveland Orchestra . . . and with the Metropolitan Opera compel me to ask you to reduce my tenure with the Philharmonic to only four weeks."[133]

Szell's Cleveland contract gave him six weeks' leave during the season. He had just committed to the Metropolitan Opera for the 1954–55 season for a production of *Salome* and tried to keep the door open with the Philharmonic, even perhaps nudging it a bit wider. Szell suggested a longer guest period in the future and requested more than one season's commitment; along these lines, he was willing to "make some basic changes" in his arrangements with Cleveland. How far the changes might have gone was not to be tested. More serious was his flirting with Chicago from time to time. The Met? That would depend on his relationship with Edward Johnson's replacement as general manager, Rudolf Bing, with whom Szell already had a run-in, in Glyndebourne in 1947.

7

George Szell and Rudolf Bing (1953–54)

In 1948, a year after the Glyndebourne fiasco, Bing sounded Szell out about the possibility of his and the Cleveland Orchestra's participation in the Edinburgh Festival. It did not work out, but no hard feelings arose. So it was not entirely surprising that a few years later, Bing invited Szell to conduct at the Metropolitan Opera, of which Bing had become general manager in 1950.

Szell was not Bing's first choice for the Met, but Bing found himself in a bind. He had tried unsuccessfully to engage other leading conductors for his fourth Met season, 1953–54, including Erich Kleiber, Hans Knappertsbusch, and Guido Cantelli. Wilhelm Furtwängler, though available, was politically unsuitable and therefore ruled out. With the imminent departure of Fritz Reiner to take over the Chicago Symphony in 1953, and with Bing's own contract due to expire, he had to produce positive results. He signed Pierre Monteux for three French operas and George Szell for a new production of *Tannhäuser*. These distinguished additions to the Met roster helped assure Bing's immediate future at the house.[1]

Monteux, at seventy-eight, had retired the previous year from a seventeen-year tenure with the San Francisco Symphony. Max Rudolf, the Met's staff conductor and artistic administrator, brought Monteux to Bing's attention.[2] Although Monteux had extensive opera experience—he had conducted at the Met in 1917–19—Bing initially felt reluctant to consider him. Rudolf also recommended Szell.

Szell would stay in New York for four weeks during his annual Philharmonic guest appearances. The Philharmonic engaged him for twelve performances, from December 3 through January 10. At the Met, he would conduct five performances of a new production of *Tannhäuser* between December 26 and January 17, and one or two additional dates between January 18 and April 17. Szell now commanded the Met's top fee at that time—$1,000 per performance—a considerable improvement over his first Met contract, which paid $400 a week for his first ten weeks.[3] There would be several Met performances on tour, including one in Cleveland in April. Because of a tight schedule, Szell tentatively accepted a tour performance in Boston on the condition he would be "in perfect physical condition and flying weather . . . favorable."[4]

The stage director of the new *Tannhäuser* production was Herbert Graf, who had collaborated with Szell at the Met in the 1940s. In the spring and early fall of 1953, their discussions about set design, casting, and schedules went through Rudolf. Szell expressed various concerns about the production, especially the shape of the set of Act 2, in the Hall of Song. He had reluctantly accepted cast changes during the run of the opera, negotiating replacements with Rudolf.[5]

Graf, believing Szell's criticism of the Act 2 plan was for acoustic reasons, wrote to Rudolf: "The traditional ground plan of this act (Vienna or Bayreuth) is by far less favorable for the vocal sonority than the plan we are proposing. The 'Halle' in those productions was by far deeper. . . . Our present plan is really a very favorable angle . . . and is extremely shallow." On that basis, Graf felt certain that Szell would ultimately "be very happy with the acoustics of this act."

Szell's misgivings, however, were not acoustical: he was concerned that the triangular shape of the stage would give the impression of a "square box which has been cut in half diagonally." At the bottom of the letter, he sketched two plans, labeling them "good" and "not so good"—the "not so good" was the design for the Met with two equal sides, the "good" showed one side longer than the other.[6] Whether Szell's objection was addressed is not known, but the rehearsals went on without outward signs of trouble.

Tannhäuser opened on December 26, 1953, to considerable acclaim. Ramon Vinay in the title role headed the strong cast, with Jerome Hines, Margaret Harshaw, and Astrid Varnay. Virgil Thomson called it "a distinguished piece of work, even brilliant," and credited Szell: "Saturday night's audience held him responsible . . . and gave him a real ovation for his achievement."[7] Two more performances followed on December 29 and January 9, the latter attended by Percy and Helen Brown. In the third performance, a technical breakdown backstage during a scene change delayed the performance. Szell later deplored this lapse, but said nothing at the time.

The day before his fourth *Tannhäuser,* Szell abruptly resigned from the Met, effective after the next day's performance. He wrote to his manager, Bruno Zirato:

> After careful consideration and under the impression of my recent experiences with present conditions at the Metropolitan Opera, I have decided not to accept their invitation to conduct there again during the season 1954–55.
>
> Furthermore, I request you to obtain a release from all performances scheduled for me the remainder of the current season, both in New York and on tour, with

the exception of the performance of *Tannhäuser* tomorrow night, Thursday, January 14, 1954.[8]

The New York newspapers announced Szell's resignation the day of his last *Tannhäuser*. At the beginning of each act that night, the audience gave Szell an "unusually hearty demonstration. There were cries of 'Bravo, Szell,' and 'Don't leave us!'"[9]

There had been no public manifestation of any prior difficulty between Szell and the Met. The press eagerly sought to discover reasons for Szell's action. Tenor Charles Kullman had to substitute in the title role on three hours' notice for the indisposed Vinay, but this likely did not present sufficient cause; a critic observed that Kullman "was remarkably effective as Tannhaeuser," and his "was no three-hour-notice Tannhaeuser; it told of years of study." Another critic ruled out friction between Szell and the orchestra. In the absence of concrete reasons for his precipitous action, other than the "present conditions," Szell was criticized as being too vague. Conjecture turned to his possible unhappiness with Graf's stage direction. Graf countered that the problem was not his staging, but that Szell had been unhappy with the set design; a fact, but not the heart of the matter.[10]

There had been the inevitable irritations and frustrations attendant on opera production, and the set-change breakdown created friction. More to the point: Szell and Bing had been engaged in a power play over artistic control of the casting of *Salome*, which Bing had invited Szell to conduct next season. In light of his troubles with *Tannhäuser*, Szell wanted complete control over artistic matters regarding *Salome* and asked Rudolf to convey this request to Bing through Zirato.[11] Szell evidently had used the threat of leaving the Met on several earlier occasions as leverage to get his way.[12] On January 4, with Rudolf present, Bing told Szell that he would "not grant him the right of final decision" and, furthermore, he wanted Szell to promise that "under no circumstances would he threaten [him] again with a 'walk out.'" But in what Szell might have considered a small victory, Bing agreed to consult with the conductor on all artistic matters, in particular casting. Although Szell's word would "weigh heavily" with him, "all final decisions must rest with Management."[13] In the discussion that followed, the sides reached agreement on casting the roles of Herod and Salome. Later, Szell had second thoughts about it, which Rudolf passed on to Bing, a normal channel of communication considering Rudolf's position as artistic administrator.

Bing knew of Szell's reservations. On Monday, January 11, "a day of heavy snowfall," in the middle of an urgent meeting between Bing, Rudolf, and several others related to "an important Met premiere" of *Boris Godunov*, Szell, "without being announced, stormed in and without taking any notice of the situation began to talk loudly about the *Salome* cast. Bing politely said we were in the midst of a meeting but that he would be glad to discuss the matter the next day, which did not impress George at all. He simply could be an ill-mannered person . . . and on this occasion, behaved abominably."[14] Only with difficulty did Bing persuade Szell to leave. Bing was so bothered that he made up his mind to "withdraw [his] invitation," to Szell for the coming season, and instructed Zirato to inform Szell. "I have to put up with the whims of prima donnas," he told Rudolf. "I need singers, but conductors are not so important."[15]

To set Szell's insensitive intrusion into context, though not to excuse it, since coming to New York in December, he had, for some weeks, operated in the midst of intense activity between the Met and the New York Philharmonic. Between December 3 and 17, 1953, he led the Philharmonic for two weeks with two different soloists and concertos each week, plus rehearsals. Met rehearsals began during this period, and *Tannhäuser* opened on Saturday, December 26. Its second performance on Tuesday, December 29, came as he began rehearsals for additional Philharmonic concerts on December 31 and January 1 and 3: an all-Wagner first half and Brahms's First Piano Concerto, with Leon Fleisher, after intermission. Szell recorded the Wagner pieces on the fourth, followed by the Philharmonic on the seventh, eighth, and tenth (all-Beethoven: *Egmont* Overture, the Violin Concerto with Isaac Stern, and the Fifth Symphony). Shoehorned in on the ninth was his third *Tannhäuser*.

Reviews of Szell's New York concerts noted his opera prowess, and reviews of his opera performances noted his formidable concert presence. He was applauded, complimented, riding high. In this whirlwind of activity Szell was also pushing himself physically and mentally. Elwell reported that Szell attended as many as six parties in one evening, "all celebrating his remarkable achievement."[16]

Szell's final Philharmonic Sunday matinee came on the tenth and his final Met performance on the fourteenth. Before and after these engagements, Szell had some free days to deal with plans for *Salome*. But he remained wound up from his month of intense activity. Szell had *Salome* on his mind, and he charged ahead regardless of Bing's urgent meeting. The repercussions went inexorably on.

After Zirato informed Szell of Bing's disinvitation, Szell wrote his letter of resignation, simultaneously sending copies to the newspapers. The scene backstage after the performance of *Tannhäuser* resembled a Marx Brothers comedy: the critics ran from a hastily called press conference by Bing to hover outside Szell's closed dressing room door. Szell, stringing them along, revealed little. Harriett Johnson provided the flavor of the occasion:

> The Metropolitan Opera was generating all kinds of excitement last night, not the least of which was the provocative contrast in personalities provided backstage by conductor George Szell and general manager Rudolf Bing.
>
> Szell, who wants a release from his contract because he objects to "present conditions," was grumpy and curt to the press after his performance of *Tannhäuser*.

> He handed out a short written statement to the effect that he would be happy to report to the board of directors what was on his mind if the board so desired. Then he slammed the door shut and in a few moments was playing some Mozart on the piano. He refused to tell us through the door what Mozart it was. "You ought to know, you're critics," he shouted.
>
> Back in the press room, Bing, never in a more affable mood, said, "Szell's tired, that's all." Previously Bing had apparently enjoyed exchanging quips with a few of us regarding the Szell problem. "I'm determined not to say anything unpleasant," he said with a sly laugh, "and critics, of course, are always right." "What about conductors?" we queried. "I am grateful to Dr. Szell for his distinguished contribution to this season and I regret his departure," answered the momentary master of diplomacy. When asked if Szell's decision to leave was final, he replied, "Dr. Szell will always be welcome at the Metropolitan."[17]

The fallout spread in the press, and an exchange of letters among Bing, Szell, and Zirato followed; by then, Szell and Bing were no longer on speaking terms. Bing circulated copies of some of their correspondence to the Met board. A letter from Bing to Szell, attempting to ameliorate the effects of Szell's defection, shows Bing as a master diplomat and psychologist:

> Dear Szell:
>
> I gather you have strong feelings and I am not suggesting that we should discuss matters at this stage. You have made it perfectly clear that you do not wish to return here next year and you know that although I regret it I am inclined to feel this is a wise decision. But we both, alas, are beyond the school boy age; does it give you any particular satisfaction to hurt the Metropolitan as your walking out this season inevitably would? Why can you not do your remaining two performances in New York and at least the one performance in Cleveland? Would you permit me to tell the press tonight that I have asked you to reconsider, that you have reconsidered and that you will fulfill the rest of your contract?
>
> I know it requires a bit of greatness to reverse oneself. The decision, of course, is yours but in any case please accept my thanks for a brilliant contribution to this season.

Szell, back in Cleveland, was unmoved by Bing's diplomacy. Referring to Bing's question, "Does it give you any particular satisfaction to hurt the Metropolitan as your walking out this season inevitably would," Szell countered in a letter by asking, "Did Bing not say that it would not be much trouble to replace him?" Szell tried to make a distinction between Bing's considering his action "walking out" as opposed to merely asking for a release. If Bing would not grant a release, Szell would conduct his remaining performances, but under those circumstances, "it would be inevitable that the questions of artistic principles and professional competence which separate us be aired in public. I leave the decision to you."

If, in fact, Szell was only asking for a release from present and future agreements, he had no need to attack Bing publicly. His bald threat to air "questions of artistic principles and professional competence" was as crude a tactic as Bing's demeanor during this incident was diplomatic. Szell's arguments contained elements of a smoke screen. He admitted no fault on his side—his bad manners at the meeting, and his preemptive resignation to being uninvited—but, perhaps rightly, blamed Bing for a stage mishap at a performance.

In his letter Szell recalled that after the first piano rehearsal with the cast of *Tannhäuser,* he went to Bing's office "to express my joy to do opera again." Szell's euphoria was short-lived: "This joy, however, gave way very soon to unhappiness." In Szell's view there existed a "distressing lack of general efficiency and of coordination between the various departments." He felt these not only "hampered" his work, but "resulted in unnecessary waste of time and money." Szell reminded Bing that he had warned him about this the previous spring during the planning of the *Tannhäuser* sets, which he opined were undertaken "in an amazingly sloppy fashion." In a parenthesis, Szell specifically exempted the Met's "excellent musical staff" from this criticism. But he described the dangerous incident of the ninth:

> The scandalous mechanical breakdown of the change of scenery in Act I of the performance of Saturday afternoon, January 9th, is only one of the symptoms of disorganization. In a normally well-functioning set-up this incident might be classed among the freak mishaps that occur inexplicably once in a long time. In the present instance, however, it was directly due to the fact that the top technicians were on leave and that the head of the department is not in the habit of attending performances and that no provision had been made to assure smooth functioning of this change of scenery that particular day. After this catastrophe, it was decided to rehearse that change before the performance, with the result that it functioned smoothly Thursday, the 14th. This is what I call improvident and disorganized.

Szell suggested that the real damage to the Met was not his withdrawal, but rather that "The Metropolitan is really 'hurt'—and very seriously—by your own improvidence and casualness, your many errors of judgement and by the dilettantism and incompetence I have encountered and observed in various departments during the past few weeks." Szell added that he regretted this turn of events and that he was "not insensitive to [Bing's] personal charm and . . . gentlemanlike behaviour, but those pleasant qualities have nothing to do with the artistic issue that separates us."

Szell sent a copy of this letter to George A. Sloan, chairman of the Met board, which further incensed Bing. "I certainly cannot reciprocate Mr. Szell's declaration of not being insensitive to his personal charm or gentleman-like behavior," Bing wrote Sloan. "I feel he has behaved like a cad and I will under no circumstances repeat my mistake of inviting Szell again wherever I may work to the end of my days." Next, Bing attempted to discredit Szell, hoping to defuse the possibility that Sloan and the board might want to hear Szell's criticisms of him:

> I really have only myself to blame because Szell walked out on me once before at Glyndebourne and he is known all over the world as one of the most unpleasant men, ruthless, impertinent, ill-mannered and completely oblivious to any kind of moral or other obligations.
>
> Mr. Szell's comments on my work at the Metropolitan leave me cool. I am completely disinterested in his artistic judgement on stagecraft. . . . Mr. Szell, before emigrating to this country, worked at a medium class German theatre in Czechoslovakia and since then has never seen or done opera outside the Metropolitan. His knowledge on the subject is of no consequence.

Bing could hit below the belt when pressed: the Prague German Opera enjoyed a considerable reputation in Europe, and not mentioning Szell's years at the Berlin Opera was undoubtedly a calculated omission; Bing knew—he moved to Berlin in 1927. Szell had conducted performances of *Der Rosenkavalier* at the Salzburg Festival in 1949, which Bing was sure to have known. "Outside the Metropolitan" was a crafty ploy to minimize Szell's four-year association with the great company, during which he served as de facto music director. Before Glyndebourne, Bing himself had served only in provincial European theaters. But he hit close to the mark on Szell's sometime behavior.

Bing, by now "getting a little tired of the whole affair," reminded Zirato that he did tell him that he would be happy to have Szell bow out for "lack of time or any other reason he could think up."[18] What seemed to worry him most was how his board might react. He need not have worried, however, for they stood behind him. What concerned Bing also was the need to quash further attention to the matter by the press, which might give Szell a forum to express his disagreement with him. Bing had his answer ready, but good sense at last prevailed and the threats on both sides were not implemented. That exchange of private letters served the last salvo in the battle. Szell stayed in Cleveland, Max Rudolf took over his Met performances for the season, and Bing remained at the Met until his retirement in 1972.[19]

In spite of his vow not to invite Szell again, "wherever I may work to the end of my days," Bing attempted to engage him in 1967 for *Götterdämmerung*, which Szell had led often at the Met in the 1940s.[20] But Szell declined, as he had long given up opera. The *Tannhäuser* of January 14, 1954, remained Szell's operatic finale in this country. The wheel came full circle: *Tannhäuser* had been on his first Met season, and his rift with Bing occurred in the course of planning for *Salome*, Szell's Met debut opera twelve years before.

In the back of Szell's 1966 pocket date book, he wrote: "Rudolf Bing and I have a tacit understanding that we do not discuss each other publicly. Since he has observed this courtesy for these many years, I intend to do the same." Szell likely crafted this statement in response to a magazine journalist who had contacted him for an unrelated article.[21]

Szell continued to conduct opera in Europe into the 1950s: at the Salzburg Festival he conducted *The Abduction from the Seraglio* (1956), the world premieres of *Penelope* (1954) and *School for Wives* (1957) by Rolf Liebermann, and *Irish Legend* (1955) by Werner Egk. At the Vienna State Opera, Szell conducted *Salome* in December 1957 and *Ariadne auf Naxos* in January 1958. He occasionally considered concert performances of opera in Cleveland but was unable to assemble casts that would have satisfied his standards. The closest the Cleveland Orchestra audience got to Szell's opera mastery were a smattering of opera overtures and preludes; orchestral excerpts from the *Ring*, which were subsequently recorded; and a November 1953 concert version of the first scene of *Die Walküre*, with Ramon Vinay, tenor, Astrid Varnay, soprano, and Lubomir Vichegonov, bass.

Although Szell did not make even one commercial opera recording, a few of his Met appearances were broadcast and eventually found their way into the body of pirated performances. They also remain in the Met's broadcast archives awaiting resurrection. A noncommercial recording of a live performance of *Die Zauberflöte* at the Salzburg Festival in 1959 was later released on CD and provides teasing evidence of what his recorded opera legacy might have been. It is stylish, spirited, and magnificently paced. Written at the end of his beloved Mozart's life, it is fitting that it was the last opera Szell ever conducted.

There would be no future engagements at the Met, but Szell would still return to the New York Philharmonic. He had given them a list of pieces and soloists to be reserved for 1954–55. Zirato normally dealt with programming, but the day after Szell's first Beethoven program with the Philharmonic, Arthur Judson wrote Szell concerning one of the next season's programs. At the end, he made a statement that Szell would have valued more than any review: "You gave a superb performance last night. I never heard the Beethoven Fifth done better!"[22]

A sign of Szell's troubled state of mind over the Met episode was that on the way home from the train station, he left his briefcase full of important papers in the taxi. A call to the Yellow Cab Company quickly located the driver, who was directed to deliver the case to Severance Hall. His name was Luther T. Sell.[23]

In spite of his effort to make up with George Szell, Rudolf Bing remained bitter, leading him to utter an immortal quip: told by a colleague that Szell was his own worst enemy, Bing retorted, "Not while I'm alive!"[24] Szell was well aware of Bing's *bon mot*. Years later a visitor to the Szell's home heard Helene Szell say to her husband, "George, you're your own worst enemy." To which he answered, "Not while Rudolf Bing is alive."[25]

8

Keeping the Promise

"Second to None" (1954–57)

George Szell began 1954 in Cleveland with an all-orchestral program: Beethoven's *Leonore* Overture no. 3 and Symphony no. 8, and Tchaikovsky's *Pathétique* Symphony. In the audience were the participants in a ten-day conducting workshop, a project of the American Symphony Orchestra League, supported by a grant from the Kulas Foundation. The workshop aimed to provide up to thirty conductors the opportunity to observe a major professional orchestra in operation, to hone their skills in baton technique, and to deepen their understanding of the repertoire. They attended ten orchestra rehearsals, four concerts, and two chorus rehearsals. The attendees themselves conducted the orchestra in rehearsal, under Szell's tutelage.[1]

Szell's colleague, Max Rudolf, who had recently written one of the most important texts on conducting, addressed them. Rudolf recalled that Szell had spoken highly to "one of the Schirmer gentlemen" about his book, and this helped gain its publication. Szell also wrote the foreword to the first edition. Composer William Schuman, head of publications for Schirmer at the time, readily accepted the manuscript, saying, "Schirmer will lose money on this book but I think it should be published." "Of course," Rudolf gleefully said, "it made money." The book has since become a classic, going through several printings.[2] Rudolf himself became a classic—artistic administrator and conductor at the Metropolitan Opera, conductor of the Cincinnati Symphony for a decade, teacher of conducting at the Curtis Institute of Music, and mentor to generations of young conductors, as well as generous consultant to managers, musicologists, and musicians on several continents.

The participants were supplied with Rudolf's text and other study materials, including a fascinating but all-too-brief essay of advice to young conductors by Richard Strauss. It contained maxims such as: "If you think the brass is not strong enough, tone them down two points further," and "Remember that you do not make music for your own amusement, but for the pleasure of your audience."[3] Strauss spoke of a conducting tradition that went back to Wagner, Liszt, and Mendelssohn and gave specific examples of tempi, phrasing, and beating handed down from these estimable forerunners. This was also Szell's tradition.

Szell gave surprising advice from a conductor with a reputation for cold precision. A participant remarked, "In Beethoven's Fifth, Szell had slowed the tempo at a given point, to excellent effect, and he ascribed the liberty to an unaccountable momentary impulse. 'An inspirational and improvisatory style of conducting is returning today after a period of putting music in a strait-jacket,' Szell observed." Other points Szell made resided in the mainstream of his aesthetic: "Among possible misconceptions in our profession is an overemphasis on extra-musical things such as public relations, the position of the orchestra in the community, and so forth. Important as these things are, what comes first is the music. Bringing the music to life is our primary technique. And to project the music one must first understand the composer. To be clear to the audience, his message must be clear to you. The driver of a sightseeing bus must first know the way himself."[4]

Szell hosted a luncheon for the conductors. Planning the menu, his correspondence was almost as lengthy as in planning the workshop. The event appeared more a dinner than a luncheon; the menu began with shrimp cocktail and, besides roast beef, included vegetables, salad, celery and olives, rolls and butter, coffee, and strawberry sundae.

Throughout the workshop, Szell was genial, relaxed, accessible to questions, and brilliantly demonstrating and explaining conducting technique, stimulated by the young colleagues to give them all he could in the short time together. One of the conductors was a fine musician, possessing extraordinary skill at realizing full scores at the piano almost as well as Szell himself. The young conductor, however, had no companion gift for the musical gesture, and when in front of the orchestra courted a major disaster. Szell, respecting the man's honest musicianship, though he lacked the talent for conducting, tactfully curtailed his turn, with the excuse that they were running short of time.[5]

During the workshop, the participants ranged freely through Severance Hall. In rehearsals they staked their posts in the balcony, the boxes, on the main floor, and on stage behind and within the orchestra. At the end of every rehearsal they surrounded Szell, eager to question him on all they had observed. He, just as enthusiastically, answered all their questions patiently, with good humor. The workshop was the experience of a lifetime for the participants, and they thanked Szell profusely. Many wrote letters expressing their gratitude, and how it had tangibly helped them on their return to their own orchestras. To all, Szell wrote individual replies.

A Progressive Programmer

The season continued with old and new works: Gottfried von Einem's *Capriccio for Orchestra*, Stravinsky's *Synphony of Psalms*, Hindemith's *Sinphonie Die Harmonie der Welt*, the Symphony in E by Ulysses Kay, Barber's Violin Concerto with Gingold, Fourth Symphonies of Schumann and Sibelius, Brahms's First, Haydn's Symphony no. 104, and the season's grand finale—Beethoven's Ninth. Mack Harrell, a new bass, joined the same trio of singers as twice before.

That spring *Musical America* noted Szell's attention to new music. It published the results of a questionnaire on programming contemporary music sent to conductors of major orchestras, which Szell and six others answered: Charles Munch, Boston; Eugene Ormandy, Philadelphia; Vladimir Golschmann, St. Louis; Thor Johnson, Cincinnati; Alfred Wallenstein, Los Angeles; and Erich Leinsdorf, Rochester. A comparison of the season's programming showed that Szell programmed more contemporary music, 36 percent, than any of the others. In reporting on the article, Herbert Elwell pointed out that the questionnaire failed to define "contemporary music." A composer himself, he was sensitive to the issue, and found significant differences in attitudes among the seven. A minority of one, Wallenstein claimed that the public was indifferent to new music. Johnson claimed that the expense of producing new works was "often enormous," an opinion with which six of the conductors did not agree. Elwell found that Johnson's answers "suggest hedging and indecision." Munch's and Ormandy's answers "suggest greater feeling of responsibility toward ultra-conservative audiences than a willingness to exert initiative in behalf of the contemporary composer. Golschmann, Szell, and Leinsdorf, on the other hand, give the impression of feeling genuine responsibility toward modernism and show that they are ready to do something about it, if and when they can." Although Szell led the group, he took "a rather resentful poke at American composers who have failed him on commissions." "Of five to whom he has offered commissions only two came through satisfactorily. But he says he is not discouraged and that he will go on commissioning new works."[6]

The summer of 1954 held less vacation for Szell than had many in recent years. Except for a month's rest in Crans, he spent practically the whole time rehearsing or conducting. A week after the Beethoven Ninth, the Szells took a train to New York, flew to Paris to pick up their automobile, and motored to Rome. Szell broadcast two concerts with the RIA Orchestra there on May 25 and 29. While in Vienna to conduct a concert, he held preliminary rehearsals for the world premiere of Rolf Liebermann's opera *Penelope*, scheduled for Salzburg in August. Szell had a number of special batons made for Bruno Walter by the property man of the Vienna Symphony, a Herr Helmer, who also fashioned some for Szell. Back in America, he mailed them to Zirato, who gave them to Walter.

Szell told a Cleveland interviewer that orchestras throughout the United States were experiencing the same problem: deficits. He predicted that America would have to subsidize music: "It will have to come and I'm certainly in favor of it." Szell proved prophetic: the National Endowment for the Arts would become a reality in his lifetime, although he would have to wait more than a dozen years for it. He also showed political astuteness, demonstrated by the anguish the endowment suffered at the turn of the twenty-first century by the politicization it had successfully avoided for the first twenty-five years. Szell perceptively hit on an issue that came to the fore then: "I'd rather see the cities or states give the money, it's much better if it's decentralized." He pointed to the European example as a model for the United States: "America should have a national theater, a national opera, a national symphony. Every civilized, every cultured nation has a ministry of enlightenment and education to promote these arts."[7]

A sign of the orchestra's growing stability was the small number of new players this season: six. An editorial in the *Cleveland Press* pointed out that it was cause for civic pride that the newcomers had been first-chair players in other orchestras and had left those posts to join Cleveland's. The editorial also found the flow of former players to the larger major orchestras a "tribute to the orchestra's quality."[8] One of the six was a future first-chair player, French hornist Myron Bloom, former principal of the New Orleans Symphony. Bloom, a native of Cleveland, played third horn for his first season. He had studied with the orchestra's second horn, Martin Morris. When Bloom became first horn, he and Morris became a matchless pair for almost twenty years. Szell's team was taking on increasing permanency. First flute Maurice Sharp, first bassoon George Goslee, and timpanist Cloyd Duff dated from Szell's first season. First clarinet Robert Marcellus had joined the orchestra the previous season and would stay the course. Marc Lifschey was first oboist from 1950 to 1965.[9]

Guest conductor Leopold Stokowski made his fourth consecutive appearance in two programs. Two other conductors made their orchestra debuts with one program each: Jonel Perlea and Max Rudolf. Soloists were mostly familiar pianists and violinists. Three significant young pianists made Cleveland debuts: Paul Badura-Skoda, Grant Johannessen, and Van Cliburn, the recent winner of the Leventritt Competition. First violist Abraham Skernick and two singers were the only soloists outside the piano/violin axis (although Maurice Sharp was featured in the Bach Suite no. 2). Frances Yeend and Mack Harrell sang in Brahms's *German Requiem*, which ended the season.

More than half of the concerts featured music new to Cleveland. This ranged from Mozart piano concertos to first Cleveland performances of works by Georges Bizet, Ernest Bloch, Henry Cowell, Henri Dutilleux, Paul Hindemith, Bernard Rogers, and Josef Suk. Ravel's G Major Piano Concerto, with Johannessen, was a first, along with Suk's Fantasy for Violin with Gingold. Szell also conducted Theme and

Variations, op. 81, by Charles Mills, a North Carolinian, commissioned by Dimitri Mitropoulos, who had premiered it with the New York Philharmonic.

Szell conducted the New York Philharmonic for two weeks in both December and January. On January 3, 1955, the American Composers Alliance honored him with its Laurel Leaf Award: "In recognition of his distinguished achievement in fostering and encouraging American music and American composers. . . . In the past season, Mr. Szell, with his orchestra in Cleveland, performed more scores by contemporary American composers than were programmed by any other major American orchestra."[10]

Szell spent ten days in Zurich for a Mozart program as conductor and piano soloist (Symphony no. 40, Piano Concerto in A Major, K. 488, and Symphony no. 41). On the flight from New York the pilot, a Mr. Maslin—who had flown the first commercial transatlantic flight seventeen years before—showed him around the cockpit. In Zurich, he practiced piano every day, and proudly reported his healthy menus to Helene, who had remained at home. There, visitors included composer Werner Egk, whose opera, *Irische Legende*, he would premiere at Salzburg in August, and Szell "had a very satisfactory phone talk with Ian Hunter—all program questions settled—*no* Tschaikowsky."[11]

The *Baseler Nationalzeitung* reported "Szell is an excellent conductor who needs no oratorical skills to convince the musicians of the rightness of his interpretations." Leading from the keyboard, "following the examples of Weingartner, Furtwängler, and Walter . . . Szell is the perfect Mozart player. . . . His piano playing is fluently clear and of exceptional rhythmic precision," and he and the orchestra achieved "a collaboration of rarely experienced unity." *Die Tat* found "a very interesting-sounding effect" in Szell's including in the piano part the unwritten generalbass, which "indeed went without saying in Mozart's time," and asked "whether in the Mozart Year that brings us a step further in performance practice?"[12] Szell always opened himself to concepts that brought him closer to the composer.

Szell returned to Cleveland to conduct nine of the remaining eight subscription pairs from January to April; Max Rudolf made his debut with the orchestra, conducting one program in March. Soloists included Rudolf Serkin, Paul Badura-Skoda, Zino Francescatti, Arthur Rubinstein, Joseph Szigeti, and, making his Cleveland debut, Grant Johannesen. The second workshop for conductors ran for two weeks in March.

A loss to the Cleveland Orchestra family was Carl Vosburgh's death on March 28, 1955, at the age of fifty-nine. Vosburgh had been orchestra manager for twenty-two years. He had worked effectively with the board and enjoyed a warm personal relationship with Szell, as well as a smoothly functioning professional one. Szell conducted Mozart's *Masonic Funeral Music*, K. 477, in his memory in two benefit concerts for the orchestra's pension fund on March 31 and April 2. Arthur Rubinstein played the first piano concertos by Tchaikovsky and Brahms.

Newly signed orchestra-related contracts included: a three-year pact with the musicians union, the first of that length in the orchestra's history; a contract with Epic Records, as the first American orchestra to sign with that offshoot of Columbia Records; and the engagement of a new manager, William McKelvey Martin. The musicians' contract provided a $10 increase in the weekly minimum scale over the three years, to $125. The terms guaranteed every member an additional $300 in recording income in the contract's first year. Also guaranteed were sixteen hours of recording a year for five years, a four-fold increase over the former Columbia contract. Recording sessions were scheduled for the following fall and spring.

Martin, forty-seven, former manager of the Pittsburgh Symphony for three years, met Szell fifteen years earlier in Los Angeles, and they had seen each other a few times since. Although not a musician, Martin's background encompassed twenty-five years in music management. His appointment bypassed George H. L. Smith, acting manager after Vosburgh died, and who had hoped to be named to the job permanently.[13]

Ed Sullivan's gossip column in the *New York Daily News* carried an item reporting that George Szell was "seriously ill." Betty Randolph Bean of the Philharmonic staff immediately wrote the paper that she had talked with Szell in Cleveland just an hour before. He was arranging his guest appearances with the Philharmonic in Edinburgh the coming September, he was in perfect health, and the report was completely erroneous. She added, "the true state of his health . . . has never been better. Not only did he conduct his regular schedule of five rehearsals and four concerts last week but he is in the midst of five rehearsals and preparations for four performances this week. . . . He will conduct at the Holland, Salzburg and Edinburgh Festivals this summer." Szell told her: "I was out for the first time yesterday on the driving range practicing for my summer's golf. In fact I hit some sixty balls with a few modest drives of up to two-hundred yards!"[14]

Former Musical Arts Association president Thomas L. Sidlo died on May 27 at the age of sixty-seven. He had been a lawyer, civic leader, and ardent supporter of music and opera in Cleveland during his long and distinguished career. In death he was again a benefactor. His will left 35 percent of his million-dollar estate to Western Reserve University and the Cleveland Orchestra.

The Szells on Holiday

Szell took time in June for his annual health regimen: his fifty-eighth birthday found him at the Privatklinik Bircher-Benner in Zurich. His first concert of the summer was with the Concertgebouw in Amsterdam on July 14. Clara Haskil, a fellow student of Richard Robert in Vienna, was soloist in Mozart's Piano Concerto in F Major, K. 459. The program opened with Henk Badings's *Die Nachtwacht* (*The Nightwatch*, named after Rembrandt's famous painting), and ended with Sibelius's Second Symphony.

His concert held the place of honor, ending the Holland Festival. Two weeks later Szell made his debut with the Munich Philharmonic. In an expression that Szell was fond of using, the program consisted of "specialties of the house": *Oberon* Overture, Haydn Symphony no. 88, and the Schubert Symphony in C Major, "The Great."

The peripatetic Szells drove from Munich to Salzburg, and settled down for seven weeks. Szell rehearsed and performed his second world premiere opera there in two seasons, Werner Egk's *Irische Legende* (*Irish Legend*), based on William Butler Yeats's play, *Countess Cathleen*. The English press panned the opera: "a work of well-nigh spotless mediocrity," wrote Hans Keller in the *Sunday Times*, although not for want of Szell's trying. Peter Heyworth in the *Observer* wrote that the opera "certainly was given the benefit of every doubt by a distinguished cast and the highly competent conducting of George Szell."[15] The German press took the opera and its sinner-finding-redemption-through-redeeming-other-souls more positively, but the music received mixed reviews. On the same day of the premiere of *Irische Legende* in Salzburg—August 17, 1955—a Cleveland newspaper reported that the Cleveland Orchestra would make its first European tour in the spring of 1957.[16]

Szell joined the New York Philharmonic for concerts at the Edinburgh Festival. A reviewer from Switzerland disliked the Philharmonic's "orgy of sound with which Dimitri Mitropoulos burdened the Vaughan Williams Fourth Symphony," and found the same in Guido Cantelli's performance of *Daphnis et Chloé*, which "went beyond what is musically bearable." But under Szell, "the noble qualities of the orchestra came fully to fruition. . . . When such a ripe, knowingly-responsible conductor who is capable of grasping such a work of musical integrity and such an orchestra come together, problematical things in works of the every-day repertoire sound as never before."[17]

Szell's Tenth Anniversary Season

Szell returned to a season of anniversaries and celebrations: 1955–56—his tenth anniversary in Cleveland, the twenty-fifth of the building of Severance Hall, the orchestra's thirty-eighth season, and musical birthdays of two hundred for Mozart and ninety for Sibelius. Szell summed up his decade with the orchestra and looked to the future:

> The Cleveland Orchestra was a fine orchestra when I first heard it. When I took over, some of the best members had left and I made it my business to get them back.
>
> Since 1946 the orchestra has greatly developed, both in numbers and in quality, and while the peak of perfection is ever elusive, the orchestra today is an instrument of artistic expression ranking with the best in the world, and with certain special qualities I do not find in any other orchestra at the present moment.

Szell proudly told of the season's extension from twenty-eight to thirty weeks and of subscription concerts from twenty to twenty-four pairs, with the summer season also increased. But he said that he "will not be satisfied until we are able to have a summer season for the full orchestra comparable to the orchestras on the eastern seaboard." For that ideal summer season he envisioned "a large attractive open-air area with a fine music shed and adequate parking space." Szell also mentioned a "substantial" pension fund and "more and more broadcasting on a nation-wide network." When asked about reviving the opera performances that Cleveland still remembered from the 1930s, Szell said he "would be happy to consider opera productions with the Cleveland Orchestra if I could find a sponsor who would meet the very large cost which is several times greater than when opera was last done at Severance Hall."[18]

A newspaper article, in the context of the bicentennial of Mozart's birth that season, tantalizingly mentioned that "A concert version of *Così fan tutte* has been weighed."[19] Unfortunately, it did not happen, nor would Szell conduct a concert version of any full opera in Cleveland; cost and casting were the major problems. Szell wanted only the best international singers for each important role. Those singers' schedules were set years in advance, mostly with the world's major opera companies. At various times Szell tried to work out opera recording projects, but that added the complication of singers' commitments to one or another recording company, further limiting the field.

Nine years later the Lake Erie Opera Theatre (L.E.O.T.) was formed to produce two fully staged operas a season with the Cleveland Orchestra in Severance Hall. It operated for seven seasons from 1964 through 1970. Louis Lane served as musical director, and the author as associate musical director. Szell attended one L.E.O.T. performance every year but the last.[20]

Szell had an ambitious wish list. With each new accomplishment, he challenged himself and the orchestra to new goals. In the next decade, he would accomplish most of them. A dozen new players this season would help him on the way. No principal chairs changed that season. Present and future key players included assistant concertmaster Anshel Brusilow and two other string players who would some day lead their sections, Lawrence Angell, double bass, and Daniel Majeske, violin.

The opening concert, customarily all-orchestral, was familiar in form and content: a French first half—Berlioz's overture to the opera *Benvenuto Cellini*, two Nocturnes by Debussy, and the Second Suite of Ravel's *Daphnis et Chloé*—and Brahms's Second Symphony after intermission. The second concert featured two section leaders, Josef Gingold and Abraham Skernick, as soloists in Mozart's Symphonie Concertante for Violin and Viola. The Symphonie Concertante was the first of eleven works by Mozart that season celebrating the two hundredth anniversary of his birth. It was also one of several that season featuring orchestra members. Two other Mozart works would fill that bill: the Divertimento in D, K. 131 for Flute, Oboe, Bassoon, Four Horns, and Strings (with Maurice Sharp, Marc Lifschey, George Goslee, Myron Bloom, Martin Morris, Richard Mackey, and Ernani Angelucci) and the Clarinet Concerto (with Robert Marcellus). William Hebert was soloist that season in the Vivaldi Piccolo Concerto and George Goslee soloist in Mozart's Bassoon Concerto in a special concert for the Friends of the Cleveland Orchestra in March. Szell granted solo opportunities to members who he felt could hold their own on turf otherwise occupied by artists of international stature. This helped attract and retain top talent. By singling out individual players, it also showed the audience the extent and depth of the talent within the orchestra.

Szell was the guest of honor at a civic luncheon for three hundred at the Hotel Statler, sponsored by the Musical Arts Association, the Cleveland Advertising Club, and the Chamber of Commerce. The mayor of Cleveland, Anthony J. Celebrezze, read a resolution by the city council honoring Szell on the occasion of his tenth season and proclaimed a George Szell Week. Guests included James H. Fassett of New York, supervisor of music for the Columbia Broadcasting System. "His name is a household word in all the musical circles of the United States," said Fassett, who asked if Americans realized the importance of the music festivals in Europe, "where Szell has performed to great acclaim." Szell used the occasion to stress some serious points. "There is not a single European country, regardless of the form of its government," he noted, "that does not give music an important place in its life—not only by the individual citizen but by city, provincial and state governments."[21]

A record five guest conductors appeared that season: Sir Thomas Beecham, Eduard van Beinum, Fernando Previtali, Thomas Schippers, and Igor Stravinsky. Stravinsky conducted his *Petrouchka* and *Le baiser de la fée*; van Beinum, a work of his countryman Hendrik Andriessen; Schippers, Hindemith's *Symphonia Serena*, a Cleveland first; and Previtali, Busoni's incidental music to Gozzi's *Turandot*. Beecham introduced Sibelius's tone poem *Tapiola*. Szell conducted a dozen twentieth-century works, including two concertos by Bartók, Concerto Grosso no. 2 and *Schelomo* by Bloch, *Two Movements for Orchestra* by Gottfried von Einem, *Sinfonia Sacra* (Symphony no. 5) by Howard Hanson, *Three Gospel Hymns* by Everett Helm, Khachaturian's Piano Concerto, *Furioso* by Rolf Liebermann, Symphony no. 6 by Martinů, *Music for Orchestra* by Wallingford Riegger, and Charles Turner's *Encounter*.

A New York Philharmonic Hiatus

Szell went to New York for the entire month of December. For the past twelve seasons since 1943, his longest absence from the Philharmonic guest list had been two consecutive seasons—1948–49 and 1949–50. The concerts in December 1955 were Szell's last with the Philharmonic for six seasons to come, until February 1963.

Reasons given for his desertion of or by the Philharmonic vary. Some have said that Szell's harsh manner so irritated the Philharmonic musicians that they implored management to stop engaging him.[22] Another rumor suggested that Szell was brought up on charges before the musicians' union, although inspection of the minutes of the executive board of Local 802 of that time found no evidence of that. Most likely, Szell's Philharmonic absence stemmed from negative criticism in the press about the reappearance of the same guest conductors (Walter, Cantelli, and Szell were specifically mentioned), and the Philharmonic board responded to that criticism.[23] The press's chief target was Arthur Judson, then both manager of the Philharmonic and head of Columbia Artists Management, a glaring conflict of interest. The Philharmonic itself was undergoing changes in leadership both upstairs and downstairs. The gentle Mitropoulos was superseded by the dynamic young Bernstein. Judson resigned his position at the Philharmonic, but was replaced by his former assistant Bruno Zirato, seen by many as tantamount to no change at all.

This 1955 season at the Philharmonic Szell began with an all-Beethoven program. Howard Taubman, in the *New York Times*, benignly stated: "It was clear from the opening 'Coriolanus' Overture that everything would be ship-shape. Mr. Szell, who has been almost a permanent guest conductor of the Philharmonic, is at home with the men, and they with him. He had them playing throughout the evening with a scrupulous regard for detail and with a sense of vitality."[24]

Some members of the Philharmonic would have disputed Taubman about Szell being "at home with the men, and they with him." Winthrop Sargeant's review of the opening concert of Szell's third week discussed the Philharmonic's problematical state of health, with emphasis on the conducting staff, only in the last paragraph getting around to the concert. It first mentioned its administrative head, Arthur Judson, the powerful impresario who guided the orchestra's destinies. Then the article patronizingly turned to the conducting staff, which, "when one considers its members individually, does not appear to be by any means the worst one possible." Bruno Walter and Pierre Monteux were "two respected veterans, both of whom are artists of considerable stature," and this "also includes Dimitri Mitropoulos, who has his points as an interesting interpreter of emotionally supercharged music." "George Szell," Sargeant said, is "a conscientious disciplinarian who has a conservative and precise approach to the classics," and finally, "Guido Cantelli, a young Italian whose claims to distinction as a symphonic maestro have always seemed to me rather dim but who makes a handsome appearance on the podium."

The critic's main point was "not that [this group] lacks competence but that it is far too numerous and disparate in its methods of conducting." Walter and Monteux, mature musicians, "are no longer men of sufficient personal forcefulness to whip an orchestra into brilliant technical shape. This leaves the whipping to be done by Mr. Mitropoulos and Mr. Szell, and they approach the problem from diametrically opposite points of view." The review presented a valid comparison citing Boston and Philadelphia, "both of which have the advantage of a single chief [Munch and Ormandy, respectively]." Sargeant's impression was "that the orchestra, torn between the hot inspirationalism of Mr. Mitropoulos and the cool, methodical, and exacting style of Mr. Szell, may have given up in despair."[25] The Philharmonic's next music director after Mitropoulos received no mention in the writer's catalog of conductors—at the time, Leonard Bernstein was not a contender.

When reviewers applied the term "conscientious" to Szell, it implied a musicality tinged with pedantry. Szell himself used the word often; to him, it stood for an admirable quality of a self-respecting musician. It encompassed always seeking the composer's intentions before all else, soul-searching for every musical decision, and especially, not serving the conductor's ego.

The Choral Dream Is Realized

Just before the New Year 1956, Szell appointed thirty-nine-year-old Robert Shaw to the staff as associate conductor, replacing Rudolph Ringwall. Shaw, a world-renowned choral conductor, in his twenties had prepared choruses for Toscanini and toured worldwide, also recording extensively with his own Robert Shaw Chorale. In Cleveland Shaw would conduct subscription concerts, the Twilights, as many as thirty-five children's concerts, and would direct the Cleveland Orchestra Chorus. The *Cleveland Press* covered his first visit in early January: "Here for a long weekend of meeting the musicians he will conduct and hearing them perform, the personable young man with a crew cut outlined his ideas: 'I'd like to audition 600 singers right after Labor Day, choose 200 of them and start right away on chorus work,' he said. 'I'd like to have the group ready for the orchestra's first concert if I can.'"

Ambitious choral works planned for the coming season included Beethoven's *Missa solemnis*, Stravinsky's *Symphony of Psalms*, and, at the final concert, the Verdi Requiem. "I want to build the best chorus in the United States," Shaw said. Szell wanted the chorus, and now he had found the man to transform it into a vocal instrument comparable to the orchestra he had built. Shaw viewed the job in Cleveland as "the greatest learning opportunity in the world."[26] Shaw actively maintained his outside career and spent long stretches away from Cleveland, although he did not tour with his Robert Shaw Chorale in his first season with the orchestra. Louis Lane, who had been with Szell ten years, was promoted to assistant conductor.

On February 2, 1956, the orchestra and city celebrated the twenty-fifth anniversary of the opening of Severance Hall. The inaugural program on February 5, 1931, had been Bach's Passacaglia and Fugue in C Minor, Charles Martin Loeffler's *Evocation*, commissioned for the occasion, and Brahms's First Symphony. The 1956 program book was bound in heavy gray paper and decoratively bordered in silver ink. A ceremony preceded the concert; speakers included the president of the Musical Arts Association, Frank E. Taplin Jr.; board chairman, Percy W. Brown; and Cleveland's mayor, Anthony J. Celebrezze. The concert did not echo that of 1931, but highlighted the orchestra's enormous artistic growth since. It began appropriately with Beethoven's Overture to *The Consecration of the House*—a first performance by the orchestra—followed by Schumann's Cello Concerto and Strauss's *Don Quixote*, with Pierre Fournier.

New York audiences gave the orchestra a wildly enthusiastic reception on their eastern tour. Reviews of the first New York concert of this tour surely gratified Szell: "A packed Carnegie Hall played host last night to one of Ohio's proudest musical possessions—the Cleveland Orchestra—and its brilliant conductor, George Szell," Louis Biancolli wrote. "It has been two years since this stalwart ensemble was last heard in this city, and the thought was widely expressed that its visits have been too few and too far between. With that sentiment this reporter is in complete accord. The Cleveland unit is one of the country's major concentrations of musical skill and power. The all-Beethoven program was a good way to prove it."[27]

In March, Szell signed another three-year contract. Covering the seasons 1956–57 through 1958–59, it would take him through his thirteenth season with the orchestra. He was closing in on Sokoloff's record of fifteen years as music director. The contract's terms paralleled those of his previous one.

In March and April, the orchestra performed special concerts for labor groups. The brainchild of new manager William Martin, they had proven successful in Pittsburgh. For the first concert in March, tickets sold in blocs and 1,600 were sold—a success! Attendance was disappointing, however; the hall was less than half full. The April labor concert, billed as "Railroad Night at the Symphony," was sponsored by the Railroad Community Committee of Cleveland, representing six railroads and three union brotherhoods. Its announcement came with amusing photos. In one, Szell was wearing a railroad engineer's cap while the Railroad Committee chairman held a baton; in another, the committee chairman, still holding a baton, wore the engineer's cap while Szell, looking at a pocket watch, sported a railroad conductor's cap.

In the spring of 1956, George Smith was promoted. Up to the last concert of the 1955–56 season, Smith served as associate manager. In the program for the April 19, 21, and 22 concerts, the program listed Smith's title as "co-manager," a sign of dissatisfaction with Martin.

Szell's accomplishments in his first decade in Cleveland were overwhelmingly positive. By careful selection of new players and constant attention to minute detail, yet never losing sight of the artistic whole, he had built the orchestra into a cohesive, brilliantly responsive ensemble. By touring within the United States and increasing the catalog of recordings, the good news was spreading in ever-widening circles. Appearances on both coasts met with eager anticipation and unqualified admiration. Szell's promise, "second to none," had clearly been kept. The final stamp of approval came soon thereafter. Capping the climax of the 1956–57 season would be the orchestra's first tour of Europe.

The summer of 1956 found Szell in Europe as usual. In Zurich in June, Szell attended to a "minor ailment," a hernia operation. He took time for rest before and recuperation after. His first music-making came on July 25 at the Salzburg Festival, conducting Mozart's *The Abduction from the Seraglio*. On August 5 Szell conducted an all-Mozart program with the Vienna Philharmonic in Salzburg's Mozarteum. It consisted of the composer's last two symphonies and the A Major Piano Concerto, K. 488, with Szell as piano soloist for the last time anywhere. In early September Szell conducted a concert with the Philharmonia Orchestra of London at the Lucerne Festival, in which Elisabeth Schwarzkopf sang Strauss's "Four Last Songs."

Later that month Szell returned to Cleveland for his eleventh season. It was business as usual, which did not preclude important extracurricular musical responsibilities. The orchestra cohosted another workshop for conductors with the American Symphony Orchestra League. For eighteen days, beginning before the season's opening concert and concluding in the second week, a dozen conductors led rehearsals of the orchestra under Szell's scrutiny and attended his rehearsals and concerts, as well as special seminars with Szell, section leaders, and management.

Overlapping the conductors' workshop was a three-day music critics' workshop, also cosponsored by the orchestra and the ASOL. Its schedule was coordinated so that music critics could attend the Saturday performance of the opening concert as well as observe the young conductors. Paul Henry Lang wrote a column comparing the Cleveland Orchestra favorably with the New York Philharmonic, which had "chosen the status quo" when it replaced longtime manager Arthur Judson with his longtime assistant, Bruno Zirato. Lang extolled the Cleveland Orchestra, "trained to perfection" under Szell, and praised the "intelligent and progressive program making" that included twenty contemporary composers, half of them American, without slighting the "usual proportion of 'classics.'" It showed, according to Lang, "good taste and a desire not only to please the public but also to lead it."[28]

Szell traveled to London in November for two concerts with the Philharmonia Orchestra, followed by a concert with the Orchestra of the Southwest German Radio in Baden-Baden. He returned at the end of December for two weeks with the Chicago Symphony. In London, a review of Szell's performance of Brahms's Fourth Symphony "revived memories of Toscanini's last visit" to the British capital.[29]

In Cleveland William McKelvey Martin resigned as manager in December, effective at the end of March, two months before his contract ran out, the culmination of months of conflict between Martin and Szell. George Henry Lovett Smith, named comanager the past year, would take over as manager after Martin's departure.[30] Smith had been hoping for this, but, as it turned out, the promotion proved the wisdom of the old proverb, "Be careful what you wish for as you might get it." Smith would be on deck for the highly charged European tour in May and June. The rest of the season before the European tour consisted of a succession of concerts, including the February eastern tour. Of one Carnegie Hall concert, Howard Taubman wrote, "this was a grand night for Cleveland, as impressive in its way as if the Indians had beaten the Yankees for the pennant."[31]

On the eve of the tour, Elwell assessed the orchestra's progress in the decade since Szell took charge. The composer-critic sat in a unique position to do so: he compared its playing that season of his own *Pastorale* with its traversal nine years earlier. The conductor and soloist were the same, many players were not. Elwell had found the 1948 performances "good . . . but they could not hold a candle" to the performances of the 1956–57 season. "What has developed," he wrote, "was a kind of empathy, an ability on the part of the players to identify themselves so completely with the style and purpose of the music that it might almost appear as though they themselves had taken part in the composing of it. . . . Now it was a sort of contagion that spread from the conductor to the entire orchestra." The key to it all was that "the members have learned in a remarkable way to listen to one another just as chamber music players do. . . . The result is an enormous increase in refinement and flexibility." Elwell asked, if "the orchestra has grown in interpretive stature, in skill, in adaptability, and in powers of assimilation, has not something similar happened to the conductor?" He answered his own question, "Emphatically yes! In every advance he has constantly been two or three steps ahead of the orchestra itself, and he is still plotting and planning for more and greater improvements."[32]

With a "remarkable tribute to Ludwig van Beethoven" (*Leonore* Overture no. 3 and Symphonies 2 and 5), the orchestra closed its subscription season in "top form." "It was an evening of wondrously expert execution and studious penetration. . . . There was a unity of style which bespoke the utmost integrity. . . . Szell exercised complete domination, inspired complete awareness and commanded complete response from the players."[33] They were ready for Europe.

Triumph: Bringing Cleveland to Europe

George Szell and the Cleveland Orchestra had been acclaimed at home, throughout the Midwest, and on both coasts. The international arena would stand as the ultimate proving ground. Szell had often returned as a guest conductor to the great orchestras in the European capitals, where he had begun his career. Now, after eleven seasons in Cleveland, he would bring with him the American orchestra he could fully call his own.

The stakes for Szell were the highest of his career. America had become his artistic home but his roots remained in Europe. He felt, accordingly, more nervous about this tour than any prior one. Szell and the orchestra had won the respect and adulation of the New York critics and audiences. Few people in Europe, mainly record collectors, were familiar with the quality of the Cleveland Orchestra. Now the orchestra faced what Szell regarded as the most discriminating audiences in the world. How would they react to a midwestern American orchestra led by an expatriate fellow European? What would they expect, what would they find, and, most important, how would they judge?

The consummate planner, Szell prepared the orchestra fully. He chose the repertoire with an eye to his and his orchestra's strengths. Standard works they had made their own over several seasons made up the core of the tour programming. Szell also included music by living American and European composers, most of which the orchestra had performed and toured with in the 1956–57 season. Works from prior seasons received careful rehearsing.

As soon as the tour was confirmed, Szell changed several Cleveland programs to accommodate repertoire they would take abroad. That spring, Elwell questioned why the orchestra was making so many program changes. Szell wrote a letter in response, which Elwell "gratefully received" and printed. Szell explained that "we had to bring back into current repertoire certain works specifically requested or even stipulated by various European festivals in which the Cleveland Orchestra will appear."[34] Afraid that the orchestra alone would not attract audiences, local sponsors asked that well-known soloists appear on selected concerts. Szell chose pianists Robert Casadesus, Leon Fleisher, and Rudolf Serkin, violinist Wolfgang Schneiderhan, and soprano Elisabeth Schwarzkopf.

The itinerary was full: in the forty-one days from the first concert in Antwerp, Belgium, on May 7, 1957, to the last concert in Scheveningen, Netherlands, on June 16, there were twenty-nine concerts, plus thirteen rehearsals, in twenty-two cities in eleven countries. The challenges of the orchestra's first foreign tour would prove much more taxing than those of the annual tours within the United States. Visiting one foreign country after another, with all the differences that foreign travel brings, and the greater distances between cities on this tour, compounded the strangeness. Different customs, currency, food, and water augmented the already considerable tensions of continuously playing important concerts. Twenty-one days out of the tour's forty-one included travel. And many days, they would fly to another city, have a rehearsal, and play a concert that night as well.[35]

Planning and preparation for the tour had begun two years earlier. Anatole Heller, director of his Paris-based Bureau Artistique Internationale, would manage the tour. In August 1955, Charlotte Flatow, Heller's assistant, visited Szell in Salzburg. Correspondence followed between Flatow, Szell, and Musical Arts Association president Frank Taplin. Projected costs of the six-week tour reached $250,000, half to come from local sponsors, and the other half split between the American National Theatre and Academy (ANTA) and the Musical Arts Association. Flatow requested at least four programs. Szell proudly replied:

> Please let me assure you that this is no problem at all for us as our repertoire is an enormous one. We can very easily have five to six different programs if necessary. Let me also say that we shall prepare to have in every concert one American work of value and importance and one work of a composer of the country in which the concert takes place. The rest of the program will be standard repertoire, with particular attention to avoiding those compositions which have been over-exploited by the Philadelphia and the New York Philharmonic-Symphony on their European tours. I think that I should emphasize at this point that the Cleveland Orchestra, although a comparatively young one, is in every respect fully the equal of the American orchestras heard up to now in Europe and, in some respects, even superior to them, in particular as far as warmth of tone, subtlety of ensemble playing, general artistic attitude, and mastery of the various styles of music is concerned.

In rehearsal, Szell almost never talked about tone. Yet, this statement shows that he considered it one of his orchestra's important characteristics. Szell passed on Taplin's request that Flatow "make a special effort to get some bookings in West Berlin because that territory is considered especially important by our State Department."[36]

The orchestra and staff, numbering 107, departed Cleveland on two chartered airplanes on Sunday and Monday, May 5 and 6. A third airplane carried baggage and instruments. (The Szells had traveled ahead.) The first plane arrived in Brussels on the sixth, the second flight on the seventh. The concerts began in Antwerp on the seventh, and Brussels on the eighth.

The orchestra flew to Bremen, Germany, on the ninth for a concert that evening. On the tenth, on to London, where they arrived shortly after noon, had a brief rehearsal at 6:00P.M., and played the concert at 8:00P.M.. Travel to and concerts in Barcelona, Madrid, Lisbon, Oporto, Bordeaux, Berlin, Stuttgart, Basel, Lugano, Geneva, Paris, and Vienna followed. After Vienna came Eastern Europe: Katowice, Poznan, Lodz, and Warsaw, Poland. In those sensitive times a few members of the orchestra who had fled Eastern Europe stayed in the West while the orchestra went behind the iron curtain, taking no chances of being detained. Then they traveled to Amsterdam for a concert at the Concertgebouw. The final concert of the tour took place on Sunday, June 16, in Scheveningen, the Dutch seaside city alongside The Hague. Szell had not previously conducted in Bremen, Stuttgart, the four Polish cities, and, surprisingly, Paris. Managers canceled concerts originally planned for Hamburg and Berlin, to make room for the Polish appearances. In October 1956 there had been an uprising against the Communist regime in Poland, centered in Poznan, and the State Department considered an American presence there of higher strategic importance than in Hamburg, or even in divided Berlin. Szell could have much regretted this: Berlin would have been one more homecoming for him. As it turned out, Prague was the city blocked. The two concerts there were completely sold out, but the Czechoslovak government canceled the orchestra's visas on short notice, without explanation. West Berlin took its place.

Tour repertoire consisted of thirty works by twenty composers. No two programs were exactly alike.[37] These concerts had an astounding effect. Until that time, not many Europeans knew about Cleveland, or even had any idea of its location. The orchestra took surprised audiences by storm; they shouted and stamped their feet. Applause reached record lengths, even after several encores. The reviews were just as ecstatic.

Berlin was typical. *Der Telegraf* wrote: "This American orchestra doubtlessly belongs to the elite of great symphony orchestras." The *Spandauer Volksblatt* reported: "Ovations without end. It turned into a festival. . . . A Berlin music spring, a surprise event and an unexpected joy." Bremen outdid itself in applause: "The festival was an overwhelming never-to-be-forgotten event. The audience of the Free Hansa City, generally considered to be somewhat cool and reserved, went into unparalleled raptures of enthusiasm."

Reviews recognized Szell as the motivating force: "The technical and artistic qualities [of the orchestra] are simply extraordinary. Unnecessary to say that this judgment is partially in respect to the conductor. Extremely dynamic and colorful, animated by a fire and an irresistible pulsation, the interpretations are coordinated by a master's hand. Szell has the gift to inflame his musicians, who are individually and collectively admirable," said the *Journal de Geneve*, Geneva.[38]

Vienna capped the tour for Szell: he brought an American orchestra that he had trained in triumph to the city considered for two centuries the center of Western music. Szell grew up and formed his musical tastes in Vienna. He was a source of pride for the city, as well. *Die Presse* claimed him for Vienna:

> What almost personally binds us with the Cleveland musicians is the fact that George Szell, who has been their conductor and artistic leader for a full ten years, can rightly be counted as one of ours. He spent his childhood and early youth in Vienna, coming from the Vienna school of Professor Richard Robert and equally early was recognized as a universally gifted musician. For the present artistic rank of the orchestra, for its high level, that background is largely responsible. When one thinks of the character of the performances, on the clear and precise manner of its musical diction, on the rhythmic exactness, on the acuteness of the dynamics and the flexible technique of the exchanges of shadings, of the transitions and preparations, so may the qualities be which rest completely with the personality of the conductor, who knows what he wants

from the music which he performs. He has a clear picture before him in which nothing is cloudy, nothing is allowed to remain approximate.[39]

On June 7, after the second concert in Vienna, Szell gave a party to celebrate his sixtieth birthday, and the tour, with the orchestra. At the party, in a suburban Viennese restaurant, the orchestra gave Szell a perfect birthday present: a first edition of *Don Giovanni*, beautifully inscribed by the musicians. For the first time, they saw tears in Szell's eyes. He was so moved that he wanted to be with the orchestra for as long as possible. Instead of taking the limousine back to his hotel, he rode in one of the buses with the musicians.

London, a city where Szell had performed since the thirties, gave no less acclaim. The Cleveland's concert caused the *New Statesman and Nation* to revise its ranking of American orchestras:

> For decades we have all firmly believed that the principal American orchestras could be classified in a fixed order of merit. Well ahead of the rest came a group of three: the Boston, the Philadelphia and the New York Philharmonic-Symphony. . . . It is time we revised our ideas. Things stay put even less in America than they do elsewhere; and the truth is that all three of these famous orchestras have passed into other hands since the days when they made their great reputations, and that not one of them now has at its head a first-rate conductor of the classical repertory. . . . It is one of the prime virtues of the Cleveland Orchestra . . . that their brilliance is entirely subordinated to strictly musical considerations. They play with the loving spontaneity of a fine European orchestra, as well as with the discipline, blend and unanimity characteristic of America.

To have an independent critic perceive and state almost in Szell's own words what his goal had been for his orchestra proved infinitely gratifying. Continuing:

> No finer orchestral playing has yet been heard in the Festival Hall, and I doubt whether anything superior is to be heard anywhere else. The particular glory of this orchestra is the smoothness, fullness and golden texture of its string tone. Passages which almost always sound harsh or scrawny came through with a comely bloom even in the far from flattering acoustics of the Festival Hall; and the theme of the finale of the Brahms's First Symphony flowed like a majestic river. The woodwind is firm and clear, there is a masterly tympanist, and the brass choir is notable for its solid resonance. . . . Such was the applause after the symphony that the orchestra gave us Berlioz's *Hungarian* March as an encore, playing now with a whiplash brilliance and bite which contrasted amazingly with their broad solidity in Brahms and Beethoven.[40]

The *London Times*' judgment of the orchestra stated that "it can now hold its own with any of the great orchestras of America, and indeed to many English ears may even be thought preferable to some of those more widely publicized. The reason for this is its mellowness. The brilliance of execution and the smartness of ensemble are both there, yet it is the golden warmth of the orchestra's tone that impresses most and differentiates it from the harder, colder virtuosity of several of its American rivals."[41]

A Casualty of the European Tour

As the tour went on, Szell grew progressively more nervous. Given the extended pressures on all, flare-ups were to be expected. What transpired was an upheaval of volcanic proportions. In Berlin, Charlotte Flatow forgot to order buses to transport the orchestra from the hotel to the airport. She realized her mistake and frantically phoned the bus company; the buses arrived, but later than scheduled. Szell mistakenly blamed manager George Smith, and in Stuttgart the next day launched into a devastating tirade in front of the orchestra. Smith gave notice of his resignation—effective a week later when the orchestra reached Paris—to Musical Arts Association president Frank Taplin, who was accompanying the orchestra. Taking Szell's side completely, Taplin fired Smith on the spot.[42]

Szell had admired Smith's musical judgment in discussions about programming and program changes, his erudition in his program notes, and his understated Bostonian manner. Szell's relationship with Vosburgh had been respectful but also warm and friendly. Vosburgh could handle Szell's tantrums; Smith did not have that capacity. Although he might have survived under normal circumstances, the first European tour was far from that.

Szell was hyper for most of the tour. A reviewer in the *Tribune de Lausanne*, who went by the nom de plume "Florestan," commented on his rapid tempi and harked back to the glory days of the American "big three." The headline translates itself: "Un splendide ensemble: l'Orchestre de Cleveland." Florestan's florid praise compared Szell and Cleveland favorably with Stokowski and Philadelphia, Koussevitzky and Boston, and Toscanini and New York. The reviewer heard the orchestra in Lugano, where Szell "sometimes allow[ed] himself to be caught up in a frenzy of tempi which transcend the golden mean." This occurred, as the critic noted, in the scherzo of Schumann's Second. Long used to the atmospheric *La mer* of Ansermet, the critic was less impressed with the clarity of Szell's interpretation. Florestan considered the Creston *Dance Overture* no more than movie music, but ended his review by saying, "but that is not an essential; what Lugano revealed to us was that this is indisputably one of the first orchestras of our time."[43]

Poland saw another triumph. Visitors from the West were as welcome as they were rare. The Poles seemed to cheer an American orchestra as an opportunity for a political demonstration against their oppressive regime; the cheers also showed appreciation for the truly overwhelming artistic experience that the Cleveland concerts represented. The newspaper *Swiat* in Warsaw wrote, "The Cleveland Symphony . . . brought about a complete change among the Polish listeners of their opinion of musical culture in the United States." Such a formal tone may have been necessary in those delicate times, especially in the Polish capital, but the State Department's efforts could not have been more fully rewarded. In Katowice, the press was less constrained: "Without a doubt, on June 9, we enjoyed one of the finest symphony orchestras that ever appeared at Slansk, the American Cleveland Orchestra. I have heard many renowned orchestras, but this orchestra is the finest I have ever heard."[44]

The plight of musicians behind the iron curtain was brought home to the members of the Cleveland Orchestra. They received generous invitations to musicians' homes. The orchestra invited local musicians to rehearsals; concert tickets were relatively expensive and given first to loyal Communist Party members. The Cleveland musicians shared supplies as much as they could spare. In an article, Frank Taplin told how, in Katowice, the first trumpeter of the orchestra had tried endlessly to obtain a new instrument through channels, but without success. Desperate, he offered to buy one of the Cleveland's trumpets. Louis Davidson, Cleveland's principal trumpet, had brought along an extra instrument, and he and his colleagues in the section acted. At dinner afterward, concertmaster Josef Gingold presented Davidson's trumpet to the Katowice Symphony conductor as a gift from the members of the Cleveland Orchestra to his orchestra. The Polish first trumpeter, Francisek Stokfiscz, thanked them: "You have changed my life." Taplin reported, "This simple gesture made an enormous impression, and word of it had already reached Cracow before our orchestra's arrival there the next day."

Taplin noted that the French stomped their feet and cheered "in one of the warmest welcomes we received." But the Poles topped all:

> For sheer heat and intensity this surpassed anything I have ever experienced in this country or Europe. It alone was the justification for the entire tour. After the performance of Brahms's First Symphony, the entire hall stood and cheered, stomped and screamed. George Szell then announced in Polish that the orchestra would play Ravel's *Daphnis et Chloé* [Suite no. 2] as an encore. This virtuoso performance, projected not only with technical perfection, but with great warmth, again set off a sizzling ovation, to which Szell responded with Berlioz' *Hungarian* March. That evening was the emotional climax of the entire trip, and no one who was there could doubt that George Szell and the Cleveland Orchestra accomplished magnificently the mission entrusted to them by the United States Government.[45]

Szell changed another Polish musician's life. He became taken with the thirty-three-year-old conductor of the Warsaw Philharmonic, who he invited to be a guest conductor in Cleveland. For that young man, Stanislaw Skrowaczewski, it was the beginning of his American and international career.

A Dutch Contretemps

An alarm sounded in Cleveland at the end of May, during the tour. The Concertgebouw Orchestra of Amsterdam announced that Szell would serve as "co-conductor" of that orchestra for three seasons beginning September 1, 1958. The *Cleveland Plain Dealer* wrote, "After next season, Szell will conduct the Concertgebouw Orchestra there for longer periods, probably two months, officials told the International News Service in Amsterdam. Amsterdam spokesmen said Szell would be considered 'second conductor,' equal in status to Eduard van Beinum, present conductor of the orchestra." It added that the Dutch concert public "might be reminded of the days when eminent French Conductor Pierre Monteux and Dutch Maestro Willem Mengelberg alternately conducted the orchestra."[46]

"George Szell," read the *Cleveland News*' report, "has been engaged by the Amsterdam Concertgebouw Orchestra as its second regular conductor for three years, it was announced today in Amsterdam according to Associated Press dispatches." The article reported, "Word of the engagement caught members of the board of directors of the Musical Arts Association here by surprise, since Szell recently signed a three-year contract to conduct the Cleveland Orchestra."[47] Szell evidently had not informed the Cleveland board or management. He may have thought it unnecessary, as it concerned only his regular time away in midwinter and in the summer, which did not threaten his Cleveland position. But that would not be generally known in Cleveland, and the timing of the announcement while Szell was away seemed especially alarming.

Frank E. Joseph, secretary of the Musical Arts Association, handled damage control at home. He "pointed out that Szell is at liberty to conduct where he wishes during his regular mid-season leave of six weeks," and "assumed" that "the extra performances that he might conduct in Amsterdam would be during the summer . . ." and would not conflict "with his duties as director of the Cleveland Orchestra in its regular season."[48]

Szell had been cultivating his Concertgebouw association for some time. In Europe in July 1954, he had lunch with its general manager, Dr. H. J. Waage, to discuss his future involvement. In November Szell followed up with a letter to Waage, advising him of his availability between December 2, 1956, and about January 15, 1957. Szell received an answer from Marius Flothuis that the Concertgebouw's schedule would not work out for that season.[49] (Although he held the title musical director, Flothuis's position was managerial. He coordinated guest conductors, soloists, programs, and schedules, while other administrators handled business details.)

In May Szell wrote van Beinum a fan letter from the French resort Eze Bord de Mer: "Yesterday evening I turned on my radio and heard from Paris such an enchanting performance of the 'Miracle' [Symphony, no. 96 in D] by Haydn that I was full of curiosity as to who this master conductor with the great orchestra could be." It was a recording by van Beinum and the Concertgebouw. "Bravo, bravo," Szell wrote.[50] Van Beinum replied to Szell, then rehearsing with the Concertgebouw for the Holland Festival: "With your letter . . . you have given me great joy." Van Beinum wrote that he loved that Haydn symphony "with all his heart."[51] Szell invited van Beinum to perform as guest conductor for a week in Cleveland in December 1955. Szell's appointment initially referred to "first conductor, next to and with Mr. Eduard van Beinum." The title was not acceptable to Szell. In Europe that rank was considered subordinate to the music director. The official letter of agreement called Szell "co-conductor to Mr. van Beinum."

Szell's 1957 European Summer; Changes in Cleveland

The orchestra returned to Cleveland to a hero's welcome in June. The Szells remained in Europe for the rest of the summer. They spent a week in Paris, picked up their automobile stored there, and motored to Switzerland for three weeks of rest. From July 20 to August 28, Szell conducted the world premiere of Rolf Liebermann's *Die Schule der Frauen (School for Wives)* at the Salzburg Festival. It featured a stellar cast and was "the most successful premiere of a new opera in the history of the Salzburg Festival."[52] Szell conducted a Mozart concert with piano soloist Leon Fleisher and an orchestra composed of forty-five members of the Berlin Philharmonic. Audience and critics greeted the performance with acclaim for conductor and soloist, who was making his Festival debut.

The following week, van Beinum, who was to conduct the Berlin Philharmonic, took ill, and Szell was called on to conduct. Younger than Szell by four years, van Beinum was in failing health. Szell took over van Beinum's program intact, except for changing its order: Debussy, *La mer;* Mendelssohn, Violin Concerto (Nathan Milstein); and Beethoven, *Eroica.* It proved an artistic triumph for Szell, who conducted as usual without scores. The reviews praised him to the skies, noting that with "virtually no rehearsal," he imparted his interpretations and produced infinite shadings of color in the Debussy, accompanied and partnered Milstein brilliantly, and led a magnificent *Eroica.* One reviewer noted that in the Beethoven, Szell "never for a moment got bogged down in details and nuances, for all that he lavished great love and attention on them." And in the Debussy, Szell had the Berliners produce colors "more firmly and more keenly than usual."[53] This was Szell's reunion with the Berlin orchestra after a gap of over four decades, and he would be a regular guest conductor thereafter.

Alfred Beverly Barksdale, supervisor of music for the Toledo Museum of Art, had been hired as assistant manager to George Smith, to begin in the fall. With Smith's firing, Barksdale found himself promoted before he put in a day's work. He became manager of the Cleveland Orchestra on July 15, and was sent to Salzburg in mid-August to work with Szell for ten days.

The organization would undergo another crucial change that summer. Frank E. Taplin accepted the position of assistant to the president of Princeton University, and he stepped down as president of the Musical Arts Association. Frank E. Joseph, a Cleveland attorney, who had been a trustee since the 1952–53 season and then secretary of the association, replaced him. Joseph's wife, Martha, had already been a trustee for two years because she was president of the Women's Committee.

From Crans in July, Szell welcomed Barksdale warmly: "I want to wish you the very best of luck in a job which at this point might perhaps be termed an unenviable one. At the same time I want to assure you that I shall do everything in my power to help making it in the shortest possible time a very enviable one." Stressing his availability in his most diligent musical director mode, he added, "call on my help at any time, vacation or no vacation." Barksdale appreciated Szell's assurance: "I am sure that with such help that will come to pass." Aware of past tensions, Szell wrote Barksdale that he looked forward to seeing him in Salzburg and that he was "altogether looking forward very much to working with you, trusting that you will reestablish at Severance Hall the cheerful and friendly atmosphere which has been absent since Vosburgh's death,—even after Martin's leaving."[54]

Szell knew how important the European successes were to the Cleveland Orchestra's reputation and touring fees at home. He wrote Joseph about exploiting "to the utmost, the simply incredible success of the Orchestra in Europe. Impress upon the AMERICAN,- not only the Cleveland,- public the fact that the C.O. has definitely been recognized internationally as one of the very very top ranking Orchestras of the world. This has to be pounded in, kept alive, reiterated, in the most effective way, or else, the European success will have been squandered."[55] Szell suggested printing a special brochure, and told Barksdale that he possessed "a practically complete collection of European reviews and would suggest we take one or two sentences or a characteristic paragraph, IMPECCABLY TRANSLATED, from each town."[56] On the personal side, Szell gave Barksdale advice on house hunting, recommending a real estate agent. This established a sound beginning. Barksdale would work effectively with Szell for the next thirteen years.

9

The Golden Years (1957–65)

The 1957 European tour had been phenomenally successful. Cleveland could now believe that its orchestra was the equal of the best in the world. This was not just local pride, but a fact. Through Szell's training and his addition of great players, the orchestra had become a great instrument.

At his apartment in New York in late September, Szell auditioned a prospective violinist.[1] First-chair musicians were, naturally, critically important. Szell chose them with care not only for their musical excellence, but also for their attitude and leadership potential. He selected section players just as carefully; audiences might not note their presence, but their individual and collective contributions prove vital to the quality and depth of the entire ensemble. Among those engaged for the 1957–58 season included Leonard Samuels, violin, and Donald White, cello.[2]

Samuels's story illustrates a part of Szell's musical prowess and also his pride in his orchestra and the conductor's understanding of the powerful effect it makes on a new player. In both Samuels's audition and first day on the job, he experienced an element of shock. In his audition, it came while he played the first movement of Mozart's Violin Concerto no. 5, in A Major.[3] Starting at the solo violin's entrance in the pause after the orchestral introduction, Samuels concentrated intensely, with eyes closed, to play as beautifully as he could the two notes leading to the reentrance of the orchestra. Hearing the orchestra part played on the piano startled him, unaware that Szell had quickly and silently moved a distance over the carpet to the keyboard. Opening his eyes, Samuels saw Szell playing while still standing. Quickly recovering, he continued, with Szell accompanying without score. Szell did not tell Samuels to stop, so the violinist continued. A battle of wills ensued as to who would stop first, and they played on to the end of the movement. Samuels passed the audition and took his place as one of only six new players that season.

Samuels never forgot his first day in the orchestra, which might have turned out to be his last. The first rehearsal began with the overture to Weber's *Euryanthe*. Szell gave a vigorous upbeat while looking at the first violins, who play the theme, a difficult, fast arpeggio passage, supported by a solid chord in the rest of the orchestra. Samuels, who had heard the orchestra only from the outside, was completely unprepared for the power of its sound from within and was struck motionless. He thought, "I've really done it, I'll be the first person to lose his job with the orchestra without having played a note." Szell noticed, of course, but said nothing. He just stopped and began again. This time Samuels played. At the rehearsal break, Szell left the podium and walked straight toward Samuels, looking at him all the while. Expecting to be fired on the spot, Samuels thought, "Now here it comes." Szell stopped directly in front of him, paused, and with understanding and pride said: "Isn't this a wonderful orchestra!"[4]

In 1957, White's appointment made the news. The *Cleveland News*'s headline read: "Orchestra Here Signs First Negro." The *Plain Dealer* headlined: "Negro Cellist in City Orchestra"[5] Both articles echoed the press release's assurance that White "has met the rigid requirements of musicianship demanded by Conductor George Szell." He had indeed; White stayed in the orchestra until his retirement in the 1990s.

White did not know at the time, but later found out, that a poll had been taken of the orchestra members to learn if they objected to his joining them. Four voted against White, but Szell hired him. Thirty-five years later, White was interviewed for a periodical serving African American symphony musicians:

> George Szell hired White and was his principal supporter. "Szell had a reputation for being a martinet—brutal and ruthless, which he was," says White. "But on things political, he was a liberal. When I first got into the orchestra—when I'd go out to warm up, he'd be out checking bowings or something, and he would just put his hand on my shoulder. He wouldn't say anything, but it was a gesture of support that meant more to me than words." On a tour of Europe [1965], the orchestra was supposed to play music representative of American composers. Szell did something that was unheard of in those days—he took along a work by African-American composer, William Grant Still, *In Memoriam: The Colored Soldiers Who Died for Democracy*. White says, "He made an effort to be *really* representative of American composers."[6]

Hiring White then showed a measure of courage that was tested in an incident eight years later. In Birmingham, Alabama, in March 1961, attendants at the stage door refused White admittance until several orchestra members identified him. The auditorium manager told Barksdale of "a city ordinance prohibiting the appearance of blacks and whites together in any public place." Barksdale told him that "they either played with all members present, or would not play at all." Barksdale conferred with Szell, who completely agreed. At the suggestion of the hall manager, Barksdale phoned the mayor and told him of their ultimatum. The mayor gave permission to proceed with the concert. "There were no incidents," Barksdale wrote, and "at the end of the concert, several people came backstage to thank us for taking this courageous stand."[7]

The Fortieth Anniversary Season: 1957–58

The 1957–58 season, Szell's twelfth and the orchestra's fortieth, presented nine of the works commissioned for the anniversary. A tenth, by Henri Dutilleux, would come several seasons late.[8] Szell did not let the commissioned works completely supplant his custom of offering works new to Cleveland. He had established this practice in his first season, but there were, naturally, fewer of them than usual.[9]

The first subscription pair on October 10 and 12 began traditionally, with Weber's Overture to *Euryanthe* and Beethoven's Seventh Symphony. Setting the tone for the season, after intermission came the first commission: American composer Alvin Etler's *Concerto in One Movement*. It ended with the flamboyant *Capriccio espagnol* by Rimsky-Korsakov. Szell had placed this on his recording agenda—not until February–March—but evidently he felt it fit well in this program. The second program surrounded Paul Creston's *Toccata* with Haydn's Symphony no. 99 and Schubert's "Great" C Major Symphony, both soon to be recorded. Elwell termed the Creston a "high point . . . a dazzling show piece of remarkable skill and fluency, allotting to almost every instrument and section of the orchestra some bit of ingenious technical display."[10]

On the sixth program, the orchestra played Boris Blacher's *Music for Cleveland*, an anniversary commission. Cello soloist Pierre Fournier appeared in two works: Saint-Saëns's Cello Concerto and Strauss's tone poem *Don Quixote*. Fournier was Szell's favorite for the Strauss, as he possessed the subtlety and technical command for that great curiosity, a tone-poem-concerto for cello. From late November 1957 through early January 1958, Szell divided his time away between the Concertgebouw of Amsterdam and the Vienna State Opera. Guest conductors Paul Paray and William Steinberg each led a subscription pair, and Robert Shaw presided over four.

Selections from Szell's reviews with the Concertgebouw and the Vienna Opera appeared in the Cleveland Orchestra program book on his return. The Dutch quotes were ecstatic: "The joy over George Szell's work with the Concertgebouw Orchestra remains undiminished." "With a program of Mozart and Sibelius this conductor played his highest trump cards." "To hear an orchestra play in this fashion leads one almost to the conclusion that there are no bad compositions, only good and bad conductors."[11]

Szell had conducted what was essentially the Vienna Opera at the Salzburg Festival, but this would mark his debut with the opera in its and his hometown. He conducted two Richard Strauss masterpieces with which he had been associated since his youth: *Salome*, on December 30, 1957, and *Ariadne auf Naxos*, on January 5, 1958. Extracts from reviews appeared in the orchestra's program booklet. For *Ariadne auf Naxos*: "The dramatic essence, admirably transparent . . . yet woven with highest intensity unfolded under Szell's hands to perhaps the most superb tapestry ever found by 'Ariadne'"; "Only a conductor as outstanding as George Szell is able to add new highlights to this opera." For *Salome*, most of the press was positive: "George Szell for the first time at the State Opera but henceforth, we hope, a regular guest, has interpreted the 'Salome' music magnificently, with dramatic tension and most careful tonal balance." The *Die Presse* reviewer attributed the glow of the orchestra's response to Szell to his absorption of the Vienna style and tradition from his childhood and youth there. The *Bild-Telegraf* said, "It was a fast *Salome* but not a hectic one.[12] One review, not quoted in the Cleveland Orchestra program, disagreed: "It was the fastest and loudest *Salome* in a long time. . . . Normally one understands hardly the half of what is sung in an opera evening. Yesterday evening there were at most five sentences whose meaning was clear, and these in two supporting roles."[13]

In Amsterdam Szell met with the Concertgebouw administration and agreed that he would increase his engagement in 1959–60 and 1960–61, contingent on Cleveland's schedule. Szell and the Concertgebouw's Marius Flothuis carried on a lively correspondence about music and soloists. Kindred spirits, they shared a sense of humor, love of music, and deep respect for each other's musical knowledge. Flothuis was considerate and thoughtful, suggesting that Szell make changes in a program for logistical reasons, but from Szell's reply, he realized that two of the works were not congenial to him. Flothuis then looked for other solutions, so Szell would not have to conduct two works on a program "*contre-coeur.*" Szell wanted his favorite soloists as much as possible, once writing Flothuis that he would very much like to have Leon Fleisher: "I consider him the finest musician on the piano of his generation."[14]

Szell's first concert on returning to Cleveland, January 16 and 18, 1958, featured Erica Morini in the Beethoven concerto. He wrote ecstatically of her to Flothuis: "It was the noblest, purest and maturest rendition of this piece I have experienced in many years and I think it is unmatched by any other violinist today." "I wonder whether you have engaged definitely Schwarzkopf," he also wrote. "If she should not be available, or if for some other reason her engagement should fall through, would that not alleviate the budgetary situation so as to make it easier to engage Morini?"[15] Brahms's Third on the first half of the program impressed not only Elwell, but the orchestra: "Szell obviously, was in his element with the Brahms Third. . . . There was much applause, and some of it came even from the musicians themselves, in spontaneous admiration for Szell's accomplishment."[16]

January held premieres of several 40th anniversary commissioned works, two of which were also played on tour: Howard Hanson's *Mosaics* and William Walton's *Partita for Orchestra*. The only commissioned work for solo instrument and orchestra was Peter Mennin's Piano Concerto, with Cleveland pianist Eunice Podis. Mennin, a thirty-three-year-old American on the composition faculty of the Juilliard School of Music, recalled that in 1947 he learned that Szell had programmed his Third Symphony for Cleveland the following year. He attended one of Szell's New York Philharmonic rehearsals and introduced himself. In the midst of another program and long before the scheduled Cleveland performance, Szell asked him several questions and impressed Mennin with his knowledge of the score; for example, "Near the end of the first movement, which do you want to hear more, the trumpets who play the first theme or the broad line in the strings?"

Six years later, while Szell prepared Mennin's Seventh Symphony for its 1964 world premiere with the Cleveland Orchestra, he and the composer had a lengthy correspondence about musical details and analysis of its structure. According to Mennin, "He really knew the piece, knew it as well as I did." Szell suggested saving a fortissimo marking for the real climax of the piece, holding it down in an earlier spot where Mennin had marked double forte. Szell also suggested doubling a horn line exactly as Mennin had originally written but on second thought had taken out. Szell instinctively confirmed his first idea, and Mennin put it back; so it stands in the printed score. Mennin felt deeply impressed that Szell knew the score in advance, not learning it in rehearsal. Asked if that was not the way with most conductors, Mennin said, "In my experience, no."[17]

Arthur Loesser described Mennin's Piano Concerto: "It is a true concerto in the post-Baroque meaning of the term. The solo instrument plays a dominant role, pitted against the orchestra. The solo part takes the amplest advantage of the larger resources of the piano; and it is written to suit the capacities of a performer of virtuoso caliber—in this case, specifically of Eunice Podis who is soloist in the world première."[18]

The concerto was first performed in Cleveland on February 27 and March 1, 1958; and its first New York performance was on March 7. Podis encountered much excitement with the premiere. The score arrived late. "The concerto was scheduled to be performed about February," Podis said, "and I was supposed to have it the preceding fall and Peter kept writing to say it was on the way." She continued learning the complicated score backward, because Mennin was composing the work in reverse order. Rehearsing the concerto with Szell at a second piano, Podis remarked, in amazement: "From a manuscript score [he] played the orchestral accompaniment on a second piano up to tempo, in a way that was absolutely staggering to me." Her husband, Robert Weiskopf, a competent amateur conductor, turned the pages: "The minute [Szell] would get to the last line of the page he would say 'turn' because he was obviously reading ahead five or six bars at a time. Bob had never seen the like."[19]

Elwell found the concerto "exciting," the performance by Podis, Szell, and the orchestra "amazingly brilliant," and he described the "enthusiastic applause, which the composer was present to acknowledge with the performers," with "several recalls." The New York critic Gid Waldrop, editor of the *Musical Courier,* found the concerto "an effective audience piece, an ideal vehicle to display the pianist's technical virtuosity and is excitingly scored. But judging from a single hearing it is more than this. It is a good piece of music, something relatively rare among concertos by contemporary composers." Podis, he said, "has technique to burn, a big powerful tone and fine sense of nuance. It was clear that she had a complete understanding of the composer's intent."[20]

On April 21, 1958, Szell signed his sixth Cleveland contract; it covered four seasons, 1958–59 through 1961–62. A new provision stated that after leaving the orchestra, Szell would continue for some years in a paid advisory status. Szell ended the orchestra's fortieth season with Mozart's Fortieth Symphony and Beethoven's Ninth. He soon left for an active summer of conducting in Europe, with time for vacation, golfing in Crans the first three weeks of July.

Szell conducted Concertgebouw concerts at the Holland Festival in Scheveningen at the end of July, and in Salzburg in early August. Earlier he had exchanged contentious letters with the Concertgebouw over the rehearsal schedule of its Salzburg segment. Wolfgang Sawallisch would conduct the first concert in Salzburg, all-Mozart, using a small orchestra. Szell followed with two concerts: one all Mozart, the other all twentieth-century, with full orchestra. The proposed schedule allotted Szell less rehearsal than he considered necessary for his second Salzburg program. He threatened to withdraw, but the Concertgebouw management added an extra rehearsal.

In August Szell tried a new mountain retreat, the Kurhotel Montafon in Schrung, Austria, and returned at the end of the month to an old favorite, the Dolder Grand Hotel in Zurich. He wrote then to the Concertgebouw with some inside information from Switzerland: "You might well be pleased to know [underlined by Szell] that the Lucerne Festival Board has decided to invite the Concertgebouw for 1960. The official decision will be made public tomorrow and you will hear from them almost immediately."[21]

In the third week of September Szell led two performances of Beethoven's Missa Solemnis at La Scala. He wrote: "Good chorus, fair soloists, rather indifferent orchestra, big success."[22] On September 27 the Szells flew from Paris to New York, leaving only a week before Szell began rehearsals for the forty-first season opening on Thursday, October 9, 1958.

A New Sound at Severance Hall

Szell returned to a new sound in Severance Hall. During the summer months, construction of acoustic renovations he had long identified as a necessity had taken place. As early as 1947 Szell had asked a consultant, Clifford M. Swan, for an acoustical evaluation of Severance Hall. Swan succinctly summed it up: "Your auditorium has far too much absorption to please the musical ear."[23] But no changes were made at that time.

A few years later Szell met Robert Shankland, professor of physics at the Case Institute of Technology. Shankland had naively recommended his friend, pianist Grant Johannesen, for a solo engagement with the orchestra. Szell replied that he knew Johannesen, "and I think we'll have him but I'd like to have you come over and talk to me about architectural acoustics." Shankland and Szell each learned from the other: Szell gave Shankland detailed analyses of the sounds of the many halls in which he conducted, and Shankland gave Szell the scientific vocabulary and bases of understanding of his observations. Szell's extraordinary hearing, buttressed by scientific principles from Shankland, enabled him to speak the language of acoustical engineers in several later design or renovation projects.

At Szell's request Shankland studied the acoustics of Severance Hall and provided recommendations for improvement.[24] The following summer, and again in November, modifications according to Shankland's design were made to the stage shell; mainly, it was covered with one-eighth-inch plywood panels with "thin muslin glued to the surface." Shankland recommended further alterations, including changing the angle of the shell's sides and top, removing carpeting in the hall, and increasing the area of wood paneling.

Szell's grasp of physics greatly impressed Shankland, especially his acute perceptions of the acoustical properties of halls and the reasons for their differences: "I found Dr. Szell to be extremely understanding of problems of physics. Now he didn't use the vocabulary that we use but the concepts and how they relate, the properties of the hall . . . what you hear and how you change the character of the sound generated by an orchestra. . . . He was a genius in that respect. I really believe had Szell gone in any other line of work besides orchestral conducting, including physics, he'd have gone clear to the top."

Reverberation time had been the gold standard in concert hall acoustics for years: "a concert hall to be good was supposed to have two seconds reverberation time." Szell told Shankland that reverberation "is not the whole story by a long shot." Shankland realized that Szell's understanding went beyond the conventional wisdom of the time. The physicist related, "The important things in a hall are what we would now call diffusing elements for sound." Shankland saw that Szell instinctively understood the principle of diffusion and its effect but did not know the term for it. "He was very, very conscious of the shape of the halls and was convinced that the rectangular shape was ideal as in Boston, Vienna, or Washington."[25] Shankland was a physicist and not an acoustician, so he did not expect responsibility for the changes to Severance Hall. Szell later recommended him for designing concert shells for the

Toledo Museum of Art and for Cleveland's suburban Lakewood and Parma, which he performed very competently. Their pleasant and mutually instructive friendship continued until Szell's death.

In 1957 Szell directed the hiring of Heinrich Keilholz, of Hamburg, to carry out his conception of the sound he wanted for Severance Hall. The Salzburg Festival had engaged Keilholz, professionally a recording engineer, to design the acoustics of the new Festspielhaus, under construction in 1957. Beverly Barksdale supervised the 1958 implementation of Keilholz's acoustic renovation of Severance Hall. In spite of a building-industry strike, the project took only ten weeks. The firm of Sam W. Emerson served as general contractor. Keilholz made drastic changes to the Hall, setting its acoustical personality for the next forty-two years.[26]

Swan's, Shankland's, and Keilholz's analyses agreed on the essentials of the problem. The old acoustics were clear but dry and not reverberant, and the sound of the strings was distant. The shell with flat sides, a back, and a roof surrounded the orchestra. A proscenium curtain—when open it draped at the sides of the stage—and carpeting in the auditorium's aisles absorbed the sound.

Keilholz designed a massive permanent wooden shell in place of the old wood and canvas one. A new curtain opened from the center and retracted completely out of sight. The thick blue carpeting in the aisles was replaced by blue flooring of a slightly rubbery texture. Sound now traveled along the angled top of the shell and reflected from its surface into the auditorium. Recessed ranks of high-powered bulbs spread light evenly from the back of the shell to the front; the front row of lights was set into the new curved proscenium. Metal reflectors increased the bulbs' brightness. Maple veneer over top-grade plywood composed the shell. Horizontal sections had a convex shape, to mix and spread the sound frequencies before they reflected into the house—"diffusion." Workers filled the hollow shell with sand to a height of nine feet. A rigid steel frame anchored to the stage floor braced the shell from behind and above.

The acoustic change was spectacular. The shell acted as an amplifier, strengthening the weakest sound and thrusting it directly into the hall with tremendous energy. The sheer power of the orchestra had been not only fully unleashed, but amplified. Bain Murray wrote that Szell and the orchestra "made musical history last night when Cleveland's great conductor and his distinguished musicians opened the orchestra's 41st season." He liked the "handsome, modernistic shell," which "has made Severance Hall one of the most acoustically perfect concert halls in the world." He understood Szell's programming, which "displayed rich sonorities, new, live sounds and mellow blendings to perfection."[27]

Szell's program showed a wide variety of styles and sounds. In the first half came the Prelude to *Die Meistersinger* and Brahms's Fourth. The second half featured two brilliant twentieth-century works: Walton's *Partita*, a repeat from the previous season, and Stravinsky's 1919 suite from the *Firebird*. Five more subscription programs followed. Soloists included Dietrich Fischer-Dieskau, Elisabeth Schwarzkopf, Robert Casadesus, and Guiomar Novaës. Szell also presented new music by Barber and Krenek, and Copland's *Appalachian Spring* ballet suite for his first (and only) time in Cleveland. Szell never felt comfortable with music containing rapid meter changes, and several sections of the Copland score are notorious for that. Szell would bring it to the Concertgebouw, so he worked it out first at home.

Szell spent most of December with the Concertgebouw, marking his twenty-fifth anniversary in Holland. Arthur Rubinstein, who had been the soloist when Szell made his Dutch debut with the Hague Orchestra in 1933, performed Tchaikovsky's Piano Concerto no. 1. Szell included two Cleveland fortieth anniversary commissions: Walton's *Partita* and von Einem's *Ballade*. Besides the Copland, he introduced *Music for Orchestra*, by Wallingford Riegger.

The death of Szell's friend Percy Brown in December deeply affected him. As a memorial tribute, Szell dedicated an entire January Cleveland program chosen from Brown's favorites: Bach *Brandenburg* Concerto no. 3, Mozart Symphony no. 40, and Beethoven's Sixth. Szell's interpretation of the Beethoven in his first guest concert in 1944 in Cleveland had won Brown over. Brown's widow, Helen, remained powerfully moved, thirty years later, by her memory of that occasion.[28]

In 1959 the orchestra's eastern tour split into two parts. The first two Carnegie Hall concerts took place in early February. On February 4 it consisted of all Beethoven: the Overture to *Coriolanus*, Symphony no. 6, and the Piano Concerto no. 5, with Clifford Curzon. The February 10 concert received reviews by Harold C. Schonberg, Paul Henry Lang, and Louis Biancolli. Schonberg wrote, "One can do no more than echo the current critical opinion about the high state of the Cleveland Orchestra. It is a superbly disciplined organization; it has by now a burnished tone, and its solo playing is of high caliber. In short, it is one of the world's very great orchestras." "How glorious this great orchestra sounds," Lang wrote, "all color and power, yet capable of the most delicate timbres." Biancolli wrote, "Most stupendous of all was the reading of Strauss' 'Death and Transfiguration.' The power of the young Strauss was astounding; no less so was that of George Szell last night."[29]

Mozart's E-flat Piano Concerto (K. 271), with Rudolf Firkusny, exemplified a Szell precept. "Part of the training of the Cleveland Orchestra," Szell said a few years later, "lay in the choice of soloists, who have been, and remain, not only the best but, among the best, those who hold similar views to mine in their attitudes towards performance. The great instrumentalists who have played with the orchestra have stimulated and inspired the orchestra in the same direction in which I am working."[30] Szell's Mozart pianists were Badura-Skoda, Casadesus, Curzon, Eschenbach, Firkusny, Fleisher, Istomin, Loesser, Schnabel, Serkin, and Szell himself.

Earlier that season Herbert Elwell had devoted a Sunday column to Szell's observation that "there has been a marked change in the attitude of symphony concert audiences toward new music." He quoted Szell as saying "Ten years ago people complained when I programmed a new work. Today they complain if a symphony program does NOT contain a new work." Elwell concurred in principle, observing that "a general interest in new works is certainly reflected in applause at Severance Hall, when new works are performed there; also in the fact that box office intake does not suffer when a new work is programmed."[31] This surely owed to Szell's long-term efforts at playing a continuous representation of contemporary orchestral music along with standard fare. He privately made it clear that this was not out of love but out of a sense of duty, for the orchestra, the audience, and for the future of music itself.

In an article at the end of March, Szell discussed training the audience. The interviewer mentioned the Dvořák G Major Symphony, the first Epic Records release of music recorded in the acoustically remodeled Severance Hall. It began with the premise, "Sometimes it's the audience that has to be trained. And conductor George Szell . . . thinks Cleveland audiences are pretty well trained by now. 'They will listen attentively to whatever we play. It's really more a question of playing what I think is the best music; but, over a period of years. They're an ideal audience.'" "He is proud of his orchestra, particularly of the way it could 'shift gears' from one style of music to another." The article asserted that the orchestra "plays more modern works than most orchestras." Szell added: "That is part of an orchestra's job."[32]

In February 1959 Szell conducted the world premiere of the Second Symphony by George Rochberg. Rochberg had studied composition with Szell at the Mannes School of Music in the 1940s. The Philadelphia Orchestra, under Ormandy, performed his first symphony, written in 1948–49. Rochberg composed his Second Symphony, a twelve-tone work, in the fifties. He told how Szell came to play it: in 1958, the composer was walking on Chestnut Street in Philadelphia, when he heard his name "bellowed out at the top of this man's voice only the way one man in my life has pronounced my name, CHROOOSHSHBERG! You could have heard him three or four blocks away in any direction. And I turned and there was Szell . . . looking like a million bucks. He had on this wonderful kind of Homburg. He had this winter coat with a fur collar. He looked positively elegant." Szell was in town to guest conduct the Philadelphia Orchestra.

Szell asked Rochberg to bring the scores to a meeting the next day. Rochberg took him to the nearby offices of the publisher, Theodore Presser, for whom he was working at the time. Years later the composer remembered that an invitation "to a young composer from a great conductor . . . is enough to help you grow eagle's wings in five seconds." Ten days later Szell called the composer and, without preliminaries, said, "I am going to play your Second Symphony."

The symphony, in Rochberg's words, is "very chromatic, very atonal, very intense, and . . . uncompromising. . . . It literally doesn't give an inch." After the first rehearsal, Szell confided: "You know, eleven years ago I could not have performed this with this orchestra. I had to train this orchestra so that they would be able to do such a work." The composer felt more than pleased: "Did they play it! God, it was fantastic!" It came across "ferocious, because you know the kind of masculine drive that that man had, the kind of compact, solid pressure. . . . It was like something of enormous power that knew how to put pressure just at the right spots and they would take on this ferocious solidity."[33]

After the death of Percy Brown, another sad event darkened that season. On April 13, 1959, Flothuis wired Szell: "regret have to announce you passing of eduard van beinum during todays rehearsal." The next day, at the end of a dictated letter to Flothuis on routine matters, Szell said: "I cannot close this letter without saying once more what a shock it was for all of us to learn of van Beinum's death. The only comfort is that he died in action—the most desirable death anyway."[34]

After a little less than a week in New York, the Szells left for Europe. They spent a day in Amsterdam on Concertgebouw business en route to Hamburg for Szell's first concerts of the summer. Pierre Fournier was soloist in a program of Mozart, Haydn, and Brahms. From there Szell traveled to Prague for the first time since 1937. It was a sentimental journey, made doubly poignant by the Czech authorities' previous cancellation of planned concerts on the 1957 Cleveland Orchestra European tour. It was possibly too sentimental for Helene: she remained in England visiting her sister. On June 3 and 4, 1959, Szell led Beethoven's Ninth Symphony with the Czech Philharmonic in the closing concerts of the Prague Festival. The applause continued for twenty-two minutes (longer than the choral finale takes to perform), and Szell "was recalled to the stage 16 times after the second concert," Beverly Barksdale reported.[35]

Szell returned to Paris, where he picked up his automobile, celebrated his 62nd birthday, and drove to Zurich. There he entered the Bircher-Benner Clinic for a health regimen. By June 22, he could write Helene: "Tomorrow I leave here very comfortably a total of 8–9 pounds lighter, with shrunken stomach and lessened appetite, otherwise well and fresh."[36] Most of Szell's letters to Helene dealt with their own concerns: a visit from an old friend, information about their bank accounts in Zurich, which were doing well, and miscellaneous news about musical and business matters. In one letter, he reported sitting through an entire performance of *Das Rheingold* to hear a singer in the role of Erda as a favor for a friend who knew the singer's father. "Musically only average," he judged.

From June 25 to July 15 Szell enjoyed his favorite golfing retreat in Crans. En route he made contact with the Lucerne Festival, thus he could write a PPPPPS: "Luzern perfect. 6 Sept. 60 with the Berlin Philharmonic." He loved the Hotel du Golf, writing Helene on June 26, "All is of the best, board already in the bed, the most considerate reception, old personnel." He told her of his travels from Zurich: "Wengen is a miserable little village full of the jargon of tourists from Northern Germany." He spent the night in a chateau in the Berner Oberland, then traveled via Lausanne, where his auto received its ten-thousand-kilometer servicing, to stay overnight in Villars and visit Igor Markevitch. Szell had heard the Markevitch concert that preceded his in Prague ("Sacre, what else") and met him afterward. Markevitch "gushed on about the evening spent in our house [on a Cleveland visit]. . . . He said there was a HERRRRliches piece of ground near him and I should come and see it and also his house. . . . [It is] really very beautiful if also a bit overdecorated, with wonderful old things, then we saw some building plots of land for sale. Villars lies much as Crans, high over the Rhone Valley, BUT,—no comparison . . . in addition thousands of horseflies. So let's get that out of our heads." The letter was one of many signed by the Szells with nicknames for each other: "Mugi" (hers), "Pussi" (his). The typewritten message included PS, PPS, PPPPPS additions in handwriting on three of its margins, and at the bottom in all caps: KANSTMARAUCHMALSCHREIBM! (Loose translation: Can't you also write once in a while!)[37]

Szell opened the Salzburg Festival on July 26, 1959, with a new production of *Die Zauberflöte*, directed by Gunther Rennert, with the Vienna Philharmonic and a stellar cast. He wrote his own review in a letter to Barksdale: "The Magic Flute last night went extremely well. The main feature was the new production which was so imaginative and of so light a touch, and so well integrated that I must say I never saw or heard anything better. Musically it went to perfection."[38] There were four more performances. A recording reveals Szell at his Mozartean best, with elegance, wit, lively pacing, and noble majesty.[39] It was the last staged opera he would conduct. On August 3 Szell led a Haydn-Mozart concert with the National Orchestra of the French Radio and Erica Morini.

Szell's European musical summer ended on September 28 with Beethoven's Ninth with the West German Radio Orchestra and Chorus in Bonn. It was the concluding event in the inaugural celebration of the rebuilt Beethoven Concert Hall. Marius Flothuis and Jacob Krachmalnick made a brief visit to Szell at his hotel in Cologne; they drove there from Amsterdam and back the same day. Before the performance, Szell received a cable from Amsterdam: "wish you a beautiful performance tonight best regards," signed "piet jake tibor herman flot" (Heuwekemeijer, Krachmalnick, two principal players from the orchestra, and Flothuis).[40]

The Szells then flew back to New York, where he judged the twentieth Leventritt competition that year for pianists. Other jurors were Rudolf Firkusny, Leon Fleisher, Gary Graffman, Eugene Istomin, Leopold Mannes, Nadia Reisenberg, and Rudolf Serkin. The winner, Malcolm Frager, would appear as soloist in Cleveland in spring.

By Monday, October 5, Szell had begun rehearsals for the opening week of the Cleveland Orchestra's forty-second and his fourteenth season (1959–60). The obligatory beginning-of-season interview took a culinary as well as musical turn, picturing Szell in a poetic and nostalgic mood: "An eminent musician is George Szell. And he is also a gourmet." Szell said: "I am at this moment thinking of [great food]. But

I have not time for it. No time for it when you are busy. It is a pity. . . . After all most great musicians have liked fine food. Have not music and food always been together? I think so." Szell said he did not do much cooking anymore because he was busy, "But my wife complains whenever I am cooking. I suppose I disarrange her kitchen. She prefers that I do not do cooking," except "When she is ill . . . I do well and she is pleased. Yes, she is pleased then." A dish Szell liked to prepare was boeuf bourguignon, "'Ah, but a salad,' he said happily. 'Like an orchestration.' And he made his hands move in graceful arcs over an imaginary bowl." A question about his composing seemed to ruffle Szell, yet his answer sounded almost poignant: "The 62-year-old conductor said he had not himself composed a piece of music lately. 'That was 35 or 40 years ago,' he said impatiently. 'It was something for orchestra. Since I concentrate so much on the works of others, I cannot concentrate on anything of my own.'"[41]

Ten new members joined the orchestra that season, among them Arnold Steinhardt, Jerome Rosen, and Alfred Genovese. Steinhardt had been the Leventritt violin competition winner the previous year. Through that prize, Steinhardt appeared as soloist the previous season but was now the new assistant concertmaster, replacing Anshel Brusilow, who took the concertmaster chair in Philadelphia. Rosen, a finalist in the Leventritt violin competition won by Steinhardt, joined the orchestra as apprentice conductor.[42] Genovese, principal oboe of the St. Louis Symphony, replaced Marc Lifschey, who had joined the Metropolitan Opera Orchestra.

The Cleveland Orchestra was now the largest in its history with 104 musicians. The first concert of the forty-second season, on October 8, 1959, was unique: a soloist appeared on the opening concert—the eighteen-year-old violinist Jaime Laredo. "An extraordinary honor accorded by George Szell," read the program.[43] A native of Bolivia, Laredo was already well known in Cleveland as a scholarship student at the Music School Settlement, aided by the Cleveland Chapter of the Society for Strings. A former student of Ivan Galamian and Josef Gingold, Laredo had just won the prestigious Queen Elizabeth of Belgium International Music Competition that May. His vehicle in the opening concert was the thorny Sibelius Concerto.

Szell received an international honor at the trustees' party in the Severance Hall Board Room following the opening concert. Dr. Margarethe Bitter, consul at Cleveland, presented the Commander's Cross of the Order of Merit of the Federal Republic of Germany to Szell. The certificate accompanying the award had been signed by Theodore Heuss before his retirement as German president. Instituted in 1951, the award recognized contributions to the peaceful rehabilitation of Germany. In her speech, Dr. Bitter noted that Szell had "masterfully interpret[ed] music from Germany, including works by contemporary composers," and "participat[ed] in the Festival for the Inauguration of the Beethovenhalle in Bonn, conducting the 9th Symphony of Beethoven," had engaged German artists to perform in Cleveland,

and "performed in Germany with the famous Cleveland Orchestra." Dr. Bitter asserted that Szell "has contributed signally in creating an atmosphere of friendship and understanding for Germany, thus helping its rehabilitation after the darkest period of its history." There is a lovely photograph of Mrs. Szell admiring the medal, which Szell wore around his neck.

The second program was all orchestral. Two years after the fortieth anniversary season, Szell continued to introduce new music; now he programmed the first Cleveland performances of the Symphony no. 2 by Benjamin Lees. Lees's Symphony had been commissioned and premiered by the Louisville Orchestra. Szell gave the work a "carefully defined performance," according to Elwell, who "could feel the emergence of an important talent."[44]

In the four weeks between October 19 and November 15, 1959, the orchestra played thirty-five services—nineteen rehearsals, eight subscription concerts, five concerts not in Severance Hall (two in the western suburb of Lakewood, one in Oberlin, one in Public Auditorium for the Northeast Ohio Teachers' Association, and one in Detroit), three children's concerts (two of which were in Lakewood)—plus seven recording sessions. Counting the recording sessions, there were forty-two services in twenty-eight days! Szell conducted all but the children's and the N.E.O.T.A. concerts. The schedule was no small feat for a man of sixty-two.[45]

In November the orchestra announced the resignation of concertmaster Josef Gingold, effective at the end of the 1959–60 season, his eleventh. "Mr. Gingold's decision to give up orchestral playing in favor of teaching," Szell remarked, "fills me with the very deepest personal regret." Gingold's replacement was announced at the same time: Rafael Druian, concertmaster of the Minneapolis Symphony. Rumors circulated that Gingold's resignation had been requested and that he was bitter. To dispel those rumors, Szell said, "This is a move which he had planned years ago for a certain period of his life."[46] Szell had stung Gingold by numerous small slights over many years. For example, he cancelled the Roy Harris Violin Concerto in 1951, which Gingold took as a personal insult, and never forgave Szell.[47]

Nevertheless, Gingold often stated that he learned more from Szell about violin playing than from all of his teachers, among whom stood a number of all-time greats.[48] Gingold was fifty years old. He would become professor of music at the Indiana University School of Music, where he enjoyed a vigorous old age, teaching generations of violinists and future concertmasters.[49] He continued teaching and giving master classes in many countries until his death at age eighty-four in 1994.

Following the sixth subscription concert, Szell went to the Concertgebouw for his second season as coprincipal conductor. Only one guest conductor, André Cluytens, had been engaged in Cleveland that season. When Cluytens cancelled his American tour, Szell chose Stanislaw Skrowaczewski as his replacement. Heuwekemeijer had been inquiring of Szell about Skrowaczewski since the previous summer. Szell returned from Amsterdam in time to hear his concert and wrote Heuwekemeijer about it: "I was very much impressed and can sum up my opinion very simply by saying that I find him musically, technically, and intellectually first rate." (Szell added by hand: "Perhaps I should say: a first rate talent, for there is still much development in him, I believe.") "I can recommend him warmly for the Concertgebouw. The one thing I cannot predict is how he would cope with certain questions of orchestral discipline, because the Cleveland Orchestra, being impeccable and ideal in this respect, gave him no opportunity to make an informative showing in this field."

Heuwekemeijer thanked Szell for the recommendation, adding with his sly wit, "Please accept my congratulations with the fact that Mr. Skrowaczewski did not have the opportunity to show his abilities in the field of orchestral discipline. Of course we hope that our Orchestra will not give him this chance either."[50] Flothuis reported to Szell in March 1960 that Skrowaczewski's debut at the Concertgebouw proved a success. The 1959 Cleveland engagement was an important showcase for Skrowaczewski. Representatives of the Minneapolis Symphony Orchestra scouted him there. In February 1960 he was appointed music director and conductor.[51]

Back for the New Year 1960, Szell and the orchestra recorded the Schumann and Grieg piano concertos with Leon Fleisher, and performed them in subscription concerts. David Oistrakh played three famous violin concertos—Bach A Minor, Beethoven, and Tchaikovsky—in a special concert on January 13 for the benefit of the 1959–60 orchestra maintenance fund. Arthur Rubinstein returned for a subscription pair with the Brahms Concerto no. 2. In that concert Szell repeated Rochberg's Symphony no. 2; it would have its New York premiere on the forthcoming tour. The final program in January, the last before the tour, was Mozart's Symphony no. 39 in E-flat and *Das Lied von der Erde*, in commemoration of the one hundredth anniversary of Mahler's birth (which was actually July 7), with soloists Maureen Forrester and Ernst Haefliger. That program was the tour de force in the first Carnegie Hall concert, on February 1. Howard Taubman noted the "buoyant and transparent reading of the Mozart E flat major Symphony" and called the "radiant performance" of Mahler's *Das Lied von der Erde* "one of the season's memorable events."[52]

The next two Carnegie Hall concerts received equal appreciation. Benjamin Lees's Symphony no. 2 was, according to Louis Biancolli, "definitely a symphony I for one want to hear again. A compelling impetus and design make its scherzo one of the best of its kind in American concert music, and its adagio finale is boldly imaginative." The concert closed with "a truly magnificent reading of Beethoven's Fifth Symphony. Bravissimo, maestro!" Leon Fleisher's performance of Mozart's C Major Concerto, K. 503, was "such as I never expect to hear bettered in my lifetime," wrote Jay S. Harrison. He found Rochberg's Symphony no. 2 "a major symphony . . . no doubt of that. . . . There is mastery to it everywhere."[53]

A Chapter Closes in Amsterdam but Reopens in New Amsterdam

In February Heuwekemeijer notified Szell that the Concertgebouw planned to appoint two first conductors, Bernard Haitink and Eugen Jochum, as of September 1961. He expressed regret that Szell had not had more time in the three seasons of his coconductorship as they had planned. He added, "We sincerely hope, however, that also after the next season, we shall have the pleasure in welcoming you regularly at Amsterdam."

Szell replied magnanimously, congratulating the Concertgebouw "most warmly on the solution of the conductors problem," but could not refrain from a slight correction of Heuwekemeijer's dates:

> I want you to know that I sincerely share your regret that it has not proved possible for me to put a longer period per season at the disposal of the Concertgebouw Orchestra and I am sorry to have disappointed you in this respect after what we both had envisaged in our talks in Berlin in 1957 (not 1958). At that time it was impossible for me to foresee the spectacular further growth of the Cleveland Orchestra's fame and prestige. This development had, among other consequences, the result that touring has become an ever-increasingly important part of our operations from the point of view of finances. In this connection, we found that touring engagements of the Orchestra with me as conductor were increasingly in demand, while the Orchestra without me was very difficult to sell. You will readily understand that under the circumstances I could not ask my Board to release me for a longer period than provided by my contract.

Szell enclosed a four-page, glossy, program-sized reprint of reviews, mostly from New York.[54]

A most significant development for Szell came out of the blue in April. A letter from George E. Judd Jr., managing director of the New York Philharmonic, told of the Philharmonic's move into its new hall in Lincoln Center intended for the 1961–62 season, and invited Szell for a week as one of the guest conductors with past associations with the orchestra. This came as a timely and pleasant surprise to Szell, whose ties with the Concertgebouw were at that very moment loosening. He had begun with the New York Philharmonic in 1943. The invitation would end a six-year hiatus in Szell's association; his most recent concert with it had been on Christmas Day in 1955. His Philharmonic appearances would now continue annually for the rest of his life. He accepted the invitation with delight and noted that the 1961–62 season was the first time in four years that he would be available during the winter for guest conducting in America.[55]

Cleveland Orchestra associate conductor Robert Shaw led the season's final subscription concerts—three performances of Bach's *Passion According to Saint Matthew*. Coming up afterward was what Szell rightly termed "a long and arduous tour"—twenty-nine concerts in twenty-six cities in the thirty days between April 23 and May 22. The tour reached eleven states: Ohio, Indiana, Illinois, Missouri, Kansas, New Mexico, Texas, Arizona, California, Oregon, and Washington.

His fourteenth season in Cleveland satisfyingly ended, Szell arrived in Europe on June 1, 1960, for a restful summer, although not without a few concerts. Driving from Paris, the Szells arrived in Zurich by the tenth. Szell might have spent his sixty-third birthday en route at any number of three-star restaurants in his favorite wine region, Burgundy. He conducted the West German Radio Orchestra in Cologne on the twenty-seventh, but was not conducting in Salzburg that summer nor did he have any other concerts until September. To keep Mrs. Szell happy and with him for the long vacation, they tried a new venue in Crans, the Châtelet Gentinetta, spending two months there from June 29 until August 31.

Pierre Boulez Enters the Conversation

Szell and the Concertgebouw were in communication about his stint in the fall, the third and last year of his coconductorship. Flothuis returned from the International Society for Contemporary Music (I.S.C.M.) festival in Cologne, where he heard Pierre Boulez perform. Szell had invited Flothuis and his wife to visit the Szells in Switzerland, but Flothuis replied that they planned to spend time in Alsace and Italy so would not be able to meet in Crans. Szell replied: "A pity we cannot meet. . . . I would have *loved* to hear more from you about Mr. Boulez' new work about which, I understand, you were wildly enthusiastic . . . and about some other chefs d'oeuvres." Those are the first records of Szell's awareness of Pierre Boulez, then known as a composer who also conducted.

The day after his Cologne concert, Szell and Flothuis had a long telephone conversation in which Szell proposed the first European performance of Walton's Second Symphony and asked Flothuis to tell him more about the I.S.C.M. festival. At Crans Szell received a letter from Flothuis accepting the idea of the Walton and filling in more details about the festival: "As for Boulez: I was fascinated by his 2 Improvisations sur Mallarmé, when I heard them last year in Rome. He has now changed and extended the score; in Cologne, however, it was not entirely ready for performance, so I heard it in an incomplete state. But anyway, he is a composer of unusual talent."[56]

The Salzburg Festival went on in August while Szell rested in Switzerland. He followed it in the newspapers with special interest in the production of *The Magic Flute* that he had conducted the previous summer, now under the leadership of Joseph Keilberth. Szell clipped and saved reviews of the opening, which compared it very unfavorably with his well-remembered performances in 1959.[57]

In September, catching Szell in Florence, Flothuis forwarded the suggestion of Walton's publisher to invite the composer to rehearsals and performances. On September 7, Szell conducted the closing concert of the Lucerne Festival: Berlioz's *Benvenuto Cellini* Overture, Mahler's *Kindertotenlieder* with Dietrich Fischer-Dieskau, and the Schubert C Major Symphony. On the twentieth he led Cherubini's *Missa Solemnis* at the Sagra Umbria Festival in Perugia, Italy, and on September 26 and 27 Szell repeated the work to open the concert season at La Scala, Milan. After two months' rest and a month of concerts, he was warmed up for his fifteenth season in Cleveland. Rehearsals would begin just six days after his second Scala concert.

Poor weather had not stopped Szell from his favorite nonmusical recreation. After his first rehearsal in Cleveland, he told a reporter that on his vacation he "played golf and looked out," then interpreted that he meant "it rained a lot." Szell also said, "For the first time in 20 years I had a real rest." It had not been easy to achieve. Asked how he managed to be free of conducting engagements for two full months, Szell answered: "By being completely stubborn and refusing to accept any engagements. I just said No!" The reporter observed, "He added [this] with gusto and a flourish of his arms in a podium-like gesture."

The forty-third season, 1960–61, consisted of twenty-four subscription concerts—seventeen of which Szell conducted—no increase over the previous season. Szell said, "Last year, however, we did so much we could do no more this year." Always aware of the box office, Szell "found the advance or guaranteed sales of tickets 'tremendously encouraging. We're all very enthusiastic about it,' he said. 'We have a following of increasing appreciation and size. The people of Cleveland have been conditioned to the best in music.' He pointed out that advance sales were ahead of last year's and suggested there might be 'a better story downstairs (in the box office).' . . . He concluded the interview as he began it, with a burst of his tremendous physical agility. He leaped to his feet, landing in the center of the room, and shook hands firmly. He is 63 and demonstrates that conducting (like golf) is 'good exercise.'"

The interviewer found box office manager Larry Pitcock busy selling single performance tickets, which went on sale Saturday after the season subscribers bought their tickets. "'This is my 33rd season,' he related. 'I've never seen anything like it. We sold 300 more seats by the season this year. Many people buying single tickets are sorry they didn't get season tickets.'"[58] That success continued for most of the next ten seasons.

In addition to the twenty-four pairs of subscription concerts, the orchestra "has its usual schedule of fifty-two children's concerts, seven twilight concerts and the West Shore series in Lakewood [western suburb of Cleveland]." Though it was "usual" for the Cleveland Orchestra to have as many as fifty-two children's concerts in a season, it was not customary for many of its major orchestra counterparts. Founders had established the orchestra for educational as well as artistic reasons, so the large number reflected its historical interest in education. The orchestra could perform so many concerts in part thanks to the Kulas Foundation, which underwrote two full weeks of ten concerts each. The orchestra itself subsidized the balance . A nominal charge for students covered considerably less than the income realized from concerts for adults.[59]

In Szell's first concert of the season, Elwell detected "a degree of tension that somehow prevented [the Schumann 3rd] from realizing in the fullest the warm romantic flavor of the music."[60] He was not the first to make that observation. Ted Princiotto's interview with Szell earlier that week had also alluded to some difficulties: "After mildly chiding a reporter for speculating that the first rehearsal, perhaps, did not go off smoothly, [Szell] related: 'It went very smoothly.'"[61]

The problem might have concerned the new personnel in the first stand of the first violins. Rafael Druian made his debut as concertmaster, with former assistant concertmaster Jacob Krachmalnick as his stand partner. Krachmalnick was substituting for Arnold Steinhardt, off four weeks fulfilling his Army reserve obligation. Druian lacked Gingold's easygoing personality but matched Szell's intensity with his own. Between the two of them, they generated enough tension to make the whole orchestra nervous. Although Krachmalnick was a known quantity to Szell and obviously his choice to replace Steinhardt, his larger-than-life personality added to the tension at just this delicate juncture. No wonder Elwell noticed some discomfort. The tension Elwell felt in the first concert had been resolved by the third. The Schumann Second in that concert showed "true devotion and fidelity expressed with traditional fervor faithfully adhered to in every detail. The instrumental color, the beauty of phrase and the sincerity of purpose were things greatly to be admired, and they were applauded with the enthusiasm they deserved."[62]

1960 was the 150th anniversary of Robert Schumann's birth, on June 8, 1810. The first program reprinted an article about Schumann's orchestral music by Szell, first published in the *New York Times*.[63] The occasion provided the opportunity for Szell to complete a recording cycle of the four symphonies.

Nestled on a Friday between Thursday and Saturday subscription programs was a concert for the benefit of the orchestra's pension fund, with one of the most famous violinists in America—comedian Jack Benny. The sixty-six-year-old Benny and the sixty-three-year-old Szell had reached the height of their respective professions. From vastly different worlds, they could come together because of Benny's sincere concern for music and generosity of spirit. Szell realized its importance to the orchestra, and was a good sport. Benny and Szell posed for a photograph for a *Press* article headlined "Benny Gives Szell Some Tips." Benny appears in the background serenading Szell, who strikes a thoughtful pose, a slight smile on his face, his chin resting on his hands, his forefinger pressed to his cheek. Perhaps he really wanted to put his fingers in his ears, but that was as near as he dared place them.[64] Szell found that Benny was a legitimate violinist, but Szell was no comedian. Dudley S. Blossom Jr., cochairman of the benefit concert, stopped by Severance Hall when Szell and Benny were rehearsing, and told his wife that he heard Szell say: "'Jack, you're doing all right, you can play that violin. You've got to teach me how to ham it up a little bit. I can't.' They were laughing and joking and playing and Szell was just marvelous."[65]

Frank Hruby observed: "For the many Benny fans . . . it must have been a surprise to learn and hear that their man did have something of a violin soloist's technique. . . . Sometimes, though, when the going got rough, he would get help from the concertmaster or other violinist of the orchestra, after which the helper would be summarily 'fired.' . . . But it was all done in fine spirit and good fun, and it should be noted that the Messrs. Benny, Szell, Shaw, Lane, and the entire orchestra donated their services for the concert."[66] Besides the enjoyment of a capacity audience, the benefit grossed $45,370 for the orchestra's pension fund.

This was a good time for Szell to make his temporary seasonal exit for the five weeks from November 9 to December 10, 1960, at the Concertgebouw, Szell's last time as coconductor. In Amsterdam Szell and Walton met for the first time—for the continental premiere of his Second Symphony—even though Szell had been championing Walton's music since the 1930s. He and Szell had been in close correspondence since Szell's commission and performance of Walton's *Partita for Orchestra* in 1958. The composer felt "overjoyed with the performance" of his symphony in Holland, Szell related to a Cleveland reporter, and "promised me the world premiere of his next work for the Cleveland Orchestra."[67] The new work would be *Variations on a Theme by Hindemith*. Walton himself conducted the world premiere in England; Szell gave its United States premiere in April 1963.

Back in Cleveland, Szell found a letter from Flothuis with the English translation of the program notes for Ton de Leeuw's *Mouvements rétrogrades*, which Szell had conducted in Holland. The letter also included his and the Concertgebouw's thanks for playing the composition several times with the Concertgebouw and introducing the work of "a young and, as we believe, gifted Dutch composer to an American audience." Szell answered in the same vein with a "thousand thanks for your kind thoughtfulness in sending the material concerning Ton de Leeuw and thank you also for your kind words about our collaboration, which now has come to what I hope will be only a temporary suspension and not a complete close." Szell included a personal note of respect for Flothuis's musical erudition.[68] In the final concert of 1960, Elwell was not as impressed with Walton's new symphony as he had been with his *Partita*, but literally thanked God for Walton's "ability still to do something interesting within the diatonic system." He duly reported that "Druian won a resounding ovation for his playing of the Prokofiev Concerto [no. 2]."[69]

New Year 1961 began on a Sunday, with the presentation of the three Kulas Foundation conductors in a Twilight Concert.[70] The first subscription concert of the year included the world premiere of Easley Blackwood's Symphony no. 2 and the American debut of twenty-five-year-old French pianist Eric Heidsieck. Both men were sons of famous fathers: the composer's was the bridge expert and the pianist's the Champagne magnate. Heidsieck "won a resounding ovation" for the Franck Symphonic Variations and the reviewer's thanks for introducing the Fauré *Fantasie* (composed in 1919) in Cleveland. Blackwood's Symphony—one of several works commissioned by the music publishing firm G. Schirmer, celebrating its one hundredth anniversary—fared less well with Elwell, who found it "not so clear or spontaneous as his First Symphony," which had been played just the season before. Elwell stated: "it seems unlikely that the composer will have a better performance."[71]

January held only two more subscription concerts because a week was dedicated to ten young people's and children's concerts in Cleveland and Akron. Subscription concerts featured the American debut of Hungarian pianist Annie Fischer, Mahler's Symphony no. 4 with soprano Saramae Endich, and a subscription pair titled "A Rubinstein Festival," with the venerable artist playing three concertos: Mozart's G Major, Chopin's F Minor, and Liszt's E-flat. It was the first time Rubinstein performed each of the three concertos in Cleveland. The occasion marked his eighteenth appearance with the orchestra and his seventy-fifth birthday. "The hall was sold out, even to standing room, and the applause was thunderous," a stunned Elwell related. "The only trouble with it is that it leaves one wide-eyed, stupefied and speechless. You can say to yourself such keyboard artistry is impossible to achieve. But there it is. He did it, the very thing you had scarcely dared to imagine."[72]

The National Philharmonic of Warsaw and its conductor, Witold Rowicki, in Cleveland on an American tour, attended the dress rehearsal at Severance Hall on Thursday morning. They cheered at its conclusion. The Warsaw gave a concert on the Friday between the Cleveland's subscription pair, and Rubinstein hosted a luncheon for the orchestra from his homeland at the Hotel Sheraton Cleveland that day.

On January 30 the orchestra began a fifteen-concert eastern tour. Always on their toes in New York, the orchestra was again in top form, as the reviews attest. "I had heard several performances of [Haydn's Symphony no. 102] that were indifferent," Winthrop Sargeant wrote, "leaving one with the impression that it was just another Haydn symphony. In Mr. Szell's hands, however, it became a revelation, set forth with incredible polish and with every phrase exquisitely adjusted to its context, so that all the delicate details of its elegant classical structure became microscopically clear to the listener." Harold Schonberg expressed surprise at the reception Szell's Mozart "Posthorn" Serenade received: "At the end of the performance the audience burst into cheers. For a Mozart Serenade!" Biancolli was as impressed by the Haydn: "One was left wondering if he had ever really heard this symphony before. That is Mr. Szell's gift."[73]

A performance by Szell put forth an eloquent argument for any score, and many composers felt fortunate to receive one. As Biancolli put it: "On performance alone, the New York premiere of Sir William Walton's Second Symphony was a resounding triumph." And giving Szell, who "conducted brilliantly," full credit: "He has created for himself one of the finest orchestras in the world, and it is an extension of his own personality by now." In a later Cleveland radio interview, Szell told how much that recording meant for the fate of the Walton Symphony:

> This piece at its first performance in London with the Royal Philharmonic for whose anniversary it was composed, did not find great favor with the London critics. When our record came out over there, they changed their mind completely, and one of the critics made the issue of live performance versus recorded performance the subject of a very long article in which he stated that if a recorded performance is so superior, then it very often reveals the scope and extent and quality of a work much better than a mediocre live performance on which they had originally based their judgment. So our recorded performance . . . changed their mind about the work itself.[74]

Small wonder that, as Biancolli told it, Sir William, "could scarcely have dreamed of a performance like last night's. On that count—plus the response of the crowd—he had every right to beam with pride and pleasure when brought out for a bow."[75]

Szell and the orchestra had given fifteen concerts in fifteen consecutive days, traveling each day and playing a concert each night, without a day off. They returned home on Tuesday, rehearsed, and were playing the first of another subscription concert pair by that Thursday. Friday provided the first free day in eighteen. The plus of continuous playing, set against the factor of fatigue, kept them in top form. It was a young orchestra and Szell remained vital at sixty-three years old. Management viewed a day off on tour as unproductive, as it produced no income. By 1965 the union contract stipulated a free day every week.

The program Szell chose on the return was one that they could perform well in a short time: the *Firebird* Suite, Prokofiev's Violin Concerto no. 1, with Henryk Szeryng as soloist, and Tchaikovsky's Symphony no. 4. Not a light program from the standpoint of orchestral demands, but after the tensions of the tour, it offered the musicians a sense of relaxation and enjoyment of familiar music.

Szell intended the Walton recording to be definitive, so he programmed the work on the second subscription pair after the tour. The orchestra had performed it just after Christmas, again on tour including the Carnegie Hall performance, and on the same season less than two months after the first Cleveland performances. The recording took two sessions, February 24 and March 3, and the results and the response spoke for themselves.

The Beethoven concertos were recorded piecemeal with Leon Fleisher in a complicated series of sessions, most tacked on to those of larger works. The results cohered because Szell's and Fleisher's unified stylistic approach had ripened over repeated rehearsals and performances. Fleisher recalled that in recording the genial second concerto, Szell felt unsatisfied with the opening tutti, even after repeating it several times. Fleisher told Szell that he thought he had the solution to what Szell was trying for, and suggested that it "needs to be more debonaire." Szell gleefully repeated "more debonaire" to the orchestra. They played it with just the character he sought, and the recording went on from there.[76]

A fourteen-concert, two-week southeastern tour in March progressed from Ohio Wesleyan at Delaware, Ohio, to Washington, D.C. The Beethoven and the Walton figured on the Washington concert, the first time the Cleveland Orchestra performed in that city. Paul Hume, music critic of the *Washington Post,* had been told three years earlier by Sir Thomas Beecham that the Cleveland Orchestra was the finest in the United States. Hume wrote, "I see now why he thought so. Washington found Szell and the Cleveland Orchestra a thrilling and satisfying combination." They played Walton's Second Symphony, Beethoven's Second Piano Concerto with Fleisher, and Schumann's Third Symphony there.

Hume mentioned some of the qualities that thrilled audience and critic: "The solidity with which George Szell has built [the] orchestra on those sound ingredients which are possessed only by the world's greatest orchestras, a musicality throughout the ensemble which communicates itself in the most disciplined response, a virile and lustrous quality of sound in every department, and the embodiment of classic orchestral technique and proportion. . . . Szell's authority, experience and taste are rivaled by precious few conductors today."[77]

In Cleveland the next week, Szell shared the podium with Robert Shaw, who conducted the orchestra and chorus in Schubert's Mass in G. Before intermission Szell conducted the "Good Friday Spell" from *Parsifal* in observance of the Easter season, the Glazounov Violin Concerto with assistant concertmaster Arnold Steinhardt, and *Mouvements rétrogrades* by Ton de Leeuw. The work impressed Elwell, with its ten short movements played without pause, and he wrote: "The fact that the melodies were played both forward and backward need not concern us. In new music these days one can be grateful for anything that is recognizable as melody. This work had fresh sounds and colors, as well as something attractively communicable."[78]

The season ended with Beethoven's Ninth Symphony. A third performance on Sunday quickly sold out. Elwell, along with the audience, was "thrilled . . . by an interpretation of such nobility and strength as is always offered by Szell and the chorus superbly trained by Robert Shaw. Both received a long standing ovation at the close. It was as though the audience could not express appreciation enough for them, the orchestra, chorus and soloists."[79]

Troubles were developing. In March members of the orchestra filed suit in federal court complaining that their union local deprived them of their right to vote to accept or reject their contract with the Musical Arts Association. A judge ruled against them on the grounds that the Landrum-Griffen Act "does not require a labor union to submit agreements to its members for a vote."[80] In June they again filed suit against the union to try to block a contract that had been signed in May, arguing that they were not sufficiently consulted in the negotiation process. The new suit was based on another principle, "that an agent has the obligation to obey the wishes of a principal he represents."[81] This conflict would continue to play out over the next several years.

After concerts in London, Ontario, on April 29 and 30, the Szells flew to New York. By May 8 they were with Helene's sister at Walton-on-Thames in Surrey. The couple stayed for only a week, sufficient time for Szell to conduct the Philharmonia of London on May 12. A week later, on the nineteenth, he conducted the West German Radio Orchestra in Cologne, and a week after that, on the twenty-sixth, he led the Swiss-Italian Radio Orchestra at the Lugano Festival.

The Szells spent a few days at the Dolder Grand Hotel in Zurich. Returning to Paris to pick up the automobile, they drove leisurely back to Switzerland and stayed for a week while Szell prepared a concert on July 4 with the Tonhalle Orchestra. Ready for a rest, they retired to Crans for three weeks.

In August Szell climbed back in the saddle for two concerts—the first on the sixth with the Dresden State Orchestra at the Salzburg Festival. On the twenty-third he conducted an all-Beethoven concert with the Swedish Radio Orchestra in Stockholm. Sweden seemed to him little changed since he had been there twenty-six years ago. Sweden's World War II neutrality had left it untouched by the conflict. The ravage of Europe, however, he had found "almost staggering." From Sweden the Szells returned to the relatives in England, caught up with their car left on the Continent, and drove south for ten relaxing days at the Lido in Venice.

They soon had the adventure of the summer. A tire blew out as they were driving at high speed on an Italian superhighway outside Milan. Szell stopped the car safely but had no luck flagging down help. "Cars were going by at breakneck pace," he told a Cleveland reporter, "I signalled for help but they rushed on past." They were rescued at last by a chauffeur-driven car. In fluent Italian, Szell communicated with the car's owner, the wife of a banker in Rome. She turned out to be a good friend of the Italian actress Marta Abba, the first wife of Severance A. Millikin. Millikin was a nephew of John Long Severance, former Musical Arts Association president and great Cleveland Orchestra benefactor. After the lady's chauffeur changed the tire, she invited the Szells to dinner in her eleventh-century palace on her estate.[82]

The Szells motored north again, destination Paris via Switzerland. Driving through the Alps, they stayed at Montreux, and there on September 10 Szell discussed his return to the Concertgebouw for two weeks in November 1962 with Flothuis and Heuwekemeijer. To celebrate its seventy-fifth anniversary season, the

Concertgebouw engaged three guest conductors who had worked extensively with the orchestra: Rafael Kubelik, Hans Rosbaud, and Szell.

Far-Flung Opportunities

At the end of summer 1961, Szell was asked to make a momentous decision regarding his future in Cleveland. During Szell's first fifteen years there, frequent but unfounded rumors of his leaving arose. They were mainly based on Szell's guest conducting the Concertgebouw, the New York Philharmonic, and the Metropolitan Opera. In his early years a few trustees thought he might leave Cleveland for the Chicago Symphony Orchestra. In 1961, however, Szell received an offer served up on a silver platter. In midyear Eric Oldberg inquired if Szell would consider the Chicago post, soon to be vacated by Fritz Reiner when he moved to the Metropolitan Opera.

Wrestling with the momentous decision, Szell put off answering. In August Oldberg sent a letter to Szell to jog him into replying. Finally, in early September, Szell wrote Oldberg a long and thoughtful letter, which began, "You are entitled to a final answer by now. I have delayed it on purpose, hoping that the stay in Europe and distance as well as absence from Cleveland will put things into perspective. . . . It appears that destiny does not want me and Chicago to get into any kind of permanent arrangement. . . . I, temporarily disgruntled with my then President, hinted at my possible availability. You made a decision which went the other way and proved eminently right,- and I understood. Now I am asking you to understand." Szell would have declined this Chicago Symphony offer "without much hesitation," explaining, "only the fact that the offer came from you with the prospect of working with you and living in the same city with you and Hilda put me into this terrible dilemma." He felt "more convinced than ever that the resolve not to accept a permanency after leaving Cleveland—taken years ago—is the correct one."

Szell did not feel up to starting all over again, nor could he part with the orchestra he had "nursed and trained for 15 years, and which has become the near-perfect instrument for what I wish to express in music. . . . I cannot break faith with a President and a Board of Trustees who have fulfilled every one of my wishes regardless of cost. . . . I want to lighten the load of work after this coming season, not to increase it by taking on a new burden which is bound to be heavier because it is new,- regardless of absolute quantity of work."[83] If Chicago had been offered in 1953, when Rafael Kubelik left, the fifty-six-year-old Szell might have taken it. But he had turned a corner; he would be sixty-five by the fall of 1962, and his decision not to begin in Chicago, confirmed his "resolve . . . taken years ago."

The Szells arrived in Paris on September 14, 1961, and New York on the twenty-first, where an interviewer found Szell:

> Dictators, it is said, are rarely happy. But for the dictator of the baton (as conductors are sometimes called), George Szell, there is not much he could add to his happy situation in Cleveland where he has been more than a decade and a half, and he has no inclination to leave. "Why should I," he asked rhetorically the other afternoon over tea. "I am happy with the management, with the directors, with Severance Hall and, of course," he added as a modest afterthought, since the last was pretty much his own creation, "with my orchestra."

Szell mentioned future guest conducting in Chicago and Los Angeles, but added that Cleveland "is the last attachment" he expected to hold. His problem, rather, "is to cut down." About younger conductors, Szell said, "They are still moving up too fast," recalling that when he started to conduct internationally, he was in his mid to late thirties. About recording an opera: "'In '64 I think,' he replied with a smile. 'It will take time to get the right cast, because it is something big. But I am hopeful.'"[84] It never came to fruition.

Not all was going as smoothly as Szell averred. As musically excellent as the orchestra was, its musicians were in court fighting for a say in their contract. In retaliation the union threatened to expel those on the orchestra committee when the objections had first been raised, further spurring the players' opposition. The conflict was escalating. A later court ruling pronounced that the musicians could not sue the union—one of two parties in the contract negotiation—without including the other party, the Musical Arts Association, the parent body of the Cleveland Orchestra. The musicians accordingly filed a new suit. The costs in money, time, and frayed nerves posed a danger that they would affect the music. Szell would not accept lowering its quality; his contract permitted him to resign at any time. In regular meetings, the orchestra committee updated members about the lawsuit. The musicians engaged in discussion and debate. Old friendships became strained. The court ruled that the union possessed authority to negotiate contracts for its members. The legal battle continued for several years.[85]

In the forty-fourth season, 1961–62, Szell's sixteenth, he led eight subscription pairs from October to early December, with occasional local concerts.[86] The season began on October 5 and 7, 1961, with three diverse works by Italian composers "dedicated to the Centenary of the Italian Unification," and Brahms's Symphony no. 2. Rehearsals for this concert began on October 2. This was the author's first day as apprentice conductor and its impact remains vivid to this day. In a brief speech to the orchestra, Szell told them how much he had missed them all summer (they had last performed together on April 30) and wished them well for the coming season. He began with the Brahms and conducted it through nonstop. I sat there in the semidarkened hall and marveled at the playing: it seemed more perfect and glorious than any performance I had ever heard. For the rest of that week, Szell worked on the Brahms in bits and pieces, dissecting it, polishing every facet of its complexity, reexamining it as though discovering it for the first time even though it was the ninth season he had programmed it since his first season in 1946.

Orchestra players would complain that they knew the Brahms and other standard works so well that Szell need not have gone into such detail every time. Working that way proved frustrating, so that by performance time they were eager to play it uninterrupted. But through all the nagging details, Szell worked toward a unified and personal vision of the piece's overall shape. As he later explained it: "Conducting is anticipating. Music making, in the good sense of the word, is anticipating. . . . When you start the first note of a piece you must already know where the arc that vaults from the first note to the last will descend." Asked how much of the work he thinks of in advance: "Twice. The whole work. And then, from moment to moment anticipating the next split second with everything it entails. Knowing that this instrument, that this particular spot, has a tendency to come in late or early and parry it with your beat, with your eye, lead it, guide it, mold it. All the time."[87]

The Italian Consul in Cleveland, Dr. Vieri Traxler, attended the concert. Verdi and his music had been a rallying point in the Italian unification, but Szell chose music by Rossini, Casella, and Respighi: the overture to *La gazza ladra*, *Paganiniana*, and *Fontane di Roma*, respectively. The concert was televised locally. In bold type, the program page stated: "The Musical Arts Association records with deep sorrow the passing on August 5 of its devoted Trustee and warm friend, Dudley S. Blossom, Jr. We shall continue to be inspired by the outstanding service he gave to The Cleveland Orchestra."[88]

Szell possessed a prodigious memory, but he was human after all (although some orchestra members might have contested that), and could have momentary lapses, if very rarely. The first one I witnessed occurred at this first concert as apprentice conductor. Szell used no score in the performance, although he routinely used the score in rehearsals until the dress run-through the morning of the concert.

Szell had presented the Casella and Respighi in Cleveland eleven and ten seasons earlier, respectively. He negotiated the complicated Casella from memory without incident. The lapse occurred in a static spot in the Respighi. At the end of the second fountain, the third horn holds a note for several bars, then the English horn and two bassoons have the upbeat to begin the third fountain. Szell gave the three winds the cue to begin one bar early. In that split second, the three instinctively and rightly decided to follow the conductor and not stubbornly hold their ground. Immediately understanding what had happened, the rest of the orchestra followed along and seamlessly joined in. The piece went to its conclusion without further incident.

I was on stage playing the celesta and could see Szell's face. He must have felt some strange electricity from the orchestra at that moment, and he immediately realized what he had done, as shown by his briefly startled expression; but he quickly recovered his composure. When he came to that place in the Saturday repeat of the concert, Szell deliberately and very pointedly marked the bar he had previously skipped with three firm, clear beats as if to say, "Yes, I know what I did and here's the bar I owe you." The musicians showed their appreciation of Szell's honesty in that spontaneous moment by a discreetly quiet shuffling of their feet.

Szell's only other lapse that I observed happened during the first rehearsals of the 1966–67 season, in a similar place. Near the end of the second movement of Beethoven's Fifth Symphony, Szell indicated an extra bar before cuing a wind entrance. In that indefinable subliminal area in which communication between conductor and orchestra takes place, the winds sensed what was happening and waited until Szell cued them, as did the rest of the orchestra in turn. At the conclusion of the movement, pleased with the beauty of the passage just described, Szell combined a compliment with an admission: "It should be that nice also if I don't wait another extra bar for the A-flat chord."

These two examples of Szell's memory lapses give a clue to the nature of his memory. Both occurred during static moments, where a note or a chord was being held. Musical memory is a balance between visual and aural, the proportion of these elements varying with each musician. If Szell's memory was preponderantly visual, it might well not have slipped in those instances. That suggests that his musical memory operated best when there was movement. Szell never made these slips again, nor any others in the nine years I observed him.

A comment Szell made showed his awareness of his possibility to err. He had invited a young conductor to conduct the first work on what was otherwise Szell's concert. It was a complex Stravinsky work, conducted brilliantly from memory. The young conductor came off the stage mad at himself. He told Szell, who was backstage waiting to go on, "Damn it, I had a memory lapse!" Szell's knowing reply was, "It won't be your last."[89]

Highlights of the 1961 fall season included Britten's *Cantata Academica*, Haydn's "Oxford" Symphony, Tchaikovsky's *Pathétique*, Bartók's *Concerto for Orchestra*, Janáček's *Sinfonietta*, *Tod und Verklärung* by Strauss, and the first Cleveland performance of Honegger's Symphony no. 3, *Liturgique*. Concerto performances included the Mendelssohn Violin Concerto with Zino Francescatti; Beethoven's "Emperor" Concerto with Leon Fleisher; two Mozart piano concertos, K. 491 and K. 467, with Robert Casadesus; and the Mozart Clarinet Concerto and Strauss Horn Concerto no. 1, with two orchestra principals, Robert Marcellus and Myron Bloom. The Mozart piano concertos would be recorded, as would the clarinet and horn concertos.

Elwell opined: "It is conceivable that if the Cleveland Orchestra were cut off from all outside sources of supply for soloists, it could easily fill the gap with artists within its own ranks." Of the orchestra's first performance of the Strauss horn concerto, Elwell wrote: "Bloom carried [it] out with flawless technique, extraordinary beauty of tone and superb musicianship." The clarinet concerto equally impressed him: "Marcellus is an artist to his fingertips, and he brings the clarinet as close to the domain of great vocal artistry as any instrument can be. No more finely styled Mozart has been heard here, but it was not style alone that distinguished the performance."[90]

On Wednesday, November 1, the Berlin Philharmonic, conducted by Herbert von Karajan, gave a concert in Severance Hall, a special event for the benefit of the Cleveland Orchestra's maintenance fund. The program consisted of Bach's Suite no. 2 for Flute and Strings, Stravinsky's Symphony in C, and *Also sprach Zarathustra*, by Strauss. Stylistically and personally very different, Szell and Karajan remained on mutually cordial and respectful terms. Knowing of a future Berlin Philharmonic tour, Szell had invited Karajan the year before to perform in Cleveland. Karajan accepted with pleasure and recalled the Cleveland Orchestra concert in Vienna: "I not only hear you but I see you before me with the extraordinary enthusiasm with which you made music then. When I sometimes have the time, it would be an exceptional joy for me to be allowed to stand before this magnificent ensemble." Karajan signed the letter to Szell "all love to you and to your wife and heartfelt greetings."[91]

Elwell's review of the next Cleveland Orchestra concert obliquely compared Szell and Karajan. He found Szell's collaboration with Robert Casadesus in two Mozart concertos "at one, and at ease, in their realization of the Mozartean style." (He also found Casadesus's playing "crystalline, pure and virile.") Obviously thinking of Karajan, the critic mused, "I wonder if we could not ask Szell to conduct more from a position of confidence than of constant fear that someone might goof. Man for man our players are probably as good as those of the Berlin Philharmonic. This might be more apparent if they were not so minutely conducted. Comparisons are odious, but the Musical Arts Association asked for it."[92] Szell might have seen Elwell's criticism as impertinent, and taken umbrage. But he might also have taken it constructively, because in the very next program, featuring Britten's *Cantata academica—carmen basiliense*, Elwell could write "The playing was just as finely controlled as ever, but noticeably more relaxed rounded and freer than on some occasions."[93]

Earlier that fall, correspondence with Piet Heuwekemeijer led to a contentious situation. In a meeting in Montreux in September 1961, Flothuis, Heuwekemeijer, and Szell had agreed on the terms of Szell's November 1962 Concertgebouw engagement. Szell would receive the same fee as the previous year, $850 per concert, for a total of seven concerts. Heuwekemeijer summed up the agreement in a letter to which Szell replied, "I am accepting the conditions. . . . I assume that you will send me a formal letter of agreement at your convenience." A month later, Heuwekemeijer sent Szell a schedule for six concerts and their rehearsals. Szell answered that he found the schedule "completely acceptable." But when Szell received the contract, he saw red and replied testily to Heuwekemeijer. It had slipped by Szell that the "completely acceptable" schedule included just six concerts, which he only realized when the contract arrived. Not admitting his oversight, but with some justification, Szell blamed Heuwekemeijer for not calling that to his attention. Szell returned the contract and set a deadline for the amended contract, or he would consider that they did not value his participation.

Heuwekemeijer sent a diplomatic reply by special delivery, apologizing for the misunderstanding and pointing out that some of the difficulty in finding a seventh concert was because Szell had shortened his original availability by four or five days. He reminded Szell that he had said he might welcome as few as two concerts, and "we did not expect that you, once having agreed to a certain fee per concert, would have done this apparently only on the basis of 7 concerts."[94]

Szell replied with a contrite answer. Although not able to resist a barb or two, he backed off as gracefully as he could: "I appreciate your very nice letter of November 17th in reply to my angry one. . . . I will attest that you acted in perfectly good faith, but what got my goat, as we say in American slang, was the tacit, I would almost say furtive, reduction in the number of concerts after we had agreed on a reduced fee for a given total. I think you know me by now well enough to understand that it was the question of principle and procedure, not the question of dollars and cents, which annoyed me."[95] Heuwekemeijer marked that last sentence with a line in the margin, beside which he wrote "oj!" With a few exchanges of telegrams and letters expressing mutual appreciation, they put the matter behind them.

With the Chicago decision made, Szell signed his seventh Cleveland contract in December 1961. It would extend over three seasons: 1962–63, 1963–64, and 1964–65, and postponed his advisory status until 1965–66, to continue for seven years through 1971–72. In mid-December 1961 Szell guest-conducted three weeks of concerts in Chicago. His first program was all Beethoven, with Erica Morini playing the Violin Concerto, preceded by the Overture to *Leonore* no. 3 and the *Pastoral* Symphony. The Walton Second was a novelty, surrounded by the *Roman Carnival* Overture and Tchaikovsky's Fourth Symphony. Szell left them with Haydn's "Oxford" Symphony, the Schumann First, and Mozart's G Major Piano Concerto, K. 453, with Arthur Rubinstein. Szell also led members of the Chicago Symphony in two television broadcasts, now on DVD.

After Christmas Szell returned to Cleveland for the annual New Year's Eve subscription pair—Schubert's Overture to *Rosamunde* and the Beethoven Violin Concerto with assistant concertmaster Arnold Steinhardt. With the strains of *On the Beautiful Blue Danube*, 1961 came to a graceful close.

Szell conducted the next four subscription pairs. In January the orchestra presented two special concerts for the benefit of the orchestra's pension fund, with the indefatigable Arthur Rubinstein, who turned seventy-six that month, playing all five Beethoven piano concertos. January 1962 saw three premieres: the world premiere of Howard Hanson's *Bold Island* Suite, the United States premieres of André Jolivet's

Les amants magnifiques, and Zoltán Kodály's only symphony. The Hungarian pianist Tamás Vásáry made his United States debut, and the Kulas Foundation conductors of the season shared a Twilight Concert. Written in the composer's eightieth year, Kodály's symphony was commissioned by the Swiss Festival Orchestra of the Lucerne Festival. The world premiere took place there in August 1961 under the baton of his former pupil, Ferenc Fricsay, with the composer in attendance. It is a strong and attractive work in its material and form and use of the orchestra. Between conducting the Dresden State Orchestra in Salzburg and the Swedish Radio Orchestra in Stockholm, Szell attended the Lucerne premiere and immediately secured the rights to the United States premiere from the publisher, Boosey & Hawkes.

This season's Carnegie Hall programs were solid Szell repertoire, with new offerings of works and a new soloist among the tried and true.[96] Critics reviewed the concerts in the *New York Times*, the *New York Herald Tribune*, the *New York Post*, and the *Saturday Review*. The critics disagreed on the Kodály's lasting merits, and two reviews of Curzon's Brahms diverged so much that one wonders if the critics attended the same performance. Szell and the orchestra were unanimously acclaimed as the prime elements of the series' great success. And the reviewers' varied takes on aspects of the performances testified to the richness of the interpretations.

Schonberg wrote of Szell's Mozart Fortieth: "nor was he interested in pretty sound for the sake of sound." Johnson, on the other hand, wrote of the Mozart: "The manner in which he brought varied color and mood to each theme was a delight." Schonberg characterized Szell's "way with Mozart" as having "[a] lean texture, clarity, forthright rhythm and impeccable ensemble." Lang took Szell to task for a "token" string reduction: "the illusion of a balanced small orchestra was created, still, there were spots where the harmonies in the woodwinds were only faintly audible." It appealed to Schonberg that "the big aspects of the G minor Symphony were emphasized. . . . It was a propulsive reading, even in the slow movement."[97]

In Carnegie Hall a large wood and canvas structure was then suspended at an angle over the stage, lower than halfway between it and the ceiling. It reflected sound into the hall and gave the strings an especially warm tone, acoustically favoring the front of the stage. That, however, put the Mozart Fortieth's nine winds—one flute, two oboes, clarinets, bassoons, and horns—at a disadvantage against Szell's reduction to fifty strings: fourteen first violins, twelve seconds, ten violas, eight cellos, and six double-basses.

Rehearsing the Mozart on the morning of the first concert, Szell was aware of the potential balance problem, and this caused him extreme concern. He kept turning around and asking Louis Lane and the author if one or another wind could be heard. After several balance adjustments in the rehearsal quieting the strings, the winds became audible, but, under the pressure of the concert, they were often covered, as Lang observed.

On Morini, the critics generally agreed: "One of the world's great violinists was heard at the top of her form," Schonberg wrote. Yet the critic lamented "the fact that Szell continues to present the same old Haydn symphonies on his programs," but found it "hard not to be intrigued by the expertness of the playing on this occasion." Lang, the musicologist and musician, appreciated Szell as being "one of the few conductors of our age [who] are equipped either musically or technically to cope with [the Haydn 'Oxford' Symphony]." Not only the Haydn, however, impressed Lang: "The Bartók Concerto for Orchestra," he wrote, "received an unusually vital performance."

The "unusually vital performance" occurred in an intense atmosphere typical of Szell's nervous state on eastern tours, and in New York in particular. In addition to the concern over the wind/string balances in the Mozart Fortieth, in the first of the three Carnegie Hall concerts, Szell had been fretting about the solo side drum part in the second movement of the Bartók. He was convinced that the percussionist who had played the part in Severance Hall was not up to the task. Once Szell convinced himself of anything, it became next to impossible to change his mind.

At a Severance Hall rehearsal that January, Szell had each member of the percussion section play the part one at a time. It was an audition of sorts for Szell to judge to whom he might reassign the part. But he so intimidated them that each percussionist began making errors he normally would never have made, from misplaying a rhythm to a small unevenness in the diminuendo at the end of the movement. The head of the section, tympanist Cloyd Duff, remembered: "You can imagine him looking at every note you play with his special eyes, it scared the daylights out of you." Duff normally would only play tympani, never other percussion. But under the pressure of the tour and fretting about the snare drum in the Bartók, Szell called Duff in to see him a week before the Carnegie Hall performance, and said: "Cloyd I want you to play that snare drum part. I remember how you played these things in Philadelphia [over twenty years earlier at the Robin Hood Dell, when Szell was guest conductor and Duff was a student at Curtis]." Defending his men, Duff became incensed. He told Szell: "You're ruining the whole section. Nobody can make a diminuendo to please you because they're so nervous. Every one of those men are capable of doing that." Duff felt that Szell was making it impossible. Szell prevailed, but Duff laid down one condition: "Okay, I'll play it for you, but don't you dare look at me." "So when I played it, I played it louder than they had played it before so I had more room to make a diminuendo. Everybody was a little bit shocked that I played it quite as loudly as I did. But Szell, true to his word, looked away, didn't look at me once and I didn't look at him under the circumstances."[98]

An interview with Szell then appeared in the *New York Post:* "That the Cleveland Symphony Orchestra ranks as high as it does is due largely to the brilliance of its 64-year-old conductor, George Szell." It described Szell as one who never could be mistaken for a native of the region in which he has chosen to work:

> His manner remains Prussian. Erect in bearing, he grants no absolution for the sins of sloppiness, nor does he indulge in the fine art of wasting time with extravagant motion. He is precise and exact and demands that musicians under him be the same. Off the podium Szell is unchanged. The air he brings to the training of his orchestra, an ensemble which critics enjoy likening to championship fighters or runners about to set off on a four-minute mile, is the same in conversation. In an interview, Szell conducts it. "Too many people write music and then consider themselves musicians. . . . most of the great composers of the past were distinguished performers and conductors themselves . . . if contemporary composers were also fine performers and conductors that might be a solution both to their economic situation and the practicability of their work. . . . The overwhelming number of brilliant young string players I have come in contact with seem to have only a rather narrow knowledge of their own instrument, having been drilled primarily in a few concert show pieces, and are very weak in knowledge of the sonata and chamber music literature in general. . . . The complete mastering of the later Beethoven quartets would put a violinist not only musically and spiritually, but also technically, on a far higher plane."[99]

The Notorious San Francisco Flap

Two West Coast orchestras, the Los Angeles Philharmonic and the San Francisco Symphony, engaged Szell to conduct for two weeks each. The Los Angeles engagement—March 1, 2, 8, and 9—featured an all-Tchaikovsky program of the Fourth Symphony and First Piano Concerto with Van Cliburn, and an all-Beethoven program of the Overture to *Coriolanus*, followed by the Sixth and Fifth Symphonies.

Later in March Szell would conduct two programs with the San Francisco Symphony. The first week, Szell gave them the *Oberon* Overture, the Kodály Symphony, and the Tchaikovsky Fourth. *San Francisco Chronicle* music critic Alfred Frankenstein expressed gratefulness to Szell for "the honor of sharing his latest enthusiasm" (the Kodály), and found it one of the composer's finest works.[100]

The first week went seemingly without incident, but two days after the final repetition of the first concert, the management sent out a press release stating that Szell "has requested, and been granted, a release from his forthcoming obligations in view of the fact that he is in need of rest due to an extremely heavy season's schedule." It went on to say that Szell's program—Beethoven's Sixth and Brahms's Second—would not change, but that the orchestra's musical director, Enrique Jorda, would conduct. Jorda received a superlative review from Frankenstein, especially for his Brahms.[101]

The matter might have rested there, but it did not. A brouhaha was precipitated by Frankenstein's letter to Szell in which he wrote: "There has been a grand crop of rumors all over the country about your withdrawal from the local scene" and that "this has not been at all good for the San Francisco Symphony. It would therefore be a just, proper and pleasant gesture," he continued, "if Mr. Jorda could be invited to serve as guest conductor in Cleveland next season." This enraged Szell, who wrote back: "Up until this moment I have tried to be as polite and discreet as possible about my early departure from San Francisco. Your letter of March 24, however, contains a tactless provocation which compels me to step out of my reserve. Since you have reopened this question, which I had thought closed, and because it is a matter of public interest, I reserve the right to make our correspondence accessible to other persons."

Szell criticized Frankenstein's "delicate dual position as music critic of The Chronicle and program annotator for the San Francisco Symphony, which in itself is liable to cast grave doubts upon your objectivity, [and] should have prompted you to exercise particular restraint in this matter." He deemed it "entirely out of order" for the music critic to suggest "my taking a step designed to be interpreted as implicit approval" of what he had found to be "the saddest state of musical affairs I have encountered in any American or European city during the almost fifty years of my active conducting career." When challenged, Szell told reporters that the reason given for his request for release, "fatigue," was just "the polite excuse."[102]

Szell made his letter public, and the *San Francisco Chronicle* reported on it in a front-page article on the twenty-eighth, to a storm of protest. The *New York Times* gave a balanced report the next day. The president of the San Francisco Symphony Association, James D. Zellerbach, said, "We have high musical standards. I never have heard this kind of criticism from any other guest conductor."[103]

The next day, the *Chronicle* struck out at Szell in an editorial: "The Tantrum of Maestro Szell." It took him to task for "the airy vagueness of this incredible indictment, plus Szell's refusal to specify or enlarge, seriously diminishes its validity." It brought up other well-known Szell walkouts, as with the Metropolitan Opera in 1954, and even recalled the Glyndebourne incident in 1947. It concluded, "We suggest that George Szell owes profound apologies to the San Francisco Symphony, Director Jorda and Mr. Frankenstein."[104] Whether Szell's criticism had influence, the season after next, the board replaced Jorda with Josef Krips. When Szell told his old friend Max Rudolf about the matter, Rudolf strongly advised him to drop it and not go public. Szell said that he expected Rudolf to say this, so he had mailed the letter before calling him.

Szell returned to Cleveland at the end of March to conduct four of the last five concerts of the season (Shaw led Bach's *Passion According to Saint John* in the next-to-last subscription pair). The Leventritt prizewinner, American pianist Malcolm Frager, gave a brilliant first Cleveland performance of Prokofiev's massive Second Piano Concerto, and veteran Rudolf Serkin did the same for Bartók's equally daunting First Piano Concerto, which was recorded. They also revived Alvin Etler's *Concerto in One Movement*, commissioned for and performed in the fortieth season in 1957 and scheduled for the opening of Lincoln Center in September. Jean Casadesus, son of pianists Robert and Gaby, played the Fifth Piano Concerto of Saint-Saëns, and Rudolf Firkusny graced the final program with an elegant traversal of Mozart's B-flat Piano Concerto, K. 456. The season ended with Schubert's Symphony in C Major, "The Great."

Szell's summer of 1962 began in Paris, where he conducted the Orchestre National de Paris at the Champs Elysées Theater, with Arthur Rubinstein playing the Brahms First Piano Concerto. He motored to Switzerland in his 1958 black Cadillac, where he spent most of June and all of July, with a full month in Crans in the middle. For a week in August, Szell attended concerts in Salzburg. There he met with Heuwekemeijer and Flothuis to discuss his programs with the Concertgebouw for the September 1963 Edinburgh Festival.

Visiting Stockholm in August, Szell conducted two concerts with the Swedish Radio Orchestra: one all Mozart, the other all Brahms. He flew to Zurich, then went to Lucerne, where on August 29 he led the Lucerne Festival Orchestra in Walton's *Partita for Orchestra*, Brahms's Symphony no. 1, and the Beethoven Piano Concerto no. 2 with Leon Fleisher. Szell checked into the Privatklinik Bircher-Benner from the thirty-first until September 10 for a health routine and rest. By the fourteenth, he was ensconced at the Savoy Hotel in London for his final two summer concerts with the London Symphony Orchestra, one including Walton's *Belshazzar's Feast* and the other with Mozart's D Minor Piano Concerto with Annie Fischer, on Sunday September 23.

An American Musical Force

On that same day, the New York Philharmonic, under Leonard Bernstein, presented the opening concert in Philharmonic Hall at Lincoln Center for the Performing Arts. On the Monday and Tuesday following, the Boston Symphony, conducted by Erich Leinsdorf, and the Philadelphia Orchestra, led by Eugene Ormandy, would take part in that opening week. On Wednesday night, the New York Philharmonic performed another concert. To complete the opening celebration, the Juilliard Orchestra under Jean Morel, with cellist Leonard Rose, performed on Friday the twenty-eighth.

That Wednesday, only three days after his last London concert, Szell rehearsed the Cleveland Orchestra in New York City for its Lincoln Center debut. Cleveland was the only non–East Coast orchestra honored with an invitation to Lincoln Center's opening week; not only was the orchestra a regular presence in New York's concert life, but the invitation also recognized Szell's stature among conductors in America. Their program presented the first New York performance of Etler's

Concerto in One Movement, Schubert's C Major Symphony, and the Brahms Violin Concerto with Isaac Stern.

Szell would never leave such an important occasion to chance. Even though the Brahms had been performed in February and the Schubert and Etler the previous May, one rehearsal in Philharmonic Hall would not have been sufficient to adequately repolish them to Szell's standards and at the same time to adjust to the hall's erratic acoustics. Szell chose to have two rehearsals the day before the Lincoln Center debut. But where? Philharmonic Hall was constantly occupied: Bernstein and the New York Philharmonic were rehearsing on Wednesday morning for their evening concert, and, in the afternoon, the New York Pro Musica would rehearse for its 5:30 P.M. concert. Szell had few choices—New York City, for all of its cultural leadership, has precious few venues where a symphony orchestra can rehearse.

Unthinkable as it may seem today, at one crucial time, the prospect of New York City without Carnegie Hall seemed a certainty. With the coming of Lincoln Center, commercial forces were dictating the demise of the great old concert hall. Isaac Stern led the crusade to save Carnegie Hall. He proved a distinguished and natural, if ironic, choice for Cleveland's Lincoln Center program. The two preliminary rehearsals, fittingly, were held on stage at Carnegie Hall (in the auditorium destined to carry Stern's name).

Questions of tempo, phrasing, and ensemble had long been well settled, but these rehearsals still could not prepare the orchestra for the acoustics of the new hall. Szell could set the balances only in Philharmonic Hall itself. He scheduled three hours instead of the usual two-and-a-half for that crucial rehearsal. Skeptical by nature and steeped in the principle of "guilty until proven innocent," Szell characteristically did not jump on the bandwagon. Some other orchestras had switched future New York concerts from Carnegie Hall to Philharmonic Hall before testing its acoustics. Word had gotten out that Philharmonic Hall presented great difficulties. It lacked sufficient reverberation, the bass was near nonexistent, and the sound differed drastically from one location to another.

Immediately after his arrival from London, Szell heard the Boston, Philadelphia, and New York orchestra's concerts in Philharmonic Hall. Before his Thursday rehearsal, he made a quick but accurate assessment of its acoustical characteristics. He had already studied the hall's design and discussed it with Robert Shankland. The so-called "clouds" were an unusual feature, hanging from the ceiling and moveable for acoustic flexibility. Shankland recalled: "I talked to Szell about the clouds and how they should have the effect of making the intensity of a single instrument on the stage be very different as you went across, through [a row of seats], or up and down an aisle. And so while the orchestra was there, Szell conducted an experiment with some first chair people. He walked back and forth while a man was playing scales. . . . [When] Szell returned he described how [widely] the intensity varied.

This was as beautiful a physics experiment as I have ever been party to. . . . It was just exactly what you'd expect theoretically from clouds in the ceiling."

Shankland remarked that it would have taken a couple of hours to explain to a physics student how to observe the acoustics of Philharmonic Hall, but that "with Dr. Szell it took about five minutes.[105] That knowledge helped Szell compensate for the hall's difficulties. It called for drastic measures. To overcome the bass deficiency, he ordered boxes quickly constructed to raise the basses and cellos and to increase their resonance. Szell also told the orchestra that he would ask them to play in ways that may seem crazy to them, but that the extreme problem demanded an equally extreme solution. For example, he asked the low strings to play unusually loudly. The final effect justified their efforts and made the Cleveland Orchestra's concert come off acoustically best of the orchestras.

Ultimately, the concert proved supremely satisfying. "In the Lincoln Center parade of orchestras through Philharmonic Hall this week," wrote Miles Kastendieck, "the Cleveland Orchestra fared best. Its concert last night proved the most exciting musically, not because of the standard repertory played but because of the superb music-making under George Szell's direction." Kastendieck granted that Szell had reaped the benefit of earlier orchestras' experiences, and the constant "tuning" of the hall, "for the acoustical adjustments have continued daily," but he added: "The kind of sound created last night brought the hall into focus and made the evening truly memorable." Most remarkably, he stated: "Mr. Szell towered over the other conductors of the week [and this] helps explain why the concert was so satisfying. He helped clarify how fine the new hall really is."

Szell's private opinion, which he did not shrink from making public, was that the hall was a disaster and they had best tear it down and begin all over again. But his uncanny technical instinct and musical greatness even made the hall appear good. Harriett Johnson began, "Philharmonic Hall settled into its musical stride last night with a magnificent concert by the Cleveland Orchestra. For the initial time the extracurricular aspects of opening week at Lincoln Center receded into the background," and ended, "the sound varies in different parts of the hall, [but] it was obvious that the Clevelanders had triumphed, no matter what."[106]

The *London Times*'s review credited Szell for "the balances, [which] for the first time, were right, and the sound of the ensemble marked by the same clarity and clean definition of line associated with the orchestra's performances at home." The reviewer noted that Szell had rehearsed the program in New York rather than "on the road as his Boston and Philadelphia colleagues had done."[107] Louis Biancolli touched on a Szell essence in describing the Schubert C Major Symphony and its effect:

> Those who, like myself, thought they were through with Schubert's [Ninth] Symphony had a jolt in store for them—a jolt of rediscovery. Here was a masterpiece all over again, new as the day it was born in Schubert's mind.

> That was the secret, perhaps, of this extraordinary visionary on the podium—the inhuman power of delving into the living essence of the music in hand and shaping it in its maker's image.
>
> The implicit drama, the bounty of melody, the ceaseless throb of tension, all were in this performance—the first I have ever heard to efface the memory of Arturo Toscanini.[108]

Hearing Szell and the Cleveland Orchestra for the first time at its Lincoln Center opening concert made an indelible impression on a young musician studying conducting at Juilliard with Jean Morel. The event would influence the course of music history. James Levine remembered his impressions: "What an eye-opener! I realized that here was an orchestra that was trained, knew what they were doing. . . . From that moment and the next two years I got all their records I could and bought a series ticket for the New York concerts."[109] In just two years, Levine would join Szell and the orchestra as apprentice conductor, and later, assistant conductor.

The Monday following the Lincoln Center concert, October 1, the program repeated in Cleveland for the benefit of the orchestra's pension fund. It was billed as "An Extraordinary Concert" and a "Lincoln Center Encore." The program noted, "Mr. Stern, Mr. Szell, and the members of the orchestra are generously donating their services for this concert."[110]

In addition to the prestigious opening of Lincoln Center, the orchestra's forty-fifth and Szell's seventeenth season, 1962–63, was distinguished by its increase of two subscription pairs to twenty-six. Szell's thoroughness continued in the new season; he used all nine services every week.[111] On the Saturday morning of the first subscription pair, Szell called a string sectional rehearsal for the Bruckner Symphony no. 7, scheduled for performance three weeks later. This was the first of three extra rehearsals for the Bruckner. Although not a premiere by the orchestra, it was not exactly a repertoire piece either—it had been performed only four times by them: twice before Szell's time in 1938 and 1945 and twice by him, in 1949 and 1953. Many new players had since joined the orchestra, and Szell was concerned that this singular music would not be adequately absorbed by the players during the week of the concert alone.

Szell rarely called sectional rehearsals, but the unfamiliarity of the Bruckner called for them. On Friday morning of the second week, he held a rehearsal for the brass section, on which Bruckner makes special demands. In addition to the usual four French horns, three trumpets, three trombones, and tuba, Bruckner's Seventh calls for two pairs of Wagner tubas.[112] Finally, on Saturday morning, the full orchestra rehearsed the Bruckner.

The first recording of the season took place in the third week—Brahms's Second Piano Concerto with Leon Fleisher, the major work on the concert that week. Its preparation utilized all five rehearsals. A sixth rehearsal for a reading of Strauss's

Sinfonia Domestica, slated for the sixth week, was squeezed in by adding a rehearsal on Monday afternoon to the usual one on Wednesday afternoon. A "runout" to Akron on Tuesday night filled the ninth service of the week. The recording sessions did not count toward weekly services. They were subject to the orchestra's contract and prevailing national musicians' union rules, which had their own arcane regulations.[113]

Before leaving for Europe, Szell included the *Symphonia Domestica* on November 8 and 10. Dietrich Fischer-Dieskau, who Szell invited to sing in the concerts, cancelled. For a replacement soloist, the conductor took the recommendation of Max Rudolf and introduced the twenty-five-year-old German violinist Edith Peinemann in Cleveland.

Born in Mainz in 1937, Peinemann was the daughter of the Mainz orchestra's concertmaster, with whom she studied until the age of fourteen. She later studied with Max Rostal in London. In 1956 Peinemann won first prize in the International Competition of the German Radio in Munich. One of the judges of that competition, William Steinberg, invited her to make her American debut with the Pittsburgh Symphony in 1962. Word of her talent spread among elder German conductors, including Max Rudolf in Cincinnati. Peinemann made a great success with her well-chosen Cleveland debut piece, the Dvořák Violin Concerto.

So began a very close friendship between the young violinist and the older conductor. She was talented, German, and attractive. Szell took Peinemann under his avuncular wing—she always referred to him as "Uncle George." Szell invited her to perform with him at the Concertgebouw, the Berlin Philharmonic, and the New York Philharmonic, and often coached her in advance on the concertos.

Szell beneficently sought sponsors who would buy her a fine violin, which he then helped her select. When Erica Morini cancelled an appearance with Szell in Cologne in 1964, he had the orchestra engage Peinemann. At a party after the concert, Szell talked to several wealthy businessmen, who agreed to buy an instrument for her. "In December just before Christmas in 1964," Peinemann recalled, Szell "was in Zurich and I had my violin dealer from Bern who had a lot of fine instruments come to Zurich. We went to the concert hall there and Mr. Szell went into the audience and I played to him five fine violins: two Guarnieri, three Stradivari. And he chose the one I have now, a Guarnieri. . . . He was marvelous to young musicians."

Peinemann studied and performed the Beethoven concerto with him, and in 1967 the Bartók Violin Concerto no. 2. Two years later, he paid her the supreme compliment by asking her to perform a Mozart concerto (the G Major), a composer he reserved for his favorite and most mature artists. He worked "a long time" with her on it as well.

Szell's advice proved not always beneficial, however. Peinemann felt that his meddling in negotiations for a pending recording contract caused the deal to fall through, which she felt set her career back. But this matter did not affect her friendship with both Szells, and she remained close to Helene after George Szell's death.[114]

Recognition for Szell

In 1963 an article in *Newsweek* and a cover story in *Time* noted Szell's fiftieth anniversary as a conductor. *Newsweek* recounted the old chestnuts—Szell as a child striking his mother's hand when she played a wrong note at the piano, and Rudolf Bing's immortal retort, "Not while I'm alive." The magazine quoted several members of the orchestra, some by name, others not. One said, "Szell is a dictator, but that's the nature of the conductor. He has to be. Szell is demanding, but he gives of himself as much—if not more. That's why our team is on top now." The article pointed out the Lincoln Center opening triumph and characterized the orchestra: "In style, the Cleveland Orchestra reflects its master, for it plays with stunning clarity, precision, and balance. No section stands out (as do the sonorous strings in the Philadelphia Orchestra, for example); the entire ensemble is smoothly coordinated." The director of the Dutch Education Ministry, Henk Reinink, remarked: "He has done a world of good for our Concertgebouw Orchestra," but members of that orchestra "jokingly refer to a rehearsal with Szell as *Szellstraf*, from the Dutch *celstraf*, meaning solitary confinement." The article revealed Szell's sentimental side: "The death of Dimitri Mitropoulos hit him hard, and so did the heart condition that caused the retirement of Fritz Reiner."

The *Time* article took another slant, noting the shifting balances of musical excellence over time; from Europe to America, from the American East to the Midwest. Mahler noted: "My orchestra [the New York Philharmonic] is the genuine American orchestra, phlegmatic and without talent." But at present, *Time* maintained, "of all Europe's orchestras, only the Berlin Philharmonic and the London Philharmonia are the occasional equals of the five leading American orchestras." Cleveland's excellence owed to Szell, according to a "young Western conductor who once studied with [Szell] and now says, 'Szell is one of the world's great musicians and a cold, cold sonofabitch.'" The article postulated: "Szell harbors a hidden fondness for musicians, but he keeps it under perfect control." And, "Szell's few close friends in Cleveland say that success has mellowed him, but only rarely do hints of this change drift out to the world at large. On forays into guest-conducting, he always bags a new enemy or two for his trophy room."

Some orchestra members felt that Szell "rehearses so much that they pass their peak before concert time. 'If you really want to hear how good we are, come to rehearsal,' says a Cleveland violinist." Also, "A few players complain of his cruelty, hinting darkly that he has driven a musician or two into emergency mental care." (Szell actually kept at least one emotionally troubled player on the payroll because he believed in his talent, and anonymously helped pay for his treatment.) *Time* ran an "almost Aristotelian" quote from Szell: "Music is indivisible. The dualism of feeling and thinking must be resolved to a state of unity in which one thinks with the heart and feels with the brain."[115]

January 1963 was packed with activity: five subscription pairs and four recording sessions in the first two weekends of the year. The Symphony no. 4 of Gustav Mahler was a highlight of the month. Metropolitan Opera soprano Judith Raskin, the exquisite soloist, sang in the fourth movement. Raskin's phrasing, diction, musicianship, and beautiful sound made an appropriately heavenly conclusion. She also sang Mozart's Motet *Exsultate, jubilate* elegantly in the first half of the concert.

Raskin was one of Szell's favorite soloists. She had begun her musical training on the violin and, besides having a lovely voice, was a first-rate musician. The orchestra loved her. One critic wrote that Szell should designate her "first-chair soprano" of the orchestra. Her purity of sound, perfection of pitch, and understanding and projection of the words combine in only a few artists in any generation. By dint of being married to a Doctor Raskin, no prior relation, orchestra wags joked that her name, therefore, was Judith Raskin Raskin. A warm and gracious person, Judith Raskin tragically died of cancer in 1984 at age fifty-six.

Szell stayed in New York after the February East Coast tour, taking a week off before a sixteen-concert stint with the New York Philharmonic from February 28 to March 24, 1963, his first appearance since 1955. Clifford Curzon, Rudolf Firkusny, Leon Fleisher, and Erica Morini performed as soloists.

Irving Kolodin noted the gap since Szell's last appearances. He observed that the Philharmonic "gave its guest perhaps not quite the front-of-the-seat attention that he gets from his own men. . . . This was clear indication that they, if not the audience, were well aware of the turn in the road represented by the presence of Szell." Szell and his soloist, Curzon (in the "Emperor" Concerto), "specialists in the restoration of nineteenth-century masterpieces, played perfectly into each other's hands."[116]

Schonberg discerned that it took Szell until the second concert for things to jell, but when they did, "what resulted was the kind of Szell performance that is heard when he conducts his own orchestra in Cleveland." Kastendieck also noted the period of adjustment between Szell and the Philharmonic: "George Szell completed his month with the Philharmonic, a conquering hero in every way. Once the musicians had adjusted themselves both to his uncompromising discipline and intense musicianship, they became again a great orchestra sensitively responsive to the direction of a great conductor. Each week the concerts became more exciting musically."[117]

Szell returned from New York for his final four concerts of the Cleveland season with a week of concerts conducted by Shaw in the middle. On April 4 Flothuis wrote Szell about the coming summer concerts, adding a P.S.: "Could you give me some confidential information about Guiomar Novaës?" Szell replied: "Let me first express my surprise that she should be so completely unknown in your parts. While I have not played with her during the past few years and while it is not completely indelicate to say that she is now a rather elderly lady [she was sixty-seven, a little more than a year older than Szell!], it must be emphasized that she is an exceedingly artistic and poetic pianist and can give an audience a quite incomparable thrill when playing the literature best suited to her personality, such as Chopin F minor Concerto, Schumann Concerto and one or the other Mozart concerto."[118]

Szell's programs at the end of the season bowed to recording requisites. An all-Beethoven concert, *Leonore* Overture no. 3, Piano Concerto no. 3, with Annie Fischer, and Symphony no. 4 provided material. The Fourth Symphony had been first recorded by Szell and the Cleveland Orchestra in April 1947. This was part of a new series of the complete Beethoven Symphonies for Epic, released in both stereo and monaural. The next-to-last program saw the United States premiere of Walton's *Variations on a Theme by Hindemith*, Mozart's Violin Concerto no. 5 in A Major,with Isaac Stern, and Brahms's Symphony no. 3. The subscription concert year ended with the Symphony in B-flat, op. 18, no. 2, of Johann Christian Bach, and the seventh of eight seasons' traversals of Beethoven's Ninth.

The Szells landed in Paris on May 26, 1963. By the thirtieth they had motored to Zurich, and on June 4 arrived in Vienna. On the seventh, Szell's sixty-sixth birthday, and again on the twelfth, he conducted the Vienna Philharmonic in the Vienna Festival. Next, they traveled back to Zurich for a few days, then on to the Maggio Musicale in Florence, where Szell conducted a concert on the twenty-second. From then to July 24, they stayed at the Hotel du Golf for the annual vacation. Szell returned to work in August with a sentimental reunion with the Czech Philharmonic at the Salzburg Festival, a concert with the Swedish Radio Orchestra in Stockholm, and an appearance with the Concertgebouw in Scheveningen. He rejoined the Concertgebouw at the Edinburgh Festival for concerts on September 6 and 7. Discussions about his next Concertgebouw engagement in November 1964 concerned two different programs, for which Szell requested Curzon and Peinemann as soloists. After two more weeks in Switzerland, he returned to the United States, and eight days later led the first rehearsal of the Cleveland Orchestra's forty-sixth and his eighteenth season, 1963–64, for the opening concert on October 3, 1963.

The season began with the usual hoopla, and the local NBC station, KYW-TV, broadcast the opening concert live. Squeezed in between big romantic works—beginning with Berlioz's *Roman Carnival* Overture and ending with Szell's hallmark interpretation of Sibelius's Symphony no. 2—were Walton's *Variations on a Theme by Hindemith* and a miniature gem, Ravel's Introduction and Allegro for Harp, Flute, Clarinet, and String Quartet. Szell doubled the string quartet, but it still presented an enormous contrast to the other pieces on the program. Orchestra harpist Alice Chalifoux played a beautiful account of the virtuoso part, and Maurice Sharp and

Robert Marcellus gave the wind parts a special distinction. At a Musical Arts Association reception after the opening concert, Szell received the honorary rank Commander of the Order of the British Empire (C.B.E.), "in recognition of his services to British Music and the furthering of Anglo-America cultural relations."[119]

Two symphonies made up the entire second concert—Beethoven's Fifth and Bruckner's Third. The orchestra recorded half of the Beethoven that week, and the rest two weeks later. That fall, Szell and Flothuis corresponded about repertoire for his November 1964 Concertgebouw appearances. Philips was interested in having Szell record the Bruckner Fourth with the orchestra, but they could not agree about which version—Philips wanted the original, Szell a later revision.

A national tragedy, the shooting of President John F. Kennedy, took place on Friday, afternoon November 22. At the time, Szell was conducting an all-Beethoven concert at the New York Philharmonic. An announcement interrupted the concert to inform the audience that President Kennedy had been shot, and canceled the remainder. In the Saturday and Sunday repetitions, the orchestra replaced the scheduled *Leonore no.* 3 with the second movement of the *Eroica*, the *Marcia funebre*, in the late president's memory.

On November 28 Szell conducted the United States premiere of Polish composer Tadeuz Baird's *Four Essays*, which he later brought to Cleveland. Standard Szell repertoire included Dvořák's G Major Symphony, Schumann's Second Symphony, Haydn's Ninety-third, and Bach's Suite no. 3 in D. Lev Oborin was soloist in the Tchaikovsky First Piano Concerto, Erica Morini played Mendelssohn's Violin Concerto, and Jeanne-Marie Darré played Liszt's Second Piano Concerto. In that program, which began with the Haydn symphony, Szell countered the French pianist playing music of a Hungarian composer with two French works—Debussy's *Afternoon of a Faun* and *La mer*—led by a Hungarian-born conductor.

At the end of December Szell led the first Cleveland performance of Stravinsky's *Monumentum pro Gesualdo*, following it with Sibelius's *Swan of Tuonela*, featuring the orchestra's English horn player, Harvey McGuire, Mozart's *Sinfonia concertante* for violin and viola, with first chair players Rafael Druian and Abraham Skernick, and Brahms's Second Symphony.

January 1964 was a brilliant month; two of America's leading composers heard their works performed. Samuel Barber attended the first concert of the New Year for the Cleveland premiere and first recording of his piano concerto, played by John Browning, for whom it was written. Szell was much taken by the work and its soloist. Browning appeared as soloist with Szell in other repertoire thereafter, and the orchestra played the Barber work on the international tour in 1965. At a lunch at his home, Szell made a gesture that touched Barber and amazed Browning. He served them a bottle of Montrachet, a rare and fine Burgundy. Remarkably, in the first act of Barber's opera *Vanessa*, the title character is given a wine list and she selects a

Montrachet. Szell never conducted the opera but he knew it and remembered to make the connection for the occasion.[120]

In the third week, Peter Mennin was on hand for the world premiere of his Symphony no. 7, *Variation Symphony*, composed for Szell and the Cleveland Orchestra. In addition to three Czech-born soloists also slated for New York (Rudolf Firkusny—Mozart K. 450, Josef Suk—Dvořák Violin Concerto, and Ivan Moravec—Beethoven Piano Concerto no. 4), Arthur Rubinstein played a marathon pair of concerts for the benefit of the orchestra's pension fund. The busy month also included the recording of Strauss's gigantic tone poem *Sinfonia Domestica* and William Schuman's *A Song of Orpheus*, with cellist Leonard Rose.

Rubinstein, that seventy-seven-year-old wonder, played Mozart's D Minor Piano Concerto, K. 466, and Beethoven's "Emperor" Concerto on the first concert and the Schumann A Minor and Tchaikovsky B-flat Concerto on the second. Late in his long career, he added the Mozart to his repertoire, and they carefully rehearsed it. The Schumann and Tchaikovsky each had been allotted rehearsal time but it ran out before the Beethoven, and Szell told the orchestra that they all knew it and would perform it without rehearsal.

Rubinstein, with his noble profile, sat calmly at the keyboard, playing with his unique depth of tone and elegant phrasing, in full command of his remarkable technique. The thrilling event was what had not been rehearsed: the "Emperor." It is an axiom that too little rehearsal is much more dangerous than none at all. Complacency from some rehearsal can lead to inattention and routine; but no rehearsal at all puts everyone on their mettle. And so it happened: that performance unfolded not only technically letter perfect, but it marked an artistic high point of the kind that Toscanini—after his historic performance of *Die Meistersinger* at the Salzburg Festival in 1936—called in honest amazement, "a dream." The "Emperor" was magical, poetic, and powerful.

During this busy period Szell auditioned candidates for assistant concertmaster to replace Arnold Steinhardt, who announced his departure to form the Guarnieri String Quartet. First violin section member Daniel Majeske won the chair. Szell also made time to coach Edith Peinemann for January performances in Cleveland. She had played the Beethoven Concerto with the Concertgebouw in Rotterdam in December 1963, but Flothuis reported to Szell that they did not think her mature enough for it. Peinemann told Szell that she encountered an incompetent provincial guest conductor, only one rehearsal—and that not in the concert hall—and missing key members of the orchestra. After Szell coached her, he wrote Flothuis relating Peinemann's explanation and stating that he felt convinced that "she will give a very fine performance indeed."

With an eye to possible inclusion on one of Szell's forthcoming Concertgebouw programs, Flothuis sent Szell a selection of scores by Dutch composers to consider. A week before Peinemann came to Cleveland, Szell wrote Flothuis, "I shall have a look at them as soon as possible but I am afraid this will probably not be before sometime during the latter part of February." But a week later, in a handwritten letter the day of the first pension fund concert, he wrote, "Contrary to expectations I did have a little time to look at the Dutch scores." Of that period, Szell confided: "I am just passing through the most insanely loaded and complicated schedule of my life."[121]

The 1964 eastern tour consisted of thirteen concerts anchored by three Mondays in Carnegie Hall. After the first, they forged north, ending in Boston on Sunday. Concerts in New York, New Jersey, and Pennsylvania led to the second Sunday in Washington, D.C., a concert followed by a gala reception in Szell's honor at the U.S. Department of State. The *Plain Dealer* told Cleveland about the concert, the reception with its distinguished guests, and the warm tribute to Szell from President Lyndon Johnson on the occasion of Szell's fiftieth anniversary as a conductor and in anticipation of the coming international tour. A dramatic photograph showed Szell with the huge world globe in the lobby of the State Department. The newspaper also reprinted a glowing review by Paul Hume.[122]

After the tour, Szell returned to Cleveland on the overnight train, arriving on Tuesday morning. After two rehearsals on Wednesday and one on Thursday morning, he led the seventeenth subscription concert of the season—Strauss's Serenade for Winds, op. 7, Bach's Cantata 51, *Jauchzet Gott in allen Landen* (with soprano Maria Stader), and Brahms's First Symphony.

Szell next appeared in New York for fifteen concerts with the New York Philharmonic. In an interview by Raymond Ericson for the *New York Times,* Szell spoke candidly: "Complimented on his performances with the New York Philharmonic of the recent Wagner-Bruckner program, Mr. Szell said without affectation or malice: 'It takes about three weeks to pull the men out of improper playing habits, to sound like the great orchestra they can be. Once they're playing well they take a real pride in what they're doing and they enjoy it.'"[123]

Outspoken on other musical matters, Szell threatened to write an article on "architects and acousticians of today's concert halls," which he termed "murderers in music." He resigned himself to his reputation of being "a fearsome autocrat of the baton, whose earthy, cutting comments have reportedly reduced orchestral musicians to near prostration." "Discussing this reputation the other day," Ericson wrote, "the conductor could not have been more courteous and affable. 'I might as well live up to this image of me,' he said smilingly. 'I don't know what I could do about it and it does not matter really. What bothers me,' he went on more seriously, 'is the number of inaccuracies. . . . I shudder when I think of researchers a hundred years from now depending for their information on today's material.'"

Szell told Ericson of his finding time to serve on contest juries and for occasional coaching. "He enjoys both because he can 'always learn something' from watching and listening to others.'" The experience of auditioning many young conductors for the Ford Foundation-Peabody Conservatory of Music Conductors' Project he found "magical—miraculous—to hear how the sound of an orchestra changes after about the third bar under a different conductor. It doesn't matter whether it is for better or for worse. What is fascinating is analyzing the cause and effect involved, what really happens to produce this change." In connection with his private coaching of "professional artists—'you would recognize their names'—he said he does that for his own pleasure but that he learns much from that also. He has the heretical notion that 'teachers should pay their pupils' instead of the other way around."

Szell's Philharmonic engagement was to have closed with a pension fund benefit concert with Arthur Rubinstein playing the two Brahms piano concertos, but Szell contracted a viral infection, and Alfred Wallenstein conducted the concert in his place. The Ericson article appeared two days before the concert, and this caused some to link Szell's withdrawal to it. He arranged to meet with Marius Flothuis in New York on the twentieth of the month, where the Concertgebouw would be on tour; and the sixty-six-year-old conductor continued to pursue a hectic schedule.[124]

The final Cleveland concert of the season presented the Verdi *Requiem*, with soprano Phyllis Curtin, mezzo-soprano Regina Sarfaty, tenor Jan Peerce, and bass-baritone Thomas Paul. It left a profound impression in a memorable year. The orchestra recorded *Exsultate, jubilate*, with soprano Raskin, on the Monday after the final concert. Raskin had performed it the previous season, but the recording was delayed until a suitable organ for the continuo was restored.[125]

Szell's 1964 summer concerts in Europe began with the West German Radio Orchestra in Cologne on June 11. He led a Richard Strauss centennial concert with the Concertgebouw at the Holland Festival on June 19 and 20 and a concert with the Berlin Philharmonic in Salzburg on July 10. Between concerts he rested in Zurich, Crans, and the Engadine. The first week in September, Szell appeared at the Montreux Festival to conduct the Czech Philharmonic. After storing his automobile in Paris, he flew to Cleveland. On Sunday the thirteenth, Szell attended the final performance of the Lake Erie Opera Theatre's premiere season in Severance Hall, a double bill of two-thirds of Puccini's *Il trittico*.[126]

The formation of the opera company required Szell's blessing. It proved useful at the time. The orchestra was not yet on a fifty-two-week contract, and management welcomed employment for inactive weeks. An opera board, formed under the leadership of Musical Arts Association trustee Dorothy Humel, raised money for production costs. The Musical Arts Association provided the orchestra and hall and received the ticket income. A wise limitation prevented duplicating repertoire brought by the Metropolitan Opera on its annual spring tours. To prevent confusion with the Northern Ohio Opera Association, the local organization sponsoring the Metropolitan Opera's Cleveland appearances, the name avoided the juxtaposition of "Ohio," "Opera," and "Cleveland," thus the ambiguous name, "Lake Erie Opera Theatre." Opera theater it was, but "Lake Erie" was misleading, and it gave no indication that opera performances took place in Severance Hall with the Cleveland Orchestra in the pit.

For institutional, budgetary, and political reasons, the opera only recruited singers among present or former Ohioans. The college- and university-rich state offered much vocal talent, and many former Ohioans had gone on to professional careers. In the seven years of its operation, a nucleus of singers appeared in L.E.O.T. productions, combining versatility and vocal and dramatic artistry. Another prime tenet of the company involved presenting operas in English, therefore the singers acquired skilled English diction and L.E.O.T. took on all the best qualities of a repertory company. When the orchestra signed its first fifty-two-week contract in 1967, the opera's relatively modest production costs came to be seen as a drain on funds needed by the orchestra, now greatly increased by the year-round contract. Three years later, the opera gave its last performances.

Szell attended a performance of each L.E.O.T. season except the last, which took place after he died. In a way, he controlled the opera's lifeline, and evidently he approved what he saw and heard. Szell not only accepted L.E.O.T., he complimented it publicly.[127]

Details of an Epic Tour Are Announced

The opening concert of the 1964–65 season, Szell's nineteenth, on Thursday, September 18, appeared live on local television.[128] A U.S. State Department representative, Charles Ellison, attended the concert and announced details of "one of the longest international concert tours" sponsored by the department. At the end of this season, the orchestra would tour the Soviet Union, Scandinavia, and western Europe.[129]

The second Cleveland program presented the first soloist of the season, Daniel Majeske, newly promoted to first assistant concertmaster, playing the Brahms concerto. Violinist Leonid Kogan's and pianist Ann Schein's appearances in this season constituted their sole appearances with the Cleveland Orchestra. Schein chose the Chopin F Minor to present herself to best advantage in her Cleveland debut, but she could not have known that the Chopin concerti were among Szell's least favorite works to conduct. After a Tuesday performance with Szell in Akron, Szell relegated the Chopin to a very junior staff conductor for the subscription pair on Thursday and Saturday. Schein felt surprised, disappointed, and puzzled as to why Szell made that last-minute assignment. If she had a crystal ball, the change might have seemed better than it did at the time. Her collaborator was that season's new twenty-one-year-old apprentice conductor, James Levine.

Szell rested for a week in November before traveling to Holland, where he would conduct concerts and a recording with the Concertgebouw. In September Heuwekemeijer had sent a contract for that November's concerts "for good order's sake." Szell wrote back, "Thanks for your letter and please find the contract, duly signed, here enclosed. You see, my relationship to you is so close and my confidence so great that I would have come without a signed commitment so I didn't press you for one although I had noticed that it was still missing." This appeared a calm contrast to their previous contract contretemps.[130] In Amsterdam, Szell introduced Walton's *Variations on a Theme by Hindemith*, conducted the Beethoven Violin Concerto with Edith Peinemann, and made his only commercial recording of the Sibelius Symphony no. 2. He then journeyed to Vienna for a concert with the Vienna Symphony.

A Seismic Shock

An upheaval occurred in Szell's first Cleveland rehearsal of the new year, upsetting the balance of his painstakingly crafted orchestra leadership. A long-standing situation had worsened the previous fall. During the seven weeks of Szell's absence, principal oboist Marc Lifschey's behavior in rehearsals had become increasingly problematic. Shaw and Lane had noticed this in their rehearsals, as had guest conductor Lukas Foss. Lifschey was clearly unhappy, but the reason remained unclear. Sometimes in rehearsal when he was not satisfied with some musical matter, he would play a sour note or two, disturbing to his colleagues and disconcerting to the guest conductor unfamiliar with the highly sensitive player.

On Szell's return in December, Barksdale, Lane, and Shaw alerted him to the situation. His first week back was uneventful. In the first rehearsal of his second week, on January 4, 1965, Szell began with a speech wishing the players a happy and healthy New Year, and expressing hope that they have only pleasant things to write in their new calendar books. (The orchestra librarians had distributed Szell's annual Christmas present, the handsome, leather-bound pocket diary by Frank Smythson of Bond Street.)

He began with Prokfiev's Symphony no. 5, important for the coming foreign tour. The opening Andante went satisfactorily and without incident, as did the Allegro marcato; then came the beautiful Adagio. In its mournful oboe passage underscored by the bassoon, Lifschey was obviously not happy with something, because he ever so slightly soured a note or two. Szell said nothing and kept going. As though he had not made the point sufficiently the first time, when the passage came around again, Lifschey went very sour. Szell, warned and on his guard, stopped the orchestra and asked in a calm tone of voice, "Now Marc, what's wrong with the pitch?" That simple question seemed to unlock all of Lifschey's pent-up emotions. He replied, "That's the pitch I'm playing and if you don't like it, you can get someone else."

A collective gasp preceded an eerie silence, frozen in time and space for seconds that seemed like minutes. Szell then said, "Very well, will you please leave." Holding his oboe in front of him with its case under his arm, Lifschey left the stage cursing under his breath. Some orchestra members clucked disapproval and some made vocal sounds of "hush." Szell indicated to assistant first oboist Robert Zupnik, who was playing a doubling part, to move into Lifschey's chair.[131]

The rehearsal went on almost as though nothing had happened. But something had, and its ramifications were lasting. Although Lifschey told friends afterward that he did not remember saying what he was heard to say and tried to apologize, it was impossible. No one could talk so disrespectfully to George Szell, especially in public. Szell could not back down. As great a player as Lifschey was, he seemed to have been unhappy for a long time. Conjecturally, the unplanned outburst may have accomplished what Lifschey may have wanted in his heart but did not otherwise know how to do—to quit. The situation was no longer healthy for him and therefore for the orchestra, as Szell must have realized.

Lifschey's midseason departure could not have come at a less opportune time. The next month, the orchestra faced the eastern tour and, in the spring, the eleven-and-a-half-week tour of the Soviet Union, Scandinavia, and western Europe. Zupnik was a fine oboist but felt content in his role as assistant principal. With a mercurial principal such as Lifschey, Zupnik knew that he might have to take over for a concert at a moment's notice. He told Szell that he did not want the whole responsibility for the entire repertoire and coming tours, but would gladly share it with another qualified player. Szell asked the New York Philharmonic's first oboist, Harold Gomberg, for a recommendation among his recent students. Gomberg proposed Adrian Gnam, whom Szell hired for the rest of the season. As "acting co-principal," Gnam would split the first oboe book with Zupnik for the rest of the season, while the orchestra conducted a national search for Lifschey's permanent replacement.

Szell's soloists after the New Year included Erica Morini, Gina Bachauer, Edith Peinemann, Clifford Curzon, Leon Fleisher, and John Browning. Vocal soloists in Beethoven's Ninth were Saramae Endich, Jane Hobson, Ernst Haefliger, and Thomas Paul. Szell programmed the Beethoven in the first week of February instead of at the end of the season, because it would lead off a Beethoven series of three Carnegie Hall Mondays. The orchestra transported its Cleveland Orchestra Chorus to New York for that event.

Dutilleux's *Cinques Métaboles* received its first New York performance on a program with Haydn's Symphony no. 31, "With the Horn Call," Hindemith's *Metamorphosis*, and Schumann's Fourth. Two twentieth-century masterpieces occupied the other Carnegie Hall concert: Bartók's *Concerto for Orchestra* and Prokofiev's Fifth Symphony, later joined for posterity on a Sony CD. The orchestra dedicated that concert, on February 21, 1965, to the memory of Leopold Mannes, who died the previous August.[132]

Szell remained always mindful of the New York audiences and critics. On a visit to Cleveland, Schuyler Chapin, then head of Columbia Records' Masterworks Division, heard the Beethoven Ninth. Completely awed, he told Szell backstage afterward: "My God, this was really one of the most extraordinary experiences of my life." And Szell "cocked his head" and answered him, "Yes," he said, "we'll show them in New York; our little country orchestra, we'll show them." Alan Rich agreed, writing that it "was one of this listener's great experiences of a lifetime of concertgoing. It was a realization of Beethoven's sovereign score as close to ideal as one could ever dare to dream of hearing."[133]

The critical reaction to Szell's eastern tour performance of Bartók's *Concerto for Orchestra* revealed much. Sometime in the 1950s, Szell made a big cut in the finale.[134] When he played it before in New York, no reviewer noticed. Now that Szell's recording (with cut) had come out, when he played it this time in concert, they did notice.

Pierre Boulez's Cleveland Debut

In March, Pierre Boulez made his United States major orchestra debut conducting a Cleveland subscription pair and a runout to Oberlin. Unknown to Boulez, Szell had taken an interest in him for some time through reports from Marius Flothuis. Just after Boulez's Concertgebouw concerts in December, Flothuis had prophesied: "Perhaps someday Boulez will turn out to be a greater conductor than composer."[135] Although he had not personally observed Boulez conduct, Szell invited him, to Boulez's great surprise.[136] Boulez's program, on March 11 and 13, 1965, featured the United States premiere of his *Figures, Doubles, Prismes* and two first performances in Cleveland: Rameau's *Concerts en Sextour,* nos. 3 and 6, and Debussy's *Jeux.* Also played were *Gigues* and *Rondes de printemps* from Debussy's *Images* for Orchestra, and Stravinsky's *Chant du Rossignol,* based on the opera.

Boulez made an impression on the orchestra and staff completely in accord with Flothuis's assessment. He had the scores securely in his head, he knew what he wanted in rehearsal, and from the start impressed one and all. Boulez boldly began working on intonation with an orchestra whose tuning ran as close to perfection as Cleveland's, but his acute ear was up to the task.

Off or on the podium, he was absolutely consistent in manner. Boulez showed himself soft-spoken, polite, articulate, interesting, and interested in everything, plus approachable and gentlemanly. So he remained in all his many subsequent visits. He did not use a baton. Boulez's beat was clear and his rhythm rock solid. To music of the classical period, he was less committed, but in twentieth-century and French music, he was superb. (And today he is freer in a wider repertoire.) Boulez's unorthodox style, thorough rehearsal technique, and the repertoire he performed to perfection was fresh, impressive, stunning. The headline of Robert Finn's *Plain Dealer* review on March 12 read, "Boulez Bowls 'Em Over."[137]

Szell did not meet Boulez when he made his Cleveland debut. In February, Szell checked into University Hospital in Cleveland for a benign obstructing urinary tract procedure, also described as a benign prostate hypertrophy (B.P.H.). The operation came between the February eastern tour and the Russian-European tour in April and May. Doctors assured Cleveland that Szell would recover well in time for that tour. The operation took place on February 26 and Szell was discharged from the hospital on March 15, two days after Boulez's last concert, and was in fine form by his next concert pair on April 1 and 3.

On March 25, Szell signed a "lifetime" contract. The terms made it ongoing until terminated by either party. The photo in the *Plain Dealer* showed Szell at the signing with Frank Joseph, Louis Lane, and Beverly Barksdale.[138] Szell conducted the last two subscription pairs as planned in the first two weeks of April. Fleisher and Browning were to be soloists on the Soviet/European tour, Fleisher in Mozart's C Major Concerto, K. 503 and Browning in the Barber. They were soloists in the last two concerts of the season. Fleisher's problem with his right hand is now well known, but at the time just beginning and sadly obvious. He played the subscription concerts but, after consultation with Szell, withdrew from the tour. Szell replaced him with Grant Johannesen, playing another Mozart piano concerto, K. 491 in C Minor. Two days after the last subscription concert, the orchestra departed on tour for the Soviet Union. They would return seventy-five days later.

10

The Cleveland Orchestra in the World (1965–68)

Touring the Soviet Union and Europe, 1965

The exchange of performing artists, including soloists, dance companies, and orchestras, played a role in the post–World War II world ideological struggle between the United States and the Soviet Union. The American National Theatre and Academy (ANTA), which had managed the Cleveland Orchestra European tour in 1957, had come under the new Cultural Presentations Program of the United States Department of State. The Boston Symphony Orchestra (1956), the Philadelphia Orchestra (1958), and the New York Philharmonic (1959) had already visited the Soviet Union. For its tour in 1965, the State Department chose the Cleveland Orchestra from seven organizations proposed by its Music Panel, chaired by Leopold Mannes.

The Cleveland tour of Europe and the Soviet Union would be the longest foreign tour yet undertaken by an American orchestra—eleven weeks, from April to June 1965. The orchestra and its members were ambassadors not only for Cleveland but for the nation as well. Tensions with the Soviet Union had eased somewhat since Stalin's death in 1953, but the cold war continued. A representative of the State Department, Terrence Catherman, briefed orchestra members on tour etiquette. We were cautioned not to wander too far from hotels and not to photograph what the Soviets considered military targets, including railroad stations, airports, and any views from an airplane. The Soviet authorities could confiscate film and cameras and could make arrests for infractions of their rules with the slightest provocation. Currency restrictions were strictly enforced and black market activity severely punished. These conditions added to the pressures of performing.[1]

Szell exerted a strong hand in planning the itinerary and limiting the number of concerts. Unlike 1957, he would have relief: Louis Lane and Robert Shaw would conduct a few concerts. Both local concert sponsors and the State Department urged more concerts in more cities and travel on concert days to increase profits for the former or political capital for the latter. Szell limited the number of concerts and made sure of sufficient rest after travel, so the orchestra would stay at top form. He succeeded so well that at the last concert of the long tour, Szell could say to a Cleveland reporter: "I feel better than ever and actually fresher than at the end of a regular Cleveland season. So does the orchestra—as they told me. Although we are just finishing what amounts to a 42-week season, the weeks of the European Tour were interspersed with many and well-spaced rest days and rest periods so that everybody is actually feeling fresher at the end of the tour than at its beginning, where the fatigue of the regular season was still being felt."[2]

In advance of the tour, Szell had to deal with numerous local sponsors' requests for entire programs, specific works, and even conductors. At the beginning of his vacation in Switzerland on June 22, 1964, Szell was not pleased. Without a secretary, he wrote several letters and sent copies of some he received to Barksdale: "Just arrived in Zurich (Helene is already in England), I find on this supposedly first day of my vacation more mail than ever and have been drudging at the typewriter for hours. Well, never mind. Here is the news." He was still drudging in August when he wrote his friend Margareta Ebert, who had relayed the dissatisfaction with Szell's Stockholm program of her boss, the Swedish impresario Helmer Enwall, and his suggestion of a few "sure fire" works, such as a Tchaikovsky symphony or Dvořák's *New World*. Szell stated that they would not have any Tchaikovsky symphony in their tour repertoire. The Dvořák was Lane's Soviet repertoire alone. Szell remarked: "This piece, beautiful as it is, has in America distinctly receded into the 'Pops' category and we cannot tour with it [there]. Altogether it must be remembered that we do not and cannot play all the time those 3–5 hackneyed Symphonies which the managers consider 'sure fire' and which 'bring down the house' no matter which conductor and which orchestra is playing them. Our task is, on the contrary, to show that we can have that kind of audience success with pieces that are not necessarily considered 'sure fire' but are great music and will be uniquely performed."

Szell suggested a compromise of *Meistersinger* Prelude, Barber Piano Concerto, "(sensational piece, very Public-like and yet interesting, STUNNINGLY played by Browning)," Brahms's Third, "a revelation to those who have never heard a first-rate performance of it, which almost never occurs," and the second suite from Ravel's *Daphnis et Chloé*, "(SURE FIRE)." There would also be encores, "of course."[3] At the top of the copy of this letter that he sent to Barksdale, Szell wrote by hand: "You see how tough it is!!"

Enwall noted that the orchestra would have two free days before the single concert in Helsinki, and suggested that Szell move the Helsinki concert a day earlier so that he could add another income-producing concert after Stockholm in Gothenburg.

"The explanation for the extra free day in Helsinki," Szell replied, "is the necessity to give the orchestra an extra day to recover from 5 weeks in Russia, which are likely to be more strenuous and less comfortable than average touring in western countries."[4] The extra day of rest in Helsinki remained and was most welcome.

The State Department wanted the orchestra to play in as many places behind the iron curtain as possible, including Prague and West Berlin, then still an enclave surrounded by communist East Germany. Pressures were also exerted at home and abroad about the programming of American music. The music panel wanted Szell to include more of the "serious" American works he had played and, in some cases, commissioned. Szell answered each diplomatically, offering some flexibility.

Goskonzert, the Soviet concert agency, determined the itinerary within the Soviet Union: Moscow, Kiev, Tbilisi, Yerevan, Sochi, and Leningrad. For the Scandinavian/European half of the tour, there was much discussion and correspondence with the State Department, eventually settling on Helsinki, Stockholm, Warsaw, Hamburg, Paris, Bergen, Berlin, Prague, Bratislava, Vienna, London, and Amsterdam.[5]

The Viennese sponsor, Peter Weiser, wanted American music for all four concerts. Szell told him: "Four consecutive concerts with only American works or works written in America would be neither advisable nor completely feasible for us." Instead he offered, "an all-Gershwin program under the baton of my associate, Louis Lane, who does this sort of thing superbly (and not only this sort of thing)." He promised to include an "important American work" in each of the other three programs, but added, "You must not forget that the State Department sponsors these tours not only to display American composers, but eminently American performers, and these performers must insist on measuring themselves against their colleagues of other nations, also in some works of the great standard literature. . . . A week of concerts without anything of the standard repertoire where my orchestra can display its qualities and I mine as interpreter with my instrument, would be of very little interest to me."

In a cable two days later, Szell added: "The cultural purpose of these State Department sponsored tours is to convince the Europeans of the artistic maturity, not only of the already known high technical proficiency, of American performers. For this reason we must play in Europe everywhere some of the standard works to show the Europeans that their facile prejudice about Americans being able to play only loud and fast but not having any feeling, inwardness, or 'real musical culture,' is completely unjustified."

Weiser did not recognize Lane's name, and suggested that Stanislaw Skrowaczewski conduct the Gershwin program. In a P.S., Szell added: "Additional information on the Gershwin program under Louis Lane. Louis Lane is a native American [American-born] and an excellent conductor who will also conduct part of our tour through Soviet Russia. He has been with me for 18 years and is an absolutely first-rate talent. Skrowaczewski would be completely out of place in a Gershwin program; besides, he is not one of our conductors on this tour."[6]

Mannes transmitted the concerns of the Music Panel for the State Department Cultural Affairs to Szell, conceding that he "would be less than frank if I did not say that I think that they made a valid point." Because they knew that Szell had performed "many serious and substantial American works by such composers as Rochberg, Lees, Blackwood, and others, several members wondered why there were not more works of this nature for the American choices." The panel, "of course, completely approved the Mennin Symphony, the Barber Piano Concerto, Copland's *Appalachian Spring*, Elwell's *The Happy Hypocrite*, and the William Grant Still." They felt, however, that four Gershwin works and the Bernstein Overture to *Candide* gave "too much of a pops weighting to the American offerings," and objected that Sessions's *The Black Maskers* was not representative of the composer and that the *White Peacock* "is pure French Impressionist." Mannes understood the special Gershwin program but thought that "the American repertoire would be more impressive" if Szell would add "two or three of some of the more serious pieces" they had already performed. Mannes added, "I hope you will not resent the Panel's comment on this subject and will be able to make them a little happier by some additions of your own choosing."

Szell felt that the panel's requests were "well taken," and asked Mannes to transmit this message:

> 1. The Gershwin works will appear only on an All-Gershwin Program specifically requested by USSR and Vienna (in the latter case it was a condition for the whole 4-nights-engagement) and nowhere else—unless especially requested,—which I consider unlikely.
> 2. The "Candide" Overture can easily be omitted.
> 3. I have full sympathy for the Panel's views on the "Black Maskers" and the "White Peacock" but they - both works - happen to be in Robert Shaw's repertoire, not in mine. He will conduct a number of concerts in USSR, nowhere else.

Szell recognized the panel's "justified ideas," and tried "to work one of the Blackwood Symphonies into the Cleveland programs so it can be taken on tour." However, he regretted that "the Rochberg or the Lees,—interesting as they were in themselves,—are, alas, impracticable because of the extreme difficulty and trickiness which make it impossible to give acceptable let alone finished performances with long intervals and no rehearsal possibilities in between,- which is unfortunately the rule on such long tours."[7] The Blackwood did not find its way into the tour repertoire, but there were works by Copland, Dutilleux, Elwell, Hindemith, Mennin, Still, Stravinsky, and Walton in addition to standard favorites, and the *New World* was also dropped.[8]

Ultimately, Shaw did not go on the tour, ending that repertoire problem. The reason was "unpleasantly characteristic of Szell's weaker side," according to Louis Lane. Shaw's previous tour of the Soviet Union with his Robert Shaw Chorale had been a brilliant success. Some of his musical friends in Moscow proposed that he prepare a Russian chorus in Beethoven's Ninth, which they wanted him to conduct with the Cleveland Orchestra on tour. Shaw asserted to Szell that since the orchestra played the Ninth so frequently, it would require only one rehearsal to put it together in Moscow. Szell appreciated the interest shown in Shaw's choral work, but said that would be completely out of the question. Szell wanted to keep emphasis on the orchestra and insisted that Shaw do an all-orchestral program. Shaw felt that under the circumstances, he would not be successful, and told Szell he would drop out. Szell seemed relieved.[9] Even though there had been many logistical problems in the 1957 tour, the same management, Anatole Heller's Paris-based *Bureau Artistique Internationale* was engaged for this one.[10]

The orchestra took off from Cleveland in a state of great excitement and no little anxiety. Even for those who had been on the 1957 European tour, this would prove an entirely new experience. For Szell, it would mark a return to Russia after thirty years—he had conducted eight concerts in Leningrad in 1935. The orchestra departed Tuesday evening, April 13, and landed in Moscow on Wednesday afternoon.[11] The orchestra played its first concert in the beautiful, historic Bolshoi (Large) Concert Hall of the Moscow Conservatory on April 16. Not coincidentally, the program was identical to that of the last subscription pair: *Roman Carnival* Overture, Barber Piano Concerto, Schubert Ninth. That performance took place on Saturday, April 10; on Monday, April 12, there were two rehearsals for the tour in Cleveland. On the morning of the first concert in Moscow, the orchestra rehearsed in the concert hall. Szell left little to chance.

Fears about their reception were not immediately assuaged. A large audience packed the hall, and Szell and the orchestra played at maximum concentration. Browning played the Barber brilliantly, as had the orchestra the Berlioz, but to moderate applause. What were they doing wrong, they wondered? The Schubert Ninth after intermission received a thunderous ovation. This was the first encounter with what they later learned to expect: polite applause during the concert and a torrent at the end. Then clapping began at random but quickly coalesced into a rhythmic unison of great power. This was the Russian style of approval, and it appeared that it was never going to let up. It had taken influence and cost to get tickets for the concerts—and there was not an empty seat—and the audience wanted maximum recompense: encores galore. And that is what they got. Such enthusiasm was intoxicating. Szell could not have been more pleased. He knew the charming Russian custom of the performer applauding the audience and did so with equal enthusiasm.

The second night, following *La gazza ladra* Overture and Mennin's Symphony no. 3, Grant Johannesen played the Mozart C Minor Concerto, K. 491. His was an elegant and sophisticated traversal of the dark masterpiece. But only after the final work, Mussorgsky's *Pictures at an Exhibition* as orchestrated by Ravel, did the audience strike up its unison approval.

Formal manifestations of the goodwill mission marked the tour in the Soviet Union: visits to the local conservatory to hear students perform, invitations to the local Composers' Union to meet its members—in Tbilisi, George Balanchine's brother was among them—and on free nights, banquets with the traditional vodka toasts. The festivities included several long-spun-out jokes about the legendary longevity of villagers in the nearby Caucasus Mountains and a riotous impromptu vocal serenade to Szell and the head table by a well-toasted group of local composers. The relaxed informality in Soviet Georgia was outstanding.

Goskonzert arranged many guided sightseeing tours. The musicians—many of whom had studied Russian for months—were fascinated to see pieces' and composer's names transliterated in the Cyrillic alphabet. In this, too, Szell had a hand. Long before the tour, he sent Barksdale "the correct transliteration of my name in Cyrillic letters," telling him to pass it on to the State Department.[12]

Szell was an enthusiastic sightseer and went on most of the trips arranged for the orchestra. The visit to the Hermitage Museum in Leningrad included a private viewing of the treasures of Scythian gold, in addition to the magnificent public collection of paintings. At the Summer Palace of the Czars, an eighteenth-century structure about twenty miles from Leningrad on the Gulf of Finland, they viewed the painstaking restoration, according to original plans, from severe damage inflicted by German officers who had made it their headquarters. In Sochi, a resort on the Black Sea, Szell and the orchestra enjoyed a ride in a huge hydrofoil passenger ferry, which skimmed the water at high speeds on "wings" fastened beneath its hull.

In each city the same wild audience reception greeted the orchestra. In some—such as Yerevan and Tbilisi—there were public near-riots by those who could not get in. In Yerevan, during the concert, musicians and audience could hear the great noise set up by the unhappy people outside. In Tbilisi not only were all seats taken—many with two people squeezed into one—but the house was chock-full with people sitting on balcony steps and squeezed into the aisles. There the orchestra experienced the only power outage of the tour, caused by a torrential hailstorm, which could be heard pounding on the theater's roof. In the middle of *Daphnis et Chloé*—during the famous flute solo, an exposed passage—the lights flickered and went out, came back on, and then all stayed out for what seemed like a long time but was probably just a couple of minutes. In complete darkness, the orchestra kept on playing, even though they could not see the conductor or their music. They finally stopped just seconds before the lights came back on. Szell gave them a rehearsal number and they continued near where they left off. Stormy applause followed.

The Philharmonic Hall of Leningrad, with its two rows of white pillars, elaborate chandeliers, and ornamental plaster, is one of the most elegant looking and acoustically magnificent in the world. The pillars resemble marble but are wood. After the rigors of the tour so far, these five last concerts in the Soviet Union were a fitting reward. Szell conducted four of them and heard Lane's from one of the seats in the hall's side sections, outside the row of columns.

The *Cleveland Plain Dealer*'s Fred W. Coleman quoted the Leningrad edition of *Pravda*, the Communist Party newspaper, which "called the Cleveland Orchestra's tour here 'a great success . . . in many ways distinct from those American orchestras which have already appeared in the Soviet Union.'" *Pravda* continued: "The orchestra plays with freedom and suppleness, as if in one breath. The rendition of each work is distinguished by coherence and warmth. The orchestra's technique is irreproachable, but, most important, it is never flaunted for its own sake. Everything is subordinated to the artistic concept which is always profound and reasoned. This is the achievement of George Szell, the musical director and first conductor of the orchestra and an outstanding musician educated in the best traditions of European musical culture."[13]

Szell gave the Soviet audiences a good review. He said: "The only comparable manifestation of enthusiasm I recall from previous tours was in Poland in 1957. . . . It has been most gratifying and exhilarating simply because of the incredible enthusiasm, the vociferous manifestations on the part of the audiences." Szell continued, "The Russians are . . . emotionally involved with music. Music plays such an important role in their lives. They have a great wealth of listening experiences. . . . The enthusiastic reaction to certain works which are not the obvious applause-drawing sorts have been most gratifying." Szell emphasized the success of the tour: "It is the only contact that functions even when political relations are bad. It is the best means of teaching people to know and appreciate each other, despite all the dividing factors, and show them that in a higher sense they all belong together."[14] After five and a half weeks in the Soviet Union, however successful, all were ready for a change. As the train from Leningrad to Helsinki slowly crossed the border, a collective sigh of relief quietly resonated through the orchestra's reserved cars.

Helsinki seemed like paradise after the Soviet Union, where food had not been bad, but there was little variety. In the Finnish city, an abundance of delicious food of the finest quality was available in great variety. A Scandinavian country, Finland has its unique style: a rugged but exuberant sense of design and color in the materials of everyday living, sharply contrasting with the drab surroundings of the past five weeks. The orchestra arrived on May 20; the first concert in the West would come on the twenty-third. On the two free days, protected by Szell, the musicians made up for lost time, eating delicacies long missed, shopping where stores offered beautiful merchandise, and paying respects to the deeply moving Sibelius monument in a city park: a metal construction resembling a huge cluster of organ pipes, slightly melted as if of wax—abstract, understated, yet powerful. Nearby, as a concession to more popular taste reluctantly added by the artist, stood a bust of the composer—literal, but apart enough to allow undistracted contemplation of the monument's body and soul. Several members of the orchestra visited Sibelius's home, where his daughter received them.

The Helsinki Festival celebrated the one hundredth anniversary of Sibelius's birth, and Szell honored it by playing his Seventh Symphony. The concert began with the *Meistersinger* Prelude, then the Sibelius. Following intermission, Browning played the Barber concerto, and the concert ended with *Till Eulenspiegel.* In a gracious speech, the Finnish Ambassador to the United States, Olavi Munkki, presented Szell with the Order of the Lion of Finland on behalf of the president of the Finnish Republic. Szell expressed his "sincere and humblest thanks," for "this very high distinction."[15] The tour continued to Stockholm, Warsaw, Hamburg, and Paris. Receptions were continuously enthusiastic, even though the houses in Stockholm and Hamburg were the first not completely full.

The Bergen Festival was in full swing the first week in June. Crisp air from the sea lay on that bustling Norwegian town, with its busy port and beautiful views from the mountains around, and it teemed with tourists and festivalgoers. The first concert presented *Die Meistersinger,* Barber Piano Concerto, and the *Eroica.* The second program honored one of Bergen's favorite sons and Norway's national heroes, Edvard Grieg, whose piano concerto was played by Grant Johannesen, American-born of Norwegian ancestry. He had been playing that work all his life, and he offered an authoritative and loving performance, with all the élan and dash the score demanded, but also with the lilting poetic sense it evokes. The reception in Bergen was enormous. Millions throughout Europe and Scandinavia viewed the televised concert. The orchestra visited Grieg's home in the hilly and wooded suburb of Troldhaugen, where they heard a concert of his songs sung in his parlor accompanied on his piano.

The last part of the tour took Szell to many of the most important cities of his musical youth and maturity: Berlin, Vienna, Prague, London, and Amsterdam. It was the crowning glory of his life's achievement to show off his great American orchestra in these cities. Berlin's Neue Philharmonie is visually striking and acoustically challenging. It is music in the not-quite-round. The orchestra sits at the bottom of an irregular bowl that slopes upward and around. Rows of seats for the audience, in rising angular facets of the bowl, surround the orchestra. The overall acoustic is rather dry and the blend and balance is completely dependent on where any particular member of the audience is seated. Szell knew the hall, having conducted the Berlin Philharmonic there. He scheduled a rehearsal onstage the afternoon before the first concert. The rehearsal was partly for the television crew, but Szell also used it to point out to the orchestra the unusual acoustics and adjust to them accordingly. The orchestra came through as usual under tricky new circumstances and received twenty-five curtain calls.

The day he arrived in Berlin, Szell met an old friend from Prague, Willy Trenk-Trebitsch, who had performed with him in the 1930s. Trenk-Trebitsch gave Szell a memento from their past: an autographed montage of two photographs—one of the handsomely ornate façade of the Prague theater lit at night, the other of the cast of Brecht-Weill's *The Rise and Fall of the City of Mahagonny*. Trenk-Trebitsch had played the role of Jim Mahoney, and he posed with Szell, other cast members, and stage director Max Liebl. In the photo, Szell sported a white handkerchief folded in points, one dangling from his breast pocket; he had a much rounder face than in his older age and, naturally, more hair. After the first concert, Monday, June 7, Szell celebrated his sixty-eighth birthday and invited the entire orchestra to a party. He was as animated and happy as the orchestra had ever seen him.[16]

The orchestra played one concert each in Prague and Bratislava, followed by bows numbering in double digits. Szell loved Prague and had found love there. He had chosen Czech citizenship as early as 1919, and spent eight years as chief conductor of Prague's German Opera House. Szell had also conducted the Czech Philharmonic in concerts in Smetana Hall, where the Cleveland Orchestra played. The house where Helene Szell had lived with her first husband and two sons still stood in its prominent downtown neighborhood. Her memories stayed strong and deep—early in her time in Cleveland, she had cried on seeing a picture of the city with her house in it.[17]

The orchestra spent the tenth week of the tour in Vienna, city of Szell's childhood and the scene of many of his past concert and opera performances. He and the Cleveland Orchestra had enjoyed a triumph in the two performances they gave there in 1957. Eight years later, they presented four concerts in the Vienna Konzerthaus. Of the four concerts, the all-Gershwin program, conducted by Lane with soloist John Browning, sold the most tickets. Two festivities for the orchestra took place the day of the Gershwin concert, a free day for Szell: a reception for the entire orchestra by the city of Vienna after the morning rehearsal and a supper after the concert for the entire orchestra, sponsored by Szell's good friend, Musical Arts Association trustee Carl N. Osborne.

Each concert was warmly received, but at the end of the fourth and final one, the *Plain Dealer* reported, "The fans surged forward, grabbing Szell's hands and shouting, 'vielen dank, auf wiedersehen . . . ' The applause rolled on for nearly 20 minutes, until the orchestra plunged into Richard Strauss's symphonic poem 'Till Eulenspiegel' as an encore." The critic of the Austrian press agency praised the orchestra for achieving "a miracle of precision, adaptability and beauty."[18]

The orchestra flew from Vienna to London on a Saturday, enjoyed a completely free day on Sunday, and appeared fresh for a rehearsal the morning of its first of two concerts in the Royal Festival Hall on Monday. Reviewer David Cairns chided the London audience for not filling the hall—it was three-quarters full, but its seating capacity is 3,500, almost three times the size of many European halls. Cairns "did not find at last night's concert any suggestion of a soulless routine underneath the obvious mastery of their playing, though it might almost have been forgiven at the end of an arduous European tour [forty-five concerts up to that point]." His assessment of the orchestra: "Among the crack ensembles of the world they are one of the least showily glamorous. One is above all aware of them as a single unit. The brass never blast, the strings play with a grainy naturalness that has no hint of padding, of thick-pile tone cultivated for its own sake, the woodwind tone is big and rich but never thrust at us for us to admire. There is a remarkable sense of intense concentration on the job in hand, which is musical expression."

Andrew Porter, writing in London's *Times*, agreed with the general opinion that in America the Cleveland is "reckoned to be 'the best.'" Of the Bartók *Concerto for Orchestra*, Porter wrote "I don't think I have ever heard so unflashy, so unforced, or so intensely musical a performance." He admired the whole concert but felt "it is for the Bartók that last night's concert will be remembered: for the alert, sterling tone from each department, for the precision and intelligence of the playing, for the suppleness of phrasing, the rhythmic vivacity in tempos both slow and fast, and the chamber-musical finesse with which the lines were woven."

Porter, later music critic of *The New Yorker*, knew America firsthand and judged "the character of the orchestra is somehow that of Cleveland itself, the most cultivated of American cities. A Szell performance makes a Karajan one seem vulgar; the classical finesse of his orchestra can make the Berlin Philharmonic, straining at the climax of some Strauss tone-poem with supercharged strings and bursting brass, seem brash."[19]

The final stand of the long tour occurred in another of Szell's musical homes, the Netherlands. The orchestra appeared in the Holland Festival, where Szell had often led the Concertgebouw Orchestra. The first concert took place in the Concertgebouw: Prelude to *Die Meistersinger,* Barber Piano Concerto, and Schubert's Ninth, and is preserved in the orchestra's broadcast archives. The Wagner and Schubert, Szell signature works, benefited handsomely from the warm acoustics. At the peroration of the Wagner, the three themes emerged in complete clarity, yet they were thoroughly blended. The Schubert glowed with vitality. It sang and danced and ended with a mighty burst of energy in the monumental finale.

The tour's finale might well have been an anticlimax, played in the antiquely charming concert hall of the grand old Kurhaus Hotel in The Hague's ocean resort city with the near-unpronounceable name, Scheveningen. Beginning with *La gazza ladra* and continuing through Mennin's Symphony no. 3, the Mozart C Minor Piano Concerto (Johannesen), and ending with the Schumann Fourth, it was memorable in its own way. Perhaps it owed to Szell's iron will and strength. Perhaps it was because of the pride he instilled into the orchestra from day one of his tenure. Perhaps, too, it resulted from their dedication and love for music that the concert sounded still fresh and overcame the hall's less than flattering acoustics. As ready as all were to have the tour end, none would allow a letdown. Szell gave a party for the orchestra after the concert, joined by his old colleagues and friends from the Concertgebouw administration, Piet Heuweckemeijer and Marius Flothuis.

The tour seemed to have gone on forever, yet paradoxically, perhaps because it had been so busy and exciting, it also seemed short. At its end in Amsterdam, Ethel Boros asked how the audience reception compared with eight years earlier. Szell replied simply, "They were even more enthusiastic than in 1957."[20] The earlier tour surprised the Europeans, perhaps even the orchestra itself, that it was so much better than expected. In 1965 there was no longer the element of surprise, but for the European audiences, the memory of 1957 and of subsequent recordings had raised high expectations. Just as Szell himself felt pleasantly surprised after a summer apart by the reality of the orchestra's playing, Europe experienced a similar jolt hearing it after a longer interval.

As in 1957, the Szells stayed in Europe after the tour and did not take part in the welcoming festivities staged by the city of Cleveland and the orchestra. Ten busloads of families and friends came out to meet the orchestra, joined by a crowd of 5,500 fans headed by Cleveland mayor, Ralph S. Locher, and vice president and general manager of the Hotel Sheraton-Cleveland, Allen J. Lowe, who planned the welcome. A letter from the vice president of the United States, Hubert Humphrey, saluted the orchestra. Barksdale and Lane accepted a scroll of congratulations "signed by congressional leaders from Cleveland," on behalf of the orchestra. Barksdale seized the moment to say, "We hope to see all of you at the Pops." Each member of the orchestra walked down the steps from the plane onto the red carpet to introductions and cheers from the crowd. It resembled the homecoming of a championship team, which, indeed, they were. In its lead editorial the same day as the page one story, "A Bouquet for the Orchestra," the *Plain Dealer* wrote, "Welcome home, members of the orchestra. You're an unexcelled Cleveland institution. The city is grateful and proud."[21]

A Quiet but Productive Summer

The Szells began their vacation in Paris. Crossing the Swiss border near Geneva on July 1, they motored to Zurich before the regular three weeks in Crans. Szell wrote Barksdale, "The weather up here is cold and it was rainy. Driving Paris-Zurich and Zurich-Crans took place mostly in thunderstorms. Happily I had a chauffeur along Paris-Zurich and did it in two comfortable days. Otherwise I feel very well and relaxed." Although Szell allowed himself the luxury of a chauffeur on the long drive, he would have dictated every turn of the route. In that letter, Szell bids Barksdale to compare notes with him about the reviews that they were collecting: "I must say they are overwhelming. Let us check what you and I have so we can pick the most striking quotations."

For some time, Szell had been thinking of another—much shorter—tour. "Talks with my friends in Switzerland make me believe that it is not unrealistic to think of a short tour in 1967 (or 68 at the latest) covering only the Festivals in Lucerne, Edinburgh & Salzburg, about 2–3 weeks. All we really seem to need from the outside is the money for the transportation." As money sources, Szell suggested either businesses in Cleveland or, failing that, the State Department. He continued, "But if indeed we should tour between say August 15th and Sept. 15th, what becomes of the Opera?" The Lake Erie Opera Theatre had concluded its first season only that past September, and as musical director of the Cleveland Orchestra, Szell recognized the possible schedule conflict, and was concerned as to how the tour might impinge on the orchestra's other valuable activity.

Another idea of Szell's came out of a happenstance: "On my arrival here," he wrote Barksdale, "I was greeted at tea-time in the bar by a re-broadcast of the Paris concert of June 2nd over the Swiss Telephone-Radio System. Complete with all applause, right to the end. A quite good job of monitoring, apart from some monkeying with the piano-orchestra balance in the Mozart. If we have indeed all tapes of all the European broadcasts, could we not occasionally utilize them over American stations?"

Szell's idea was expanded that fall. Near the end of July, Barksdale reported that they "can launch a taping program [of the orchestra's concerts] for the benefit of the Pension Fund at the beginning of the approaching season. Over the weekend Bob Conrad of WCLV and I developed a plan somewhat along the Boston [Symphony] lines which can be implemented without the aid of a national sponsor and which can be physically handled by the station with certain assistance from our office."[22]

The summer Pops had seen its best days. Barksdale wrote Szell, "I am developing the feeling that the Pops are declining and that the general public seems to want more of the full orchestra in standard fare. All the more reason for pushing hard for the summer festival."[23]

Looking to Szell's Future

The orchestra's activities were increasing, but Szell wanted to reduce his. He began to reconsider the practice of one to three guest conductors a season. He wrote Barksdale, "I think we should stick to this plan for the season after next [1966–67] but—should think and explore immediately what more promising plans for the future in terms of one very fine man, who could take a more substantial part of the season, might be developed." Szell expressed another area of concern, regarding soloists: "Re the 66–67 season I shudder to think HOW far ahead we now have to plan. (Carlos [Moseley of the New York Philharmonic] is already engaging Soloists!)."[24]

Szell's summer after the strenuous tour called for just one concert—with the Dresden State Orchestra at the Salzburg Festival on August 2. Szell told Barksdale, "The concert last night was sold out and hugely successful—a bit beyond just deserts to my way of thinking for the Dresden Orchestra, although basically very fine and working like beavers, revealed some painful weaknesses in the winds. Curzon played beautifully."[25] Five weeks of Szell's summer remained, three spent in Bad Ragaz, Switzerland, and a visit to Berlin at the end of August. Szell wound up in Paris to put the automobile in storage for the winter. He arrived in Cleveland in time to hear the Lake Erie Opera's second-week production, Prokofiev's *The Love for Three Oranges*.[26]

Glories at Home

The orchestra's opening concert of 1965–66 was the first of three televised that season. It offered something for everyone: it ended with Tchaikovsky's Fourth Symphony; the first half included Wagner's *Rienzi* Overture, the first Cleveland performance of *Four Essays for Orchestra* by Polish composer Tadeuz Baird, and—as a vehicle to introduce the new principal oboist, John Mack—*Le tombeau de Couperin* by Ravel. The Cleveland Orchestra Syndication Service broadcast the second program of the season. FM radio station WCLV broadcast it locally on Sunday, October 3, 1965. On the thirty-first, after tape duplication and distribution, national broadcasts on subscribing radio stations began.[27] That concert saw the return of the orchestra's "First Soprano," Judith Raskin. She had sung the Mahler Fourth three seasons earlier in Severance and Carnegie Halls and on tour. Szell performed it with genial warmth and deep understanding. Also on the program was Mozart's Twenty-eighth Symphony, K. 200, in C.[28]

Szell conducted only four Cleveland subscription weeks, plus a week of touring in Ohio and Michigan before his annual departure, this time for four weeks with the New York Philharmonic. The four Cleveland weeks were characteristically busy and included recording three works, the Mahler Fourth and Mozart Twenty-eighth Symphonies, and the craggy *Sinfonietta* by Leoš Janáček. Szell had a deep affinity for this work. He introduced it in Cleveland in his first season in 1946 and played it again in 1954 and 1961. Now in 1965, he would play it for the last time and record it. Harking back to a long Bohemian tradition of brass music, the *Sinfonietta* requires many additional instruments. Among others, it calls for two tenor tubas, two bass trumpets, and twelve trumpets, although it can be played with "only" nine, which Szell did. Outside players had to be hired to augment the orchestra regulars, and so much of the piece involved brasses, Szell called a brass sectional for the Saturday morning of the week before the first performance.

With its many short, repeated motifs of rapid rhythmic figures and its abrupt changes of tempo and mood, the work evokes Janáček's unique atmosphere. The piece also presents major difficulties for the strings, and for the first violins in particular. They have to navigate in the upper reaches of their range and run a gamut of passages with awkward leaps and intervals, a cruel exposure for all but the most virtuoso of orchestras. A recording of a 1946 performance shows a brave attempt at these passages but exhibits some obvious scrambling. The Cleveland violins of the 1960s could execute the fiendish demands with aplomb. The recording made in one session on October 15 sounded exactly how they played it live.

Szell conducted the New York Philharmonic for four weeks. Major works included Seventh Symphonies of Bruckner and Dvořák, Tchaikovsky's Fifth, and Berlioz's *Harold in Italy*, with the Philharmonic's principal violist, William Lincer. Concerto soloists and works were: Graffman, Prokofiev's Third; Curzon, Mozart K. 595; Johannesen, Ravel G Major; and Rostropovich, Dvořák. In a broadcast interview, Szell turned the tables on interviewer James Fassett by asking him why musicians were expected to talk, saying "Why don't they just let us make music?" When asked if audiences have changed over the last decades, Szell replied that as recently as fourteen years earlier, critics "attacked" him in Detroit for playing Bartók's *Concerto for Orchestra*, and now it is "old hat, like *Scheherazade*." Szell's concert on November 6, 1965, was the Philharmonic's 7000th.

Back in Cleveland, Szell led an all-Sibelius concert commemorating the 100th anniversary of the composer's birth. The program consisted of the haunting tone poem *En Saga*, the extraordinary Fourth Symphony, and the Violin Concerto with Christian Ferras. One of Szell's most unforgettable performances took place in the eleventh subscription pair. He presented the work from outside the symphonic repertoire proper—Schubert's sublime Octet, scored for two violins, viola, cello, double bass, clarinet, French horn, and bassoon. Szell enlarged the string quintet to a total of eight first violins, six seconds, four violas, three cellos, and three basses. Perhaps Schubert's "heavenly length" (said of the Ninth Symphony, but the Octet is also about fifty minutes' duration) had something to do with its neglect. But with such superb forces as the Cleveland Orchestra strings, wind players Robert Marcellus, Myron Bloom, and George Goslee, and with Szell guiding it overall, there was pure poetry in Severance Hall those nights. Nowhere more than in this Schubert could one witness Szell's musical nobility. Shaping phrases, choosing flexible tempos that allowed the music to sing without sagging, giving the solo winds leeway to involve themselves in a true chamber music experience of give and take, and keeping in mind the grand scheme of Schubert's idiosyncratic architecture, Szell was in his element. A Szell commemorative CD set issued by the orchestra included the performance. After intermission the Casadesuses—Robert, Gaby, and their son, Jean—appeared in two triple concertos: Robert's, written for his family, and Mozart's *Lodron* Concerto for three pianos.

Szell gave apprentice conductor James Levine the chance to shine in the next-to-last concert of the year. He began the twelfth subscription concert pair (December

23 and 25) with the Divertimento from Stravinsky's ballet *Le baiser de la fée*. Szell conducted the rest of the program: Mozart's Piano Concerto in B-flat, K. 456, with Rudolf Firkusny, and Beethoven's Seventh. Shaw and the chorus ended the old year and greeted the new with a joyous rendition of Haydn's genial oratorio *The Seasons*.

1966 began more calmly than had 1965, with its exit of principal oboist Marc Lifschey and the nervous preparation for the long international tour. There were two recording sessions in January and one each in March and April. In one concert, Gary Graffman performed Prokoviev's Piano Concertos Nos. 1 and 3 back-to-back after intermission (Bartók's *Concerto for Orchestra* occupied the first half).

A striking rarity in January was Busoni's massive Piano Concerto—programmed in honor of the one hundredth anniversary of the composer's birth. It runs for fifty minutes and calls for male chorus in addition to the solo piano (played by Italian pianist Pietro Scarpini). Szell also scheduled it for Carnegie Hall in February. Scarpini played magnificently and created a sensation in New York, including coverage in *Time* magazine. For its article on the Busoni, *Time* requested an interview with Szell. After that magazine's 1963 cover story had misquoted him, Szell was wary and refused the interview. "For a scandal [sheet] it isn't scandalous enough, for accurate reporting, it isn't accurate enough," he told the orchestra's New York–based publicist, Edgar Vincent. He charged Vincent to keep him out of the two magazines that practiced "collective journalism."[29] But *Time* persisted, saying it would settle for a quote from Szell. He countered with conditions formulated to make them drop the matter: 1. The questions were to be submitted in writing; 2. Quotes were to be used *not* out of context; 3. Quotes not to be edited. *Time* accepted, but could not refrain from tampering. To the question "What do you think of the Busoni Concerto?" Szell answered that it was "a monstrosity full of genius." In spite of agreeing to Szell's terms, *Time* tried to change Szell's metaphor in a way that it turned against him. *Time*'s tentative version quoted: "When asked what he thought of the Busoni Concerto, Szell muttered 'It is monstrous,' but that he had to agree with the critics that it was also a work of genius." Besides twisting Szell's statement, the word "muttered" implied that it had been verbal instead of written. A member of *Time*'s staff contacted Vincent for Szell's okay of the draft. Shocked and angered, Vincent told the representative to immediately call Szell, which she did. His original answer appeared in the published article. Vincent said of this incident, "He was right to insist that the printed word be accurate because a man dies but his words live on after him. I was so fond of that man!"[30]

In Carnegie Hall, John Browning was soloist in Brahms's First Piano Concerto. Its only preparation consisted of a rehearsal the previous afternoon in Hartford, Connecticut, where Szell and the orchestra later played a concert, not including the concerto. This signified Szell's increasing confidence in Browning. The pianist felt "so buoyed up by the experience that [he] wrote Mr. Szell a letter and said is there any possibility of doing some work with you?" Szell replied immediately: "I will be in Switzerland for my holiday and nothing would give me greater pleasure."[31]

The Second Western Tour, 1966

The orchestra toured the West from April 17 to May 15, its second since 1960. Twenty-four cities heard twenty-eight concerts—twenty-two conducted by Szell, four by Lane, and two by the author. Beginning in DeKalb, Illinois, the tour took the orchestra to Iowa, Kansas, Colorado, Utah, Arizona, California, Oregon, Washington, Minnesota, Wisconsin, and back to Illinois (Wheaton), ending in Indianapolis, Indiana. The halls ranged from surprisingly good (a gymnasium at the University of California, Irvine) to expectedly excellent (the striking new Gammage Memorial Auditorium of the University of Arizona in Tempe, designed by Frank Lloyd Wright with acoustician Russell Johnson), but also to very poor (Smith Field House of Brigham Young University at Provo, Utah). The audiences were unanimously fine.

After the tour the Szells returned to Europe. In June Szell conducted the Vienna Philharmonic at the Vienna Festival on the fourth and the West German Radio Orchestra in Cologne on the twenty-fourth, turning sixty-nine years old between them. The Szells flew to Paris to retrieve their automobile and drove toward Switzerland, stopping at Baden-Baden to have lunch with Pierre Boulez. There Szell invited Boulez to conduct in Cleveland for three weeks in November-December 1967.[32] Szell accepted an invitation from Leonard Bernstein to serve as one of five guest conductors of the New York Philharmonic in the 1967–68 season, celebrating the orchestra's 125th anniversary. In a follow-up letter, Carlos Moseley wrote, "Good news from Bernstein," and told Szell, "You have first choice" of dates. They took Szell's only available dates, March 28 to April 1.[33]

Listening to the radio in Crans, Szell heard a Concertgebouw broadcast of a symphony he did not recognize, and wrote to Flothuis the next day:

> I heard last night over the short wave radio a very pleasant post-classical, pre-romantic Symphony which [Karel] Ančerl performed with your orchestra at the [Holland] Festival—but could not catch the name of the (presumably Czech—perhaps [or not] Mannheimer Czech) composer. Please let me know his name—also the Nr. of the work and whether the orchestra material is available in print or as rental . . .
>
> P.S. Most of it sounded rather like early XIX century.

Flothuis answered: "With your natural shrewd insight, you had already practically determined the symphony you heard on the radio. It was the Symphony in D Major by Jan Hugo Voříšek (1791–1825), published by Artia in Prague. The material can be rented."

"Beethoven thought highly of this composer, who had some influence on Schubert. Among other functions, Voříšek assumed the one of conductor of the 'Gesellschaft der Musikfreunde' in Vienna. He died exactly three years before Schubert."[34]

Barksdale kept Szell informed of the work in progress on the future summer home of the Cleveland Orchestra. It was becoming clear that the structure would not be completed in 1967 as planned, but would definitely be ready in 1968. This cleared the way for the European tour in 1967.

July and August were vacation months for Szell in Switzerland, interrupted briefly by a concert with the Berlin Philharmonic at the Salzburg Festival on August 1. During this time he worked intensively with John Browning, who rented a chalet and ordered a Steinway concert grand shipped in. Browning recalled:

> We went through practically everything, almost all the major concerti, classical and late Schubert Sonatas, [Beethoven opus] 110, both Brahms concerti. We met about three times a week, three- to four-hour sessions. And then we would talk afterwards or he would play a little bit himself, incredible things like his arrangement of *Till*. It was quite extraordinary. We would have fun. Of course I was always very respectful, but I would say, "All right, Mr. Szell, now isolate the viola part for the Mozart string quartet such and such" and, by God, he could after twenty years of not having given a crack at the score. He probably had the greatest musical mind.[35]

The summer bore fruit for Browning. Szell paid him his highest compliment: he chose a Mozart concerto for Browning's next appearance in January 1968, not only in Cleveland, but in Carnegie Hall. The Mozart Szell selected was his own youthful calling card, K. 488. And in October 1969, Browning played Prokofiev's Third Piano Concerto at Severance Hall. At the end of his summer, Szell had one more engagement in Europe: on September 3 he led a concert with the Vienna Philharmonic at the Lucerne Festival. Then he flew to New York from Paris five days later.

Cleveland's opening concert of the 1966–67 season was documented for posterity, this time by a team sent by the Bell Telephone Hour—producer Henry Jaffe, director Nathan Kroll, and writer/narrator Irving Kolodin. The hour-long show, broadcast nationally in early December, included portions of rehearsals and of the season's first concert. The program was Brahms's *Academic Festival* Overture, Berg's Violin Concerto with concertmaster Rafael Druian, and Beethoven's Fifth. Kroll tried to talk Szell out of the Beethoven as being too well known, but Szell insisted, saying "You will hear it like you've never heard it before."[36]

Included in the broadcast was a piano rehearsal of the Berg in Szell's studio, with Szell playing the score as effortlessly as if it were a Mozart concerto. In another segment, Szell and Louis Lane discussed Lane's forthcoming recording of Mendelssohn's First Symphony. Szell gave a conducting lesson to "the young conductors": Kulas Fellowship conductor Stephen Portman and staff conductors James Levine and the author. This is the only surviving televised Szell Cleveland Orchestra concert, if only partial. It has been commercially preserved.

Szell conducted five out of the first six Cleveland subscription programs (Lane conducted the fifth) before joining the Concertgebouw for three weeks. His repertoire with both orchestras was driven in part by recording obligations, mainly of Beethoven and Brahms. In March 1966 Szell received from Waage in Amsterdam a copy of a very positive German review of his Sibelius Second recording ("the ideal presentation") along with the news that there were also many favorable comments about it in the Dutch press. (New York and London newspapers also published laudatory reviews.) Szell wrote back, thanking Waage "for your thoughtfulness in sending me that outstanding review," and added, "If you find other reviews of the same kind, I should be much interested in seeing them."[37]

In Amsterdam from November 9 to 30, Szell led seven Concertgebouw concerts, beginning with a Mozart/Beethoven program containing the two symphonies to be recorded at the end of his stay. Arthur Rubinstein played the Beethoven Piano Concerto no. 4, the work of their first collaboration thirty-three years earlier in The Hague, Szell's debut in Holland. One reviewer found Rubinstein's playing "sublime" but Szell's Fifth Symphony overdriven. The headline read: "Armored musical temperament by Szell in Beethoven's Fifth" (within the review it reads "armored against sentimentality"). The reviewer admitted that doubling winds was in accord with Szell's conception of the Symphony's titanic nature, but said that Szell let it degenerate into noise, "breaking the sound barrier."[38] Szell led the Dutch premiere of the Dutilleux *Cinq métaboles* on three programs.[39]

Szell made a comment in an interview in *De Telegraaf* on November 24 that caused an uproar. The headline read: "George Szell, Guest Conductor of the Concertgebouw Orchestra 'American Orchestras are the best.'" The lengthy article, illustrated with sketches of Szell in rehearsal and with a photograph of his "good friend" Rubinstein, also quoted Szell: "American musicians work much harder than their colleagues here . . . because of the strong element of competition in the American society." The rest of the article talked about the planned Blossom Music Center, the coming "very short, very elegant tour," and Szell's inviting Pierre Boulez, a frequent Concertgebouw guest, to conduct contemporary music in Cleveland.[40]

Seeking to mollify the situation, Szell wrote in Amsterdam to the orchestra chairman that his stay there "has, through my work with your orchestra, given me very great pleasure - frankly, more than ever before. This is due not only to the artistry of its members but very specially to the spirit of genuine cooperation and the excellent discipline which prevailed both at the rehearsals and at the recording sessions." Szell asked him to pass those comments on to his colleagues in the orchestra. Szell also wrote a more specific disclaimer about the article, making three points as to what he actually said:

> 1) In matters of intonation, precision and beauty of sound the American Top-Orchestras are unbeatable.

2) The average American orchestra musician works perhaps fewer hours but works with more efficiency than his European counterpart.
   [Szell explained that that was because of the competitive nature of American life, and that salaries are not fixed as in Europe, but can be negotiated individually] and:
3) I did say that between the Concertgebouw and myself there are ties of long friendship (my first appearance was in 1936) which was *not* printed.

That letter was reported in the press. Nothing more about it occurred during Szell's stay, but the matter was not over.[41]

Szell introduced the young American Peter Serkin, who played Beethoven's Second Piano Concerto. He had written Flothuis from Cleveland in 1965 about him: "Peter Serkin, the son of Rudolf Serkin . . . is an exceedingly gifted musician and beautiful pianist, having already a very considerable career of his own both in America and in Europe. He has never played in Holland yet, whereas he has played in England, France, Italy, etc. It would give me great pleasure to introduce him to the Amsterdam audiences. He is one of the rare exceptions to the rule about sons of outstanding fathers. Incidentally, he is playing with me and the Cleveland Orchestra this season, both here and in New York."[42]

Feeling that the controversial interview in *De Telegraaf* had hurt his friend Piet Heuwekemeijer, Szell wrote him: "I should like to take this opportunity to tell you that I enjoyed my stay with the Concertgebouw this time very much indeed, and very much more than ever before." In reply Heuwekemeijer politely chided Szell about interviews that do not do the Concertgebouw any good when seeking support from the city or federal governments. He suggested that they "both forget all about it." Szell answered, "Far from minding your frankness, I appreciate it as genuine proof of friendship."[43] Szell left Holland the day after recording K. 338 and Beethoven's Fifth.

Blowup in Cleveland

After the New Year Szell conducted five consecutive programs in Cleveland. During a rehearsal for a concert prior to the eastern tour, Szell blew up at the orchestra, using rather coarse language. The players were so incensed that at the break they stayed in the locker room and refused to return to the stage unless Szell apologized. After some backing and forthing, Szell agreed to address them. In complete silence the orchestra filed in and sat not on stage but in the hall and waited to hear Szell, who came out on the stage. Without really doing so, he came as close to apologizing as any diplomat or politician might. He hemmed and hawed, made excuses and the like. In the end the musicians took his contrition as an apology and the rehearsal continued.

The last subscription concerts before the tour, on February 2 and 4, offered Beethoven's *Missa solemnis*. Fresh from rehearsals and two performances, Szell brought it to Carnegie Hall the following Monday. Szell's sense of structure and clarity and penetrating insight into this knotty score produced a taut, intense performance. Rafael Druian's extended violin solo in the Sanctus was ethereal. Robert Shaw had developed a powerful and responsive chorus in Cleveland. The Beethoven Ninth in 1965, the Busoni Piano Concerto with male chorus in 1966, this *Missa Solemnis* in 1967, and the Verdi Requiem in 1968, manifested Szell's eagerness to show New York this magnificent choral complement to his orchestra. Shaw himself took more than behind-the-scenes credit for his accomplishment when, a day after the 1966 Busoni, he led Haydn's oratorio *The Seasons* in Carnegie Hall.

Winthrop Sargeant wrote in *The New Yorker:* "Since the time of Toscanini, I have not heard Beethoven's 'Missa Solemnis' done in a way that convinced me that it is one of his masterpieces. . . . Here was a great conductor with an array of forces that hold the present championship in things of this sort." Harold C. Schonberg also mentioned the older conductor: "But the big hero was the conductor. . . . The outstanding feeling of the performance was controlled exaltation. . . . One must go back to Toscanini for this kind of 'Missa Solemnis.'"[44]

The eastern tour always included three successive Monday evenings in Carnegie Hall, sponsored by the orchestra. In 1965 Carnegie Hall had sponsored two more concerts in its International Series of Visiting Orchestras. One year later, Carnegie Hall again sponsored two concerts on its series and the orchestra sponsored four—three Mondays conducted by Szell and the Tuesday on which Shaw conducted Haydn's *The Seasons*. In 1967 they returned to five—the three Mondays plus two on the Carnegie series—and this stayed fixed through Szell's tenure. Benjamin Lees's Concerto for String Quartet and Orchestra was the novelty of the tour.

After the tour Szell took advance vacation time for that lost to the coming August tour of three festivals—Salzburg, Edinburgh, and Lucerne. Shaw, Lane, and guests Georges Prêtre and Sixten Ehrling conducted the five subscription weeks without him. During that period, however, Szell conducted five tour concerts in Ithaca and Syracuse, New York, Burlington, Vermont, and Toronto and London, Ontario. The University of Western Ontario in London arranged a special convocation to coincide with Szell's presence at their spring festival and conferred an honorary doctorate on him.

In April and May Szell conducted the final four subscription concerts and a pension fund concert with Rudolf Serkin. He took part in a week called the "New Music Program," sponsored by the Rockefeller Foundation. In it, the orchestra performed compositions by five American composers in Severance Hall and at Oberlin and Kent, Ohio.[45]

Immediately after the final Severance concert, Szell made a brief trip to Cincinnati for a May Festival concert. As Szell described it, leaving town was like a scene in a Mack Sennett comedy. Owing to a downtown power failure, the Szells were stranded on a high floor of their hotel. Members of the Cincinnati festival board came to the rescue, climbing the stairs and helping carry the Szells' baggage down. They missed their flight to New York but took a later one. The passage to Paris went smoothly; they arrived on May 20.[46] A little over two weeks later Szell celebrated his seventieth birthday (June 7, 1967) in Zurich.

That same day, Druian met with Pierre Boulez in London and wrote about it to Barksdale, who passed it on to Szell. Boulez's presence was perfect timing: just as the orchestra's activity was expanding and moving toward a fifty-two-week contract for the orchestra, Szell was looking to reduce his load. Boulez indicated to Druian that he would happily consider a principal guest conductor–type of arrangement with Cleveland. On July 4 Szell had a "very friendly phone talk . . . with Boulez" in Baden-Baden. As Szell informed Barksdale, Boulez was "delighted to reserve for us all of March plus half April 1970 and promised to instruct at once Hartog, his general agent, not to book him for this period and to advise the Hurok office accordingly."[47]

Columbia Records' John McClure inquired to Szell about European orchestras "not on exclusive contract to other companies" with which he would like to make opera and symphony records. Szell "at once sidetracked the question." He sensed that the Boulez situation might serve as a possible wedge of advantage with Columbia for the Cleveland Orchestra. "I think you know," he wrote Barksdale, "that I find recordings important mainly as a source of income for the orchestra members. Personally I am not too keen on making many myself. I am afraid, however, that Columbia will more and more shift orchestral recordings (both Opera and Symphony) to Europe where talent costs are plus-minus half of what they are in the States." "So far as I am concerned," he continued, "and particularly if you can exploit this versus Columbia Records, the more Boulez, the merrier." But Szell also instructed Barksdale to see if "some discreet intimation should be leaked by third persons, to say, [RCA] Victor, that the C.O. might become available." But realistically, Szell was "just afraid that they may not be any more idealistic than Columbia" was then.[48]

Szell's seventieth birthday "could not be kept unnoticed," he wrote in a chatty letter that June to Frank Joseph. In it he assured his friend that he and his wife were "very well," and that he was "enjoying a quiet and lazy time of unprecedented duration. (You see, I take your advice to heart.)" With modest pride he related, "Especially in Europe the radio stations had special programs, the newspapers carried articles and I got so many dozens of wires, letters, etc. that it will take me weeks to answer just part of them. Pleasant surprises among them were congratulatory wire messages from the memberships of orchestras such as Vienna, Berlin etc. and even the Austrian Minister of Education, Art and Science sent a long cable."[49]

In an endearing letter from Hans Gal in Edinburgh, his older friend welcomed him to the "club of the 70-year-olds," which Gal had joined seven years before. He wished Szell all possible luck and good things but, above all, that Szell would make his life a bit more comfortable. As Gal himself had discovered for the past two years, he was experiencing the relief of no longer making time in having to do unwelcome things out of duty.[50] Szell wrote Joseph his regrets at not being able to attend the groundbreaking ceremony for the Blossom Music Center on Sunday, July 2: "I would appreciate it if you would convey to all present my warmest wishes for the future of this so significant new departure and my gratitude to all who so generously have made it possible to start it. May it be the opening of a new, glorious chapter in the history of the Cleveland Orchestra!"[51]

Szell wrote Barksdale from Zurich about hearing Arthur Rubinstein in concert "with the (very decently playing) local orchestra,- Beethoven G major, Brahms 2nd Concerto and as a 'little' encore Chopin's Scherzo in B-flat. He played simply incredibly, in every respect, including mechanical control. After the concert at a big party he was as hearty an eater and conversationalist as you can imagine. After the rehearsal (same day) we saw him at the Grill of the [Hotel] Baur au Lac where he put away two huge helpings of Curried Lamb, etc. . . . He will be 82 next January, as you know."

In July, Szell wrote Barksdale, "I haven't had my sweater out of my golf-bag yet this year here! About my golf the less said the better but it makes me walk 3 hrs in the morning." In the same letter he offered more thoughts about Boulez: "I am quite in favor of Boulez for 6 weeks in 69–70 starting March 2nd and suggest you 'sew up' these dates right now. Also, I would find it attractive if he were to take over a few concerts on the [1970] tour to Japan."[52] With the next foreign tour only a month away, Szell was already making plans three years in the future.

Tour of Three European Festivals, 1967

Cleveland's 1965 tour to the Soviet Union and western Europe was one of the longest foreign tours ever undertaken by an American orchestra; this tour in the summer of 1967 would be one of the shortest. Within three weeks the orchestra would appear in three of the most prestigious music festivals: Salzburg, Edinburgh, and Lucerne. Not sponsored by the State Department, it received private funding by the Musical Arts Association and the festivals themselves.

Returning from Europe, Szell stopped in New York on July 30 to record four Mozart violin and piano sonatas with Rafael Druian. On the sixth he flew to Cleveland for two rehearsals on the seventh and eighth and one on the ninth. Szell and the orchestra left Cleveland the night of the tenth, and arrived in Salzburg on Friday, August 11. Szell's programs were signature: *Oberon* Overture, *Don Juan*, and the *Eroica*; Brahms's Second; Mozart's Fortieth; and the Second Suite of *Daphnis et Chloé*. Completely rested and out to show off his orchestra, Szell was primed to the maximum. Their brilliant performances were tumultuously received by audiences and critics.

Salzburg is Mozart's for eternity. In 1967, it seemed to belong to Herbert von Karajan—"In Karajanopolis, the former Salzburg . . ." began a review in a Munich newspaper.[53] Whatever their differences in musical style and substance, and whatever Szell thought of his activities during the war, he had cultivated Karajan, who seemed genuinely to admire Szell. Their letters would fit a mutual admiration society. Without Karajan's approval, the Cleveland Orchestra would surely not have appeared in Salzburg nor, most likely, Lucerne. Karajan conducted his program in both festivals. The orchestra was intrigued to experience the Karajan mystique in person.

Karajan appeared at rehearsal in a black turtleneck and black trousers, surrounded by a large entourage with whom he seemed to be discussing important business up to the last minute. When he began conducting Prokofiev's Symphony no. 5, the Clevelanders were galvanized by his energy, his forceful beat, and the intensity of his expression. After the break, the orchestra took their seats to continue, but there was no Karajan. They sat there, fidgeting but trying to be patient, trained by Szell not to waste a minute of precious rehearsal time. Ten minutes late, Karajan sauntered in, engaged with his entourage, busier than before. He had changed his clothing completely—he now wore all white: trousers and turtleneck. He looked fresh and might have even showered. He appeared oblivious to the general bewilderment.

In the concert, Karajan did as he was wont to do: he conducted with eyes closed. Accustomed to vital visual communication, the orchestra became uneasy and the performance was, if not shaky, at least tentative, compared with the dynamic energy felt in the rehearsals. By Lucerne, they were prepared, but did not completely overcome their unease. Before intermission Karajan had been one of the three piano soloists in Mozart's Concerto for Three Pianos, along with Jörg Demus and Christoph Eschenbach, the latter two making their Salzburg debuts.

Although Demus shouldered the lion's share of the work, Szell was taken with the young Eschenbach, who showed his eagerness to learn from the master. That attitude, besides Eschenbach's obvious talent, endeared him to Szell. They met for a session on two pianos in Lucerne while Karajan conducted. Szell coached the pianist on the Schumann Piano Concerto and the Mozart Piano Concerto K. 459. "I had a most enjoyable hour with Eschenbach on two pianos," Szell wrote to Barksdale. "He is a really great talent, of promise and uncommon sensitivity, who understands suggestions and can put them into reality at the drop of a hat." Szell agreed to more coaching in November in Vienna, "which shows his interest and affinity." A year earlier, on the basis of the pianist winning the Lucerne Prize in the Clara Haskil Competition, and many verbal recommendations, Szell asked Barksdale to arrange with Eschenbach's management for his United States debut in Cleveland and first appearance in New York in the 1968–69 season, without actually auditioning him, "Opinions about him . . . are so favorable that I am inclined to take the chance before having heard him."[54] Szell's contact with the young pianist in August 1967 confirmed his earlier decision.

Because the tour was cosponsored by the festivals and the orchestra, there were no constraints on repertoire. Szell bowed to the twentieth century with four pieces, only one of them recent: Walton's *Variations on a Theme by Hindemith*, two Stravinsky classics, the Suites from the ballets *Pulcinella* and *The Firebird* (1919), and the Second Suite of Ravel's ballet *Daphnis et Chloé*, masterpieces but not new. Szell's soloists were Robert Casadesus, in Mozart's C Major Piano Concerto, K.467; Leonid Kogan, in Mozart's Violin Concerto in A Major, no. 5; and Clifford Curzon, in Beethoven's Piano Concerto no. 5 in E-flat Major, "The Emperor." Szell's standard repertoire consisted of the *Eroica*, Mozart's Fortieth, *Don Juan*, Schumann's Third Symphony (*Rhenish*), and Brahms's Second. The tour was a distillation and celebration of twenty years of Szell and the orchestra, and each performance thrilled all who heard it.

The Cleveland Orchestra opened the twenty-first Edinburgh Festival, playing four concerts on four consecutive days. The theme of the Festival was Bach and Stravinsky, and Szell obliged with as conservative choices as possible—Bach's Orchestral Suite no. 3 in D and Stravinsky's 1919 *Firebird* Suite, for which the press took him and the festival to task. As a further gesture, Szell added Walton's *Variations on a Theme by Hindemith*. Programming choices aside, the press was, with very few exceptions, ecstatic.

The second concert conflicted with an opera opening. Neville Cardus remarked that the majority of his colleagues "had been unable to resist the attraction down the street . . . of Stravinsky's 'The Rake's Progress.' In any case, any one of my colleagues could have argued, why should a critic nowadays attend a programme so hackneyed as the Cleveland Orchestra's on this occasion—the Oberon Overture, the Eroica Symphony and the C Minor piano concerto of Mozart." He answered his own question:

> The concert, in fact, was a sort of revelation. George Szell is musically one of the most thoroughly equipped of living orchestra conductors, and also his mind is constantly creative. Routine disperses in his presence. Though he is somewhere near his seventieth birthday, the impression he gives is of tireless curiosity, vigilance, and energy. He is of the old school of conductors who "make music." He does not "put it over." His gestures on the rostrum are intense and mobile, yet musically concentrated, without obvious audience appeal. . . . This concert proves yet again a favourite saying of mine: "There are no hackneyed masterpieces, only hackneyed listeners and hackneyed music critics."

Of Szell's performance of the *Eroica*, Cardus wrote, "Not since Toscanini have I heard this greatest of all symphonies explored and unfolded with so much power of dramatic illumination, with so firm and comprehensive a vision." His review ended, "A concert to cherish." Cardus was long familiar with Szell. In his review of the first

Edinburgh concert, he confessed that, "decades ago, I tried to push [Szell] into the position vacated by Hamilton Harty as director of the Hallé Orchestra."[55]

Author and critic Peter Heyworth astutely observed: "For here is a great orchestra, at whose head has stood a conductor of real stature, not for a handful of concerts a year, but throughout the better part of each season for a period of more than two decades. It may be that the Boston woodwind is more elegant, that Chicago's string tone is warmer and Philadelphia's more silky. But what makes the Cleveland Orchestra unique in both Europe and America is this old-fashioned sense of identity with its formidable conductor and the ensemble that stems from it."

Perhaps because the ubiquitous Karajan was coming to this season's festival with the Berlin Philharmonic (just three days after his Cleveland Orchestra concert in Lucerne), Heyworth made this comparison: "It is a sobering thought that George Szell, who at the age of 70 is, with Klemperer, the last survivor of that great generation of Central European conductors who grew up before the holocaust of 1914–18 and for which Karajan and Co., with all their achievements, are no substitute. . . ." The old Klemperer was active in London then and Heyworth would write his biography. Heyworth also noted that Szell had briefly been conductor of the Scottish National Orchestra. That was the orchestra now in the pit for *The Rake's Progress*, of which Cardus wrote.[56]

Desmond Shawe-Taylor took as his theme the "cautious coming of age" of the Edinburgh Festival in its twenty-first season. He regretted the conservative programming of all the participating ensembles, not just Cleveland, and remarked that the Cleveland played "not one note of American music." But he "cheerfully avow[ed] that the American orchestra has provided some of the finest music-making heard in the Usher Hall, or anywhere else for that matter. . . . To his superb capacities as an orchestral trainer," Shawe-Taylor continued, "Mr. Szell adds a ripe and secure classical musicianship of precisely the type that we miss in the work of his leading rivals at Boston, New York and Philadelphia. . . . He attends to the composer's thought as well as to his sonorous effects. Without fuss, but with unceasing vigilance, he makes music—and seems happiest when, for a few bars, he can hover like a motionless eagle and let the music make itself." The critic "was not . . . the only listener who was irresistibly reminded of Toscanini."[57]

From Edinburgh the orchestra went to London for two days, on the second of which they recorded Beethoven's *Fidelio* and *Leonore* no. 1 Overtures and Mozart's Fortieth Symphony for Columbia. The next day, the orchestra traveled to Lucerne for the tour's last week. There, among other friends of the orchestra from Cleveland, violinist Edith Peinemann visited the group. As Milstein, Francescatti, and Morini grew older, Peinemann was becoming one of Szell's favorite violinists.

The Lucerne programs contained some works played for the first time on the tour—Schumann's Third, Mozart's C Major Piano Concerto (K. 467) with Robert

Casadesus, and Berlioz's *Roman Carnival* Overture. The finale of the tour was a repeat of Karajan's Mozart/Prokofiev program. Reviews were as ecstatic as for Salzburg and Edinburgh: one critic reported "orgiastic applause at the close of the concert." But not everyone in Lucerne was eager to hear the orchestra. One of the orchestra's violists, Edward Ormond, met Vladimir Golschmann there on the street. Ormond had played for years in the St. Louis Symphony under Golschmann, and Szell's former rival expressed surprise when Ormond told him that he was there with the Cleveland Orchestra. Golschmann said, "Don't tell Szell you saw me. I'm not going to the concert tonight and I don't want him to know I'm here."[58]

Strife in the Orchestra

The orchestra returned to Cleveland on September 1. From Europe Szell kept a watchful eye on events. The first strike in the orchestra's forty-nine-year history posed a distinct possibility. In May the orchestra voted seventy-eight to thirteen to reject the five-year contract offer worked out by management and the Musicians Union. This, in effect, was a vote to strike, but it would not take effect until after the present contract ran out in early September.

The Lake Erie Opera Theatre suffered as chief casualty of the labor strife. Orchestra members did not wish to jeopardize the fledgling company's existence and were willing to play the opera season even if the contract remained unsettled by September. But the opera's producer, Howard Whittaker, and its board felt unable to risk losing the considerable amount of money and effort entailed in preparing a season. Without the guarantee of a contract by the end of May, they cancelled the fall production, planned as a double bill of Ravel's *L'heure espagnol* and Stravinsky's *Oedipus rex*.

Throughout the spring, mounting tension over the three-way struggle—orchestra musicians, Musical Arts Association, and Musicians Union Local 4—had been reported in local papers. By September 11, with no settlement and only a few days to go before the season's opening performance, the *New York Times* reported that orchestra members were seeking "a $300 weekly minimum wage, a better pension plan, improved overtime provisions, a sick-leave program and other fringe benefits." The *Times* explained this as no ordinary situation, but one that expressed the orchestra members' wish to circumvent the union and deal directly with the Musical Arts Association. This had been smoldering since the last contract negotiations and was now coming to a head. The *Times* stated: "Many people here believe that if the orchestra does not begin its season as scheduled, Mr. Szell will either guest conduct in the United States or Europe, or even accept another conducting post."[59] This was an especially crucial year for the Musical Arts Association: it was the orchestra's fiftieth anniversary, and a special celebration was planned.

The musicians believed that the local chapter of the union neither understood nor was sympathetic to their needs. They hired a lawyer, Bernard Berkman, to represent them in negotiations. The local claimed to function as sole bargaining agent for the musicians, as reaffirmed in recent court decisions. The union argued that a lawyer for the musicians must be mutually agreed upon, and they banned Berkman from the negotiating sessions. In protest, the orchestra committee boycotted further sessions. The newspapers carried extensive coverage of the tense situation. One erroneously reported that because of the uncertainty, twenty-five players had left the orchestra. The actual turnover stood at sixteen, still a significant number. All but two of the sixteen played strings. At least four would have left under any circumstance: one violinist left to become concertmaster of another orchestra, two violinists left to join the Philadelphia Orchestra, and another went to the Boston Symphony. Szell harbored two main concerns: that the artistic control he had always insisted upon would erode and that the orchestra's playing would be adversely affected.

When it returned from the tour, the orchestra was technically on strike. Picketing began on September 11. On the fifteenth, however, Barksdale informed Szell that a contract had been mailed to the orchestra the night before, and that he was mailing Szell a copy. It covered the next three years, not the original five, and was presented as final. "There is no thought of any further offer," Barksdale said. The orchestra was set to vote on it on Sunday the eighteenth, and Barksdale wrote Szell that he would telephone him the results "as soon after as I can." He and Lane had gone over the new contract and they felt that "neither your rights nor artistic matters are affected."[60] Representatives informed the musicians arriving to vote on the contract that the union had "interpreted" the number of votes needed to end the strike as a simple majority, rather than the 60 percent required to call the strike. Ratification under the old rule would have required fifty-six votes. The vote of fifty for and forty-two against came to 55 percent of the vote. In October the musicians asked Berkman to file a suit declaring the contract null and void, but in the meantime they agreed to play under its terms.

The *Plain Dealer*'s Robert Finn heard that if "the union simply let the vote go ahead under the old rules the majority for ratification would have been considerably higher, and no court case would have been necessary. It seems that some of the men who had intended to vote for ratification were so enraged by the union's action that they switched sides." By November, twelve of the sixty-two plaintiffs had withdrawn from the lawsuit against the contract, and this season and the next two proceeded as scheduled. But the seeds of real grief had been sown. Finn warned prophetically, "Assuming that this three-year contract runs its course, perhaps that time can be used to seek some resolution of the bitterness between the players and their union. This is essential if we are to avoid even bigger trouble in 1970."[61]

The new contract did not weaken Szell's position, but he sensed the changes in the wind and felt concern about future erosion of orchestral quality and working conditions. The musicians received a sizable raise but not all they sought. They were not entirely happy, but would, for the first time, be paid for fifty-two weeks. "Good

News for Music World," read the headline of the *Plain Dealer* editorial hailing the accord: "Now it is up to Greater Cleveland and indeed much of Northern Ohio to get behind the orchestra management financially to help pay the higher bills growing out of the new contract."[62] The estimated cost of the new contract, over three years, came to one and a half million dollars more than the old contract.

The Fiftieth Anniversary Season, 1967–68

The orchestra was on top of the world. Its third international tour, only two years after its previous one, had been brilliantly successful, and the union contract had been settled. In the summer of 1968 it would inaugurate the Blossom Music Center. Expectations ran high that extra concerts would attract new audiences. A gradual effort toward a three-performance subscription structure began this season. There seemed to be an audience for a third performance—the Thursday/Saturday series had long been virtually sold out. The question, however, concerned whether it would work better to have the third performance on the Friday between the old pair or on the Sunday following. The popular old Twilight series and occasional third performances of high-drawing-power programs had played on Sunday afternoons. But there might also exist an audience for a Friday repetition. This season was a test: the orchestra announced six Friday evenings and six Sunday afternoons. Audiences were offered a subscription of either six or twelve concerts (six for the price of five, twelve for the price of ten), and later, single sales.

It was unrealistic to assume that the extra concerts would immediately sell out. They did not, producing disappointment and consternation. The public had long been accustomed to subscriptions being all but sold out, so it would take years for the new availability to be recognized. Many Thursday/Saturday subscribers switched to better seats in one or the other of the new series, but far fewer new subscribers materialized than expected. There were three fairly well-attended but not sold-out houses for each concert. Other major orchestras around the country that had expanded their subscription series were experiencing the same phenomenon. Some of the grumbling over the moderate ticket sales even hinted that Szell's long tenure might be the cause. The possibility that better promotion and public preparation might have been the problem was conveniently overlooked by those on the staff on whom the blame would otherwise have fallen.

The season's opening program leaned toward the twentieth century. It began with the Prelude to *Die Meistersinger* and continued with the *Prelude to the Afternoon of a Faun* and the Walton *Partita for Orchestra*. After intermission came Prokofiev's Fifth Symphony. It was perhaps no coincidence that the orchestra had just performed it twice on the European tour—with Karajan. Could it be that Szell wanted to purge the orchestra of the other conductor's musical influence?

The season opened as planned, and this brightened Finn's reception of the opening concert. In "Orchestra Opens on Happy Note," Finn wrote, "A festive air prevailed. There was a gold cover on the program, a post concert champagne reception, a standing ovation for George Szell, and other indications that everything, for the nonce, is in proper order." Frank Hruby remained unconvinced. "The bloom is off," he wrote, "as opening nights go . . . the rather bitter wrangling centering around the strike, regardless of its merits was bound to have some psychological effect on those in attendance. It was reflected in the perfunctoriness of the now traditional standing greeting given to the conductor and his men on opening night. It was also reflected in the fewer than usual number of recalls for Szell at the close, this in spite of the fine performance of the Prokofiev 5th."[63]

The fortieth anniversary had brought forth ten commissioned works, but there were only two for the fiftieth, neither conducted by Szell: *Christmasmusic*, by Cleveland composer Donald Erb, conducted by Louis Lane; and *Magnificat*, by composer-in-residence Russell Smith, conducted by Robert Shaw. Costs were mounting: the Blossom facility had large construction cost overruns, the new contract called for hefty salary increases, and the budget would soon require even greater increases. Thus began a new era for the Cleveland Orchestra and the Musical Arts Association. This degree of labor unrest represented a new and uncomfortable phenomenon. Unaccustomed to running a deficit, the board would be facing that beast from now on. As a reminder of past glories, and to try to make up for not conducting either of the new commissions, Szell programmed three of the fortieth anniversary commissioned works in programs of the fiftieth: Walton's *Partita for Orchestra*, Walter Piston's *Symphonic Prelude*, and the Dutilleux. A sense of uneasiness hung over the orchestra.

In its uncertainty, the board did what corporations and other orchestras do: it undertook a study. It engaged the McKinsey Company, a management consultant firm, to investigate its problems and recommend solutions. McKinsey would provide the results to the board the following season.

Meanwhile, life and concerts went on. Szell led the first five concerts. Newly appointed associate concertmaster Daniel Majeske joined the list of familiar soloists, including Robert Casadesus and Pierre Fournier. Szell devoted an all-orchestral, single-work program to Mahler's Symphony no. 6, *Tragic*, a first time in Cleveland.

In New York, the Philharmonic announced that Szell had been named "Music Advisor and Senior Guest Conductor," to begin in the 1969–70 season. No permanent successor to the retiring Leonard Bernstein was named; Szell would serve as interim conductor. William Steinberg, senior guest conductor of the Philharmonic for the 1966–68 seasons, had been expected to be appointed, and "was said to be extremely bitter," as Barksdale wrote Szell. He related that "Steinberg did not learn of this until the day the announcement was being given to the newspapers."[64] Repercussions in Cleveland, according to Barksdale, were "a mixture of pride and apprehension," about which Frank Joseph and he had to do "a lot of reassuring."[65] At age seventy, Szell was not about to leave Cleveland for New York, but it must have given him great satisfaction to be guiding the New York Philharmonic's destiny, if only temporarily and so late in his career.

Szell left for six weeks for two programs each with the Berlin and Vienna Philharmonics, from November to early December.[66] He chose Zurich as his European port of entry and exit, arriving there on October 31. He wrote to Barksdale the next day, "I reached [Walter] Legge and [Elisabeth] Schwarzkopf last night at Geneva, in a hotel, where they are waiting to move into their newly acquired palatial villa with 240 ft. of waterfront." The contact was more than social; it would decide the repertoire for Schwarzkopf's two appearances in the Blossom Music Center's first season. Szell continued, "It will be a group of Strauss songs with the Mahler IV and a group of Mozart arias with the Strauss [Four] Last Songs."[67]

A review of Szell's Berlin Philharmonic concerts said that Szell makes "a mighty and powerful appearance, a man of distinction and authority, a Kapellmeister in the supreme sense of the word. One senses not only his complete familiarity with the world of forms, but the act of spiritual co-creation. There are no tricks, no effects. Szell needs no willful deviations from tradition, but the way in which he transmits tradition holds also the connoisseur, perhaps especially the connoisseur, in the spell of his mastery."[68]

Boulez's role in Cleveland was increasing. Plans were in the works to involve him more and more with the orchestra in the future. Also rising were the fortunes of the assistant manager, Michael Maxwell, a New Zealander who Szell met in London. Like Boulez's, Maxwell's timing proved excellent. Good looking, seemingly efficient, and with a suave British accent, Maxwell charmed Szell so that with the orchestra's activities expanding, a place was made for Maxwell beginning with the 1966–67 season. Barksdale was named general manager, George P. Carmer's title changed from assistant manager and comptroller to assistant general manager and comptroller, and Maxwell became assistant manager. His duties were to deal directly with the orchestra, and it soon became apparent that his style was confrontational.

Szell's final four subscription concerts of the Cleveland season held a few novelties amid old familiars. A genial April program presented the Overture to Bach's *Easter Oratorio* (a first on subscription concerts), and with a bow to the season, the "Good Friday Spell" from *Parsifal,* followed by Beethoven's *Pastoral.* Rudolf Serkin was soloist in Brahms's First Piano Concerto, and Schumann's First Symphony was the major work on a concert that concluded with Levine conducting *Petrouchka.* The final concert, all choral, began with Mozart's Requiem and closed with Bruckner's powerful "Te Deum."

Robert Finn, writing in the *Plain Dealer,* gave the fiftieth anniversary season a mixed report card. He took Szell to task for the token anniversary commissions. In his own defense, Szell "did his bit by dismissing the whole commissioning gambit as a 'shopworn procedure.' Actually, a number of prestigious composers were approached but turned the offers down due to press of other commitments," Finn wrote. For him there were two high points of the season: "Szell's performance of the Mahler Sixth Symphony and Robert Shaw's concert performances of Handel's superb opera 'Semele.'" Boulez impressed Finn favorably, and the announcement of his increased presence at Severance Hall caused many to make "the obvious inference that Boulez is being groomed as the eventual heir to the 70-year-old Szell, a prospect which thoroughly frightened some of the Severance Old Guard to whom anybody who champions the moderns is a musical bomb-thrower." Summing up, Finn wrote, "A good season, but not the outstanding one hoped for. Now it is on to Blossom Music Center where much of the orchestral programming will be drawn from the 50th season's programs. But no Mahler Sixth at Blossom—that might not draw 15,000 customers."[69]

11

Summers at Home

Szell had firsthand experience with the summer activities of many American orchestras. In the 1940s, he conducted the Los Angeles Philharmonic at the Hollywood Bowl, the Chicago Symphony at the Ravinia Festival, and the Philadelphia Orchestra at the Robin Hood Dell. In 1943 and 1945, he conducted the New York Philharmonic in the first and third of its three wartime summer seasons at Carnegie Hall. And later he conducted in at least one summer season at the Lewisohn Stadium.[1] He never conducted the Boston Symphony at Tanglewood, but knew of Koussevitzky's brainchild in the Berkshires.[2] When he took charge of his own major orchestra in Cleveland, Szell knew what he wanted for its summer activities, but it took twenty-two years to be realized.

Szell supported the Pops as a practical necessity but disparaged its musical content. Any disturbance to the orchestra's hard-won, finely tuned precision and delicate balance presented a threat to its quality. Szell was extremely particular about the guest conductors to whom he would temporarily entrust his orchestra in the winter seasons. If he detected the slightest lessening in the orchestra's response on returning, he would bellow to Lane, like Goldilocks's papa bear, "who's been conducting MY orchestra?!"

Suffering the orchestra's winter interruptions of his ministrations was difficult for Szell, but its summer activities were even less tolerable. Repertoire was a mixture of light classics, package arrangements of Broadway show tunes for vocal soloists and chorus, dances and marches, ballet music—sometimes with dancers—and a smattering of popular concertos with less-well-known soloists than in the winter season. The physical conditions during the summer concerts also undermined Szell's standards. Extremes of heat and humidity not only affect the players' comfort, but have a disastrous effect on intonation and can damage fine instruments. Musicians who owned valuable instruments would use cheaper backups when conditions were poor. The installation of air conditioning in the Public Auditorium in 1953 provided a considerable improvement.

Associate conductor Rudolph Ringwall conducted the Cleveland Summer Orchestra, as the Pops orchestra was called, for thirteen seasons through 1951. He was well known and well liked in the city. Ringwall had much involvement with the orchestra in the winter seasons, conducting a few pairs of subscription concerts and all children's and the Sunday Twilight Concerts. Louis Lane replaced Ringwall in the summer concerts in 1952, which helped maintain Szell's musical standards, but the physical deficiencies remained.

The summer Pops was an economic necessity for the musicians, but it was no artistic experience and, from Szell's viewpoint, detrimental to its quality. Salaries compared unfavorably with those of comparably trained musicians of the great eastern orchestras—Boston, New York, Philadelphia, and their western counterpart, Chicago—a fact members soon brought up in union negotiations.

Many players elected not to play the Pops. There were more attractive summer musical opportunities, such as the Aspen Festival, the Santa Fe Opera, and the venerable Chautauqua Festival. They may have paid no better than the Pops, but the music there was mostly classical, the acoustics natural and not amplified, and the physical beauty of the settings was a tonic for the musicians and their families.

Conditions at the Pops were discouraging: The audience sat at tables on the main floor on moveable chairs that made a clatter, added to by the walking of waiters serving food and beverages. Speakers amplified the orchestra—poorly at first, better later, but never very well. Musical finesse proved impossible to achieve. The cavernous Public Auditorium itself imposed a fundamental handicap. With the tables on the main floor for the Pops, its seating capacity numbered around six thousand. (For regular concerts or for the weeklong visit of the Metropolitan Opera in its annual spring tour, with rows of chairs on the main floor plus the oval balcony, it seated more than ten thousand.) Impressive in size and adequate for meetings and other public purposes, Public Auditorium seemed better suited to housing zeppelins than orchestras.

In summertime, "the livin' wasn't easy," particularly for the majority of the orchestra, who earned minimum scale set by the prevailing union contract. Until the first fifty-two-week contract, in the 1967–68 season, musicians were paid per week for the winter subscription series, much less for the variable number of summer Pops weeks, and not at all for the remaining inactive weeks. They needed to supplement their incomes, and did so in a surprising variety of ways.

In July 1952 an article in the *Cleveland Press* listed the different outside jobs held by orchestra members so they could afford to play in the orchestra. It told a human interest story. But the article only pointed up the embarrassingly low pay the players put up with. It was indeed a financial sacrifice to be a member of the Cleveland Orchestra for at least the first forty-five years of its existence.

If some players depended on outside jobs, it meant they spent that much less time at their art, less time practicing their instrument, less time learning the orchestra's new repertoire, and they had less time and money needed for healthy recreation. The orchestra was part-time but musicians' needs were full-time. To support themselves and their families, they had to work throughout the calendar year just to make ends meet, and that not well enough. The principal players naturally earned more than section players, but more than half of the orchestra earned just minimum scale.

The article credited the information about the orchestra's extracurricular jobs to a survey "undertaken during the orchestra's recent contract negotiations to find out how many members do not live by music alone. Apparently 60% did not." The writer listed forty different types of outside nonmusical jobs orchestra members held. "The orchestra's new contract raised minimum salary to $108 a week for the Severance season of 30 weeks. That comes to $3240 a year."[3] For artists at the top of their profession, who invested a lifetime of education and experience to qualify for membership in this top organization, that offered meager compensation.

When Public Auditorium closed in the summer of 1953 for repairs and the installation of air conditioning, it appeared that the summer concert season would be totally lost. Szell felt "extremely worried . . . not only for the sake of continuity but for the sake of the orchestra men, it is terribly important we have pops going in the summer." He pointed out that the players would then be unemployed from May to October and could "drift away to more musically active communities." Moreover, the orchestra would not play together for almost half of every year. Szell conceded that it was better to be playing something than nothing at all.[4]

The solution was to have the orchestra give twelve short concerts at the Cleveland Stadium between June 2 and August 10 before the Cleveland Indians' home baseball games.[5] Workers erected a stage, and installed a sound amplification system, reportedly the best available. At the first concert, two thousand baseball fans, a respectable number for the early hour, arrived in time to hear the orchestra, their numbers swelling to around seven thousand by game time. On double-header Sundays, the orchestra played concerts between games. In this stopgap manner, the summer season was saved. When Szell returned in the fall, however, he must have heard many complaints because, at his first rehearsal, he apologized to the orchestra for the conditions under which they had had to play.[6]

Szell wanted to attract and keep the best players. From the first, his demands of the board were for the orchestra rather than for himself. Throughout his tenure he requested raises for the players and more weeks of employment. The more the orchestra played together, the higher standards they could achieve and maintain. Szell talked about the need for proper summer activities with Frank E. Joseph as early as the late 1950s. Szell conveyed his urgent belief that the orchestra should play classical concerts year-round.

After successful but difficult union negotiations in 1964 for the coming summer seasons, the orchestra trustees realized that a fifty-two-week contract loomed not far in the future, and that the summer offered the best possible opportunity for expansion. With board approval, Musical Arts Association president Frank Joseph wrote the musicians' union that the board would appoint a committee to study that expansion and "will also give full consideration to the possibility of a permanent summer home for the orchestra."[7]

Seven months later, the board approved funds to undertake "a preliminary survey of needs and possible sites." It issued a press release: "Musical Arts Association Trustees Approve Proposal for Summer Home for Cleveland Orchestra," and the press reported it the next day.[8] By 1965 five other major orchestras had concluded fifty-two-week contracts, and Cleveland, whose present contract called for forty-eight paid weeks, felt pressure to follow suit.

Szell was struck by the contrast between the European summer music scene and what was happening in Cleveland. On the principle that great music cannot be made in poor surroundings, he concentrated first on the facility, writing Barksdale, "I have given the matter much thought and I think I have some distance to the problem now. While it is of course IMPERATIVE to have such an installation for the summer, it seems to me even more important to have it turn out to be exceptional, absolutely first rate, terribly attractive, and not merely a provincial imitation of Tanglewood et al." He reasoned:

> In view of the fact that we are at a disadvantage, geographically as well as demographically and not over blessed with striking scenic beauty in our immediate vicinity, I consider it of vital importance to have the chosen area and its "furnishing" as beautiful, attractive and functionally perfect as possible. If this goal should be jeopardized by having to rush to meet a deadline we might find ourselves with something on our hands that costs enough money but is not the really right thing. . . . I do feel that we should think and act on a large scale and with as much quality-fanaticism as possible. It may well be that for something along big lines money is easier to get than for something that would strike the prospective donors as an imitation of something other orchestras have and have had for years.[9]

The summer home was essential for the future of the orchestra. The cost of having an "attractive" summer facility was later partially offset by the freedom from the costs of rent for the Pops and would enable the orchestra to sponsor other money-making musical events. It would draw larger audiences than at the Public Auditorium. Szell was exercising his strong and farsighted leadership.

In the early 1960s, Joseph and Louis Lane journeyed to Tanglewood to learn about its operation. They had a four-hour meeting with Boston Symphony manager Thomas "Todd" Perry, heard rehearsals and concerts, and inspected the grounds and facilities. There were several more facilities in operation from which to learn. When the Detroit Symphony's Meadowbrook Festival opened in the mid-1960s, Lane and Barksdale made a scouting visit. It was on a smaller scale than what Cleveland needed, but they gathered useful operating information. Barksdale wrote Szell in Europe in August 1966, "Tanglewood remains an ideal not only for the natural beauty of the surroundings but the fact that the old shed permits a close relationship between the environment and the performance."[10]

At just that time, the Ford Foundation offered a two-million-dollar matching grant usable toward the summer festival. A family of prominent Clevelanders, the Blossoms, made a generous gift of $1,350,000. This gift provided the spark for a campaign to raise the estimated seven million dollars needed to complete the summer home, later named the Blossom Music Center.

The Blossom family had been long affiliated with the Musical Arts Association. Dudley S. Blossom and his wife were among the founders of the orchestra. Blossom, a longtime member of the board, had been active in the development and building of Severance Hall and was president of the Musical Arts Association from 1936 until he died in 1938.[11] Later, his wife, Elizabeth, served on the board, in time along with their son, Dudley S. Blossom Jr., until his untimely death in 1961 at age forty-nine. The $1.35 million gift to the orchestra by Mrs. Blossom Sr., Dudley Jr.'s widow, Emily, and other members of the family honored the memory of their late husbands and identified the family name with the orchestra for posterity. The initial gifts served as a vital impetus. Szell played an active part in raising the considerable amounts still needed.

Szell was guest of honor at a "Leadership and Corporate Dinner" held on April 20, 1967. Leading businesspeople of the entire northeastern Ohio region were present to kick off the Half Century Fund for Blossom Music Center (1967–68 was the orchestra's fiftieth season). Musical Arts Association trustees James Nance and Walter Bailey introduced Szell. He was both modest and imperious, mixing in a few choice colloquialisms as he spun his wheels: "Honored guests," he began, "now it's my turn to be overawed." Humble in the face of "this impressive and imposing assembly of distinguished leaders of commerce," he called himself "a simple musician." He "realized . . . that [he'd] been asked to talk to you for a few seconds practically only so that you will have an idea what kind of a guy it is whom you occasionally see from the back but very rarely from the front." Szell pointed out that Blossom would serve a wider area, including "vast areas of northeastern Ohio," and, he hoped, "many, many listeners who drive even further." And its seating capacity would more than double that of Severance Hall.

Szell as a fund raiser was very direct. He boldly challenged them in their pocketbooks: "When I discussed with a friend the list of the distinguished people invited to this assembly, he said to me, 'Oh, well, these people, if they really want to, can get all the money in one place in twenty-four hours.' Well, I'm not qualified to judge whether he was right. I, for my part, can say twenty-four *days* will do me very, very nicely."[12]

Joseph appointed a task force to develop the project. First came the challenge of finding the best location for the facility and choosing its architectural and acoustical design. They had to decide the type of building they wanted, its size and location, whether or not there would be a school in conjunction with the summer concerts (such as at Tanglewood, Aspen, and Meadowbrook), and how to fund it.

The Musical Arts Association needed to address the growing needs of the orchestra in its Severance Hall season, keeping solvent while the orchestra moved toward a fifty-two-week contract with the players, and its exploding budget for staff and orchestra and general operating costs. Up to a point, the winter staff could carry a great deal of the summer work, but running Blossom would require a full-time operation, especially when management booked package shows and pop entertainment for Mondays and Tuesdays—the orchestra concerts would take place from Thursdays to Sundays. The Blossom staff would oversee the running of a full week of ballet at the end of the summer season. The Severance Hall staff, meanwhile, would be at the height of its activity of planning and getting ready for the winter season. The board hired Marshall Turkin as Blossom's manager.

If Szell were to give up part of his annual European vacation to involve himself with the orchestra in northern Ohio in the summer, he would have to be satisfied with the facility. The orchestra deserved a first-class physical plant, but the enterprise would incur an enormous expense in a very short time. Szell held strong ideas, and he made them known. He set forth fourteen comprehensive points to Joseph. The first concerned the corridors approaching the area's airports: Cleveland-Hopkins, Akron-Canton, and a few noncommercial ones. Szell insisted that the summer site be at least five miles from the center of any existing or future flight path. Planes could fly five miles on either side of a designated path, making each corridor ten miles wide. This immediately eliminated almost 75 percent of the territory. Szell directed that the facility sit far enough away from interstates and other major highways to avoid vibration transmitted through the ground (he had often felt the subway rumble at Carnegie Hall). But the facility required access roads to permit large numbers of automobiles to arrive and leave in a reasonable time, with sufficient capacity for huge audiences for the popular attractions. The site would have to be located near enough to Cleveland for accessibility for the orchestra and staff, yet central to the largest possible population concentration in the northern Ohio area. Summer facilities need roofs for the stage and seated audience but are open on the sides and back for those on the lawn. A flat lawn—as at Ravinia and, to some extent, Tanglewood—creates poor sight lines; sloping ground is ideal.

With all the sky seemingly fair game for airplanes, the matter could have ended right there. With considerable clout, the orchestra negotiated feasible flight paths at rehearsal and concert times. Against the odds, they came closer to an ideal facility than would have been thought possible, but there were many problems along the way.

The board engaged William A. Gould and Associates as site selection consultants. By mid-1966, after an eleven-month search over a five-county area, the company found no acceptable location. Joseph took it on himself to continue the search in person, along with Barksdale and Lane. They followed every tip, but nothing seemed to meet even a small part of their requirements. In despair, Joseph was just about to report to the board that a satisfactory site did not exist: "Then a young architect by the name of Siebert, who is a graduate of Kent [State University] School of Architecture, asked if he could show us a parcel in Northampton Township. . . . So he took us to this property, and it was all covered with bramble and forest, and he took us to the top of that hill where you could look down and see the natural bowl. It was almost carved just exactly the way we wanted it. The bowl was there, the hills were there, the shell would just fit perfectly. I remember looking at Louis and saying "'Moses has led us to the promised land.'"[13]

Szell's approval was necessary before all major decisions. Musical Arts Association trustee Peter Reed, chairman of the Site Development Committee, visited the site with the Szells and Barksdale, and recalled: "Mr. Szell walked around with his overshoes through the thicket and the brush and finally turned to us and said: 'This is a great site and we should go ahead here.'"[14]

The promised land, in the bucolic township of Peninsula between Cleveland and Akron, was not just waiting to be gathered up. Joseph recalled: "Then our troubles really began. We discovered that we were talking about eleven different farms, every one of which was encumbered by mortgages, foreclosure suits, easements, rights of way, pipelines and everything else a lawyer could dream about in his wildest nightmare. . . . It took more than six months just to put all this together."

Joseph was determined that the Blossom Music Center would not suffer from small-scale planning. He had the orchestra buy more than five hundred acres when three hundred might have seemed sufficient to protect Blossom from commercial encroachment. Kent State University bought fifty-four adjacent acres for an arts center to operate in conjunction with the music festival.[15]

Barksdale wrote Szell, "We are on the brink of announcing the purchase of more than 500 acres of land in the site near Akron." Szell wrote back, "The news about the summer site is GREAT. Frank cabled me and I cabled my grateful congratulations back. Now we have to do quick- but GOOD- work." Using the Tanglewood term,

Szell asked, "Who is to do the first draft of the shed?" The parallel important area was acoustics. "How soon do you want to get [Christopher] Jaffe in," Szell wrote, "(on a tentative basis)? Let me have all the details available. How are the surrounding grounds to be developed? If it is really high class and reasonably priced, I might not be disinclined to buy a piece of land myself."[16]

A setback occurred regarding the water supply. Assured by engineers that because of the nearby Cuyahoga River there was sufficient water for the site, the board bought it. But well after well came up dry, at $40,000 a try. Effective political maneuvers brought Akron city water to Blossom, and this saved the day.

The Cleveland firm of Schafer, Flynn, and van Dijk won the design contract, with partner Peter van Dijk as chief architect. The board hired Pietro Belluschi as architectural advisor. The acoustical challenge would prove many times greater than building a Severance Hall. With open sides and back, every molecule of sound would have to be squeezed out of the shell around and above the orchestra and from the resonance of the stage floor. Seating planned for more than four thousand exceeded two-thirds that of Tanglewood's extraordinary shed, but provided twice the capacity of Severance Hall. With no balcony possible, the seating would have to cover a much greater area than the main floor of an indoor hall. For symphony concerts, no amplification would be used under the roof; there would have to be a sophisticated sound system for the outdoors. The amplified sound needed a time delay exactly calculated to meet the live sound as it traveled the distance from the stage, and to blend seamlessly with it.

Szell had Blossom Music Center much on his mind. Sleeping on the plane to Zurich at the end of October 1966, he had a nightmare about Blossom, about which he wrote to Barksdale: "Blossom was opened, most things worked fairly well, except that the audience could not be got back in after intermission. Signal provisions for the outside area had been forgotten. . . . I hope this nightmare won't prove ominous." He instructed Barksdale, "The outside loudspeakers—let alone inside installations—should provide for long-carrying power signals. A tape with a fanfare should be played as such." Barksdale assured Szell, "We have planned all along to have some kind of P.A. system on the lawn area for summoning the audience in."[17]

Szell was deeply involved in the vital choice of acoustician. The one he knew best was the German Heinrich Keilholz, the designer of the 1958 acoustic renovation of Severance Hall and who he was urging the New York Philharmonic to hire for Philharmonic Hall's acoustic renovation. Apparently, Szell always had Keilholz in mind, but at first he had the board turn to the American Christopher Jaffe. Szell wrote his reasons to Barksdale: "You will have noticed that I have not mentioned Keilholz yet in this connection. The reason was simply that for a speed-job such as ours I cannot see a team-member who lives on a different continent and because I have heard much favorable opinion about Jaffe who seems to specialize in this sort of assignment. But I think it might not be a bad idea to get Keilholz in at some point in a loose, advisory function."[18]

Keilholz, it seems, had gotten wind of the project. A friend tipped him off that Blossom was in the works. In a telephone conversation in Europe, Keilholz brought it up to Szell. "He apparently expected me to make some overtures to him regarding acoustical work," Szell wrote, "but I pleaded ignorance of any detail, saying that the matter is in the hands of our Trustees." But Szell was hooked and, true to his pattern, he would find fault with Jaffe as an excuse to switch to Keilholz.

In Amsterdam in November 1966, a month before a meeting with Jaffe and the architects, Szell appeared to be working himself up to an explosion; he was in a foul mood in general, devastatingly critical about the orchestra's new stationery, in particular. He felt that things were progressing much too slowly, and he wrote Barksdale details of what he expected each party to bring to the meeting: "I leave it to you to drive these people enthusiastically to work and to work out more than just approximate sketches. Frankly, I am getting concerned about the slow pace of progress and would regret it if my disappointment would force me to dissociate myself from the whole project, but I am determined not to waste much more time on it if the others proceed at snail's pace and talk instead of work." Szell was not satisfied with Jaffe's plans at the meeting. Leaving Cleveland afterward, Jaffe read in the newspaper of Keilholz's appointment as "advisor to the Blossom Music Center project." When Jaffe tried to clarify the situation, he realized that he would lack the authority to make final decisions on acoustical matters, and he reluctantly resigned. In the end, Keilholz was titled "acoustical engineer," but Jaffe received credit for "preliminary acoustical design."[19]

During the orchestra's tour of the three European festivals in August 1967, orchestra representatives attended a luncheon meeting with Keilholz, who had a summer home near Salzburg. Attendees included Musical Arts Association trustee Peter Reed, who had taken a leading hand in Blossom's funding and construction; general manager A. Beverly Barksdale; associate conductor Louis Lane, representing Szell; and the author, to translate. Keilholz staged the luncheon to perfection. It took place at an inn in the mountains some miles from Salzburg, on an outdoor terrace with views of breathtaking scenery. The party dined on venison from deer hunted by the inn's host, who had supervised its preparation and who warmly greeted the arriving guests. The parties agreed in principle that Keilholz would do the job and would come to Ohio for the final touches before the opening. He was difficult to pin down as to his exact plans for the acoustic treatment of the facility, and even more vague about his compensation. One wonders what Szell would have done had he attended that meeting.

The official ground-breaking ceremony had taken place on Sunday, July 2, 1967, with several generations of Blossoms on hand. The oldest and youngest—Mrs. Blossom Sr., and her namesake, granddaughter Elizabeth—turned the first shovels of earth. Frank Joseph served as master of ceremonies and the State of Ohio was represented by its director of development. From Europe Szell wrote Joseph his regrets at not attending: "I would appreciate it if you would convey to all present my warmest wishes for the future of this so significant new departure and my gratitude to all who so generously have made it possible to start it. May it be the opening of a new, glorious chapter in the history of the Cleveland Orchestra!"

Szell saw to it that his plan would reach fulfillment. He constantly asked Barksdale for details and bombarded him and Joseph with ideas for construction and improvements. He told Barksdale that he had telephoned Joseph and "urged him to seek maximum and novel steps in creature-comfort for the shed, to serve as examples to all other summer music places." He was also thinking about outdoor climate control: "I wonder whether anything can be done about at least partial Air Conditioning in a not completely hermetically sealed-off space. If there is anything, it might be THE most valuable innovation we could contribute. Our beastly summers really should be dealt with in an imaginative way if at all possible."

Barksdale wrote of visiting the new Saratoga summer concert facility with the Cleveland design team, Flynn, Van Dijk, Jaffe, and Gould. There they met Paul S. Veneklasen, its architect, who Barksdale found "quite aloof and uncommunicative, although polite." Szell was not surprised: Veneklasen "was in the original repair committee at Lincoln Center which accomplished nothing. He could not have liked my having pushed Keilholz later into the actual repair work."

Szell felt uneasy about outdoor music-making. He related to Barksdale: "Curious duplication of events: During 'my' Pastoral in Salzburg, in the most solid new Festival Theater there was, during the 'Scene at the Brookside' already, such a tempestuous Thunderstorm outside that it not only was audible inside the Hall but threw more than once the whole electrical system on to the emergency-current, which was noticeable by blinking and, for fractions of a second, ceasing of the lights. . . . But in our case we could beat the Good Lord's unfair competition. A distinct advantage of indoor music-making."

Szell continually stressed the performers' comfort: "Looking again at the Blossom rehearsal schedule I see that *all* concerned will need a place to rest between rehearsals and concerts. Will you [Barksdale] please transmit to Messrs. Reed and Van Dijk my concern that in the locker-room as well as in all soloists rooms + concertmaster room there is not only adequate furniture to hang + store changes of suits etc but some comfortable chairs, preferably,- in the single rooms,- easy chairs with ottomans (as in mine) where one can stretch out + rest. This is nothing to economize on—I cannot be expected to deliver good performances with tired + disgruntled personnel. This is an earnest concern of mine." He was well aware of concertmaster Rafael Druian's extreme sensitivity: "Of course, my car & driver should be at the disposal of the Guest Conductors,- also my dressing room. I warn, however, not to neglect the other dressing rooms, including that of the *concertmaster*, so no bad blood is artificially generated." Another detail to which he attended, "Regarding the walk-way [between the ancillary building and the backstage area], a good canvas cover should be adequate,- just don't forget to string up a few light-bulbs."[20]

Barksdale related an anecdote from his visit to Saratoga:

> No doubt you have heard that Mr. Ormandy visited Saratoga in the early summer and was annoyed by the waterfall nearby. He demanded that some means be found of silencing it during rehearsals and concerts of the orchestra. A sluice had to be built around the fall so that the water could be gently lowered during these times and restored to its natural state at other times. Balanchine did not see the place until the day of the opening. He was escorted to his room which has a view overlooking a stream. He stood for a long time in meditation and finally turned to [the manager of the facility] and asked "Is this the waterfall?" Assured that it was he meditated for a few moments longer and then said: "It would be better to turn Ormandy off."

Barksdale had not foreseen that Szell's sympathy to Ormandy's legitimate musical objections outweighed his enmity toward him. "I had not heard the Balanchine-Ormandy story before," Szell wrote, "and find it mildly amusing. That a Ballethound cannot understand a musician's reluctance to have the sound he has to watch and to work with drowned out by extraneous noise is par for the course. But what would you have said to the drowning out of the music by the tap-dance noises of an 80-member Spanish Ballet-Group in Karajan's production of 'Carmen' ??-"[21]

Construction of Blossom came under pressure: only one year separated ground breaking from scheduled opening. The Turner Construction Company worked throughout the Ohio winter. In the early summer, when Keilholz came to fine-tune his work, he expressed amazement at the enormous structure that had grown from nothing in just a year, and exclaimed, "Only in America!"

The architectural design concept created one of the most striking arts buildings of its time. It not only perfectly provided a summer venue for hearing a great orchestra perform great music, it is an impressive work of art on a grand scale, contemporary yet organic, sweeping yet warmly inviting, and beautifully harmonious with its natural setting. The structure is also a bold work of engineering. Imagine the top half of a huge inverted scallop shell covered with shingles, supported by a giant horseshoe of a steel girder. Thus the pavilion of Blossom Music Center.

Not all parts of the facility were completed, but enough were ready to make it possible to open on time on Friday, July 19, 1968. At the opening ceremony, Mrs. Dudley S. (Emily) Blossom Jr., who had been instrumental in winning the family over to the project, represented them. Frank Joseph, who led the campaign to find, fund, and build the center, represented the Musical Arts Association, of which he was president. Who would serve as the featured speaker?

The committee in charge of the ceremonies wanted someone well-known and respected, a person who would speak appropriately and briefly, and maintain composure in the face of the size of the audience and the occasion's importance. It was not a political occasion, and the committee did not want a political figure. Emily Blossom introduced the idea to ask Szell. At first, that produced laughter, but the logic of it persuaded the committee. The public would see his face, which they only glimpsed otherwise on his entrances and exits from the stage, and during his bows, and also they would hear his impressive voice—the silent member of the orchestra would be heard.

Blossom's next task was to persuade Szell to do it. She had gotten to know him very well during the planning of Blossom Center. Before she committed the family's gift, she met Szell to learn how much the project meant to him, and the extent of his future concert commitment there. In their meetings at her house, Szell had been delighted with its spacious and well-kept grounds. They shared an interest in gardening. She nevertheless felt quite nervous on this mission. Meeting Szell, they discussed the aspects of the facility and the opening. When Szell asked her about the speaker, she responded:

> You know we have to consider that very carefully and that's one of the main reasons why I am here. You know we have to be so careful in choosing a speaker because we don't want someone who is going to make a political speech, we don't want someone who is just going to get carried away in front of a large audience and spoil your program for you, I said, yet we need someone who is an international person because this is a big thing and we can't have just some little local someone, and he said, "Yes, I understand that." I said this person has to be a very colorful person and it isn't too hard to find one. He said, "I know that, damn it, but who?" I said, Oh, I was thinking of you. He said, "ME?" I don't know of anyone else who fills these qualifications. He thought a minute and said, "I guess I could do that, and if I do it, I'll make it very short," and he did.[22]

Even so, the gala opening almost did not take place. Racial unrest in the cities marked the summer of 1968. On the day of the opening, John Ballard, the mayor of Akron, called Frank Joseph and told him that he would have to postpone the opening. Joseph replied that he could not, for he expected distinguished guests from all over the world. With the threat of riots, Ballard said he could not spare one deputy sheriff. Then, the governor of Ohio told Joseph to close down until they could get proper protection. Joseph asked if that was an official order or just the governor's opinion.[23]

In spite of the risk, the opening went ahead. A curfew had been modified to allow people from Akron to attend the Blossom opening, and by the time the concert ended the curfew had been lifted. The pavilion was full and 1,300 on the lawn heard the opening program. Beethoven's overture, *The Consecration of the House*, began the event, followed by the speeches of Emily Blossom, Frank Joseph, and Szell. Blossom presented the spade used at the ground breaking just a year before, now gold-plated, to the Musical Arts Association. Joseph spoke briefly, then introduced Szell, who rose to the occasion as expected:

> To accomplish what you, ladies and gentlemen, what you see here tonight, requires mainly three ingredients, three qualities: vision, generosity, and talent. Vision is represented by our president, Frank Joseph, who, from the first moment of planning on, years ago, until literally this minute, took care of the grand design and of every detail and drove things through. Generosity is represented by the Blossom family, without whose action and example we couldn't be here tonight. Talent is represented by so many people who worked to accomplish this that it is impossible to name them all. But I feel I have to mention, primarily, Peter Van Dijk, the architect whose creative design you are here enjoying. Next to him is Heinrich Keilholz, the famous acoustician who was our consultant also on this center. And difficult to enumerate all of them—all the members of our board and our various committees with their leaders and administrative talent, who have toiled and worked at this project. And all the workmen, without exception, in all branches of endeavor, who worked with an incredible devotion and efficiency. I feel that I am not speaking for myself only but for every member of this distinguished orchestra, if I offer all of these personalities the expression of our high admiration and deep gratitude. Let's give them a hand![24]

After tumultuous applause, the honorees left the stage and Szell conducted Beethoven's Ninth. The performance was powerful and moving, and it brought the audience of 5,963 to their feet cheering. Blossom was an artistic and acoustical success.[25]

Harold C. Schonberg, chief music critic of the *New York Times*, covered the event in a long article. He devoted only its final paragraph to the music. To say that he reviewed the facility would be more accurate. Here, in its entirety, is Schonberg's review of the music: "For the record: The Beethoven Ninth was sung by Phyllis Curtin, Jane Hobson, Ernst Haefliger and Thomas Paul, with the Cleveland Orchestra Chorus. The music received a typical Szell interpretation—taut, tensile, logically shaped and powerful in its impact. One had expected no less."[26]

Blossom Center had a great visual impact on Schonberg, as it does for everyone seeing it, not only the first time, but with every walk up the path from the main entrance as the roof and then gradually the rest of the building come into view. Schonberg described it in his Sunday column a week after the concert: "It is a big structure, and a breathtaking one. Peter van Dijk, the chief architect, sank some massive girders into the earth and swung them around the entire building, and the entire mass is at once rooted in the ground and taking off into the sky. The outside is covered with gray asbestos shingles, while the stage and shell, designed by Heinrich Keilholz, uses natural cedar. . . . It already is a major addition to the American musical scene. The Cleveland Orchestra and its distinguished conductor are among the world's greatest, and the auditorium is a visual triumph."

Large it is—there are 4,642 seats under the massive roof. The interior measures 328 feet from front to back and 310 feet from side to side. For comparison, a football field is 300 feet long. Vertical girders support the great curved girder around its edges, but no internal columns block the audience's view. The warmth of the wood shell surrounding and covering the stage seems to translate directly to the sound. As evening comes on, the lighted shell begins to glow. The effect is beautiful, but most important, the sound is remarkably present for such a large, partly open space. There is the right amount of reverberation and the bass response is strong and clear.

Schonberg interviewed Szell and reported that he "will exercise complete artistic control. He will select the guest conductors ('those I can trust') and soloists, scan the programs, and 'keep an eye on the school.' This summer the conductors he has trusted are Stanislaw Skrowaczewski, Louis Lane, William Steinberg, Robert Shaw, Aaron Copland and Karel Ančerl."[27] The Blossom Festival School first convened at Kent State University—jointly administered by Kent State and the orchestra—and, after the facility's construction, on Kent State's grounds adjacent to the orchestra.[28]

Szell led all six programs in the opening two weeks. Rehearsals began at air-conditioned Severance Hall for comfort and to save the travel time of forty-five minutes to an hour. That first summer was exceptionally hot. Rehearsing outdoors in the afternoons presented a hardship for the performers and proved to be bad for instruments and intonation. Three different programs in one week contrasted with one in the winter, repeated two or three times, could only cause a rehearsal crunch unless the repertoire came mainly from the winter concerts.

The opening weekend was all Beethoven: the Third and Fourth Piano Concertos with Rudolf Firkusny, and the Seventh and Ninth Symphonies. There were three completely different programs the second weekend. On Friday and Sunday, Elisabeth Schwarzkopf was a commanding presence, if a bit less vocally powerful than in her prime. Friday's program consisted of Haydn's Symphony no. 93, Strauss songs with orchestra, and Mahler's Fourth Symphony. Sunday's first half was the "Jupiter" Symphony and arias from Mozart operas. The second half presented Strauss's *Four Last Songs* and *Death and Transfiguration*. Saturday was all Brahms: *Academic Festival Overture*, the Violin Concerto with Edith Peinemann, and the First Symphony.

Controlling the Outdoor Climate

The extreme heat in northern Ohio that first summer made one necessity evident. The natural construction that makes a stage a perfect collector and reflector of sound makes it also a perfect collector and keeper of heat. In a corner protected from the elements, the orchestra was far from summer breezes. Stage lights added to the heat, and the humidity in that part of the country is notorious. Szell said that if he were to be involved again, something would have to improve. But how to air condition the outdoors?

The ingenious and practical solution was to circulate air on the stage, from which the moisture has been extracted, through vents installed across the front of the wide stage. Vents at the back took up the air for recirculating. The initial construction included the vents and the room for the air drying machinery. Because of cost overruns, installation of the machinery itself had been postponed.

After the Blossom opening, Szell traveled to Salzburg to conduct concerts with the Berlin and Vienna Philharmonics. He cabled "Can do final blossom week 1969," to the relief of all. In a letter a few days later, Szell qualified the "can do": "I am writing to inquire . . . whether you have received my cable indicating that I *could* do the final week at Blossom?"

Getting wind of delays in completing the air system, Szell resorted to his sometime characteristic threatening mode. "Your reply to my comments I found disappointing," Szell wrote Barksdale. "The least I had expected was some sympathetic concurrence. Instead of that you fobbed me off with one of those non-committal, elusive answers you have taught me during the years to suspect and distrust. Frank was at least candid enough to tell me 'The so-called authorities are not in favor of Airconditioning on stage.' Whereupon I wrote him that this leaves me no choice but to ask him to instruct all concerned to remove forthwith my name from all printed matter etc. connected with Blossom."

Barksdale replied with a handwritten letter; he wanted to keep this matter contained. He apologized that his remarks had such a negative effect and told Szell that he then circulated a 1967 memo stating that the air system would be postponed until after the first Blossom season, but if found necessary he would have it installed by the second. Szell kept up the pressure: "As I don't consider myself its Musical Director until such time as I have concrete assurance that the Air-cooling work on stage has actually started, I am not in a position to either write Casadesus [about a repertoire choice] or give you authoritative opinions, approvals or disapprovals." But, not wanting a wrong choice to be made, he softened in the next sentence: "All I can do is to give friendly personal advice to you,"[29] and answered many pending questions.

The air drying system proved a lifesaver for the orchestra players and also ensured Szell's participation in the second season. Gary Graffman wrote Szell that it was the only outdoor concert he played where the piano keys were not slippery and did not stick. Szell expressed his gratitude to the engineer for the "very definite relief" of the dehumidifying installation, but added "we have not had this summer the worst extremes of heat and humidity."[30] In later years, the system conditioned the air to an icy blast.

Szell guided the orchestra into creating a living monument to itself—one of beauty and esthetic grandeur. He would grace it for only its first two seasons, 1968 and 1969, but his high aims inspired this handsome setting, a tangible and lasting legacy, and a fitting summer home for the great orchestral instrument he nurtured.

12

Finale

Cleveland, Japan, Korea, Anchorage, Cleveland (1968–70)

George Szell had reached the pinnacle of his career: the Cleveland Orchestra was universally acknowledged to be among the greatest, and the Blossom Music Center was a brilliant success. Szell and the orchestra continued to record for both Columbia and Angel Records, and the syndicated broadcast concerts were enrolling an increasing number of stations nationwide. The international tours of 1965 and 1967 had solidified the West's high perception of the orchestra. Szell was in demand as a guest conductor with the majority of the greatest European orchestras, and he guided the New York Philharmonic while it sought a successor for Leonard Bernstein. In November 1967, the Cleveland Orchestra announced a May 1970 tour to Japan.

For Blossom, Szell had to change his summer routine, making sure that his sacrifice was duly appreciated. The final Severance Hall concert of the 1967–68 season took place on May 12. Two weeks later, Szell arrived in Switzerland for a month of golf while Helene visited her sister in England. He picked her up en route to New York on July 12; they arrived back in Cleveland two days later. Blossom opened on the nineteenth. After his two weekends at Blossom, Szell returned to a rainy Salzburg Festival for one concert each with two of the finest orchestras on the Continent. To Barksdale he wrote that the first one, with the Berlin Philharmonic early in August, "was something of a sensation (with just Haydn, Mozart + Beethoven)" (Haydn Symphony No. 93, Mozart Symphony K. 201, Beethoven Eighth). Two weeks later, he led Beethoven and Bruckner with the Vienna Philharmonic ("Emperor" Concerto, Curzon; Bruckner Seventh). He wrote Barksdale that on his arrival at the Oesterreichischer Hof, the head concierge said: "'You may know that both your concerts have been sold out for weeks - I need desperately some 24 tickets, could you help me?' - I couldn't." After the first Vienna rehearsal, Szell found the musicians "remarkably cooperative and eager to rehearse properly (!)"[1] The reviews were stunning, and two mentioned figurative physical effects on volatile audiences: "The public melted," and "The public exploded." Gottfried Kraus of the *Salzburger Nachrichten* was thankful that Szell put Beethoven's Eighth at the center of attention, revealing its greatness, when so often its "undeserved Cinderella-placement" puts it in the shadows of its mighty neighbors, the Seventh and Ninth.[2] In Salzburg Szell privately coached pianist Christoph Eschenbach, who expressly came for the sessions. Szell asked Barksdale to take a further hold on him for the season after the next one ("to be exercised after his appearances with us").[3]

The Szells took two weeks of vacation at Bad Ragaz, Switzerland, and a week in Paris. Flying to England, there Szell conducted the opening concert of the London Symphony Orchestra's sixty-fifth season. The program noted that Szell had appeared with that orchestra as piano soloist and composer sixty years earlier, in 1908, at the age of eleven. The concert—*Prometheus* Overture, Mozart's A Major Piano Concerto, K.488 (which Szell had played in 1908) with Clifford Curzon, and the *Eroica*—was summed up by Joan Chissell in the *Times* of London: "It was virtuoso orchestral playing; it was certainly virtuoso conducting." She observed: "Dr. Szell contrived to give every single note a life of its own, weighing it, colouring it, blending it—with gestures at once expressive, clear and concise."

Of Szell's *Eroica*, Colin Mason in the *Daily Telegraph* was almost put off by Szell's forceful approach:

> In Beethoven's "Eroica" Symphony the conductor's assertion of his remarkable musical personality was somewhat more controversial and the result could have been revolting if it had not been magnificent.
>
> He has shown himself a conductor who is not afraid to improve on the work of the masters. And here he amplified and adjusted Beethoven's instrumentation to secure a sound which was euphonious and thrilling beyond the composer's wildest dreams, at times nothing short of Mahlerian.
>
> But the true magnificence lay not in this, which could easily have been tawdry, but in the complete commitment and devotion with which it was put to the service of the music.
>
> Not an ounce of showmanship or desire for self-glorification showed in the performance, which beyond and above all its marvels of sound and execution gave an impression of complete absorption in the music and intentness on communicating all the teeming multiplicity of its genius.

The *Financial Times*' Ronald Crichton began his review, "Would that the LSO could capture George Szell more often! There is surely no other living conductor who to such an extent combines wisdom and experience, fanatical care for detail and galvanic energy." Crichton accepted Szell's tempo fluctuations in the *Eroica* with understanding: "But none of this really weakened the total effect because the playing had such fire, strength and conviction."

Szell returned to Cleveland for the first four programs of the orchestra's fifty-first season—his twenty-third. Within those four Cleveland weeks there were seven recording sessions for Columbia Records. The recording of the *Ring* excerpts was a special case: their complexity, their use of large orchestra with extra instruments, including the fussy "Wagner tubas," and their importance to Szell. One of the world's leading Wagner conductors, Szell had conducted only a concert version of the first act of *Die Walküre* in Cleveland. He had recorded excerpts with voices and many of the overtures, but not one of Wagner's music dramas complete. The previous spring, Szell had made the carefully marked music available to the musicians, as it was difficult and unfamiliar. From the intensity with which he conducted the rehearsals, performances, and recording sessions, Szell clearly felt as passionate about the work then as earlier.

Back in London in November, Szell presented two characteristic concerts with the New Philharmonia: Weber, Mozart, and Schumann. The second concert was Beethoven's Eighth and Ninth Symphonies. London reviewers found Szell's Eighth a "revelation," much as had those who heard it in his Salzburg concert.

Szell was indeed at the pinnacle. His only competition seemed to be with himself and with the great Arturo Toscanini. Desmond Shawe-Taylor alluded to that when discussing the Ninth: "We do not get from Szell, it is true, the sense of a brooding cosmic mystery at the beginning of the symphony, or the heart-easing contentment of lyrical song in the flowering variations of the slow movement; but we get such a scherzo as I have hardly heard since Toscanini, with an irresistibly pulsing rhythm and titanic interventions from Denis Blyth's timpani, which allowed us to understand very clearly the reaction of the first Vienna audience, as recounted to the young Weingartner by an old lady who had sung in the chorus on that occasion: 'at this unprecedented stroke,' she said, 'bursts of excited applause ran around the house.'"[4]

According to more than one reviewer, Szell had raised the level of the Philharmonia Orchestra's playing, but, as Edward Greenfield observed: "If the playing was hardly polished enough to be mistaken for that of another Cleveland Orchestra, Szell kept making one wonder what miracles would result from a whole course of his training."[5] Szell himself felt dissatisfied: "The New Philharmonia Orchestra I found in a pitifully run-down condition," he wrote Barksdale. "After one week of drudgery things are improving. The first concert was most enthusiastically received - with 7 or 8 recalls after the 'Rhenisch' and splendid notices; and today's rehearsal for the 9th (fine chorus - *superb* soloquartett - [Heather] Harper - [Janet] Baker - [Ronald] Dowd - [Franz] Crass - Dowd the relatively weakest) was encouraging - but sometimes I wonder whether this sort of elementary tuition to 'self-governing' orchestras is worth my while + effort." Writing from Paris a few days after London, Szell added a P.S. to Barksdale: "The London concerts were howlingly successful but the New Philharmonia is a very run-down outfit—it took me more than a week to pull them together. . . . Their chorus, however, is sensationally beautiful in sound + training."[6]

The previous May, Szell had told Edward Greenfield: "Of the progress made in British orchestral playing since [Szell] worked in Glasgow, he is very appreciative, but still feels that the sum total of first-rate British orchestral players is too thinly spread." Szell implied that there were too many orchestras for the number of fine players and that self-governance had its weaknesses for achieving top quality. About Cleveland, Szell explained: "As [Szell] sees it, his greatest achievement in Cleveland is the habit he has instilled into the players of listening to each other. It is not for the individual, he says, to play just his own part and count bars in between. Whether the orchestral musician is actually playing or not, he must always be 'involved in the totality' of the music. As an afterthought Szell emphasizes the importance of phrasing and articulation—'good sound, good intonation, and good ensemble being taken for granted.' At least in Cleveland."[7]

Correspondence with Barksdale in Cleveland and Moseley in New York was not always limited to programs, soloists, contracts, and orchestra players. The latest women's fashion at home was the miniskirt, the thought of which brought out Szell's prudery in full force. He felt affronted by the exposure of so much leg and was concerned that the skimpy apparel would shatter decorum at Severance Hall. Szell often chided Barksdale for softness in keeping his staff in line. To bolster his resolve, Szell sent him a clipping from *Time*. A New York bank chose attractive young women for its tellers and provided them with designer dresses—"career-coordinated ensembles"—but, as Szell underlined, "<u>no miniskirts allowed</u>."[8] Szell wrote in the margins of an advertisement on that page: "→ABB! You see it is not as you said that 'They do it in all offices.' You <u>can very well</u> put down rules of attire + deportment. Members of our board + Women's Committee object also to Miniskirts worn by Severance Hall personnel. If I see a single one on my return, There will be a scandal; I shall be insulting to the utmost of my ability. If you have no sense of propriety or no guts to enforce it, others must press you. I, for one, am nauseated by what I have sometimes to see. G.S." And below, he added, "P.S. They can go half naked during their own time if they so desire, but <u>at work, in the hall,</u> they must be made to conform with certain standards of appearance!!" In his reply Barksdale added by hand in the margin: "re office dress: offenders told no shorter than top of knee." Szell responded about a few points of business. Then, in his last paragraph, he wrote, none too elegantly, "Thanks for the good news that I shall not be exposed any further to nausea by the exposition of elephant trotters up to the genitals."[9]

Szell next conducted two programs with the Vienna Philharmonic, then returned to New York. On December 10 he met Carlos Moseley for lunch and auditioned

French horn candidates for the Philharmonic. Two days later, he arrived in Cleveland to conduct in mid-December.

In January, Szell received and signed a letter of agreement with the New York Philharmonic as senior music advisor and principal guest conductor. It may seem odd that they waited fourteen months after the announcement of his appointment, and even after he began working in his advisory capacity, carrying on extensive correspondence, planning meetings, and auditioning players, to commit the agreement in writing. Both sides exhibited good will and trust and no pressing need. Bernstein remained music director in 1968–69, conducting twelve weeks. Szell conducted the Philharmonic in only one concert that season—a pension fund benefit in April with Arthur Rubinstein.

Under the new agreement, Szell would conduct the Philharmonic for nine weeks the following season (1969–70), thirty-four concerts. Szell was to be paid for the nine weeks of guest conducting in 1969–70, but "Dr. Szell will not be paid any compensation for his services as Music Advisor, which he is offering as a token of esteem for the Society and of affection for its President [Amyas Ames] and its Managing Director [Carlos Moseley]," a generous gesture by Szell to the Philharmonic. He would only be reimbursed for his out-of-pocket expenses "in connection with this phase of his activities."[10]

On Monday, January 6, 1969, Szell began rehearsing for subscription concerts and repertoire for Cleveland's East Coast tour in February and recordings of the suites from *Háry János* by Kodaly and *Lieutenant Kijé* by Prokofiev, Mozart's Serenade no. 9 in D, K. 320, "With the Post Horn," Haydn's Symphony no. 95, and the Tchaikovsky Piano Concerto no. 1 with Gary Graffman.

Tour repertoire also included Brahms, Mahler, Mozart, Schumann, and Tchaikovsky. Soloists slated for Carnegie Hall were Clifford Curzon, James Oliver Buswell IV, Gary Graffman, Leonid Kogan, and—making his United States, Cleveland, and New York debuts—Christoph Eschenbach. Kogan missed the Cleveland performances because of illness, joining the orchestra in New York only. In Cleveland, Szell memorialized the beloved Arthur Loesser with Brahms's *Tragic Overture*. During the forty-two years Loesser had lived in Cleveland, he was frequent piano soloist with the orchestra, taught piano, lectured brilliantly on music, and wrote entertaining and informative books, articles, concert reviews, and program notes.[11]

Eschenbach made a successful debut, the benefit of private coachings with Szell in Salzburg and Vienna. In Vienna Eschenbach arrived at the appointed time at the studio with two pianos and heard Szell, who had come early, practicing the orchestra tuttis (passages the orchestra plays without the soloist). The building's concierge remarked, "Professor Szell was here practicing for hours yesterday, too."[12]

After the Cleveland tour, Szell heard auditions at the New York Philharmonic in March and conducted its pension fund concert in April. During his six-week absence, Lane and Shaw led the Cleveland concerts, with guests Georges Prêtre, Hans Schmidt-Isserstedt, and Pierre Boulez, who also led the orchestra on a one-week tour. In March 1968 Pierre Boulez was engaged as a guest conductor of the Cleveland Orchestra for five seasons from 1967–68 through 1971–72. The following February, Boulez was named principal guest conductor. He would be in residence for five weeks in 1969–70 and eight weeks each in 1970–71 and 1971–72.

Szell recognized that Boulez was in a special category among conductors. In 1968 Barksdale wrote Szell that he was encountering difficulties working out 1969 Blossom programs with Boulez that would be sufficiently mainstream to draw the summer audiences. Szell wrote back, "I don't know what can be done about it. The reason for it all is that he is a most interesting specialist and an attractive personality but not a professionally trained and seasoned conductor in the orthodox sense, and that his repertoire is an 'off-brand' one and extends only very slowly. He recently added the Beethoven 5th and his performance of it was promptly dubbed 'MINI-FIFTH." If I were you, I'd go—during the summer brutally, but not indecently, for sure-fire-income and leave the riskier things for the inter-season—although there are some financial hazards as well." Boulez himself felt misgivings about conducting the Fifth at Blossom and wrote respectfully, "Do you think that people would accept the Beethoven no. 5 from me when they have 'at home' a master who does it so magnificently?"[13] He did conduct it, to a mixed reception.

Boulez's appointment had Clevelanders wondering if he were the heir apparent to Szell. Some would have welcomed that, but others were concerned that his appointment would have meant a modern bias in repertoire. They need not have worried: Boulez accepted a bid from the New York Philharmonic. Carlos Moseley recalled Szell's comment: "I had intended to recommend Boulez for Cleveland but you beat me to it and I won't interfere."[14]

Boulez met more than once with Szell in New York to discuss the Philharmonic position before accepting it. He felt that it would be absurd for him not to meet the challenge. Additionally, he said that he wanted Szell's advice on many matters and hoped to meet further in New York or in Europe. Boulez made it clear to Szell and to the Philharmonic that he would honor his commitments to Cleveland through 1971–72.[15]

The last three weeks of the season were full: Brahms's German Requiem; concerts with Mstislav Rostropovich in the Dvořák Cello Concerto and Brahms's Double Concerto with Jaime Laredo; and the final program, with Erica Morini playing the Mendelssohn Violin Concerto and Brahms's Second Symphony.

Amid the hectic activity, concertmaster Rafael Druian left abruptly that May, a momentous change in the orchestra's personnel. A minor mix-up precipitated this move. The orchestra had to cancel a recording session scheduled for a Monday morning because the recording equipment had been mistakenly sent to St. Louis.

At the previous Saturday night's concert, the personnel manager had posted notice of the cancellation in the musicians' locker room, on the floor below stage level. But he neglected to inform Druian, whose dressing room was on stage level on the side opposite the musicians' room. When Druian arrived on Monday, he stormed up to Barksdale's office, beat on the desk with his fists, shouting invective against the poorly managed orchestra, and told Barksdale, "You can tell Mr. Szell if he wants me to be at the recording session tomorrow, he can call me."

Szell instructed Barksdale to have any call from Druian directed to assistant manager George Carmer, who should tell Druian to call Szell, and if he did not choose to come to the recording session, he "will be in violation of [his] contract and it will be abrogated forthwith." When Druian called the office, Carmer gave him that message. He chose not to call Szell and did not come to the recording session. Afterward, Carmer called Druian: "I am sorry to tell you that you are no longer a member of the Cleveland Orchestra." Szell directed assistant concertmaster Daniel Majeske to move into the concertmaster's chair, and shortly afterward officially appointed him to the position. Years later Druian confided that he regretted his actions, wistfully recalling, "Mr. Szell went out of his way to be nice to me."[16]

Szell turned seventy-two that June. He spent a week in Zurich, Vienna, Berlin, and again Zurich before retiring to Crans for most of July. Barksdale wrote him of the successful first test of the new air system on the Blossom stage and sadly reported the death by suicide of soprano Saramae Endich. "She was to have left the next day for Santa Fe," Barksdale wrote, "where she had several leading roles. What a pity." Szell replied: "What a shame about Saramae. Poor thing! She must have dreaded something more than death; what could it have been? We shall probably never know."

Szell reported to Barksdale: "The 'Ninth' in Vienna was the usual affair with interminable applause (and an honest-to-goodness splendid Soloquartet- Janowitz Dickenson Häfliger Berry) but the orchestra was rather spotty, especially in the woodwinds. Last night's concert here confirmed to me again the higher quality of the Berlin Philh. as Symphony Orchestra, but it, too, has its weak spots and bad habits, on the other hand it has a few superior players not matched by anybody in Vienna."

Barksdale sent Szell a copy of a letter from artist manager Constance Hope proposing they engage Edouard Van Remoortel as guest conductor. Barksdale told Szell, "I have taken the liberty of replying that we have completed the engagement of conductors for that period. I am sure that you would be just as thrilled as I to have Van Remoortel conduct here, and even more so to do business with this charming lady." Barksdale knew Hope as the person who wrote Adela Prentiss Hughes in the 1940s, saying, "let us conspire together" to engage Leinsdorf in Cleveland over Szell. Szell answered Barksdale, "In the matter of Remoortel-Hope you were again a perfect mind-reader. . . . Poor girl, always backing the wrong horse,- what a come-down from Leinsdorf via Efrem Kurtz to Remoortel!"[17]

Larger internal events were in motion. A press release by the orchestra on September 24, 1969, announced Barksdale's resignation as general manager. Faced with a deficit that would reach a million dollars by the following season, the orchestra's fund raising clearly had not kept pace with its rapid recent growth. The buck stopped at the administrative head's desk. With his musical background and administrative experience at the Toledo Museum of Art and his polished southern manners, Barksdale had worked well with Szell for a dozen years. The only discernible fault Szell found with him was his gentleness and reluctance to enforce discipline in his staff and to be firm with the orchestra in contract negotiations. But the report of the management consultant firm McKinsey and Company showed that the deficit had mushroomed on Barksdale's watch, and he had not taken measures to anticipate it. It was not McKinsey's policy to make a direct recommendation, but one could infer that from the report. Szell stated in the press release: "It is with the greatest regret that I learn of ABB's decision not to continue beyond this season as General Manager of The Cleveland Orchestra. We have been closely associated during the last twelve years and his knowledge and dedication were of extraordinary help to me. His resourceful contribution to the present public image of our orchestra will remain unforgotten and my warmest wishes will be with him in his future plans."[18] Szell was truly fond of Barksdale, and their working and personal relationship remained cordial to the end.

If Szell had supported Barksdale, he might well have remained, but there was a consensus that the situation called for a more managerially oriented man, and Szell was already sold on his replacement. They did not have far to look: Barksdale's assistant, Michael Maxwell, had joined the staff in 1966 and would succeed him at the conclusion of the Far East tour in May 1970.

Barksdale first mentioned Maxwell to Szell in July 1966: "He catches on very fast."[19] As assistant manager Maxwell worked hard to impress Szell and the trustees with his ability and efficiency. But in the time between the announcement of his appointment and Szell's hospitalization, Szell came to realize that Maxwell was confrontational to the orchestra, not as business-wise as it had appeared before he had the responsibility for policy decisions, and that he maneuvered to put himself between Szell and all other staff members. On his deathbed Szell confided to Louis Lane, "I fear I have made a terrible mistake with Michael Maxwell."[20]

In July 1968, Barksdale had written Eugene Ormandy at Saratoga, on Szell's behalf, inviting him to open the 1969 Blossom season. (Szell was planning to conduct only the last week in 1969.) Ormandy declined: "Since we, like other orchestras, now operate on a fifty-two week basis, I have only six weeks each year for a 'working vacation,' which includes the month of July. For this reason, as much as I regret it, I cannot accept any invitations during July. However, I do appreciate your inviting me." Ormandy visited Blossom in the spring of 1969, and Szell invited him again, this time by a very cordial personal letter.[21] Ormandy's reply is not on record, but the arrangement did not work out then. Although he did not conduct at Blossom, he opened the 1970–71 Severance Hall season in October 1970 with performances of Beethoven's Ninth Symphony, "dedicated to the memory of George Szell."[22]

In August 1969 Peter Andry of EMI Records told Szell that Oistrakh and Rostropovich, with whom he had recorded the Brahms Double Concerto, were going to record the Beethoven Triple Concerto with pianist Sviatoslav Richter and Herbert von Karajan and the Berlin Philharmonic for a combination of the EMI and DGG record companies. "He [Andry] was very apologetic about this when he told me the fact in Salzburg," Szell wrote Barksdale in September, "but said (rightly) that as I would not be available until 1970 or 71 and as it is very difficult to get the 3 Russians together anyhow he could not put a brake on the matter when Karajan heard about the possibility and just jumped at it. They want to do it in 2 sessions, Karajan has no time for preliminary understanding with the soloists and just wants them to agree among themselves . . ." [Szell's ellipsis].[23] Szell would not have recorded such an important, nonstandard repertoire work without a performance, but Karajan accepted that condition. It seems natural, if also ironic, that Szell's Brahms Double and Karajan's Beethoven Triple are now eternally wedded on a commercial CD.[24] Szell met with Andry to discuss future Cleveland Orchestra recordings for EMI. He instructed Barksdale to press Columbia Records to abandon exclusivity "with no strings attached other than the usual 5-year work-reserve clause, which in case I am conducting should be reduced, in view of my age, to 2 or 3 years."[25] Szell was beginning to put a time frame on his retirement, or at least on reducing his activity.

After Crans, Szell conducted a Beethoven concert with the Monte Carlo Orchestra. The orchestra had no permanent music director at the time and the acoustics of its hall were problematical. The other guests that season were Sir John Barbirolli and Paul Kletzki. "Inevitably," wrote Priscilla Witter for the *International Herald Tribune*, "Mr. Szell's leadership was the most successful."[26]

Szell returned to Cleveland for the final week of the Blossom Music Festival, with soloists Robert Casadesus, James Oliver Buswell IV, and Geza Anda. He flew immediately back to Salzburg for a Beethoven concert with the Vienna Philharmonic, including the Third Piano Concerto with Emil Gilels. In the recording of that concerto made in Cleveland a year earlier, Gilels and Szell had expressed strong differences about the tempo of the first movement. Gilels played slower than Szell liked and stubbornly held his ground. Szell had no choice but to go with him. Some of the tension of the recording may have carried over in this Salzburg concert, producing positive sparks. "The concert event of this summer," read the *Salzburger Nachrichten*'s headline; "The zenith of musical happenings," read the *Salzburg Press*. To Franz Endler in the latter, Gilels played "as clearly as glass" and was in best form. Although he had not always been so well received as in this concert, Endler observed, Gilels was not always in the company of such an animated partner as Szell.[27]

A week later, Szell led an all-Dvořák program with the Czech Philharmonic at the Lucerne Festival: "Dvořák im Blut" ("Dvořák in the Blood") read one review's headline, noting Szell's heritage and musical activity in Prague, and his attention to the tiniest detail without losing sight of the totality: "Szell absolutely is among the really great interpreters," stated another.

But perhaps the most telling review of the concert came from the orchestra itself. The soloist, Rudolf Firkusny, spoke with a number of the orchestra members and recalled: "of course they know this music backwards because they've played it so many times since their childhood. And they told me when [his] rehearsals were over they were very unhappy. They wanted it to go on because it was so fascinating and they learned so many new things that they just would like it to continue. I told him and he was very touched."[28]

Szell took another two-week holiday in Bad Ragaz, Switzerland, then returned to Cleveland for the 1969–70 season, his twenty-fourth. The masthead of the personnel page for the Cleveland Orchestra's fifty-second season, 1969–70, listed six conductors: George Szell, *Musical Director and Conductor;* Louis Lane, *Associate Conductor;* Pierre Boulez, *Principal Guest Conductor;* Michael Charry and James Levine, *Assistant Conductors;* and Margaret Hillis, *Director of Choruses.* This was the first of two years for Hillis. She commuted from her post as director of the Chicago Symphony Chorus, which she had founded at Fritz Reiner's invitation. Hillis was a superb musician and supremely organized, with unbounded energy.

The season began with a program of Szell favorites: beginning with the Overture to *The Bartered Bride* and continuing with the *Prelude to "The Afternoon of a Faun."* The first half of the concert closed with Haydn's Symphony no. 97 in C, scheduled for recording. The Wagner-Strauss second half included the *Siegfried Idyll* and *Till Eulenspiegel.*

Credited in the program notes as "the first at these concerts and probably the first in Cleveland" was Richard Strauss's *Metamorphosen,* A Study for 23 Solo String Instruments, paired in the fourth program with Mozart's Serenade no. 10 in B-flat Major for 13 Wind Instruments, K. 361 (called *Gran Partita*).[29] A titular coincidence not noted by program annotator or reviewers was the proximity of Hindemith's *Symphonic Metamorphosis on Themes of [sic] Carl Maria von Weber* and Strauss's *Metamorphosen* on the third and fourth programs, respectively. Whether Szell intended a deeper meaning—referring to the evolving change in leadership of the orchestra—is conjectural, but on reflection it was happening. Szell told Columbia Records' producer Andrew Kazdin about his coming performances of the Mozart Serenade, saying, "It is probably the last time I will ever do it, and I'm offering it to you if you want to record it." Kazdin regretfully had to inform Szell that Columbia turned it down.[30]

Szell's fifth Cleveland concert at the end of October was his last until the New Year. For the first half of the program, a young Belgian, François Huybrechts, conducted. He served as a conducting fellow that season and would remain for another year as conducting assistant. Huybrechts led Mendelssohn's Third Symphony, the *Scottish*, preceded by the overture to Mozart's *The Abduction from the Seraglio*. Szell honored Robert Casadesus's seventieth birthday in the second half of the program, presenting him as both piano soloist and composer. This was the first Cleveland performance of Casadesus's Suite for Orchestra in B-flat Major, and Casadesus performed Mozart's Piano Concerto no. 24 in C Minor, K. 491. Szell then conducted Casadesus's Suite with the New York Philharmonic in November, in one of his four subscription weeks. This was Casadesus's twentieth season as soloist with Szell in Cleveland, the record for any soloist (Serkin came in next at nineteen seasons). Szell and Casadesus were looking forward to their next collaboration, in 1971, the Mozart Concerto no. 21 in C Major, K. 467, which they had played together four times in Cleveland. But in 1971, it was Boulez who conducted. The greatly saddened Casadesus missed Szell deeply, saying then that he and Szell were, from the first time *d'accord* ("in agreement"), and they were so close, "like brothers."[31]

Advisor to the New York Philharmonic

In November Szell began his stewardship of the New York Philharmonic. His first concert was for the orchestra's pension fund: Mozart's Fortieth and Piano Concerto in C Major (K. 467), with Rudolf Serkin, who also played Beethoven's Piano Concerto no. 4 after intermission. For his opening subscription program, Szell chose all Beethoven—*Leonore* Overture no. 2 and the Ninth Symphony, with a fine quartet of vocal soloists: Heather Harper, soprano; Jane Hobson, mezzo-soprano; Ernst Haefliger, tenor; and Thomas Paul, bass.

Schonberg wrote, "It was an evening of large-scale musicmaking, and that included the Mozart. . . . Classic proportions were observed, as they invariably are when Mr. Szell conducts Mozart, and there was almost a ferocious emphasis on clarity of texture and line. But the sound was big throughout, and the interpretation verged on the romantic, as befits this particular symphony, which does verge on the romantic." Szell had been "strenuously rehearsing the orchestra," Schonberg remarked, and the results as he observed in the concert had "the musicians . . . leaning forward in their seats and listening to one another, to obtain the cohesive kind of ensemble demanded by Mr. Szell." Schonberg found it "always a thrill to observe two such thoroughbreds as Mr. Szell and Mr. Serkin working together. They have parallel ideas about the music, though Mr. Serkin has perhaps a little more freedom in his approach." In the Beethoven Fourth Piano Concerto there occurred another case of complementary talents. Schonberg called Serkin "a musician who respects the composer, yet who has enough confidence in his own instincts to add his own personality to the playing. The same can be said of Mr. Szell, and thus it is no wonder that between the two there emerged a performance of the concerto that will be one of the criteria against which all performances are measured."

Of Szell conducting the Ninth, Schonberg wrote: "He stands up there in complete control, economical in gesture but with every clear stroke of the baton meaning something. . . . His job is to guide a large number of performers through this difficult score, making sure that everything is heard, that everything is smooth and well shaped, and that the combination of power and tenderness in the music is brought out. . . . If there was one way to describe it, the adjective would be 'big.' . . . It was a superb performance." Schonberg appreciated Szell's including the less played *Leonore* Overture no. 2: "Here again Mr. Szell conducted the kind of organized, balanced, meaningful Beethoven that is all but in a class by itself."[32]

"Being the elder statesman of the conducting profession in America, and in many ways the champion in the field," Winthrop Sargeant wrote, "George Szell can present programs of pretty conventional character on the ground that nobody else can conduct conventional music quite as well as he can." Sargeant found himself in a quandary: "Everything was performed with the utmost spit and polish. . . . The trouble with Mr. Szell from a concert reviewer's point of view is that he is predictable—always fastidious, always in control of every scrap of detail, always able to project the larger architecture of a composition; in short, he is a great conductor." Irving Kolodin, in the *Saturday Review,* attributed biblical status to the conductor in his review titled: "The Gospel of Beethoven as Szell Is His Prophet."[33] Szell flew to Vienna to record Beethoven's incidental music to Schiller's play "Egmont" with the Vienna Philharmonic. Before leaving Cleveland, he had obtained the text from the Public Library.

Since January 1969, Szell had been corresponding with Flothuis about a future engagement with the Concertgebouw, for March 1971. Until November 19, 1969, Szell continued to refine the three planned programs. But on January 3, 1970, Szell wrote Flothuis the bad news: "I am only halfway through the first of two seasons of double duty (Cleveland Orchestra plus New York Philharmonic), but I feel already more exhausted than ever before in midseason. This extremely heavy schedule will be going on until the end of the calendar year 1971 and in reviewing the whole situation, I have most reluctantly come to the conclusion that it would be extremely unwise and quite possibly even dangerous for me to take on any additional intensive concert schedule during the winter season '70–'71."

Szell asked, "with extreme reluctance and regret," to postpone the March 1971 engagement to "another mutually convenient date in the more distant future." He added: "I would hate to embarrass you by a cancellation at short notice in consequence of a possible breakdown." And he ended with the hope that the postponement, "which is dictated by absolute necessity on my part and by my consideration for you, will not affect my close relationship to you and to the orchestra." Flothuis immediately offered dates in the 1971–72 season. Szell thanked Flothuis and begged the organizers to postpone further, until the 1972–73 season, "particularly since the period of March 1st to 21st, '72, is promised to the New York Philharmonic." That was Szell's last letter to the Concertgebouw.[34]

"Dangerous," "possible breakdown," these were unusual words from Szell and perhaps ominous indicators of worse to come. The strain showed, and his physical stamina was not serving him as in the past. At the end of December 1969, he faced the Cleveland concerts and East Coast tour, more Philharmonic concerts and administrative duties, a return to Cleveland to record as well as close the season at home, and preparation for a short but strenuous tour to Japan.

After the holiday, Szell led Schubert's "Unfinished" and Mahler's *Das Lied von der Erde*, with mezzo-soprano Janet Baker and tenor Richard Lewis—repeated on Monday in Carnegie Hall two days later. Szell had conducted *Das Lied von der Erde* in Cleveland in 1947, 1960, and 1967. The 1960 performances of the Mahler were in honor of the one-hundredth anniversary of the composer's birth, and the orchestra again played it in Carnegie Hall the Monday after, as now ten years later. Over the course of the years, the vocal soloists had shifted and overlapped. In 1960 they were Maureen Forrester and Ernst Haefliger, and in 1967 Richard Lewis joined Forrester, and in 1970 Lewis partnered with Janet Baker.

This was one of the great works that Szell felt profoundly but never commercially recorded because of a sad progression of circumstances. Columbia Records, learning that Szell was scheduled to perform *Das Lied von der Erde* in 1970, explored the possibility of recording it. The major problem revolved around the tenor soloist. For the concert, Szell was able to engage only half of his dream team of Janet Baker and Jon Vickers. Vickers was unavailable, so Szell settled for his second choice, Lewis, and was willing to make the recording with him and Baker. But Lewis had recently recorded the work for Columbia with Ormandy and Philadelphia. If Columbia was to record it with Szell, they wanted a completely different cast. They considered having Lewis sing the performances, and Vickers sing for the recording. Szell was agreeable, on the condition that they hold a full rehearsal with Vickers prior to the recording session.

A musicians' union rule held that a rehearsal solely for recording and not associated with a specific performance had to be paid at the full recording rate. This entailed considerably more expense than allocating one of the weekly services for a rehearsal. Columbia appealed to the union, which said if the orchestra musicians voted to waive the rule, Columbia could do it.

At a recording session in October 1969, Columbia Records producer Andrew Kazdin spoke to the orchestra to explain the situation and to ask for their permission to allow a rehearsal with Vickers not under recording rates. A musician asked, "Why should we subsidize Columbia Records?" Kazdin replied that he could not answer that question, only that he hoped the musicians would agree to the rehearsal. Szell retired to the control room, where he heard Kazdin's speech over the microphones. As soon as a player asked Kazdin a question, Szell gestured sharply to the engineer to cut the sound. He could recognize individual voices and did not want to know who was against the proposal.

The musicians turned down the request. Neither Columbia Records nor the Musical Arts Association agreed to the extra expense, and Szell refused to go into a recording session unprepared. The recording was never made. Kazdin observed, "All the things he wouldn't do were usually to his or the music's best interest."[35] Szell would rather forego a recording than lower his standards in making it. In this case the Fates were ultimately kind: the broadcast recording of the concert performance of *Das Lied von der Erde* was included in the CD set produced by the orchestra commemorating its seventy-fifth anniversary.

The East Coast tour was a continuing triumph for Szell and the orchestra. Sold-out houses, enthusiastic audiences, and good reviews had become routine. After the final Carnegie Hall concert, Szell stayed in New York. From mid-March to mid-April he conducted sixteen concerts in four weeks with the New York Philharmonic. The Cleveland season was drawing to a close, and Szell and the orchestra made several recordings. On April 30, 1970, as a bonus filler for one record, they recorded two Slavonic Dances, Op. 46, no. 3 and Op. 72, no. 2, thereby completing an historic circle—both of these dances appeared in the first recordings Szell and the orchestra made twenty-three years before, on April 21, 1947. After the fact, they were billed as "Szell's last recordings," and there is good evidence that he knew they would be his last.

Ominous Signs

People often raise the question as to when or whether Szell knew he was terminally ill. He was planning for the 1971–72 season and beyond with Cleveland, the Concertgebouw, and the Vienna and New York Philharmonics, but clearly he was considering his age in some negotiations. With the New York Philharmonic he worked out a "non-appearance" clause for 1969–70, stipulating that in case he was unable to conduct any concerts by reason of incapacity, he would still be paid 50 percent of his regular fee. (The Philharmonic took out an insurance policy to cover that eventuality.) And he was in the process of buying an apartment in Zurich, not only for holidays, but for eventual retirement.

On April 30, 1970, a luncheon and Convocation at Baldwin-Wallace College in Berea, Ohio, west of Cleveland, honored the late musicologist Hans David, who had willed his large collection to the Bach Institute Library there. Szell and Max Rudolf were scheduled to speak. At the last minute, Szell cancelled. Helene

Szell read a statement her husband had prepared. He had not been feeling well. Just a few days earlier, Szell underwent an examination by his doctor, who gave him most distressing news. Szell learned that he had cancer, and the illness was probably terminal. It so unsettled him that he could not immediately face such a public event. After the ceremony, Helene Szell told Max and Liese Rudolf the seriousness of the situation.[36]

Szell nevertheless went ahead with the Japanese tour. For a "swan song," the program was as fitting as one could imagine: Weber's Overture to *Oberon*, Mozart's Fortieth, and the *Eroica*. They were pieces Szell identified with and that were identified with him throughout his life. Szell was facing a personal tragedy, and a national tragedy occurred nearby that week—members of the National Guard had shot students at Kent State University. Before the concert, Szell delivered a solemn speech: "Ladies and Gentlemen, my gratitude for your warm reception is very deep and very genuine. But now, I would like to ask of you a favor. Would you please join us in standing silently for a few moments, in simple human recognition of the tragic events of this week. . . . Thank you."

Knowing his condition, the concert held even more significance for Szell: it was the last concert of the season, preparation for an important international tour, and his last performance in Severance Hall. He invested in it all the insights his wisdom and love for this music embodied. After the *Eroica*, he allowed himself a rare bit of self-praise, saying: "Now, *that* was a performance!"[37]

The season in Cleveland ended on a Friday instead of the usual Saturday, to give the orchestra a free day before departure for the tour to the West Coast, Japan, Korea, and Alaska; it was Szell's and the orchestra's first tour to the Far East. To everyone associated with Szell, it would remain special, as soon would become sadly apparent.

Szell's Final Tour: 1970

The tour began in familiar places: Portland, where the orchestra played in 1960, and Seattle, where it performed in 1966. Repertoire was also familiar. The Portland program consisted of the *Oberon* Overture, Mozart's Fortieth, and the Sibelius Second. In Seattle there was Berlioz's *Roman Carnival* Overture, Schumann's Fourth Symphony, Walton's *Variations on a Theme by Hindemith*, and the Second Suite of Ravel's *Daphnis et Chloé*. After the concert, Szell and staff members attended a reception at the home of Seattle Symphony conductor Milton Katims.[38] Until then, the tour had been routine. But the next part did not begin well.

Since his delight at his first transatlantic jet flight on Pan American World Airways, the airline had remained Szell's choice for personal travel and for many of the orchestra's international tours. On this trip, the airline was showing signs of the trouble to which it eventually succumbed. At the Seattle airport, the orchestra received word that their chartered plane to Osaka would be hours late. Because of this delay, the plane arrived over Japan after the Osaka airport had closed for the night, and had to divert to Nagoya. The party rode to hotels in Osaka—Szell in an automobile, the orchestra in buses—adding three hours to the trip. If the musicians were exhausted from the combination of the long flight with unscheduled delays on both ends, the ailing Szell had his endurance stretched to the limit. And the most intense part of the tour was just beginning.

The orchestra enjoyed a free day after arrival, but not Szell, who had to attend the obligatory press conference. There were four concerts in as many days in Osaka: Szell conducted the first two on May 15 and 16, and Pierre Boulez led the next two. Szell faced other difficulties. Incumbent general manager Michael Maxwell had made the hotel assignments. The in-house tour booklet listed rehearsals, programs, and travel details. It used a two-letter code for Szell's, Boulez's, and the staff's hotel assignments in each city. It was not immediately obvious that Szell's secretary, Margaret Glove, had not been assigned to his hotel because she did not receive a letter code. When Szell missed her and learned that Maxwell had assigned her to a remote hotel, he immediately demanded that Maxwell move her to his hotels for the remainder of the tour.[39]

On the podium, Szell's energy and iron will did not flag, but when he came off stage, Barksdale sometimes had to support him for a moment. If no longer indefatigable, Szell remained an enthusiastic tourist, eager to experience Japan's artistic riches. Szell's friend, Sherman Lee, director of the Cleveland Museum of Art, had told Szell of the most important temples and museums to see. These he visited—often with Gary Graffman, who is an expert on Asian art, and his wife, Naomi.

Carlos Moseley accompanied the orchestra as a guest. He was acting as advance man for the New York Philharmonic's pending Japanese tour. Deeply fond of Szell, Moseley had been instrumental in Szell's return to the Philharmonic in the early 60s, and championed Szell for the advisory position that he then held.

Soloists on the tour were Graffman, who played four performances of the Prokofiev Concerto no. 3, and concertmaster Daniel Majeske, who played one performance of Bartók's Concerto no. 2 under Boulez. Boulez brought some of his specialties—*Images* and *La mer* of Debussy and the 1910 *Firebird* of Stravinsky—along with some unexpected associations—Schubert's Symphony no. 5 and the Prelude to *Parsifal*. To Boulez's further credit, he also brought Ives's *Three Places in New England*.

Szell's repertoire revolved around the *Eroica* and Sibelius's Second, with Mozart's Fortieth and Schumann's Fourth, prefaced by an overture: *Oberon*, *The Bartered Bride*, or *Roman Carnival*. The orchestra played Osaka—the site of Japan's 1970 Expo—Kyoto, Nagoya, Tokyo, Sapporo, and again Tokyo. From Nagoya to Tokyo the orchestra traveled on the New Tokaido Bullet Train, at speeds of up to 180 miles per hour.

The concert of the tour took place in Tokyo on May 22. Television station NHK-TV broadcast the sold-out performance at the Uno Buna Kaikan Hall, and Szell and the orchestra rose to the occasion. A wildly enthusiastic audience heard Weber, Mozart, and Sibelius. At the climax of the last movement, the video director superimposed Szell's image over that of the full orchestra, a moving effect, routine by now, but new then and very powerful. At the end of the concert, on a stage festooned with flowers, two young girls, exquisitely dressed in traditional costume, presented Szell with bouquets. Szell took his bows with these girls, and Majeske and other orchestra members beamed seraphically on them.[40]

Szell hosted a postconcert dinner for the Japanese tour sponsors at the premier geisha house in Sapporo, whose culinary specialty was king crab. Guests sat on the floor around a large rectangular table, each attended by a geisha in elaborate dress. As host, Szell was accorded the honor of being attended by the head geisha. He felt put out because he did not get a younger, more attractive one, and he was shocked by the bill.

After Japan there were two more concerts: Seoul, Korea—with the same program as televised in Tokyo—and Anchorage, Alaska. Anchorage ended the tour, and it was also Szell's last concert. Pan Am stayed true to form, and the orchestra arrived in Anchorage almost five hours late.

The next day, the musicians had a little time to see Anchorage and its surroundings. Visiting the site of the great earthquake of a few years before, the group saw vivid evidence that the ground had been rudely heaved up. But nature was already mending and softening its own blow, and the rifts were filling up with earth in the cracks, and vegetation slowly took hold. The orchestra's own world was about to experience an upheaval as well.

The concert was scheduled for broadcast recording, but the equipment supplied proved so primitive that no useful tape could have resulted. Perhaps clairvoyantly, the cover of the program book was an ominous, solid black. High school auditorium notwithstanding, and tour fatigue likewise, the orchestra gave a better performance than the dreadful acoustics should have allowed. Szell, at his energy's end, and the orchestra, at the last gasp of the tour that had come hard upon the full season, never gave less than their best.

The scheduled program included *Roman Carnival* Overture, Walton's *Variations on a Theme by Hindemith*, and the *Eroica*. Owing to a further intervention of fate caused by the indisposition of a key brass player, Szell substituted *Oberon* Overture for the Berlioz, and Mozart's Fortieth for the Walton. Thus the last concert of Szell's life duplicated his last in Severance Hall. The larger circle closed even more emphatically: on Szell's first program as musical director and conductor of the Cleveland Orchestra, on October 17 and 19, 1946, that concert had begun with the *Oberon* overture and ended with the *Eroica*. The Beethoven had been a touchstone for Szell all his life. He programmed it in his first concert in Holland in 1933 and almost everywhere he conducted. And Szell played it in twelve of his twenty-four seasons in Cleveland. It was a fitting *finale*.

On Saturday, May 30, after an eight-hour flight, the orchestra landed at Cleveland Hopkins Airport. On June 10, three days after his seventy-third birthday, Szell checked into University Hospital. In front of the hospital, he encountered Robert Shankland, the Case Western Reserve physics professor with whom he had discussions over the years on concert hall acoustics. Shankland's wife was ill at the time and also under the care of Szell's doctor, Gerald Kent. In the spring Shankland had talked over his plans with Szell to measure the acoustics of St. Peter's Church. He hoped to see Szell again, but learned from Barksdale of his illness.

Meeting coincidentally, Szell seemed as eager to learn of Shankland's findings as he was amazed that he had obtained permission from the Vatican to make measurements. Shankland noticed that Helene Szell appeared "a bit nervous," but her husband seemed "as alert as ever." As Szell excused himself to go, he shocked Shankland with his parting words: "You know, it's easier to get in here, I understand, than to get out."[41]

In the hospital, doctors discovered that Szell had cancer of the bone marrow. On June 18 he suffered a heart attack. Officials cautiously announced his condition. Szell withdrew from his Blossom Festival concerts for the summer, but at first, word surfaced that he would open the subscription season in September. The press failed to note the cancelled summer engagements in Salzburg, Lucerne, and Edinburgh until a month after Szell's heart attack. Although the attack was relatively mild, it had weakened his heart, and this prevented aggressive treatment of the cancer. Late in July, an announcement conceded that he could not open the Cleveland season.

With Szell in the hospital, regulars Boulez and Louis Lane held forth on the Blossom podium, along with guest conductors Bernard Haitink, André Previn, Aaron Copland, Morton Gould, Sixten Ehrling, Rafael Frübeck de Burgos, Stanislaw Skrowaczewski, and Leonard Bernstein. To open the Blossom season, Bernstein made his Cleveland Orchestra début in a "special benefit concert" of Mahler's Symphony no. 2, *Resurrection*. Bernstein tried to visit Szell in the hospital. He "swept in wearing a white suit with a lavender tie, followed by a bowing and scraping Michael Maxwell." When he approached Helene Szell, she said, "You can't see him," which shocked Bernstein and "practically gave Maxwell a fit."[42] When I met Bernstein later that day before the rehearsal, he was in tears. "I've just come from the hospital, where I tried to see George but couldn't," he cried, "and I'm afraid I'll never see him again."[43] The Mahler, on July 9, was especially moving.

Thursday, July 30 appeared a typical summer day in northern Ohio, hot and humid. At Blossom, the evening concert, conducted by Boulez, consisted of Handel's Concerto Grosso in C Major, Brahms's Piano Concerto no. 1 with Mischa Dichter, and, after intermission, Prokofiev's *Scythian Suite*. It was a long first half and a short second. The concert began a little after 8:30. The Brahms ended near 10:00 P.M. At intermission Lane received a call from the hospital reporting that Szell had died.[44] After the concert, the orchestra was called to a meeting, where Barksdale told them the news. The unimaginable had happened.

A small, private, Catholic funeral service was held. On Monday, August 3, the orchestra performed a public memorial concert at Severance Hall. The concert attracted dignitaries from all over and telegrams and letters poured in. Flowers adorned the stage. The program began with the Air from Bach's Suite no. 3 in D, played by the strings without conductor. The beautiful playing heightened the solemn occasion, and where eyes had for years focused on the conductor, there stood a vacant podium. Lane led the rest of the program.[45]

Szell's body was cremated and Helene Szell kept the urn with his ashes. She lived for twenty more years, until 1990. At first she resided in the apartment in Zurich and traveled regularly, spending a few months in England with her sister, then making long visits to old friends in Cleveland. She continued to travel while able, but was not happy anywhere, and her friends despaired of her visits. She moved to Atlanta to live near her son, John Teltsch, and his family; she gave up Zurich, and eventually no longer traveled.

For sentimental reasons, Helene kept some scores with her that Szell loved best—Mozart's Fortieth and Schubert's Ninth—rather than including them with the rest of his books, scores, and orchestra parts that he deeded to the orchestra. A fire in her apartment when she was away destroyed everything there. Some of her belongings, at her son's house, were unaffected. Szell's scores survived, and John Teltsch returned them to the orchestra after his mother's death. One of the fine paintings they had collected, and a portrait of Helene at age twenty-one by the fashionable Viennese painter Viktor Tischler, also survived.[46] Helene Szell was buried in Atlanta, together with the urn containing George Szell's ashes. The grave is marked with both their names.

Epilogue

A month after Szell's death, Irving Kolodin, who had reviewed Szell concerts over the years and had written the script for the 1966 Bell Telephone Hour featuring Szell and the Cleveland Orchestra, prophesied Szell's future place in the pantheon of musicians: "The size of his figure," Kolodin wrote, "will grow as time recedes and the magnitude of his accomplishment emerges in ever greater grandeur against its background."[1]

Szell's achievement with the Cleveland Orchestra will associate him with that ensemble for all time. Shortly after Szell died, a concert review by Frank Hruby bore a telling headline: "Szell's Spirit Hovers Over Concert."[2] To this day, Szell's influence has persisted even as the number of musicians who played under him diminishes; eventually there will be none left. But the fierce pride and ethic of excellence that Szell instilled was passed on from the generation of orchestra musicians who played under him to the next generation, who did not. And that next generation is passing on Szell's powerful tradition to the generation that follows.

Donald Rosenberg noted in 1994 that "many observers believe the ghost of Szell . . . still haunts Severance Hall," and argued that after ten seasons of Lorin Maazel and ten of Christoph von Dohnanyi, it was time "to bid the ghost of Szell goodbye."[3] Rosenberg opined that the orchestra was superior to that of Szell's day, and that one should no longer dwell on the past. But Szell's stewardship that raised the orchestra to the ranks of world class is a unique legacy that many believe remains unmatched.

Whether Szell's ghost still haunts Severance Hall, his memory and influence is instilled in musicians and in music lovers around the world—in the many cities where he conducted, wherever broadcasts of his concerts are still heard, where his recordings excite and inform new generations of listeners. Someone once asked Szell what major lessons musicians, especially young musicians, can learn from

Toscanini. His answer was as much a personal credo as a summing up of Toscanini's example: "Self discipline, highest degree of competence, relentless dissatisfaction with everything including oneself . . . based . . . on a sufficient amount of talent."[4]

Szell led by force of his authority and experience, but most of all, by example. Knowing full well his enormous talent and depth of knowledge, he remained humble in the face of great music and respectful of the composers who wrote it. A year before he died, the seventy-two-year-old conductor, reflecting on his life, summed up this key to his greatness: "I started as a pianist, actually I was a prodigy pianist, and also started composing at seven and went on until my occupation with other composers' music became so intensive that there was no concentration left for my own music. I was a pretty finished musician at the age of twelve. I kept on learning and I keep on learning and I hope to keep on learning until my last days."[5] Szell learned and he taught—and his example will continue to teach us far beyond his last days.

All the Cleveland Orchestra's technical proficiency alone would not have set it apart from any other top-notch orchestra. Any one of their many virtues—the impeccable precision of ensemble and intonation, the finely calculated balances, the gradation of dynamics, the power—was matched at various times by one or another of their peer orchestras: the Chicago under Reiner or the Berlin with Karajan, for example. What made the Szell-Cleveland collaboration special and unique was the combination of all those virtues, plus Szell's stylistic insight and depth of musical understanding, which he infused into the orchestra. The orchestra's deep involvement in the music and caring about the standards that Szell set created a climate of dedication and hard work in which all gave their best to achieve the best. If some grumbled over Szell's tediously detailed rehearsals of thrice-familiar works—and they did—the results were cause for individual and collective pride. At times, some players left Cleveland for higher and better-paying positions in other orchestras, but many who could have left stayed for the rewards of music making there. It was a golden age, not found elsewhere or at another time, and those who were aware of that knew how fortunate they were to have been a part of it.

In Szell's Words

In life, George Szell always had the last word, so it seems entirely fitting that his biography should end with a collection of his own words. They show the depth of his thinking and feeling about moral leadership for conductors, his artistic integrity, and his passion for music—his "hobby"—and his life.

"I was too young to really choose my profession. Rather it chose me."[1]

"Finally, something extremely essential, which I will call the moral responsibility of the interpreter of an art. Part of our instruction must be emphasis of the need of self-forgetfulness in the face of the conductor's obligation to the music that he interprets. This is not merely artistic decency. It would be recommendable if only on the grounds of enlightened self-interest. The temptations to vanity and vainglory where conducting is concerned are many and dangerous. The artist is impregnable whose knowledge is genuine and whose conscience is in his task."[2]

"Many thanks for your kind note which gave me great pleasure and satisfaction. May I ask you to tell your friend of the Rotary luncheon who is surprised that a man whose lifetime has been spent in working out problems would be willing to share his knowledge, that I have never conceived my profession as that of a businessman who will not leak trade secrets to competitors, but rather as that of an artist or scientist or discoverer who considers it his duty to share his knowledge in the interest of general progress and improvement."[3]

"Between conductor and orchestra, a great deal must occur below the conscious level. There must be an understanding that is mystical and even occult. The freshness of the eyes, the mood—each movement must transmit itself to the players as an unmistakable musical signal."

"It is perfectly legitimate to prefer the hectic, the arrhythmic, the untidy, but to my mind, great artistry is not disorderliness."[4]

"It is my conviction that the characteristics commonly associated with chamber music can be achieved in symphonic orchestras far more readily than is customarily imagined. It is a matter, first, of the excellence of the players themselves, and second of the manner in which they are trained to listen to what others are doing and to make their individual part contribute to the ensemble synthesis."[5]

"I am not a Wagner 'specialist.' In fact, I have conducted more operas by other composers than Wagner. Neither am I an opera 'specialist,' for I have conducted more symphony concerts in my life than operatic performances. I am simply a musician who loves music and tries to perform good compositions of many different styles, forms, nations and periods to the best of his abilities."[6]

What turns a merely good orchestra into a great one?

"There are two sides to this question—spiritual and material. To accomplish greatness, one must love music more than himself. First there must be love of music on my part, and then what is being asked of them for love of music must be infused into the players."

"It is a matter of artistic morality. It is necessary to find and bring in players who have artistic morality and, of course, have the funds to afford them. It is necessary to keep the musicians interested in the music for its own sake, and it is my job to inspire them every day at the rehearsal period from 10 to 12:30 with a sense of selfless devotion to the musical purpose."

Can a great orchestra be created simply by having "star" performers in key positions?

"Star quality, yes, but without star mentality. But first-chair men are not the whole solution. Unless there is excellence in depth, there is no genuine excellence."

"A good conductor should first of all be a good musician and a traditionally trained composer, but above all he must be a leader type who is able to communicate his desires to other people."[7]

"I love to learn. There is no single instance that I can remember in which, directly or indirectly, I haven't learned something from a concert or a recital I've attended. If one listens with an open mind and open ears, one will always profit."[8]

"There's very little that does not interest me. I don't live in the past. My happiest moments have been those where I have succeeded in doing some justice to the great works I am permitted to perform."[9]

"His idea is to 'slip into the skin of the composer.'"[10]

"After a few bars, I forgot that this was a rehearsal. To me, the term 'orchestra rehearsal' had always conjured up a scene of slack playing and casual attitudes, of musicians going reluctantly through the motions, looking bored, chatting, and making life hard for the conductor. But there was nothing casual about this rehearsal. No one looked bored, and there was none of the kidding and horseplay that musicians often inject into a dull rehearsal. The players sat on the edges of their chairs, and they played with a happy intensity that reminded me of a successful performance by a string quartet. Everybody played as though this were an important concert, and the players obviously *enjoyed* making the music. Later, Szell said to me, 'The Cleveland Orchestra plays seven concerts a week and admits the public to the final two.'"[11]

"My aim in developing the Cleveland Orchestra has been to combine the finest virtues of the great European orchestras of pre–World War II times with the most distinguished qualities of our leading American orchestras"[12]

"Remember, gentlemen, great music is great music no matter where it is played."[13]

APPENDIX A

On the 150th Anniversary of Schumann's Birth

GEORGE SZELL

NEW YORK TIMES, SUNDAY, MARCH 13, 1960

Robert Schumann has not been faring too well at his recent anniversaries. In 1956 the centenary of his death was overshadowed by the bicentenary of Mozart's birth. This year he has to share his 150th birthday with Chopin, who, as the only great composer of his nation, has a whole country and its government behind him.

Schumann deserves better. For me he is the greatest purely romantic composer and his music the exponent of the more affecting traits of German character, nobly representative of a people of "Dichter und Denker," before their fatal unification and their ominous entry into the arena of world politics. The originality of his musical thought and design, his imagination and his warmth, his tenderness and his fire, his solemnity, and also his frolicsome boisterousness, the infinite variety of characters populating his musical stage, have secured Schumann a place in the heart of every sensitive musician and music lover.

While his position as a composer of piano music, of songs and also of chamber music seems established beyond doubt, I find Schumann's merits and his influences as symphonic composer sadly underrated. I see in him the originator of the Romantic symphony, the inventor not just of lovely tunes, but of interesting, novel designs of harmony and formal structure which have influenced and stimulated great composers after him.

Berlioz' device, prompted by a poetical idea, to link the various movements of a symphony by the red thread of a "leitmotiv" was taken over by Schumann, transformed and enriched and given purely musical motivation. In this, as in certain turns of phrase, Schumann's influence on Brahms is too obvious to need further elaboration.

Less obvious, but equally provable, is Schumann's influence on Tchaikovsky—for better or worse. I could never help feeling that the device of sequential repetition, and the trend to rhythmical stereotype in some of Tchaikovsky's development sections, are due to the influence of Schumann, who for this mannerism has come in for severe strictures from pundits and pedants for more than a hundred years.

But Schumann's influence on Tchaikovsky goes even deeper and can be shown in a striking similarity between the middle sections of two symphonic movements. The middle section of the second movement of Schumann's Third Symphony ("Rhenish"), with its throbbing tympani-pedal built on the third of the relative minor chord, and its harmonization which oscillates between this chord and its neighboring diminished seventh, has indubitably inspired the corresponding middle section of the *Allegretto con grazia* movement of Tchaikovsky's "Pathétique." The similarity of mood and of harmonic device are far too striking to be pure coincidence.

* * *

I want to say a few more words about the most misunderstood and misrepresented Schumann—the Schumann of the four symphonies.

These four symphonies, full of the most glorious music, have occupied and should again occupy a permanent place in the ever-shrinking repertory of unhackneyed symphonies. They undergo eclipses not because of their intrinsic weaknesses, which are negligible, but because of the fallacy that Schumann did not know how to write for the instruments of the orchestra, that his scoring is "muddy," and that it is "inflated pianoforte music with mainly routine orchestration," as the contributor to the last edition of Grove's dictionary puts it.

This opinion is too fatuous to merit refutation. Schumann's symphonies are orchestrally conceived, if not altogether expertly realized, and the inspiring image of orchestral sound can be found often enough even in his piano works.

To be sure, a Schumann score is not as foolproof, as "self-rising," as a score of Wagner or Tchaikovsky or Richard Strauss, nor has the musical substance of a Schumann symphony the kind of inexorable propulsion of some Beethoven symphonies, which will survive even a shabby performance relatively unharmed. But is it really Schumann's fault that it takes a little trouble on the part of conductor and orchestra to make his symphonies come off? I know from experience, both as a performer and as a listener (remembering unforgettable performances under Weingartner, Furtwaengler and Bruno Walter), that each one of the Schumann symphonies can be a thrilling experience to both performers and audiences if Schumann's case is stated clearly and convincingly through the proper style of interpretation.

* * *

That Schumann didn't know how to write for the instruments of the orchestra is simply not true. His imagination of characteristic phrases or passages for the individual instrument is vivid and accurate. Let us only remember the oboe melody in the *Adagio* of his Second Symphony, the clarinet tune in the third movement of the "Rhenish," the innumerable bravura passages for horns in all the symphonies, the use of the brass choir in the fourth movement of the "Rhenish," the horn and flute cadenza in the First, the dazzling, moto-perpetuo-like strings in the scherzo of the Second—to mention only a few examples.

Schumann's shortcoming as orchestrator—apart from minor lapses due to inexperience—is his inability to establish balances. This can and must be helped with all means known to any professional conductor who professes to be a cultured and style-conscious musician. Much soul-searching and discrimination in the choice of the remedies has to be applied. They cover the whole range from subtle adjustment of dynamic marks to the radical surgery of reorchestrating whole stretches. The wholesale reorchestration of the Schumann symphonies by Gustav Mahler, however, I must consider a most unfortunate mistake on the part of a great conductor. Mahler adulterates the character of these works by wrapping them in a meretricious garb of sound completely alien to their nature and in some instances even goes so far as to change the music itself.

The delicate question of how far to go in orchestral retouches must be settled by each conductor in accordance with his own conscience and taste. At this anniversary and in conclusion, may I make this plea to my younger colleagues: Take a loving interest in Schumann's four masterpieces! You will be richly rewarded not only with deep musical satisfaction, but, if you do your job well, with just as much applause as after a Tchaikovsky symphony.

APPENDIX B

Staff and Kulas Foundation Conductors under George Szell

Associate and Assistant Conductors:

Rudolph Ringwall,*associate conductor 1946–56
Robert Shaw, associate conductor 1956–67
Louis Lane, assistant conductor 1956–61, associate conductor 1961–70
Michael Charry, conducting assistant 1965–67, assistant conductor 1967–70
James Levine, assistant conductor 1967–70
*Ringwall became assistant conductor in 1926 and associate conductor in 1934.

Principal Guest Conductor:

Pierre Boulez, 1969–70

Directors of the Chorus:

Russell L. Gee, 1951–56
Robert M. Stofer, 1951–56
Robert Shaw, 1957–67
Clayton H. Krehbiel, 1967–69
Margaret Hillis, 1969–70 (stayed until 1971)

From 1970–1972, Pierre Boulez was music advisor, Louis Lane was resident conductor, and Michael Charry was assistant conductor

Kulas Foundation Apprentice Conductors:

John Boda, 1946–47
Theodore Bloomfield, 1946–47
Louis Lane, 1947–49

Seymour Lipkin, 1947–48
Jerome Rosen, 1959–62
Michael Charry, 1961–65
James Levine, 1964–67
Kulas Foundation apprentice conductors were chosen by Szell by audition (see appendix C for qualifications); Conducting Fellows were chosen on the basis of credentials and references.

Kulas Foundation Conducting Fellows:

Bernard Goodman, 1959–60
Maurits Sillem, 1959–60
Evan Whallon, 1959–60
Vladimir Benic, 1960–61
David Epstein, 1960–61
Michel Haller, 1961–62
Peter Erös, 1962–63
Yoshimi Takeda, 1962–64
George Cleve, 1964–65
Stephen Portman, 1966–67
Edo de Waart, 1967–68
In 1969–70 Matthias Bamert, Shunji Aratani, and François Huybrechts were with the orchestra on various non-Kulas grants.

APPENDIX C

Apprentice Conductor Qualifications

From the announcement for the revival of the apprentice program—American Symphony Orchestra League bulletin dated November 21, 1958:

To be considered for audition, a candidate for the apprenticeship had to be an American or Canadian citizen under twenty-five years old and have impeccable musical credentials. The applicant "must be an accomplished pianist. . . . Facility on some orchestral instrument is desirable but not obligatory." Applicants must have "thorough knowledge of harmony, counterpoint, composition and orchestration," and had to submit recommendations "from teachers or musicians of repute" as well as "a brief summary of musical studies." Those selected to come to Cleveland had to pass an extensive audition, personally administered by Szell, described as follows:

> Applicants will be asked to play a piano piece of the classical repertory, conduct from memory the first movement of a symphony by Brahms, Beethoven or Mozart (not with orchestra, but by humming or singing the leading voice); play an orchestral score on sight; transpose from piano or orchestral score at sight; orchestrate a page of piano music; realize at sight a figured bass; and will be examined in hearing, rhythm and musical memory.

Those chosen for this honor received a stipend from the Kulas Foundation, the amount of which was set at the equivalent of the prevailing union "scale," that is, the minimum weekly salary at which a member of the orchestra was paid. During the 1946–47 season, scale was $85 a week for twenty-eight weeks. The program was revived in 1959. When the author became apprentice conductor in 1961, scale was $130 a week for thirty-six weeks.

APPENDIX D

1957 European Tour Repertoire

Barber, *Music for a Scene from Shelly*
Bartók, *Concerto for Orchestra*
Beethoven, Symphony no. 3, *Eroica;* Symphony no. 5; Symphony no. 6, *Pastoral;* Piano Concerto no. 5, "Emperor" (Leon Fleisher)
Berlioz, *Roman Carnival* Overture
Brahms, Symphony no. 1; Violin Concerto (Wolfgang Schneiderhan)
Creston, *Dance Overture*
Debussy, *La mer*
Hindemith, *Symphonic Metamorphosis on Themes of Weber*
Martinů, *The Frescoes of Piero della Francesca*
Mozart, Symphony no. 41 in C, "Jupiter"; Three Arias (Elisabeth Schwarzkopf); Piano Concerto in D Minor, K. 466 (Rudolf Serkin); Piano Concerto in C Minor, K. 491 (Robert Casadesus)
Ravel, symphonic excerpts from *Daphnis et Chloé*
Riegger, *Music for Orchestra*
Rossini, *La gazza ladra* Overture
Schuman, *New England Triptych*
Schumann, Symphony no. 2; Symphony no. 4
Smetana, *The Moldau*
Strauss, *Don Juan;* Three Songs (Elisabeth Schwarzkopf)
Stravinsky, Suite from the *Firebird* (1919)
Wagner, Prelude to *Die Meistersinger; Tannhäuser* Overture
Weber, *Oberon* Overture
Thirty works by twenty composers (counting groups of arias as one work)

APPENDIX E

1965 European Tour Repertoire

Szell conducting unless otherwise noted

Barber	Piano Concerto (Browning)
Bartók	*Concerto for Orchestra*
Beethoven	Symphony no. 3, *Eroica*
	Symphony no. 5, C Minor (Lane)
	Symphony no. 6, *Pastoral*
Brahms	Piano Concerto no. 1 (Lane/Browning)
	Symphony no. 3
Berlioz	*Roman Carnival* Overture
Copland	*Appalachian Spring*, Suite (Lane)
Debussy	*La mer*
Dutilleux	*Cinque Métaboles*
Elwell	*The Happy Hypocrite*, Suite (Lane)
Grieg	Piano Concerto (Johannesen)
Gershwin	*An American in Paris* (Lane)
	Cuban Overture (Lane)
	Piano Concerto in F (Lane/Browning)
	Porgy and Bess (symphonic picture, Lane)
	Rhapsody in Blue (Lane/Browning)
Haydn	Symphony no. 31
	Symphony no. 88
Hindemith	*Symphonic Metamorphosis*
Mennin	Symphony no. 3
Mozart	Piano Concerto in C Minor, K. 491 (Johannesen)
	Symphony no. 39 in E-flat
Mussorgsky/Ravel	*Pictures at an Exhibition*

Prokofieff	Symphony no. 5
Ravel	*Daphnis et Chloé*, Suite no. 2
Rossini	*La gazza ladra* Overture
Sibelius	Symphony no. 5 (Lane)
	Symphony no. 7
Schubert	Symphony no. 9
Schumann	Symphony no. 4
Smetana	*The Moldau*
Still	*In Memoriam: The Colored Soldiers Who Died for Democracy*
Strauss	*Till Eulenspiegels lustige Streiche*
Stravinsky	*Firebird*, Suite (1919, Lane)
Wagner	Prelude to *Die Meistersinger*
Walton	*Variations on a Theme by Hindemith*
Weber	*Oberon* Overture

Thirty-eight works by twenty-nine composers

APPENDIX F

Szell's Repertoire

Szell Cleveland Orchestra Repertoire (Twenty-seventh to Fifty-second Seasons, 1944 to 1970)

[1] Commissioned work
[2] World premiere
[3] United States premiere
[4] Cleveland premiere
[5] First performance at subscription concerts
N Nonsubscription performance
R Recorded (see Discography for details)
R* Recorded but not released
(R) Recorded that season but not performed in concert

A complete database of Cleveland Orchestra concerts has been made by the Cleveland Institute of Music and is available on line. Its Web address is: http://www.cim.edu/library/locate/programnotes.php

Albéniz, Isaac
 Iberia, orch. E. Fernandez Arbós, 51–52, 60–61
Babin, Victor
 Concerto no. 2 for Two Pianos and Orchestra [2], 56–57 Vitya Vronsky, Victor Babin
Bach, Johann Christian
 Symphony, B-flat, op. 18, no. 2, 62–63
Bach, Johann Sebastian
 Cantata no. 51, *Jauchzet Gott in allen Landen* [5] 63–64 Maria Stader, soprano
 "Weichet nur, betrübte Schatten," [5] from Cantata no. 202, *Wedding* [5] 53–54, Maria Stader, soprano
 Brandenburg Concerto no. 1, F, 48–49

Brandenburg Concerto no. 3, G, 50–51, 58–59
Concerto for Violin and Orchestra, G Minor [4] (Reconstructed by Gustav Schreck from Clavier Concerto, F Minor, ed. Joseph Szigeti), 49–50 Joseph Szigeti
Concerto for Violin, A Minor, 66–67 James Buswell
Concerto for Violin, E, 52–53 Zino Francescatti
Three Fugues from *The Art of the Fugue*, transcribed for orchestra by Robert Scholz [2] 49–50
Sinfonia from *Christmas Oratorio* 52–53, 59–60
Overture to the *Easter Oratorio* [5] 67–68
Suite no. 1, C [5] 49–50
Suite no. 2, B Minor [5] 54–55 Maurice Sharp, flute
Suite no. 3, D [5] 46–47, 49–50, 54–55, 66–67

Baird, Tadeusz
Four Essays for Orchestra [4] 65–66

Barber, Samuel
Concerto for Piano and Orchestra, op. 38 [4] 63–64*R* John Browning 64–65 Browning
Concerto for Violin 53–54 Josef Gingold, 61–62 Jaime Laredo
First Essay for Orchestra [4] 46–47
Intermezzo from the Opera *Vanessa* (1958) [4] 58–59
Music for a Scene from Shelley 56–57
Night Flight, op. 19a [2] 64–65
Symphony no. 1, revised version [2] 48–49, 48–49 (repeat)
Overture to *The School for Scandal*, op. 5, 48–49, 50–51, 59–60

Barraud, Henry
Rhapsodie Cartesienne [3] 61–62
La Symphonie de Numance [4] 57–58

Bartók, Béla
Concerto for Orchestra [4] 45–46, 49–50, 52–53, 56–57,61–62, 64–65*R*, 65–66
Concerto for Piano no. 1 [4] 61–62*R* Rudolf Serkin
Concerto for Piano no. 2 55–56 Géza Anda
Concerto for Piano no. 3 [5] 59–60 Jacob Lateiner, 66–67 Anda
Concerto for Violin no. 2 66–67 Edith Peinemann
Divertimento [4] 50–51, 51–52
Portrait no. 1 for Violin and Orchestra, op. 5 [4] 55–56 Szigeti
Rhapsody no. 1 for Violin and Orchestra 60–61 Johanna Martzy

Beethoven, Ludwig van
Concerto for Piano no. 1, C, op. 15, 48–49 Arthur Loesser, 53–54 Serkin, 60–61*R* Leon Fleisher, 63–64 Serkin, 67–68 Rudolf Firkusny (67–68*R* Emil Gilels)
Concerto for Piano no. 2, B-flat, op. 19 53–54 Fleisher, 56–57 Glenn Gould, 60–61*R* Fleisher, 69–70 Grant Johannesen (67–68*R* Gilels)
Concerto for Piano no. 3, C Minor, op. 37, 47–48 Leonard Shure, 49–50 Gary

Graffman, 57–58 Seymour Lipkin, 59–60 Theodore Lettvin, 60–61 Firkusny (60–61*R* Fleisher), 62–63 Annie Fisher, 66–67 Gilels (67–68*R* Gilels)

Concerto for Piano no. 4, G, op. 58, 46–47 Artur Schnabel, 49–50 Schnabel, 54–55 Eugene Istomin, 55–56 Fleisher, 56–57 Robert Casadesus, 57–58 Firkusny, 58–59*R* Fleisher, 59–60 Serkin, 60–61 Casadesus, 62–63 Firkusny, 63–64 Ivan Moravec, (67–68*R* Gilels), 69–70 Joseph Kalichstein

Concerto for Piano no. 5, E-flat, op. 73, "Emperor" 45–46 Serkin, 47–48 Firkusny, 49–50 Curzon, 51–52 Serkin, 52–53 Curzon, 55–56 Casadesus, 58–59 Curzon, 59–60 Malcolm Frager, 60–61*R* Fleisher, 66–67 Curzon, (67–68*R* Gilels)

Concerto for Piano, Violin, and Violoncello, C, op. 56, 50–51 Beryl Rubinstein, Gingold, Ernst Silberstein; 65–66 Stern, Rose, Istomin

Concerto for Violin, D, op. 61 47–48 Szigeti, 48–49 Ginette Neveu, 50–51 Heifetz, 51–52 Morini, 54–55 Szigeti, 56–57 Francescatti, 57–58, 59–60 Morini, 61–62 Arnold Steinhardt, 64–65 Peinemann, 66–67 Morini

Missa Solemnis, D, op. 123 66–67 Saramae Endich, soprano, Florence Kopleff, contralto; Ernst Haefliger, tenor; Ezio Flagello, bass

Overture: *The Consecration of the House*, op 124 [4] 55–56

Overture: *Coriolan*, op. 62 48–49, 54–55, 58–59, 66–67*R*

Overture: *The Creatures of Prometheus*, op. 43 46–47, 49–50, 51–52, 53–54, 57–58, 62–63, 64–65

Overture: *Egmont*, op. 84 45–46, 53–54, 59–60, 66–67*R*, 67–68

Overture: *Fidelio*, op. 72b 51–52, 55–56, 66–67 (London 1967R)

Overture: *King Stephen*, op. 117 [4] 50–51, 63–64, 66–67*R*, 69–70

Overture: *Leonore* no. 1, op. 138 64–65, 66–67 (London 1967R)

Overture: *Leonore* no. 2, op. 72a 66–67

Overture: *Leonore* no. 3, op. 72 46–47, 47–48, 53–54, 56–57, 62–63*R*

Romanza for Violin and Orchestra, F, op. 50 [5] 64–65 Leonid Kogan

Symphony no. 1, C, op. 21 51–52, 54–55, 64–65*R*

Symphony no. 2, D, op. 36 47–48, 49–50, 52–53, 56–57, 58–59, 63–64, 64–65*R*

Symphony no. 3, E-flat, op. 55, *Eroica* 46–47, 47–48, 49–50, 52–53, 53–54, 55–56, 56–57*R*, 60–61, 62–63, 64–65, 66–67, 69–70

Symphony no. 4, B-flat, op. 60 46–47*R*, 54–55, 57–58, 60–61, 62–63*R*

Symphony no. 5, C Minor, op. 67 46–47, 48–49, 50–51, 52–53, 54–55, 55–56*R*, 56–57, 57–58, 59–60, 61–62, 63–64*R*, 66–67

Symphony no. 6, F, op. 68, *Pastoral*, 44–45, 47–48, 48–49, 50–51, 52–53, 54–55, 56–57, 58–59, 61–62*R*, 64–65, 67–68, 69–70

Symphony no. 7, A, op. 92 45–46, 47–48, 49–50, 51–52, 57–58, 59–60*R*, 65–66, 67–68

Symphony no. 8, F, op. 93 46–47, 50–51, 53–54, 55–56, 57–58, 58–59, 60–61*R*, 62–63, 65–66

Symphony no. 9, D Minor, op. 125 50–51 Frances Yeend, soprano; Jane Hobson, mezzo-soprano; David Lloyd, tenor; Oscar Nitzka, bass; 51–52 Frances Yeend, soprano; Jane Hobson, mezzo-soprano; David Lloyd, tenor; Hans Hotter, bass;

53–54, 55–56, 57–58 Yeend, Hobson, Lloyd, Mack Harrell, bass; 60–61*R* Adelle Addison, Hobson, Richard Lewis, Donald Bell, 62–63 Sara Endich, Hobson, Haefliger, Jerome Hines, 64–65 Endich, Hobson, Haefliger, Thomas Paul

Berg, Alban
  Violin Concerto 66–67 Rafael Druian

Berlinski, Jacques
  Kenaan [2] 48–49

Berlioz, Hector
  Three Excerpts from *The Damnation of Faust* 48–49, 50–51, 53–54, 58–59, 61–62, 65–66
  Grand Messe des Morts, op. 5 [4] 58–49 Leopold Simoneau, tenor
  Overture: *Béatrice et Bénédict* [4] 48–49
  Overture: *King Lear,* op. 4 [5] 52–53
  Overture: *Roman Carnival* op. 9 46–47, 49–50, 51–52, 56–57, 57–58, 59–60, 61–62, 63–64, 64–65, 69–70
  "Queen Mab" Scherzo from *Romeo et Juliet*, op. 17 54–55
  Symphony, *Harold in Italy*, op. 16 50–51, 54–55, 68–69 Abraham Skernick

Bizet, Georges
  Suite from the incidental music to Daudet's Play, *L'Arlesienne* 52–53
  Roma, Orchestral Suite no. 3 [4] 54–55
  Symphony, C 51–52

Blacher, Boris
  Music for Cleveland, op. 53 [1] 57–58, 62–63
  Variations for Orchestra on a Theme by Paganini, op. 26 [3] 53–54

Blackwood, Easley
  Symphonic Fantasy, op. 17 [4] 66–67
  Symphony no. 1, op. 3 [4] 59–60
  Symphony no. 2, op. 9 [2] 60–61

Bloch, Ernest
  Sinfonia Breve [3] 53–54
  Three Jewish Poems 50–51
  Two symphonic interludes from *Macbeth* [4] 54–55

Borodin, Alexander
  "Polovtzian Dances" from *Prince Igor* 53–54 (with chorus), 57–58

Brahms, Johannes
  Academic Festival Overture, op. 80 49–50, 53–54, 56–57*R*, 59–60, 60–61, 66–67*R*, 67–68
  A *German Requiem* 54–55 Yeend, Harrell 68–69 Gundula Janowitz, Tom Krause
  Concerto for Piano no. 1, D Minor, op. 15 46–47, 48–49*R* Serkin, 50–51 Curzon, 52–53*R* Serkin, 56–57 Graffman, 57–58*R* Fleisher, 58–59 Serkin, 61–62 Curzon, 67–68*R* Serkin, 69–70 Bruno Leonardo Gelber
  Concerto for Piano no. 2, B Flat, op. 83 46–47 Rubinstein, 49–50 Serkin, 52–53 Rubinstein, 55–56 Serkin, 56–57 Moura Lympany, 57–58 Serkin, 59–60 Rubinstein, 62–63*R* Fleisher, 65–66*R* Serkin

Concerto for Violin, D, op. 77 46–47 Szigeti, 49–50, 53–54 Morini, 56–57 Henryk Szeryng, 61–62 Morini, 64–65 Daniel Majeske, 67–68 David Oistrakh

Concerto for Violin and Violoncello, A Minor, op. 102 46–47 Adolf and Hermann Busch; 52–53 Gingold, Silberstein; 65–66 Stern, Rose; 68–69 Laredo, Mstislav Rostropovich (68–69*R* Oistrakh, Rostropovich)

Symphony no. 1, C Minor, op. 68 45–46, 47–48, 49–50, 50–51, 52–53, 53–54, 55–56, 56–57*R*, 57–58, 59–60, 60–61, 63–64, 66–67*R*, 67–68

Symphony no. 2, D, op. 73 46–47, 47–48, 49–50, 51–52, 53–54, 55–56, 57–58, 59–60, 61–62, 63–64, 66–67*R*, 68–69

Symphony no. 3, F, op. 90 46–47, 48–49, 50–51, 52–53, 54–55, 57–58, 58–59, 60–61, 62–63, 64–65*R*, 67–68, 69–70

Symphony no. 4, E Minor, op. 98 46–47, 48–49, 50–51, 51–52, 53–54, 56–57, 58–59, 60–61, 62–63, 65–66*R*, 68–69

Tragic Overture, op. 81 51–52,57–58, 66–67*R*, 68–69

Variations on a Theme by Haydn, op. 56a 47–48, 50–51, 52–53, 55–56*R*, 61–62, 63–64, 64–65*R*, 68–69

Britten, Benjamin

Cantata Academica—Carmen Basiliense, op. 62 [3] 61–62

Three Sea Interludes from *Peter Grimes* [4] 46–47

Bruckner, Anton

Symphony no. 3, D Minor [4] 49–50, 63–64, 65–66*R*

Symphony no. 7, E 48–49, 52–53, 62–63

Symphony no. 8, C Minor 48–49, 47–48, 54–55, 69–70*R*

Symphony no. 9, D Minor 51–52, 57–58

Te Deum, C 67–68

Busoni, Ferrucio

Concerto for Piano and Orchestra with final chorus for male voices, C, op. 39 [4] 65–66 Pietro Scarpini

Casadesus, Robert

Concerto for Piano, E, op. 37 [4] 54–55 Casadesus

Concerto for Two Pianos, op. 17 [4] 63–64 Robert and Gaby Casadesus

Concerto for Three Pianos and String Orchestra, op. 65 [4] 65–66 Robert, Gaby, and Jean Casadesus

Three Dances [4] 60–61

Suite for Orchestra, B-flat [4] 69–70

Casella, Alfredo

Paganiniana, op. 65 [4] 50–51, 61–62

Chabrier, Emmanuel

Bourrée fantastique, transcribed by Mottl 50–51

Chasins, Abram

Period Suite [4] 50–51

Chausson, Ernest

Poème for Violin and Orchestra 48–49, 58–59 Gingold

Diamond, David
The Enormous Room [2] 49–50
Music for Shakespeare's "Romeo and Juliet" [4] 53–54
Rounds for String Orchestra [4] 46–47
Symphony no. 4 [4] 51–52
Donatoni, Franco
Concerto for Strings, Brass, and Solo Tympani [3] 56–57 Cloyd Duff
Dukas, Paul
Fanfare to *La Péri* [4] 61–62
La Péri 46–47, 49–50, 54–55, 61–62
Dutilleux, Henri
Cinque Métaboles for Orchestra [1] 64–65, 67–68
Symphony [4] 54–55
Dvořák, Antonin
Carnival Overture, op. 92 52–53, 62–63*R*, 64–65
Concerto for Violoncello, B Minor, op. 104 48–59 Silberstein, 51–52 Rose, 53–54 Paul Tortelier, 58–59 Rose, 62–63 Pierre Fournier, 68–69 Rostropovich
Concerto for Piano, G Minor, op. 33 [5] 53–54*R*, 66–67 Firkusny
Concerto for Violin, A Minor, op. 53 46–47 Samuel Thaviu, 51–52, 60–61 Nathan Milstein, 62–63 Peinemann, 63–64 Josef Suk
Slavonic Dances
op. 46, nos. 1, 3, 4, 8; op. 72, nos. 2, 7 46–47*R*
op. 46, nos. 1, 3 51–52
op. 46, no. 3; op. 72, nos. 2, 7 53–54
op. 46, nos. 1–8 55–56
op. 72, nos. 1–8 56–57
op. 46, nos. 1, 3; op. 72, nos. 2, 7 62–63*R*
op. 46, nos. 2, 4–8; op. 72, nos. 1, 3–6, 8 (64–65*R*)
op. 46, no. 3; op. 72, no. 2 69–70
Symphony no. 7, D Minor, op. 70 50–51, 59–60, 67–68
Symphony no. 8, G, op. 88 47–48, 54–55, 58–59*R*, 60–61, 63–64, 65–66, 69–70*R*
Symphony no. 9, E Minor, op. 95 *From the New World*, 46–47, 51–52*R*, 53–54, 58–59*R*
Einem, Gottfried von
Ballade for Orchestra [1] 57–58
Capriccio for Orchestra [4] 53–54
Meditations, Two Movements for Orchestra, op. 18 [4] 55–56
Elgar, Edward
Variations on an Original Theme, op. 36, *Enigma* 47–48, 51–52
Elwell, Herbert
The Forever Young, A Ritual for Solo Voice and Orchestra, based on the poem by Pauline Hanson [2] Marie Simmelink Kraft 53–54
Ode for Orchestra [4] 50–51
Pastorale for Voice and Orchestra [2] 47–48, 56–57 Marie Semmelink Kraft

Etler, Alvin
  Concerto in One Movement [1] 57–58, 61–62
  Passacaglia and Fugue [4] 49–50
Falla, Emanuel de
  Three Dances from *The Three-Cornered Hat* 49–50
  Nights in the Gardens of Spain 54–55 Curzon, 66–67 Casadesus
Fauré, Gabriel
  Ballade for Piano and Orchestra in F-sharp Minor, op. 19 58–59 [5] Casadesus, 60–61 Anton Kuerti, 64–65 Johannesen
  Fantasie for Piano and Orchestra, op. 111 [5] 60–61 Eric Heidsieck
  Suite from *Pelléas et Mélisande*, op. 80 52–53, 59–60
Foote, Arthur
  A *Night Piece* 46–47
  Suite in E Major for String Orchestra, op. 63 52–53
Franck, César
  Symphonic Variations 53–54 Casadesus, 56–57*R* Fleisher, 60–61 Heidsieck, 64–65 Casadesus
  Symphony, D Minor 47–48, 49–50, 53–54, 55–56
Gabrieli, Giovanni
  Canzon duodecimi toni for Double Brass Choir [4] 58–59
  Two *Canzoni a 12* 51–52
Gal, Hans
  A *Pickwickian Overture*, op. 45 [3] 48–49
Geminiani, Francesco
  Concerto Grosso, G Minor, op. 3 no. 2 [5] 56–57, 66–67
Gilbert, Henry
  Comedy Overture on Negro Themes [4] 51–52
Ginastera, Alberto
  Pampeana no. 3, A *Pastoral Symphony* [4] 56–57
Glazounov, Alexander
  Concerto for Violin, A Minor, op. 82 53–54 Morini, 60–61 Steinhardt, 67–68 Majeske
Goldmark, Carl
  Concerto for Violin, A Minor, op. 28 51–52 Gingold
Grieg, Edvard
  Concerto for Piano, A Minor, op. 16 49–49 Menahem Pressler, 56–57 Curzon, 59–60 Fleisher
Handel, George Frederic
  Concerto Grosso, D, op. 6, no. 5 [5] 58–59
  Concerto Grosso, B Minor, op. 6, no. 12 [5] 52–53
  Concerto for Oboe, B-Flat [5] 58–59 Marc Lifschey
  Overture to the Opera *Agrippina* [4] 48–49
  "Si tra treppi" from *Berenice* [5] 58–59 Dietrich Fischer-Dieskau
  Suite from *Water Music*, arranged by Harty 50–51

Hanson, Howard
Bold Island Suite [2] 61–62
Mosaics [1] 57–58, 58–59
Serenade for Flute, Harp and Strings, op. 35 [5] 60–61
Sinfonia Sacra (Symphony no. 5) [4] 55–56
Suite from the opera *Merry Mount* [4] 48–49
Haydn, Franz Josef
Concerto for Cello, D 52–53 Fournier
Concerto for Violin, C [5] 54–55 Szymon Goldberg
Mass, D Minor, *Missa in angustiis* [5] 63–64
Symphony no. 31, D ("With the Horn Call") 58–59, 64–65
Symphony no. 86, D [4] 52–53
Symphony no. 88, G 48–49, 51–52, 52–53, (53–54*R*), 54–55, 58–59, 64–65
Symphony no. 92, G "Oxford" 46–47, 48–49*R*, 56–57, 61–62*R*, 66–67
Symphony no. 93, D [4] 53–54, 58–59, 66–67, 67–68*R*
Symphony no. 94, G, "Surprise" [5] 52–53, 66–67*R*
Symphony no. 95, C Minor 68–69*R*
Symphony no. 96, D, "Miracle" 68–69*R*
Symphony no. 97, C 47–48, 49–50, 54–55, 57–58*R*, 69–70*R*
Symphony no. 98, B-flat [5] 69–50*R*
Symphony no. 99, E-flat 48–49, 57–58*R*, 65–66
Symphony no. 102, B-Flat 50–51, 60–61
Symphony no. 104, D, "London" 51–52, 53–54*R*
Helm, Everett
Three Gospel Hymns [4] 48–49
Hindemith, Paul
Ballet Overture, *Cupid and Psyche* [4] 67–68
Chamber Music no. 4 for Violin and Chamber Orchestra, op. 36, no. 3 [4] 54–55 Goldberg
Concert Music for String Orchestra and Brass Instruments, op. 50 [4] 49–50, 61–62
Concerto for Orchestra, op. 38 [4] 51–52
Concerto for Piano [2] Jésus María Sanromá 46–47
Concerto for Woodwinds, Harp, and Orchestra [2] 60–61
Symphonie Mathis der Maler 48–49
Symphonic Metamorphosis of Themes by Carl Maria von Weber [4] 44–45, 47–48*R*, 52–53, 56–57, 59–60, 64–65*R*, 65–66, 69–70
Symphonie Die Harmonie der Welt [4] 53–54
Honegger, Arthur
Concerto da Camera for Flute, English Horn, and String Orchestra [4] 50–51
Monopartita [4] 52–53
Symphony no. 3, *Liturgique* [4] 61–62
Ibert, Jacques
Concerto da camera, for Alto Saxophone and Small Orchestra [4] 57–58 Sigurd Rascher

d'Indy, Vincent
Symphony on a French Mountain Air 49–50 Casadesus
Ives, Charles
The Unanswered Question [4] 56–57
Jacobi, Frederick
Music Hall, Overture for Orchestra [4] 49–50
Janáček, Leoš
Sinfonietta, op. 60 [4] 46–47, 54–55, 61–62, 65–66
Jirak, Karel
Symphonic Variations, op. 40 [3] 50–51
Jolivet, André
Les Amants magnifiques, Variations on Themes by Lully [3] 61–62
Symphonie de danses (choreographic piece in one movement) [3] 58–59
Kabalevsky, Dimitri
Overture: *Colas Breugnon*, op. 24 63–64
Kay, Ulysses
Symphony in E [4] 53–54
Kelly, Robert
A Miniature Symphony [4] 51–52
Khachaturian, Aram
Concerto for Piano 55–56 Eunice Podis
Kodály, Zoltán
Suite from the Opera *Háry János* 68–69R
Symphony (1961) [3] 61–62
Lajtha, László
Symphony no. 5, op. 55 [3] 59–60
Lalo, Eduard
Symphonie espagnole, for Violin and Orchestra, op. 21 47–48 Gingold, 57–58 Anshel Brusilow, 67–68 Milstein
Lees, Benjamin
Concerto for String Quartet and Orchestra [4] 66–67 Druian, Goldschmidt, Skernick, Lynn Harrell
Symphony no. 2 [4] 59–60
Leeuw, Ton de
Movements rétrogrades [3] 60–61
Liadov, Anatol
The Enchanted Lake 49–50, 63–64
Liebermann, Rolf
Furioso [4] 55–56
Geigy Festival Concerto for Side Drum and Orchestra (A Fantasy on Basel Tunes) [3] 58–59
Liszt, Franz
Concerto no. 1 for Piano and Orchestra, E-flat 60–61 Rubinstein, 61–62 Támás Vásáry

Concerto no. 2 for Piano and Orchestra, A [5] 51–52 Casadesus, 68–69 Casadesus
Second Episode from *Faust* [5] 48–49

Mahler, Gustav
Das Lied von der Erde 47–48 Louise Bernhardt, Set Svanholm; 59–60 Maureen Forrester, Ernst Haefliger; 66–67 Forrester, Richard Lewis; 69–70 Janet Baker, Lewis
Lieder eines farenden Gesellen [5] 58–59 Fischer-Dieskau
Symphony no. 4, G 50–51 Kraft, 55–56 Stader, 60–61 Endich, 62–63 Judith Raskin, 65–66*R* Raskin
Symphony no. 6, A Minor, *Tragic* [4] 67–68 (posthumous recording)
Symphony no. 9 [4] 48–49, 63–64, 68–69 (posthumous recording)
Symphony no. 10, F-sharp Minor, op. Posth. [4] 58–59*R* (movements 1 and 3)

Martin, Frank
Concerto for Seven Wind Instruments, Timpani, Percussion, and String Orchestra [4] 50–51
Concerto for Violin [4] 52–53 Szigeti
Concerto for Violoncello [3] 67–68 Fournier
Six Monologues from *Jedermann* [4] 65–66 Gerard Souzay

Martinů, Bohuslav
Concerto for Piano no. 3 [4] 50–51 Firkusny
Symphony no. 6, *Fantaisies symphoniques* [4] 55–56
The Frescoes of Piero della Francesca [3] 56–57
Rhapsody-Concerto for Viola and Orchestra [2] 52–53 Jascha Veissi
The Rock, Prélude symphonique [1] 57–58

Mendelssohn, Felix
A Midsummer Night's Dream, Incidental Music:
Overture: 47–48, 53–54, 55–56, 60–61, 61–62, 66–67
Scherzo: 66–67 Nocturne: 66–67
Concerto for Piano no. 1, G Minor, op. 25 57–58 Kuerti
Concerto for Violin, E Minor, op. 64 46–47 Morini, 47–48 Joseph Fuchs, 51–52 Berl Senofsky, 54–55, 61–62 Zino Francescatti, 64–65 James Oliver Buswell IV, 68–69 Morini
Overture: *The Hebrides* ("Fingal's Cave"), op. 26 50–51, 59–60, 61–62
Symphony no. 3, A Minor, op. 56, *Scottish* 59–60
Symphony no. 4, A, op. 90, *Italian* 47–48, 49–50, 57–58, 58–59, 62–63

Mennin, Peter
Concertato for Orchestra, *Moby Dick* [4] 62–63
Concerto for Piano [1] 57–58 Podis
Symphony no. 3 [4] 47–48, 64–65
Symphony no. 7 in One Movement, *Variation Symphony* [2] 63–64

Messiaen, Olivier
L'Ascension, Four Symphonic Meditations [4] 47–48

Mills, Charles
Theme and Variations, op. 31 [4] 54–55

Moevs, Robert
Symphony in Three Movements [1] 57–58
Mussorgsky, Modest
Pictures at an Exhibition (orch. Ravel) 50–51, 52–53, 58–59, 63–64*R*
Prelude to *Khovantchina* 46–47, 50–51, 51–52, 56–57, 57–58*R*, 62–63, 64–65, 67–68, 69–70
Mozart, Wolfgang Amadeus
Adagio for Violin and Orchestra, E, [5] K. 261 65–66 Suk
Arias: "Et incarnatus est" from Mass, C Minor, K. 427, "Vorrei spiegarvi," K. 418, "Voi avete un cor fidele," K. 217 [5] 55–56 Stader
Recitative and Aria: "Ch'io mi scorda di te," "Non temer, amato bene," for Soprano and Orchestra with Piano Obbligato, K. 505 [5] 58–59 Elisabeth Schwartzkopf
Concerto for Clarinet, A, K. 622 [5] 55–56, 61–62*R* Marcellus
Concerto for Piano, E-flat, K. 271 49–50 Istomin, 58–59 Firkusny, 65–66 Claude Frank, 68–69 Peter Frankl
Concerto for Piano, A, K. 414 [4] 54–55 Casadesus (1955R Casadesus)
Concerto for Piano, E-flat, K. 449 [4] 51–52 Serkin, 65–66 Istomin, 69–70 Firkusny
Concerto for Piano, B-flat, K. 450 [5] 47–48 Schnabel, 63–64 Firkusny, (1968R Casadesus)
Concerto for Piano, D, K. 451 [4] 56–57 Serkin
Concerto for Piano, G, K. 453 [4] 47–48, 54–55 Serkin (1955R Serkin), 60–61 Rubinstein, 65–66 Peter Serkin (1968R Rudolf Serkin)
Concerto for Piano, B-flat, K. 456 [4] 49–50 Leonard Shure (1956R Casadesus), 61–62, 65–66 Firkusny
Concerto for Piano, F, K. 459 [4] 51–52 Loesser, 57–58 Paul Badura-Skoda (1961R Serkin), 68–69 Christoph Eschenbach
Concerto for Piano, D Minor, K. 466 50–51 Serkin (1956R Casadesus), 56–57 Serkin, (1961R Serkin), 63–64 Serkin
Concerto for Piano, C, K. 467 47–48 Casadesus, 54–55 Serkin, 58–59, 61–62*R*, 66–67 Casadesus
Concerto for Piano, E-flat, K. 482 [4] 47–48 Serkin, 54–55 Badura-Skoda (1959R Casadesus), 60–61 Annie Fischer, 66–67 Frankl
Concerto for Piano, A, K. 488 51–52 George Szell (1959R Casadesus), 60–61 Casadesus, 67–68 Browning
Concerto for Piano, C Minor, K. 491 47–48 Schnabel (1954R Casadesus), 54–55 Curzon, 61–62*R*, 69–70 Casadesus
Concerto for Piano, C, K. 503 [4] 50–51 Serkin (1955R Serkin), 58–59*R*, 64–65 Fleisher
Concerto for Piano, D, K. 537, *Coronation* 49–50, (1954R Casadesus), 62–63*R*, 67–68 Casadesus
Concerto for Piano, B-flat, K. 595 47–48 Casadesus, 52–53 Szell, 62–63*R* Casadesus, 64–65, 68–69 Curzon

Concerto for Two (or Three) Pianos, F, K. 242, *Lodron* [5] 56–57, 62–63, 64–65 Vitya Vronsky and Victor Babin, 65–66 Robert, Gaby, and Jean Casadesus
Concerto for Two Pianos, E-flat, K. 365 (1955R Robert and Gaby Casadesus), 55–56 Ward Davenny and Arthur Loesser, 59–60 Robert and Gaby Casadesus, 61–62 Rudolf and Peter Serkin
Concerto for Violin, G, K. 216 [4] 51–52 Arthur Grumiaux, 55–56 Betty-Jean Hagen, 60–61 Johanna Martzy (1961R Stern), 69–70 Peinemann
Concerto for Violin, D, K. 218 48–49 Jacob Krachmalnick, 55–56 Szigeti, 56–57 Brusilow, 63–64 Steinhardt
Concerto for Violin, A, K. 219, "Turkish" 49–50 Goldberg, 52–53 Senofsky, 53–54 Morini, 59–60 Steinhardt, 61–62 Druian, 62–63*R* Stern, 64–65 Kogan
Divertimento, D, K. 131[4] 48–49, 55–56, 62–63*R*
Motet, "Exsultate, jubilate," K. 165 [5] 53–54 Stader, 62–63 Raskin (1964R Raskin)
Masonic Funeral Music, K. 477 50–51, 52–53, 54–55
Marches: D, K. 335; C, K. 408 [5] 67–68
Overture: *The Impresario*, K. 486 47–48, 57–58, 59–60, 65–66*R*, 68–69
Overture: *The Magic Flute*, K. 48–49, 53–54, 61–62
Overture: *The Marriage of Figaro*, K. 492 50–51, 51–52, 57–58*R*, 60–61, 63–64, 68–59
Requiem Mass, D Minor, K. 626 67–68 Raskin, Kopleff, Haefliger, Paul
Serenade, G, "Eine kleine Nachtmusik," K. 525 53–54, 60–61, 68–59*R*
Serenade, D, "Posthorn," K. 320 50–51, 60–61, 68–69*R*
Serenade, B-flat, for 13 Wind Instruments, K. 361 [5] 69–70
Sinfonia concertante for Violin and Viola, K. 364 50–51;Krachmalnick, Skernick; 55–56 Gingold, Skernick; 63–64*R* Druian, Skernick
Symphony no. 28, C, K. 200 65–66*R*
Symphony no. 29, A, K. 201 [5] 56–57
Symphony no. 33, B-flat, K. 319 [5] 50–51, 58–59, 62–63*R*
Symphony no. 34, C, K. 338 57–58, 63–64, 68–69
Symphony no. 35, D, K. 385, "Haffner" 46–47, 54–55, 59–60*R*
Symphony no. 38, D, K. 504, "Prague" 59–60, 65–66*R**
Symphony no. 39, E-flat, K. 543 46–47*R*, 51–52, (1955R), 59–60*R*, 64–65
Symphony no. 40, G Minor, K. 550 48–49, 53–54, 55–56*R*, 57–58, 58–59, 61–62 (1967R London), 69–70
Symphony no. 41, C, K. 551, "Jupiter" 47–48, 49–50, 55–56*R*, 63–64*R*, 66–67

Paganini, Nicolo
Concerto for Violin no. 1, D, op. 6 47–48, 59–60 Francescatti
Concerto for Violin no. 1, D, Wilhelmj version [5] 49–50 Gingold

Pascal, Claude
Concerto for Violoncello [3] 61–62 André Navarra

Pergolesi, Giovanni Battista
Concertino for Strings no. 2, G Minor [4] 58–59

Piston, Walter
Symphonic Prelude [2] 60–61, 67–68
Toccata [4] 48–49

Poulenc, François
Sinfonietta [3] 49–50
Prokofiev, Sergei
Concerto for Piano no. 1, D-flat, op. 10 59–60 Podis, 65–66*R* Graffman
Concerto for Piano no. 2, G Minor, op. 16 [4] 61–62 Frager
Concerto for Piano no. 3, C, op. 26 [4] 52–53 Graffman, 64–65; Gina Bachauer, 65–66*R* Graffman, 69–70 Browning
Concerto for Violin no. 1, D, op. 19 49–50 Szigeti, 54–55, 57–58 Senofsky, 60–61 Szeryng
Concerto for Violin no. 2, G Minor, op. 63 49–50 Krachmalnick, 52–53 Francescatti, 60–61 Druian, 68–69 Buswell
Lieutenant Kijé, Suite for Orchestra, op. 60 68–69*R*
Symphony no. 1, D, op. 25, *Classical* 55–56, 61–62, 68–69
Symphony no. 5, B-flat, op. 100 [4] 46–47, 46–47 (repeat), 52–53, 54–55, 59–60*R*, 64–65, 67–68
Symphony no. 7, op. 131 [4] 53–54
Rachmaninoff, Sergei
Concerto for Piano no. 2, C Minor, op. 18 55–56 Daniel Wayenberg
Concerto for Piano no. 3, D Minor, op. 30 55–56 Van Cliburn, 59–60 Bachauer
Rhapsody on a Theme by Paganini, op. 43 44–45 Rubinstein, 53–54, 56–57*R* Fleisher, 60–61 Graffman
Ravel, Maurice
Bolero 53–54
Concerto for Piano, G [4] 54–55 Johannesen
Piano Concerto for the Left Hand 53–54, 59–60, 63–64 Casadesus
Daphnis et Chloé, Suite no. 2 53–54, 54–55, 55–56, 56–57, 58–59, 59–60, 61–62, 64–65, 65–66, 66–67
"Don Quichotte à Dulcinée," Three Songs 65–66 Gerard Souzay
Introduction and Allegro for Harp, Strings, Flute, Clarinet 63–64 Alice Chalifoux, Maurice Sharp, Marcellus
Pavane pour une Infante défunte 48–59, 62–63*R*
Le Tombeau de Couperin 51–52, 59–60
Tzigane 51–52 Grumiaux
La Valse 45–46, 48–49, 56–57, 59–60
Respighi, Ottorino
The Birds 59–60
The Fountains of Rome 51–52, 61–62
Riegger, Wallingford
Music for Orchestra, op. 50 [4] 55–56, 56–57
Rimsky-Korsakoff, Nikolai
Capriccio espagnole, op. 34 57–58*R*
Overture: *The Russian Easter*, op. 36 55–56
Scheherazade, Symphonic Suite, op. 35 50–51

Rochberg, George
  Symphony no. 2 [2] 58–59, 59–60
Rogers, Bernard
  Dance Scenes [4] 54–55
  Portrait for Violin and Orchestra [2] 56–57 Gingold
  Three Japanese Dances [4] 52–53
Rossini, Gioachino
  Overture: *The Italian Woman in Algiers* 51–52, 55–56, 60–61 (1967R)
  Overture: *The Silken Ladder* 50–51, 55–56, 58–59, 61–62 (67R)
  Overture: *The Thieving Magpie* 56–57 (1958R), 61–62, 64–65 (1967R)
  Overture: *Semiramide* [5] 49–50
  Overture: *The Turk in Italy* [5] 65–66 (1967R)
  Overture: *The Voyage to Rheims* [4] 58–59 (1967R)
Roussel, Albert
  Bacchus et Ariane, op. 43, Suite no. 2 63–64
  Suite in fa, op. 33 52–53
Rózsa, Miklós
  Concerto for Violin, op. 24 [4] 57–58 Krachmalnick
Ruggles, Carl
  Organum [4] 50–61
Saint-Saëns, Charles Camille
  Carnival of the Animals 62–63, 64–65 Vronsky and Babin
  Concerto for Piano no. 2, G Minor, op. 22 61–62 Lorin Hollander
  Concerto for Piano no. 4, C Minor, op. 44 57–58 Casadesus, 64–65 Johannesen
  Concerto for Piano no. 5, F Minor, op. 103 61–62 Jean Casadesus
  Concerto for Violin no. 3, B Minor, op. 61 48–49, 62–63 Francescatti
  Concerto for Violoncello, A Minor, op. 33 57–58 Fournier
  Introduction and Rondo Capriccioso, op. 28 56–57, 58–59 Gingold
Schnabel, Artur
  Rhapsody for Orchestra [2] 47–48
Schoenberg, Arnold
  Theme and Variations, op. 43B [4] 46–47
Schubert, Franz
  Octet for Clarinet, French Horn, Bassoon, and String Quintet, F, op. 166 [5] 65–66 (posthumous recording)
  Overture: *Rosamunde* [5] 61–62, 66–67*R*
  Symphony no. 2, B-flat 51–52
  Symphony no. 5, B-flat [5] 49–50
  Symphony no. 8, B, "Unfinished" 47–48, 50–51, 54–55*R*, 59–60*R*, 61–62, 65–66, 69–70
  Symphony no. 9, C, "The Great" 46–47, 48–49, 50–51, 52–53, 57–58*R*, 59–60, 61–62, 64–65, 67–68, 69–70*R*
Schuman, William
  A Song of Orpheus, Fantasy for Violoncello and Orchestra [4] 63–64*R* Rose

Spohr, Ludwig
  Concerto for Violin no. 8, A Minor, op. 47 48–49, 59–60 Gingold
Still, William Grant
  In Memoriam: The Colored Soldiers Who Died for Democracy [4] 46–47, 64–65
Strauss, Johann II
  Annen Polka [5] 61–62
  New Pizzicato Polka, op. 449 [3] 60–61
  Overture: *Die Fledermaus* 51–52, 57–58
  Tritsch-Tratsch Polka, op. 214 61–62
  Perpetuum Mobile, A Musical Joke, op. 257 [5] 48–49, 60–61
  Waltzes: *Austrian Village Swallows* [5] 48–49
  Waltzes: *By the Beautiful Blue Danube*, op. 314 [5] 52–53, 61–62
  Waltzes: *Delirien*, op. 212 [5] 51–52, 61–62
  Waltzes: *The Emperor*, op. 437 52–53, 60–61
  Waltzes: *Tales from the Vienna Woods*, op. 325 51–52
Strauss, Johann II and Josef
  Pizzicato Polka 61–62
Strauss, Richard
  Aus Italien, Symphonic Fantasy, op. 16 [5] 49–50
  Burleske, D Minor 53–54 Serkin
  Concerto for Horn, E-flat, op. 11 [5] 61–62*R* Myron Bloom
  Der Bürger als Edelmann, Orchestral Suite, op. 60 51–52, 68–69
  Four Last Songs [5] 51–52 ("Fruhling" omitted) Kirsten Flagstad, 58–59 Elisabeth Schwarzkopf
  "Dance of the Seven Veils," from *Salome* 47–48
  Don Juan, op. 20 46–47, 47–48, 49–50, 50–51, 52–53, 55–56, (1957R) 58–59, 60–61, 62–63, 64–65, 66–67
  Don Quixote, op. 35 48–49 Edmund Kurz, Marcel Dick; 50–51, 52–53, 55–56, 57–58, 60–61*R*, 67–68 Fournier, Skernick
  Ein Heldenleben, op. 40 51–52
  Metamorphosen, A Study for 23 Solo String Instruments [5] 69–70
  Serenade for Winds, op. 7 51–52
  Sinfonia Domestica, op. 53 62–63, 63–64*R*
  Till Eulenspiegels lustige Streiche, op.28 44–45, 46–47, 48–49*R*, 51–52, 54–55*R*, 56–57*R*, 59–60, 64–65, 69–70
  Tod und Verklärung, op. 24 47–48, 49–50, 53–54, 56–57*R*, 58–59, 61–62, 65–66
Stravinsky, Igor
  Capriccio for Piano and Orchestra, [5] 50–51 Beryl Rubinstein
  Concerto for Violin, D 66–67 Buswell
  Firebird, Suite 1919 45–46, 51–52, 53–54, 55–56*R*, 58–60, 60–61*R*, 66–67
  Fireworks, Fantasy for Orchestra, op. 4 59–60
  Monumentum pro Gesualdo [4] 63–64
  Suite from the Ballet, *Pulcinella* 51–52, 62–63, 66–67
  Symphony of Psalms [4] 53–54

Suk, Josef
  "A Fairy Tale," Suite after the Incidental Music to *Radúz and Mahulena*, op. 16 [4] 49–50, 64–65
  Fantasy for Violin and Orchestra, op. 24 [4] 54–55 Gingold, 65–66 Josef Suk
  Meditation on the Saint Wenceslas Chorale [4] 57–58
Sullivan, Arthur
  Overture: *Di Ballo* [4] 49–50
Tchaikovsky, Piotr Ilyich
  Capriccio Italien, op. 45 [5] 57–58
  Concerto for Piano no. 1, B-flat, op. 23 48–49 Rubinstein, 54–55 Cliburn, (1955N) Rubinstein, 61–62 Bachauer, 62–63 Michel Block (1969R Graffman)
  Concerto for Violin, D, op.35 46–47 Joseph Knitzer, 48–49 Morini, 54–55 Milstein, 55–56 Morini, 56–57, 58–59 Milstein, 59–60 Stern, 63–64 Morini, 69–70 Regis Pasquier
  Romeo and Juliet, Overture-Fantasia 58–59
  Symphony no. 4, F Minor, op. 36 48–49, 51–52, 53–54, 56–57, 58–49, 60–61, 62–63, 67–68
  Symphony no. 5, E Minor, op. 64 46–47, 50–61, 54–55 (1955N) 57–58, 59–60
  Symphony no. 6, B Minor, op. 74 45–46, 47–48, 49–50, 52–53, 53–54, 55–56, 61–62, 68–69
  Variations on a Rococco Theme, for Violoncello and Orchestra, op. 33 53–54 Tortelier
Thompson, Randall
  Symphony no. 3, A Minor [4] 49–50
Thomson, Virgil
  Suite from *Louisiana Story* [4] 49–50
Toch, Ernst
  Hyperion, A Dramatic Prelude, op. 71 [1] 47–48
Turner, Charles
  Encounter [2] 55–56
Vaughan Williams, Ralph
  Symphony no. 5, D [4] 46–47
  Symphony no. 6, E Minor [4] 50–51
  Symphony no. 8, D Minor [4] 56–57
Verdi, Giuseppe
  Overture: *La forza del destino* [5] 47–48, 52–53, 55–56, 62–63, 67–68
  Overture: *I vespri Siciliani* 50–51
  Requiem Mass 52–53 Herva Nelli, Nell Rankin, Jan Peerce, Nicola Moscona 56–57 Eileen Farrell, Rankin, Richard Tucker, Moscona 63–64 Phyllis Curtin, Regina Sarfaty, Peerce, Thomas Paul 67–68 Gabriela Tucci, Janet Baker, Pierre Duval, Martti Talvela
Vieuxtemps, Henri
  Concerto for Violin, no. 5, A Minor, op. 37 [4] 50–51 Michael Rabin

Viotti, Giovanni Battista
  Concerto for Violin no. 22, A Minor 64–65 Morini
Vivaldi, Antonio
  Concerto for Piccolo, A Minor [5] 55–56 William Hebert
  Concerto for Four Violins, B Minor, op. 3, no. 10 [5] 54–55 Gingold, Senofsky, Ernest Kardos, William Barrett
  Concerto for Violoncello, E Minor [5] 60–61 Fournier
Wagenaar, Bernard
  Song of Mourning [4] 51–52
Wagner, Richard
  A Faust Overture 54–55, 65–66*R*
  A Siegfried Idyll 47–48, 50–51, 53–54, 57–58, 69–70
  Die Walküre Act I 53–54 Vinay, Varnay, Vichegonov
  Overture: *Flying Dutchman* 48–49, 59–60, 63–64 (1965R)
  Overture: *Rienzi* 49–50, 54–55, 57–58, 65–66*R*
  Overture: *Tannhäuser* 48–49, 49–50, 51–52, 52–53, 55–56, 56–57, 59–60, 61–62*R*, 66–67
  "Daybreak and Siegfried's Rhine Journey" from *Götterdämmerung* 56–57*R*, 68–69*R*
  "Immolation Scene" from *Götterdämmerung* 51–52 Flagstad, 56–57, 68–69 Margaret Harshaw
  "Siegfried's Funeral Music" from *Götterdämmerung* 50–51, 56–57*R*, 68–69*R*
  Prelude to Act I of *Lohengrin* 47–48, 52–53, 59–60, 62–63, 63–64, 65–66*R*
  Prelude to Act III of *Lohengrin* 60–61
  Prelude to *Die Meistersinger von Nürnberg* 48–49, 49–50, 51–52, 54–55, 56–57, 58–59, 59–60, 61–62*R*, 64–65, 67–68
  Excerpts from Act III of *Die Meistersinger* 50–51
  "Good Friday Spell" from *Parsifal* 47–48, 55–56, 57–58, 60–61, 67–68
  Prelude to *Parsifal* 48–49, 54–55, 55–56
  Excerpts from *Der Ring des Nibelungen*, "Entrance of the Gods" from *Das Rheingold*, "Forest Murmers" from *Siegfried*, "Magic Fire Music" and "The Ride of the Valkyries" from *Die Walküre* 68–69*R*
  "Prelude and Love-Death" from *Tristan und Isolde* 47–48, 49–50, 51–52 Flagstad, 56–57 Harshaw, 58–59, 61–62
Walton, William
  Concerto for Violin and Orchestra 58–59, 67–68 Francescatti
  Partita for Orchestra [1] 57–58, 58–59*R*, 59–60, 67–68
  Symphony no. 2 [3] 60–61, 60–61*R* (repeat performance)
  Variations on a Theme by Hindemith [3] 62–63, 63–64, 64–65*R*, 66–67, 69–70
Ward, Robert
  Euphony for Orchestra [4] 62–63
Weber, Carl Maria von
  Konzertstück, F Minor, op. 79 [5] 51–52*R* Casadesus, 60–61 Kuerti, 64–65 Casadesus

Overture: *Euryanthe* 47–48, 51–52, 57–58, 62–63, 67–68
Overture: *Der Freischütz* 49–50, 59–60, 65–66, 68–69
Overture: *Oberon* 46–47, 48–49, 56–57, 60–61, 62–63R, 63–64, 64–65, 68–69, 69–70

Webern, Anton
Passacaglia, op. 1 61–62
Six Pieces for Orchestra, op. 6 [4] 58–59

Wieniawski, Henri
Concerto for Violin no. 2, D Minor, op. 22 57–58 Gingold, 58–59 Steinhardt

Whittaker, Howard
Two Murals for Orchestra [2] 59–60

Orchestra repertoire not conducted in Cleveland

Australia: 1938, 1939
Benjamin: *Overture to an Italian Comedy*
Boccherini: Cello Concerto B-flat, Edmund Kurtz
Delius: *On Hearing the First Cuckoo in Spring*
Elgar: *Falstaff*
Jenkins, Cyryl: *Welsh Suite*
Larsson: Concerto for Saxophone, Rascher
Mozart: Three German Dances
Rimsky-Korsakov: Piano Concerto, C-sharp Minor, Spruhan Kennedy
Schubert: Entr'acte no. 2 from *Rosamonde*
Stravinsky: Divertimento *Jeu de cartes*
Sutherland, Margaret: *Suite on a Theme by Purcell*
Vaughan Williams: *Fantasy on a Theme of Tallis*
Walton: Symphony no. 1

Chicago Symphony
Mahler: Symphony no. 8, February 28, March 1, 1949

Concertgebouw Orchestra
Andriessen: *Ricercare*, December 1958
Henkemans: *Barcarola fantastica*, November 1964
Otterloo: *Sinfonietta for 16 Wind Instruments*, December 1959
Pijper: *Six Adagios*, December 1958
Wagenaar, Johan: Overture: *The Taming of the Shrew*, November 1959

New York Philharmonic
Barber: *Second Essay for Orchestra*, December 21 and 22, 1944
Foss: *Ode to Those Who Will Not Return*, March 15 and 16, 1945
Gershwin: *Rhapsody in Blue*, Eugene List, July 11, 1943
Kalliwoda, Johann Wenzel: Overture, D, December 6, 1951
Tartini-Szigeti: Violin Concerto, D Minor, Szigeti, March 1945

St. Louis Symphony: 1930, 1931
Gershwin: *An American in Paris*
Szell, George: *Variations on an Original Theme*

London Symphony Orchestra
Walton: *Belshazzar's Feast*, September 1962

Lucerne Festival
Berlioz: Overture: *Benvenuto Cellini*, September 7, 1960

NBC Symphony
Piston: *The Incredible Flutist*, March 22, 1941

Residence Orchestra of The Hague 1937–1939
Borodin: *On the Steppes of Central Asia*
Dohnányi: *Ruralia Hungarica*
Liszt: *Tasso*
Krenek, Ernst: Fragment from the opera *Jonny spielt auf*
Glazounov, Alexander: *Stenka Razin*
Reger, Max: *Variations and Fugue on a Theme by Mozart*
Szell, George: *Variations on an Original Theme*
Wagenaar, Johan: Overture: *Cyrano de Bergerac*
Walton: Symphony no. 1

Sagra Umbria Festival, Perugia Italy
Cherubini: Stabat Mater, September 20, 1960

Scottish Orchestra: 1936–39
Auber: Overture: *Fra Diavolo*
Babin, Victor: Konzertstück for Violin and Orchestra (Temianka)
Bantock: Overture: *Pierrot of the Minute*
Bax: Tone Poem, *Tintagel*
  The Garden of Fand
Bizet: Suite, *Fair Maid of Perth*
Bliss: *Introduction and Allegro*
Boildieu: Overture: *La Dame blanche*
Busoni: Konzertstück for Piano and Orchestra, op. 31a
Chisholm, Eric: *Scottish Suite*
Davis, Cedric Thorpe: *Fantasia on Four Scottish Tunes*
Debussy: *Petite Suite*
Delibes: Suite, *Coppelia*
Delius: *On Hearing the First Cuckoo in Spring*
  In a Summer Garden
  The Walk to the Paradise Garden
Dohnanyi: Suite from *Ruralia Hungarica*
Donizetti: Aria from *La Favorita* (Risë Stevens)

Dukas: *The Sorcerer's Apprentice*
Dvořák: Overture: *Hussitska*
  Symphonic Poem, *Waldtaube*
Elgar: Symphonic Study for Orchestra in C Minor, op. 68, *Falstaff*
  Symphony no. 2 in E-flat, op. 63
Gal, Hans: Ballet Suite
German, Edward: *Welsh Rhapsody*
Glazounov: Tone Poem: *Stenka Razine*
Grainger, Percy: *Country Gardens*
  Over the Hills and Far Away
Grieg: March from *Sigurd Jorsalfar*
  Two Melodies for Strings: "Herzwunden," "Letzter Frühling"
Handel: Concerto Grosso in G Minor
Handel-Beecham: *The Gods Go A-Begging*
Handel-Harty: *Introduction and Rigaudon*
Haydn: Symphony no. 7, *Le Midi*
Hindemith: Concerto for Viola (Hindemith)
Humperdinck: Overture: *Hänsel und Gretel*
Ireland: Overture: *London*
Kilburn, Clifton Parker: *Rumba for Orchestra*
Kodály: *Dances from Galanta*
Korngold: Suite: *Much Ado About Nothing*
Liszt: Symphonic Poem: *Tasso*
Mendelssohn: Overture: *Ruy Blas*
Mengelberg, Rudolf: Violin Concerto (Temianka)
Moeran, E. J.: Two Pieces for Small Orchestra
Nicolai: Overture: *The Merry Wives of Windsor*
Paumgartner, Bernhard: *Five Old English Dances*
Prokofiev: March from the opera *The Love for Three Oranges*
Purcell: *Trumpet Voluntary*
Respighi: *The Birds*
Reger: *Variations and Fugue on a Theme by Mozart*, op. 132
Reznicek: Overture: *Donna Diana*
Rossini: Overture: *The Barber of Seville*
Scott, George Francis: Overture *Renaissance*
Shostakovich: Symphony no. 1
Schubert: Rondo for Violin and Strings (Temianka)
Smetana: Overture: *The Two Widows*
  Symphonic Poem: *Vyšehrad*
Szell, George: Variations on an Original Theme
Tchaikovsky: Overture: *1812*
  Suite: *The Nutcracker*

Vaughan Williams: Overture: *The Wasps*, op. 38
A Norfolk Rhapsody, no. 3
Walton: Symphony no. 1
Wolf: *Italian Serenade*

Szell's Opera Repertoire

German Opera House Prague, 1929–37
Standard repertoire including: *Carmen*, *Fidelio*, *Le Nozze di Figaro* (the rest unknown), plus:
Berg: *Lulu*
Krenek: *Jonny Spielt Auf*
Weill: *Aufstieg und Fall der Stadt Mahagonny*

Salzburg Festival
Egk: *Irische Legende* (Irish Legend) (world premiere) 1955
Liebermann: *Penelope* (world premiere) 1954
Liebermann: *Die Schule der Frauen* (School for Wives) (world premiere) 1957
Mozart: *Die Entführung aus dem Serail* 1956
Mozart: *Die Zauberflöte* 1959
Strauss: *Der Rosenkavalier* 1949

Budapest: (audition)
Carmen (2) February 13 and 24 1920
Tannhäuser (1) February 20, 1920

Berlin State Opera: 1924–29
Aida(4), *Ariadne auf Naxos* (1), *Der Barbier von Bagdad* [Cornelius] (4), *Der Barbier von Seville* (20), *La Bohème*(8), *Boris Godunov* (30), *Carmen* (4), *Andrea Chenier* (4), *Così fan tutte* (18), *Le Nozze di Figaro* (2), *Götterdämmerung*(4), *Contes d' Hoffmann* (15), *Der Fliegende Hollander* (7), *Intermezzo* (30), *Josephslegende* (1), *Lohengrin* (14), *Die Meistersinger von Nürnberg* (17), *Otello* (20), *Palestrina* [Pfitzner](6), *Parsifal* (2), *Das Rheingold* (4), *Rigoletto* (1), *Der Rosenkavalier* (24), *Die Rose vom Liebesgarten* [Pfitzner] (3), *Salome* (24), *Siegfried* (6), *Tannhäuser* (23), *Tosca* (23), *Die tote Stadt* [Korngold] (10) (Berlin premiere), *La Traviata* (2), *Tristan und Isolde* (3), *Der Vampyr* [Marschner] (4), *Der Waffenschmied* [Lortzing] (2), *Die Walküre* (12)
371 performances of thirty-four operas
Five performances of two ballet productions

Metropolitan Opera: 1942–46
Boris Godunov (9), *Don Giovanni* (7), *Götterdämmerung* (9), *Die Meistersinger von Nürnberg* (11), *Otello* (4), *Das Rheingold* (4), *Der Rosenkavalier* (16), *Salome* (7), *Siegfried* (4), *Tannhäuser* (10), *Die Walküre* (8)
Eighty-nine performances of eleven operas by five composers:
Mozart (2), Mussorgsky (1), Strauss (1), Verdi (1), Wagner (6)

Discography

This discography focuses on George Szell's commercial recordings on 78-rpm discs and 33-rpm LPs. With a few important exceptions so noted, no attempt is made to keep current with numerous reissues on CD, which is constantly changing, or releases from concerts. The third discography listed below does include many of these.
There are three previously published discographies of George Szell, listed below with descriptions.

1. Frederick P. Fellers and Betty Meyers, *Discographies of Commercial Recordings of the Cleveland Orchestra (1924–1977) and the Cincinnati Symphony Orchestra (1917–1977)*, Greenwood Press, Westport, Conn., 1978. Deals with Cleveland Orchestra recordings only, giving dates of recording, recording companies, multiple releases, and matrix numbers. Chronological listing by recording sessions, which are numbered; and alphabetical by composer.
2. *Le Grand Baton*, Journal of the Sir Thomas Beecham Society, February–May 1972, "A George Szell Discography," by Jack Saul, president, and Rabbi Howard J. Hirsh. This covers Szell's career from first recordings through his death in 1970. Listed by composer, work, dates of recording, multiple releases, and matrix numbers.
3. *Hungarians in Exile: Reiner, Dorati, Szell,* Discographies compiled by John Hunt, published by John Hunt, 1997, 2009. This discography is the most up-to-date, and includes recent CD reissues and concert recordings, multiple releases, and matrix numbers. Available in paperback.

Szell's earliest recording is uncredited; he conducted the first two of the four 78-rpm sides of the first recording of Richard Strauss's *Don Juan*. The last two sides were conducted by the composer, who is credited for the entire recording.

Key to abbreviations:

ORCHESTRAS

CO	Cleveland Orchestra
CSO	Columbia Symphony Orchestra
RCO	Royal Concertgebouw Orchestra
LPO	London Philharmonic
LSO	London Symphony
MASO	Music Appreciation Symphony Orchestra
NYPh	New York Philharmonic

RECORD COMPANIES

AAL	U.S. Columbia 10" mono LP
Ang.	U.S. Angel 12" stereo LP
BC	U.S. Epic 12" stereo LP
BSC	U.S. Epic 12" stereo LP set
C	U.S. Columbia 12" 78-rpm
CM	U.S. London 12" mono LP
CS	U.S. London 12" stereo LP
CSS	U.S. Columbia special products 12" stereo LP
D	English Decca 12" mono LP
D3L	U.S. Columbia 12" mono LP set
D3S	U.S. Columbia 12" stereo LP set
E	Parlophone 12" 78-rpm
GM	English HMV 12" 78-rpm set
HMV	His Master's Voice (English Gramophone Co.)
LA	U.S. London 12" 78-rpm set
LLP	U.S. London 12" mono LP
LC	Epic mono LP
LCT	U.S. RCA Victor 12" mono LP
Lon.	London (U.S. import of English Decca)
LS	Epic stereo LP
LX	English Columbia 12" 78-rpm set and individual recording(s)
LXT	Decca 12" mono LP
M	U.S. Columbia 12" 78-rpm set—manual sequence
M	U.S. Columbia 12" stereo LP
M	U.S. RCA Victor 12" 78-rpm set—manual sequence
MAR	U.S. Music Appreciation Recording 12" mono LP
MARS	U.S. Music Appreciation Recording 12" stereo LP
MG	U.S. Columbia 12" stereo LP set
MJA	U.S. private release
ML	U.S. Columbia 12" or 10" mono LP
MM	U.S. Columbia 12" rpm set—automatic sequence

MS	Columbia stereo LP
M2	U.S. Columbia 12" stereo LP set
M2L	U.S. Columbia 12" mono LP set
M2S	U.S. Columbia 12" stereo LP set
Od.	European Odeon 12" 78-rpm
P	European Parlophone 12" 78-rpm
PHM	U.S. Philips 12" mono LP
PHS	U.S. Philips 12" stereo LP
R.N.	Radio Nederland (noncommercial recording for radio broadcast)
S	U.S. Angel 12" stereo LP
SC	Epic mono 12" mono LP set
SE	Angel LP set
Van.	U.S. Vanguard 12" LP

Recordings are by the Cleveland Orchestra unless otherwise noted

Andriessen, Hendrik
"Ricercare"
RCO (ca. 1965–66) R.N. 109 225

Anonymous
"Deck the Halls with Boughs of Holly"
"Joy to the World"
"Patapan"
(5/12/66) CSS 547/MS 7322

Auber, Daniel François
Overture: *Fra Diavolo*
1. Grand Symphony Orchestra (ca. 1926–27) P E 10687
(Orchester des Staatsoper Berlin)
2. (11/2/57) LC 3506

Bach, Johann Sebastian
Concerto for Violin no. 2, E, BWV 1042
Zino Francescatti
Columbia Symphony Orchestra (NYPhil?) (1/6/53) ML 4648

Concerto for Violin, G Minor, arr. from Clavier Concerto BWV 1056
Josef Szigeti
Columbia Symphony Orchestra (NYPhil?) (1/13/54) ML 4891
Suite no. 3, D, BWV 1068
MASO (CO) (12/24/54) MAR 26B

Badings, Henk
Symphonic Prologue
RCO (1955) R.N. 109240

Barber, Samuel
Concerto for Piano, op. 38
John Browning (1/3/64) ML 6038/MS 6638

Bartók, Béla
Concerto for Orchestra
(1/15–16/65) ML 6215/MS 6815
Concerto for Piano no. 1
Rudolf Serkin
CSO (CO) (4/20–21/62) ML 5805/MS 6405

Beethoven, Ludwig van
Concertos:
Piano no. 1, C, op. 15
1. Leon Fleisher(2/25/61) LC 3788/BC 1136
2. Emil Gilels (5/1/68) Ang. SE 3731/S 36027

Piano no. 2, B-flat, op. 19
1. Leon Fleisher (4/16/61) LC 3789/BC 1137
2. Emil Gilels (4/29–30/68, 5/1/68) Ang. SE 3731/S 36028

Piano no. 3, C Minor, op. 37
1. Leon Fleisher (3/4/61, 4/14/61) LC 3790/BC 1138
2. Emil Gilels (4/29/68) Ang. SE 3731/S 36029

Piano no. 4, G, op. 58
1. Leon Fleisher (1/10/59) LC 3574/BC 1025
2. Emil Gilels (4/30/68) Ang. SE 3731/S 36030

Piano, no. 5, E-flat, op. 73, "Emperor"
1. Benno Moiseiwitsch LPO (ca. 1938) M 761, Eng. HMV: GM 321
2. Clifford Curzon LPO (9/4–5/50) Lon. LLP 114/LA 123
3. Leon Fleisher (3/3/61) LC 3791/BC 1139
4. Emil Gilels (5/4/68) Ang. SE 3731/S 36031

Violin, D, op. 61
Bronislaw Huberman
Vienna Philharmonic (6/1934) C. LX 509/13/LX 8256/60 ML 4769

Egmont: Complete Incidental Music
Pilar Lorengar, soprano; Klausjürgen Wussow, speaker
Vienna Philharmonic (12/11–14/69) CS 6675

Overtures:
Coriolan, op. 62 (10/29/66) ML 6366/MS 6966
Egmont, op. 84 (10/8/66) ML 6366/MS 6966
Fidelio, op. 72 (8/25/67, London) ML 6468/MS 7068

König Stefan, op. 117 (10/29/66) ML 6366/MS 6966

Leonore no. 1, op. 138 (8/25/67, London) ML 6468/MS 7068

Leonore no. 2, op. 72 (10/8/66) ML 6366/MS 6966

Leonore no. 3, op. 72a
1. Berlin State Symphony Orchestra
   (ca. 1927) P E 10545/6 Od. 0 7502/3
2. (4/5/63) LC 3864/BC 1264

Symphonies:
no. 1, C, op. 21 (10/2/64) LC 3892/BC 1292
no. 2, D, op. 36 (10/23/64) LC 3892/BC 1292
no. 3, E-flat, op. 55, *Eroica* (2/22–23/57) LC 3385/BC 1001
no. 4, B-flat, op. 60
1. (4/22/47) M 705 (12676-79D)/ML 4008
2. (4/5/63) LC 3864/BC 1264
no. 5, C Minor, op. 67
1. (11/26/55) LC 3195
2. (10/11, 10/25/63) LC 3882/BC 1282
3. RCO (11/28–29/66) PHS 900 169
no.6, F, op. 68, *Pastoral*
1. NYPh (12/55) ML 5057
2. (1/19–20/62) LC 3849/BC 1249
no. 7, A, op. 92 (10/30–31/59) LC 3658, BC 1066
no. 8, F. op. 93 (4/15/61) LC 3854, BC 1254
no. 9, D Minor, op. 125, "Choral"
Adele Addison, soprano; Jane Hobson, mezzo-soprano
Richard Lewis, tenor; Donald Bell, bass
(4/15/61, 4/21–22/61) SC 6041/BSC 112

Berlioz, Hector
Overture: *Roman Carnival*, op. 9 (3/15/58) LC 3506

Bizet, Georges
L'Arlesienne: Suite no. 1 and "Farandole" from Suite no. 2
(3/25–26/66) ML 6277/MS 6877
Carmen: "Hier an dem Herzen treu geborgen"
("Il flor che avevi a me tu dato")
("La fleur que tu m'avais jetée") "Flower Song," sung in Italian
Tino Pattiera, tenor
Berlin State Opera Orchestra (11/1926) Od. O 7526
Carmen: "Votre toast!" ("Toreador song") sung in German
Michael Bohnen, bass-baritone
Berlin State Opera Orchestra (10/1926) Od. O 8304/O 6804

Borodin, Alexander
Prince Igor: "Polovtsian Dances"
(2/28/58, 3/1/58, 3/14/58) LC 3483/BC 1002

Brahms, Johannes
Concerto for Piano no. 1, D Minor, op. 15
1. Artur Schnabel LPO (12/1938) M 667 HMV DB 3712-3717/ DB 8614-8619
2. Rudolf Serkin (11/30/52) ML 4829
3. Leon Fleisher (2/21–22/58) LC 3484/BC 1003
4. Clifford Curzon LSO (6/5/62) CM 9329/CS 6329
5. Rudolf Serkin (4/19–20/68) MS 7143

Concerto for Piano no. 2, B-flat, op. 83
1. Leon Fleisher (10/19–20/62) LC 3853/BC 1253
2. Rudolf Serkin (1/21–22/66) ML 6367/MS 6967

Concerto for Violin, D, op. 77
David Oistrakh (5/13,16/69) Ang. SFO 36033

Concerto for Violin and Violoncello (Double Concerto), op. 56
David Oistrakh, violin; Mstislav Rostropovich, violoncello
(5/9/69, 5/12–13/69) Ang. SFO 36032

Academic Festival Overture, op. 80
1. MAR (CO) (10/19–21/55) MAR 573A/MARS 5558
2. (10/28/66) ML 6365/MS 6965

Tragic Overture, op. 81 (10/28/66) ML 6365/MS 6965

Symphony no. 1, C Minor, op. 68
1. (3/1–2/57) LC 3379 BC 1010
2. (10/7/66) D3L 358, D3S 758

Symphony no. 2, D, op. 73
1. Berlin State Opera Orchestra (1925) P E 10487/90
2. (1/6/67) (Columbia set) D3L 358/D3S 758

Symphony no. 3, F, op. 90
1. RCO (9/3/51) LL or LLP 487
2. (10/16–17/64) ML 6085/MS 6685

Symphony no. 4, E Minor, op.98 (4/8–9/66) D3L 358/D3S 758
Variations on a Theme by Haydn, op. 56a
1. Symphony Orchestra (CO) (10/19–21/55) MAR 573A
2. (10/24/64) ML 6085/MS 6685

Bruckner, Anton
Symphony no. 3, D Minor (1/28–29/66) ML 6297/MS 6897
Symphony no. 8, C Minor (10/3,6,10,13/69) M2 30070

Cornelius, Peter
Der Barbier von Bagdad: Overture (c. 1926–27)
Berlin State Opera Orchestra P E 10613

Debussy, Claude
La mer (1/11/63) LC 3863/BC 1263

Delden, Lex van
Symphony no. 3, *Facets*
RCO (12/1957) R.N. 441–2

Delius, Frederick
Irmelin: Prelude (10/28/56) LC 3330

Dvořák, Antonin
Concerto for Violoncello, B Minor, op. 104
1. Pablo Casals, Czech Philharmonic, Prague (4/1937)
M 458 (14936/40) HMV DB 3288-3292/14941-14945
2. Pierre Fournier, Berlin Philharmonic (6/1961) Deutsche Gramophon LPM 18 755/
SLPM 138 755
Concerto for Piano, G Minor, op. 33
Rudolf Firkusny (4/9, 11/54) ML 4967
Slavonic Dances:
op. 46, no. 1, C
1. (4/21/47) 12855D in M 756 ML 2023
2. (2/24, 26/56) SC 6015
3. (1/4/63) LC 3868/BC 1268
op. 46, no. 2, E Minor
1. (2/24, 26/56) SC 6015/LC 3322
2. (1/22/65) M2L 326/M2S 726
op. 46, no 3, A-flat
1. (4/21/47) 12856D in M 756 ML 2023
2. (2/24, 26/56) LC 3322/SC 6015
3. (1/4/63) LC 3868/BC 1268
4. (4/20/70) Ang. S 36043
op. 46, no. 4, F
1. (12/24, 26/56) SC 6015
2. (1/29/65) M2L 326/M2S 726
op. 46, no. 5, A
1. (12/24, 26/56) LC 3322/SC 6015

2. (1/29/65) M2L 326/M2S 726
op. 46, no. 6, D
1. (12/24, 26/56) SC 6015
2. (10/17/64) M2L 326/M2S 726
op. 46, no. 7, C Minor
1. (12/24, 26/56) SC 6015
2. (1/22/65) M2L 326/M2S 726
op. 46, no. 8, G Minor
1. (4/21/47) 12856D in M 756 ML 2023
2. (12/24, 26/56) SC 6015
3. (10/24/64) M2L 326/M2S 726

op. 72, no. 1, B
1. (3/16–17/56) LC 3322/SC 6015
2. (1/29/65) M2L 326/M2S 726
op. 72, no. 2, E Minor
1. (4/21/47) 12857D in M 756/ML 2023
2. (3/16–17/56) LC 3322/SC 6015
3. (1/4/63) LC 3868/BC 1268
4. (4/29/70) Ang. S 36043
op. 72, no. 3, F Minor
1. (3/16–17/56) SC 6015
2. (1/22/65) M2L 326/M2S 726
op. 72, no. 4, D-flat
1. (3/16–17/56) LC 3322/SC 6015
2. (1/22/65) M2L 726/M2S 326
op. 72, no. 5, B-flat Minor
1. (3/16–17/56) LC 3322/SC 6015
2. (2/11/65) M2L 326/M2S 726
op. 72, no. 6, B-flat
1. (3/16–17/56) SC 6015
2. (1/22/65) M2L 326/M2S 726
op. 72, no. 7, C
1. (4/21/47) 12855D in M 756 ML 2023
2. (3/16–17/56) LC 3322/SC 6015
3. (1/4/63) LC 3868/BC 1268
op. 72, no. 8, A-flat
1. (3/16–17/56) LC 3322/SC 6015
2. (1/22/65) M2L 326/M2S 726

Carnival Overture, op. 92
(1/4–5/63) LC 3868/BC 1268

Symphony no. 7, D Minor, op. 70 (3/18–19/60) LC 3748/BC 1111

Symphony no. 8, G, op. 88
1. RCO (9/4/51) D LXT 2461/D. K 23281/5
2. (10/25, 31/58), (11/1/58) LC 3532/BC 1015
3. (4/28–29/70) Ang. S 36043

Symphony no. 9, E Minor, op. 95, *From the New World*
1. Czech Philharmonic (1937) M 469 (12254/8)
2. (1/18/52) ML 4541/4143
3. (3/20–21/59) LC 3575/BC 1026

Franck, César
Symphonic Variations, Fleisher
(10/28/56) LC 3330

Grieg, Edvard
Piano Concerto, A Minor, op. 16, Fleisher (1/8/60) LC 3689/ BC 1080

Peer Gynt Suite no. 1, op. 46 and
"Solveig's Song" from Suite no. 2, op. 55
(1/21/66) ML 6277/MS 6877

Handel, George Frederick
The Faithful Shepherd: Minuet (arr. Beecham)
LSO (c. 1961) CM 9305/CS 6236

Royal Fireworks Suite (arr. Harty)
LSO (c. 1961) CM 9305/CS 6236

Water Music Suite (arr. Harty/Szell)
LSO (c. 1961) CM 9305/CS 6236

Xerxes: Largo (arr. Reinhard)
LSO (c. 1961) CM 9305/CS 6236

Haydn, Franz Joseph
Symphonies:
no. 88, G (4/9/54) LC 3196

no. 92, G, "Oxford"
1. (4/27/49) MM 880 (13054/6) ML 4268
2. (10/20/61) LC 3828/BC 1156

no. 93, D (4/19/68) ML 6406/MS 7006

no. 94, G, "Surprise" (5/5/67) ML 6406/MS 7006

no. 95, C Minor (1/17/69) M 30366

no. 96, D, "Miracle" (10/11/68) M 30366

no. 97, C
1. (10/25/57) LC 3455
2. (10/3, 6, 10/69) M 30646

no. 98, B-flat
(10/3, 6, 10/69) M 30646

no. 99, E-flat (10/26/57) LC 3455

no. 104, D, "London" (4/9/54) LC 3196

Henkemans, Hans
Barcarola fantastica
RCO (11/1964) R.N. 109 519

Herold, Louis Joseph
Overture: *Zampa*
Grand Symphony Orchestra (c. 1926/27) P. E 10623

Hindemith, Paul
Symphonic Metamorphosis of Themes by Weber
1. (11/25/47) MM 855 (13008/10D)/LM 4177
2. (10/10/64) MS 7166

Humperdinck, Engelbert
Hänsel und Gretel: Children's Hymn
(5/5/67) unreleased Columbia

Janáček, Leos
Sinfonietta, op. 60 (10/15/65) ML 6215/MS 6815

Kodály, Zoltán
Háry János: Suite (1/10–11/69) MS 7408

Korngold, Erich
Die tote Stadt: "Glück das mir verliebt" (4/1924)
Lotte Lehman, soprano; Richard Tauber, tenor Od. Lxx 80944

Die tote Stadt: "Ich werde sie nicht wiedersehen"
(4/1924) Richard Tauber, tenor Od. Lxx 80946

Lalo, Edouard
Symphonie espagnole, op. 21
Vienna Philharmonic, Bronislaw Huberman (6/1934) M 214 Rococo 2002

Leeuw, Ton de
Movements retrogrades
RCO (12/1960) R.N. 109 226

Liadov, Anatol
The Enchanted Lake (10/18/63) LC 3872/BC 1272

Liszt, Franz
Concerto for Piano no. 2, A
Robert Casadesus (1/20/52) ML 4588

Loewe, Johann Karl
Der Erlkönig, op. 1, no. 3, Michael Bohnen, bass;
Georg Szell, piano (10/1926) Od. 0-6818 (Matrix XXB 7499)

Prinz Eugen, der edle Ritter, op. 92 Michael Bohnen, bass;
Georg Szell, piano (10/1926) Od. 0-6818 (Matrix XXB 7498)

Mahler, Gustav
Des Knaben Wunderhorn, LSO, Elisabeth Schwarzkopf, soprano, Dietrich Fischer-Dieskau, baritone Ang. S 36547
Symphony no. 4, G
Judith Raskin, soprano, (10/1–2/65) ML 6233/MS 6833

Symphony no. 6, A Minor, "Tragic"
(10/12, 14–15/67) (from live radio broadcasts, released posthumously, 1972) M2 31313

Symphony no. 10, F-sharp Minor, op. Posth.
(Andante-Adagio and Purgatorio movements only)
(11/1/58) LC 3568/BC 1024

Mendelssohn, Felix
Concerto for Violin, E Minor, op. 64
Zino Francescatti
CSO (CO) (12/1/61) ML 6158/MS 6758

Overture: *Hebrides* ("Fingal's Cave") op. 26
(10/26/62) LC 3859/BC 1259

Midsummer Night's Dream, Incidental Music, opp. 21 and 61
Overture, Scherzo, Intermezzo, Nocturne, *Wedding March*
1. NYPhil (1/6/51) ML 4498
2. RCO (omits Intermezzo) (12/2–4/57) LC 3433/BC 1023
3. (1/7, 13/67) ML 6402/MS 7002

Symphony no. 4, A, op. 90, "Italian"
1. (11/26/47) MM 733 (72503D-05D) ML 4127
2. (10/26/62) LC 3859/BC 1259

Mozart, Wolfgang Amadeus
Concert Arias:
"Alma grande e nobil core," K. 578
"Chio mi scordi di te?" K. 505
"Nehmt meinem Dank," K. 383
"Vado, ma dove?" K. 583

Elisabeth Schwarzkopf, soprano; Alfred Brendel, piano (in K. 505)
LSO, London, (3/1968) Ang. S 36643

Concertos:
Clarinet, A, K. 622
Robert Marcellus, clarinet (10/21/61) LC 3841/BC 1241

Piano:
no. 12, A, K. 414
Robert Casadesus, CSO (CO) (12/20/55) ML 5151

no. 15, B-flat, K. 450
Robert Casadesus (10/18/68) MS 7245

no. 17, G, K. 453
1. Rudolf Serkin, CSO (CO) (11/20–21/55) ML 5169
2. Robert Casadesus (10/18–19, 21/68) MS 7245

no. 18, B-flat, K. 456
Robert Casadesus, CSO (CO) (11/11/56) ML 5276

no. 19, F, K. 459
Rudolf Serkin, CSO (CO) (4/28/61) ML 5934/MS 6534

no. 20, D Minor, K. 466
1. Artur Schnabel, NYPhil (12/1944) MJA 1971–1A
2. Robert Casadesus, CSO (CO) (11/10/56) ML 5276
3. Rudolf Serkin, CSO (CO) (4/26–27/61) ML 5934/MS 6534

no. 21, C, K. 467 Robert Casadesus (11/5/61) ML 6095/MS 6695

no. 22, E-flat, K. 482, Robert Casadesus, CSO (CO)
(11/13/59) ML 5594/MS 6194

no. 23, A, K. 488, Robert Casedesus, CSO (CO)
(11/14–15/59) ML 5594/MS 6194

no. 24, C Minor, K 491
1. Robert Casadesus, CSO (CO) (11/12, 15/54) ML 4901
2. Robert Casadesus, (11/3–4/61) ML 6095/MS 6695

no. 25, C, K. 503
1. Rudolf Serkin, CSO (CO)(11/20–21/55) ML 5169
2. Leon Fleisher, (1/9/59) LC 3574/BC 1025

no. 26, D, K. 537, "Coronation"
1. Robert Casadesus, CSO (CO) (1/12, 15/54) ML 4901
2. Robert Casadesus, CSO (CO) (11/2–3/62) ML 5803/MS 6403

no. 27, B-flat, K. 595
Robert Casadesus, CSO (CO) (11/3–4/62) ML 5803/MS 6403

Concerto for Two Pianos and Orchestra no. 10, E-flat, K. 365
Robert Casadesus, Gaby Casadesus, CSO (CO)
(12/19, 21/55) ML 5151

Violin:
no. 1, B-flat, K. 207
Isaac Stern, CSO (CO) (1/21–22/61) ML 5957/MS 6557

no. 3, G, K. 216
Isaac Stern (1/21–22/61) ML 6462/MS 7062

no. 5, A, K. 219, "Turkish"
Isaac Stern, CSO (CO) (4/19/63) ML 5957/MS 6557

Divertimento no. 2, D, K. 131 (4/20/63) LC 3873/BC 1273

Eine kleine Nachtmusik, Serenade, G, K. 525 (10/7/68) MS 7273

Exsultate, jubilate, Motet, K. 165
Judith Raskin, soprano (5/11/64) ML 6025/MS 6625

Overtures:
The Impresario, K. 486, (1/28/66) CBS M2X 787/MG 30841

The Marriage of Figaro, K. 492 (10/25/57) LC 3506

Quartet no. 1, Piano and Strings, G Minor, K. 478
Members of the Budapest String Quartet, George Szell, piano
New York (8/19–20/46) MM 773 (72624D/6D)/ML 4080

Quartet no. 2, Piano and Strings, E-flat, K. 493
Members of the Budapest String Quartet, George Szell, piano
New York (8/19–20/46) M 669 (71930D/2D)/ML 4080

Serenade no. 9, D, K. 320, "Posthorn"
(1/10, 18, 24/69) MS 7273

Sinfonia concertante, Violin and Viola, E-flat, K. 364
Rafael Druian, violin; Abraham Skernick, viola
(12/28/63) LC 3881/BC 1281

Sonatas: Violin and Piano:
no. 4, E Minor, K. 304
no. 6, G, K. 301
no. 7, F, K. 376
no. 8, C, K. 296
Rafael Druian, violin; George Szell, piano
(8/2–3/67) New York ML 6464/MS 7064

Sonatas: Violin and Piano:
no. 32, B-flat, K. 454

no. 33, E-flat, K. 481
Joseph Szigeti, violin; George Szell, piano (date unknown)
Van. S 265/7/ML 5005

Symphonies:
no. 28, C, K. 200 (10/1–2/65) ML 6258/MS 6858
no. 33, B-flat, K. 319 (10/26/62) LC 3873/BC 1273

no. 34, C, K. 338 RCO (11/30/66) PHS 900-169

no. 35, D, K. 385, "Haffner" (1/8, 10–11/60) LC 3740/BC 1106

no. 38, D, K. 504, "Prague" (10/15/65) Unreleased Columbia (1st movement only)

no. 39, E-flat, K. 543
1. (4/23/47) MM 801 (12929D/31D) ML 4109
2. "G. Szell and His Symphony Orchestra" (CO)
(10/19, 21/55) MAR 6225B
3. (3/11–12/60) LC 3740/BC 1106

no. 40, G Minor, K. 550
1. (11/18/55) LC 3287
2. CO (London) (8/25/67) MG 30368
no. 41, C, K. 551, "Jupiter"
1. (11/18/55) LC 3287
2. (10/11, 25/63) LC 3883/BC 1282

Mussorgsky, Modest
Pictures at an Exhibition (orch. Ravel)
(10/18–19/63) LC 3872/BC 1272

Nicolai, Otto
Overture: *Die Lustigen Weiber von Windsor* (The Merry Wives of Windsor)
Berlin State Opera Orchestra (ca. 1924) Od. 0-7504

Prokofiev, Sergei
Concerto for Piano no. 1, D-flat, op. 10
Concerto for Piano no. 3, C, op. 26
Gary Graffman, (3/25/66) ML 6325/MS 6925

Lieutenant Kijé Suite, op. 60 (1/17–18/69) MS 7408

Symphony no. 5, B-flat, op. 100 (10/24, 31/59) LC 3688/BC 1079

Puccini, Giacomo
La Bohème, "Wie eiskalt ist dies Händchen"
(Che gelida manina) (sung in Italian)
Tino Pattiera, tenor
Berlin State Opera Orchestra (11/1926)E 10526 Od. 0-7526
Turandot: Arias: Carl Martin Oehman, tenor (11/9, 21/26) P 9623/P 9821

Rachmaninoff, Sergei
Rhapsody on a Theme of Paganini, op. 43
Leon Fleisher (10/26/56) LC 3330

Ravel, Maurice
Daphnis et Chloé: Suite no. 2 (1/12/63) LC 3863/BC 1263

Pavane pour une Infante défunte (1/12/63) LC 3863/BC 1263

Rimsky-Korsakov, Nikolai
Capriccio espagnole, op. 34 (2/28/58) (3/1/58) LC 3483/BC 1002

Rossini, Giacomo
Overtures:
La Gazza ladra (The Thieving Magpie)
1. (3/15/58) LC 3506
2. (5/5/67) ML 6431/MS 7031

L'Italiana in Algeri (The Italian Girl in Algiers)
(5/5/67) ML 6431/MS 7031

La Scala di seta (The Silken Ladder) (5/5/67) ML 6431/MS 7031

Il Turco in Italia (The Turk in Italy) (5/5/67) ML 6431/MS 7031

Il viaggio a Reims (The Voyage to Reims) (5/5/67)
ML 6431/MS 7031

Schubert, Franz
Rosamunde: Incidental Music, op. 26, D. 797
Overture
1. Berlin State Opera Orchestra (ca. 1926–28) Od. 0-7500/1
2. RCO (12/57) LC 3433/BC 1023
3. (1/7/67) ML 6402/MS 7002

Entr'acte no. 2 (also called no. 3), B-flat
1. Berlin State Opera Orchestra Od. 0-7501
2. RCO (12/1957) LC 3433/BC 1023
3. (1/7/67) ML 6402/MS 7002

Ballet Music, no. 2, G
1. RCO (12/1957) LC 3423/BC 1023
2. (1/7/67) ML 6402/MS 7002

Symphony no. 8, B Minor, "Unfinished"
1. (11/26/55) LC 3195
2. (3/12/60) LC 3828/BC 1156

Symphony no. 9, C, "The Great"
1. (11/1/57) LC 3431/BC 1009
2. (4/27–28/70) Ang. S 36044

Schuman, William
A *Song of Orpheus*, Leonard Rose, violoncello (1/11/64) ML 6038/MS 6638

Schumann, Robert
Concerto for Piano and Orchestra, A Minor, op. 54
Leon Fleisher, piano, (1/8, 10/60) LC 3689/BC 1080

Manfred Overture, op. 115 (1/21/58) LC 3612/BC 1039

Symphony no. 1, B-flat, op. 38, "Spring"
(10/24–25/58) LC 3612/BC 1039

Symphony no. 2, C, op. 61
1. (11/28/52) ML 4817
2. (10/21, 24/60) LC 3832/BC 1159

Symphony no. 3, E-flat, op. 97, "Rhenish"
(10/21/60) LC 3774/BC 1130

Symphony no. 4, D Minor, op. 120
1. (11/26/47) MM 821 (12948D/50D)/ML 2040
2. Symphony Orchestra (CO) (11/4/55) MAR 579 MARS 5558
3. (3/11–12/60) LC 3854/BC 1254

Sibelius, Jean
Symphony no. 2, D, op. 43
RCO (11/30/66–12/4/66) PHM 500-092/PHS 900-092

Smetana, Bedřich
The Bartered Bride, Overture (3/15/58) LC 3506

The Bartered Bride, Three Dances
Polka, Furiant, Dance of the Comedians
(1/5/63) LC 3868/BC 1268

From Bohemia's Meadows and Forests
NYPhil (Dec–Jan/1950–51) MM 1004/ML 2177

The Moldau (*Vltava*), Symphonic Poem no. 2 from *Ma Vlast* (My Country)
1. NYPhil(Dec–Jan/1950–51) MM 1004/ML 2177
2. MASO (CO) (12/24/54) MAR 610 B
3.(1/4–5/63) LC 3868/BC 1268

String Quartet no. 1, E Minor, "From My Life" (orchestral version by George Szell)
(4/26/49) MM 887(13057D-60D) ML 2095

Strauss, Johann
An der schönen, blauen Donau, op. 314 (Blue Danube Waltz)
1. Vienna Philharmonic (6/1934) HMV C 2686

2. (1/5/62) LC 3858/BC 1258
Die Fledermaus, Overture (3/1/58) LC 3506

Frülingsstimmen, op. 410 (Voices of Spring)
1. Vienna Philharmonic (6/1934) HMV C 2687
2. (1/5/62) LC 3858/BC 1258

Perpetuum Mobile, A Musical Joke, op. 257 (1/5/62) LC 3858 BC 1258

Tritsch-Tratsch Polka, op. 214
Vienna Philharmonic (6/1934) HMV C 2687

Strauss, Josef
Austrian Village Swallows, Waltzes, op. 164
(1/5/62) LC 3858 BC 1258

Delirien Waltzes, op. 212 (1/5/62) LC 3858 BC 1258

Strauss, Johann, and Josef Strauss
Pizzicato Polka
1. Vienna Philharmonic (6/1934) HMV C 2687
2. (1/5/62) LC 3858 BC 1258

Strauss, Richard
Concerto for Horn no. 1, E-flat, op. 11
Myron Bloom, horn (10/27/61) LC 3841/BC 1241

Don Juan, op. 20
1. Berlin State Opera Orchestra (11/1916)
Szell (uncredited) conducted first two sides, Strauss, three and four
2. (3/29–30/57) LC 3439/BC 1011

Don Quixote, op. 35
Pierre Fournier, violoncello; Abraham Skernick, viola; Rafael Druian, violin
(10/28–29/60) LC 3786/BC 1135

Four Last Songs, op. posth. 1948
"Frühling," "September," "Beim Schlafengehen," "Im Abendrot,"
Songs:
"Freundliche Vision," op. 48, no. 1
"Die heilige drei Könige," op. 56, no. 6
"Muttertändelei," op. 43, no. 2
"Waldseligkeit," op. 49, no. 1
"Zuneigung," op. 10, no. 1
Elisabeth Schwarzkopf, soprano
Berlin Radio Symphony Orchestra (9/1965) Ang. S 36347

"Das Rosenband," op. 36, no. 1
"Ruhe, meine Seele," op. 27, no. 1

"Meinem Kinde," op. 37, no. 3
"Morgen," op. 27, no. 4
"Wiegenlied," op. 41, no. 1
"Winterweihe," op. 48, no. 4
Elisabeth Schwarzkopf, soprano
LSO (3/1968) Ang. S 36643

Symphonia Domestica, op. 53 (1/10/64) ML 6027/MS 6627

Till Eulenspiegels lustige Streiche, op. 28
1. (4/25/49) MX 327 (13047D/8D) ML 2079
2. MASO (CO) (12/24/54) MAR 610B
3. (3/29–30/57) LC 3439/BC 1011

Tod und Verklärung, op. 24 (*Death and Transfiguration*)
(3/29–30/57) LC 3439/BC 1011

Stravinsky, Igor
Firebird, Suite (1919)
1. Symphony Orchestra (CO)
(11/4/55) MAR 5611A MARS 5558
2. (1/22, 23/61) (3/3/61) LC 3812 BC 1149

Tartini, Giuseppe
Concerto for Violin and Orchestra, D Minor
Columbia Symphony (CO)
Joseph Szigeti, violin (11/15/54) ML 4891

Tchaikovsky, Piotr Ilich
Capriccio Italien, op. 45 (2/28/58) LC 3483 BC 1002

Concerto for Piano and Orchestra no. 1, B-flat Minor, op. 23
1. New Symphony Orchestra of London
Clifford Curzon, piano (9/4–5/50) D. X53059/62 D. LXT 2559
2. Symphony Orchestra (NYPh)
Vladimir Horowitz, piano 1/12/53) P 100-B
3. Gary Graffman, piano (1/24–25/69) MS 7339

Symphony no. 4, F Minor, op. 36 LSO (9/1962) SPA 206

Symphony no. 5, E Minor, op. 64 (10/23–24/59) LC 3647/BC 1064

Variations on a Rococo Theme, op. 33
Leonard Rose, violoncello NYPh (12/17/51) Col. GB-1

Verdi, Giuseppe
Rigoletto
"Freundlich blick ich" ("Questa o quella")
1. Jan Kiepura, tenor (11/1926) Od. 0-7532

2. Richard Tauber, tenor
Berlin State Opera Orchestra (5/23/27) Od. 0-4950a

"O wie so trügerish" ("La donna e mobile")
1. Jan Kiepura, tenor (11/1926) Od. 0-7532
2. Richard Tauber, tenor (5/23/27) Od. 0-4950b
Berlin State Opera Orchestra

Wagner, Richard
A Faust Overture (12/10/65) ML 6284/MS 6884

Der Fligende Holländer: Overture (The Flying Dutchman)
1. NYPhil (1/4/54) AL 55/ML 4918
2. (12/11/65) ML 6284/MS 6884

Götterdämmerung:
"Dawn" and "Siegfried's Rhine Journey"
1. (11/2/56) LC 3321
2. (10/7/68) MS 7291

"Siegfried's Funeral Music" and "Final Scene"
1. (11/2/56) LC 3321
2. (10/7/68) MS 7291

Lohengrin: Prelude to Act I (12/10/65) ML 6284/MS 6884

Die Meistersinger von Nürnberg:
Prelude to Act I
1. LPO (10/38) HMV C 2809
2. NYPh (1/4/54) AL 54/ML 4918
3. (1/26/62) LC 3845/BC 1245

"Am stillen Herd"
Carl Martin Oehmann, tenor
Berlin State Opera Orchestra (11/9/26) P E 10552

"Preisleid: Morgenlicht leuchtet"
Carl Martin Oehmann, tenor (11/9/26) P E 10552

Das Rheingold: "Entrance of the Gods into Valhalla"
(10/7/68) MS 7291

Rienzi: Overture
1. NYPh (1/4/54) AAL 54 ML 4918
2. (12/11/65) ML 6284 MS 6884

Siegfried: "Waldweben" (Forest Murmurs)
1. (11/2/56) LC 3321
2. (10/12/68) MS 7291

Tannhäuser: Overture
1. NYPh (1/4/54) AAL 55 ML 4918
2. (1/26/62) LC 3845 BC 1245

Tristan und Isolde: "Prelude" and "Liebestod"
(1/26/62) LC 3845 BC 1245

Die Walküre: "Ride of the Valkyries"
1. (11/2/56) LC 3321
2. (10/12/68) MS 7291

Die Walküre: "Wotan's Farewell" and "Magic Fire Music"
(11/2/56) LC 3321

Die Walküre: "Magic Fire Music"
(10/11/68) MS 7291

Walton, William
Partita for Orchestra (1/21/59) LC 3568/BC 1024

Symphony no. 2 (2/24/61, 3/3/61) LC 3812/BC 1149

Variations on a Theme by Hindemith (10/9/64) ML 6136/MS 6736

Weber, Carl Maria von
Der Freischütz: Overture
NYPh (1/8/52) AAL 19

Konzertstück for Piano and Orchestra, F Minor, op. 79
Robert Casadesus, piano (1/20/52) ML 4588

Oberon: Overture
1. Berlin State Opera Orchestra (1927) 12" 78-rpm German Homocord 4-9010
2. LPO (1935–36) HMV C 2826
3. NYPh (1/52) (AAL 19 GB1)
4. (1/4–5/63) LC 3859/ BC 1259

Selected CD Sets, CDs, and DVDs

CD SETS

George Szell Plays and Conducts Mozart, limited 10-CD set, Sony BMG Music, 2006. Original Jacket Edition, prerecorded and previously not recorded material
Symphonies 28, 33, 35, 39, 40, 41
Sinfonia concertante (Rafael Druian, Abraham Skernick) (12/28/1963)
Clarinet Concerto (Robert Marcellus) (10/21/61)
Piano Concerto, K. 503 (Leon Fleisher) (1/9–10/59)
Exsultate, jubilate (Judith Raskin) (5/11/64)
Symphony no. 39 (4/22/47) (mono)

Divertimento in D, K. 131 (4/20/63)
Serenade in G, K. 525, "Eine kleine Nachtmusik" (10/7/68)
Serenade in D, K. 320, "With the Posthorn" (1/10, 18, 24/69)
Four Sonatas for Piano and Violin (George Szell, Rafael Druian), New York (8/1–3/67)
Quartets for Piano, Violin, Viola, and Cello, K. 478 and 493 (George Szell, piano; members of the Budapest String Quartet), New York (8/19–20/46)

The Cleveland Orchestra Seventy-Fifth Anniversary Compact Disc Edition, 1918–1993, The Cleveland Orchestra, 1993
George Szell: discs 3–6, broadcast concerts recorded live in Severance Hall, except as noted
Sibelius: Symphony no. 3 (12/9/47)
Sibelius: Symphony no. 2 (5/22/70), Tokyo, Japan
Wagner: *Siegfried Idyll* (9/26–27/69)
Mozart: Requiem (Judith Raskin, Florence Kopleff, Ernst Haefliger, Thomas Paul) (5/9, 11–12/68)
Schumann: Introduction and Allegro passionato, G; Concertstück for Piano and Orchestra, op. 92 (Rudolf Serkin) (3/12 or 14/59)
Strauss: Orchestral Suite from *Der Bürger als Edelmann*, (10/10–12/68)
Ravel: *Le Tombeau de Couperin* (9/23, 25/65)
Prokofiev: Symphony no. 1, op. 25, *Classical* (10/17, 19/68)
Mahler: *Das Lied von der Erde* (Janet Baker, Richard Lewis) (2/5, 7/70)

The Cleveland Orchestra Szell Centennial Compact Disc Edition, 7 CDs, TCO-GS97,The Musical Arts Association, www.clevelandorch.com
Wagner: Overture to *Tannhäuser;* "Dich teure Halle," from *Tannhäuser;* "Prelude and Love Death" from *Tristan und Isolde;* "Siegfried's Funeral March and Immolation Scene," from *Siegfried* (Margaret Harshaw) (11/1/56)
Samuel Barber: *Music for a Scene from Shelley* (10/25/56)
Henri Dutilleux: *Cinq métaboles* (10/19–21/67)
William Walton: Violin Concerto (Zino Francescatti) (1/25–27/68)
Beethoven: *Missa solemnis*, (2/2, 4/67, Saramae Endich, Florence Kopleff, Ernst Haefliger, Ezio Flagello, the Cleveland Orchestra Chorus, Robert Shaw, director)
Schubert: Octet, F Major, D. 803, (12/16, 18–19/65)
Berlioz: Three Excerpts from *The Damnation of Faust*, (1/13, 15/66)
Sibelius: *En Saga;* Symphony no. 4 (12/9, 11/65), Symphony no. 7 (5/23/65), Helsinki
Mahler: Symphony no. 9 (1/30–2/1/1969)
Interviews: with John Culshaw (9/68?), BBC, London; with James Fassett, (4/12/63) WQXR, New York; with Paul Myers, (3/25/66) CBS, Cleveland; with James Fassett, (11/12/65), WQXR, New York

George Szell, "Salzburger Orchesterkonzerte 1957" (George Szell, Salzburg Orchestra Concerts 1957), 3 CDs, Orfeo C 774 083 D
Berlin Philharmonic, George Szell, conductor

August 3, 1957, 4th Orchestra Concert, Mozarteum
Mozart: Symphony no. 21, A, K. 201
Piano Concerto, C, K. 503 Leon Fleisher
Symphony no. 40, G Minor, K. 550
August 9, 1957, 6th Orchestra Concert, Festspielhaus
Debussy: *La mer*
Mendelssohn: Violin Concerto, E Minor, op. 64 Nathan Milstein
Beethoven: Symphony no. 3, E-flat, op. 55, *Eroica*

CDS

Brahms: Quintet in F Minor, op. 34, October 11, 1945; Schubert: Quintet in A Major, op. 114 (*Trout*), May 16, 1946; Budapest String Quartet: Joseph Roismann and Edgar Ortenberg, violins; Boris Kroyt, viola; Mischa Schneider, violoncello; George Szell, piano; Georges E. Moleux, contrabass in the Schubert; "Great Performances from the Library of Congress," Bridge CD 9062.

Liebermann, Rolf, *Die Schule der Frauen*, (*School for Wives*), Vienna Philharmonic, George Szell, Salzburg Festival 1957, Walter Berry, Kurt Bohme, Anneliese Rothenberger, Nicolai Gedda, Christa Ludwig, Alois Pernerstorfer; Festispiel Documente, Altes Festspielhaus, August 17, 1957, Orfeo CD C 429 9621.

Mozart: *Die Zauberflöte*, Vienna Philharmonic, George Szell, Salzburg Festival 1959, Kurt Böhme (Sarastro), Leopold Simoneau (Tamino), Lisa Della Casa (Pamina), Walter Berry (Papageno), Graziella Sciutti (Papagena), Hans Hotter (Speaker), Karl Dönch (Monostatos), Friederike Sailer (First Lady), Hetty Plumacher (Second Lady), Sieglinde Wagner (Third Lady), Gala, GL 100.502.

Mussorgsky: *Boris Godunov:* Excerpts
1. Alexander Kipnis (Boris), Kerstin Thorborg (Marina), René Maison (Dimitry), Metropolitan Opera Orchestra and Chorus (2/13/43) EJS 550, 2 CDs SIAE FT 1505, 1506
2. Ezio Pinza, Armand Tokayyan, Kerstin Thorborg, Metropolitan Opera Orchestra and Chorus EJS 561

Strauss, Richard, *Der Rosenkavalier*, Vienna Philharmonic, George Szell, Salzburg Festival 1949, Maria Reining (Marchallin), Jarmila Novotná (Octavian), Hilde Güden (Sophie), Jaro Prohaska (Baron Ochs), Andante CD 3986, 3987, 3988, 3989.

Verdi, *Otello*, Live Recording, November 16, 1946, Orchestra and Chorus of the Metropolitan Opera, George Szell, conductor, Torsten Ralf (Otello), Leonard Warren (Iago), Alessio de Paolis (Cassio), Anthony Marlowe (Rodrigo), Nicola Moscona (Lodovico), William Hargrave (Montano), Philip Insman (Herald), Stella Roman (Desdemona), Martha Lipton (Emilia), GDS 20213

Wagner, *Tannhäuser*, Live Recording, December 19, 1942, Metropolitan Opera Orchestra and Chorus, George Szell, conductor, Lauritz Melchior (Tannhäuser), Helen Traubel (Elisabeth), Herbert Janssen (Wolfram), Kerstin Thorborg (Venus), Alexander Kipnis (Hermann), John Garris (Walther), Emery Darcy (Heinrich), Osie Hawkins (Biterolf), John Gurney (Reinmar), Maxine Stellman (Shepherd) (Also included are Wagner excerpts sung by Kirsten Flagstad), Music and Arts CD-664-3

DVDS

The Bell Telephone Hour, *The Cleveland Orchestra, A Portrait of George Szell,* George Szell, the Cleveland Orchestra, "One Man's Triumph," VAI Video 69702, VAI DVD 4271.

Chicago Symphony Orchestra, Telecasts of December 10 and 17, 1961, George Szell, conductor, Beethoven: Symphony no. 5, *Leonore* Overture no. 3; Berlioz: *Roman Carnival* Overture; Mozart: Overture to *The Marriage of Figaro;* Mozart: Violin Concerto no. 5 ("Turkish"), Erica Morni, violin; Mussorgsky: Prelude to *Khovanshchina;* VAI 4222.

Notes

Chapter 1. The New Mozart (1897–1929)

1. The birth was recorded in Hungarian and Hebrew in a ledger in the Central Synagogue Archives, Budapest. His parents' marriage is reported as April 8, 1896. The ritual circumcision of the baby, whose Hebrew name was Kalonymus Zevi, ben Yakov, occurred on June 14. The infant's maternal grandfather, Lipot Hirschbein, a merchant and businessman of Ipolyság, enjoyed the honor of holding him. Explained and translated by Professor Menachem Schmelzer, Hebrew Union Theological Seminary, New York City.

2. Interview with George A. Lanyi, Oberlin, Ohio, April 13, 1976; Lanyi and his parents often visited Szell's home in Vienna.

3. Seen in 1990, the house looked substantial, though needing repair.

4. Conflicting sources put the move in either 1903 (Joseph Wechsberg, "The Grace of the Moment," *TNY*, November 6, 1965, 83), when Szell was six, or 1904 (promotional brochure).

5. Szell's Artist's Questionnaire, October 20, 1942, MOA. In it Szell gave his father's name as George Charles. Early in the 1940s in America, Szell added the final "e" to his first name. Except for direct quotations, he will be referred to here as "George."

6. Lanyi interview.

7. George Szell's boyhood friend Rudolf Serkin was a frequent guest. He recalled the Szells as "very warm, sweet people," and that George's mother was an excellent cook. The hospitality meant a great deal to the shy young Serkin, far from home, and coming from a poor family. Interview with Rudolf Serkin, July 5, 1977, Marlboro, Vermont.

8. Lanyi interview.

9. Artist's Questionnaire, 1942, MOA.

10. "George Szell talks to John Culshaw," BBC television broadcast, April 8, 1969.

11. R. de Chateleux, "My Talk with the New Mozart, an Interview with the Little Romping Boy Whose Musical Powers Have Amazed London: The Eleven-year-old Composer and the Cakes," *Daily Mail* (London), November 24, 1908, 11.

12. Questionnaire, 1942, MOA. Correcting wrong notes was a routine part of Szell's adult profession.

13. Chateleux. At that time, Richard Robert had a special reputation for his success with infant prodigies. Vera Schapira and Clara Haskil had been his pupils, and later Rudolf Serkin studied with him, making a similarly early start as a virtuoso.

14. Hans Gál (the original spelling), letter to the author with twelve-page essay, October 1, 1975. Gál (1890–1987), a prominent Austrian composer and music scholar, taught at the University of Vienna and became director of the Mainz Conservatory. He worked as joint editor of the complete edition of Brahms with one of his (and Szell's) former teachers, Eusebius Mandyczewski. In 1938 Gál left Mainz, becoming lecturer at Edinburgh University in 1945. There, he dropped the accent in his name, which usage will be followed from here.

15. "George Szell talks to John Culshaw."

16. Gal essay.

17. Szell bequest, George Szell Memorial Library, Severance Hall, Cleveland. Translation by Klaus George Roy.

18. *Neue Freie Presse*, Vienna, February 5, 1908.

19. "My Talk with the New Mozart . . ." *Daily Mail* (London), also in *Kölnische Zeitung*.

20. Wechsberg, "The Grace of the Moment," 86.

21. "George Szell Talks to John Culshaw."

22. Chateleux.

23. *Morning Leader* (London), undated (1908).

24. *Daily Mail* (London), undated, quoted in Szell's first brochure. There is no way to confirm the number of early compositions, because all family possessions were lost in the war. The Fleisher Collection in Philadelphia houses a handful of published works.

25. "Georg Széll, Representative: Concert Office Emil Gutmann, Munich," dated August 1909, with photograph of Szell in a sailor suit.

26. Gal essay.

27. Interview with Hans Heinsheimer, 1982. Heinsheimer (1900–87) worked at Universal Publishers in Vienna, and later at Boosey & Hawkes and G. Schirmer in New York.

28. Serkin interview.

29. Wechsberg, "The Grace of the Moment," 88.

30. "George Szell Talks to John Culshaw."

31. "He is perceived throughout as modern under the influence of the models of Strauss and Bruckner, and where his own invention dares to show itself, he shows a flare for melody and euphony," *Berliner Tageblatt*, undated. Reprinted in Szell's second concert brochure, author's translation.

32. "Music by George Szell," Louis Lane and Carl Topilow, conductors: *Variations on an Original Theme* (Topilow), *Lyric Overture* (Lane), Piano Quintet in E Major (Cavani String Quartet, Anne Epperson, piano), recorded in Kulas Hall, produced by the Cleveland Institute of Music, 1992.

33. "George Szell Talks to John Culshaw."

34. Wechsberg, "The Grace of the Moment," 86.

35. Gal essay. Gal did not specify where the rehearsal took place.

36. Promotional brochure, "Georg Széll, Youthful Pianist, Composer, and Conductor," 14 pp., undated, probably published by Emil Gutmann, Munich.

37. "George Szell Talks to John Culshaw."

38. Telephone interview with Louis Lane, May 8, 2002.

39. Wechsberg, "The Grace of the Moment," 88.

40. Harold C. Schonberg, *The Great Conductors* (New York: Simon and Schuster, 1967), 237.

41. Bell Telephone Hour, NBC-TV, broadcast December 4, 1966, "George Szell, The Cleveland Orchestra, 'One Man's Triumph,'" VAI DVD 4271.

42. "George Szell talks to John Culshaw."

43. Wechsberg, "The Grace of the Moment," 88.

44. Peter Heyworth, *Otto Klemperer, His Life and Times* (Cambridge, U.K.: Cambridge University Press, 1983), 1:115.

45. Interview with Olga Band Heifetz, Szell's first wife, Great Neck, New York, June 7, 1975.

46. Telephone interview with Louis Lane, May 8, 2002.

47. *Richard Strauss–Franz Schalk, Ein Briefwechsel (Richard Strauss-Franz Schalk, Correspondence)*, (Tutzing, Ger.: Hans Schneider, 1983). Author's translation, with editorial help from Max Rudolf and Katrin Bean. All following quotations are from this source.

48. Strauss to Schalk, December 7, 1918, 48.

49. Schalk to Strauss December 2, 1918, 51.

50. Strauss to Schalk, December 15, 1918, 57; Schalk to Strauss, December 20, 1918, 66.

51. Telegram, Schalk to Strauss, December 25, 1918, 72–73.

52. Strauss to Schalk, December 26, 1918, 73–74. Strauss to Schalk, December 27, 1918, 78. Leopold Reichwein was one of the Vienna Opera staff conductors whose tenure Strauss and Schalk were reviewing.

53. Strauss to Schalk, January 4, 1919, 84.

54. Schalk to Strauss, January 10, 1919, 89.

55. Strauss to Schalk, December 31, 1919, 158–59.

56. In a way, Strauss had the last word: Schalk's Vienna successor in 1929 was Strauss's recommendation, Clemens Krauss.

57. Interview with Marcel Dick, former principal violist of the Cleveland Orchestra and head of the composition department of the Cleveland Institute of Music, Cleveland, April 13, 1975.

58. Szell kept a few small posters for performances he conducted in these cities. One such was for a new staging of Verdi's *Masked Ball* on Friday, April 1, 1921 in Darmstadt.

59. Olga Heifetz interview.

60. In 1929 Olga and Wolfstahl married. He died of pneumonia two years later, at the age of thirty-one. She later married the cellist Benar Heifetz, who became associate principal cellist of the NBC Symphony.

61. Gal essay.

62. Berlin Hochschule catalog, 1927–28. Schnabel remained a close friend and, until his retirement, a performing colleague. Reznicek was a respected composer, Sachs a leading musicologist. Among the conducting students who would become known in America were Franz Allers, noted Broadway and Pops conductor, and Wolfgang Vacano, who became professor of conducting at Indiana University; other students well known in the United States were Hans Kindler, Karl-Ulrich Schnabel, and Ignatz Strasfogel.

63. The witness was the future wife of cellist Pierre Fournier (at the time married to another cellist, Gregor Piatigorsky) and mother of pianist Jean Fonda Fournier. Letter to the author from Jean Fonda Fournier, September 8, 1996.

64. Gal essay.

65. Compiled by the author at the Berlin City Archives, May 2004. See appendix F.

66. Gal essay. According to a yearbook of the theater, Szell's title was "Leitende Dirigent," literally "leading conductor," not music director, although in effect his position was the equivalent of a general music director.

67. Steinberg (1899–1978) left Germany in 1936 as cofounder, with Bronislav Huberman, of the Palestine (later Israel) Philharmonic. Known in the United States as William Steinberg, he had a long and distinguished career as conductor of the Pittsburgh and Boston Symphonies. Relations between Steinberg and Szell remained good throughout their lives. Steinberg was one of the few guest conductors Szell invited to Cleveland.

68. Max Rudolf interview with the author, Philadelphia, 1978.

69. "Prager Theaterbuch 1930," listing the personnel and events of the previous season, courtesy of Max Rudolf.

70. Schick was a staff conductor of the Metropolitan Opera in New York and later became president of the Manhattan School of Music. Adler put the San Francisco Opera on the map during his long tenure. Susskind held several important conducting posts, most notably with the St. Louis Symphony, which he built to national prominence, and also conducted the Aspen Music Festival. Halasz was a prime mover in the early days of the New York City Opera.

71. Yearbook of Das Deutsche Theater in Prague, 1931, courtesy of Max Rudolf.

72. Concert repertoire included Bach: Orchestra Suite no. 1, Beethoven: Violin Concerto and Leonore Overture no. 2, Berlioz: *Harold in Italy*, Bruckner: Symphony no. 2, Hindemith: Concerto for Viola d'amore, Mendelssohn: "Italian" Symphony, Mozart: "Jupiter" Symphony, Mussorgsky-Ravel: *Pictures at an Exhibition*, Reger: Piano Concerto (Serkin).

73. Max Rudolf interview. Also confirmed by Frederic Waldman, another former piano student of Richard Robert. He conducted opera at the Juilliard School of Music and founded and conducted Musica Aeterna in New York City. Waldman was Szell's only known conducting student. After one lesson in 1921, when Szell was on vacation at his parents' home in Vienna, Szell asked Waldman to play duets—Waldman on trumpet and Szell on horn, "I think maybe Bach Inventions," Waldman recalled. They "made such a racket that the old Mrs. Szell opened up the door and said 'what's going on here?'" When I told Waldman I was going to Cleveland in 1961 as apprentice conductor to Szell, he said, "I envy you." Interview, May 22, 1975.

Chapter 2. The Conductor Spreads His Wings (1930–38)

1. Thomas B. Sherman, "Symphony to End Its Season Tonight," *St. Louis Post-Dispatch*, (hereafter *SLPD)* March 12, 1927. It is often misquoted by orchestra players as: "There are no bad orchestras, only bad conductors." Leaving out the positive, it is a denigration of conductors, implying that only they are responsible for bad results, while orchestras are responsible for the good. Strauss properly gave conductors both the blame *and* the credit for an orchestra's quality.

2. Walter was formerly business manager of the Curtis Institute of Music in Philadelphia.

3. The six were: Enrique Fernandez Arbós, Eugene Goossens, Bernardino Molinari, William van Hoogstraten, Emil Oberhoffer, and Carl Schuricht.

4. "Symphony Manager Tells Season's Plans," *SLPD*, June 19, 1929.

5. Sherman, "Music. Szell's Debut," *SLPD*, January 25, 1930.

6. Sherman, "Music. Mozart Predominates," *SLPD*, February 1, 1930.

7. Postcard, Szell to Rudolf, February 2, 1930, courtesy of Max Rudolf.

8. Sherman, "Music. Horowitz and Szell," *SLPD*, February 15, 1930.

9. Sherman, "Echoes of Mr. Szell. The Prague Conductor's Unusual Gift for Self-Criticism," *SLPD*, February 16, 1930. When, for example, a new critical edition of Mahler's Fourth Symphony was published in 1964, Szell asked me to list all the changes the edition noted. He then incorporated every detail that he judged to be valid, modifying his interpretation accordingly.

10. Sherman, "Echoes of Mr. Szell." Szell had not yet heard Toscanini conducting the New York Philharmonic's 1930 European tour. The "Toscanini shock" demonstrated to Szell that superb orchestral ensemble could be realized without sacrificing any other musical values.

11. Sherman, "Symphony Continues Guest Leader Policy," *SLPD*, March 13, 1930. Fernando Arbós, who at age seventy was not a candidate, would begin the season.

12. Letter from Max Rudolf, January 6, 1988. Referring to his diary, Rudolf noted that on March 17, 1930, "Sz. tells M.R. that he plans to cancel St. Louis concerts in 1931."

13. Sherman, "Permanent and Impermanent Conductors, Some of the Reasons Why the St. Louis Orchestra Is Still Engaging Guests," *SLPD*, March 30, 1930.

14. "Sherman, French Conductor to Lead Symphony," *SLPD*, May 13, 1930.

15. Prague German-language daily *Bohemia*, February 10, 1930. Courtesy of Max Rudolf.

16. Sherman, "Golschmann Makes Debut With Symphony," *SLPD*, January 24, 1931.

17. Sherman, "Golschmann Charms Symphony Audience," *SLPD*, February 7, 1931.

18. Sherman, "Pianist Iturbi Wins Symphony Audience," *SLPD*, February 14, 1931.

19. Sherman, "Walter Resigns as Symphony Manager," *SLPD*, February 17, 1931.

20. Sherman, "Szell Again Directs St. Louis Symphony," *SLPD*, February 28, 1931.

21. John S. Edwards (1912–84), interview with the author, New York City, December 20, 1975. Edwards had been manager of the National, Pittsburgh, and Chicago Symphonies, and became president of the American Symphony Orchestra League.

22. Louis Lane, interview, undated.

23. Sherman, "Symphony Signs Golschmann for Next Two Years," *SLPD*, March 23, 1931.

24. March 16, 1931.

25. Sherman, "Szell Gives His Best Symphony Program: Prague Guest Conductor Finishes Season in a Blaze of Glory," *SLPD*, March 28, 1931.

26. Anne Mendelson, *Stand Facing the Stove, the Story of the Women Who Gave America "The Joy of Cooking."* New York: Henry Holt, 1996, 81.

27. Edward Murphy, interview with the author, St. Louis, October 6, 1975.

28. Letter, William E. Walter to Florence Sherman, August 16, 1932.

29. Ibid. In 1962, after a St. Louis concert led by a young American conductor who had a reputation for a quick temper, two older gentlemen, possibly trustees of the orchestra, were heard commenting in the corridor. The first one said: "He's a very talented conductor but it's too bad I understand that he's impossible to get along with." The other one answered: "Yes, but if we hadn't said that thirty-five years ago we might have had George Szell instead of Vladimir Golschmann." Overheard by Peter W. Smith, manager of the Grand Rapids Symphony, and told to the author in Chicago, June 18, 1988.

30. Arthur Rubinstein, *My Many Years* (New York: Alfred A. Knopf, 1980), 409; *My Young Years* (New York: Alfred A. Knopf, 1973). In these works he uses the first name "Arthur." In all of his Cleveland Orchestra appearances, the program book read "Artur." The pianist wrote, "In later years, my manager Sol Hurok used the *h*-less 'Artur' for my publicity, but I sign 'Arthur' in countries where it is common practice, 'Arturo' in Spain and Italy, and 'Artur' in the Slav countries."

31. The van in Beethoven's name denotes his Flemish ancestry.

32. Lane interview, undated.

33. Interview with A. Beverly Barksdale, Cleveland, April 18, 1975, who learned this from Szell's former European artist manager, Eric Simon.

34. "Szell—Champion of the Classics. Great Conductor Expounds Australia's Musical Needs. Abhors the 'Human Interest' Story," *Brisbane Telegraph*, June 29, 1938.

35. "Conducting with Touch of Genius. Scottish Orchestra's Brilliant Playing. A Triumph for Mr. Georg Szell," *Evening Times* (Glasgow), December 21, 1936.

36. *Glasgow Herald*, November 16, 1936.

37. *The Scotsman*, December 1, 1936.

38. *Edinburgh Evening News*, January 12, 1937.

39. "The Authentic 'Eroica,' Georg Szell at Queen's Hall," *Daily Telegraph* (London), November 27, 1936.

40. *Truth* (London), December 2, 1936.

41. *New Statesman and Nation* (London), December 12, 1936.

42. "An Electric Climax. Szell's Wizardry in Brahms Symphony," *Evening Times* (Glasgow), December 23, 1936.

43. "The Scottish Orchestra. Seventh Symphony of Schubert. Close of Georg Szell's Visit," *Glasgow Herald*, January 18, 1937.

44. Interview with Henri Temianka, New York, May 31, 1975; Henri Temianka, *Facing the Music* (New York: David McKay, 1972); Temianka, "My George Szell," *SR*, September 26, 1970. (About one of their recitals, the *London Observer*, November 9, 1937, wrote: "At the Aeolian Hall on Tuesday, Mr. Temianka played the violin neatly and Mr. Szell the pianoforte noisily," quoted in "My George Szell.")

45. A. Beverly Barksdale interview, April 18, 1975.

46. "Conductor of 'Scottish' Wed in City," *Glasgow Evening News*, January 25, 1938; "'Scottish' Conductor Remarries in Glasgow," *Glasgow Bulletin*, January 26, 1938; Temianka interview.

47. Temianka, "My George Szell."

48. This point is exemplified in the many letters of Mozart and his family.

49. Temianka, *Facing the Music*.

50. Temianka interview.

51. Szell to Rodriguez, November 5, 1936, ROA. All this correspondence is translated from the German by the author.

52. Rodriguez to Szell, October 31, 1936; Szell to Rodriguez, November 5, 1936, ROA. In later years Szell did conduct the *Fidelio* Overture in concert, but not often.

53. Szell to Rodriguez, October 25, 1936, ROA. The numbering of the Dvořák symphonies is especially complicated owing both to the composer's reticence about his early symphonies and his publisher Simrock's marketing machinations. The Fourth mentioned is really the Eighth. The famous Ninth, *From the New World*, was known for years as the Fifth. In the 1950s and 1960s the record was set straight: the symphonies, edited by Otakar Sourek, were published in a critical edition by the Czech State Publishing House, ARTIA, numbered in the order of composition.

54. Rodriguez to Szell, November 13, 1936, ROA. The composer Johan Wagenaar (1862–1941) was director of the Royal Conservatory of The Hague for eighteen years, until 1937. The work that Rodriguez had in mind was the overture to *Cyrano de Bergerac*, written when Wagenaar was seventy-six years old. Szell evidently liked it, because he programmed it again the following season and performed it elsewhere, as well.

55. Almost forty years later, the first musical recollection of Szell's 1930s Hague concerts by Martin Zagwijn, a former cellist in the Residence Orchestra, was of the Dvořák. The beauty of Szell's conception, and even the particular lilt of the opening of the third movement, were so vivid to him after forty years that he remembered and sang it as Szell had phrased it. Interview with the author, May 1, 1976, The Hague.

56. Szell to Rodriguez, December 27, 1936, ROA.

57. George Szell, "Toscanini in the History of Orchestral Performance," *SR*, March 25, 1967, 53, 55.

58. "Toscanini: The Maestro Revisited," Bell Telephone Hour, March 12, 1967.

Chapter 3. Musical Pioneering in Australia (1938, 1939)

1. *Melbourne Sun*, October 30, 1937. The reviews and letters quoted in this chapter were provided to the author by the ABC Archives, Sydney. Some are missing dates and/or sources.

2. "From a Special Correspondent, London, 25 February 1938," published in Australia: "Music in London. Szell," *Melbourne Age*, March 19, 1938.

3. Unidentified clipping.

4. "Musician and Good Cook, Too, George Szell, Noted Conductor, Arrives. A.B.C. Concerts," *Sydney Labor Daily*, April 28, 1938.

5. "Noted Conductor for A.B.C.," *Melbourne Herald*, April 19, 1938.

6. "His Sporting Side," *Melbourne Sun*, May 5, 1938.

7. "Conductor Who Cooks, Czech Professor Likes It," *Sydney Sun*, May 27, 1938.

8. "Conductor Czell, Caveman," unidentified and undated clipping.

9. "Szell, Champion of the Classics," *Brisbane Telegraph*, June 29, 1938.

10. "Music and Radio. 'Great Service Rendered,'" *Perth Western Australian*, April 20, 1938.

11. Unidentified clipping.

12. Gordon Kay, "Some Things the Baton Can't Do, Says Szell," *Melbourne Sun*, May 7, 1938.

13. "Professor Szell's Brilliance. Orchestral Season Opens," *Melbourne Argus*, May 9, 1938.

14. "A Floating Opera House. Conductor's Novel Suggestion," *Melbourne Argus*, May 12, 1938.

15. Thorold Waters, "Szell Orchestral Concert Another Triumph: Elgar's Falstaff Ably Performed at Town Hall," *Melbourne Sun*, May 16, 1938.

16. T. W. [Thorold Waters], "Szell's Best Brahms Performance," *Australian Musical News*, May 23, 1938.

17. Memorandum, Wickes to Moses, May 23, 1938.

18. J. R., "Szell Gives Few Surprises," *Sydney Telegraph*, June 1, 1938.

19. H. A., "Triumph of Szell's Leadership," *Sydney Sun*, June 1, 1938.

20. "Szell Conducts Again," *Sydney Telegraph*, June 6, 1938.

21. Memo: "Szell & Orchestra," Basil W. Kirke, New South Wales manager of the Celebrity Concerts, to Charles Moses, General Manager, Sydney, June 1, 1938.

22. "Georg Szell and 12 Orchestral Players Arrive," *Brisbane Telegraph*, ca. June 18, 1938.

23. Szell to Moses, July 19, 1938.

24. Interview with Szell in Sydney by an unnamed "Special Correspondent," *Brisbane Courier Mail*, June 18, 1938.

25. "From Our Sydney Correspondent," "Georg Szell Invited to Stay as Permanent A.B.C. Conductor," *Perth Broadcaster*, June 25, 1938.

26. Memorandum, from W. G. James to the General Manager, dated July 11, 1938, quoting extract of Nelson Burton's report: "Queensland Division's Music Report for the Week Ended 2nd July, 1938."

27. Ibid.

28. Szell to William James, July 23, 1938.

29. H. Brewster Jones, "Noted Czech Conductor Here, Praises Australian Orchestral Players, First Rehearsal," *Advertiser* (Adelaide), July 6, 1938.

30. Memorandum, "George Szell Season—Adelaide," L. R. Thomas, Manager for

South Australia, to The Federal Controller of Music, Australian Broadcasting Commission, Sydney, July 6, 1938.

31. "Celebrity Orchestral Season, Georg Szell's Adelaide Appearance," *Advertiser* (Adelaide), June 22, 1938.

32. Allegro, "Prof. Szell's Success, but Better Items Wanted," *Adelaide News*, July 11, 1938.

33. Memorandum: "Report on Touring Artist: Georg Szell, Conductor," from L. R. Thomas, Sydney, November 7, 1938.

34. "Szell Conducts, A. B. C. Orchestral Concert, Perth Pianist's Success," *Western Australian* (Perth), July 28, 1938.

35. Memorandum: "Orchestral Report—Western Australia—Period—29th May to 30th July, 1938," W. G. James to the General Manager, August 10, 1938.

36. Memorandum, "West Australian Programme Report—Week Ending Aug. 6," Perth, Keith Barry to The Federal Controller of Music, August 15, 1938.

37. Memorandum, "Georg Szell," C. Charlton to The General Manager, Perth, September 13, 1938.

38. Szell to C. J. A. Moses, General Manager, Australian Broadcasting Commission, July 19, 1938.

39. Szell to William James, July 23, 1938.

40. Moses to Szell, July 19, 1938. Australia's orchestras have become full-size, full-season, professional musical ensembles, in large part owing to the early and long-term efforts of the Australian Broadcasting Commission in sponsoring foreign musicians, such as Szell, and in encouraging Australian conductors and teachers to cultivate their native musical resources.

41. Szell to Moses, November 14, 1938.

42. Unidentified clipping, May 2, 1939.

43. "Music and Radio. 'Great Service' Rendered. Czech Conductor's Views," *Western Australian* (Perth), April 20, 1938.

44. "Prof. Szell's Life Is a Busy One," *Brisbane Mail*, May 27, 1939.

45. "Professor and Mrs. Szell 'Delighted to Be Back,'" *Teleradio* (Queensland), May 13, 1939.

46. "Europe Puts Guns before Music, Says Professor," *Melbourne Herald*, May 2, 1939.

47. "Professor and Mrs. Szell 'Delighted to Be Back'."

48. "Szell Brings Music to the People," *Melbourne Herald*, May 20, 1939.

49. J. E. Tremearne, "Concert-Goers Neglect Professor Szell," *Melbourne Herald*, June 8, 1939.

50. Howard Ashton, "Music Notes," *Sunday Sun* (Melbourne), May 7, 1939.

51. "Georg Szell, Second Orchestral Concert, Dissimilar Works," *Sydney Morning Herald*, July 5, 1939.

52. "Modern Music Perplexes, Reflects Troubled World," *Sydney Daily News*, July 11, 1939.

53. Max Rudolf held that conductors' places in history have been influenced by the greatness of their related composers.

54. "Rousing Farewell Concert," *Sydney Daily News*, July 28, 1939.

55. Moses to Szell, July 28, 1939; Szell to Moses, August 2, 1939.

56. Charles Buttrose, *Playing for Australia: A Story about ABC Orchestras and Music in Australia* (Sydney: Macmillan; Australian Broadcasting Commission, 1982).

57. "A Great Conductor Out of Work," December 13, 1939.

Chapter 4. New World, New Beginnings (1939–46)

1. Standing on the northeast corner of 34th Street, two blocks from the Empire State Building, Seven Park Avenue had its own notepaper with its picture, and Szell used this for his correspondence.

2. Szell to Henri Temianka, October 21, 1939. Letters provided by Temianka to the author, quotes from interview, May 31, 1975.

3. Rodriguez to Szell, November 11, 1939; Szell to Rodriguez, November 18, 1939, ROA.

4. In April 1940 Hitler's forces took Norway. In May, France, Belgium, and Holland fell to them. In July 1940 Marshal Pétain moved his government from Bordeaux to Vichy, designated the capital of the "Unoccupied Zone." By November 1942 all of France was occupied.

5. Firkusny interview, November 20, 1975; John Teltsch interview with Carol Jacobs and Dorothy Humel Hovorka, Cleveland, March 11, 1992.

6. June 18, 1940.

7. Conversation with Igor Kipnis, New York City, 1993.

8. Raymond Burrows and Bessie Carroll Redmond, *Symphony Themes* (New York: Simon and Schuster, 1942).

9. Coincidentally, these institutions were later joined—in 1989 the Mannes College of Music became a division of the New School for Social Research (now New School University). It is now called Mannes College the New School for Music.

10. More of an epiphany than, but reminiscent of, Szell's memory of the piano playing of Max Reger.

11. Twenty years later Szell performed Rochberg's Symphony no. 2 with the Cleveland Orchestra.

12. Interviews with George Rochberg, Bryn Mawr, Pennsylvania, July 28, 1989; and Ursula Mamlok, New York, May 16, 1988.

13. Salzer's system, defined in his book *Structural Hearing* (New York: Charles Boni, 1952; repr., Dover, 1962), is based on theories of Heinrich Schenker. It remains a mainstay of Mannes's renowned Techniques of Music program; interview with Hedwig (Mrs. Felix) Salzer, New York, April 23, 1996.

14. Isabel Morse Jones, "Conducting of Szell Interesting," *Los Angeles Times*, August 17, 1940.

15. Carl Bronson, "Tschaikowsky 'Pathetique' Is Highlight," *Los Angeles Express*, August 17, 1940. Szell had an affinity for this work that produced performances of passion and excitement.

16. Szell interviewed by Harvey Sachs, WCLV-FM, Cleveland, January 1965.

17. "Szell, Conductor, Makes Debut Here," March 3, 1941.

18. William G. King, "Music and Musicians. About the NBC Symphony's New Guest-conductor, Georg Szell of Czecho-Slovakia," *NYS*, March 8, 1941.

19. "T.," "Szell in an All-Czech Program," *MA*, March 25, 1941.

20. *NYHT*, March 23, 1941.

21. *NYT*, March 23, 1941.

22. Letter to the Editor, April 29, 1967. Berv's letter was a response to a somewhat critical article by Szell the previous month, "Toscanini in the History of Orchestral Performance," *SR*, March 25, 1967.

23. Alan Shulman, letter to the editor, *Keynote* magazine, July 1977.

24. NYPL, Toscanini Legacy, folder L931, brought to the author's attention by Harvey Sachs during research for his book *The Letters of Toscanini* (New York: Alfred A. Knopf, 2002).

25. Szell, "Toscanini in the History."

26. Harvey Sachs, *Toscanini* (New York: J. P. Lippincott, 1978; repr., Da Capo Press, 1981), 274–76.

27. Interviews, Max Rudolf, 1975–93. Johnson was general manager of the Met at that time.

28. Fortunately, she told the story to the conductor of the Spokane Symphony, Donald Thulean, who told it to me (in Chicago on June 10, 1988).

29. Kahn was a wealthy banker. The Metropolitan Opera was then a private corporation for profit.

30. Ziegler to Kahn, December 23, 1929, MOA.

31. Martin Mayer, *The Met, One Hundred Years of Grand Opera* (New York: Simon and Schuster, 1983); Witherspoon file: "Artists under Consideration" [for 1936–37], MOA.

32. Szell to Dorle Jarmel, New York Philharmonic press director, January 26, 1952, NYPhA.

33. *NYT*, December 10, 1942.

34. *NYHT*, December 10, 1942.

35. *NYS*, December 20, 1942.

36. *NYT*, December 20, 1942.

37. Not long after Szell orchestrated Smetana's First String Quartet, he was evidently still in the mood for arranging. He made his own arrangement of "The Star-Spangled Banner," which opened the performance of *Boris*. A complete set of parts resides in the Mapleson Music Library.

38. Olin Downes, *NYT*, December 31, 1942.

39. Virgil Thomson, *NYHT*, December 31, 1942.

40. Cyrus Durgin, *Boston Daily Globe*, January 30, 1943.

41. Rudolph Elie Jr., "Szell First Guest Conductor of Symphony," *Boston Herald*, January 30, 1943.

42. Cyrus Durgin, "Szell Guest Conductor of Symphony Orchestra," *Boston Daily Globe*, January 28, 1943.

43. February 8, 1943.

44. Durgin, "Szell Guest Conductor of Symphony Orchestra."

45. Durgin, "Szell Returns to Conduct His Favorite Boston Symphony," *Boston Daily Globe*, January 19, 1945.

46. "Conducting," *NYS*, January 26, 1945.

47. Claudia Cassidy, "Miss Lawrence Sings Radiantly in 'Tannhäuser,'" *Chicago Daily Tribune*, March 30, 1943.

48. Hans Wilhelm Steinberg, Szell's predecessor in Prague, was now Wilhelm, and eventually William.

49. *NYWT*, December 3, 1943.

50. "Szell Conducts 'Ring' Cycle," MA, March 1944.

51. Oscar Thompson, "Surprise Effect Ends 'Ring' Cycle," *NYS*, March 1, 1944.

52. Helene Szell to Hilda Oldberg, April 12, 1944, NWA.

53. *NYT*, April 9, 1944.

54. "Horrifies," very likely, but "terrifies," never!

55. *Time*, April 17, 1944.

56. NWA, August 20, 1944.

57. "Music: Liveliness and Horror," *NYHT*, November 30, 1944.

58. "The World of Music. George Szell Begins a Two-Week Guest Engagement With the Philharmonic," *NYT*, December 10, 1944.

59. Lukas Foss, interview with the author, November 21, 1996.

60. "Szell Conductor of Philharmonic. Guest on Podium, He Leads Brilliant Program Including 'Eroica' by Beethoven," *NYT*, December 15, 1944.

61. "Szell and Arrau at Carnegie Hall. Conductor and Pianist Offer Unusual Program, Including the Strauss 'Burlesque,'" *NYT*, March 9, 1945.

62. *Newsweek*, January 22, 1945.

63. Ronald F. Eyer, "Gala Performance Restores 'Meistersinger,'" *MA*, January 25, 1945.

64. Olin Downes, "New Friends Hear Szell as Pianist," *NYT*, February 26, 1945; Arthur V. Berger, "Szell as Pianist in Mozart Works," *NYS*, February 26, 1945; Jerome D. Bohm, "Szell Is Pianist at New Friends' Mozart Concert," *NYHT*, February 26, 1945.

65. NWA, March 1, 1945. The colloquial *ain't* was considered humorous by the Szells.

66. Szell to Zirato, May 2, 1945, NYPhA.

67. John Teltsch interview with Carol Jacobs and Dorothy Humel Hovorka, Cleveland, March 11, 1992; Max Rudolf interview with the author, January 23, 1992. Szell was in the hospital when John's boat docked in Philadelphia, so Rudolf accompanied Helene to meet him.

68. To Harold Spivacke, September 21, 1945.

69. Zirato to Szell, October 11, 1945; Szell to Zirato, October 13, 1945, NYPhA.

70. *NYT*, February 2, 1964.

71. Rodzinski quoted by Zirato to Szell, July 5, 1945; Zirato to Szell, July 16, 1945, NYPhA.

72. Interview with the author, April 16, 1976.

73. Downes, "Szell Features Strauss 'Quixote,'" November 2, 1945; Kolodin, "Szell in Charge of Philharmonic," November 2, 1945, NYPhA.

74. Downes, "'Otello' Returns With Ralf in Lead. Warren and Miss Roman Join in Fine Performances Before Throng—Szell at Best," *NYT*, February 24, 1946; Kolodin, "Szell Vivifies Verdi's 'Otello,'" *NYS*, February 25, 1946.

75. "Szell Conducts Philharmonic," *NYS*, February 1, 1946.

76. *NYP*, February 1, 1946.

77. "Music, Posthumous Compliment," *NYHT*, February 1, 1946.

78. "Szell Conducts Philharmonic," *NYS*, February 1, 1946.

79. MOA; backstage at the New York Philharmonic, after Bing's retirement from the Met was known in musical circles but before his successor was announced (ca. April 1970), Szell asked Edgar Vincent, "Any news about the other house? They offered me that job once." That would have been by Edward Johnson in 1947 or 1948, before Bing was engaged. Szell declined the offer, because he had only begun with the Cleveland Orchestra in 1946. He said the job could not be done by anyone with his standards. Vincent interview, July 6, 1976.

80. For Szell's total Met repertoire, see appendix F.

Chapter 5. Cleveland: Contest and Commitment (1942–47)

1. John Selby, "Cleveland Needs Symphony Leader," *Newport News* (Rhode Island), January 28, 1943.

2. Milton Widder, "Rodzinski Wants a Good Conductor as Successor," *CP*, January 23, 1943.

3. "Outlines Job for Conductor," *CP*, January 30, 1943.

4. Milton Widder, "Wallenstein, Stoessel, Leinsdorf Head List of Candidates for Orchestra Post," *CP*, February 3, 1943; "Leinsdorf to Speak at Opera Meet," *CP*, March 13, 1943.

5. Related to the author by A. Beverly Barksdale, Cleveland Orchestra Manager 1957–70, April 18, 1975.

6. Widder, "Leinsdorf to Speak . . ." March 13, 1943.

7. In 1932 Szell had been recommended by William Walter, former manager of the St. Louis Symphony.

8. Judson had told Szell that he would not have a chance. On his own, Szell contacted Sidlo; Sidlo was not available and trustee Edgar Hahn escorted Szell. Interview with A. Beverly Barksdale, April 18, 1975; entries in Percy W. Brown's diary, graciously made available by his son, Edward R. Brown.

9. Milton Widder, "Erich Leinsdorf to Conduct Operas for Metropolitan," *CP*, October 9, 1944.

10. Marcel Dick interview, Cleveland, April 13, 1975. The cellos and violas enter quietly a fifth apart on the first beat, so that the first violins can start the main theme, beginning after an eighth rest. If the cellos or violas are late or not together, the violin entrance will be shaky at best.

11. Barksdale interview, April 18, 1975; "Arthur Shepherd Writes About Szell's Conducting," *CP*, November 4, 1944.

12. "American for Symphony," *PD*, January 16, 1944.

13. "Brilliant Baton Debut for Szell," *PD*, November 3, 1944.

14. "Rubinstein and Szell Applauded," *PD*, November 10, 1944.

15. "Szell Success Stirs New Severance Hall Gossip," *CN*, November 11, 1944.

16. "Szell Gets Big Ovations Here, Also on Tour," *CN*, November 13, 1944.

17. John G. Teltsch interview, March 11, 1992, for oral history of the Cleveland Orchestra, by Carol Jacobs, archivist of the Cleveland Orchestra, and Dorothy Humel Hovorka, trustee of the Music Arts Association.

18. Szell to Vosburgh, January 17, 1945.

19. "Szell and Orchestra Win with Music of Brahms and Bartok," *PD*, January 4, 1945.

20. Milton Widder, "Music Patrons Applaud Szell's Final Concert," *CP*, January 4, 1946.

21. "George Szell Talks to John Culshaw."

22. January 23, 1946, NWA.

23. A poll of board members indicated that 85 percent of the trustees favored Szell's engagement. Minutes of the Board of Trustees of the Musical Arts Association, January 24, 1946; March 7, 1946.

24. "Cleveland's Pride," *Newsweek*, February 4, 1946. According to *Time*, "Talk about Cleveland," February 4, 1946, Szell's salary was "more than $30,000 a year, the largest ever paid to a Cleveland conductor," MAA. The $40,000 salary is reported by Donald Rosenberg in *The Cleveland Orchestra Story "Second to None"* (Cleveland: Gray, 2000), 307. In 1948 Sidlo told the trustees, "At a meeting of Symphony Orchestra Presidents in New York last week, I learned that ours was the lowest salary paid any conductor of the orchestras represented at the meeting, viz,. Boston, New York, Philadelphia, Chicago and Cleveland; that the salaries of the others ranged from $50,000 to $100,000." December 8, 1948. Leinsdorf's and Rodzinski's salaries provided in a note from Rosenberg, January 17, 2002.

25. January 24, 1946.

26. Elmore Bacon, "Szell Named Conductor of Orchestra," *CN*, January 25, 1946 (dummy paper prepared during news strike).

27. Milton Widder, "Szell Foresees 'Great' Orchestra," *CP*, May 15, 1946.

28. To Oldberg, January 23, 1946, NWA.

29. A. H. Thomas, "Szell—Champion of the Classics," *Brisbane Telegraph*, June 29, 1938.

30. Interview with Jane Bourne, a trustee of the Women's Committee at the time and later a trustee of the Musical Arts Association, August 10, 1988.

31. Sidlo, Minutes of the Musical Arts Association, January 24, 1946.

32. "Cleveland Orchestra Stands at Threshold of Great Season," *PD*, September 8, 1946.

33. "George Szell Talks to John Culshaw."

34. In St. Louis in 1930 and 1931, Szell had become acquainted with the second-oldest orchestra in the country. It was then not in a position for major growth—it lacked a fine hall of its own and the artistic and business leadership that would come some years later.

35. In his review of opening night, one critic wrote, "Even a repainted stage set transformed from blue to buff helped to strengthen the feeling that a new dispensation was to be in effect." Arthur Loesser, "Szell Proves Authority in Symphony Opener," *CP*, October 18, 1946.

36. Interview with James Barrett, Cleveland Orchestra violinist, Cleveland, 1975. Orchestra contracts today generally prohibit individual exposure of string section musicians, although principal wind and brass players play individual parts. In the normal course of rehearsals conductors may routinely ask them to play alone or in small groups, while strings are generally rehearsed by full sections.

37. "Krueger Accuses Szell of 'Pirating' Violinist," regarding Josef Gingold, *NYT*, February 21, 1947. Depending on one's point of view, orchestras that lose players call it pirating, orchestras to which players move call it recruiting.

38. E. J. Kulas was a vice president of the Musical Arts Association; he and his wife, Fynette, were trustees.

39. Olin Downes, "Apprentice to a Conductor," *NYT*, June 2, 1946. In 1946–47, John Boda and Theodore Bloomfield were apprentice conductors. Boda made an academic career; Bloomfield conducted orchestras and opera houses internationally, and returned to Cleveland as a guest conductor in 1962–63.

40. Louise Davis, "Cleveland Orchestra Women Meet Conductor George Szell," *PD*, October 15, 1946.

41. Edward Greenfield, "The discipline of the hard Szell," *The Guardian*, May 28, 1968.

42. Interview with record producer Paul Myers, Columbia Masterworks Record BTS 31.

43. Ibid.

44. Louis Lane oral history interview, January 15, 1992, for oral history of the Cleveland Orchestra, by Carol Jacobs, archivist of the Cleveland Orchestra, Dorothy Humel Hovorka, trustee, and Klaus George Roy, program annotator of the orchestra.

45. Arthur Loesser, "Szell Proves Authority in Symphony Opener," October 18, 1946. Szell's tempo of the *Marcia funebre* had been criticized by some New York critics; Loesser felt that Szell got it just right.

46. "Szell Baton Masterful in Symphony Opener," *PD*, October 18, 1946.

47. "Cleveland Orchestra Is Heard under Szell," *NYHT*, October 18, 1946. "Szell, as Conductor, Opens in Cleveland," *NYT*, October 18, 1946.

48. October 19, 1946, NYPhA.

49. Interview with Leon Fleisher, Blossom Music Center, August 6, 1988.

50. At this writing, Fleisher is making a welcome comeback to two-hand pianism. The pianist-conductor was honored with a Kennedy Center Award for excellence in the performing arts in December 2007.

51. Szell played "Dawn," "Sunday Morning," and "Storm," omitting the third: "Moonlight."

52. Some of the original discs were found by the author in 1988 in a trunk in the closet of Szell's former Severance Hall study. Among these were some from Szell's guest

conducting in 1944 and his first season as musical director in 1946; a timely record of the orchestra's ability and Szell's interpretive ideas. Some of these are included in the ten-CD set, "The Cleveland Orchestra Seventy-Fifth Anniversary Compact Disc Edition," The Musical Arts Association, Cleveland, 1993.

53. Elmore Bacon, "Szell Inspired in Czech Program Is Given Ovation," *CN*, November 1, 1946.

54. Interview with Norman Hollander, former cellist in Cleveland, Kansas City, Missouri, September 29, 1975.

55. When Tchaikovsky conducted the premiere of his Fifth Symphony in St. Petersburg in 1888, it was not a success. Nikisch's subsequent brilliant performances proved the work's greatness.

56. Milton Widder, "Notes and Sketches," *CP*, January 4, 1947.

57. Minutes of the Musical Arts Association, January 14, 1947.

58. "Thaviu Quits Position with Symphony," *CP*, January 30, 1947. Thaviu returned to the Pittsburgh Symphony, where he served with distinction for many years as concertmaster under William Steinberg, but never forgave Szell. Conversation with the author, Pittsburgh, February 1968.

59. "Longhair Brushes Stiffen as Symphony Orks Comb Out Gripes," March 8, 1947.

60. "Szell and Vosburgh Scoff at Detroit 'Pirate' Charge," *PD*, February 21, 1947; Elmore Bacon, "Artur Rodzinski's Attempt to Raid Cleveland Orchestra 'First-Chairs,'" *CN*, February 19, 1947.

61. Harvey Taylor, "Gingold Secrecy Angers Krueger," *Detroit Times*, February 21, 1947.

62. Note from Louis Lane, who heard it directly from Gingold, June 2002.

63. Farkas had left the Cleveland Orchestra in 1945 for the Boston Symphony, but Szell reengaged him for Cleveland's 1946–47 season. He later became first horn in Chicago, but at Szell's invitation, Farkas joined the Cleveland Orchestra as an extra on some of the orchestra's international tours.

64. Milton Widder, "Fuchs Quits Cleveland Orchestra," *CP*, February 15, 1947.

65. "We Ask Mr. Szell," *CP*, February 18, 1947.

66. "Letter Attacks Szell, Reveals Orchestra Unrest," *CP*, March 27, 1947.

67. Interview with Marcel Dick, April 13, 1975.

68. Carlton K. Matson, "George Szell, and the Musicians' Protest," *CP*, March 29, 1947.

69. "George Szell Talks to John Culshaw."

70. Interview, April 13, 1975.

71. Carlton K. Matson, "George Szell, and the Musicians' Protest."

72. "New Orchestra Cellist Makes Bow at Opera," *CN*, April 9, 1947.

73. In the 1959–60 season, Silberstein and Adolphe Frezin were called "co-principals," in 1960–61, Frezin held the title of principal and Silberstein was coprincipal. In 1961–62, Jules Eskin was named principal. Frezin left, and Silberstein occupied second chair, but without a title.

74. "Orchestra Glows for 9,547 Friends," *PD*, April 2, 1947; *PD*, April 18, 1947.

75. Minutes of the Musical Arts Association, April 18, 1947.

76. "Sidlo Proudly Cites Three Records Set by Orchestra," *PD*, June 26, 1947.

77. Szell's program, repeated on April 29 and 30, and May 1 and 2, consisted of: Wagner: Overture to *Tannhäuser*, Prelude to Act 1 of *Lohengrin*, Prelude and Liebestod from *Tristan und Isolde*, and Brahms's Symphony no. 2; Shanet, *Philharmonic*, 537–38.

78. Miller, *Edinburgh International Festival*, 1–2.

79. HAPPY TO OFFER YOU BOTH OPERAS MACBETH AND FIGARO NINE EACH BETWEEN AUGUST 25 SEPTEMBER 13 FIVE WEEKS REHEARSALS PRECEDING DETAILED LETTER UNDER WAY STOP SO FAR GRANDI VALENTINO AND ENGLISH BASS ENGAGED FOR MACBETH ITALO TAO [*sic*] FIGARO ELEANOR STEBER COUNTESS JOHN BROWNLEE COUNT AND *YOUR SCOTTISH ORCHESTRA* [emphasis added] STOP PLEASE ADVISE URGENTLY SUSANNA CHERUBINO STOP HAVE JUST COMMUNICATED FINANCIAL OFFER IBBSTILLETT HOPE SINCERELY YOU WILL ACCEPT, REGARDS BING GLYNDOPERA. Telegram from Rudolf Bing in London to Szell at Severance Hall, November 22, 1946. Forwarded by Day Letter by George H. L. Smith to Szell c/o Eric Oldberg in Chicago, November 23, 1946. Ibbs and Tillett was Szell's artist management in Great Britain.

80. Bing, *Memoirs*, 121.

81. Szell to Schnabel, August 11, 1947. In Edinburgh, Schnabel would give "solo recitals and a cycle of Brahms, Schumann, and Mendelssohn chamber music with Joseph Szigeti, William Primrose, and Pierre Fournier," Bing, *Memoirs*, 118.

Chapter 6. Szell, the Orchestra Builder (1947–54)

1. To Smith, August 6, 1946; September 15, 1946.

2. To Vosburgh, August 12, 1947.

3. Telephone interview with Louis Lane, June 16, 2002.

4. Ibid.

5. "Orchestra Shows Musical Mastery," *CP*, October 10, 1947.

6. "Revitalized Orchestra Thrills First-Nighters," *PD*, October 10, 1947.

7. Ernst Silberstein, cello; Bert Gassman, oboe; Bernard Portnoy, clarinet; Frank Brouk, horn were the new replacements.

8. With contralto Louise Bernhardt and tenor Set Svanholm.

9. Arthur Shepherd, former assistant conductor (1920–26), had been music critic of the *Cleveland Press*, and from 1920 to 1930 was editor of the orchestra's program notes.

10. The Toch work was not only a world premiere but had been commissioned by the orchestra under a grant from the Kulas Foundation; others were *Poem for Orchestra* by William Grant Still, *Concerto for Orchestra* by Morton Gould, and works by Lukas Foss and Randall Thompson. The foundation also funded the apprentice conductor program and underwrote many children's concerts.

11. "Orchestra's Year Is $12,000 in Red," *PD*, June 24, 1948.

12. Szell to Vosburgh, June 12, 1948. The New York Philharmonic appeared at the Edinburgh Festival in 1955, the Cleveland Orchestra in 1967.

13. December 8, 1948.

14. *NYHT*, June 27, 1948. Lane stayed on as keyboard player, and was groomed by Szell for a staff conducting position.

15. Thomas L. Sidlo, "Report on the Maintenance Fund," Cleveland Orchestra program book, October 28 and 30, 1948, 104.

16. Elmore Bacon, "Szell Contract for 1949 Poses Problem in Symphony Circles," *CN*, September 18, 1948. Bacon also reported gossip that Szell might replace Ormandy in Philadelphia or "the aging Bruno Walter" in New York. Walter had turned seventy-two three days earlier (he died in 1962 at age eighty-five).

17. Hanson to Sidlo, May 26, 1947; Sidlo to Vosburgh, May 29, 1947. The *Merry Mount* Suite was the first of five Hanson works performed by the Cleveland Orchestra in the next eleven years—one conducted by the composer, the rest by Szell.

18. Desmond Shawe-Taylor, "The Length of Mahler," reprinted from the *New Statesman and Nation*, London, April 10, 1948, Cleveland Orchestra concert booklet, October 28 and 30, 1948, 119–23. Szell's timings for the Schubert averaged fifty minutes, for the Mahler, seventy-four.

19. November 6, 1948.

20. Percy Brown diary, November 16, 1948; December 6, 1948.

21. Minutes of the Board of Trustees of the Musical Arts Association, December 8, 1948. Sidlo had learned about other conductors' salaries at a meeting of symphony orchestra presidents in New York the previous week.

22. J. C. Daschbach, "Extend Szell Contract until Spring of 1950," *PD*, December 9, 1948.

23. Szell to Oldberg, December 10, 1948, NWA.

24. "Pianist Serkin, Composer Shapero Hailed," *CP*, December 17, 1948.

25. "Serkin Sparkles in Brahms Concerto with Orchestra," *PD*, December 17, 1948.

26. Aaron Copland, *Copland on Music* (New York: Schirmer Books, 1960), 169–70.

27. Mark Swed, "40 Years Later, but It's Never too Late," *NYT*, May 8, 1988, MCA.

28. "Pianist Serkin, Composer Shapero Hailed," *CP*, December 17, 1948.

29. Smith to Shapero, December 21, 1948.

30. Shapero to Smith, January 2, 1949.

31. Lane interview, July 5, 2002. In 1992 guest conductor André Previn closed the circle, conducting Shapero's symphony in Cleveland.

32. Arthur Loesser, "American Symphony Hailed at 2nd 'Debut' Here," *CP*, February 4, 1949.

33. "National Art Group Chooses Szell for Its Advisory Board," *PD*, January 28, 1949.

34. "Szell, Orchestra Win High Praise at Carnegie Hall," February 16, 1949.

35. Szell to Smith, June 2, 1948.

36. March 5, 1949.

37. Minutes of the Meeting of the Board of Trustees of the Musical Arts Association, March 7, 1949; March 28, 1949.

38. Undated letter, probably August 1949. Vosburgh wrote Szell that season ticket

sales were going excellently, and projected that they could "improve the present total to at least $5000."

39. Roy Harris's Third Symphony had been announced, but Szell evidently had second thoughts and repeated the Barber instead.

40. W. Holden White, "Szell Pleased by His Reception in Britain," *PD*, June 19, 1949.

41. Herbert Elwell, "U.S. Music Is Gaining Abroad, Szell Finds," *PD*, September 26, 1949. An example Szell gave of what he termed the "intense craving for music in Europe" was the fact that although the top-price seats for *Rosenkavalier* in Salzburg cost 75 Austrian schillings, tickets for those seats were traded in the black market for between 400 and 800 schillings.

42. Ibid.

43. W. Holden White, "Szell Pleased. . ."

44. "Symphony Board Re-Elects Sidlo, Bright Artistic Outlook Seen, Finances Cloudy," *PD*, June 23, 1949.

45. While in Amsterdam he visited the Rijksmuseum, writing Oldberg about a painting that deeply impressed him: "When I saw Rembrandt's picture of the Brain Surgeon of which I am enclosing a photo—helas a poor one, the colored one is out of print. Do you know it? How do you like the assistant holding the skull (or do you say cranium?) in his hand and the patient seeming conscious?!" Szell to Oldberg, July 18, 1949, NWA.

46. August 26, 1949.

47. Undated, probably late August 1949.

48. Other members of the jury were Eugene Istomin, Nadia Reisenberg, Rudolf Serkin, Alexander Schneider, Lillian Fuchs, and Arthur Judson.

49. Cleveland Orchestra apprentice conductor Seymour Lipkin was the winner of the Rachmaninoff competition.

50. Graffman wrote amusingly of his experiences with Szell in his entertaining book, *I Really Should Be Practicing* (Garden City, N.Y.: Doubleday, 1981).

51. Herbert Elwell, "U.S. Music Is Gaining Abroad, Szell Finds," *PD*, September 26, 1949.

52. "Finds Gemlike Polish in Orchestra Opening," *PD*, September 30, 1949.

53. Thomas Sidlo, Cleveland Orchestra program book, September 29 and October 1, 1949, 10.

54. "Mozart's 'Jupiter' Symphony Played Radiantly," *PD*, December 30, 1949. Thomson was awarded the Pulitzer Prize for music for his *Louisiana Story* in 1949.

55. Undated interview with Louis Lane.

56. Elwell, December 30, 1949.

57. W. H. Cunningham, "Friends 40 Years. Szell, Serkin Reunited by Concert Here," unidentified clipping, ca. February 1952.

58. Virgil Thomson, "Music; Cleveland Orchestra; Wondrous Musical Beauties," *NYHT*, February 15, 1950.

59. Mitropoulos was conductor of the New York Philharmonic. Steinberg conducted the Buffalo Philharmonic. Walter was a favorite guest conductor of the New York Philharmonic.

60. April 4, 1950.

61. March 15, 1950.

62. Interview with John S. Edwards, Chicago, July 25, 1980. Edwards had been manager of the National Symphony in Washington when Szell was a guest conductor. Edwards said, when his name was put forward to replace Cleveland Orchestra manager Carl Vosburgh, who died in 1955, that Szell vetoed it.

63. Szell's contract, March 31, 1950.

64. Minutes of the Musical Arts Association, June 9, 1950. The new contract was for 1950–51, 1951–52, and 1952–53.

65. July 2, 1950; September 3, 1950.

66. James Frankel, "Szell Back for Fifth Music Season," *CP*, September 26, 1950.

67. September 3, 1950.

68. Arthur Loesser, "Music Lovers Hail Orchestra Opener," *CP* October 6, 1950.

69. *Paganiniana* (1942) was commissioned by the Vienna Philharmonic, a virtuoso orchestra, on the occasion of its one hundredth anniversary. Karl Böhm conducted its premiere. Based on fragments from the *Caprices* by its namesake, the four-movement work displays every section of the orchestra in a whirlwind of technique.

70. Arthur Loesser, "Music Lovers."

71. Witnessed by the author on more than one occasion.

72. Minutes of the Musical Arts Association, October 20, 1950.

73. Ibid. The chorus for the Beethoven Ninth was made up of the combined choruses of Western Reserve University, the Fairmont Presbyterian Church, and the Church of the Covenant, with the addition of other choral singers. It was trained by Russell L. Gee and Robert M. Stofer, two prominent local choral directors.

74. Elwell, "Audience Cheers Orchestra for Great Beethoven Ninth," *PD*, April 27, 1951; Loesser, "Beethoven Ninth Exalting at Severance," *CP*, April 27, 1951; Bacon, "Szell's Beethoven Ninth Thrills Capacity Crowd," *CN*, April 27, 1951.

75. To Zirato, October 11, 1950, NYPhA. Rabin died an untimely death in 1972, at the age of thirty-five.

76. Dick was head of the Cleveland Institute of Music's composition department.

77. January 2, 1951.

78. January 5, 1951.

79. George J. Barmann, "Think of Obligations First, Reserve Graduates Are Told," *PD*, February 3, 1951.

80. Variously reported: $42,000—"Around the Town," *CP*, May 2, 1951; $36,000—"Szell Buys a 14-Room House in Shaker Hts.," *CN*, May 16, 1951.

81. Cantrick's project was supported by the Ford Foundation through the Fund for the Advancement of Education, to which he wrote a six-page report on July 16, 1952. Included in the extensive material he furnished to the author in July 2004.

82. Szell to Cantrick, July 26, 1951, courtesy of Robert Cantrick.

83. Thompson to Szell, November 28, 1952, Cantrick material.

84. Thompson to Cantrick, December 8, 1952. Cantrick material.

85. Thompson to Cantrick, June 1, 1953, Cantrick material.

86. Cantrick died in 2006, and his family has donated a copy of this invaluable material, including his notes on conversations with Szell, to the archives of the Musical Arts Association.

87. In Szell's first season there were six new principals, in his second there were four. In only one other season during his tenure were there four changes of principal players—two or three were more usual. In Szell's twenty-four years there were seven seasons with just one change in principal players and seven with no changes in these key positions.

88. Louis Lane, telephone interview, August 2002; note, June 16, 2002.

89. Louis Lane, note, April 2002; and interview, June 16, 2002. As far as their conducting qualifications, Szell was suspicious of the musicianship of violinists, which Ormandy had been, calling them "one-line musicians." Szell favored conductors who were pianists because they play and therefore hear multiple lines, a basic feature of orchestral music. Szell would not consider anyone for apprentice conductor who was not an excellent pianist, no matter how well they played another instrument.

90. Louis Lane interview, June 16, 2002.

91. Bernard Wagenaar (1894–1971) was the son of Johan Wagenaar (1862–1941), whose overture, *Cyrano de Bergerac*, Szell had conducted with the Concertgebouw. Bernard came to the United States in 1920 as violinist in the New York Philharmonic. He then taught composition and theory at the Institute of Musical Art, predecessor of the Juilliard School of Music.

92. Louis Lane, note, July 5, 2002. Lane informed me that *Also sprach Zarathustra* was conducted by Carvalho. Szell told Lane that he had never conducted that work and never would.

93. Herbert Elwell, "Szell Has Three Roles in Concert," *PD*, October 19, 1951. Previous honorees were Serge Koussevitzky, Eugene Ormandy, Leopold Stokowski, and Alfred Wallenstein.

94. Szell to Zirato, October 22, 1951; Zirato to Szell, October 25; Szell to Zirato, October 29, NYPhA.

95. "Wagenaar Music Proves Stirring," *PD*, November 2, 1951.

96. Szell to Zirato, November 3, 1951, NYPhA.

97. Zirato to Szell, November 6, 1951; Szell to Zirato, November 13, 1951; Zirato to Szell, November 16, 1951, NYPhA.

98. December 17, 1951.

99. "Szell Back Here from N. Y. Stint; Plans to Remain," unidentified Cleveland clipping, January 1, 1952.

100. Flagstad never sang with Szell at the Met. She left in 1941 to be with her husband, Henry Johanson, in Norway, where she stayed throughout the war.

101. Elmore Bacon, "Flagstad, Szell Are Given Biggest Ovation of Season," *CN*, March 14, 1952; Herbert Elwell, "Flagstad Scores Triumph before Overflow Audience," *PD*, March 14, 1952;"Flagstad, Cleveland Orchestra, Present Notable Concert," *Toledo Blade*; March 14, 1952.

102. To Louise Fry, April 19, 1952, NYPhA.

103. "Szell Triumphs Again in Orchestra Finale," *CP*, April 25, 1952.

104. The ceremony took place in Finney Memorial Chapel, architect Cass Gilbert's 1908 Mediterranean Romanesque-style building in whose warm acoustics the Cleveland Orchestra had performed over the years, for the past six under Szell.

105. John G. Teltsch, *Sursam corda* ("Raise Up Your Hearts"), a personal memoir (privately published, 1993).

106. To Helene, July 13 and 20, 1952.

107. Szell to Zirato, July 24, 1952; Zirato to Szell, July 28, 1952, NYPhA.

108. *Die Liebe der Danae*, libretto by Josef Gregor, was written in 1938–40. It had been rehearsed at the 1944 Salzburg Festival, but there were no public performances.

109. Elmore Bacon, "Szell Sets Salzburg Precedent Batoning in White at Festival," *CN*, August 27, 1952; quoting from a letter from Szell to George H. L. Smith.

110. "Szell Back, All Set to 'Pitch' Thursday," *CN*, October 1, 1952.

111. November 3, 1952, NYPhA.

112. Schumann Symphony no. 2 and Brahms Piano Concerto no. 1 with Rudolf Serkin.

113. James Frankel, "Cleveland Orchestra Renews Szell Contract," *CP*, January 6, 1953.

114. "Compatibility in Cleveland," *Time*, January 12, 1953.

115. "Curzon Is Soloist for Philharmonic. Szell Conducts Orchestra in Haydn Symphony, Piano Concerto by Brahms," *NYT*, January 9, 1953, NYPhA.

116. Gerald Moore, *Furthermoore* (London: Hamish Hamilton, 1983), 110–11.

117. Years later, the author witnessed rehearsals and a performance of the same concerto in Carnegie Hall. The orchestra played the concerto with as much polish and style as they did the symphonies. The tuttis in outer movements of the "Emperor" had brilliance and power, while the middle movement had an ethereal air of tranquility and repose. Curzon was a dynamo of intense energy who, when called for by the music, could produce thunderous sonorities as well as extract the most exquisite delicacies from the keyboard.

118. "Szell Conducts in Carnegie Hall," *NYT*, February 11, 1953. Downes was used to the then-current seating of the Philharmonic, forgetting that ten years earlier Rodzinski had seated that orchestra with the violins together on the conductor's left.

119. Some conductors in the late twentieth and early twenty-first centuries have split the violins in their orchestras: Christoph von Dohnanyi, in the latter part of his tenure with the Cleveland Orchestra, and James Levine, at the Metropolitan Opera and the Boston Symphony.

120. "Visitors from Ohio," *NYHT*, February 11, 1953.

121. San Francisco Symphony conductors: Pierre Monteux, 1935–52, and Enrique Jorda, 1954–64.

122. "George Szell Leads S. F. Symphony," *San Francisco Chronicle*, March 28, 1953.

123. This aided Szell to perform a major segment of the literature with commensurate quality of all forces involved. The choral directors who prepared the Ninth, Robert M. Stofer and Russell L. Gee, were in charge of the new orchestra chorus.

124. Herbert Elwell, "Orchestra Gives Historic Concert," *PD*, May 1, 1953.

125. To Helene, July 15, 1953; July 22, 1953.

126. August 18, 1953.

127. Milton Widder, Interview, *CP*, September 26, 1953.
128. Mrs. Samuel Whitman, "Just What Is Vulgar?" *CP*, September 29, 1953.
129. "New Brown Team Already Scoring Musical Touchdowns," *CP*, October 3, 1953.
130. "Szell and Orchestra Win Opening Ovation," *PD*, October 9, 1953.
131. "Elwell 'Ritual' Given Stirring Debut," *CP*, October 30, 1953.
132. "Szell and Opera Singers Click in Wagner's 'Valkyrie,'" *PD*, November 6, 1953.
133. December 20, 1953, NYPhA.

Chapter 7. George Szell and Rudolf Bing (1953–54)

1. "Metropolitan Opera Engages Szell and Monteux as Conductors of German and French Sections," *NYT*, December 11, 1952, MOA.
2. Interview with Max Rudolf, July 28, 1987.
3. Szell's first Metropolitan Opera contract, signed by Szell and general manager Edward Johnson on October 16, 1942, engaged the conductor for ten weeks (from November 23, 1942, to January 31, 1943) at $400 per week, with the stipulation that he would not be asked to conduct more than four performances a week. The dates included two weeks of rehearsal, but the contract also stipulated that Szell would make himself available gratis for preliminary rehearsals from November 9, MOA.
4. Max Rudolf to H. Wendell Endicott, Boston Opera Association, December 9, 1953, MOA.
5. Szell to Rudolf, October 12, 1953, MOA
6. Rudolf to Szell, May 13, 1953; Szell to Rudolf, May 15, 1953, MOA.
7. "Music: *Tannhäuser*," *NYHT*, December 28, 1953.
8. Szell to Zirato, January 13, 1954, MOA.
9. "Szell Severs Tie with Metropolitan; Kullman Takes Role on Short Notice," *NYT*, January 15, 1954, MOA.
10. Jay S. Harrison, "Szell Conducts Tannhaeuser," *NYHT*, January 15, 1954; Paul V. Beckley, "Szell Quits Met Tonight, Hit at 'Present Conditions,'" *NYHT*, January 15, 1954, MOA. In the article, according to an unnamed member of the Met orchestra, Szell's relations with the orchestra were described as "perfect." Harriett Johnson, "Szell vs. Bing in Met Row," *NYP*, January 15, 1954, MOA. *Mise-en-scène* could mean either the stage set or the stage direction. Szell evidently had no quarrel with Graf's direction but still strongly objected to the ground plan of Act 2. That was the designer's province, but Graf had defended it.
11. Interview with Max Rudolf, July 28, 1987.
12. The last occasion was a few days before the final dress rehearsal of *Tannhäuser*. Bing called Szell's bluff and made arrangements for Rudolf to take over the conducting. Szell apologized to Bing and "eventually conducted a very successful performance," Bing to Zirato, January 18, 1954, MOA.
13. Bing to Zirato, January 18, 1954, MOA.
14. Rudolf to the author, October 10, 1987.
15. Bing to Zirato, January 18, 1954, MOA; interview with Max Rudolf, July 28, 1987. Bing was equally high-handed with singers when it suited him.

16. "New Yorkers Love Szell Even If He's Outlander," *CPD*, January 17, 1954.

17. "Szell vs. Bing in Met Row," *NYP*, January 15, 1954, MOA.

18. January 14, 1954; January 18, 1954; January 20, 1954; January 23, 1954, MOA.

19. In efforts to cover themselves against future fallout, Bing and Zirato exchanged letters regarding Bing's assertion to Zirato that he had told the manager he could tell Szell that Szell could write a letter of resignation. Zirato wrote, for the record, that Bing never told him that, to which Bing replied that indeed he did and Zirato may not have heard him. Bing had also stated that Szell made his letter public before Bing knew of it, and Zirato countered that he read Szell's letter to Bing over the telephone the afternoon before it came out, to which Bing had replied "Perfect." Bing to Zirato January 18, 1954, Zirato to Bing January 21, 1954, Bing to Zirato January 23, 1954, MOA.

20. This reconciliation is also suggested because the Szells attended a Met performance with Bing in his box. Interview with Edgar Vincent, publicist for Szell and the Cleveland Orchestra, September 14, 1976.

21. The original letter is missing, along with the rest of Szell's Cleveland Orchestra files. A copy, undated and without address, was found in the files of A. Beverly Barksdale (manager from 1957–70) in the orchestra's archives.

22. Judson to Szell, January 8, 1954, NYPhA.

23. Milt Widder, "Sights and Sounds," *CP*, January 19, 1954.

24. Rudolf Bing, *The Memoirs of Sir Rudolf Bing, 5,000 Nights at the Opera* (New York: Doubleday, 1972), 177.

25. Telephone conversation with Louis Perelman, December 11, 2010.

Chapter 8. Keeping the Promise: "Second to None" (1954–57)

1. This workshop took place January 23 to February 4, 1954; a second, March 5 to 19, 1955; and a third, September 24 to October 11, 1956. Almost all the participants were already conductors of smaller orchestras or were eventually to have their own orchestras.

2. "The Grammar of Conducting," (New York: Schirmer Books, 1950, 3rd ed., 1993). Interview with the author, Philadelphia, October 22, 1987. Rudolf reported then that well more than 100,000 copies of the first two editions had been sold.

3. "Conductors and Musicians; Ten Golden Rules," from *Recollections and Reflections*, *Symphony* magazine, November 1953, 7.

4. Herbert Elwell, "Szell Hails Role of Impulse at Conductors' Workshop," *PD*, January 24, 1954.

5. Louis Lane, telephone interview, July 21, 1991.

6. "New Music Symposium Shows Szell Leads Field," *PD*, April 4, 1954.

7. Jim Frankel, "State Will Subsidize Music, Szell Predicts," *CP*, October 1, 1954.

8. "Orchestra Gets the Best, and Offers the Best, Too," October 5, 1954.

9. Bloom would be Szell's fourth and last principal horn, and Marcellus his third and final principal clarinet. Among the winds and brasses, three men would serve as principal trumpet under Szell: Louis Davidson, Richard Smith, and Bernard Adelstein. Szell had only two first trombones: Merritt Dittert and Robert Boyd. The principal oboes were more volatile. Szell had six of them: Philip Kirchner, Bert Gassman, Emanuel Tivin,

Marc Lifschey, Alfred Genovese, and John Mack. There was similar range in the numbers of principal strings during Szell's tenure—two second violinists (Hyman Schandler and Bernhard Goldschmidt), two double basses (Jacques Posell and David Perlman), two violas (Marcel Dick and Abraham Skernick), six cellos (Harry Fuchs, Ernst Silberstein, Adolphe Frezin, Jules Eskin, Gerald Appleman, and Lynn Harrell), and four concertmasters (Samuel Thaviu, Josef Gingold, Rafael Druian, and Daniel Majeske). The position of assistant concertmaster served as a training ground and stepping stone for a succession of talented young violinists, chosen by Szell and trained by him and his concertmasters, who went on to be concertmasters in other orchestras or, in Majeske's case, the Cleveland Orchestra itself. Arnold Steinhardt, after five seasons with the orchestra, founded the venerable Guarnieri String Quartet as first violinist. The others were Jacob Krachmalnick, Berl Senofsky, Anshel Brusilow, Majeske, and William Steck.

10. "Award to Szell," *NYHT*, December 30, 1954.

11. Szell to Helene, January 14, 1955, MAA. Hunter succeeded Rudolf Bing as director of the Edinburgh Festival.

12. "Zürcher Konzerte" (Zurich concerts), February 1955; ohr, "Sechstes Abonnementskonzert" ("Sixth Subscription Concert"), Zurich, January 25, 1955, translation by the author.

13. Item, *CN*, April 4, 1955: "George H.L. Smith, acting manager of the Cleveland Orchestra, is believed to be on deck to succeed the late Carl Vosburgh—the post is to be filled at a meeting on Friday." Martin's appointment was announced three days later: "Pick New Orchestra Manager," *CN*, April 7, 1955.

14. Sullivan: "Little Old New York"; Bean letter, April 11, 1955, NYPhA.

15. "New Work at Salzburg," London, August 21, 1955; "Salzburg," London, September 4, 1955. In the 1960s, the author, as associate conductor of the Lake Erie Opera Theater, having attended a performance in Germany of the Egk opera years before, and unaware of Szell's involvement with the work, suggested presenting *Irische Legende*. Without a word, Szell wrinkled his nose as if smelling a bad odor and shook his head vigorously. The matter was dropped.

16. Jim Frankel, "Orchestra Plans Tour of Europe," *CP*, August 17, 1955.

17. h.g., "Festpiele in Edinburgh," *Nationalzeitung Basel*, September 16, 1955. Szell conducted works by Brahms, Sibelius, and Wagner.

18. Uncredited New York interviewer: "Anniversary Appraisal, Szell Seeks More Summer Music, Pension for Symphony," *Special to the Press*, *CP*, September 24, 1955.

19. "Anniversary Year," *CP*, February 19, 1955.

20. The L.E.O.T.'s board of directors represented leading northern Ohio arts organizations, headed by Dorothy Humel, who was a longtime trustee of the Musical Arts Association.

21. J. A. Wadovick, "Szell Honored on 10th Season," *PD*, October 29, 1955.

22. Including Saul Goodman, longtime timpanist of the Philharmonic. Interview with the author, August 3, 1986.

23. Howard Shanet, *Philharmonic. A History of New York's Orchestra* (New York: Doubleday, 1975), 323–24. Shanet cites Howard Taubman's "The Philharmonic—What's

Wrong With It and Why," *NYT*, April 29, 1956, and Paul Henry Lang's three Sunday articles (*NYHT*) in June 1956 on the same subject.

24. "Music: Szell Conducts Beethoven. Podium Guest Leads Luminous Program," *NYT*, December 2, 1955.

25. "Musical Events. Too Many Cooks?" *TNY*, December 24, 1955.

26. "Shaw Here to Meet Orchestra," *CP*, January 9, 1956.

27. "Cleveland Orchestra Wins Praise in Carnegie Hall," *NYWT*, February 15, 1956.

28. "Music and Musicians. Cleveland vs. New York," *NYHT*, October 14, 1956.

29. Excerpted from the *London Daily Telegraph*, program book of the Cleveland Orchestra, December 6 and 8, 1956, 304.

30. Murray Seeger, "Cleveland Orchestra Manager Quits Post," *PD*, December 22, 1956; "Smith to Manage Orchestra Here," *CN*, December 22, 1956.

31. Szell, "Cleveland Orchestra Win N.Y.," undated, United Press, printed in Cleveland newspapers.

32. "The Evolution of an Orchestra, Szell and His Men Reach Peak of Art," *PD*, March 17, 1957.

33. Herbert Elwell, "Tribute to Beethoven Is Called Remarkable," *PD*, April 19, 1957.

34. "Tour Has Forced Changes in Program, Szell Explains," *PD*, March 13, 1957.

35. In future foreign tours, Szell would place stipulations on the concert and travel schedule to make it easier on himself and the orchestra, allowing more recovery time after travel, more days off, and no concerts on travel days.

36. October 25, 1955.

37. See appendix D, 1957 Tour Repertoire.

38. European tour quotations are from materials collected, translated, and reprinted by the Cleveland Orchestra's publicity department.

39. Kr., "Musikfest im Konzerthaus: Ovationen für George Szell," Vienna, June 8, 1957.

40. "A Great Orchestra," London, May 18, 1957.

41. "Festival Hall. The Cleveland Orchestra," London, May 11, 1957.

42. Telephone conversation with Louis Lane, June 16, 2002.

43. July 28, 1957.

44. *Swiat*, Warsaw; *Trybuna Robotnicza*, Katowice.

45. Frank E. Taplin, "The Cleveland Orchestra, Musical Ambassadors," *Fine Music*, Cleveland, June 1957.

46. "Szell Signs to Conduct in Holland," *PD*, May 27, 1957.

47. May 28, 1957.

48. "Szell Signs . . ." *PD*, May 27, 1957.

49. November 2, 1954; April 22, 1955; April 25, 1955, RCO.

50. May 26, 1955, RCO, translation from the German by the author.

51. June 22, 1955, RCO.

52. Herbert Elwell, "Szell Scores in Salzburg with Liebermann Opera," *PD*, September 1, 1957. A recording of the opera was released on CD, see discography for details.

53. Heinrich Kralik, *Die Presse* (Vienna), August 13, 1957. Recorded by the Austrian

Radio, both concerts were released by the Salzburg Festival in a three-CD set; see discography.

54. July 1, 1957; July 8, 1957; July 14, 1957.

55. Quoted by Joseph to Barksdale, July 15, 1957.

56. Szell to Barksdale July 22, 1957.

Chapter 9. The Golden Years (1957–65)

1. The audition process today, regulated by union contract, stipulates that auditions must take place on site, heard by committees of members of the orchestra, and generally, at least in the first round, requires auditioners to play behind a screen. (Cleveland resisted the screen until 2007.) The conductor might not be involved until the final round.

2. Samuels previously played in the Kansas City Philharmonic and the New Orleans Symphony. The thirty-two-year-old White, from Richmond, Indiana, had studied with Dudley Powers in Chicago and had been first cellist of the Chicago Civic Orchestra, the training arm of the Chicago Symphony. White later studied with Luigi Silva and Leonard Rose in New York, and was assistant first cellist of the Hartford (Conn.) Symphony.

3. In addition to a selection of orchestral excerpts, orchestra auditions usually require one or two solos (part of a movement of a concerto or two contrasting solos), without accompaniment.

4. Leonard Samuels, interview with the author, Cleveland, August 8, 1989.

5. Ethel Boros, *CN*, October 3, 1957; *PD*, October 4, 1957.

6. *Symphonium* (For and About the Professional African-American Symphony Musician), Vol. 5, no. 2, (Spring 1993): 1

7. Memo, Barksdale to Szell: "CONCERT—BIRMINGHAM, ALABAMA, October 20, 1969." The reason for Szell requesting this report of the incident is unknown, nor is there a record of its being used for any purpose.

8. The commissioned works were: Boris Blacher, *Music for Cleveland*, Op. 53; Paul Creston, *Toccata*, Op. 68; Henri Dutilleux, *Cinques Métaboles*; Gottfried von Einem, *Ballade for Orchestra*; Alvin Etler, *Concerto in One Movement*; Howard Hanson, *Mosaics*; Bohuslav Martinů, *The Rock, Prélude symphonique*; Peter Mennin, Concerto for Piano and Orchestra; Robert Moevs, *Symphony in Three Movements*; and William Walton, *Partita*. The orchestra performed the Dutilleux in the 1964–65 season.

9. Pieces by Auber, Barraud, Debussy, Ibert, Rózsa, and Suk were played for the first time in Cleveland. Tchaikovsky's *Capriccio Italien* was a first on subscription concerts.

10. "Orchestra's Skill Shows in 'Toccata,'" *PD*, October 18, 1957.

11. Cleveland Orchestra program book, January 16 and 18, 1958, 404. Newspapers and dates were: *Maasbode*, December 2, 1957; *Telegraaf*, December 13, 1957; *Volkskraut*, December 13, 1957.

12. "New Wardrobe for the Vienna State Opera Yesterday Evening: Szell Conducted 'Salome,'" *Bild Telegraf*, December 31, 1957; "George Szell: 'Salome' in Viennese Style," *Die Presse*, January 1, 1958; "George Szell Conducted 'Ariadne auf Naxos,'" *Neues Österreich*, January 1958; "Ariadne with tones like the Gobelin wallhangings of the Vienna Opera, George Szell weaves a masterfully discrete tapestry," *Welt Presse*, January 1958.

13. Herbert Schneiber, "Salome lived and loved fast and loud," *Wiener Kurier*, December 31, 1957.

14. February 2, 1957, RCO.

15. January 17, 1958; RCO.

16. "Szell, Erica Morini Share Fine Program," *PD*, January 17, 1958. Morini had made her debut with Szell at the Concertgebouw in the 1930s.

17. Peter Mennin, interview with the author, New York, December 14, 1981.

18. Program notes, Cleveland Orchestra program, February 27 and March 1, 1958, 536. The Mennin marked Podis's fiftieth performance with the orchestra, a number she eventually doubled. A native of Cleveland, Eunice Podis held the distinction of having appeared more frequently with the Cleveland Orchestra than any other soloist.

19. Eunice Podis, interview with the author, Cleveland, April 8, 1975.

20. "Miss Podis' Mastery of New Concerto Hailed," *PD*, February 28, 1958. Reprinted in the *PD*, "Cleveland Orchestra Wins Praise in N.Y.," March 1958. Mennin thought highly of Waldrop; in 1962, as president of Juilliard, he chose Waldrop as his dean.

21. To Waage, August 31, 1958, RCO. Szell may have had something to do with the Lucerne Festival's choice; he would conduct the Berlin Philharmonic at the 1960 festival.

22. Szell to Flothuis, September 25, 1958, RCO.

23. Swan to Vosburgh, December 30, 1947. Following the lead of Harvard physics Professor Wallace Clement Ware Sabine (1861–1919), a pioneer of acoustical studies, Swan compared reverberation times in other concert halls with that of Severance: Symphony Hall Boston, 2.31 seconds (Sabine was a consultant there from 1898–1900); Leipzig Gewandhaus, 2.44 seconds; Severance Hall, 1.6 seconds filled, 1.7 seconds empty. Swan worked as design consultant for the San Francisco Opera House, Toledo Art Museum, Green Hall at Smith College, and the Music Hall for the 1939 New York World's Fair.

24. November 20, 1953.

25. Robert Shankland, interview with the author, April 14, 1975.

26. "*Entr'acte*, A New Sound and A New Look in Severance Hall," Cleveland Orchestra Program Book, October 9 and 11, 1958, 24. The next major renovation of Severance Hall, including replacing Keilholz's shell, was undertaken in 1998. The reopening took place in January 2000 and was a triumph for acoustician Christopher Jaffe.

27. "Severance Gives Szell New, Rich Sonorities," *PD*, October 10, 1958.

28. Interview with the author, April 5, 1975.

29. Schonberg, "Firkusny Is Soloist with Clevelanders," *NYT*; Biancolli, "Cleveland Orchestra Plays at Carnegie Hall," *NYWT*; Lang, "Music, Cleveland Orchestra," *NYHT*; February 11, 1959.

30. "Intangible and Misunderstood," *MA*, editorial, May 6, 1963.

31. "Audiences Now Want to Hear New Works," *PD*, October 27, 1957.

32. Dick Kleiner, "Cleveland Audiences Trained, Szell Says," *NYWT*, March 28, 1959.

33. Interview with the author, July 28, 1989.

34. Telegram, April 13, 1959; letter, April 14, 1959, RCO.

35. Bain Murray, "Szell Cuts Iron Curtain, Draws Applause in Prague," *CHSP*, July 9, 1959.

36. Szell to Helene, June 22, 1959; June 26, 1959.

37. Szell to Helene, June 26, 1959, Szell humorously exaggerated the local dialect; explicated and translated by Max Rudolf.

38. Quoted by Bain Murray, "Szell Scores Triumph in Return to Salzburg," *CHSP*, August 6, 1959.

39. See discography.

40. September 28, 1959, RCO.

41. George J. Barmann, "Fine Music, Food Are Szell's Tour Memories," *PD*, October 5, 1959.

42. Jerome Rosen was also a fine pianist; otherwise Szell would not have considered him for apprentice conductor. He later joined the Boston Symphony Orchestra as violinist, doubling on keyboard.

43. Cleveland Orchestra program book, October 8 and 10, 1959, 23. The concert opened with Weber's Overture to *Der Freischütz* and continued with Respighi's *The Birds*, followed by the concerto. The second half was Tchaikovsky's Fifth Symphony, recorded two weeks later.

44. "Orchestra Is Still Groping for Perfect Sound," *PD*, October 16, 1959.

45. There were only two completely free days in this period—recording sessions paid extra, but did not count toward the maximum number of weekly services.

46. "Concertmaster Post Resigned by Gingold," *PD*, November 16, 1959.

47. Louis Lane telephone interview, August 23, 2002. Lane said he warned Szell in advance that the orchestra parts were amateurishly copied, but Szell did not authorize him to do anything. When the rehearsal became the expected disaster, Szell cancelled the concerto. Lane later learned about Gingold's feelings from principal violist Abraham Skernick, in whom Gingold had confided.

48. Interview with the author, Bloomington, Indiana, October 11 and 12, 1975.

49. A Gingold student, William Preucil, became concertmaster of the Cleveland Orchestra in 2002.

50. Heuwekemeijer to Szell, undated telegram, presumably September 1959; Szell to Heuwekemeijer, December 31, 1959; Heuwekemeijer to Szell, January 15, 1960, RCO.

51. The Minneapolis Symphony Orchestra was renamed the Minnesota Orchestra in 1968. Szell claimed that Skrowaczewski's hiring was "very largely on the strength of my recommendation." Szell to Heuwekemeijer, December 31, 1959, RCO.

52. "Music: Glowing Mahler. Clevelanders Give 'Das Lied von der Erde,'" *NYT*, February 2, 1960.

53. "One Word Fits All: Bravo!" *NYWT*, February 9, 1960; "Leon Fleisher Is Soloist with the Cleveland Orchestra," *NYHT*, February 16, 1960.

54. Heuwekemeijer to Szell, February 23, 1960, Szell to Heuwekemeijer, March 4, 1960, RCO.

55. Judd to Szell, April 19, 1960; Szell to Judd, April 21, 1960; NYPhA. Philharmonic Hall was inaugurated on September 23, 1962, by the New York Philharmonic under Leonard Bernstein. Szell and the Cleveland Orchestra took part in the hall's opening festivities on September 27. Szell was guest conductor of the New York Philharmonic in twelve concerts from February 28 to March 24, 1963.

56. Heuwekemeijer to Szell, June 16, 1960; Flothuis to Szell, June 22, 1960; Flothuis to Szell, June 29, 1960, RCO.

57. Hans Georg Bonte, "The Magic of a Better Time, W. A. Mozart's 'Magic Flute' as the Last Opera of the 1960 Festival," unidentified clipping; Herbert Schneiber, "The High Priest in the Parish House," *Vienna Kurier,* August 13, 1960. To be fair, the cast in 1960, except for the roles of Papageno, Papagena, and the Queen of the Night, was new, although of repute. Keilberth was taken to task for sluggish tempi and thick textures already noticeable in the overture. "A very unfestival-like musical direction," Schneiber wrote.

58. Ted Princiotto, "Szell Returns after 'Good Rest' in Europe," *PD,* October 4, 1960.

59. By comparison, the New York Philharmonic, the oldest orchestra in America, founded in 1842, announced in 1994 that it had played five hundred young people's concerts in the eighty years since its first one in 1914, according to *Symphony Magazine,* 45, no. 3 (July-August 1994), 17. I tallied five hundred children's concerts given by the Cleveland Orchestra during just the eleven years of my association with it, 1961–72. Alas, the yearly number of children's concerts in Cleveland has since diminished, owing to economic pressures.

60. "Orchestra Opens 43rd Season with Familiar Works," *PD,* October 7, 1960.

61. "Szell Returns after 'Good Rest' in Europe," *PD,* October 4, 1960.

62. "Violinist Johanna Martzy Warms Severance Throng," *PD,* October 21, 1960.

63. See appendix A.

64. "Benny Gives Szell Some Tips," *CP,* November 4, 1960.

65. Emily Blossom, interview with the author, April 4, 1975.

66. "Jack Benny Sends 'Em in Pension Concert," *CP,* November 5, 1960.

67. Ethel Boros, "Szell, Lane Return with Diverse European Images," *PD,* December 20, 1960.

68. Flothuis to Szell, December 14, 1960; Szell to Flothuis, December 20, 1960, RCO.

69. "Walton Symphony Pleases; So Does Druian," *PD,* December 30, 1960.

70. "3 Young Conductors Excel but Orchestra Gets Off Easy," *PD,* January 2, 1961. Kulas Fellows David Epstein and Vladimir Benic conducted Schubert's "Unfinished" Symphony and the Franck Symphony, respectively, and Kulas Apprentice Jerome Rosen led the first two of Debussy's *Nocturnes: Nuages* and *Fêtes*. Elwell believed that the program was no test for the young conductors because the orchestra could have played the repertoire pieces "blindfolded." A common fallacy—orchestras *can* operate on automatic, but then they will sound that way. When led with authority, they will respond.

71. "French Pianist, New Symphony Applauded," *PD,* January 6, 1961.

72. "Rubinstein Perfect in Keyboard Artistry," *PD,* January 27, 1961.

73. Sargeant, "Musical Events, Szell," *TNY,* February 18, 1961; Schonberg, "Music: Walton's Second," *NYT,* February 6, 1961; "Music: Blackwood's 2nd," *NYT,* February 13, 1961; Biancolli, "Cleveland and Szell at Carnegie," *NYWT,* February 6, 1961.

74. Interview by Martin Perlich, radio station WCLV, Cleveland, undated tape.

75. "Cleveland and Szell at Carnegie," *NYWT,* February 6, 1961.

76. Fleisher interviewed by Jim Svejda, KUSC, Los Angeles, February 2008.

77. "Szell and Orchestra Enthrall Washington," *PD* (from the *Washington Post*), March 26, 1961.

78. "Szell, Shaw Fit Program to the Season," *PD*, March 31, 1961.

79. "Szell, Orchestra and Chorus Win Praise with Beethoven's 'Ninth,'" *PD*, April 21, 1961.

80. "Dismisses Suit by Orchestra over Contracts," *PD*, April 28, 1961.

81. "Musicians Seek to Block Contract with Orchestra," *PD*, June27, 1961.

82. Jan Mellow, "Szell Treasures Fix of Flat Tire in Italy," *PD*, October 1, 1961.

83. Szell to Oldberg, September 5, 1961, NWA.

84. Irving Kolodin, "A Happy Conductor," *Newark Star Ledger*, undated. He refers to David Ewen's *Dictators of the Baton* (Chicago: Alliance Book Corporation, 1943).

85. It is now usual that orchestra members have a say on a wide range of issues, including hiring a music director.

86. Seven new members joined the orchestra that season, including principal cellist Jules Eskin. Jerome Rosen was reappointed apprentice conductor for his third season and the author joined the orchestra with that title.

87. Interview with James Fassett, New York Philharmonic broadcast, April 27, 1963.

88. October 5 and 7, 1961, 11.

89. Witnessed by the author, who had come backstage to congratulate his colleague.

90. "Bravos for Our First Clarinet," *PD*, October 13, 1961.

91. Karajan to Szell, November 26, 1960. Translation by Klaus George Roy.

92. "Casadesus Wins Bravos as Piano Soloist," *PD*, November 3, 1961.

93. "Orchestra, Britten's Cantata Win Applause," *PD*, November 10, 1961.

94. Heuwekemeijer to Szell, September 25, 1961; Szell to Heuwekemeijer, September 29, 1961; Heuwekemeijer to Szell, October 28, 1961; Szell to Heuwekemeijer, November 2, 1961; Szell to Heuwekemeijer, November 10, 1961; Heuwekemeijer to Szell, November 17, 1961, RCO.

95. Szell to Heuwekemeijer, November 20, 1961, RCO.

96. The programs for the three successive Mondays were:

February 5, 1962

Mozart	Symphony no. 40 in G Minor
Kodály	Symphony (New York premiere)
Brahms	Piano Concerto no. 1—Clifford Curzon

February 12

Rossini	Overture to *La gazza ladra*
Hanson	*Bold Island* Suite (New York premiere)
Haydn	Symphony no. 92 in G Major, "Oxford"
Brahms	Violin Concerto—Erica Morini

February 19

Wagner	Prelude to *Die Meistersinger*
Bartók	*Concerto for Orchestra*
Liszt	Piano Concerto no. 1 in E-flat—Tamás Vásáry (New York debut)
Schumann	Symphony no. 4 in D Minor

97. Schonberg, "Music: Kodaly's First Symphony Is Performed," *NYT*, February 6, 1962; Harriett Johnson, "Szell Leads First of 3 Concerts," *NYP*, February 6, 1962; Lang, "Music, The Cleveland Orchestra," *NYHT*, February 6, 1962; Schonberg, "Music: Erica Morini at Top Form," *NYT*, February 13, 1962; Lang, "Music, The Cleveland Orchestra," *NYHT*, February 13, 1962, MC.

98. Telephone interview with Cloyd Duff, November 30, 1997. The unfortunate original percussionist left for another major orchestra. His replacement in the section, Richard Weiner, played the part from then on, to Szell's complete satisfaction, including the Severance Hall performances and commercial recording in January 1965 and the Carnegie Hall performance that February. In my liner notes for the Sony Classical Masterworks release of the Bartók on CD, I made a regrettable error of chronology, placing the incident in 1965 instead of 1961–62. Apologies to Weiner for my oversight.

99. Beverly Gary, "A Brilliant Conductor Gives a Creed of Musical Excellence," *NYP*, February 9, 1962.

100. "Delightful New Symphony Here," *San Francisco Chronicle*, March 16, 1962.

101. Press release, San Francisco Symphony Association, 19, March 1962; Alfred Frankenstein, "Jorda Shows His Skill in Brahms," *San Francisco Chronicle*, March 24, 1962.

102. Frankenstein to Szell, March 24, 1962, Szell to Frankenstein, March 26, 1962, "Symphony Dispute, A Bit of Discord by Conductor Szell," *San Francisco Chronicle*, March 28, 1962.

103. Lawrence E. Davies, "George Szell Angers San Franciscans," *NYT*, March 29, 1962.

104. March 29, 1962.

105. Robert Shankland, interview with the author, April 14, 1975.

106. Kastendieck, "Clevelanders Are Superb," *NYJA*, September 28, 1962; Johnson, "Szell, Stern at Philharmonic Hall," *NYP*, September 28, 1962, MC.

107. "From Our Special Correspondent," "The Arts. Trying Out the New York Philharmonic Hall," October 6, 1962.

108. "Cleveland Plays in Philharmonic Hall," *NYWT*, September 28, 1962, MC.

109. Interview with the author, New York, March 3, 1976.

110. Inserted in the program booklet was a one-page reprint of excerpts of six reviews of the Lincoln Center concert, titled: "THE CLEVELAND ORCHESTRA GREETED WITH ENTHUSIASM IN LINCOLN CENTER APPEARANCE," five from New York newspapers, and a "dispatch from Frank Hruby" to the *Cleveland Press*: "If the Lincoln Center people were looking for perfection to help test and dedicate their new hall, they found it last night in our orchestra."

111. Rehearsals and performances each count as one "service." The number permitted weekly was negotiated by union contract. Szell normally had five rehearsals and two subscription concerts a week. The remaining services were either a concert out of town ("runout"), plus a children's concert, or a Twilight Concert with its rehearsal.

112. One pair pitched in B-flat and the other in F. These instruments are named for Wagner because he "invented" them (he actually had them constructed to fulfill his

concept of sound for parts of his *Ring* cycle). Bruckner admired, or more like worshipped, Wagner, and used these instruments in the magnificent slow movement of his Seventh Symphony and near the end of the *finale*.

113. Union regulations limit the length of music used from a recording session. The audio producer tracks union regulations and the time consumed by breaks and listening to playbacks during the session.

114. Undated interviews with the author in Cleveland, Lucerne and New York City.

115. "The Autocrat on the Podium," *Newsweek*, January 28, 1963, 60–61; "The Glorious Instrument," *Time*, February 22, 1963, 58–65, MC.

116. "Szell at the Philharmonic—Menotti's 'Labyrinth,'" *SR*, March 16, 1963, NYPhA.

117. Schonberg, "Szell Continues His Miniature Beethoven Cycle: Firkusny Soloist," *MA*, March 15, 1963; Kastendieck, "Appraisal: Szell to Stokowski," *Christian Science Monitor*, March 27, 1963, NYPhA.

118. Flothuis to Szell, April 4, 1963; Szell to Flothuis, April 8, 1963, RCO.

119. The Ambassador, the Rt. Hon. Sir David Ormsby Gore, presented the insignia of the order, which also recognized Szell's fiftieth anniversary as a conductor and listed the British works, mostly of Walton, that Szell conducted in world, North American, European, and Cleveland premieres. Cleveland Orchestra press release: "George Szell Honored by Her Majesty, Queen Elizabeth, of Great Britain," October 3, 1963.

120. Interview with John Browning, October 20, 1979.

121. Flothuis to Szell, December 9, 1963; Szell to Flothuis, January 13, 1964; Szell to Flothuis, January 7, 1964; Szell to Flothuis, January 13, 1964, RCO.

122. *Cleveland Plain Dealer* bureau, Washington: "Concert Tomorrow. LBJ Writes Tribute to Szell, Orchestra," February 14, 1964; Marilyn Swanton, "Szell Honored. Cleveland Orchestra Captures Washington," February 16, 1964; Marilyn Swanton, "Washington Is Captivated. Szell Charms Dignitaries at Reception," February 17, 1964; Paul Hume, "Szell, Orchestra at Their Finest in Memorable Capitol Concert," *Washington Post*, reprinted in the *PD*, February 17, 1964.

123. "Catching Up with His Image," April 5, 1964. Reviewers Miles Kastendieck and Harold Schonberg had observed the phenomenon with the Philharmonic that Szell described to Ericson.

124. For example, on April 10 Szell went from New York to Cleveland for just one subscription concert pair on the sixteenth and eighteenth, back to New York on the twentieth for the Concertgebouw concert, meetings, and judging the Leventritt finals, and returned to Cleveland on the twenty-fourth. On the twenty-fifth, he conducted the Cleveland Orchestra in London, Ontario, at the University of Western Ontario's annual Spring Festival, and on Monday the twenty-seventh, he conducted the orchestra in Toronto's Massey Hall. Back in Cleveland, he led two rehearsals on Tuesday and Wednesday. A fifth rehearsal on Thursday morning prepared the twenty-fifth subscription pair.

125. Severance Hall's unwieldy house organ was barely adequate for the subscription performances, but a more authentic instrument was needed for the recording. Manager

Barksdale called on the venerable Holtkamp Organ Company, located in a western suburb of Cleveland, for an ideal small organ (called a portative).

126. The opening production, conducted by Louis Lane and staged by Henry Butler on September 9 and 10, 1964, was the first Cleveland performances of Stravinsky's *The Rake's Progress*. On the twelfth and thirteenth, Lane conducted *Il Tabarro* and I conducted *Gianni Schicchi*.

127. In an interview with the *Plain Dealer*'s Robert Finn at the beginning of the fifty-first season, 1968–69, Szell said of the L.E.O.T. performance of Richard Strauss's opera *Capriccio*, conducted by the author, "I wish Strauss could have heard it, the orchestra sounded just the way he would have wanted it."

128. Tragically, the tapes of these historic artistic documents of a dozen-and-a-half televised concerts were not preserved. In the mid-1970s the author brought the potential loss of these tapes to the attention of then-general manager of the Musical Arts Association, Michael Maxwell; the president of the Musical Arts Association, Alfred M. Rankin; and the chairman of the board, Frank E. Joseph. Maxwell was not interested and the others could not find the funds to purchase the two-inch-wide video tapes ($350 per one-hour reel), so they were erased and reused by the television station.

129. Judith McCluskey, "Orchestra Tour Planned 2 Years," *PD*, September 19, 1964.

130. Heuwekemeijer to Szell, September 28, 1964; Szell to Heuwekemeijer, September 30, 1964, RCO.

131. Following an established practice, Szell frequently doubled the woodwinds in large orchestral works from late Beethoven on, marking the parts clearly as to where the doubling should take place.

132. The David Mannes School of Music was founded in New York City in 1918 by David and Clara Damrosch Mannes. When David died in 1959, their son Leopold became director. The school was later renamed Mannes College of Music and is now Mannes College the New School for Music.

133. Chapin interview with the author, March 23, 1994; *NYHT*, February 9, 1965.

134. Louis Lane recalled that Szell consulted his then principal violist, Marcel Dick, a serious composer and musician he respected, about the cut. Dick was Hungarian and knew Bartók's music well. When Lane later questioned Szell's preparing the cut by repeating a bar four times as uncharacteristic of the composer, he answered that it had a distinct parallel in a passage in Bartók's First Suite (undated conversation with Lane).

135. Flothuis to Szell, December 16, 1964, RCO.

136. Pierre Boulez, interview with the author, November 16, 1999.

137. When the *Cleveland Plain Dealer*'s chief music critic, Herbert Elwell, retired in 1964, the newspaper hired the *Akron Beacon-Journal*'s Robert Finn to replace him.

138. "Long-Term Contract Is Signed by Szell," March 25, 1965.

Chapter 10. The Cleveland Orchestra in the World (1965–68)

1. Charles Hutaff of Cleveland radio station WJW asked me to document the tour with weekly five-minute taped commentaries to be relayed by phone or mail. Soviet paranoia about film or tape made me more than a little nervous about carrying a recorder on the tour, however official. MCB.

2. Ethel Boros, "Szell Frank in Jubilation after Tour," *PD*, June 29, 1965.

3. Szell to Barksdale, June 22, 1964; Szell to Ebert, August 7, 1964.

4. Enwall to Szell, September 14, 1964; Szell to Enwall, September 17, 1964.

5. On a memo from Barksdale dated October 30, 1963, Szell wrote: "NB Itinerary: It should be kept in mind that Berlin is accessible only from the West not to & from Vienna or Prague because they have no direct air connections with our (West) Berlin & Therefore a certain detour will be inevitable and Berlin might conceivably best be fitted in between London & Paris."

6. Szell to Peter Weiser, general secretary of the Vienna Konzerthausgesellschaft, October 30, 1963; Szell to Weiser, November 1, 1963.

7. Mannes to Szell, June 16, 1964; Szell to Mannes, June 22, 1964.

8. For the 1965 tour repertoire, see appendix E.

9. Louis Lane, September 15, 2002. With Shaw out of the picture, the conducting staff on tour would consist of Szell, associate conductor Louis Lane, and myself as "acting assistant conductor." Apprentice conductor colleague James Levine joined me in the keyboard section.

10. Heller was suave, multilingual, and clever, and had practically cornered the market for U.S. State Department tours. His staff included administrative assistant Margaret Flatow and two stagehands, Giovanni Esposito and Eduard Ebner, who supervised loading and unloading of baggage, music, and instruments through customs from plane or train to truck to theater and back to plane or train. Ebner's gravelly speaking voice, the loudest in or out of any opera house, could be heard in every theater giving orders in whatever language was necessary to keep local stagehands hopping. Another Heller regular, costumer Joseph James, served as Szell's valet.

11. The pocket-sized itinerary issued to the orchestra and tour staff informed them that Moscow time was eight hours ahead of Cleveland's.

12. Memo: Barksdale to Terrence Catherman, Anatole Heller, and Eugene Schelp, February 25, 1965.

13. "34 Clevelanders Join Orchestra in Leningrad," *PD*, May 19, 1965. Trustees and friends of the Orchestra joined parts of the tour.

14. "Szell Calls Soviet Acclaim 'Best,'" *PD*, undated.

15. The program included a message from Secretary of State Dean Rusk:

"The Cultural Presentation Program of the Department of State is an eloquent realization of the American people's wish to share with the rest of the world the best of our arts developed by academic as well as professional groups. . . . The culture of any country is the key to the hearts and minds of its people." Program, Cleveland Orchestra concert, Helsinki, Finland, May 23, 1965; the speech, Szell's reply, and the concert were broadcast the following season by the Cleveland Orchestra's syndication service.

16. The author interviewed Szell in Berlin for Cleveland radio station WJW. Telling of his youth in Berlin and of Richard Strauss, Szell delighted in emphasizing that as an apprentice at the Berlin Opera, he was paid "exactly zero Deutschmarks," because "the position's value to me was much greater than my value to the Opera." June 8, 1965, MCB.

17. Of the choices of citizenship Szell had in the aftermath of World War I, Czechoslovakia seemed to him to offer the brightest financial future. Interview with Louis Lane,

September 15, 2002. Helene Szell's house in Prague was reclaimed by her son, John Teltsch, who later sold it to Vaclav Havel.

18. "Viennese Shout Thanks to Szell," *PD*, June 19, 1965.

19. "Royal Festival Hall, Cleveland Orchestra," *Financial Times* (London), June 23, 1965; "Royal Festival Hall, Cleveland Orchestra," *Times* (London),June 22, 1965.

20. Ethel Boros, "Szell Frank in Jubilation after Tour," *PD*, June 29, 1965.

21. "Cheers Welcome Orchestra"; editorial, "A Bouquet for the Orchestra," *PD*, June 27, 1965.

22. Barksdale to Szell, July 21, 1965. Robert Conrad was vice president of the successful FM fine music station, WCLV. He became announcer of the broadcasts and producer of the syndication service. As associate producer, I served as liaison between Szell and the recording engineers.

23. Szell to Barksdale, July 5, 1965; Szell disclosed that "for a number of years, the Festivals of Edinburgh, Salzburg and Lucerne have expressed keen interest in appearances of the Cleveland Orchestra. . . ."; Szell to Glenn C. Wolfe, July 1, 1963; Szell to Barksdale, July 6, 1965; Barksdale to Szell, July 16, 1965.

24. Szell to Barksdale, July 22, 1965. Guest conductors for 1966–67 were Sixten Ehrling (Detroit Symphony), Jean Martinon (Chicago Symphony), and Max Rudolf (Cincinnati Symphony).

25. Szell to Barksdale, August 3, 1965.

26. The author conducted the Prokofiev, Louis Lane the first, Mozart's *The Abduction from the Seraglio*.

27. Robert Conrad of WCLV was announcer and producer, Vladimir Maleckar was audio supervisor, the author was associate producer, and Richard L. Kaye of Boston's WCRB was consultant.

28. Lane had chosen this symphony for his apprentice conductor audition with Szell in the mid-1940s, guessing correctly that Szell might not have known it well, or at all, at the time.

29. Interview with Edgar Vincent, September 14, 1976.

30. "Composers, A Bridge to the Future," *Time*, February 18, 1966; Edgar Vincent interview.

31. Interview with John Browning, November 20, 1979.

32. Szell to Barksdale, June 14, 1966; Boulez, interview with the author, November 16, 1999.

33. Bernstein to Szell, June 8, 1966. By some alchemy of the calendar, the anniversary fell within the 126th season. Szell was one of six guest conductors that season. Others were: principal guest conductor William Steinberg, Claudio Abbado, Sir John Barbirolli, Seiji Ozawa, Thomas Schippers, and Leopold Stokowski; Moseley to Szell, July 6, 1966, NYPhA.

34. Szell to Flothuis, July 7, 1966; Flothuis to Szell, July 19, 1966, RCO.

35. Interview with John Browning, November 20, 1979.

36. Nathan Kroll, interview with the author, October 20, 1993.

37. Waage to Szell, March 17, 1966; Szell to Waage, March 19, 1966, RCO. Translation by the author.

38. J. Reichenfeld, "Gepantserde musiceerdrift van Szell in Beethovens Vijfde," unidentified Amsterdam newspaper, November 30, 1966, RCO.

39. The composer later revised the score and shortened the title to *Métaboles*. Szell so informed Flothuis in a letter dated September 2, 1969.

40. Ferry Eiselin, "Georges Szell, Gastdirigent van het Concertgebouworkest, 'Amerikaanse orkesten zijn de beste,'" *De Telegraaf*, Amsterdam, November 24, 1966, RCO.

41. Szell to Karel Schouten (also the principal violist), undated; Szell to Schouten, also undated; "George Szell gaf een pluim" ("George Szell Gives a Compliment"), *De Telegraaf*, December 8, 1966, RCO.

42. Szell to Flothuis, October 8, 1965, RCO.

43. Szell to Heuweckemeijer, December 7, 1966; Heuweckemeijer to Szell, December 20, 1966; Szell to Heuweckemeijer, December 29, 1966, RCO.

44. Sargeant, "Musical Events," *TNY*, February 18, 1967; Schonberg, "Music: Szell Leads Beethoven Mass," *NYT*, February 7, 1967, MCA.

45. Lane, Levine, and the author took part, along with Szell. Soloists were assistant concertmaster Daniel Majeske and orchestra pianist Joela Jones. Composers, works, and performers were: Walter Aschaffenburg, *Three Dances* (Levine); Russell Smith, Second Piano Concerto (Szell/Jones); David Lewin, *Fantasy-Allegro* (Charry/Majeske); Edward Miller, *Orchestral Changes* (Lane); and Lothar Klein, *Musique á Gogo* (Lane).

46. Szell to Barksdale, June 1, 1967.

47. Druian to Barksdale, June 7, 1967; Barksdale to Szell, June 9, 1967; MAA. Harold Hartog was at the London concert agency Ingpen and Williams; the Sol Hurok agency was in New York.

48. Szell to Barksdale, July 5, 1967.

49. Szell to Joseph, June 17, 1967.

50. Gal to Szell, "Mein lieber Alter" ("My dear old fellow"), June 3, 1967.

51. Szell to Joseph, June 17, 1967.

52. Szell to Barksdale, June 15, 1967; Szell to Barksdale, July 13, 1967.

53. Karl Schumann, "Karajan unter fremder Flagge" ("Karajan under Foreign Colors"), *Feuilleton des Münchner Kulturberichte*, August 18, 1967, pg. 12, translation by Henry Bloch.

54. Memo: Szell to Barksdale in Lucerne, August 31, 1967; Szell to Barksdale, November 17, 1966.

55. Neville Cardus, "Georg Szell and the Cleveland Orchestra at the Usher Hall," *The Guardian*, three reviews: August 22, 23, and 25, 1967.

56. "Orchestral Greatness," *Observer Review*, August 27, 1967. In 1947 Szell almost conducted his old orchestra with Glyndebourne casts in *Figaro* and *Macbeth* at the then-new Edinburgh Festival. As the character Anne Trulove remarks in Act Two of *The Rake's Progress*, "How strange!"

57. "Cautious Coming of Age," *Sunday Times* (London), August 27, 1967.

58. Told to the author by Ormond.

59. "Members of Cleveland Orchestra Plan to Strike Beginning Today," September 11, 1967, MCA.

60. Szell to Barksdale, June 15, 1967; Barksdale to Szell, September 15, 1967.

61. "Orchestra Peace Requires Pursuing," September 24, 1967.

62. September 18, 1967.

63. *PD*, September 27, 1967; "Strike Aftermath Blunts Orchestra Opener," *CP*, September 27, 1967.

64. From their early years, Steinberg's and Szell's careers had crossed paths and had many parallels. The Philharmonic situation was an unfortunate late chapter in their otherwise friendly relationship. It continued, and Steinberg guest conducted three concerts in the opening season of the Blossom Music Center, in July 1968.

65. Barksdale to Szell, November 16, 1967.

66. Berlin: Haydn Ninety-third, Bruckner Third; *Oberon* Overture, Bartók Second Violin Concerto (Peinemann), Schumann Third. Vienna: *Freischütz* Overture, Haydn Ninety-second, Schumann Third; Mozart Symphony K. 200, Bruckner Seventh.

67. Szell to Barksdale, November 1, 1967.

68. H. H. Stuckenschmidt, "Conductor Marathon: Szell, Maazel, Karajan, Kubelik, and Steinberg in Berlin," November 24, 1967, author's translation.

69. "Excellent Orchestral Season Lacked Anniversary Touch," *PD*, May 12, 1968.

Chapter 11. Summers at Home

1. The stadium was the upper Manhattan athletic field of the College of the City of New York. From 1922 to 1966 the New York Philharmonic gave summer concerts there at low ticket prices.

2. The Tanglewood Music Festival, formerly the Berkshire Music Festival, in Lenox, Massachusetts.

3. James Frankel, "Reveals 57 of 95 Symphony Men Have Non-Musical Jobs," *CP*, July 6, 1952.

4. James Frankel, "Szell Upset over Loss of Pops," *CP*, March 27, 1953.

5. The summer solution was developed from a plan submitted by Ernest Wittenberg, "Ball Yard 'Pops' Light as Feller's," *CN*, April 2, 1953.

6. Milt Widder, "Sights and Sounds," *CP*, October 10, 1953.

7. Minutes of the Musical Arts Association, March 20, 1964.

8. Minutes of MAA meeting and press release, November 20, 1964; "Tanglewood for Cleveland. Summer Festivals in Prospect; Orchestra Pavilion Approved," *PD*, November 21, 1964, accompanied by a photo of MAA trustees Frank E. Joseph and James D. Ireland.

9. Szell to Barksdale, July 13, 1966.

10. Barksdale to Szell, August 18, 1966.

11. In 1928 John Long Severance inaugurated the campaign to build the concert hall named for his wife with a donation of $1,000,000, and the Blossoms immediately pledged $750,000, princely sums then.

12. A recording of the event.

13. Frank E. Joseph, "Magnificent Blossom," *Fine Arts*, August 2, 1968; interview with the author, April 7, 1975.

14. Peter Reed, interview with the author, April 9, 1975.

15. Frank E. Joseph, "Magnificent Blossom," *Fine Arts*, August 2, 1968; interview with the author, April 7, 1975.

16. June 23, 1966; Szell to Barksdale, June 28, 1966.

17. Szell to Barksdale, November 1, 1967; Barksdale to Szell, November 6, 1967.

18. Szell to Barksdale, August 23, 1966.

19. Szell to Barksdale, November 17, 1966; Szell to Barksdale, November 16, 1966. In January 2000 Jaffe had a triumphant vindication that more than made up for his disappointment over Blossom in 1968. His acoustical design for the extensive remodeling of Severance Hall's stage turned out to be a great success and a notable improvement over Keilholz's 1958 stage shell.

20. Szell to Joseph, June 17, 1967; Szell to Barksdale, July 5, 1966; Szell to Barksdale, August 23, 1966; Barksdale to Szell, August 18, 1966; Szell to Barksdale, August 23, 1966; Szell to Barksdale, May 27, 1968; Szell to Barksdale, June 24, 1968.

21. Barksdale to Szell, August 18, 1966; Szell to Barksdale, August 23, 1966. In Karajan's Salzburg *Carmen*, production of the third act was set on a beach instead of in the mountains, as the score called for. In another letter, Szell thought that production "strange."

22. Emily Blossom interview, April 4, 1975.

23. Frank E. Joseph interview, April 7, 1975.

24. Transcribed from WCLV's broadcast of the concert.

25. The building was to have had a second ceiling, to be installed below the framework supporting the roof. It proved unnecessary, because the sound was excellent without it.

26. "Music: The Blossom Festival Opens," *NYT*, July 20, 1968.

27. "A Festival Blossoms in Ohio," *NYT*, July 28, 1968.

28. The ancillary building, hidden just behind the main one, is connected to the backstage area by a covered walkway. This separate structure is of simple design compared to the main one, but its interior is aesthetically pleasing in its efficiency. The concrete walls are offset by wood and glass. Inside the corridor, which runs the length of the building, the shingle motif from the main building roof continues in the interior, forming the spaces for offices and dressing rooms. On this main floor is the orchestra library. Downstairs, a large lounge area looks out on a terrace and the woods beyond, also used for chorus rehearsals and warm-ups. The roof is naturally insulated for sound—it is covered with earth and seeded with grass. Downstairs, corridors lead to the main building, under which there are more dressing rooms for larger productions such as ballet or opera, and for the orchestra itself, a storage area for pianos and other instruments and a broadcast studio.

29. Szell to Barksdale, August 5, 1968; Szell to Barksdale, August 10, 1968; Szell to Barksdale, September 3, 1968; Barksdale to Szell, undated letter; Szell to Barksdale, November 3, 1968.

30. Graffman to Szell, August 10, 1969; Szell to Kelvin Smith, August 17, 1969.

Chapter 12. Finale: Cleveland, Japan, Korea, Anchorage, Cleveland (1968–70)

1. Szell to Barksdale, August 10 and 19, 1968.

2. "Melted": Gottfried Kraus, "Erlebnis des klassicschen Dreigestirns" ("Experiencing the Classical Trinity"), *Salzburger Nachrichten*, August 8, 1968; "Exploded": Herbert

Schnelber, "Zwei grosse Musiker" ("Two Great Musicians"), Vienna *Kurier*, August 23, 1968.

3. Szell to Barksdale, September 3, 1968.
4. "Peaks of Creation," *Sunday Times* (London), November 17, 1968.
5. "Royal Festival Hall. George Szell," *The Guardian*, November 8, 1968.
6. Szell to Barksdale, November 10, 1968; November 16, 1968.
7. "The Discipline of the Hard Szell," *The Guardian*, May 28, 1968.
8. "BANKING. Coffee, Tea or Money?" *Time*, November 15, 1968, MAA.
9. Barksdale to Szell, November 18, 1968; Szell to Barksdale, November 21, 1968.
10. NYPhA.
11. Arthur Loesser, August 26, 1894–January 4, 1969. Appreciation appeared in the program book, January 9 and 11, 1969, pg. 500.
12. Christoph Eschenbach, conversation with the author, February 4, 1969.
13. Szell to Barksdale, November 10, 1968; quoted in Barksdale to Szell, November 18, 1968.
14. Carlos Moseley interview with the author, February 8, 1971.
15. Pierre Boulez, interview with the author, New York City, November 16, 1999.
16. Telephone conversation with Louis Lane, September 15, 2002.
17. Barksdale to Szell, June 17, 1969; Szell to Barksdale, June 26, 1969; Barksdale to Szell, July 17, 1969; Szell to Barksdale, July 22, 1969.
18. Undated handwritten draft, signed by Szell for press release.
19. Barksdale to Szell, July 8, 1966.
20. Louis Lane, interview with the author, July 21, 1991. Maxwell held the job for six years, until September 1976, in the fourth year of Lorin Maazel's ten-year tenure as music director.
21. Barksdale to Ormandy, July 25, 1968; Ormandy to Barksdale, July 31, 1968; Szell to Ormandy, undated, probably September 1969.
22. Cleveland Orchestra program book, October 22, 24, and 25, 1970, 12–13.
23. Szell to Barksdale, September 12, 1969.
24. EMI Classics D 125446.
25. Szell to Barksdale, September 12, 1969.
26. "Guest Conductors Grapple with Monaco's Acoustics," August 6, 1969.
27. Gottfried Kraus, "Das Konzerterlebnis dieses Sommers" ("This Summer's Concert Adventure"), August 25, 1969; Franz Endler, "Zenit des musikalischen Geschenhens" ("The Pinnacle of Musical Experience"), August 26, 1969.
28. Interview with Rudolf Firkusny, New York City, November 20, 1975.
29. Cleveland Orchestra program booklet, October 16, 17, and 18, 1969, 135 and 142.
30. Andrew Kazdin, interview with the author, New York City, June 7, 1975.
31. Robert and Gaby Casadesus interview, January 15, 1971.
32. "Music: Szell Leads the Philharmonic," *NYT*, November 11, 1969.
33. "Musical Events. As It Was in the Beginning," *NYT*, December 6, 1969; *SR*, November 17, 1969.

34. Szell to Flothuis, January 16, 1970, RCO.

35. Interview with Andrew Kazdin, June 7, 1975.

36. Telephone interview with Elinore Barber, director of the Baldwin Wallace Bach Institute, January 3, 1994. Thanks to the *Cleveland Plain Dealer*'s Donald Rosenberg for the suggestion to call Barber.

37. Szell to the author backstage after his last concert in Severance Hall, May 8, 1970.

38. Katims (1909–2006), former first violist and assistant conductor of the NBC Symphony under Toscanini, had been a guest conductor in Cleveland in 1962.

39. Interview with Margaret Glove, Lake Wales, Florida, March 1, 1995. She maintained that this was part of a deliberate campaign by Maxwell to make Szell more dependent on him.

40. A photo by the author from a television screen of Szell's image superimposed on the orchestra in the Tokyo concert is included in this book's picture section (p. 17). The photo of the two young Japanese flower girls on stage with Szell and the orchestra during the bows is by Peter Hastings, official photographer on tour and longtime photographer of the Cleveland Orchestra, and was published: Peter Hastings, *Musical Images* (Shaker Heights, Ohio: Holly Publishing Company, 1981). It is also included in this book's picture section (p. 17).

41. Shankland interview, April 4, 1975.

42. Margaret Glove interview, March 1, 1995.

43. I was assigned to conduct the backstage music in the Mahler, to assist Bernstein, and to see him before every rehearsal.

44. At ten minutes before ten, disturbed by the sound of an airplane a bit closer than usual, I looked at my watch. It was during the coda of the Brahms concerto where the horn plays a rising arpeggio in D Major, a consoling passage after all the D Minor that had gone before. Nevertheless, I felt a chill at that moment. Years later, in researching this biography, I found Szell's exact time of death in his hospital record. It read: "Expired 9:50 pm." Could that eerie feeling I sensed have been a soul rising to Heaven?

45. On September 24, 25, and 28, Bernstein conducted Mahler's Ninth Symphony with the New York Philharmonic in concerts dedicated to the memory of Sir John Barbirolli and George Szell, who died within twenty-four hours of each other. Carlos Mosley thoughtfully informed Helene Szell about the tribute, NYPhA.

46. Tischler also painted a portrait of Szell, on view at Severance Hall, as well as that of Olga Band, Szell's first wife, seen by the author at her home in Great Neck, New York, June 7, 1975.

Epilogue

1. *SR*, August 29, 1970.

2. *CP*, May 7, 1971.

3. "Bid the Ghost of Szell Goodbye, It's Dohnanyi Now," *PD*, May 29, 1994. To Rosenberg's credit, he wrote an appreciation commemorating the twenty-fifth anniversary of Szell's death, headlined "Szell's Cherished Legacy, Career Still a Beacon 25 Years after

Death," *PD*, July 30, 1995. The critic is the author of *The Cleveland Orchestra Story: Second to None* (Cleveland: Gray, 2000).

4. Radio Interview with Harvey Sachs, WCLV, Cleveland, January 1965.

5. "George Szell and the Cleveland Orchestra, 1946 to 1970," Columbia Special Projects, A service of Columbia Records, C 10017, production and narration by Robert Conrad, engineering and editing by Vladimir Maleckar.

In Szell's Words

1. Beverly Gary, "A Brilliant Conductor Gives a Creed of Musical Excellence," *NYP*, February 9, 1962.

2. Olin Downes, "Apprentice to a Conductor," *NYT*, June 2, 1946.

3. Szell letter, October 30, 1956, in reply to a letter from Everett Fetter who took part in the conductors' workshop.

4. Szell quoted in *Time* magazine, February 22, 1963, 60.

5. Robert C. Marsh, "The Cleveland Orchestra, One Hundred Men and a Perfectionist," *High Fidelity*, February 1961, 38.

6. Mark A. Schubart, "Szell's Viewpoint," *NYT*, March 4, 1945.

7. Ronald Eyer, "Master Builder of Orchestras," *NYHT*, February 11, 1962.

8. William J. King, article title unknown, unidentified newspaper, during Szell's conducting of the NBC Symphony, 1941.

9. Ross Parmenter, "Man of Many Backgrounds," *NYT*, January 17, 1943.

10. J.F.T., "George Szell: The Music Comes First," *The International Musician*, date unknown.

11. Joseph Wechsberg, "Orchestra," *TNY*, May 30, 1970, 46.

12. Marsh, *Cleveland Orchestra*, foreword by George Szell.

13. Author's interview with Norman Hollander, Kansas City Philharmonic principal cellist, Kansas City, September 1976; former assistant principal cellist of Cleveland Orchestra in Szell's first two seasons, 1946–48.

Bibliography

Bing, Sir Rudolf. *The Memoirs of Sir Rudolf Bing, 5,000 Nights at the Opera*. New York: Doubleday, 1972.

Brosche, Günter, ed. *Richard Strauss—Franz Schalk: ein Briefwechsel*. Tutzing, Ger.: Hans Schneider, 1983.

Copland, Aaron. *Copland on Music*. New York: Schirmer Books, 1960.

Fellers, Frederick P., and Betty Meyers. *Discographies of Commercial Recordings of the Cleveland Orchestra (1924–1977) and the Cincinnati Symphony Orchestra (1917–1977)*. Westport, Conn.: Greenwood Press, 1978.

Graffman, Gary. *I Really Should Be Practicing*. Garden City, N.Y.: Doubleday, 1981.

Heyworth, Peter. *Otto Klemperer, His Life and Times*, Volume 1, 1885–1933. Cambridge, U.K.: Cambridge University Press, 1983.

Leinsdorf, Erich. *Cadenza: A Musical Career*. Boston: Houghton Mifflin, 1976.

Marsh, Robert C. *The Cleveland Orchestra*. Cleveland and New York: World Publishing, 1967.

Mayer, Martin. *The Met, One Hundred Years of Grand Opera*. New York: Simon and Schuster, 1983.

Miller, Eileen. *The Edinburgh International Festival, 1947–1996*. Hants, U.K.: Scolar Press, 1996.

Moore, Gerald. *Furthermoore*. London: Hamish Hamilton, 1983.

Rosenberg, Donald. *The Cleveland Orchestra Story "Second to None."* Cleveland: Gray, 2000.

Rubinstein, Arthur. *My Many Years*. New York: Alfred A. Knopf, 1980.

———. *My Young Years*. New York: Alfred A. Knopf, 1973.

Rudolf, Max. *The Grammar of Conducting*. New York: Schirmer Books, 1950, 2nd ed. 1980, 3rd ed. 1993.

Sachs, Harvey. *Toscanini*. New York: J.P. Lippencott, 1978, repr. Da Capo Press, 1980.

Salzer, Felix. *Structural Hearing*. New York: Charles Boni, 1952, repr. Dover, 1962.

Schonberg, Harold C. *The Great Conductors*. New York: Simon and Schuster, 1967.
Shanet, Howard. *Philharmonic, A History of New York's Orchestra*. Garden City, N.Y.: Doubleday, 1975.
Teltsch, John G. *Sursam corda*. ("Raise Up Your Hearts"). Privately published personal memoir, 1993. Cleveland Orchestra Archives.
Temianka, Henri. *Facing the Music*. New York: David McKay, 1972.
Turner, W. J. *Mozart, The Man & His Works*. New York: Alfred A. Knopf, 1938, repr. Greenwood Press, 1979.
Walzer, Tina, and Stephan Templ. *Unser Wien, Arisierung auf österreichish* ("Our Vienna, Arianisation in the Austrian Manner"). Berlin: Aufbau Verlag, 2001.

Index

Photo by Bachrach

MICHAEL CHARRY has conducted widely in the U.S. and internationally. He was a member of the conducting staff of the Cleveland Orchestra for nine years under George Szell and for two years after Szell's death. He is on the faculty of Mannes College The New School for Music, in New York City, where he was head of orchestral studies and music director of the Mannes Orchestra.

Only a Miner: Studies in Recorded Coal-Mining Songs *Archie Green*
Great Day Coming: Folk Music and the American Left *R. Serge Denisoff*
John Philip Sousa: A Descriptive Catalog of His Works *Paul E. Bierley*
The Hell-Bound Train: A Cowboy Songbook *Glenn Ohrlin*
Oh, Didn't He Ramble: The Life Story of Lee Collins, as Told to Mary Collins *Edited by Frank J. Gillis and John W. Miner*
American Labor Songs of the Nineteenth Century *Philip S. Foner*
Stars of Country Music: Uncle Dave Macon to Johnny Rodriguez *Edited by Bill C. Malone and Judith McCulloh*
Git Along, Little Dogies: Songs and Songmakers of the American West *John I. White*
A Texas-Mexican *Cancionero*: Folksongs of the Lower Border *Américo Paredes*
San Antonio Rose: The Life and Music of Bob Wills *Charles R. Townsend*
Early Downhome Blues: A Musical and Cultural Analysis *Jeff Todd Titon*
An Ives Celebration: Papers and Panels of the Charles Ives Centennial Festival-Conference *Edited by H. Wiley Hitchcock and Vivian Perlis*
Sinful Tunes and Spirituals: Black Folk Music to the Civil War *Dena J. Epstein*
Joe Scott, the Woodsman-Songmaker *Edward D. Ives*
Jimmie Rodgers: The Life and Times of America's Blue Yodeler *Nolan Porterfield*
Early American Music Engraving and Printing: A History of Music Publishing in America from 1787 to 1825, with Commentary on Earlier and Later Practices *Richard J. Wolfe*
Sing a Sad Song: The Life of Hank Williams *Roger M. Williams*
Long Steel Rail: The Railroad in American Folksong *Norm Cohen*
Resources of American Music History: A Directory of Source Materials from Colonial Times to World War II *D. W. Krummel, Jean Geil, Doris J. Dyen, and Deane L. Root*
Tenement Songs: The Popular Music of the Jewish Immigrants *Mark Slobin*
Ozark Folksongs *Vance Randolph; edited and abridged by Norm Cohen*
Oscar Sonneck and American Music *Edited by William Lichtenwanger*
Bluegrass Breakdown: The Making of the Old Southern Sound *Robert Cantwell*
Bluegrass: A History *Neil V. Rosenberg*
Music at the White House: A History of the American Spirit *Elise K. Kirk*
Red River Blues: The Blues Tradition in the Southeast *Bruce Bastin*
Good Friends and Bad Enemies: Robert Winslow Gordon and the Study of American Folksong *Debora Kodish*
Fiddlin' Georgia Crazy: Fiddlin' John Carson, His Real World, and the World of His Songs *Gene Wiggins*
America's Music: From the Pilgrims to the Present (rev. 3d ed.) *Gilbert Chase*
Secular Music in Colonial Annapolis: The Tuesday Club, 1745–56 *John Barry Talley*
Bibliographical Handbook of American Music *D. W. Krummel*
Goin' to Kansas City *Nathan W. Pearson, Jr.*
"Susanna," "Jeanie," and "The Old Folks at Home": The Songs of Stephen C. Foster from His Time to Ours (2d ed.) *William W. Austin*
Songprints: The Musical Experience of Five Shoshone Women *Judith Vander*

"Happy in the Service of the Lord": Afro-American Gospel Quartets in Memphis *Kip Lornell*
Paul Hindemith in the United States *Luther Noss*
"My Song Is My Weapon": People's Songs, American Communism, and the Politics of Culture, 1930–50 *Robbie Lieberman*
Chosen Voices: The Story of the American Cantorate *Mark Slobin*
Theodore Thomas: America's Conductor and Builder of Orchestras, 1835–1905 *Ezra Schabas*
"The Whorehouse Bells Were Ringing" and Other Songs Cowboys Sing *Collected and Edited by Guy Logsdon*
Crazeology: The Autobiography of a Chicago Jazzman *Bud Freeman, as Told to Robert Wolf*
Discoursing Sweet Music: Brass Bands and Community Life in Turn-of-the-Century Pennsylvania *Kenneth Kreitner*
Mormonism and Music: A History *Michael Hicks*
Voices of the Jazz Age: Profiles of Eight Vintage Jazzmen *Chip Deffaa*
Pickin' on Peachtree: A History of Country Music in Atlanta, Georgia *Wayne W. Daniel*
Bitter Music: Collected Journals, Essays, Introductions, and Librettos *Harry Partch; edited by Thomas McGeary*
Ethnic Music on Records: A Discography of Ethnic Recordings Produced in the United States, 1893 to 1942 *Richard K. Spottswood*
Downhome Blues Lyrics: An Anthology from the Post–World War II Era *Jeff Todd Titon*
Ellington: The Early Years *Mark Tucker*
Chicago Soul *Robert Pruter*
That Half-Barbaric Twang: The Banjo in American Popular Culture *Karen Linn*
Hot Man: The Life of Art Hodes *Art Hodes and Chadwick Hansen*
The Erotic Muse: American Bawdy Songs (2d ed.) *Ed Cray*
Barrio Rhythm: Mexican American Music in Los Angeles *Steven Loza*
The Creation of Jazz: Music, Race, and Culture in Urban America *Burton W. Peretti*
Charles Martin Loeffler: A Life Apart in Music *Ellen Knight*
Club Date Musicians: Playing the New York Party Circuit *Bruce A. MacLeod*
Opera on the Road: Traveling Opera Troupes in the United States, 1825–60 *Katherine K. Preston*
The Stonemans: An Appalachian Family and the Music That Shaped Their Lives *Ivan M. Tribe*
Transforming Tradition: Folk Music Revivals Examined *Edited by Neil V. Rosenberg*
The Crooked Stovepipe: Athapaskan Fiddle Music and Square Dancing in Northeast Alaska and Northwest Canada *Craig Mishler*
Traveling the High Way Home: Ralph Stanley and the World of Traditional Bluegrass Music *John Wright*
Carl Ruggles: Composer, Painter, and Storyteller *Marilyn Ziffrin*
Never without a Song: The Years and Songs of Jennie Devlin, 1865–1952 *Katharine D. Newman*
The Hank Snow Story *Hank Snow, with Jack Ownbey and Bob Burris*

Milton Brown and the Founding of Western Swing *Cary Ginell, with special assistance from Roy Lee Brown*
Santiago de Murcia's "Códice Saldívar No. 4": A Treasury of Secular Guitar Music from Baroque Mexico *Craig H. Russell*
The Sound of the Dove: Singing in Appalachian Primitive Baptist Churches *Beverly Bush Patterson*
Heartland Excursions: Ethnomusicological Reflections on Schools of Music *Bruno Nettl*
Doowop: The Chicago Scene *Robert Pruter*
Blue Rhythms: Six Lives in Rhythm and Blues *Chip Deffaa*
Shoshone Ghost Dance Religion: Poetry Songs and Great Basin Context *Judith Vander*
Go Cat Go! Rockabilly Music and Its Makers *Craig Morrison*
'Twas Only an Irishman's Dream: The Image of Ireland and the Irish in American Popular Song Lyrics, 1800–1920 *William H. A. Williams*
Democracy at the Opera: Music, Theater, and Culture in New York City, 1815–60 *Karen Ahlquist*
Fred Waring and the Pennsylvanians *Virginia Waring*
Woody, Cisco, and Me: Seamen Three in the Merchant Marine *Jim Longhi*
Behind the Burnt Cork Mask: Early Blackface Minstrelsy and Antebellum American Popular Culture *William J. Mahar*
Going to Cincinnati: A History of the Blues in the Queen City *Steven C. Tracy*
Pistol Packin' Mama: Aunt Molly Jackson and the Politics of Folksong *Shelly Romalis*
Sixties Rock: Garage, Psychedelic, and Other Satisfactions *Michael Hicks*
The Late Great Johnny Ace and the Transition from R&B to Rock 'n' Roll *James M. Salem*
Tito Puente and the Making of Latin Music *Steven Loza*
Juilliard: A History *Andrea Olmstead*
Understanding Charles Seeger, Pioneer in American Musicology *Edited by Bell Yung and Helen Rees*
Mountains of Music: West Virginia Traditional Music from *Goldenseal* *Edited by John Lilly*
Alice Tully: An Intimate Portrait *Albert Fuller*
A Blues Life *Henry Townsend, as told to Bill Greensmith*
Long Steel Rail: The Railroad in American Folksong (2d ed.) *Norm Cohen*
The Golden Age of Gospel *Text by Horace Clarence Boyer; photography by Lloyd Yearwood*
Aaron Copland: The Life and Work of an Uncommon Man *Howard Pollack*
Louis Moreau Gottschalk *S. Frederick Starr*
Race, Rock, and Elvis *Michael T. Bertrand*
Theremin: Ether Music and Espionage *Albert Glinsky*
Poetry and Violence: The Ballad Tradition of Mexico's Costa Chica *John H. McDowell*
The Bill Monroe Reader *Edited by Tom Ewing*
Music in Lubavitcher Life *Ellen Koskoff*
Zarzuela: Spanish Operetta, American Stage *Janet L. Sturman*
Bluegrass Odyssey: A Documentary in Pictures and Words, 1966–86 *Carl Fleischhauer and Neil V. Rosenberg*
That Old-Time Rock & Roll: A Chronicle of an Era, 1954–63 *Richard Aquila*
Labor's Troubadour *Joe Glazer*

American Opera *Elise K. Kirk*
Don't Get above Your Raisin': Country Music and the Southern Working Class *Bill C. Malone*
John Alden Carpenter: A Chicago Composer *Howard Pollack*
Heartbeat of the People: Music and Dance of the Northern Pow-wow *Tara Browner*
My Lord, What a Morning: An Autobiography *Marian Anderson*
Marian Anderson: A Singer's Journey *Allan Keiler*
Charles Ives Remembered: An Oral History *Vivian Perlis*
Henry Cowell, Bohemian *Michael Hicks*
Rap Music and Street Consciousness *Cheryl L. Keyes*
Louis Prima *Garry Boulard*
Marian McPartland's Jazz World: All in Good Time *Marian McPartland*
Robert Johnson: Lost and Found *Barry Lee Pearson and Bill McCulloch*
Bound for America: Three British Composers *Nicholas Temperley*
Lost Sounds: Blacks and the Birth of the Recording Industry, 1890–1919 *Tim Brooks*
Burn, Baby! BURN! The Autobiography of Magnificent Montague *Magnificent Montague with Bob Baker*
Way Up North in Dixie: A Black Family's Claim to the Confederate Anthem *Howard L. Sacks and Judith Rose Sacks*
The Bluegrass Reader *Edited by Thomas Goldsmith*
Colin McPhee: Composer in Two Worlds *Carol J. Oja*
Robert Johnson, Mythmaking, and Contemporary American Culture *Patricia R. Schroeder*
Composing a World: Lou Harrison, Musical Wayfarer *Leta E. Miller and Fredric Lieberman*
Fritz Reiner, Maestro and Martinet *Kenneth Morgan*
That Toddlin' Town: Chicago's White Dance Bands and Orchestras, 1900–1950 *Charles A. Sengstock Jr.*
Dewey and Elvis: The Life and Times of a Rock 'n' Roll Deejay *Louis Cantor*
Come Hither to Go Yonder: Playing Bluegrass with Bill Monroe *Bob Black*
Chicago Blues: Portraits and Stories *David Whiteis*
The Incredible Band of John Philip Sousa *Paul E. Bierley*
"Maximum Clarity" and Other Writings on Music *Ben Johnston, edited by Bob Gilmore*
Staging Tradition: John Lair and Sarah Gertrude Knott *Michael Ann Williams*
Homegrown Music: Discovering Bluegrass *Stephanie P. Ledgin*
Tales of a Theatrical Guru *Danny Newman*
The Music of Bill Monroe *Neil V. Rosenberg and Charles K. Wolfe*
Pressing On: The Roni Stoneman Story *Roni Stoneman, as told to Ellen Wright*
Together Let Us Sweetly Live *Jonathan C. David, with photographs by Richard Holloway*
Live Fast, Love Hard: The Faron Young Story *Diane Diekman*
Air Castle of the South: WSM Radio and the Making of Music City *Craig P. Havighurst*
Traveling Home: Sacred Harp Singing and American Pluralism *Kiri Miller*
Where Did Our Love Go? The Rise and Fall of the Motown Sound *Nelson George*
Lonesome Cowgirls and Honky-Tonk Angels: The Women of Barn Dance Radio *Kristine M. McCusker*

California Polyphony: Ethnic Voices, Musical Crossroads *Mina Yang*
The Never-Ending Revival: Rounder Records and the Folk Alliance *Michael F. Scully*
Sing It Pretty: A Memoir *Bess Lomax Hawes*
Working Girl Blues: The Life and Music of Hazel Dickens *Hazel Dickens and Bill C. Malone*
Charles Ives Reconsidered *Gayle Sherwood Magee*
The Hayloft Gang: The Story of the National Barn Dance *Edited by Chad Berry*
Country Music Humorists and Comedians *Loyal Jones*
Record Makers and Breakers: Voices of the Independent Rock 'n' Roll Pioneers *John Broven*
Music of the First Nations: Tradition and Innovation in Native North America *Edited by Tara Browner*
Cafe Society: The Wrong Place for the Right People *Barney Josephson, with Terry Trilling-Josephson*
George Gershwin: An Intimate Portrait *Walter Rimler*
Life Flows On in Endless Song: Folk Songs and American History *Robert V. Wells*
I Feel a Song Coming On: The Life of Jimmy McHugh *Alyn Shipton*
King of the Queen City: The Story of King Records *Jon Hartley Fox*
Long Lost Blues: Popular Blues in America, 1850–1920 *Peter C. Muir*
Hard Luck Blues: Roots Music Photographs from the Great Depression *Rich Remsberg*
Restless Giant: The Life and Times of Jean Aberbach and Hill and Range Songs *Bar Biszick-Lockwood*
Champagne Charlie and Pretty Jemima: Variety Theater in the Nineteenth Century *Gillian M. Rodger*
Sacred Steel: Inside an African American Steel Guitar Tradition *Robert L. Stone*
Gone to the Country: The New Lost City Ramblers and the Folk Music Revival *Ray Allen*
The Makers of the Sacred Harp *David Warren Steel with Richard H. Hulan*
Woody Guthrie, American Radical *Will Kaufman*
George Szell: A Life of Music *Michael Charry*

The University of Illinois Press
is a founding member of the
Association of American University Presses.

Designed by Kelly Gray
Composed in 10/13 Goudy Oldstyle
by Jim Proefrock
at the University of Illinois Press
Manufactured by Sheridan Books, Inc.

University of Illinois Press
1325 South Oak Street
Champaign, IL 61820-6903
www.press.uillinois.edu